The Word of God in the Child of God

The Word of God in the Child of God:

Exegetical, Theological, and Homiletical Reflections from the 119th Psalm

by

George J. Zemek

Wipf & Stock
PUBLISHERS
Eugene, Oregon

THE WORD OF GOD IN THE CHILD OF GOD
By George J. Zemek

ISBN: 1-59752-380-1

TABLE OF CONTENTS

Preface xiii

PART I: INTRODUCTORY MATTERS

Estimations of the Psalm 3
Critical Evaluations 3
Conservative Evaluations 4

Authorship and Date 7
No Superscription 7
Related Issues 7
Perspective: National, Individual, or Both? 7
Age at Composition: Young, Old, or In-Between? 9
Historical Nominees 10

Literary Vehicles 17
The Acrostic Framework 17
Description 17
Examples 17
Criticisms 20
Purpose 24
Psalm-type Analyses 25
Poetic Parallelisms 27

Textual Assessment 29
The Hebrew Text 29
The Dead Sea Scrolls 29
The Septuagint and Other Early Versions 32

PART II: OVERVIEW

Analytical Overview 35
Macro-development 35
Micro-development 38
Theological Overview: Applied Bibliology 39
Words for the Word 39
The Synonyms 39
Their Interrelations 50
Attributes of the Word 51
Their Source 51
Their Solace 52
Reactions to the Word 54
Not Pharisaic Bigotry nor Bibliolatry 54
Dependent Appropriation, Internalization, and Application 56

PART III: ANALYSIS

ALEPH Stanza (vv. 1–8) 63
Translation and Notes 63
Synopsis and Outline 65
Commentary 68

BETH Stanza (vv. 9–16) 81
Translation and Notes 81
Synopsis and Outline 83
Commentary 85

GIMEL Stanza (vv. 17–24) 97
Translation and Notes 97
Synopsis and Outline 99
Commentary 101

DALETH Stanza (vv. 25–32) 113
Translation and Notes 113
Synopsis and Outline 115
Commentary 117

HE Stanza (vv. 33–40) 131
Translation and Notes 131
Synopsis and Outline 133
Commentary 135

WAW Stanza (vv. 41–48) 145
Translation and Notes 145
Synopsis and Outline 147
Commentary 149

ZAYIN Stanza (vv. 49–56) 155
Translation and Notes 155
Synopsis and Outline 157
Commentary 158

HETH Stanza (vv. 57–64) 167
Translation and Notes 167
Synopsis and Outline 168
Commentary 170

TETH Stanza (vv. 65–72) 177
Translation and Notes 177
Synopsis and Outline 180
Commentary 182

YODH Stanza (vv. 73–80) 191
Translation and Notes 191
Synopsis and Outline 193
Commentary 195

KAPH Stanza (vv. 81–88) 205
Translation and Notes 205
Synopsis and Outline 208
Commentary 209

LAMEDH Stanza (vv. 89–96) 215
Translation and Notes 215
Synopsis and Outline 217
Commentary 219

MEM Stanza (vv. 97–104) 229
Translation and Notes 229
Synopsis and Outline 231
Commentary 233

NUN Stanza (vv. 105–112) 243
Translation and Notes 243
Synopsis and Outline 245
Commentary 247

SAMEKH Stanza (vv. 113–120) 257
Translation and Notes 257
Synopsis and Outline 259
Commentary 261

AYIN Stanza (vv. 121–128) 269
Translation and Notes 269
Synopsis and Outline 273
Commentary 275

PE Stanza (vv. 129–136) 287
Translation and Notes 287
Synopsis and Outline 290
Commentary 292

TSADHE Stanza (vv. 137–144) 305
Translation and Notes 305
Synopsis and Outline 306
Commentary 308

QOPH Stanza (vv. 145–152) 321
Translation and Notes 321
Synopsis and Outline 325
Commentary 326

RESH Stanza (vv. 153–160) 333
Translation and Notes 333
Synopsis and Outline 335
Commentary 337

SHIN Stanza (vv. 161–168) 349
Translation and Notes 349
Synopsis and Outline 351
Commentary 353

TAW Stanza (vv. 169–176) 363
Translation and Notes 363
Synopsis and Outline 365
Commentary 368

APPENDIX: DIAGRAMMATICAL ANALYSES 387

IN MEMORY OF Dr. Charles R. Smith,
mentor, colleague, Dean,
but above all, *loyal friend*.

PREFACE

The longest chapter in the Bible has proven itself to be an especially precious treasure to children of God throughout the ages. Frequent identifications with its human author through his passions, pressures, and praises offer a recognizable landscape of real life from the vantage point of the believer. As a disciple, I also have been challenged frequently to measure my personal wounds and walk by the standard of the psalmist's sublime worship.

The impetus for a more careful study of the 119th Psalm came thirty years ago when my first pastor-teacher-friend preached a series of messages on this multifaceted gem from God's Word. Ever since that time, the Lord has providentially brought into my life occasions for plumbing the depths of its 176 verses. Some of these avenues of Divine confrontation and comfort have included two life-threatening thoracic surgeries accompanied by discomforting hospital stays for a total of nearly eight months, the periodic pangs of personal criticisms and attacks, and the many pressures which attend a commitment to the ministry of "the whole counsel of God." Consequently, there have been ample opportunities to empathize deeply with the psalmist when he said, "It was good for me that I was afflicted, in order that I might learn Your statutes" (v. 71).

However, he also testified, "Let those who fear You turn to me, that they may know Your testimonies" (v. 79). By my Lord's sovereign grace I have been blessed to share the truths and treasures of this psalm with many congregations and with hundreds of students in Hebrew exegesis classes. I remain acutely aware of a Divine constraint to pass along the sacred deposit of these life-impacting verses. Consequently, this written product is offered to fellow disciples who, with me, have been called of God to walk in His pathways during the end of the twentieth century.

At various times and out of different contexts others have sensed the need to take pen in hand in order to broadcast the 119th Psalm's ever-current applicability. None less than Spurgeon grasped the baton in his era, remarking, "Several notable authors traversed this heavenly country before Mr. Bridges, and I am one of those who follow after him: the succession will not end till the Lord comes."[1]

Notwithstanding Spurgeon's prediction, a candid reader might ask, "Why another?" or, more particularly, "What special contribution is anticipated in conjunction with yet another investigation of this Psalm?" Namely this: most of the published treatments are very devotional in nature, and most of the unpublished monographs, theses, and dissertations are quite specialized and/or technical. Consequently, there is a need for a middle-of-the-road analysis of Psalm 119.

Such an analysis must pulsate with the devotional heartbeat (i.e. theme) of the psalm, which is the God of the Word powerfully internalizing the Word of God in the child of God. At the same time, it must pay due respect to the footing and foundation of this theme through a careful exegetical and theological exposure of the text. Additionally, it would seem appropriate, based upon the structure of the stanzas, to offer twenty-two outlines as working models for packaging the deep truths from this scriptural reservoir. In the light of these diverse objectives and commitments, an invitation is extended to a variety of serious Bible students to accompany this observer as we enter the "Grand Canyon" of applied Bibliology.

---

[1] C. H. Spurgeon, *The Golden Alphabet of the Praises of Holy Scripture, Setting Forth the Believer's Delight in the Word of the Lord: Being a Devotional Commentary upon the One Hundredth and Nineteenth Psalm* (Pasadena, TX: Pilgrims Publications, 1980), p. 8.

PART I:

INTRODUCTORY MATTERS

ESTIMATIONS OF THE PSALM

As one walks the corridors of the hermeneutical history of Psalm 119, two polarized estimations of it are discernible. A few observers unhesitatingly cast a negative vote against the psalm. However, most Judeo-Christian testimonies clearly extol the beauty and benefit of this scriptural monument. Rather than engaging in a detailed history of its interpretation, the following evaluations of the psalm have been selected to exemplify these antithetical reactions.

Critical Evaluations

Most, if not all, critical assessments of the psalm are fed by an invalid assumption that the psalm's acrostic format automatically and necessarily evacuates from it any significant content. Such a presupposition is obviously bound up with Sabourin's bold evaluation: "Tedious repetitions, poor thought sequence, apparent lack of inspiration reflect the artificiality of the composition."[1]

Of course, this particular assumption is part and parcel of a larger stance. When Pfeiffer dogmatically asserts that "the most dreadful example of uninspired Old Testament versification is Psalm 119,"[2] he exposes a whole platform of bibliological skepticism. The tragedy is that, under the guise of academic objectivity and superiority, such pontifications adversely affect many gullible students.

---

1 Leopold Sabourin, *The Psalms: Their Origin and Meaning* (New York: Society of St. Paul, 1969), 2:287.

2 Robert H. Pfeiffer, *Introduction to the Old Testament* (New York: Harper and Brothers, 1941), p. 640.

Anyone who might find himself becoming more and more enamored with humanistic exploits in the arena of biblical studies would do well to listen closely to the testimony and confession of Mitchell Dahood in reference to his personal study of the 119th Psalm:

> . . . artificiality of structure seems to have hindered many commentators from appreciating the variety of the contents of the psalm. Some have denied that any real connection or progress of thought is to be found in it. Thus Weiser *(The Psalms*, p. 739) writes that the formal external character of the psalm stifles its subject matter. For him this poem is a many-colored mosaic of thoughts which are often repeated in a wearisome manner. The present writer shared this evaluation until a careful analysis of the Hebrew text revealed, in verse after verse, a freshness of thought and a felicity of expression unnoticed and consequently unappreciated in earlier versions. Weiser *(The Psalms*, p. 740) appears mistaken in his conviction that "the simple form of the diction makes it unnecessary to expound the psalm in detail."[3]

Conservative Evaluation

Positive assessments of the psalm are ultimately rooted in an outlook characterized by humility, dependence, and trust, those very qualities reflected by the human instrument through whom it has come from God. From this vantage point the form of the psalm becomes an asset rather than a liability. Moll argues that "the spiritual worth and beauty of the Psalm are not impaired by its artificial form."[4] Rotherham corroborates, positively noting that "the art is so exquisite that, when familiarised, it not only

---

[3] Mitchell Dahood, *Psalms*, The Anchor Bible (Garden City, NY: Doubleday and Company, Inc., 1966), 3:172.

[4] Carl B. Moll, *The Psalms*, trans. with additions by C.A. Briggs, *et al., Lange's Commentary on the Holy Scriptures* (Grand Rapids: Zondervan, 1960), p.589.

gratifies the taste, but aids the judgment, and ministers to the hunger of the spirit."[5]

Consequently, the 119th Psalm has been rightly classified as a "giant among the Psalms."[6] Delitzsch commends the heading placed before it in the German Bible: "In our German version it has the appropriate inscription, 'The Christian's golden ABC of the praise, love, power, and use of the word of God'; for here we have set forth in inexhaustible fullness what the word of God is to a man, and how a man is to behave himself in relation to it."[7] "No part of Scripture is more deeply imprinted upon memory, especially of the young, than portions of it; nor is any Scripture more suggestive of edifying trains of thought; nor is any other Scripture of the Old Testament more saturated, so to say, with a spirit all but Christian, of humility, trust, devoted love to God, and realization of His near Presence, than this psalm: which is an epitome of all true religion, and must be studied by any one who wishes to fathom the meaning of the law."[8]

Girdlestone also dwells upon the applicability of its truths when he notes, "With exquisite beauty and with inspired depth of thought the writer of the 119th Psalm draws out these varied aspects of the Divine Truth, and presents the law of God in every light in which the experience of a godly man can regard it."[9] Consequently, it is a powerful prescription from the Great Physician for those who, as measured by their own natural resources, are finite and fallen.

---

[5] Joseph B. Rotherham, *Studies in the Psalms* (London: H.K. Allenson, Ltd., 1911), p.511.

[6] Derek Kidner, *Psalms* 73-150 (Downers Grove, IL: InterVarsity Press, 1980), p.416.

[7] F. Delitzsch, Psalms, trans. by James Martin, in *Commentary the OT in Ten Volumes*, by C.F. Keil and F. Delitzsch (Grand Rapids: William B. Eerdmans, n.d.), 3:243.

[8] Canon Cook, G.H.S. Johnson, and C.J. Elliot, "Psalms," *Bible Commentary*, vol. 4, ed. by F.C. Cook (New York: Scribner, Armstrong and Company, 1875), p. 443.

[9] Robert B. Girdlestone, *Synonyms of the Old testament* (Grand Rapids: Williams B. Eerdmans, 1973, pp. 209-10.

AUTHORSHIP AND DATE

No Superscription

Psalm 119 is one of thirty-four psalms not bearing a superscription.[1] Consequently, what may be gleaned about occasion and authorship must be harvested exclusively from internal evidence. Such being the case, two reminders are in order. First, all dogmatic conjectures should be looked upon with suspicion. As one sifts the data of Psalm 119, he should keep in mind the attitude of Origen in reference to the authorship of Hebrews—only God knows for sure.[2] Secondly, although the Psalm has no superscription, it does place before us *176 verses*, a significant amount of internal evidence! Therefore, the following survey is a legitimate and profitable exercise.

Related Issues

Perspective: National, Individual, or Both?

A few commentators (e.g. Hengstenberg) have argued that the psalmist was speaking as a mouthpiece for all the people of

[1] Superscriptions are early notations in the Hebrew texts which convey information about authorship, musical directions, historical occasion, etc. That these notations were highly respected is witnessed by the fact that Hebrew Bibles in current usage count each superscription normally as v. 1 of that particular psalm.

[2] However, this attitude should not take the form of blanket agnosticism to avoid wrestling with informed conjectures. Even Origen felt quite strongly that Hebrews was Pauline.

God at that time. In other words, its truths come forth from a corporate or national perspective rather than an individual or personal perspective. Sometimes verses 63, 74, and 79 are cited as support for this position. It is argued that the use of חָבֵר (*ḥāḇēr*, i.e. companion, associate) in verse 63 along with the phrase "the ones who fear You" (vv. 63, 74, 79) document a nationalistic interpretation. Needless to say, the evidence for this view is meager.

Besides a few commentators who have at times argued for a combined individual/national outlook,[3] most recognize the fact that this psalm is characteristically individualistic. Scroggie, working from the English text, has assembled the following tabulations: the subjective pronoun "I" occurs 142 times; the objective pronoun "me," 91 times; the possessive pronoun "my," 62 times; "myself," three times; and the third person singular circumlocution "Thy servant," 13 times.[4] Thus Alexander's dogmatism in reference to the psalm's perspective is justifiable:

> There is no psalm in the whole collection which has more the appearance of having been exclusively designed for practical and personal improvement, without any reference to national . . . relations, than the one before us, which is wholly occupied with praises of God's word or written revelation, as the only source of spiritual strength and comfort, and with prayers for grace to make a profitable use of it.[5]

---

[3] Cf. Moll, *Psalms*, pp. 588–89.

[4] W. Graham Scroggie, *The Psalms* (London: Pickering and Inglis, Ltd., 1967), p. 174.

[5] J. A. Alexander, *The Psalms* (New York: Baker and Scribner, 1851), 3:150–51. Most form–critical analyses also favor the individualistic perspective conveyed in Ps 119; e.g., Sigmund Mowinckel, *The Psalms in Israel's Worship*, trans. by D. R. Ap–Thomas (New York: Abingdon Press, 1962), 2:78.

Age at Composition: Young, Old, or In-Between?

Once the psalm is accepted as the product of an individual's outlook, there may be a need to reflect upon his age at the time of composition. Some feel strongly that he was a young man when he became the instrument of the Spirit to record these words of testimony.[6] Verses 9, 99, and 100 are consistently employed in support of this view, and less frequently, the translation of צָעִיר (*ṣāᶜîr*) by "young" in verse 141 is added as another indication.

On the other hand, a few commentators (e.g., Ewald) have been bold in insisting that the psalmist was an old man. Specific textual documentation for this position is scarce.[7] It is no wonder why so many men who mention the age issue gravitate to middle ground. For example, Perowne suggests that the psalmist had reached the "middle arch of life" when he penned these words.[8] Moll reveals a similar preference in response to those espousing the youthful view, especially as based upon their interpretation of verses 99–100:

> It is plain that the writer is not an old man. . . . But it does not follow that he is a young man. The teachers whom he had outstript may have been those whose disciple he once was, not whose disciple he still is, or he may refer to authorized teachers, to whom he listened because they taught in Moses' seat, though he felt that they had really nothing to teach him.[9]

---

[6] E.g., Delitzsch, *Psalms*, 3:243.

[7] An implicit argument is sometimes built upon the psalmist's question voiced in v. 84a.

[8] J. J. Stewart Perowne, *The Book of Psalms* (London: George Bell and Sons, 1886), 2:350.

[9] Moll, *Psalms*, p. 589.

In the light of these differing positions relating to the psalmist's age, yet another interpretation has been put forth seemingly as a compromise. It has been suggested that the psalm may have developed as a diary; different stanzas or groups of stanzas are conjectured to have been written during different periods in the psalmist's life.[10] Such a view may be questioned for legitimate reasons; however, irrespective of its pragmatic strength but obvious weaknesses, it does help to characterize the unique applicability of the 119*th* Psalm. The testimonies of the psalmist are predicated upon his actual experience of walking with God from the time of his youth up to and including however old he might have been at the time of composition. Therefore, this psalm readily applies to people of all ages.

Historical Nominees

Authorship and date go hand-in-glove; therefore, the following nominees have been assembled in a chronologically descending order. Some of the suggestions are explicit while others are generic, and some are based upon Jewish and Christian traditions while others are based upon supposedly inductive extrapolations.[11]

At the outset of every course on Psalm 119, I have asked how many students have assumed that the psalm's origin is Davidic. Invariably, about two-thirds of them raise their hands in favor of Davidic authorship; however, most of those are unable to document their assumption from historical and/or internal evidence. A few commentators have suggested that the general thrust of the

[10] Cf. Spurgeon, *The Golden Alphabet*, pp. 12ff.

[11] Those which are constructed upon critical assumptions will not be treated extensively since they are not worthy of delineation nor extensive denunciation. Most of these conjectures are dated late because of the acrostic format, but this presupposition will be exposed as invalid in subsequent discussions.

internal evidence would not contradict the parallel occasion in David's life when he was in exile (e.g. 1 Sam 27). Yet, other scenarios fit the outcast references in Psalm 119 better.[12] Although no piece of internal evidence would patently contradict this traditional Christian presupposition, it seems better to conclude with Scroggie that "the older commentators are at fault in *assuming* that this psalm is Davidic."[13]

Dahood, not intimidated by the late-date mania which characterizes his circle of scholarship, has argued that the psalm should be regarded as anonymous but *early:*

> Current scholarship tends to assign a late date of composition to this psalm, but the view that the psalm was composed for a ruler—even perhaps, a Davidic king who stood in special relation to God's law (cf. Deut xvii 18ff.; Ps xl 6–8)—does not seem improbable. Numerous poetic usages that were rarely employed in the post-Exilic period have been uncovered in the poem. These strongly favor a pre-Exilic date of composition. The period of the Deuteronomic reform (late seventh century B.C.) provides a likely background for the spirit and legal language that pervades throughout.[14]

Dahood's expertise in ancient near eastern studies and comparative Semitics arms him with a weaponry capable of inflicting heavy damage upon the invalid assumption which late-dates any passage because of its acrostic format.

---

[12] Often vv. 9, 23, 46, 141, and 161 are mentioned in support of the quite traditional Christian assumption of Davidic authorship. It should be noted, however, that the references to youthfulness could fit a host of candidates. Furthermore, the mention of king<u>s</u>, prince<u>s</u>, or ruler<u>s</u> (note the plural) could just as well, or better, support another nominee. Surprisingly, very few proponents document their argumentation by appealing to theme and content parallels in Ps 19 which is Davidic.

[13] Scroggie, *Psalms*, p. 186.

[14] Dahood, *Psalms*, 3:173.

Notwithstanding his commendable corrective, it is extremely difficult for a critical scholar to aim the arsenal of his background at his own presuppositions. Without getting involved in an extended biblical refutation of Dahood's particular assumption which undergirds his acceptance of the Deuteronomic hypothesis, it must be stated that sporadic indications of certain stylistic data do not provide a solid footing upon which to erect views concerning date and authorship.[15] The construction of isagogic hypotheses should rather be built upon the more solid foundation of a comprehensive integration of the internal and historical evidences.

Rotherham is one who has ransacked the internal evidence of both Psalm 119 and several other psalms, and he finds in them the hand of "Prince Hezekiah."[16] At times his analogies bear marks of credibility; however, they are often vague and sometimes seemingly incompatible. His reconstructions seem to have been driven by compulsion, and his dogmatically sensationalistic affirmations stifle any serious consideration of his hypothesis.

One of the best conjectures in the light of internal evidence is Daniel. It would be difficult to improve upon Thrupp's condensed synopsis of the data:

> The suggestion that the long and unique meditation to which we now proceed [i.e. Psalm 119] should be regarded as the composition of Daniel has been but recently put forward. Yet if internal evidence (and we have here little else on which to depend) is in this instance to be allowed that due weight which in proportion to its copiousness and distinctness we generally feel no scruple in according it, there seems to remain but little

[15] For some general warnings, see: R. K. Harrison, *Introduction to the Old Testament* (Grand Rapids: William B. Eerdmans, 1969), pp. 984–85.

[16] Rotherham, *Studies in Psalms*, pp. 514–16. It must be noted that some of the psalms which he attributes to Hezekiah bear Davidic superscriptions.

ground for hesitation in recognizing Daniel as the author. He, above all men whose lives are in the Old Testament recorded to us, had in his youth cleansed his way by guarding it according to God's word (cf. v. 9). Cast as a stranger and a pilgrim in a foreign land (vv. 19, 54), yet still assured that God's mercies would be vouchsafed to his servants wheresoever in the wide earth they might dwell (v. 64), he had found God's testimonies far dearer to him than all manner of worldly wealth (vv. 14, 36, 37, 72, 127). Reproached (vv. 22, 23), derided (v. 51), slandered (v. 69), and plotted against (vv. 78, 85, 86, 95, 110, 161) by the proud princes whom he had never wronged, (how vividly does the acknowledgment of the Median presidents and princes rise up before us, that they should find no occasion against Daniel except concerning the law of his God!) he yet had spoken of God's testimonies even before kings, and had not been ashamed (v. 46). He had seen an end of all perfection (v. 96); guilty Jerusalem and haughty Babylon had during Daniel's life-time, each in her turn, yielded up their spoils to their conquerors; but his trust was reposed in God's word, which abideth forever. To this he remained steadfast; and day by day and night by night he unintermittingly persevered in his practice of pious devotion, meditating in God's word, crying for God's help, and praising God's name (vv. 147, 148, 164). The whole psalm bespeaks the character of one who, like Daniel, lived in close and habitual communion with God; one habitually trained from his youth upwards in secret self-discipline, the peaceful flow of his whole saintly career was not marked by the ruggedness which would generally follow, as in the case of St. Paul, from sudden conversion, or by the fitfulness attaching to lives that, like David's, have been once disordered by acts of heinous transgression; one indeed who was not without spot, who confessed his sin, who relied only on God's grace to reclaim him from the many strayings of which he was conscious (v. 176); but

> yet "a man greatly beloved," one of the pure in heart who might see God, and whom therefore God numbered, along with the patriarch Joseph and the evangelist St. John, among the special few to whom he partially unlocked the secrets of the times and seasons of the future.[17]

Thrupp also bolsters his correlation of the internal evidence with a canonical notation arguing that Daniel's prophetical office would furnish sufficient authority for the reception of any psalm composed by him.[18]

Jewish tradition is very consistent in attributing the 119*th* Psalm to Ezra or one of his disciples,[19] and some Christian commentators follow their lead.[20] Again, nothing in the psalm would explicitly forbid such a *general* conclusion, but the *specificity* of the psalm's internal evidence would align far better with Daniel than Ezra or one of his followers.

Another option would be an anonymous author of the Persian period.[21] Conjectures after this period (e.g., Jaddo, the high priest in the time of Alexander the Great, or an anonymous Maccabean psalm) are prompted by the circular reasonings of higher criticism,[22] since textual evidence, especially coming from Qumran,

---

[17] Joseph F. Thrupp, *An Introduction to the Study and Use of the Psalms* (Cambridge: Macmillan, 1860), 2:244–45. These and other possible connections to Daniel will be highlighted as they are encountered throughout the analyses of the stanzas in Part III.

[18] Ibid., p. 245. The position of Ps 119 in the fifth book of canonical psalms might also be mentioned since incorporation into this historical grouping would readily lend itself to the consideration of it as another exilic composition. Cf. Harrison, *Introduction to the OT*, p. 985.

[19] Cf. A. Cohen, *The Psalms* (London: Soncino Press, 1968), p. 394.

[20] E.g. Herbert C. Leupold, *Exposition of the Psalms* (Columbus, OH: Wartburg Press, 1959), p. 822.

[21] Cf. Moll's argument: *Psalms*, p. 588.

[22] Note that even Ivan Engnell has expressed objections to this tendency: *A Rigid Scrutiny*, trans. and ed. by John T. Willis (Nashville: Vanderbilt University Press, 1969), p. 111.

strongly suggests that the canonical psalms were completed in the Persian period. These early manuscripts and fragments also necessitate the recognition of a fixed collection in pre-Maccabean times.[23]

If one were forced to make a choice between all of the aforementioned options, analogies from the psalm's data with historical referents more consistently point in the direction of Daniel. Therefore, if for no other reason than illustration, it is suggested that the reader "think Daniel" as we roam through this sacred territory. However, for those who still may feel reluctant to lean toward any particular historical nominee, the words of Barnes are comforting:

> All these are mere conjectures, and it is now impossible to ascertain the occasion on which the psalm was composed, or to determine who was its author. Nor is it necessary. The psalm is so applicable to the people of God at all times, so fitted to strengthen the mind in trial, so adapted to guide, comfort, and support the soul, and so true in regard to the influence and value of the law of God, that it is not needful to know when it was composed, or who its author was. It is sufficient to know that it was composed under the guidance of the Holy Spirit, and is a repository of truths which will be of inestimable value in all ages of the world.[24]

---

[23] On both points, see: Harrison, *Introduction to the OT*, pp. 984–85.

[24] Albert Barnes, *Psalms*, in *Notes on the Old Testament* (Grand Rapids: Baker Book House, 1950), 3:177.

LITERARY VEHICLES

The Acrostic Framework

Description

Psalm 119 has been appropriately labeled "the great alphabet":[1]

> This is by far the longest Psalm in the Psalter; it consists of twenty-two strophes [i.e., stanzas] corresponding to the twenty-two letters of the Hebrew alphabet. Each strophe has eight verses or *bicola* (*two-line units*), and each bicolon of a particular strophe begins with the same Hebrew letter. Consequently the whole Psalm forms a very elaborate acrostic poem . . . , since the strophes are arranged according to the alphabet sequence.[2]

Examples

Biblical and extra-biblical examples of the acrostic format abound. Full or partial employments may be found in Psalms 9–10, 25, 34, 37, 111, 112, and 145. An acrostic pattern is obvious in Proverbs 31:10–31, and some have argued for indications of one in Nahum.[3] "The Book of Lamentations," however, "stands alongside of Psalm 119 as the largest in scope and execution":[4]

---

1 *Encyclopedia of Religion and Ethics*, s.v. "Acrostic," by C. Taylor, 1:75.

2 A. A. Anderson, *The Book of the Psalms*, New Century Bible (Greenwood, SC: Attic Press, 1972), 2:805.

> All five poems in Lamentations are in one way or another shaped according to the Hebrew alphabet. This is most noticeable in the first four poems, which are alphabetic acrostics. Chapters 1 and 2 are of relatively simple type, in which each stanza has three lines, and only the first word of the first line of each is made to conform to the alphabet, so that stanza one begins with *aleph*, stanza two with *beth*, and so on through the twenty-two letters of the Hebrew alphabet. Chapter 4 is of the same type, but here each stanza has only two lines. Chapter 3 is more elaborate: each stanza has three lines, and all three lines are made to begin with the proper letter, so that there are three lines starting with *aleph*, three with *beth*, and so on. . . . Chapter 5 is not an acrostic, but has exactly twenty-two lines and thus conforms to the alphabet to a lesser degree.[5]

Outside of the canon, acrostic examples crop up in ancient Mesopotamia, Qumran, the Apocrypha, post-biblical Jewish literature (e.g. "The Alphabet of Ben Sira"),[6] and even in Hellenistic

[3] Cf. S. R. Driver, *An Introduction to the Literature of the Old Testament* (NY: Charles Scribner's Sons, 1923), p. 337; George B. Gray, *The Forms of Hebrew Poetry* (London: Hodder and Stoughton, 1915), ch. 7; *Interpreter's Dictionary of the Bible*, s.v. "Acrostic," by Norman K. Gottwald, 1:28; Richard D. Patterson and Michael E. Travers, "Literary Analysis and the Unity of Nahum," *Grace Theological Journal*, 9:1 (Spring 1988): 56–58; etc.; contr. Walter A. Maier, *The Book of Nahum* (Saint Louis: Concordia Publishing House, 1959), pp. 52–62.

[4] Norman K. Gottwald, *Studies in the Book of Lamentations*, Studies in Biblical Theology, 14 (Chicago: Alec R. Allenson, Inc., 1954), p. 23. And yet, "the scope and execution" of the poems in Lam really do not rival the device's extensive development in Ps 119; furthermore, there are metrical and sequential divergencies in these poetic oracles over Jerusalem.

[5] Delbert R. Hillers, *Lamentations*, The Anchor Bible (Garden City, NY: Doubleday and Company, Inc., 1972), p. xxiv.

[6] Cf. *The Jewish Encyclopedia*, s.v. "Acrostics," by Israel Abrahams, 1:171–72, and "Ben Sira, Alphabet of," by Louis Ginzberg, 2:678–80.

[7] Ralph Marcus, "Alphabetic Acrostics in the Hellenistic and Roman Periods," *Journal of Near Eastern Studies* 6:2 (April 1947): 109–115.

and Roman literature.[7] The examples from ancient Mesopotamia are particularly devastating to any position which contends that this poetic device is a late contrivance signifying degenerating literary productions. Lambert catalogs five of these ancient acrostic texts.[8] K 8204 is especially interesting, since "both the first and last syllables of each line form one and the same acrostic."[9] However, it is "The Babylonian Theodicy"[10] which captures the attention of students of Psalm 119. This "syllabic sentence acrostic"[11] is both extensive and intricate:

> The *Theodicy* is an acrostic poem of twenty-seven stanzas of 11 verses each. Nineteen of the stanzas are preserved either completely or sufficiently for the trend of the argument to be apparent. The other eight are either totally lost or inadequately preserved. The acrostic itself can, however, be restored completely and it reads: *a-na-ku sa-ag-gi-il-ki- [i-na-am-u]b-bi-ib ma-áš-ma-šu ka-ri-bu ša i-li ú šar-ri* "I, Saggilkinam-ubbib, the incantation priest, am adorant of the god and the king." . . . The metrical form of the work is outstanding. Each of the 11 lines of the stanzas begins with the same sign, like Psalm 119.[12]

Of great importance is the fact that "the text itself . . . was probably written about 1000 B.C."[13]

---

8 W. G. Lambert, *Babylonian Wisdom Literature* (Oxford: Clarendon Press, 1960), p. 67.

9 Ibid. For a glimpse at the text along with the transliteration and translation, see S. A. Strong, "On Some Babylonian and Assyrian Alliterative Texts," *Proceedings of the Society of Biblical Archeology*, 17 (1895): 138–39.

10 Also known as "The Babylonian Ecclesiastes" or "A Dialogue about Human Misery."

11 I.e. Marcus' appropriately descriptive designation (Ralph Marcus, "Alphabetic acrostics in the Hellenistic and Roman Periods," *JNES*, 6:2 [April, 1947]: 109).

12 Lambert, *Babylonian Wisdom Literature*, pp. 63, 66.

13 Ibid., p. 63.

From the later apocryphal writings comes the acrostic found in Ecclesiasticus 51:13–30.[14] Even before the original Hebrew text was discovered in 1897 reconstructions from the Greek and Syriac versions intimated the presence of an acrostic: "The canticle is, as Bickell perceived and as the Cairo text indicated, an alphabetic acrostic."[15] Portions of the "Third Apocryphal Psalm" (i.e. Psalm 155) from Qumran also give indications of an acrostic arrangement.[16] Skehan's seemingly reserved designation of "a broken alphabet acrostic" is appropriate, but he is adamant in his argument for the classification of Psalm 155 as unreservedly acrostic.[17] Additionally, the evidences of an acrostic arrangement are reflected in the "Apostrophe to Zion."[18]

Criticisms

Older critics, as previously mentioned, unanimously urged a late date for the biblical acrostics solely on the basis of this form. For example, Oesterley in reference to Psalm 119 casually affirmed that "the date, like all the acrostic psalms, is late post-exilic."[19] Obviously, such affirmations are incredible in the light of the Davidic acrostics and early ancient near eastern utilizations of this poetic device: "The acrostic pattern, commonly taken as a sign of lateness, appears in Pss. ix–x, which can scarcely be

[14] See R. H. Charles, ed., *The Apocrypha and Pseudepigrapha of the Old Testament* (Oxford: Clarendon Press, 1913), 1:271–80, 515–17.

[15] J. A. Sanders, *The Psalms Scroll of Qumrân Cave 11*, Discoveries in the Judaean Desert of Jordan, Vol. 4 (Oxford: Clarendon Press, 1965), p. 80.

[16] J. A. Sanders, *The Dead Sea Psalms Scroll* (Ithaca, NY: Cornell University Press, 1967), pp. 110ff.

[17] Patrick W. Skehan, "A Broken Acrostic and Psalm 9," *Catholic Biblical Quarterly*, 27:1 (January 1965): 1–5.

[18] Cf. Sanders, *Dead Sea Psalms Scroll*, pp. 123–27.

[19] W. O. E. Oesterley, *The Psalms* (London: S. P. C. K., 1962), p. 189. This assumption had been widely publicized and became normative among subsequent critics; consequently, and in spite of contrary evidence from recent discoveries, many modern critics obstinately and tenaciously hold on to this antiquated conjecture.

termed late poems, and the several Ugaritic tablets with the letters arranged in alphabetical order suggest that the acrostic pattern may have been used in the Late Bronze Age"[20] [i.e., approximately 1500–1200 B.C.]. Consequently,

> whatever the age of the individual alphabetic compositions, it is clear that the phenomenon cannot be used as a criterion for the dating of biblical texts. The word and sentence acrostic is found in at least five works in Akkadian literature. Although the only two dated examples come from the seventh and sixth centuries B.C.E., there is no reason to doubt that the principle was not in vogue in Mesopotamia much earlier. Moreover, since the traditional order of the alphabetic signs is now known to have been fixed no later than the 14th century B.C.E., there is every likelihood of its early employment in Israel in literary compositions.[21]

Allegations of inferior quality still persist among the critics. The assumption is that this so-called "monotonous and jejune" format[22] necessarily and consistently impedes the poem's content: "In consequence the sequence and substance of the thought are subordinated to the necessities of the formal structure."[23] Concerning all acrostic compositions in the Bible, it has been said that "they have an even looser order of thought than is in any case commonly true of Hebrew poetry."[24] Mowinckel's comment is also exemplary: "When a psalm was tied down to an artificial

---

[20] Dahood, *Psalms*, 3:336.

[21] *Encyclopedia Judaica*, s.v. "Acrostics (and Alphabetizing Compositions)," by Nahum M. Sarna, 2:229.

[22] I.e. Binnie's accurate characterization of their perspective (William Binnie, *The Psalms: Their History, Teachings, and Use* [London: Hodder and Stoughton, 1886], pp. 144–45).

[23] R. B. Y. Scott, *Proverbs, Ecclesiastes*, The Anchor Bible (Garden City, NY: Doubleday and Company, Inc., 1965), p. 186.

[24] Otto Eissfeldt, *The Old Testament: An Introduction*, trans. by Peter Ackroyd (New York: Harper and Row, 1965), p. 501.

'alphabetic' pattern . . . it very otfen [*sic*] resulted in a rambling and obscure train of thought and a loose composition."[25]

However, "to say that acrostics are artificial and therefore dull is to show one's prejudice against a mechanical structural formula":[26]

> Such a form is simple to execute, and allows a free movement from theme to theme without an undue loss of coherence. It is no fetter to the poet's spontaneity, as the psalm itself bears witness with its lively, persuasive invitation to share the singer's joy and learn from his experience.[27]

In addition, it should be pointed out that in the biblical acrostics the content is preeminent as indicated by fluctuations in meter[28] and unexpected deviations:

---

[25] Mowinckel, *The Psalms in Israel's Worship*, 2:77–78.

[26] A. Berkeley Mickelsen, *Interpreting the Bible* (Grand Rapids: William B. Eerdmans, 1963), pp. 330–31. He refers especially to Lam 1–4 in his refutation of the critics' invalid presupposition.

[27] Derek Kidner, *Psalms 1–72* (London: Inter–Varsity Press, 1973), p. 138. Kidner's comment was made in reference to Ps 34; however, it is just as applicable to Ps 119 and the other biblical acrostics. For similar defences, see: Dahood, *Psalms*, 3:172; Maier, *The Book of Nahum*, p. 61; Binnie, *The Psalms*, pp. 144–45; and James Muilenburg, "A Study in Hebrew Rhetoric: Repetition and Style," *Supplements to Vetus Testamentum*, vol. 1 (London: E. J. Brill, 1953), p. 103.

[28] Both Allen's notations on the meter of the individual verses of Ps 119 (Leslie C. Allen, *Psalms 101–150*, Word Biblical Commentary, Vol. 21 [Waco, TX: Word Books, 1983], pp. 126–34) and Anderson's seemingly frustrated metrical synopses (*Psalms*, 2:807) indicate that the psalmist's testimonies and arguments were not suppressed by the alphabetic framework. The acrostic device was not slavishly employed at the expense of the psalm's content.

> For we find in other alphabetic poems also, especially the older ones, many deviations from the rule, which undeniably prove that the composers bound themselves rigorously to the order of the alphabet only so long as it fitted in to the course of thought without any artificiality. . . . We reply that there is no want in these poems of a careful arrangement of thought; but that the skill of the poet, in making use of this arrangement, was not always sufficient to let him put his thoughts, corresponding to things, into the alphabetic form, without using artificial means or forced constructions; and that, in such cases, the form was rather sacrificed to the thought, than rigorously maintained through the adoption of forced and unnatural forms of expression.[29]

Throughout the forthcoming exposition of Psalm 119 it will be seen that the acrostic format, rather than being a detriment,[30] "is a remarkable adjunct to didactic poetry."[31]

Needless to say, for these and other reasons, the use of the acrostic framework as a basis for suggesting textual transpositions and conjectural emendations is exceedingly presumptuous. Even Freedman, noted for his metrical analyses, is careful to publish similar warnings; see: David Noel Freedman, "Acrostics and Metrics in Hebrew Poetry," *Harvard Theological Review*, 65:3 (July 1972): 367–92; and "Archaic Forms in Early Hebrew Poetry," *Zeitschrift Für Die Alttestamentliche Wissenschaft*, 72 (1960): 101–07. Cf. Hans Kosmala, "Form and Structure in Ancient Hebrew Poetry," *Vetus Testamentum*, 14:4 (October 1964): 423–45.

[29] Carl Friedrich Keil, *The Prophecies of Jeremiah*, vol. 2, trans. by James Kennedy, in *Commentary on the Old Testament in Ten Volumes*, by C. F. Keil and F. Delitzsch (Grand Rapids: William B. Eerdmans, n.d.), pp. 338–39; cf. Delitzsch, *Psalms*, 3:388.

[30] Even in the *Hē* and *Wāw* stanzas, which would respectively anticipate causatives and sequences, the author's message is obviously not thwarted by the alphabetic guide; cf. Kidner, *Psalms 73–150*, p. 417.

[31] Harrison, *Introduction to the OT*, p. 968.

Purpose

Many purposes have been suggested for the employment of this literary device in biblical poetry. Unacceptable conjectures include the magical and pedagogical viewpoints.[32] A partially viable suggestion would be the artistic motivation.[33] Ryken has appropriately connected the skillful format and content of Psalm 119 by arguing that "this orderliness reinforces the meaning of the poem, which is the law of God. The poem thus illustrates on an artistic level the beauty of order that it declares to exist on the moral level."[34] However, one should not regard this artistic motivation as constituting the *exclusive* or *primary* purpose for the employment of the device in biblical examples. As a matter of fact, "it is likely that more than one motive was involved" in connection with scriptural occurrences.[35] It may be best to look upon a combination of the next two suggestions also as viable motives for the employment of the device without denying a corollary artistic impetus.

Based upon various utilizations of the acrostic device, Sarna has concluded that "frequently, it must have been used as a mnemonic aid."[36] Apart from some minor objections,[37] the suggestion that this particular format was employed as an aid to the memory is more or less acceptable when applied to the various biblical examples. Nevertheless, it is the suggestion of "exhaustive com-

---

[32] Both of these suggestions are built upon apparently eccentric post–biblical data; for delineations and refutations, see: Hillers, *Lamentations*, p. xxvi; Engnell, *A Rigid Scrutiny*, p. 100; Gottwald, *Lamentations*, pp. 25–26; Harrison, *Introduction to the OT*, p. 1068; and Otto Kaiser, *Introduction to the OT*, trans. by John Sturdy (Minneapolis: Augsburg Publishing House, 1975), p. 355.

[33] E.g. Engnell, *Rigid Scrutiny*, p. 100.

[34] Leland Ryken, *The Literature of the Bible* (Grand Rapids: Zondervan, 1974), p. 153.

[35] Hillers, *Lamentations*, p. xxvi.

[36] Sarna, "Acrostics (and Alphabetizing Compositions)," p. 230; cf. Gottwald, *Lamentations*, p. 32; and Dahood, *Psalms*, 1:54.

[37] Cf. *Encyclopedia Judaica*, s.v. "Mnemonics or Memora Technica," by Louis Isaac Rabinowitz, 12:187; and Harrison, *Introduction to the OT*, p. 1068.

pleteness"[38] which aligns with most of the biblical data: "One of the most plausible explanations for the motif behind the alphabetic arrangement is the idea of completeness. As the writer exhausted the letters of the alphabet, so he exhausted his subject."[39] In addition to several extra-biblical models,[40] the affirmations about our Lord recorded in Revelation 1:8; 21:6; and 22:13 lend their weight to the essence of this proposal. Consequently, the student of biblical acrostics should be aware of the potentiality for mixed motives (i.e. completeness, memory assistance, and corollary artistry) undergirding the employment of this device in the various poems.

Psalm-type Analyses

Some form critics and genre analysts have associated the acrostic format exclusively with the general category of wisdom literature.[41] However,

> any simple theory about the origin and usage of the poetic forms of ancient Israel is likely to be a fallacious one. It is apparent that the poet exercised great freedom in employing diverse forms and images to serve his purpose. Lamentations, with its firm anchorage in the his-

---

[38] Keil's terminology (*Jeremiah*, 2:337).

[39] Maier, *Nahum*, p. 58; cf. Gottwald's summation: "Those who entertain this idea of completeness, therefore, instinctively feel that in naming the whole alphabet one comes as close as man may to a total development of any theme or the complete expression of any emotion or belief. If the subject is to be exhausted, the alphabet alone can suffice to suggest and symbolize the totality striven after" (*Lamentations*, p. 29).

[40] E.g., "in a Midrash we find . . . 'Adam transgressed the whole law from *Aleph* to *Taw*,' and again, 'Abraham kept the whole law from *Aleph* to *Taw*'" (Gottwald, *Lamentations*, p. 30).

[41] E.g., J. Kenneth Kuntz, "The Canonical Wisdom Psalms of Ancient Israel: Their Rhetorical, Thematic and Formal Dimensions," in *Rhetorical Criticism: Essays in Honor of James Muilenburg*, ed. by Jared J. Jackson and Martin Kessler (Pittsburg: Pickwick Press, 1974), p. 210.

> torical events of the sixth century B.C., might very well be used as a touchstone for reconsidering various theories about the literary types of Israelite poetry, notably those advanced by Hermann Gunkel, Rudolph Smend, and Sigmund Mowinckel. It would appear now that the views of these critics, so instructive in many respects, were too rigid to do justice to the sovereign freedom of the poet and the catalytic impact of historical circumstance.[42]

Although one may say that the 119th Psalm is "essentially a didactic poem," he must also acknowledge that it "takes the form of a personal testimony. . . . Its main purpose is to glorify the Tôrâ."[43]

Soll offers one of the best *technical* analyses concluding that "Ps. 119 is both an individual lament and a meditation on Torah at the same time, throughout."[44] Nevertheless, "this Psalm incorporates many elements of different psalm-types, e.g. blessing (verses 1–3), lamentation (verses 153–60), thanksgiving (verse 7), and assertion

---

[42] Norman K. Gottwald, "Studia Biblica: XXX. Lamentations," *Interpretation*, 9:3 (July 1955): 327.

[43] Kyle M. Yates, Jr., "Psalms," in *Wycliffe Bible Commentary*, ed. by Charles F. Pfeiffer and Everett F. Harrison (Nashville, TN: Southwestern Company, 1962), p. 539.

[44] William Michael Soll, "Psalm 119: The Hermeneutic of an Acrostic Lament," unpublished Ph.D. dissertation (Nashville, TN: Vanderbilt University, 1982), p. 122; cf. his whole argument in chapter four entitled "The Individual Lament Genre and Psalm 119," pp. 121–152. The following excerpts document the essential objectivity of his research: "The most basic forms within the individual lament are *petition* and *lament*. . . . Sixty verses in Ps. 119 (over a third of the verses) contain a petition, either in the jussive mood . . . or, more frequently, in the imperative mood. . . . The form of the lament occurs in thirty–eight verses of Ps. 119. . . . All in all, ninety verses (more than half the number in the psalm) contain either petition, lament or both. . . . While genre cannot be established on this kind of statistical basis, this substantial recurrence of petition and lament makes a good *prima facie* case for considering other speech forms in Ps. 119 in the light of the individual lament tradition" (ibid., pp. 135–37).

of innocence (verses 97–106)."[45] Allen concurs and well concludes that in reference to forms the psalmist was quite eclectic:

> There is the description characteristic of the complaint, concerning the speaker, e.g. vv 25a, 143a, and concerning his enemies, e.g. vv 51a, 85, the confession of trust, e.g. vv 57a, 137a, and prayer for help, e.g. vv 94a, 149. Assertions of innocence as motivations for Yahweh to intervene appear in the form of devotion to the Torah, e.g. vv 30, 61, and obedience, e.g. vv 31a, 51b. The vow of praise associated with the complaint has become a vow of future obedience, e.g. vv 34, 44, 57b. The confession of trust is often Torah-centered, e.g. vv 20, 105. This orientation toward the Torah is also evident in the wisdom elements of the psalm, such as beatitudes, vv 1-3, and comparative sayings, vv 72, 127. The psalm's hymnic praise can often be included in the element of confession of trust, but often it is too strongly accentuated to be subordinated to the complaint in this way. Accordingly Ps 119 may best be described as a medley of praise, prayer and wisdom features.[46]

Poetic Parallelisms

Psalm 119 is obviously poetic, and therefore, the normal varieties of Hebrew parallelism should be anticipated. These conceptual interrelationships will be highlighted throughout the analyses of the stanzas in Part III.

---

[45] Anderson, *Psalms*, 2:806; from this, he concludes, "It is quite possible that the intention of the author was to produce a Wisdom poem in the widest sense of the word, without imitating any particular psalm–type" (ibid.).

[46] Allen, *Psalms 101–150*, p. 140.

TEXTUAL ASSESSMENT

The Hebrew Text

The traditional Hebrew text (i.e. Masoretic text [MT]) of Psalm 119 does not preoccupy the exegete with a plethora of textual enigmas and problems. When Hebrew manuscripts and the early versions are compared a high degree of confidence in the traditional text ensues. Almost all the variations are phenomena of optional spellings or differences in singulars and plurals.

The Dead Sea Scrolls

Confidence in the MT of the 119th Psalm has been bolstered through the Qumran discoveries. Fragments of the psalm were found in caves one, four, and five; however, it was the *Psalms Scroll* from cave eleven which has yielded 65% of the text of Psalm 119.[1] Concerning the variants, "there are about a dozen points of interest in the scores of minor variants to Psalm 119 in the *Psalms Scroll*, but only a few command attention."[2] It may be helpful to divide the variants into two classes for the purpose of brief analysis, those which are likely to have been actual and those which are apparently deliberate.

---

1 Sanders, *Dead Sea Psalms Scroll*, p. 17. From this textual representation, Sanders rightly concludes that "certainly one of the most popular psalms at Qumran was the one hundred and nineteenth" (ibid.).

2 Ibid.

Most of the actual variants "are orthographic and important only to those scholars who are interested in clues to the pronunciation of Hebrew in antiquity, and such matters."[3] One of the more significant variants, however, occurs in verses 37, 40, 88, 107, 132, 156, and 159.[4] While the MT exhibits forms built upon the root חיה (*ḥyh*) in these verses, the Qumranic text displays appropriately inflected forms of the root חנן (*ḥnn*).[5] The former root has to do with making or preserving alive (e.g. "revive me"), and the latter connotes acting graciously (i.e. "be gracious to me"). "Contextually," it must be admitted that the חונני of the manuscript from Qumran "is a possible reading in each case where it stands."[6] However, this does not furnish an automatic precedent for emending the MT.[7] As a matter of fact, the ancient Greek version, the Septuagint (LXX), in this particular case would indicate that it was reflecting an early Hebrew textual tradition which stood in agreement with the MT by a ratio of six to one. Apart from these and other relatively technical considerations, it should be observed that both roots convey essentially the same thought and that either would be in accordance with the immediate and larger circles of context doctrinally.

---

[3] Ibid., p. 15. Almost all of these relate to full or defective spellings; for example, "generally speaking *ḥolem, shureq, qibbuṣ*, and *qameṣ ḥaṭuf* are indicated by *waw*" (Sanders, *The Psalms Scroll of Qumrân Cave 11*, Discoveries Judaean Desert, 4:9). This is true also of its employment of *yoḏ*. In Eng such a phenomenon could be illustrated by a document which would consistently employ the spelling judg*e*ment rather than judgment. Pronominal suffixes usually follow the precedent of historically longer forms.

[4] Sanders is correct in assuming "that the scribe reliably transmitted what he received" (*The Psalms Scroll of Qumran Cave 11*, 4:11).

[5] Both are obviously to be construed as masculine singular imperatives with first person singular suffixes.

[6] Sanders, *The Psalms Scroll of Qumran Cave 11*, 4:11.

[7] "While the Psalms Scroll is considerably older than the medieval Leningrad text [cf. the MT], it contains some errors, recognizable as such without debate. The fact that it affords us a copy of some of the psalms much older than any we had heretofore does not mean that every reading in it is always to be preferred to those in younger manuscripts" (Sanders, *Dead Sea Psalms Scroll*, p. 15).

The outlook and theological presuppositions of the Qumranic community quite obviously stand behind those few occurrences of deliberate variations. Sanders' examples and evaluations are illuminating:

> In two verses in Psalm 119 verbs are read as active where in other manuscripts they are passive:
>
> It is good for me that *I was afflicted,*
> that I might learn thy statutes.
> [119:71—RSV]
>
> It is good that *thou didst afflict me,*
> that I might learn thy statutes.
> [119:71—11QPs[a]]
>
> For *I have become* like a wineskin in the smoke,
> yet I have not forgotten thy *statutes.*
> [119:83—RSV]
>
> For *thou hast made me* like a wineskin in the smoke,
> yet I have not forgotten thy *steadfast love.*
> [119:83—11QPs[a]]
>
> In both instances God is seen, in the scroll's readings, as the active agent of the psalmist's condition. Theologically the variants are very interesting in the light of the expectations of most Jewish sects in the first century . . . that God was the cause of the afflictions which were seen as prelude to the dramatic events of salvation soon to be supernaturally introduced into history. It is perhaps the same light in which a further variant should be read:
>
> The unfolding of thy words gives light;
> *it* imparts understanding to the simple.
> [119:130—RSV]
>
> Unfold thy words, and enlighten him
> *who* imparts understanding to the simple.
> [119:130—11QPs[a]]

> These look like purposive changes in the text made perhaps by someone . . . whose teachings and sufferings were viewed under a strong belief in divine sovereignty.[8]

The Septuagint and Other Early Versions

Most of the variants in the LXX involve disagreements in number. For example, the Greek version may have a plural noun at a juncture where the MT exhibits a singular. This common phenomenon is almost always immediately clarified by contextual associations in the Hebrew text and is therefore not a matter of consequence. Any individual variations in the Greek text of a more conspicuous nature will be dealt with upon occurrence in the forthcoming translation notes. Periodic references to variations from other early versions, ranging from the Latin Vulgate to the Aramaic Targum,[9] will be offered mainly for their hermeneutical rather than textual interest.

8 Ibid., pp. 17–18. Sanders goes on to show how the sect's basic teachings would corroborate his evaluations; nevertheless, he wisely cautions against utilizing historically constructed scenarios for the purpose of rejecting or possibly even accepting some of these variants (ibid.).

9 Generally speaking, the Targum of Ps 119 is surprisingly literal in vocabulary and reduplicated syntax.

PART II:

OVERVIEW

ANALYTICAL OVERVIEW

Macro-development

A variety of opinions have surfaced throughout hermeneutical history in reference to the progression of thought or lack of it in Psalm 119. Most observers will concede periodic inter-strophic continuities (i.e. within each eight-verse stanza); however, they would characteristically challenge the existence of any kind of definitive intra-strophic progression.[1] On the other hand, there have been some commentators who have fabricated elaborate developments from the first verse right on through the 176th.[2] Based upon prolonged meditations over the psalm as a whole, it is apparent that the truth lies somewhere in between these poles of contention. This great psalm evidences a continuity of thought that could well be described as general, variable, and sporadically transparent.[3]

---

1 Obviously, some have objected to any kind of continuity; cf. Artur Weiser, *The Old Testament: Its Formation and Development*, trans. by Dorothea M. Barton (New York: Association Press, 1968), p. 25. This has even been true of a few conservatives (e.g. Hengstenberg and Barnes).

2 Cf. Delitzsch, *Psalms*, 3:244; and Thrupp, *The Psalms*, 2:248–52.

3 Kidner's statement reflects this kind of conception: "While different thoughts tend to predominate in different stanzas, . . . they are mingled with others that constantly recur" (*Psalms 73–150*, p. 417).

One of the most pleasing analyses of inter- and intra-strophic continuities comes from Soll. The following excerpts reflect his commitment to inductivity:

> The question of the coherence of the psalm must still be addressed. . . . That the psalm has a strong unity of subject matter has long been noted, and this, combined with unity of genre, may be said to constitute a reasonably unified poem by Hebrew standards. . . . The degree of logic within each strophe varies; sometimes the argument is quite clear. . . . The *Aleph* strophe serves as a prologue to the psalm. . . . Not all the strophes are as tightly wrought as this one, but at least we have grounds to expect some progression of thought, and in many cases the careful reader will not come away empty-handed. . . . Fully granting the repetitive and concentric nature of thought in Ps. 119, the psalm may nonetheless be said to have a certain order and argument. . . . The *Aleph* and *Beth* strophes function as a kind of prologue to the psalm, stating the problem and the means whereby the problem will be addressed. With the *Gimel* strophe, the lament proper begins. . . . The letter *lamed* can provide a turning point in alphabetic acrostics (see especially Pss. 9–10, 34) since the second half of the alphabet begins with it. . . . If the conventional lament motifs enter the psalm with the *Gimel* strophe, they positively dominate the *Kaph* strophe. The increase of these motifs in this strophe is dramatic, and one may fairly see this strophe as the nadir of the psalm. By contrast, the first three verses of the *Lamed* strophe constitute the psalm's zenith; we are transported to the heavens and to the beginning. . . . The *Lamed* stanza ends with the psalmist's assertion that, while everything he has seen has a limit, Torah is "exceedingly broad" . . . . In the *Mem* stanza, the psalmist gives himself leave to enjoy that breadth. . . . The strophes that follow (*Nun* through *Shin*) are not markedly different from *Gimel* through *Yod*, except that

they are more confident and forward-looking. . . . Two characteristics of the *Taw* strophe make it appropriate for the conclusion of the poem: the vow of praise (vv. 171–2) and the jussive petitions (vv. 169–70, 173–5). . . . The following outline summarizes the argument of Ps. 119:

I. *Aleph–Beth*: Prologue
Aleph—The problem
Beth—The method

II. *Gimel–Yod*: Initial Prayer Section
Gimel–He—Petition and lament
Waw—Promises (dependent on initial petition)
Zayin–Yod—Personal retrospective, consolation
(Yod—first collection jussive prayers)

III. *Kaph–Mem*: Central Section
Kaph—Intense lamentation
Lamed—Consolation through an "eternal" perspective
Mem—Enjoyment of Torah

IV. *Nun–Shin*: Second Prayer Section
More confident and forward-looking

V. *Taw*: Conclusion

Vow of praise and final jussive prayers . . .

The psalm may be said to have an argument. It is an argument of prayer and meditation, not of analytical demonstration. Like an arch or a Shakespearean tragedy, it reaches its climax in the middle, and lets the subsequent strophes function as a return to normalcy. One returns, it is hoped, with a greater measure of resolve and understanding than one had at the beginning.[4]

---

[4] Soll, "Psalm 119," pp. 152–53, 155–57, 161–65.

In other words, the psalmist's emotional affirmations and petitions may be plotted, as they rise and fall, along an acrostic parabola. And yet, through its subtlety of incorporation and development, there is no encroachment upon spontaneity.

Micro-development

Although "each separate verse possesses a certain completeness in itself . . . , the very structure of each strophe, when fairly examined, will generally show that its eight several verses cannot be regarded as independent of each other."[5] Consequently, "we may reasonably assume . . . that within each stanza . . . there must at the least be a general suitability of one thought to another."[6] This is quite consistently confirmed by the surfacing of a major burden within each eight-verse stanza. Such emphases are bonded together within the strophes by all kinds of literary glue.[7] The major burden and development of each stanza will be addressed in Part III under the heading "Synopsis and Outline."

---

[5] Thrupp, *The Psalms*, 2:246–48; he elaborates by arguing that "without necessarily conforming to the law of strictly logical consecutiveness, the different parts of a meditation may yet be moderately connected; and it seems reasonable to suppose that in the working out of each separate strophe a train of thought would generally suggest itself to the psalmist's mind" (ibid.). Or in the words of Kaiser, "The question of whether it is possible to group lines of Hebrew poetry into stanzas or strophes was stimulated by the work of Friedrich B. Köster in 1831. While some scholars remained skeptical, it is plain from the existence of acrostic poems such as Psalm 119 that such an arrangement is not only possible, but actually required. Hence, what the paragraph is to the exegete of prose, the strophe is to the exegete of poetry" (Walter C. Kaiser, Jr., *Toward an Exegetical Theology* [Grand Rapids: Baker, 1981], p. 214).

[6] Leslie S. M'Caw, "The Psalms," *The New Bible Commentary Revised*, ed. by D. Guthrie and J. A. Motyer (Grand Rapids: William B. Eerdmans, 1970), pp. 526–27; cf. Charles Augustus Briggs, *A Critical and Exegetical Commentary on the Book of Psalms*, vol. 2, ICC (New York: Charles Scribner's Sons, 1911), pp. 409–10.

[7] E.g. poetic parallelisms and other structural indicators.

THEOLOGICAL OVERVIEW: APPLIED BIBLIOLOGY

Words for the Word

Psalm 119 is a veritable gold mine on Bibliology. However, prior to synthesizing any theological conclusions, it is wise to examine the psalm's bibliological data inductively. This procedure not only assures statistical accuracy but also lends credibility to subsequent theological formulations.

The Synonyms

Although all agree that God's special revelation is the gemstone of these 176 verses, there has been disagreement over the number, frequency, and distribution of words which may be regarded as quasi-technical terms for the Word.[1] When the various Hebrew roots are carefully evaluated in their contextual settings, it seems best to conclude that *eight* synonyms for God's Word surface.[2] It should be noted that

> there is no regularity in their use. All eight occur once in four strophes, *ḥeth*, *yod*, *kaph* and *pe*, while the *waw* stro-

[1] For example, some would regard an attribute *of* or a response *to* God's Word as a technical term thereby concluding that there should be a total of nine or ten synonyms. Masoretic tradition claims that there is a synonym in every verse except one (i.e. v. 122). Others would vie for a distribution of technical terms for the Word in all but two, three, or four verses. Tabulations also vary on the number of verses which exhibit more than one quasi-technical term.

[2] "The number of lines seems to have been determined by the use of eight synonyms for the focus of the psalmist's interest, the 'Torah.' Five of these occur too in Ps 19B, upon which this psalm may be dependent" (Allen, *Psalms 101–150*, p. 139).

> phe uses one term twice . . . . The other strophes exhibit seven or six of the synonyms, using them from seven to nine times in each case. The psalmist did not strive for symmetrical perfection: two synonyms appear per line in vv 16, 48 (in MT), 160, 168 and 172 . . . .[3]

Seven verses are devoid of quasi-technical employments of these roots as bibliological terms.[4] The following tabulations are presented in the order in which the terms are introduced in the psalm. Preliminarily, it should be pointed out that each of the root connotations reflects a nuance of the Word and/or its relationship to the believer. Nevertheless, the terms are true synonyms in the sense that each ultimately comes to represent biblical revelation in toto.

תּוֹרָה (*tôrâ*)

In verse one we encounter the first word for the Word, תּוֹרָה (*tôrâ*). Throughout the remainder of the psalm it recurs twenty-four times.[5] This feminine singular noun, variously rendered as "direction, instruction, law,"[6] is derived from the root ירה (yrh) which in the Hiphil stem denotes the functions of pointing out, di-

---

[3] Ibid.

[4] In vv. 3 and 37, דֶּרֶךְ (*derek*) should not be regarded as a term for the Word of God per se but as a designation for the ethical consequences which emanate from both God's person and His precepts. מִשְׁפָּט (*mišpāṭ*) in the context of v. 84 is a reference to Divine retribution, and the occurrence of the same root in v. 132 should be regarded as part of an idiomatic prepositional phrase. The אֱמוּנָה (*'ĕmûnâ*) of v. 90 conveys an attribute of God. Neither of the two terms in v. 121 is being used as a direct designation for the Word of God, and of course, all are in agreement that v. 122 contains no synonym.

[5] Its 25 occurrences are as follows: vv. 1, 18, 29, 34, 44, 51, 53, 55, 61, 70, 72, 77, 85, 92, 97, 109, 113, 126, 136, 142, 150, 153, 163, 165, 174.

[6] Francis Brown; S. R. Driver; and C. A. Briggs; eds., *A Hebrew and English Lexicon of the Old Testament* (Oxford: Clarendon Press, 1962), p. 435. Hereinafter this source will be cited as BDB.

recting, teaching, or instructing.[7] Girdlestone legitimately builds upon this semantical foundation when he argues:

> The verb (ירה) whence it is derived signifies to project, and hence to point out or teach. The law of God is that which points out or indicates His will to man. It is not an arbitrary rule, still less is it a subjective impulse; it is rather to be regarded as a course of guidance from above. The verb and the noun are found together in Exod. 24:12, 'I will give thee a law, and commandments which I have written, that thou mayest teach them.' It is generally, though imperfectly, represented in the LXX by the word νόμος.[8]

Although not discussed by him, Girdlestone's last observation is of great theological significance. It seems that the Septuagint's rendering has paved the way for subsequent legalistic conceptions of תּוֹרָה and, in reaction, for periodic antinomian responses which have unfortunately emanated from the Body of Christ. Dodd quickly diagnoses the root of the problem when he notes that νόμος (*nomos*) "is by no means an exact equivalent for תּוֹרָה and its substitution for the Hebrew term affords an illustration of a change in the ideas associated with the term—*a difference in men's notion of what religion is*" (emphasis added).[9]

However, in the light of the broader connotation of תּוֹרָה in the Book of Deuteronomy,[10] some scattered but very similar occur-

---

[7] Ibid. It is interesting that the Targum of Ps 119 renders תּוֹרָה by אוֹרַיְתָא (*'ôrayᵉtâ*) which has the meanings of "instruction, the Law, Bible-verse" (Marcus Jastrow, ed., *A Dictionary of the Targumim, the Talmud Babli and Yerushalmi, and the Midrashic Literature* [New York: Pardes Publishing House, 1950], 1:34).

[8] Girdlestone, *Synonyms*, p. 206.

[9] C. H. Dodd, *The Bible and the Greeks* (London: Hodder and Stoughton, 1935), p. 25; emphasis added.

[10] Soll well argues that in Deuteronomy תּוֹרָה is "a comprehensive designation for the entire body of legislation deriving from Yahweh and given through Moses" ("Psalm 119," pp. 69–71).

rences of תּוֹרָה / νόμος in other books of the Old and New Testaments,[11] and its consistent usage in Psalm 119, "law" should be understood as also demonstrating a biblically documented wider connotation of "an immanent or underlying principle of life and action"[12] rather than merely a narrowly and legalistically perceived code of mandates. Consequently, תּוֹרָה in such contexts refers to "Scripture as a whole,"[13] and furthermore, "as canonical scriptures in which God has made known his character and purpose for his people. It is hailed as Yahweh's communication of moral truth and demonstration of his grace and guidance."[14] Therefore, "the 'law' which the poet describes in Ps. 119 is not a yoke which 'neither our fathers nor we have been able to bear' (Ac. 15:10). To the Psalmist the *tôrāh* is a gift of God, which was both preceded and followed by divine grace."[15]

In review, תּוֹרָה in Psalm 119 is not to be taken restrictively, but as a comprehensive designation for the totality of God's precep-

[11] E.g. Isa, Jer, Prov (cf. Allen, *Psalms 101–150*, p. 141); also note the *law's* comprehensive scope in John 10:34, quoting Ps 82:6 (also notice the parallelism with "Scripture" in v. 35); John 15:25, quoting Ps 35:19; Rom 3:19, quoting passages from the Pss and Isa in vv. 10b–18; 1 Cor 14:21, quoting Isa 28:11; etc.

[12] Dodd, *The Bible and the Greeks*, p. 25. After much substantive argumentation (cf. pp. 25–40), he concludes that there is an area of affinity between the two terms when each is viewed in its broadest context: תּוֹרָה (*tôrâ*) "in its widest sense means divine teaching or revelation: νόμος in its widest sense means a principle of life or action" (ibid., p. 40).

[13] Kidner, *Psalms 73–150*, p. 418.

[14] Allen, *Psalms 101–150*, pp. 141–42.

[15] Anderson, *Psalms*, 2:808; cf. 1 John 5:3. Our psalmist demonstrated the transdispensational truth so well articulated by Kaiser: "Biblical law and the gospel of God's grace are not archrivals but twin mercies given by the same gracious Lord who did not wish his people in any age to be impoverished but to enjoy life to the fullest" (Walter C. Kaiser, Jr., "God's Promise Plan and His Gracious Law," *JETS* 33:3 [Sept 90]: 302). The validity of both Anderson's and Kaiser's assertions will be documented through forthcoming discussions.

tive directions.[16] And yet, תּוֹרָה refracts a special hue through its semantical facet on this scriptural gemstone; it depicts God's special revelation as a gracious gift which points out or *shows the way* through life's twisted highways and byways.

עֵדָה / עֵדוּת (*ᶜēḏâ / ᶜēḏûṯ*)

Verse two introduces us to a second bibliological word group.[17] Including verse two, there are twenty-three occurrences of feminine nouns from this word group in Psalm 119.[18] Throughout the Bible, these nouns are well rendered by "testimonies" (or "testimony" for the singulars),[19] since their parent verb עוּד (*ᶜûḏ*) means "to bear witness."[20] The inference is that "the law of God is His testimony, because it is His own affirmation concerning His

---

[16] Soll well concludes that "in general, the word seems to indicate God's overall direction for Israel" ("Psalm 119," pp. 71–72). It should also be noted that via poetic parallelisms and conceptual juxtapositions with תּוֹרָה, all the other words for the Word in Ps 119 participate in this wholistic emphasis (even though only תּוֹרָה and אִמְרָה [*'imrâ*] are employed consistently in the singular).

[17] BDB, p. 730, suggests that some plural forms derive from a conjectured feminine noun עֵדָה, while the others come from its sister noun עֵדוּת. For argumentation that all the occurrences are related to עֵדוּת, see Soll, "Psalm 119," p. 84.

[18] The composite distribution is as follows: vv. 2, 14, 22, 24, 31, 36, 46, 59, 79, 88, 95, 99, 111, 119, 125, 129, 138, 144, 146, 152, 157, 167, 168. It should be noted that all are inflected as plurals except the form in v. 88 which is singular (cf. Ps 19:8 [v. 7, Eng]).

[19] Because of some conspicuous parallelisms with בְּרִית (*bᵉrîṯ*) "covenant," and a substantial amount of extra-biblical evidence relating this word to vassal treaty contexts, some would prefer the more nuanced meaning of "covenant stipulations," etc. (e.g. Dahood, *Psalms*, 3:173).

[20] Eddleman comments, "The word is the same as that used for court room procedure. It is the highest revelation of God available to man. Sometimes used to refer to the Ten Commandments, 'testimony' . . . can mean either the direct claims of God about himself or the evidence set forth in the Scriptures concerning him" (H. Leo Eddleman, "Word Pictures of the Word: An Exposition of Psalm 19," *Review and Expositor*, 40 [1952]: 418). It should also be noted that throughout Ps 119 the LXX renders these Hebrew nouns with appropriate forms from the μάρτυς (*martys*) word group.

nature, attributes, and consequent demands."[21] Another member of this semantical family, עֵד (*ᶜēḏ*), sharpens the bibliological focus even more: "Israel was told to place the book of the law beside the ark of the covenant, 'that it may be there for a witness ('ē*d*) against you' (Dt. 31:26). The outspokenness of Scripture, with its high standards and frank warnings (e.g. Dt. 8:19, using this root), is implied in this expression . . . ."[22] The Word of God as "testimonies" emphasizes both the authority of their source in the LORD and the accountability of their reception by men.

פִּקּוּדִים (*piqqûḏîm*)

Occurring third, commencing in verse 4,[23] is a masculine noun derived from the verb פָּקַד (*pāqaḏ*).[24] This verbal root exhibits several semantical fields such as to attend to, to visit, to muster, and to appoint.[25] The last activity is of primary significance for the noun פִּקּוּד (*piqqûḏ*), a thing appointed, a charge.[26] Eddleman correctly emphasizes the connection when he argues:

---

[21] Girdlestone, *Synonyms*, p. 209.

[22] Kidner, *Psalms 73–150*, p. 418; cf. Koehler and Baumgartner's renderings of "monitory sign, reminder" for עֵדוּת (L. Koehler and Walter Baumgartner, eds., *Lexicon in Veteris Testamenti Libros* [Leiden: E. J. Brill, 1958], p. 683). Hereinafter this lexicon will be referred to as KB.

[23] Remembering that v. 3 exhibits no quasi-technical synonym.

[24] Twenty-one out of this noun's 24 biblical occurrences are found in Ps 119; cf. vv. 4, 15, 27, 40, 45, 56, 63, 69, 78, 87, 93, 94, 100, 104, 110, 128, 134, 141, 159, 168, 173. All the forms cited above are plural constructs, and all but one (i.e. v. 128) have second masculine singular suffixes referring to the LORD (i.e. He is the sovereign source of these orders).

[25] BDB, p. 823.

[26] Ibid, p. 824; and yet Kidner has a point when he stresses another dimension of semantical background: "This is a word drawn from the sphere of an officer or overseer, a man who is responsible to look closely into a situation and take action (cf. Je. 23:2, where God will 'attend to' (*pōqēḏ*) the shepherds who have not 'attended to' the flock). So the word points to the particular instructions of the Lord, as of one who cares about detail" (*Psalms 73–150*, p. 418).

> This reference to the Word of Yahweh as "precepts" savors of oral or written declarations as to what he expects of man. The original meaning carries the idea of fix, appoint, designate; here is an intimation of the sovereignty of Yahweh. While the word in itself does not carry the idea of arbitrariness, it is obvious that Yahweh had the right and power to make such declarations and statements regarding man's obligations toward him. While the chief note of these verses is that the "law" is good and of friendly purpose, it is not wholly devoid of the idea that man must submit to it or suffer the consequences.[27]

Consequently, acceptable renderings for these פִּקּוּדִים (*piqqûḏîm*) would be the "precepts,"[28] "orders,"[29] or "charges"[30] which flow from man's Master.

---

[27] Eddleman, "Word Pictures of the Word," p. 419.

[28] BDB, p. 824. This traditional rendering will be retained throughout the forthcoming translation.

[29] KB, p. 774.

[30] Allen, *Psalms 101–150*, pp. 126–34. Soll opts for "instructions" based upon the following reasoning: "The traditional translation of *piqqudîm* is 'precepts,' but 'charges' would be more accurate, conveying as it does both a sense of trust and of a particular task to be discharged. However, other connotations of 'charges' make it an unwise choice for a translation. The term 'instructions' will be used in the present translation, since it is at least more applicable to the carrying out of an appointed trust than 'precepts,' which often simply refers to general rules of conduct" ("Psalm 119," p. 87).

חֹק / חֻקָּה (*ḥōq* / *ḥuqqâ*)

Masculine plurals and one feminine plural (i.e. v. 16) from this noun group occur a total of twenty-two times throughout the psalm.[31] That these nouns convey "something prescribed, a statute or due"[32] is confirmed by their derivation from the root חקק (*ḥqq*). "This word comes from a root which means to hew, cut in, engrave, inscribe; and so comes to mean what is ordained, decreed, prescribed, enacted."[33] The common denominator is revelational and applicational indelibility; these "statutes" have been "written down and preserved for permanent observance."[34] Isaiah 30:8 provides a graphic context for this root's bibliological significance of "the binding force and permanence of Scripture."[35]

מִצְוָה (*miṣwâ*)

This fifth term for special revelation in Psalm 119 occurs as a feminine plural noun 21 times and also as a feminine (collective) singular in verse 96.[36] "Commandment" is an appropriate translation based upon its semantical heritage: "The most general word for command or commandment is some form of *tsavah* (צוה), which appears to signify literally *to set up* or *appoint*. It is used from Gen. 2:16 onward, and applies to any order, human or divine."[37] "This word emphasizes the straight authority of what is

---

[31] See vv. 5, 8, 12, 16 (feminine form), 23, 26, 33, 48, 54, 64, 68, 71, 80, 83, 112, 117, 118, 124, 135, 145, 155, 171.

[32] BDB, p. 349.

[33] Scroggie, *Psalms*, p. 172; Dodd passes along a common perception concerning this association: "חֹק or חֻקָּה is derived from חָקַק = to cut, because, it is said, statutes were engraved on tablets of stone or metal" (*The Bible and the Greeks*, p. 27). Note also that Dodd offers some appropriate observations on δικαίωμα (*dikaiōma*) which is the preferred Greek rendering for these Hebrew words throughout Ps 119 (ibid., pp. 27–28).

[34] Allen, *Psalms 101–150*, p. 134.

[35] Kidner, *Psalms 73–150*, p. 418.

[36] The combined references are vv. 6, 10, 19, 21, 32, 35, 47, 48, 60, 66, 73, 86, 96, 98, 115, 127, 131, 143, 151, 166, 172, 176.

[37] Girdlestone, *Synonyms*, p. 207. Throughout Ps 119 the LXX renders the Hebrew nouns by appropriate forms of the Greek noun ἐντολή (*entolē*).

said; not merely the power to convince or persuade, but the right to give orders."[38] Therefore, as a designation for the Divine commandments inscripturated it "expresses the insistent will of a personal God who is Israel's Lord."[39]

מִשְׁפָּט (*mišpāṭ*)

Various forms of this masculine noun occur 23 times throughout the psalm's 176 verses,[40] and many, but not all of these, may be viewed as quasi-technical terms for God's Word. Contextual ambiguities arise because of the background and nature of the root שפט (*špṭ*). The verb שָׁפַט (*šāpaṭ*) from which the noun derives means "to judge,"[41] with the whole family bearing this forensic freight.[42] Consequently, a מִשְׁפָּט may denote "an act of judging, or its result, a judgment."[43] At times, the psalmist employs מִשְׁפָּט as a request for Divine intervention, a beneficent act of judgment,[44] while in other contexts he refers to the Judge's "revealed decisions or judgments" (i.e. His inscripturated ordinances).[45] Both

---

[38] Kidner, *Psalms 73–150*, p. 418.

[39] Allen, *Psalms 101–150*, p. 134.

[40] Survey vv. 7, 13, 20, 30, 39, 43 (should be construed as a plural), 52, 62, 75, 84 (singular should be understood as "justice"), 91, 102, 106, 108, 120, 121 (this singular also refers to "justice"), 132 (a singular which is part of an idiomatic prepositional phrase), 137, 149 (should be construed as a plural or possibly as a singular in an idiomatic prepositional phrase), 156, 160 (best taken as a collective singular), 164, 175 (should be construed as a plural). It should be stressed, however, that "the singular is never used to refer to an individual ordinance" (Soll, "Psalm 119," p. 81).

[41] Cf. BDB, pp. 1047–49.

[42] Cf. Allen, *Psalms 101–150*, p. 134.

[43] Dodd, *The Bible and the Greeks*, p. 29; cf. the significance of the LXX's preference of κρίματα (*krimata*) for מִשְׁפָּט (ibid.).

[44] Cf. Scroggie's "a judicial decision or sentence" (*The Psalms*, p. 171) and Eddleman's "a statement of the law resulting from its application to an individual case" ("Word Pictures of the Word," p. 422), i.e. a "ruling" (Allen, *Psalms 101–150*, p. 126).

[45] Delitzsch, *Psalms*, 3:249.

sub-categories of usage[46] "point to rules of righteous administration."[47]

דָּבָר (*dāḇār*)

"The most general term for God's communication of His will to man" is דָּבָר (*dāḇār*).[48] Etymological conjectures[49] are generally stretched and practically fruitless. Singular or plural forms[50] of this very common noun refer to the "Word of God, as a divine communication in the form of commandments, prophecy, and words of help to his people" about 400 times in the OT.[51] Focusing on the bibliologically significant occurrences in our psalm, Anderson observes that "*dāḇār* is the divine word which proceeds from the mouth (or lips) of God. . . . Consequently, this word or words

---

[46] Kidner interrelates these categories of occurrence in the following manner: "These [i.e. מִשְׁפָּטִים (*mišpāṭîm*)] are better known in the Old Testament as 'judgments': the decisions of the all-wise Judge about common human situations (cf. Ex. 21:1; Dt. 17:8a, 9b), and hence the revealed 'rights and duties' appropriate to them (as RSV puts it in I Sa. 10:25). Scripture, then, as the standard given for fair dealing between man and man, is a predominant sense of this term" (*Psalms 73–150*, pp. 418–19).

[47] Girdlestone, *Synonyms*, p. 209. An ethical emphasis is discernible throughout the Bible (e.g. מִשְׁפָּטִים are generally "verdicts of the divine judge concerning moral issues" [Allen, *Psalms 101–150*, p. 134]) and especially in the 119th Ps: "The word *mišpāṭîm* emphasizes, for our psalmist, the moral dimension of the law: six times they are described as *ṣedeq* ('righteous,' vv. 7, 62, 75, 106, 160 . . . , 164), once as *ṭôb* ('good,' v. 39), and once as *yāšār* ('right' or 'fair,' v. 137)" (Soll, "Psalm 119," p. 81).

[48] A. F. Kirkpatrick, *The Book of Psalms* (Cambridge: University Press, 1939), p. 704.

[49] Cf. Edmond Jacob, *Theology of the Old Testament*, trans. by Arthur W. Heathcote and Philip J. Allcock (New York: Harper and Row Publishers, 1958), p. 128; *Theological Dictionary of the New Testament* [hereinafter: *TDNT*], s.v. "λέγω, λόγος," by A. Debrunner, *et al.*, 4:92; etc.

[50] Often in the MT it is difficult to determine, in the light of textual evidence, which are to be construed as true singulars; this is especially true in reference to this term's occurrences in the psalm before us.

[51] BDB, p. 182; cf. Kidner, *Psalms 73–150*, p. 419. In Ps 119, note the following 24 occurrences of this word for "word": vv. 9, 16, 17, 25, 28, 42 (x2), 43, 49, 57, 65, 74, 81, 89, 101, 105, 107, 114, 130, 139, 147, 160, 161, 169.

may also signify divine commands . . . ; so the 'ten words' (Exod. 34:28) is the Decalogue. . . . *Dāḇār* may indicate not only a particular message of Yahweh . . . , but also the sum total of his revealed will. . . ."[52] In a few contexts within the psalm דָּבָר takes on the nuanced connotation of "promise" (cf. אִמְרָה below).[53]

אִמְרָה (*'imrâ*)

The last word for the Word introduced in Psalm 119 is (*'imrâ*),[54] best rendered generally in biblical contexts as "word" but also conveying the idea of "promise."[55] Both the general meaning of "word" and the more focused rendering of "promise" are documented in Psalm 119.[56] The significance of God's Word as promise, whether conveyed by אִמְרָה or דָּבָר, cannot be overestimated: "Our psalmist, as a member of the Israelite community who keeps faith, appropriates these promises personally. . . . This dimension of Torah as promise is crucial for an understanding of the comfort and support the psalmist receives from Torah."[57]

---

[52] Anderson, *Psalms*, 2:812; cf. his panoramic summary of דָּבָר on pp. 811–12.

[53] For an excellent discussion of this phenomenon, see: Soll, "Psalm 119," pp. 75–77.

[54] All 19 occurrences in Ps 119 are singular in form: vv. 11, 38, 41, 50, 58, 67, 76, 82, 103 (some early versions construe as a plural), 116, 123, 133, 140, 148, 154, 158, 162, 170, 172.

[55] Again, most etymological studies are not profitable (e.g. Jacob, *Theology of the OT*, p. 128); however, a few aid in placing the root within its wider Semitic context (e.g. *Theological Dictionary of the Old Testament*, s.v. "אָמַר," by S. Wagner, 1:328; and KB, p. 63).

[56] "In Ps. 119 it often means the law of God in general, or his promises in particular . . ." (Anderson, *Psalms*, 2:812); for example, the "RSV has 'promise' thirteen times, but allows it a more general sense (mostly 'word') six times (verses 11, 67, 103, 158, 162, 172). This probably strikes the right balance between the general and the particular in this word, which is derived from the verb 'to say'" (Kidner, *Psalms 73–150*, p. 419).

[57] Soll, "Psalm 119," pp. 76–77.

Their Interrelations

In reference to these eight quasi-technical words for the Word, Leupold has appropriately cautioned that "though they are distinctive terms that convey the many-sidedness of the Word of God [i.e. like the various reflective facets on a gemstone], the specific connotation of the root meaning of the Hebrew word dare not always be pressed too precisely."[58] There is an obvious unselfish contribution of each to the total bibliological impression. Kidner's synopsis strikes a balance as it illustrates this phenomenon:

> Like a ring of eight bells, eight synonyms for Scripture dominate the psalm, and the twenty-two stanzas will ring the changes on them. They will do it freely, not with a bell-ringer's elaborate formulae, and they will introduce an occasional extra term. But the synonyms belong together, and we should probably not look for each to show its distinct character at each occurrence, but rather to contribute, by its frequent arrival, to our total understanding of what Scripture is.[59]

The total impression of "what Scripture is" is also advanced by an investigation into the attributes of special revelation.

---

[58] Leupold, *Psalms*, p. 822. Poetic parallelisms, internal and external to Ps 119, justify such a cautious approach; cf. Soll, "Psalm 119," pp. 87–91; Cook, "Psalms," p. 443; etc.

[59] Kidner, *Psalms 73–150*, p. 417.

Attributes of the Word

Their Source

The attributes of the Word of God do not emanate merely, mechanically, or mystically from embossed characters on writing materials but from a vital association with their Author, the God of the Word:

> The *attributes* applied to the Law should also be studied. Like its Author (v. 137, cp. Deut. xxxii.4) it is perfectly righteous. The note of righteousness is constantly repeated; in all its aspects the Law answers to that perfect standard which God is to Himself for all His works and words. Its faithfulness and truth correspond to the faithfulness and truth of His nature; it is sharply contrasted with all that is false in belief and conduct.[60]

By explicit parallelisms[61] and implicit associations which surface throughout the psalm, the Word of God functions characteristically as a mirror reflecting the image of its ultimate Divine Source.

---

[60] Kirkpatrick, *Psalms*, p. 704.
[61] These shall be noted throughout the exposition in Part III.

Their Solace

The root אמן (*'mn*)

In verse 86a the psalmist extols the אֱמוּנָה (*'ᵉmûnâ*), the "faithfulness" of God's Word, and in verses 142b (cf. John 17:17), 151b, and 160a he testifies to its אֱמֶת (*'emet*), "truth." The common semantical denominator of the root אמן, from which these nouns derive, is "to confirm, support, uphold" as manifested in the Qal stem and "to be established, be faithful" in the Niphal.[62] The stress is upon "fidelity, security, firmness, stability, trustworthiness; and these qualities characterize the Law of God."[63]

The root ישׁר (*yšr*)

The psalmist recognizes that God's "judgments are *upright*," i.e. יָשָׁר (*yāšār*), in verse 137;[64] therefore, through his testimony recorded in verse 128, he "considers right,"[65] i.e. יִשָּׁרְתִּי (*yiššārᵉtî*), God's precepts in application to everything.[66] His ethically upright response to the *rightness* of God and His Word might well be contrasted with the make up of the ungodly one of Habakkuk 2:4a: "Behold, his soul is swollen; *it* is *not upright*," i.e. לֹא־יָשְׁרָה (*lō' yāšerâ*).

---

[62] *Theological Wordbook of the Old Testament* [hereinafter: *TWOT*], s.v. "אָמַן (*'āman*)," by J.B. Scott, 1:51. In the Hiphil it takes on the color of "to be certain," meaning "to believe in" (ibid.).

[63] Scroggie, *Psalms*, p. 173.

[64] This masculine singular adjective often bears ethical freight, pointing to that which is "straightforward, just, upright" (BDB, p. 449; cf. *TWOT*, s.v. "יָשָׁר (*yāshār*)," by D. Wiseman, 1:417). The significance of the psalmist's ethical pronouncement regarding the Word is enhanced by the parallelism with God's personal righteousness, i.e. צַדִּיק (*ṣadîq*), in the first line of the v.

[65] Allen's appropriate rendering (*Psalms 101–150*, p. 132).

[66] This Piel verb in ethical contexts means "to esteem right, approve" (BDB, p. 448).

The root צדק (*ṣdq*)

This root crops up in noun forms within verses 7, 123, 144, and 172.[67] The majority of cognates relates the root to that which is straight, perfect, excellent, true, clear, etc.[68] "*Ṣeḏeq*, then, refers to an ethical, moral standard and of course in the OT that standard is the nature and the will of God."[69] "These words mean what is right, just, equitable, virtuous; and these qualities characterize the Law of the LORD."[70] Consequently, the Word of God presents to the child of God an unwavering ethical standard as it flows from its *just* Giver.

---

[67] These should be construed as functioning adjectivally in reference to the various terms for Scripture.

[68] Cf. BDB, p. 841.

[69] *TWOT*, s.v. "צֶדֶק (*ṣeḏeq*)," by H. Stigers, 2:752; for excellent developments of the significance of this point see: C. E. B. Cranfield, *The Epistle to the Romans*, 2 vols., ICC (Edinburgh: T. & T. Clark, Ltd., 1979), 1:94; and David Hill, *Greek Words and Hebrew Meanings: Studies in the Semantics of Soteriological Terms*, Society for NT Studies Monograph Series, 5 (Cambridge: University Press, 1967), pp. 96–97.

[70] Scroggie, *Psalms*, p. 173.

The inseparable preposition כְּ (k^e)

Some of the psalmist's boldest prayer requests are predicated upon the fidelity of God's inscripturated promises. A primary meaning of the preposition כְּ is "according to" expressing "conformity to a standard or rule."[71] Its occurrences in verses 25, 41, 58, 65, 107, 156, and 169 suggest that the psalmist is employing it idiomatically as an appeal to various Divine precedents. This contention is corroborated by the כְּמִשְׁפָּט (*k^emišpāṭ*) idiom of verse 132: "Turn to me and have mercy on me, *as you always do* to those who love your name" (NIV, emphasis added). It is interesting that the Targum renders כְּ by הֵיךְ (hêḵ) which is usually translated by "as, so," or "even as," but, at times in Jewish literature the obvious significance had become "even as you read in the Scriptures."[72] The psalmist's principle for prayer was: "Your Word says that You act graciously and faithfully according to inscripturated precedents; that's why I ask this way—boldly."[73]

REACTIONS TO THE WORD

Not Pharisaic Bigotry nor Bibliolatry

It has been said that "it is possible to deduce from the psalm a full-fledged 'theology' of the law, in *both* its *theoretical and* its *practical* aspects" (emphasis added).[74] This is true. However, most observers fail to maintain the psalmist's own intricate balance between the "theoretical" and the "practical." Often, because of our hermeneutical myopia, the penman of the 119th Psalm has been falsely accused of bigotry and/or bibliolatry.

---

[71] BDB, p. 454; in the context of its occurrences in Ps 119 the LXX appropriately utilizes κατά (*kata*) with the accusative case.

[72] Cf. Jastrow, *Dictionary*, 1:345.

[73] For a more thorough interaction with the data pertaining to this usage of כְּ, see Soll, "Psalm 119," pp.75–76, 79–80.

[74] Weiser, *The Old Testament: Its Formation and Development*, p. 740.

For example, some of the bold statements made by this mature man of God have been lifted out of their immediate and larger contexts in an attempt, be it conscious or unconscious, to discredit his testimony. Such statements as those recorded in verses 23, 51, 61, 69–70, 78, 83, 87, 95, 109–110, 113, 141, 143, 157, and 161 are so intimidating[75] that it is tempting to allay our conviction through an allegation of pharisaic braggadocio. However, these and other bold affirmations[76] must be evaluated in the light of the psalmist's overall perspective on his painful but productive experiences of affliction[77] and persecution,[78] the acute awareness of his own frailty[79] and fallenness,[80] and, most importantly, on the basis of his total dependence upon Divine fellowship and resources.[81]

---

[75] The convicting affect of these astounding affirmations is amplified by the fact that they are contained within antithetical couplets which capsulize the psalmist's dire circumstances. All but five of these parallelisms are phrased without a conjunction adding even more amplification through stylistic accentuation. In the light of such an adverse life situation, we would have expected "normal human" reactions to have been the opposite of those claimed by this child of God.

[76] E.g. vv. 14, 24, 30, 54–56, 57, 59, 63, 97–101, 106, 121a, 128, 163, 167, etc.

[77] For helpful synopses regarding his affliction, see: Scroggie, *Psalms*, pp. 173–78; and Kirkpatrick, *Psalms*, p. 702.

[78] There seem to have been two sources of persecution: godless men (i.e., vv. 23a, 51a, 61a, 69a, 78a, 84–87, 95a, 109a, 121b, 122b, 134a, 150a, 157a, 161a), and apostate men (i.e., vv. 21b, 53b, 113a, 126b, 136b, 139b, 158b).

[79] E.g. vv. 25, 28a, 41, 76–77, etc.

[80] E.g. vv. 10, 29, 67, 176, etc.

[81] E.g. vv. 5, 8b, 12b, 18–19, 28b, 32b, 33–39, 66a, 68b, 73, 125, 144, 145a, 147a, 169, 173a, etc.

Dependent Appropriation, Internalization and Application

Every statement by the psalmist, including the boldest ones, ultimately breathes in an atmosphere of dependency. His motivations are energized by Divine Presence and privilege, not by human pressure and pretense. Therefore, conformity to the law of God is proportionally and progressively realized through communion with the God of the law. In the light of these undeniable emphases, all accusations of bibliolatry miss, ignore, or deny the psalmist's overriding theocentric orientation.

This mature disciple's commitment to the marriage of Bibliology and theology proper is exemplified in various ways. First, the words for the Word should be re-examined noting especially their second person suffixes referring to God; it is unequivocally *God's* Word which preoccupies the psalmist. Other second person references add even more weight to the psalm's theocentricity.[82]

Secondly, there is an emphasis upon not only the attributes of the Word but also upon the attributes of its Divine Author. God's fidelity[83] and righteousness[84] are singled out especially, and His

[82] Tallying these references and including the occurrences of "God" (i.e. אֱלֹהִים) and the 21 vocative employments (out of 24 occurrences) of "LORD" (i.e. יהוה), Scroggie arrives at a total of 152 (*Psalms*, p. 174)!

[83] I.e. חֶסֶד (*ḥesed*); cf. vv. 41a, 64a, 76a, 124a. For some appropriate commentary, see: Nelson Gleuck, *Ḥesed in the Bible*, trans. by Alfred Gottschalk, ed. by Elias L. Epstein (Cincinnati: Hebrew Union College Press, 1967), p. 91; and *TWOT*, s.v. "חסד (*ḥsd*)," by R. Harris, 1:305–07.

[84] I.e. the root צדק; cf. vv. 40b, 137a, 142a. For the significance of this root, see the previous discussion under "Attributes of the Word."

sovereignty, in its general[85] and personal[86] dimensions, is consistently acknowledged. A third category of evidence for the bond between God and His Word comes from the interesting and significant parallelisms drawn between the two throughout the psalm.[87]

Finally, all of the psalmist's prayer requests magnify his utter dependence upon God and His grace. One particularly recurrent plea (v. 12, *et al.*) clearly reveals that for the psalmist God must efficiently apply the Word to his life; growth and maturity are not the products of unaided human efforts.[88]

Quite obviously, since the psalmist has wedded theology proper and Bibliology, he also naturally includes as a part of that union God's salvation. He views the Scriptures as God's soteriological *instrument*. God is the one who saves and spiritually revitalizes; yet, the primary vehicle for both imparting life and preserving life is His special revelation.[89] Verse 93 is illustrative: "I never forget Your precepts [i.e. a word for the Word], because *by means of* them [i.e. the precepts as God's instrument] *You* have given [i.e. a second person verb referring to the LORD] me life."[90]

---

[85] It must be admitted that the psalmist "recognizes the will of God which he discerns at work everywhere" (Oesterley, *Psalms*, p. 487).

[86] The psalmist personally recognized the providential beneficence of Divine discipline; cf. vv. 50, 67, 71, 75.

[87] For example, in v. 2 there is an obvious conceptual parallelism between obeying God's Word and pursuing Him, in v. 38 there is an affirmation that the Word was given as an instrument for the fear of God, in v. 81 the LORD's salvation and His Word are placed in parallelism (cf. v. 123), etc.

[88] Cf. Phil 2:12–13; Hengstenberg long ago observed that "a characteristic feature of our Psalm is the deep conviction that we have nothing to do with human strength in keeping the commandments of God, but that God alone must create the will and the power to perform" (*Psalms*, 3:385).

[89] Cf. the contexts of the 11 occurrences of the root חיה (*ḥyh*) in vv. 25, 37, 40, 50, 88, 93, 107, 149, 154, 156, and 159 along with other soteriological reminiscences and expectations. On the theological impact of חיה in the OT, see Hill, *Greek Words and Hebrew Meanings*, pp. 165–68.

[90] See the commentary on v. 93 in Part III for the reasoning for viewing this as historical retrospect on his initial salvation.

These and other theocentric observations should serve as a corrective to superficial conceptions of the psalmist's bold affirmations regarding human effort. Since they are a highly significant part of the fabric of the psalm, they should be utilized in not only understanding the content of his various statements but also for gaining some access into that mature heart from which they have arisen.

Long before Paul wrote 2 Timothy 2:15 our psalmist epitomized the model student of the Word of God. For him diligent study as approved by God must include not only memorization (i.e. v. 11) but also internalization and application. In verses 45 and 94 he uses the verb דָּרַשׁ (dāraš) to characterize his study as seeking with application, following, or practicing,[91] and when he looks upon his scriptural preoccupation as "meditation"[92] he emphasizes a deep process of internalization with an applicational goal within the context of the painful pressures of real life. At the same time, he was able to be infused with a deep-seated contentment, a biblically mediated joy which transcended his circumstances.[93] These attitudes help to provide a framework for synthesizing his overall conception of the Word of God: "This law is neither an intolerable burden, nor a mere reference book, but a gracious gift of God, which is the faithful man's delight and joy, his comfort and the source of the fulness of life."[94]

---

[91] BDB, p. 205.

[92] Note the noun form of the root שׂיח (*śyḥ*) in vv. 97 and 99, and see especially the verbal occurrences in vv. 15, 23, 48, 78, and 148. BDB, pp. 966–67, notes that several Semitic cognates view such study as a diligent or eager occupation.

[93] Cf. his introductory appeal to blessedness and happiness as a deeply anchored contentment conveyed through his employment of the root אשׁר (*'šr*) in vv. 1–2, his frequent affirmations of stabilizing delight as indicated by the repetition of the root שׁעשׁ (š*ᶜᶜ*: vv. 16, 24, 47, 70, 77, 92, 143, and 174), and his periodic assurances of hope (cf. Soll, "Psalm 119," pp. 75–77).

[94] Anderson, *Psalms*, 2:807; unlike those governed by a pharisaic outlook, the psalmist understood to a surprising degree that God's Word was a "law of liberty" (cf. Jas 2:12) and, as such, it was to be looked upon as regulative but certainly *not* to be regarded as a Divine albatross that had been hung upon his neck (cf. 1 John 5:3).

Beyond study, the psalmist was concerned about life-style obedience. Rotherham, in commenting on the psalmist's frequent references to the words for the Word, has correctly concluded that

> there is one restriction to be placed on all these synonyms; and that is, that they must be held to have a regulative bearing on human character and conduct. The manner of the man they make is always an essential question throughout the psalm. The psalmist's one absorbing passion is to be conformed to Jehovah's will.[95]

He never questioned the priority of obedience[96] but understood that it must be qualified by proper attitudes and motives.[97] Consequently, this man of God never besought God merely to teach him His Word but to form within him the *way of* that Word.[98] The psalmist recognized that the application of the Bible to behavior, the commandments to conduct, would require a divinely bestowed insight and illumination for which he prayed incessantly (cf. vv. 18, 27, 33–34, 73, 125, 144, 169). Spurgeon appro-

---

[95] Rotherham, *Studies in the Psalms*, p. 513. Kirkpatrick describes this passion as follows: "The Psalmist is one whose earnest desire and steadfast purpose it is to make God's law the governing principle of his conduct, to surrender all self-willed thoughts and aims, to subordinate his whole life to the supremely perfect will of God, with unquestioning faith in His all-embracing Providence and unfailing love" (*Psalms*, p. 700).

[96] The root נצר (*nṣr*: to guard with fidelity, keep, observe) occurs 10 times and its near synonym, שׁמר (*šmr*), occurs 19 times in the sense of keeping God's Word; e.g., vv. 2, 4, 5, 8, 33b, 106, 129, 145, (cf. Jesus on the priority of obedience in John 14:15, 21, 23; etc.).

[97] E.g., cf. his emphasis on wholeheartedness as a necessary prerequisite for genuine obedience, noting לֵב (*lēḇ*), "heart," in vv. 7, 11, 32, 36, 80, 111, 112, 161; and כָּל־לֵב (*kol-lēḇ*), "whole heart," in vv. 2, 10, 34, 58, 69, 145.

[98] He uses the words דֶּרֶךְ (*derek̲*; cf. vv. 1, 3, 5, 14, 26, 27, 29, 30, 32, 33, 37, 59, 168) and אֹרַח (*'ōraḥ*; cf. vv. 9, 15, 101, 104, 128), "road" or "way," as commonly employed biblical metaphors: "Either word implies that man's course of life, thought, and desire ought to be brought into harmony and made coincident with God's" (Girdlestone, *Synonyms*, p. 209; cf. Scroggie, *Psalms*, p. 172). In addition, he uses נָתִיב (*nāṯîḇ*), "pathway," in v. 35 in a similar fashion.

priately characterized the psalmist when he said, "The man of God exerts himself, but does not trust himself."[99]

All of this, once again, has brought us full circle but with some new insights into the heart of the psalmist. His consuming interest in God's Word may not be regarded as pharisaic bibliolatry:

> This untiring emphasis [upon the Scriptures] has led some to accuse the psalmist of worshipping the Word rather that the Lord; but it has been well remarked that every reference here to Scripture, without exception, relates it explicitly to its Author; indeed every verse from 4 to the end is a prayer or affirmation addressed to Him. This is true piety: a love of God not desiccated by study but refreshed, informed and nourished by it.[100]

May we emulate this mature man of God even now as we embark upon an excursion through the twenty-two stanzas of this great psalm.

---

[99] Charles H. Spurgeon, *The Treasury of David* (New York: Funk and Wagnalls, 1892), 6:33.

[100] Kidner, *Psalms 73–150*, p. 419.

PART III:

ANALYSIS

א

ALEP STANZA (vv. 1–8)

Translation and Notes

1 O how blessed[a] are those whose way is blameless,
those who walk[b] in the law of the LORD.[c]

2 O how blessed are those who keep[a] His testimonies;
they seek Him[b] wholeheartedly.[c]

3 Furthermore,[a] they do not practice[b] wrongdoing;
they walk[b] in His ways.[c]

4 You[a] have commanded Your precepts[b]
that *they should be* kept[c] diligently.[d]

5 Would that[a] my ways be established
to keep Your statutes.

6 Then[a] I shall not feel shame
when I look[b] upon all of Your commandments.

7 I shall give You thanks with an upright heart[a]
as I learn[b] Your righteous judgments.[c]

8 I shall keep Your statutes;
do not[a] utterly[b] forsake me.

1:a Cf. this ascription in Pss 1:1; 2:12; 34:9 (v. 8, Eng); 40:5 (v. 4, Eng); 84:6 (v. 5, Eng); 84:13 (v. 12, Eng); 112:1; 128:1; 146:5; etc. where the common denominator for its employment is an unflinching dependence upon the LORD.

1:b Lit., "the ones who are walking," i.e. the articular participial phrase in apposition to "the blameless of way" (lit.) stresses their characteristic life-style.

1:c Or possibly, "*by* the law of the LORD" as the standard for conduct; cf. NIV, "who walk according to the law of the LORD," or Allen's, "whose conduct is based on Yahweh's Torah" (*Psalms 101–150,* p. 126).

2:a Again, the substantive is a durative participle calling attention to a characteristic activity of these individuals.

2:b The imperfect tense, like the participle, often denotes continuity of action, habituality; these individuals are *characteristically seeking* the LORD.

2:c Lit. "with a whole heart."

3:a אַף (*'āp̱*), a "conj. denoting addition, . . . *also, yea*" (BDB, p. 64), inextricably binds this fidelity to community (v. 3) with their commitment to God and His Word (vv. 1–2).

3:b The perfect verbs, translated above as presents, arrest the reader's attention since they come after the imperfect (v. 2b) and the participles (vv. 1–2): "In verse 3 the description of those who are counted blessed is carried further. Perfects, as *denoting that which is habitual,* alternate with futures used as presents" (Delitzsch, *Psalms,* 3:245 [emphasis added]).

3:c Or, "by His ways" (cf. note 1:c above); note that there is no textual justification for an emendation of בדרכיו (*b<u>d</u>r<u>c</u>yw*) to בדבריו (*b<u>db</u>ryw*) as argued for by Soll (cf. "*Psalm* 119," pp. 94–95, 172).

4:a Emphatic אַתָּה (*'atâ*).

4:b See under the commentary section for a discussion of the syntactical options concerning this verse.

4:c The text contains only the *active* infinitive construct לִשְׁמֹר (*lišmōr*), "to keep"; therefore, a smooth translation must conceptualize the rendering based upon the thrust of the whole verse.

4:d מְאֹד (*m^e'ō<u>d</u>*), "n.m. muchness, force, abundance, exceedingly" (BDB, p. 547), is a commonly employed OT idiom of intensity or perpetuity (cf. the pleonastic עַד־מְאֹד in v. 8b); also, cf. מְאֹד in the great *Shema* (Deut 6:5).

5:a On this rare optative particle (only here and 2 Kgs 5:3 in the OT) see A. B. Davidson, *Hebrew Syntax* (Edinburgh: T. & T. Clark, 1901), ¶ 134 R2; the Ugaritic *ahl* has provided some further insight (cf. Dahood, *Psalms,* 3:174).

6:a Delitzsch rightly labels this אָז (*'āz*) as "retrospective" (*Psalms*, 3:245), since all that follows (vv. 6–8a) depends upon the logical protasis voiced in v. 5.

6:b It seems best to take this infinitive construct with temporal בְּ (b^{e}), along with the one in v. 7, as a durative, i.e. "as I continue to look into" the whole of Your Word.

7:a בְּיֹשֶׁר לֵבָב (b^{e}*yōšer lēḇāḇ*), another idiom for sincerity (cf. כָּל־לֵב in v. 2), i.e. "out of an honest heart" (Allen, *Psalms 101–150*, p. 126).

7:b Cf. 6:b above on the nature of this infinitive; it could well be rendered "as I go on learning" (Anderson, *Psalms*, 2:810).

7:c Lit. "the judgments of Your righteousness," i.e. one of many adjectival usages of the construct state in this psalm.

8:a The subjective negation, אַל (*'al*), likely plugs into the larger context of the psalmist's currently experienced acute persecution.

8:b "Deletion of ^{c}*aḏ m*^{e}*'ōḏ* (as suggested by Kraus, Gunkel, NEB, and JB) is not necessary. The phrase may mean, 'I am in affliction, and therefore "forsaken" now, but do not let me continue in my affliction' (so Anderson); it may be differential, or intended as a motive for the prayer ('if you forsake me, I am utterly forsaken')" (Soll, "Psalm 119," p. 172).

Synopsis and Outline

Both the theme and development of the *Aleph* stanza are quite transparent.[1] In this opening stanza of our psalm the roots דרך (*drḵ*) and הלך (*hlḵ*), common OT metaphors for the pathways of life, occur five times. In conjunction with this phenomenon, the roots נצר (*nṣr*), שׁמר (*šmr*), דרשׁ (*ḏrš*), and פעל (*p̄'l*), which frequently emphasize obedience, occur six times. Quite obviously, when this data is combined, the thematic glue of these introductory verses reveals itself to be life-style obedience.

[1] The relationship of this stanza to the rest of the psalm is similar to the relationship of Ps 1 to the rest of the Psalter; there is an introductory emphasis upon life-style obedience.

The unfolding of this theme grows progressively more personal. This may be noted in the grammatical shift from a third person orientation in verses 1–3, to a second person orientation in verse 4, and ultimately, to the first person orientation in verses 5–8.

In the first three verses the psalmist utilizes the "they" perspective on this priority of obedience. It must be admitted that it is easier for us as individuals to address our responsibilities before God from the more comfortable context of community (be it expressed either "we" or "they"). However, these broad-sweeping generalizations about the fellowship of the faithful were an integral part of the psalmist's keen awareness of his own personal responsibilities relating to character and conduct.

The perspective of verse 4, God's own perspective, is the fulcrum of this stanza. As Soll astutely notes concerning this "You" perspective, "v. 4 provides an important link between vv. 1–3 and v. 5: the condition described in vv. 1–3 is not only desirable, it is commanded."[2] With this acknowledgment of the LORD's will for the conformity of man's conduct to His Word, the psalmist's responsibility takes a quantum leap. The magnitude of God's expectation is subsequently contemplated from the most intimate perspective in the verses which follow.

His "my" and "I" perspective in verses 5–8 neither underestimates God's awesome requirement nor overestimates his own finite resources and fallible estate. This man of God, understanding both the will of the LORD and the woe of man, rushes to the God of grace beseeching His enablement (v. 5; cf. 8b). Verse 5 is both the logical protasis and the theological prerequisite upon which the results of verses 6–8a may be realized. Through this concluding perspective we are able to sense how this very practical priority is intimately personalized.

---

[2] He appropriately continues: "This gives added urgency to the wish in v. 5, but also gives him some reason to expect help (v. 8b). Both vv. 6 and 7 are conditional statements (note their parallel structure) that are part of the wish in v. 5, elaborating what would happen if the desire expressed in v. 5 were to be fulfilled" (Soll, "Psalm 119," p. 156).

It, therefore, behooves us to investigate these three interrelated perspectives on the priority of obedience:

1A. (vv. 1–3) The perspective of all the faithful on the priority of obedience.
  1B. (vv. 1–2) They experience the happiness of obedience.
    1C. (v. 1) This happiness comes from conformity to God's Word.
    2C. (v. 2) This happiness comes from knowing God through His Word.
      1D. (v. 2a) Knowing the Word of God.
      2D. (v. 2b) Knowing the God of the Word.
  2B. (v. 3) They experience the practicality of obedience.
    1C. (v. 3a) This practicality is first expressed negatively.
    2C. (v. 3b) This practicality is then expressed positively.
2A. (v. 4) The perspective of God on the priority of obedience.
  1B. (v. 4a) His standard concerning obedience.
  2B. (v. 4b) His burden concerning obedience.
3A. (vv. 5–8) The perspective of the psalmist on the priority of obedience.
  1B. (vv. 5–8a) His positively phrased plea for enablement points to the priority of obedience.
    1C. (v. 5) The potential of this plea for enablement.
    2C. (vv. 6–8a) The products of this plea for enablement:
      1D. (v. 6) The immediate product: maturing integrity.
      2D. (vv. 7–8a) The related products:
        1E. (v. 7) Formal worship.
        2E. (v. 8a) Practical worship.
  2B. (v. 8b) His negatively phrased plea for communion points to the priority of obedience.

Commentary

The repetition of the exclamation אַשְׁרֵי (*'ašrê*) at the outset of verses 1 and 2 launches the psalm on a positive note. This repetition calls attention to the fact that those demonstrating a pattern of consistency in obeying God's directives for life correspondingly experience a deeply rooted joy. The LXX and the Latin Vulgate provide a providential link to NT truth by their respective renderings of μακάριοι (*makarioi*) and *beati*.[3] The faithful of all ages experience a transcendent joy internalized, a happiness defined by God's standards and values, not by the world's. Consequently, Anderson's paraphrase of "How rewarding is the life of those . . . ,"[4] captures the impact of this twofold אַשְׁרֵי in its significantly revelational context.

God's faithful people are designated תְמִימֵי־דָרֶךְ (*ṯᵉmîmê-ḏereḵ*), "blameless of way," in verse 1. דֶּרֶךְ (*dereḵ*), it will be remembered, is commonly employed as a metaphor for life's roadway, as here. It is, however, the substantive adjective from תָּמִים (*tāmîm*) which characterizes their faithfulness along that "way." As a matter of fact, this word conveys God's goal for all those called by His grace. He commanded Abraham in Genesis 17:1, "Walk in My presence, and *be*[5] *blameless*" (i.e., תָּמִים). Of Job it was said, "There was a man named Job in the land of Uz and that man was *blameless* (תָּם)[6] and upright . . ." (Job 1:1). In the book of Proverbs, a book with which our psalmist was apparently exceedingly famil-

---

[3] Cf. some of the "Beatitudes" of the NT: Matt 5:3–11; 11:6; 13:16; 16:17; Luke 1:45; 6:20–22; 7:23; 10:23; 12:37, 43; 14:14, 15; John 13:17; 20:29; Rom 4:7 (quoting Ps 32:1); Jas 1:12; Rev 1:3; 14:13; 16:15; 19:9; 20:6; 22:14; etc.

[4] Anderson, *Psalms*, 2:807; currently there is a trend to associate אַשְׁרֵי (*'ašrê*) with privilege, e.g. "'to be envied'" (Bruce K. Waltke and M. O'Connor, *An Introduction to Biblical Hebrew Syntax* [Winona Lake, IN: Eisenbrauns, 1990], ¶ 40.2.3b).

[5] Note that both "walk" and "be" are imperatives in Gen 17:1.

[6] Another adjectival form (cf. Job 1:8; 2:3; etc.).

iar,[7] we read: "The perverse in heart are an abomination to the LORD, but the *blameless* in *their* walk [i.e., תְּמִימֵי דָרֶךְ] are His delight" (Prov 11:20, NASB; cf. 13:6). God's ethical objective for our lives is integrity of character and conduct and that is precisely the thrust of תָּמִים.[8] It should also be pointed out that His expectation ultimately rests upon Divine models of fidelity: "*In reference to* God, His way [i.e., דֶּרֶךְ] is *perfect* [i.e., תָּמִים]" (Ps 18:31 [v. 30, Eng]); and "the law [i.e., תּוֹרָה] of the LORD is *wholesome* [i.e., תְּמִימָה]" (Ps 19:8 [v. 7, Eng]).

Most English renderings, such as "undefiled" (AV) and "blameless" (e.g. NASB, NIV, NAB, etc.), fail to reflect the thoroughly positive connotation of תָּמִים in the OT. However, "O how blessed are the ones having integrity of manner of life" would certainly not commend itself as a smooth translation. Additionally, there may be some intratestamental justification for these more negatively expressed English renderings. The LXX opened the conceptual door with its rendering of תָּמִים by ἄμωμοι (*amōmoi*).[9]

---

7 Many other allusions to Proverbs will be pointed out.

8 The verbal root from which these adjectives derive means to "be complete, finished" (BDB, p. 1070) in telic contexts and connotes maturity in ethical contexts, i.e. to be "sound, unimpaired" (ibid.). The noun form conveying "completeness" or "fulness" in ethical contexts comes across as "integrity," and the adjectives are variously rendered as "complete, perfect, sound, wholesome, morally innocent, having integrity" (ibid., pp. 1070–71).

9 The α privative plus the adjective μῶμος (*mōmos*) is rendered "without blemish, blameless" (cf. Henry George Liddell and Robert Scott, *A Greek-English Lexicon*, rev. and aug. by Henry Stuart Jones and Robert McKenzie [Oxford: Clarendon Press, 1968], p. 96; hereinafter this work will be referred to as LSJ).

This has seemingly provided a semantical bridge to some very significant occurrences in the NT. In Ephesians 1:4; 5:27; Philippians 2:15; Colossians 1:22; and Jude 24 the appropriate forms of ἄμωμος reveal that the goal of God for those whom He has chosen is that they become unblemished (i.e. blameless).[10] That goal, although expressed through a negatively formulated term in NT Greek, is identical *theologically* to that of תָּמִים in OT Hebrew. It is no wonder that the psalmist affirms that those who are committed to making God's goal of blamelessness their preoccupation experience transcendent blessing.

The second part of verse 1 further describes those who demonstrate integrity along life's pathway (i.e. דֶּרֶךְ; cf. the Vulgate's *via*). Their movement along that circuitous road is picked up by the appositionally substantive participle הַהֹלְכִים (*hahōlᵉḵîm*). The faithful consistently walk[11] "in the law of the LORD."[12] All facets of their lives are recognized as being governed by the preceptive will of God. Consequently, in conjunction with a maturing conformity to God's Word, they taste true happiness.[13]

---

[10] Once again, God's expectation is grounded upon a Divine model; this time it is Christ (cf. ἄμωμος of Christ in Heb 9:14 and 1 Pet 1:19). In reference to Christ, the sacrificial contexts of this term in the LXX provide another rich dimension of background (cf. W. E. Vine, *An Expository Dictionary of New Testament Words* [Old Tappan, NJ: Fleming H. Revell, 1940], 1:130, 132).

[11] The participle emphasizes habituality (cf. Barnes, *Psalms*, 3:178). On the metaphorical impact of הָלַךְ, see "Walking in the Way(s) of Yahweh": *TDOT*, s.v. "הָלַךְ (*hālakh*)" by F. Helfmeyer, 3:396–401.

[12] Metaphorical continuities come not only through דֶּרֶךְ (i.e. way) and הָלַךְ (i.e. walk) but also from the root of תּוֹרָה (i.e. ירה: it is God's "law," direction, instruction which *shows* or *points out* the correct way). It must be remembered that "here, as in Pss i and xix, *torah* signifies 'law' in its widest sense, including all divine revelation as the guide of life . . ." (Dahood, *Psalms*, 3:173; cf. Cohen, *Psalms*, p. 394).

[13] As the psalm develops there will be no possibility of interpreting this as any kind of self-satisfying complacency; the larger context shows it to be a deep-seated contentment which is graciously mediated.

The obedience that verse 1 addresses through metaphor is conveyed more directly in verse 2. A substantive participle from נָצַר (i.e. *nāṣar*: to watch, guard, keep[14]) stands in construct with "God's testimonies"[15] signifying that those who characteristically obey[16] His Word are the ones who experience the special blessing of a transcendent satisfaction.

That knowledge, even the applicational knowledge of "His testimonies," may not be conceived as an end in itself is confirmed by the synthetic parallelism of verse 2b. *Seeking Him* provides the ultimate context for *keeping His Word* (also, cf. Ps 24:6 in its context). This habitual imperfect from דָּרַשׁ (*dāraš*), to seek,[17] has as its object none but the LORD (i.e. "Him").[18] As argued previously, bibliolatry is ruled out, since the Word of God is the vehicle by means of which we are to wholeheartedly pursue Him.[19] The purpose of knowing the Word of God is to know the God of the Word.

The practicality of obedience is painted with bold strokes in verse 3 largely through the employment of two perfect tense verbs.[20] These perfects are panoramic landscapes which stand

---

[14] BDB, p. 665.

[15] I.e. עֵדֹתָיו (*ᶜēḏōṯāyw*), "rules of conduct which attest the Divine will" (Cohen, *Psalms*, p. 394).

[16] The thrust is consistently *guarding with fidelity, keeping, observing*, etc. (cf. BDB, p. 665).

[17] See category #3 for seeking God, and cf. category #6 for seeking with application, studying, following, or practising His Word [note vv. 45, 94, 155; cf. Ezra 7:10] in BDB, p. 205. It is interesting that the LXX uses an intensified form (i.e. ἐκζητέω) meaning "to seek out, search for, investigate, scrutinize" (Joseph Henry Thayer, *Greek-English Lexicon of the New Testament* [Grand Rapids: Zondervan Publishing House, 1962], p. 195).

[18] "Note here what is implicit throughout the psalm, that Scripture is revered for being *his* (or 'thy') sayings, and God's servants thereby seek *him*, not the book for its own sake" (Kidner, *Psalms 73–150*, p. 424).

[19] Cf. דָּרַשׁ plus בְּכָל־לֵבָב (*bᵉkol־ lēḇāḇ*) from the standpoint of God's intention in Deut 4:29.

[20] There is no textual justification for emending the first of these to another substantive participle based upon the οἱ ἐργαζόμενοι (*hoi ergazomenoi*) of the LXX.

against the animated background provided by the durative participles and the habitual imperfect of verses 1 and 2. As such, they depict, first with negative hues and then with positive tones, the concrete realities of obedience demonstrated in the horizontal context of community.

First, when the whole of the life of the faithful is synoptically viewed, they "do not practice wrong."[21] The word עַוְלָה (*ᶜawlâ*) is variously rendered as "wrong, unrighteousness, injustice" or more concretely as "violent deeds of injustice."[22] The common denominator is recognizable wrongdoing; consequently, a bird's-eye view of their life vindicates them from accusations of social malpractice.

Phrased more positively and through contrast, verse 3b reads, "they walk in (or by means of) His ways." This recalls the affirmation of verse 1b, both employing הָלַךְ ethically; however, there is an advancement. The first verse speaks generally of living (lit., "walking") in or by means of the Word of God while verse 3 is somewhat more personal and applicational by its reference to the Source and ethical intentions of that Word, i.e. "His ways" (בִּדְרָכָיו [*bidrākāyw*]).[23] Therefore, it is to be understood that all these earmarks of sanctification (vv. 1–3) are deeply couched in the theological contexts of both Bibliology and theology proper. The theocentric and ethical clarification of verse 3b provides a fitting transition to the vertically-oriented perspective revealed in the next verse.

This theocentric perspective becomes even more conspicuous with the emphatic אַתָּה (*'attâ*, i.e. "*You*") which stands at the head of verse 4. In reference to this, Anderson appropriately com-

---

[21] Alexander's rendering of פָּעַל (*pāᶜal*) with the objective negation (*Psalms*, 3:152); cf. the assertion of 1 John 3:9a in its larger theological context.

[22] BDB, p. 732; the LXX utilizes ἀνομία (*anomia*), "lawlessness," which conspicuously resurfaces in the NT (cf. esp. 1 John 3:4), and the שִׁקְרָא (*šiqrā'*, lit. "the lie") of the Targum should probably be looked upon as an illustration rather than a translation.

[23] For a thorough discussion demonstrating that דֶּרֶךְ is not a word for the Word in Ps 119, see Soll, "Psalm 119," pp. 91–93.

ments, "The use of the second person, when referring to God, can indicate that the author was primarily concerned with the Giver of the law rather than merely with law itself."[24] The effect of this upon the psalmist, and hopefully upon us, is that as this theocentric awareness catapults so does an acute sense of personal responsibility.

Revelation about the heart of God in relation to the law of God and the people of God has never been lacking. Consequently, verse 4 could be viewed as a theological abstract of those many passages which make known the LORD's intention in giving His Word to His people. For example, Leviticus 18:4 states, "You are to perform My judgments and keep My statutes, to live in accord with them; I am the LORD your God" (NASB). Similarly, a major theme within the Book of Deuteronomy is "observe to do," i.e. obedience to God through compliance with His Word.[25]

A word needs to be said about the difficult syntax of this verse. The whole verse may be taken as a run-on affirmation, or it may be construed as an affirmation clause followed by a subordinate purpose statement.[26] Dahood argues for the former;[27] however, based upon the most natural word order and the syntactical

---

[24] Anderson, *Psalms*, 2:809.

[25] E.g., Deut 4:13 uses צִוָּה (*ṣiwwâ*) plus an infinitive of עָשָׂה (*ᶜāśâ*), and Ps 119:4 uses the same leading verb plus an infinitive of a synonymous word for obedience, שָׁמַר (*šāmar*). Generally speaking, in Deut the verbs to observe and to do are coordinated 10 times, and the combination of *observe to do* occurs another 16 times.

[26] It must be acknowledged, however, that either option will direct one to the basic significance of the verse.

[27] "The verse becomes syntactically explicable when read as a run-on line, that is, as an instance of enjambment; . . . In the infinitival phrase *piqqūḏeḵā lišmōr* (which is the direct object of the verb *siwwītāh*), *piqqūḏeḵā*, 'your precepts,' parses as the direct object of the construct infinitive *lišmōr*. In this unusual piece of syntax we have the object preceding the infinitive expressing the idea of obligation . . . , but this usage is not as uncommon as previously thought" (Dahood, *Psalms*, 3:173–74).

parallelism of verse 5, the latter option is preferred. As such, the verse emphasizes first the authoritative status and then the consequential intention of God's "particularized rules."[28]

Because the LORD has "commanded"[29] His Word, it is invested with His authority, and because that Word is an infallible standard for man concerning obedience, submissive response ought to be axiomatic. The psalmist was deeply convicted of this as the immediate arrival of the purpose clause לִשְׁמֹר מְאֹד (*lišmōr mᵉʾōḏ*) indicates.[30] "God's precepts are given with the very idea in mind that they may be kept, and kept diligently."[31]

Indeed, if that is God's heart, it must become the psalmist's heart also.[32] That holy desire constitutes the nucleus of his own perspective on the priority of obedience. Having sensed the burden of God deeply (i.e. v. 4), he is consumed with documenting that desire personally (i.e. vv. 5–8).

The initial אַחֲלַי (*ʾaḥᵃlay*) of verse 5 introduces an optative clause[33] which becomes the conceptual protasis of verses 6–8a. In its context, this passionate exclamation pulsates with conviction, strong desire, and an acute awareness of dependence. Although

---

[28] Cohen's (*Psalms*, p. 394) condensed concept of פִּקֻּדֶיךָ (*piqquḏeyḵā*, "Your precepts"). Cf. Alexander, *Psalms*, 3:153.

[29] צִוָּה (*ṣiwwâ*), "*lay charge* (upon), *give charge* (to), *charge, command, order*" (BDB, p. 845), is used of a variety of binding injunctions coming from superiors to inferiors. This word is sometimes used of God's *creation* of the world (e.g. Ps 33:9) and His establishment of covenant (e.g. Ps 111:9). Cf. the lexical significance of the LXX's ἐντέλλω (*entellō*), "*to order, command to be done, enjoin*" (Thayer, *Lexicon*, p. 218).

[30] Delitzsch astutely observes that "in ver. 4 לִשְׁמֹר expresses the purpose of the enjoining, as in ver. 5 the goal of the directing" (*Psalms*, 3:245).

[31] Leupold, *Psalms*, p. 824; cf. Kirkpatrick, *Psalms*, p. 706.

[32] The semantical, syntactical, and stylistic parallels enhance the concentric burdens of God and the psalmist in vv. 4 and 5.

[33] See Williams on "Desiderative (Optative) Clauses" (Ronald J. Williams, *Hebrew Syntax: An Outline* [Toronto: University of Toronto, 1976], §§ 546–551). In the LXX, the combination of ὄφελον (*ophelon*) with the optative κατευθυνθείησαν (*kateuthuntheiēsan*), "would that . . . they be made straight (i.e. guided, directed)" commendably captures the passion of the psalmist's statement in the MT.

the psalmist was an exemplary member of the faithful ones described in verses 1–3, he understood to the very core of his being that there was no room for complacency in the LORD's presence. Therefore, this transparent request, born out of a holy dissatisfaction with anything less than a life which consistently conforms with God's ways (i.e. בִּדְרָכָיו, v. 3) and will (i.e. v. 4), turns the spotlight on his own ways (i.e. דְרָכָי [*d^erāḵay*], v. 5).[34]

His plea is expressed succinctly through the combination of דְרָכָי with יִכֹּנוּ (*yikkōnû*). It is interesting that this same combination occurs in the second line of Proverbs 4:26: "Make level the wagon-tracks [i.e. a vivid metaphor for life's course] of your feet, then all of *your ways will be directed aright*."[35] The passive verb יִכֹּנוּ, a Niphal imperfect coming from כּוּן (*kûn*),[36] shows his exclamation to be a plea for Divine enablement.[37] Possible meanings of the Niphal in such contexts would be "to be established, fixed, arranged, set in order," or "directed aright."[38] Through circumlocution, the psalmist dependently petitions the Source of enablement to pilot his life toward the *goal* of obedience (i.e. לִשְׁמֹר חֻקֶּיךָ [*lišmōr ḥuqqeyḵa*]). With confidence in the potentiality of a positive Divine response, he makes a transition to some sample products of anticipated enablement (vv. 6–8a).

---

[34] I.e. his own character manifested in "daily conduct" (Cohen, *Psalms*, p. 395).

[35] A quite literal rendering of the MT. Note the semantical parallelism of Prov 4:26b (i.e. וְכָל־דְּרָכֶיךָ יִכֹּנוּ) with Ps 119:5a (i.e. אַחֲלַי יִכֹּנוּ דְרָכָי).

[36] This root demonstrates a great variety of usages in Biblical Hebrew and other cognate languages; for a credible survey see *TWOT*, s.v. "כּוּן (kûn)," by J.N. Oswalt, 1:433–34. Several semantical fields will be displayed within the 119th Ps itself.

[37] Theologically, this should be viewed as a Divine passive; he is obviously depending upon God to actively direct his ways.

[38] BDB, pp. 465–66. Alexander suggests to be "settled, fixed, confirmed, established, in opposition to capricious vacillation and unsteadiness" (*Psalms*, 3:152); however, although his comments reflect an important truth, they may be overly reliant upon conjectural etymology. The same critique would be appropriate in reference to Anderson's paraphrase: "Oh that my obedience might be unwavering" (*Psalms*, 2:810).

"Then" (i.e. upon the condition of God's benevolent intervention), he says, "I shall not feel shame when I look unto all of Your commandments." It may be beneficial to examine the latter part of the verse first, since it outlines the occasion wherein no shame might overwhelm him. This subordinate infinitival phrase functioning temporally[39] is as bold as it is brief. The psalmist looks upon that occasion collectively, those frequent personal encounters with the *totality* of God's special revelation.[40] Characteristically, these were not superficial encounters as indicated by the combination of נָבַט (*nābaṭ*) plus אֶל (*'el*).[41] In this and similar contexts, נָבַט denotes "a careful, sustained, and favorable contemplation."[42] The NT saint is reminded of the response of the doer of work, in contrast with the forgetful hearer, illustrated in James 1:22–25. The man of God wants to never[43] be ashamed as he exposes his life to the penetrating totality of God's preceptive declarations.

Shame was the ultimate disaster in the ancient Near East.[44] "Dishonor" seems to be the semantical common denominator of בּוֹשׁ (*bôš*) among the cognate languages of Hebrew.[45] Usages in the OT fall into various subcategories; however, "the primary meaning of this root is 'to fall into disgrace, normally through failure,

---

[39] Note how the LXX mimics the syntax of the MT with its articular infinitive from ἐπιβλέπω (*epiblepō*) governed by ἐν (*en*) and followed by ἐπί (*epi*), "when I gaze upon." It should also be noted that v. 7b follows the same pattern both in the MT and LXX.

[40] The כָּל־מִצְוֹתֶיךָ (*kol-miṣwōṯeykā*) is deliberately all inclusive; his deep desire is that, as he encounters all the Scriptures, not one part of them would convict him of disregard.

[41] Lit., "to look unto."

[42] *TWOT*, s.v. "נָבַט (*nābaṭ*)," by L. Coppes, 2:546; cf. Perowne, *Psalms*, 2:350; Alexander, *Psalms*, 3:52–53; etc. This intensified nuance is corroborated by the LXX's ἐπιβλέπω ἐπί (*epiblepō epi*).

[43] The objective negation לֹא (*lō'*); cf. the LXX's emphatic negation οὐ μή (*ou mē*).

[44] This phenomenon is illustrated even today in the basic mindset of Eastern cultures.

[45] Cf. *TDOT*, s.v. "בּוֹשׁ (*bôsh*)," by H. Seebass, 2:50–60.

either of self or of an object of trust.'"[46] Although most contexts would suggest that a public exposure was in view, the occurrence of בוֹשׁ in the verse before us shows its impact to be a very private *feeling* of shame. The psalmist dreaded the worst kind of disgrace, an internal and painful exposure of scriptural nonconformity in the presence of an omniscient God.[47] Consequently, when God graciously provides the resources for the psalmist's walk to conform with His Word (v. 5), then he will not feel the pangs of disgrace as he looks into the full mirror of special revelation. Phrased positively, he is hoping that God's enablement will produce in him new levels of personal integrity.

God's gracious enablement would also energize both formal (v. 7) and practical (v. 8a) worship. Genuine praise sincerely offered[48] will habitually accompany (v. 7a) his growth as a disciple (v. 7b). The leading verb אוֹדְךָ (*'ôḏ*^{e}*ḵā*),[49] from יָדָה (*yāḏâ*), denotes either confession or praise.[50] Herein, it is the later field of usage which is in view; the psalmist commits himself to praising God, to giving thanks to Him.[51]

Sincere thanksgiving is an appropriate accompaniment to the anticipated growth indicated by בְּלָמְדִי מִשְׁפְּטֵי צִדְקֶךָ (*b*^{e}*lomḏî mišpeṭê ṣidqeḵâ*). לָמַד (*lāmaḏ*) is a key verb in our psalm, and for good reason; it is the word which signifies discipleship in the OT.[52] In the

---

[46] *TWOT*, s.v. "בוֹשׁ (*bôsh*)," by J. Oswalt, 1:97; cf. Seebass' similar generalization: "Thus *bosh* means to be disgraced for something that has been undertaken" (*TDOT*, 2:53).

[47] On the implied synergism between the God of the Word and the Word of God, see Heb 4:12–13 for sharper resolution.

[48] I.e., the impact of בְּיֹשֶׁר לֵבָב (*b*^{e}*yōšer lēḇāḇ*) as it qualifies אוֹדְךָ (*'ôḏ*^{e}*ḵā*).

[49] A Hiphil imperfect 1 c s with 2 m s suffix.

[50] BDB, p. 392.

[51] "A vow of praise, usually expressed through a voluntative 1st person singular hiphil, concludes individual laments (Ps. 7:18 [Eng. v. 17]; 28:7; 35:18; 42:6, 12 [5, 11]; 43:4f.; 52:11 [9]; 54:8 [6]; 57:10; 71:22; 86:12; 109:30; 119:7). The supplicant can also use an infinitive construct to describe the vow of praise. The voluntative may be retained, as in Ps. 119:62: 'I will rise to praise,' . . ." (*TDOT*, s.v. "ידה" by G. Mayer, 5:431).

Qal stem this root means "to learn," and in the Piel it means "to teach."[53] Both stems are interrelated throughout the 176 verses which stretch out before us. The psalmist's continued learning (e.g., vv. 7, 73) was dependent upon a sustained Divine enlightenment, usually expressed by his anticipation of God teaching him (e.g., vv. 12, 26, 64, 66, 68, 108, 124, 135, 171). Although the psalmist was very mature (e.g., vv. 98–100), he was always aware of the fact that he had not arrived.[54] He must keep on learning[55] God's "righteous judgments,"[56] and as he does, praise directed to the Master Teacher will consistently flow through his lips from an undivided heart.

---

[52] Note that the LXX appropriately renders בְּלָמְדִי by ἐν τῷ μεμαθηκέναι (*en tō memathēkenai*). Μανθάνω (*manthanō*) furnishes a linguistic bridge to the NT's thorough development of the child of God as μαθητής (*mathētēs*). In the light of Ps 119 and other key passages in the OT the *preoccupation* of our Lord's Great Commission (i.e., μαθητεύσατε, making *disciples* in Matt 28:19–20) had been fully anticipated.

[53] BDB, p. 540. Cf. Kaiser's brief synopsis: "As one of the twelve words for teaching in the OT, *lāmad* has the idea of training as well as educating. The training aspect can be seen in the derived term for 'oxgoad,' *malmēd*. In Hos 10:11 Ephraim is taught like a heifer by a yoke and goad. . . . The principle use of this verb is illustrated in Ps 119. Here is repeated the refrain, 'Teach me thy statutes' or 'thy judgments'. . . . While Greek uses two different words for 'to learn' (*manthanō*) and 'to teach' (*didaskō*), each having its own content, goal, and methods, Hebrew uses the same root for both words because all learning and teaching is ultimately to be found in the fear of the Lord (Deut 4:10; 14:23; 17:19; 31:12, 13). To learn this is to come to terms with the will and law of God" (*TWOT*, s.v. "לָמַד (*lāmad*)," by W. Kaiser, 1:480).

[54] "The psalmist knows that he has not yet attained to a complete knowledge of God's revealed Will; but he gives thanks for every advance. The will to obey (vv. 5, 6) is the condition of progress (cp. John vii.17); and throughout the Psalm he prays repeatedly for teaching and direction" (Kirkpatrick, *Psalms*, p. 706).

[55] The force of the infinitive construct in this context (cf. Anderson, *Psalms*, 2:810; Alexander, *Psalms*, 3:153; Allen, *Psalms 101–150*, p. 126).

[56] The "'judgments of Thy righteousness' are the decisions concerning right and wrong which give expression to and put in execution the righteousness of God" (Delitzsch, *Psalms*, 3:245).

The אֶת־חֻקֶּיךָ אֶשְׁמֹר (*'et ḥuqqeykā 'ešmōr*) of verse 8a picks up the infinitives of שָׁמַר encountered earlier in verses 4b and 5b.[57] His desire for obedience, predicated upon the hope of Divine assistance (v. 5), now manifests itself as an expression of commitment (v. 8a). Thus the apodosis begun in verse 6 culminates in this statement of practical worship, "I shall consistently obey Your statutes."[58] His strong volitional stance should not be minimized, but it must be couched in the same context in which he viewed it (cf. both v. 5 and v. 8b which immediately follows). Alexander well captures the significance of that context with the following reminder: "The fixed resolution to obey is intimately blended with a consciousness of incapacity to do so, unless aided by divine grace."[59]

A dramatic shift occurs at the middle of verse 8 with the words אַל־תַּעַזְבֵנִי עַד־מְאֹד (*'al taᶜazbēnî ᶜad¯meʼōd*). If taken only in its immediate context the statement seems to be a perplexing paradox;[60] however, this exclamation, "Do not completely abandon me,"[61] is a harbinger of the many references to the perilous predicament of the psalmist.[62] It is astutely noted by Allen that "this is the first hint that the author-disciple is no dilettante composing poetry in an ivory tower but caught up in a situation of tension and distress, which he asks Yahweh to resolve with his helping presence."[63]

---

57 This linguistic inclusio is a part of the thematic integration of these verses.

58 Stressing the thrust of the imperfect.

59 Alexander, *Psalms*, 3:153.

60 Cf. the startling impact of the very last verse of the psalm (i.e. v. 176).

61 I.e., Allen's pleasing translation (*Psalms 101–150*, p. 126).

62 The subjective negation אַל (*'al*) normally draws attention to a specific occasion, particular circumstances. In this case it would be those pressures and persecutions which were avalanching the psalmist.

63 Allen, *Psalms 101–150*, p. 142.

The magnitude of the threatening situation in which he found himself is reflected in his choice of the verb עָזַב (*ᶜāzab̲*), to leave, abandon, forsake.[64] It is the same word that is used by David in Psalm 22:2 (v. 1 in the Eng text) and picked up by the Greater David while bearing our sins upon the cross.[65] Our psalmist qualifies his own sense of personal abandonment by עַד־מְאֹד.[66] From the vantage point of his persecutions they were becoming more acutely painful; therefore, deeply sensing his vulnerability, he pleads with the LORD not to leave him completely or permanently. Without unbroken communion with his God he was rightly convinced that there was no hope for him to live obediently.

---

[64] BDB, pp. 736–37.

[65] The LXX employs the appropriate inflection of the strengthened verb ἐγκαταλείπω (*enkataleipō*), "*to abandon, desert, . . .* i.e. *to leave in straits, leave helpless*" (Thayer, *Lexicon* , p. 166), to render עָזַב, and the Aramaic Targum uses שְׁבַק (*šᵉb̲aq*) which closely parallels the Hebrew verb in meaning. What is significant is that Christ's crying out from the cross brings all of these strong terms for abandonment together. It is also interesting that Heb 13:5 similarly employs the strong ἐγκαταλείπω with an emphatic negation (i.e. οὐ μή σε ἐγκαταλίπω). This calls to remembrance Deut 31:6, 8; Josh 1:5; etc., passages which may have been reverberating in the psalmist's mind (also cf. Ps 37:25, 33).

[66] This idiomatic prepositional phrase (lit. up to abundance) functions adverbially: "to a great degree, exceedingly" (BDB, p. 547).

ב

BETH STANZA
(vv. 9–16)

Translation and Notes

9 How[a] can a young man keep his way pure?[b]
By keeping[b] *it* according to Your Word.[c]

10 I have wholeheartedly[a] sought You;
Do not let me stray[b] from Your commandments.

11 I have treasured up Your Word[a] in my heart
in order that I might not sin against You.

12 You are blessed, O LORD;
teach me[a] Your statutes.

13 I have declared[a] with my lips
all the judgments of Your mouth.[b]

14 I have rejoiced in the way of[a] Your testimonies
as *one does* over[b] all wealth.

15 I will[a] meditate on Your precepts,[b]
and I will[a] pay attention to Your ways.[b]

16 I delight myself in Your statutes;
I shall not forget Your Word.[a]

9:a Lit. "with what" (i.e. by what means).
9:b See the commentary section on this syntactical option.
9:c The LXX has a plural reading.
10:a Again, בְּכָל־לֵב , this time with 1 c s suffix.
10:b A very strong expression: the Piel means to "make stray" or "lead astray" (cf. BDB, p. 993).

11:a The LXX and Syriac Versions have plural readings.

12:a There is no textual justification for rejecting this imperative (i.e. strong petition) in preference for an imperfect or participle (i.e. statement of affirmation). Ascriptions or affirmations (e.g. v. 12a) are frequently followed by bold petitions (e.g. v. 12b) throughout the psalm.

13:a ספר (*spr*) in the Piel (i.e. to recount, rehearse); cf. the creation's *publishing* (i.e. מְסַפְּרִים [*m^e^sapp^e^rîm*]) of God's glory in Ps 19:2 (v. 1, Eng).

13:b The parallelism between בִּשְׂפָתַי ("with *my lips*") at the beginning of the verse and פִּיךָ ("Your [God's] mouth") at the very end is striking.

14:a The first of those significant occurrences of דֶּרֶךְ (*dere<u>k</u>*) in construct with a word for the Word (cf. the previous survey on applied Bibliology).

14:b The terse כְּעַל (*k^e^ʿal*) phrase has generated much discussion usually catalyzed by the Syriac's reading which renders it as a comparative (i.e. מֵעַל [*meʿal*]). Soll's comments are instructive: "Syriac reads 'I have rejoiced *more than* in all wealth.' Kraus and Gunkel suggest emendation from *kaph* to *mem*, and NEB, BCP, and JB all follow this by indicating that the psalmist's joy in Torah is greater than in wealth. This he does in fact say in vv. 72 and 127, but we must not be so fastidious as to deny him the use of a common simile here (so also in v. 162)" ("Psalm 119," p. 172). The other occurrence of כְּעַל in 2 Chr 32:19 along with parallel renderings of the MT in the LXX, the Targum, etc. at Ps 119:14 strengthens the case for it being a simile rather than a comparative.

15:a Both cohortatives expressing strong volition.

15:b The parallelism between the *Word* of God and the *ways* of God sheds even more light upon the theological theme of applied Bibliology.

16:a Both the *Dead Sea Psalms Scroll* (Cave 11) [hereinafter DSS (Q11)] and the LXX support a plural reading (i.e. דבריך [*dbryk*]).

Synopsis and Outline

Thematic and structural parallels with the *'Ālep̱* stanza are evident. The ethical thrust of those first eight verses continues in verses 9–16. Personal sanctification is the psalmist's burden throughout this *Bêt* stanza. The root זכה (*zḵh*), a primary term for purity, in verse 9 functions as a thematic heading.[1] The rhetorical question which frames this root (v. 9a) and the abbreviated answer which follows (v. 9b) are both didactic and experiential.[2] Stylistic threads are intricately woven together forming the smooth fabric of this stanza; for example, "the question [is] asked 'how?' . . . The rest of the strophe replies, 'with heart, lips, eyes,' and so on."[3] These eight verses in the context of the whole psalm might be looked upon as a positive corollary of Ecclesiastes 12 in its largely negative setting.

Like the *Ālep̱* stanza, the *Bêt* stanza reflects a change in persons, and not just coincidentally, the second person reference to God is central. In verses 1–8, it came at verse 4, and within verses 9–16, it comes at verse 12. Slightly different from the initial strophe, this second stanza employs the first person in both the verses which come before (i.e. vv. 9–11)[4] and those which follow verse 12 (i.e. vv. 13–16), perpetuating the psalmist's personal orientation launched back in verse 5. This two party intimacy will continue throughout the remainder of the psalm's 176 verses with only a few side glances at third party involvements.

---

1 Cf. Spurgeon, *Treasury of David*, 6:38; Yates, "Psalms," *Wycliffe Bible Commentary*, p. 540; Leupold, *Psalms*, p. 825; M'Caw, *New Bible Commentary Revised*, p. 527; etc.

2 "From the heartfelt prayers of the surrounding verses it would seem that the *young man* is the psalmist himself in the first place. . . . He is praying rather than preaching" (Kidner, *Psalms 73–150*, p. 424).

3 Soll, "Psalm 119," p. 159.

4 Although the rhetorical question of v. 9 is strictly in the third person, there is an implicit reference to the psalmist.

Based upon these brief thematic and structural observations, Psalm 119:9–16 presents three crucial ingredients in reference to personal sanctification:

1A. (vv. 9–11) The first ingredient: the right attitude.
  1B. (v. 9) It is an attitude characterized by awareness.
  2B. (v. 10) It is an attitude characterized by acknowledgment.
    1C. (v. 10a) A crucial acknowledgement of the God of the Word.
    2C. (v. 10b) A crucial acknowledgment of the Word of God.
  3B. (v. 11) It is an attitude characterized by accrual.
    1C. (v. 11a) The testimony of this accrual.
    2C. (v. 11b) The target of this accrual.
2A. (v. 12) The second ingredient: the right Source (i.e. God).
  1B. (v. 12a) The character of this Source.
  2B. (v. 12b) The capability of this Source.
3A. (vv. 13–16) The third ingredient: the right effort (i.e. a balanced view of human responsibility).
  1B. (v. 13) The right effort is demonstrated in oral testimony.
  2B. (v. 14) The right effort is demonstrated in proper priorities.
  3B. (v. 15) The right effort is demonstrated in diligent study.
    1C. (v. 15a) The burden of this diligent study.
    2C. (v. 15b) The by-product of this diligent study.
  4B. (v. 16) The right effort is demonstrated in unwavering resolution.
    1C. (v. 16a) The positive side of this resolution.
    2C. (v. 16b) The negative side of this resolution.

Commentary

Attention is arrested concerning the priority of purity through the vehicle of a rhetorical question. Two translations of the verse are possible. One would regard the whole verse as the strophe's introductory question.[5] Such a translation lends itself to a more statistically normal rendering of the infinitival phrase (i.e. v. 9b). However, the other option which aligns itself with the psalm's basic genre is preferred based on the following argument:

> The second strophe opens with a question and answer—a style reminiscent of Wisdom writings (see Prov. 23:29f.; . . . cf. Ps. 25:12f., 34:12f. (M.T. 13f.), 107:43). Also the "young man" (verse 9a) reminds us of the "my son" of the sapiential literature.[6]

It should be pointed out that, no matter which syntactical option is chosen, "the question, in the form that it is asked, is never fully answered in the psalm."[7] Yet, much significant data may be gathered in this and the remaining stanzas toward the formulation of an implicit answer. As a matter of fact, in the psalm all the basics of personal sanctification are variously integrated into the curriculum of real life: God, the gracious Teacher; the psalmist, the dependent disciple; and the Textbook, the sufficient Word.

As previously noted the verb יְזַכֶּה (*y^e^zakeh*) sets the tone for what follows. The word in the Qal stem means to be pure, clean or innocent.[8] The Piel form, as here, takes on a causative nuance, to make or keep clean, pure.[9] The root carries with it heavy ethical

---

[5] I.e. "How might a young man purify his way so as to keep it according to Your Word?" (e.g. Alexander, *Psalms*, 3:153; Soll, "Psalm 119," p. 158).

[6] Anderson, *Psalms*, 2:811; cf. Allen, *Psalms 101–150*, pp. 126, 135; etc.

[7] Soll, "Psalm 119," p. 159.

[8] Combining the literal and metaphorical sub-categories as developed in: *TDOT*, s.v. "זָכָה (*zākhāh*)," by A. Negoiță and H. Ringgren, 4:62; for a synopsis of important synonyms see Girdlestone, *Synonyms*, pp. 150–51.

[9] BDB, p. 269.

freight as its occurrences in passages such as Job 15:14; 25:4;[10] Proverbs 20:9;[11] and Isaiah 1:16[12] demonstrate.[13] In our verse there is a special stress upon the youthfulness of the subject; he is designated נַעַר (*naᶜar*), a boy, lad, youth.[14] The focal point (i.e. object) of a youth's cleansing should be "his way" אָרְחוֹ (['*orḥô*]), another figurative term which refers to character and/or conduct.[15] Putting these few words together with the instrumental interrogative בַּמֶּה (*bammeh*) which precedes them results in one powerfully significant question: "How might (i.e. should, can)[16] a youth purify his way?"

A concise answer is returned: לִשְׁמֹר כִּדְבָרֶךָ, "by keeping[17] *it* according to Your Word." A detailed explanation, for the time being, is by-passed in preference for the primary measurement[18] which itself is part of God's gracious means (i.e. His Word). The next verse along with the remaining 166 model both the dedication and dependency involved in making the answer of verse 9b a progressively realized experience of life.

---

[10] Both in parallelism with the root צדק (*ṣdq*); cf. the adjective זַךְ (*zak*) in parallelism with the root ישׁר (*yšr*) in Job 8:6; also, cf. Prov 20:11b and 21:8b.

[11] In parallelism with the root טהר (*ṭhr*).

[12] In parallelism with the ethical signification of רחץ (*rḥṣ*).

[13] Based upon the contexts of these occurrences, Soll concludes that such purity is "an unattainable moral ideal" ("Psalm 119," p. 159). This is correct in the light of hamartiological considerations, but that does not abrogate a disciple's human responsibility of working toward that goal. Our psalmist was acutely aware of his own inability; however, at the same time, he exerted himself with a 1 John 3:3 type of exertion.

[14] BDB, p. 655.

[15] BDB, p. 73; cf. the synonym דֶּרֶךְ in v. 1ff. It is to be remembered that "either word implies that man's course of life, thought, and desire ought to be brought into harmony and made coincident with God's" (Girdlestone, *Synonyms*, p. 209).

[16] The imperfect should be understood as functioning subjunctively.

[17] Another occurrence of שָׁמַר (cf. vv. 4, 5, 8; to keep, watch, preserve) emphasizing practical obedience; cf. the NIV's rendering of v. 9b: "*by living* according to your word."

[18] The preposition כְּ (*kᵉ*), "according to," expresses "conformity to a standard or rule" (BDB, p. 454).

Verse 10a individualizes the truth already observed in verse 2b.[19] It is to be remembered that the verb דָּרַשׁ (*dāraš*) usually conveys an intense pursuit[20] and is frequently used in the OT to express a variety of ethical relationships.[21] Here that relationship is intensely personal, since it is God Himself (i.e. the 2 m s pronominal suffix) who is being pursued by the psalmist.[22] Furthermore, he characterizes himself as having done this "with utmost sincerity."[23]

Suspicions of arrogance are immediately allayed in verse 10b. Spurgeon well understood the significance of the relationship of the latter part of this verse to the former:

> The man of God exerts himself, but does not trust himself. His heart is in his walking with God; but he knows that even his whole strength is not enough to keep him right unless his King shall be his keeper, and he who made the commands shall make him constant in obeying them.[24]

Consequently, being petrified of "the danger of wandering,"[25] he cries out to God, "Make me not stray!"[26]

---

[19] There is an obvious correlation of vv. 2b and 10a as indicated by occurrences of the root דרשׁ (*drš*) and the qualifier בְּכָל־לֵב.

[20] Cf. its "Theological Use" in *TDOT*, s.v. "דָּרַשׁ (*dārash*)," by S. Wagner, 3:298–304.

[21] "When man is the subject, the object of *darash* may be God (Yahweh), or a place or text (law, command) belonging to God, or an abstract idea (justice, peace, good) connected with man's relationship to God" (ibid., 3:298).

[22] The Targum expectedly emends the subject to אוּלְפָּנָךְ (*'ûlᵉpānāk*; i.e. "Your instruction") in keeping with its theological presuppositions. Contra. the LXX which appropriately utilizes the intensified ἐξεζήτησα with σε as object.

[23] Anderson's (*Psalms*, 2:812) pleasing synopsis of בְּכָל־לִבִּי (*bᵉ kol libbî*).

[24] Spurgeon, *Treasury of David*, 6:33; cf. Alexander: "While the first clause alleges his sincerity in seeking God, the second and third owns his dependence on him for success and safety" (*Psalms*, 3:154).

[25] Scroggie, *Psalms*, p. 180.

[26] Dahood's rendering of this strong negative command (*Psalms*, 3:175).

The verb שָׁגָה (*šagâ*; to go astray, err[27]) occurs here as a Hiphil imperfect[28] conveying literally "to lead astray."[29] Obviously, this is "a rather strong expression; cf. Dt. 27:18: 'Cursed be he who misleads a blind man on the road' and Isa. 63:17: 'why dost thou make us err from thy ways . . .' (cf. also Mt. 6:13). Verse 10b might be understood from Prov. 19:27, which states that when a man ceases to obey instructions he begins 'to stray from the words of knowledge.'"[30] Consequently, sensing the pressure of his acute circumstances,[31] the psalmist bares his soul imploring God's effectual intervention so that he might not stray from the Divine commands.[32]

In verse 11 the child of God reminisces over a life which has been dedicated to a purposeful accruing of Divine dividends. His commitment to treasuring, storing up the Word[33] illustrates an exemplary response to the intention of such passages as Psalm

---

[27] BDB, p. 993; in its Qal form (i.e. שָׁגָה) the primary significance seems to be related "to deliberate, not unconscious, sin" [cf. vv. 21, 118 of our psalm] (Allen, *Psalms 101–150*, p. 135).

[28] Its second person masculine singular inflection shows that the LORD is the subject of this action, and the first person singular pronominal suffix identifies the psalmist as the personal object of that action.

[29] BDB, p. 993.

[30] Anderson, *Psalms*, 2:812; because of this data, Anderson appropriately concludes: "So 119:10 is a recognition of man's dependence upon God" (ibid.). The LXX captures the force of this powerful expression with an appropriately inflected form of the verb ἀπωθέω (*apōtheō*), "to thrust away, aside; drive away; drive back; repel"; etc. (LSJ, p. 232).

[31] Cf. above on the significance of the negative אַל (*'al*) in v. 8b; "the *'al* prohibitive . . . covers a wide spectrum. At its weakest it expresses a wish or request; it may heighten into a plea, an earnest entreaty, a supplication; then to an exhortation, a solemn admonition, a stern warning; and finally, to a direct negative command, an order. . . . The *'al* prohibitive expresses a specific command for a specific occasion . . ." (John Bright, "The Apodictic Prohibition: Some Observations," *JBL*, 92:2 [June 1973]: 186–87).

[32] I.e. מִמִּצְוֹתֶיךָ (*mimmiṣwôṯeyḵā*).

[33] צָפַן (*ṣāp̄ān*) is better rendered after this manner than the potentially misleading idea of *hiding* (e.g. the LXX's ἔκρυψα [*ekrypsa*]).

37:31; Proverbs 2:10–12; 7:1; and Colossians 3:16.[34] בְּלִבִּי (*bᵉlibbî*), "in my heart," is the noteworthy repository of these dividends. לֵב (*lēḇ*) is a preeminently significant anthropological term because of its comprehensibility. Extending far beyond the emotional characteristic which is usually associated with the English word, "heart" in the Bible very frequently stands for "the seat of [man's] rational functions."[35] Also, "from the heart comes planning and volition," and "religious and moral conduct is rooted in the heart."[36] It is no wonder that the heart is the "symbol for the focus of life."[37] The psalmist understood all these anthropological truths vividly as documented by his life-time task of accrual.[38]

He also painfully understood the hamartiology of the heart[39] as the ensuing purpose clause (i.e. v. 11b) indicates.[40] His sights were set high, the target being "in order that I might never sin

---

[34] Prov 7:1 even employs the root צפן (*ṣp̄n*); Kidner parallels Ps 119:11a with Prov 2:10–12 and Col 3:16 concluding "that the mind which stores up Scripture has its taste and judgment educated by God" (*Psalms 73–150*, p. 424).

[35] See "לֵבָב/לֵב in the OT" in *TDNT*, s.v. "καρδία," by F. Baumgartel, 3:606–07.

[36] Ibid.; cf. Hans Walter Wolff, *Anthropology of the Old Testament* (Philadelphia: Fortress Press, 1974), pp. 40–55. It must be noted that although the Greek NT has an arsenal of explicit noetic and volitional terms, καρδία (*kardia*) continues to function similarly to OT לֵב in a significant number of passages (e.g. Matt 9:4; 13:15; 24:48; Mark 2:6–8; 7:21; Luke 1:51; 2:19; Acts 5:4; 11:23; 1 Cor 4:5; 2 Cor 9:7; Heb 4:12, etc.). Therefore, καρδία also "is the seat of understanding, the source of thought and reflection"; additionally, it "is the seat of the will, the source of resolves. . . . Thus the heart is supremely the one centre in man to which God turns, in which religious conduct is rooted, which determines moral conduct" (*TDNT*, s.v. "καρδία," by J. Behm, 3:611–13). For an excellent anthropological synopsis, see *NIDNTT*, s.v. "Heart," by T. Sorg, 2:182–83.

[37] J. Barton Payne, *The Theology of the Older Testament* (Grand Rapids: Zondervan Publishing House, 1962), p. 225.

[38] It must not be concluded that the psalmist was speaking merely of memorization, since "understanding and personal transformation, not knowledge and memory, are the issue here" (Soll, "Psalm 119," p. 160).

[39] E.g., cf. לֵב/καρδία in Gen 6:5; Jer 17:9–10; Mark 7:18–23; Eph 4:17–18; etc.

[40] BDB argue that לְמַעַן (*lᵉmaʿan*) "is always *in order that*, never merely *so that*" (BDB, p. 775); on this telic conjunction see also Davidson, *Hebrew Syntax*, § 149.

against You."[41] The verb חָטָא (*ḥāṭā'*), building upon its literal usage in Judges 20:16, portrays sinning as missing the bull's-eye; sin is thereby viewed as a failure, a deviation.[42] Such failure must never be generalized and consequently minimized. In its biblical framework, חָטָא is a very personal offense *against* God,[43] and the man of God conceives of it accordingly. To be noticed also is another (e.g. v. 2) implicit parallelism between the God of the Word (i.e. לָךְ [*lāḵ*]) and the Word of God (i.e. אִמְרָתֶךָ [*'imrāṯeḵā*]). The truths in this verse are deep and wide; nevertheless, Scroggie's brief anecdote commendably summarizes them: "The best thing, hidden in the best place, for the best purposes."[44]

The person of God again stands at the center of this stanza (i.e. v. 12; cf. v. 4 amidst vv. 1–8). Verse 12a in its immediate context indicates that "Yahweh is celebrated as the wisdom teacher par excellence."[45] The blessing formula proceeding from an inferior to a superior is comparatively rare but certainly not without precedent.[46] As such, it indicates personal indebtedness:[47] "The Israelite who knows that his whole life is in the hands of the Creator can-

---

[41] The objective negation לֹא (*lō'*) with אֶחֱטָא־לָךְ (*'eḥᵉṭā'-lāḵ*) is deliberately ambitious. This psalmist never sacrificed upon an altar of complacency or mediocrity in the light of God's holy demands. Yet he knew that his only hope for advancement was grounded in the goodness and grace of his LORD to whom he would flee directly (i.e. v. 12) and persistently.

[42] See Girdlestone, *Synonyms*, pp. 76–77, for a brief synopsis; cf. *TDOT*, s.v. "חָטָא (*chātā*)," by K. Koch, 4:309–19; and *TDNT*, s.v. "ἁμαρτάνω, ἁμάρτημα, ἁμαρτία," by G. Quell; G. Bertram; G. Stählin; and W. Grundmann, 1:267–316. For surveys of חָטָא, the most general and inclusive OT term for sin (cf. Job 34:37), and other hamartiological terminology, see: Payne, *Theology of the Older Testament*, pp. 194–213; and Millard J. Erickson, *Christian Theology*, (Grand Rapids: Baker Book House, 1986) 2:564–80.

[43] Cf. חָטָא לְ (*ḥāṭā' lᵉ*) in 1 Kgs 8:46 and Ps 51:6 (v. 4, Eng).

[44] Scroggie, *Psalms*, p. 180.

[45] Allen, *Psalms 101–150*, p. 142.

[46] On "a laudatory commendation to the deity" see *TDNT*, s.v. "εὐλογέω, etc.," by H. W. Beyer, 2:758–59; cf. Gen 24:48; Deut 8:10; Judg 5:2, 9; Pss 15:7; 33:1; 67:26; Dan 3:57ff. [4:34ff., Eng.]. Beyer tabulates a total of 32 occurrences after this fashion.

[47] Cf. *TDOT*, s.v. "בּרךְ (*brk*)," by J. Scharbert, 2:279–308, on the significance of Semitic blessing formulas.

not find any better expression for his faith and gratitude and hope than by giving God the glory."[48]

However, this doxology bursts forth from the psalmist's lips not only because of God's historic beneficence but also in anticipation of further endowments of Divine sufficiency. Although בָּרוּךְ אַתָּה יהוה (*bārûk 'attâ YHWH*) and similar laudatory expressions are "generally followed by an explanation as to why God should be praised (as in [Pss] 28:6, 31:21 (M.T. 22), 66:20, 68:19 (M.T. 20), etc.),"[49] herein "the poet makes his way through adoration to petition."[50] Consequently, the affirmation (i.e. v. 12a) "implicitly urges Yahweh to comply with the request of v. 12b and expresses the psalmist's reason for it."[51]

That passionate request is phrased very strongly through the vehicle of a Piel imperative: לַמְּדֵנִי חֻקֶּיךָ (*lammᵉdēnî ḥuqqeykā*), "Teach me Your statutes!"[52] It certainly indicates great boldness, but it, all the more, shows the psalmist's absolute dependence. The learner/disciple (cf. the Qal of למד in vv. 7, 71, 73) is publishing his declaration of dependence in the presence of the Source of all knowledge and wisdom.

Verses 13–16 are bound together by subtle features,[53] and they, in the light of their larger contextual setting, echo the testimony

---

48 *TDNT*, 2:758.

49 Anderson, *Psalms*, 2:812; he continues, "consequently some scholars read, '(for) you teach me . . .' (*tᵉlammᵉdēnî*) (cf. verse 171)" (ibid., 2:812–13).

50 Delitzsch, *Psalms*, 3:246.

51 Allen, *Psalms 101–150*, p. 135; cf. Alexander, *Psalms*, 3:154; Kirkpatrick, *Psalms*, p. 707; Leupold, *Psalms*, p. 825; etc.

52 This is the first of 10 occurrences of the root למד (*lmd*) in the Piel stem, all of which emphasize teaching (cf. vv. 12, 26, 64, 66, 68, 99, 108, 124, 135, 171). Concerning the Piel imperative directed to God, Soll well points out that "this verse introduces the petition 'teach me your statutes,' which becomes something of a refrain in the psalm; the verse thus introduces the conception of God himself as teacher" ("Psalm 119," p. 159).

53 E.g. "Meditation, which had been referred to in v. 11, is again part of the method (vv. 13 and 15), but now delight has been brought in as well (vv. 14 and 16). These four verses are highly patterned: they alternate between meditation and delight (ABAB) and perfect and imperfect tense (AABB)" (Soll, "Psalm 119," p. 160).

of a balanced view of human responsibility. In verse 13 the treasure house of the heart (v. 11a) issues not only private (i.e. v. 11b) but also public dividends.[54] The psalmist had "publicly declared"[55] or "proclaimed"[56] all of the LORD's judgments.[57] Special attention is directed to the source of the Scripture being God's own mouth (cf. Deut 8:3; Matt 4:4; etc.). Consequently, this disciple-servant viewed himself as a mouthpiece (cf. the introductory בִּשְׂפָתַי [*biśp̄āṯay*], "with my lips") for everything which had issued from God's own mouth.[58]

Proper priorities are exemplified in verse 14 through the use of a simile.[59] This verse, with שַׂשְׂתִּי (*śaśtî*), introduces another set of conspicuous milestones, an array of terms conveying the psalmist's deep-seated delight. The verb שׂוּשׂ / שִׂישׂ (*śûś/śîś*) means to exult, rejoice,[60] and herein, it is complemented by the preposition עַל in the latter half of the verse.[61] The object of this transcendent contentment is not merely identified as the Word of God but

---

[54] Cohen has well noted that "in addition to laying them up in his heart (verse 11), he took every opportunity to speak of them for the instruction of others" (*Psalms*, p. 396); cf. Alexander, *Psalms*, 3:154. Verses such as v. 79 also possibly refer to a period in the psalmist's life when he had a public hearing as a teacher.

[55] Leupold, *Psalms*, p. 826.

[56] Dahood's rendering of the root ספר (*sp̄r*) in the Piel (*Psalms*, 3:175); other renderings would be to recount, rehearse, or to declare (BDB, p. 708). The LXX renders the Hebrew verb with the appropriately strong term ἐξαγγέλλω (lit. to tell out; i.e. to publish); for its only NT occurrence see 1 Pet 2:9.

[57] That such activity should be considered normal for believers is attested in both Testaments (e.g. Deut 6:7; Rom 10:11ff.; etc.). It is likely that the psalmist had had many opportunities to emulate Ps 40:10–11 (vv. 9–10, Eng).

[58] Barnes' synopsis of the verse captures this interrelationship: "With my mouth I speak those things which have proceeded from thine" (*Psalms*, 3:182).

[59] Cf. the suggested translation above along with the textual notation for v. 14.

[60] BDB, p. 965.

[61] Cf. שׂוּשׂ plus עַל in Deut 28:63 (2x) and Zeph 3:17 (note the parallelisms in this verse).

as the *way of* His testimonies.[62] Furthermore, the man of God illustrates the magnitude of his joy in personal transformation through a comparison with the exuberance of someone in possession of כָּל־הוֹן (*kol-hôn*), "all wealth" or "all sufficiency."[63]

Obviously, the psalmist had understood the Scriptures' teaching on the priority of spiritual treasure above literal wealth.[64] He had already intimated this in verse 11; now he states it directly. This affirmation takes on an even greater depth of reality if the source of it indeed be Daniel.[65] For a *few* people scattered throughout the course of the history of belief (e.g. Joseph, Moses [cf. Heb 11:24–26], Daniel) such a commitment was tested in the context of great potential for personal gain. Consequently, these men stand as examples since they commendably responded to the LORD's challenges in reference to an eternal perspective and proper priorities (cf. Matt 6:33 in its context). Verse 14 is not a pietistic façade; this man of God had really discovered the way to *genuine* contentment. Kidner's comments well serve as a review of the testimony of verse 14 in its largest context:

> A persistent theme is the *delight* these sayings bring. The first references to this, in verses 14 and 16, set the tone of much that will follow, by the words they use for delight

---

[62] It must be remembered that דֶּרֶךְ (*dereḵ*) in construct with a word for the Word (cf. also vv. 27, 32, 33) or as it is used in other ethical constructs (e.g. vv. 29, 30, etc.) emphasizes the application and documentation of God's will into the fabric of man's ways (i.e. an infiltration into character and conduct). The terminology reflects "a life governed by your commands" (Anderson, *Psalms*, 2:813); however, the psalmist's balanced outlook prohibited a gravitation into legalism.

[63] BDB, p. 223; the semantical common denominator of the root הוּן (*hûn*) from which הוֹן derives is "to be easy" (ibid.; cf. Delitzsch, *Psalms*, 3:246).

[64] E.g. Job 28:12–19; Prov 2:4; 3:13–15; 8:10, 11, 19; 10:22; 11:4; 16:16; etc. Kutsch has appropriately concluded that "the psalmist prefers a life according to the will of Yahweh above all riches (Ps 119:14); for riches offer no protection against the wrath of Yahweh, but only righteousness . . ." (*TDOT*, s.v. "הוֹן (*hôn*)," by E. Kutsch, 3:368).

[65] Cf. the introduction on candidates for the authorship of Ps 119, and also note Dan 2:46–48; 5:16–17, 29; etc.

> and by the comparison of Scripture with the riches it outshines (cf. the "thousands of gold and silver pieces" in verse 72; see also verses 111, 127, 162). This is not merely a scholar's pleasure (though it has this aspect, 97) but a disciple's, whose joy is in obedience: "*in the way* of thy testimonies" (14; cf. verse 1 which sets the whole course of the psalm).[66]

His recognition of the satisfaction of true riches issues in the resolves of verse 15.[67] He commits himself to meditating upon, studying God's Word (i.e. "precepts"),[68] and to paying attention to God's ways.[69] Inter- and intra-verse parallelisms enhance these strong affirmations. First, the four words of the Hebrew text unfold chiastically with the verbals standing on the inside (i.e. in positions 2 and 3). Standing on the outside (i.e. in positions 1 and 4) are the respective objects of God's precepts and God's paths.[70] Secondly, the first two words taken together relate to the last two synthetically. Personal contemplation (v. 15a) is complemented by personal commitment (v. 15b), and the *Word* of God is recognized

[66] Kidner, *Psalms 73–150*, p. 420; cf. Alexander, *Psalms*, 3:155; Leupold, *Psalms*, p. 826; Perowne, *Psalms*, 2:351; Cohen, *Psalms*, p. 396; etc.

[67] Both cohortative verbs, אָשִׂיחָה (*'āśîḥâ*) and אַבִּיטָה (*'abbîṭâ*), should be taken as strong volitional commitments.

[68] This verb (i.e. שִׂיחַ [*śîaḥ*]) occurs in vv. 15, 23, 27, 48, 78, 148, and its cognate feminine noun in vv. 97, 99.

[69] The verb from נָבַט (*nābaṭ*) was previously encountered at v. 6 wherein, as here, and again in v. 18, it points to a deep penetration into the Word and ways of God. Cf. the respective renderings of the LXX and the Targum; κατανοέω (*katanoeō*) conveys a consideration which has as its goal understanding and apprehension (LSJ, p. 24), and the Aramaic root סכל (*skl*) regularly conveys "to look at" with reflection so as to become wise (Jastrow, *Dictionary*, 2:990–91). Also note the respective paraphrases in Delitzsch and Allen (*Psalms*, 3:246; *Psalms 101–150*, p. 126).

[70] V. 9 introduced אֹרַח (*'ōraḥ*) as a synonym of דֶּרֶךְ (*derek*); on this root as a comprehensive metaphor for life-style see also vv. 101, 104, 128. Delitzsch well notes that the plural form of v. 15 with its second person singular pronominal suffix refers to "the paths traced out in the word of God" (*Psalms*, 3:246).

as the source of the *ways* of God. This truth had been anticipated in that both God's Word (v. 15a: פִּקֻּדֶיךָ [*piqqudeykā*], "Your precepts") and God's ways (v. 15b: אֹרְחֹתֶיךָ [*'orḥōteykā*], "Your ways") were viewed in stereo in verse 14a (i.e. בְּדֶרֶךְ עֵדְוֹתֶיךָ [*bᵉderek ᶜēdwōteykā*], "in the way of Your testimonies").

The psalmist's resolves continue in verse 16.[71] In so doing, he returns to the concept of delight; however, this time it is not antecedent (cf. the perfect tense of v. 14) but anticipatory (i.e. the imperfect tense of v. 16a). Herein, he utilizes the reflexive stem of the verb שָׁעַע (*šāᶜaᶜ*),[72] meaning to delight oneself,[73] as a synonym of the previously employed שׂוּשׂ / שִׂישׂ (i.e. v. 14a).

This continuous commitment to find ultimate satisfaction in God's statutes stands in a parallel relationship with his pledge never to forget (i.e. לֹא אֶשְׁכַּח [*lō' 'eškaḥ*]) God's Word. The impact of the verb שָׁכַח (*šākaḥ*) in its familiar biblical setting is highlighted by Anderson when he notes that

> this involves not only one's memory but also a deliberate act of the will (cf. 13:1 (M.T. 2), 44:24 (M.T. 25), 74:19, 77:9). In the OT to forget God means much more than an inability to remember; it can be described as a guilty forgetfulness (cf. 106:13, 21), or as being false to his Covenant (44:17 (M.T. 18)), and as turning to other gods (44:20 (M.T. 21)).[74]

Such volitional forgetfulness, being a harbinger of all kinds of apostasy, was to be diligently avoided; consequently, the psalmist boldly committed himself to guarding against it (cf. vv. 61, 83, 93, 109, 141, 153; contra. v. 139).

---

[71] This time they are not conveyed through the vehicle of cohortative verbs, but through a reflexive affirmation immediately followed by an objectively (i.e. לֹא [*lō'*]) phrased denial.

[72] Cf. this root in vv. 47, 70; also see Ps 94:19.

[73] I.e. "delight or enjoy myself, seek my pleasure, find my happiness" (Alexander, *Psalms*, 3:155).

[74] Anderson, *Psalms*, 2:813.

ג

GIMEL STANZA (vv. 17–24)

Translation and Notes

17 Deal bountifully[a] with Your servant that[b] I may live,
then I will keep[c] Your Word.[d]

18 Uncover my eyes,
then I will behold wonderful things out of Your law.[a]

19 I am a sojourner in the land;
do not conceal Your commandments from me.

20 My soul is crushed[a] with longing
for Your judgments at all times.

21 You have rebuked *the*[a] insolent, *the*[a] cursed,
who stray[b] from Your commandments.

22 Roll away[a] from me reproach and contempt,
for I have kept Your testimonies.

23 Although officials have sat down *and*[a]
spoken together[b] against me,
Your servant meditates on Your statutes.

24 Moreover, Your testimonies are my delight;
they are[a] my counsellors.[b]

17:a The DSS (Q11) reads גמור from גָּמַר (*gāmar*), *to end, come to an end, complete* (cf. BDB, p. 170), so Sanders translates this lead-off imperative "fulfill thy purpose for" (*Dead Sea Psalms Scroll*, p. 46). However, the LXX uses an appropriately inflected form of ἀνταποδίδωμι (*antapodidōmi*) which closely parallels the semantical fields of the MT's גְּמֹל (*gāmal*); this pattern, which demonstrates both positive and negative applications of "requital," continues from biblical Greek through NT usage (cf. Thayer, *Lexicon*, p. 49). Also, the Targum's שְׁלֵם טָב (*šᵉlēm ṭāḇ*) aligns itself well with the MT's גְּמֹל.

17:b Some Hebrew manuscripts and the DSS (Q11) exhibit a *waw* conjunction attached to אֶחְיֶה (*'eḥyeh*), but the asyndetonic form of the MT is reflected in the LXX, Targum, etc. The absence of the *waw*, however, would not prohibit taking this verbal as conveying purpose (cf. Davidson, *Hebrew Syntax*, ¶ 65–65); he cites Exod 7:9; Isa 27:4; Job 9:32, 33, 35; Pss 55:7; 61:8; 118:19; 119:17 as examples (ibid., p. 92).

17:c The *wāw* on this cohortative introduces a volitionally charged apodosis (cf. Delitzsch, Psalms, 3:233, 246).

17:d Several manuscripts, the DSS (Q11), and the LXX have plural readings.

18:a The DSS (Q11) renders as a plural, but this has no other support in manuscripts and early versions.

20:a There are no significant semantical differences between the MT's גרס (grs) and the DSS's גרשׂ (grś).

21:a Both the masculine plural adjective, זֵדִים (*zēḏîm*), and the masculine plural Qal passive participle, אֲרוּרִים (*'ᵃrûrîm*), are anarthrous emphasizing their nature and status, "insolent ones" and "cursed ones" respectively.

21:b Due to the previous anarthrous constructions and the juxtaposition of this articular participle, several syntactical options for the verse are possible; for example, in addition to the translation above, at least two others are possible: "You have rebuked *the* accursed proud *ones*, who wander from Your commandments" (i.e. אֲרוּרִים modifying זֵדִים attributively); and, "You have rebuked *the* insolent ones; cursed are the ones who stray from Your commandments" (i.e. אֲרוּרִים functioning in a predicate relationship with הַשֹּׁגִים [*haššōḡîm*]). For a quite complete discussion, see Soll, "Psalm 119," pp. 173–74. It should be stressed, however, that no matter which option is preferred the basic thrust of the verse is clear.

22:a The MT's גַּל (gal) has quite frequently been repointed as גֹּל (*gōl*) from the root גלל II (*gll*), to roll, roll away (BDB, p. 164).

This option has been corroborated by the DSS (Q11) text which reads גול (gwl; i.e. *gôl*). Some still prefer (e.g. Dahood, *Psalms*, 3:176) construing גל as a masculine singular imperative from גלה (*glh*), to uncover, remove (BDB, pp. 162–63; cf. its occurrence in v. 18) instead of from גלל II. Both roots convey vivid scriptural metaphors; the former depicts a heavy weight being rolled off, and the latter a garment being divested. Again, although a preference for the former option has been indicated through the translation above, either option is in keeping with both the Hebrew consonantal text and the general thrust of the psalmist's affirmation.

23:a The second perfect tense verb is asyndetonic.

23:b I.e. to speak with one another; a quite rare occurrence of the Niphal reflexive of the root דבר (*dḇr*).

24:a The text is structured as a simple apposition, lit. "Your testimonies *are* my delight, *the* men of my council." Obviously, he is far more concerned with what the Word of God says to and about him (v. 24b) than with what powerful plotters are speaking against him (v. 23a).

24:b The LXX adds τὰ δικαιώματά σου (*ta dikaiōmata sou*) to the end of this verse; however, other early sources do not agree with it.

Synopsis and Outline

Indications of the occasion for this psalm manifest themselves in the *Gimel* stanza. As Soll stresses, "We meet up with 'the enemies' for the first time in this strophe ('the arrogant' of v. 21 and the 'princes' of v. 23). In the first two strophes, all danger came from within the psalmist; beginning with the *Gimel* strophe, it comes largely from without."[1] That these eight verses are paradigmatic for much of that which shall follow them is pointed out by Allen when he argues that

---

1 Soll, "Psalm 119," p. 161; therefore, "the lament proper begins with this strophe" (ibid., p. 174).

> distressing circumstances, specifically persecution, v 23, prompt a double prayer characteristic of the whole psalm, for deliverance and for deeper insight into Yahweh's will for his life revealed in the Torah. . . . He prays out of a strong sense of religious and moral values and a deep love of Yahweh's revelation, but is conscious of the gap between his faith and his spiritual ambition.[2]

Alternately, his pains and prayers enter and exit center stage. This stanza unfolds in a subtle fashion. He implicitly draws two sets of contrasts between himself and his persecutors in verses 20–21 and 23–24. Then in anticipation of those contrasts he lays down his petitions in verses 17–19 and 22. A schematic of this structure could be drawn as follows:

vv. 17–19: requests
    vv. 20–21: contrast (order: the psalmist; his enemies)
vv. 22: request
    vv. 23–24: contrast (order: the enemies; the psalmist)[3]

By drawing these observations together the following proposition and outline capture the essence and expression of verses 17–24.

The man of God's prayers for Divine intervention are ignited by two painful contrasts:

1A. (vv. 17–21) His prayers for relief are ignited by a painful contrast between his anticipation and the apathy of his enemies.
    1B. (vv. 17–19) He voices the prayers for relief.
        1C. (v. 17) He prays generally for personal intervention.
        2C. (vv. 18–19) He prays specifically for propositional intervention:

[2] Allen, *Psalms 101–150*, p. 142.
[3] Note the chiastic welding between these sets of contrast: psalmist, enemies (vv. 20–21); enemies, psalmist (vv. 23–24).

1D. (v. 18) First he phrases his request positively.
2D. (v. 19) Then he phrases his request negatively.
2B. (vv. 20–21) He voices the painful contrast between:
1C. (v. 20) How his anticipation draws him to God's Word.
2C. (v. 21) How his enemies' apathy repels them from God's Word.
2A. (vv. 22–24) His prayer for respect is ignited by a painful contrast between the slander of his enemies and his satisfaction.
1B. (v. 22) He voices the prayer for respect.
2B. (vv. 23–24) He voices the painful contrast between:
1C. (v. 23a) How his enemies have slandered him.
2C. (vv. 23b–24) How God's Word has satisfied him.

Commentary

A petition in the form of a Qal masculine singular imperative from גָּמַל (*gāmal*) launches this passionate stanza. "The verb used here means to do, or show, or cause good or evil to any one; and then to reward, or to recompense, either good or evil."[4] Although some have argued for the more specific connotation of requital,[5] "here it seems to be used in a general sense of doing good, or showing favor."[6] In its present contextual setting it therefore becomes an obvious plea for deliverance.[7] The psalmist designates himself as the benefactor of God's anticipated intervention not by

---

[4] Barnes, *Psalms*, 3:182; it is obvious that גמל exhibits two basic semantical fields, and correspondingly, two antithetical applications (cf. the wide-spectrum usage pattern of פקד [*pqd*] in the OT).

[5] E.g. Dahood, *Psalms*, 3:175.

[6] Barnes, *Psalms*, 3:182–83; he supports his conclusion with references to Pss 13:6; 116:7; and 142:7 (v. 8, Eng); cf. Prov 11:17 for a different contextual setting. For גָּמַל complemented by the preposition עַל (*ʿal*), as here, BDB suggest "to deal bountifully with" (p. 168).

[7] Cf. *TDOT*, s.v. "גָּמַל (*gāmal*)," by K. Seybold, 3:30–32; Anderson, *Psalms*, 2:814; etc.

means of a normal pronominal indicator but by means of the graphic עַבְדְּךָ (*ᶜab̲dᵉk̲ā*), "Your servant."[8]

The specific consequence and content of a gracious intervention is made clear by the אֶחְיֶה (*'eḥyeh*), "*that* I may live."[9] The basic significance of חָיָה (*ḥāyâ*) for the OT believer was not merely a hanging on to physical existence; neither was it viewed as something exclusively spiritual in an eschatological sense. Based upon key OT passages, it was an abundant life that was in view, "a fulness of life in his [i.e. God's] favour."[10] As such, it alluded both to covenantal blessings[11] and to a qualitative relationship with the Bestower of all such blessings. Kidner, in stressing this latter dimension, has well commented: "*That I may live* is the first of many such prayers . . . . While some of them could refer simply to surviving an illness or an attack, others are clearly qualitative, speaking of life that is worthy of the name, or in our terms, spiritual life in fellowship with God: e.g. verses 37, 50, 93, 144, and probably others. It is a familiar Old Testament concept (cf., e.g., Pss. 16:11; 36:9; Dt. 8:3)."[12]

---

[8] Sometimes this serves a circumlocutionary device for the pronoun; however, it may convey, in the light of the surrounding context, something stronger herein. For example, Anderson argues, "'Thy servant' is more than a poetic variation on the first person pronoun 'I'; . . . it emphasizes the God-man relationship, and alludes to the Covenant concept" (*Psalms*, 2:814). Concerning the use of עֶבֶד throughout the Psalms, Kraus argues for the following basic emphasis: "their whole life is committed to the Lord" (Hans-Joachim Kraus, *Theology of the Psalms*, trans. by Keith Crim [Minneapolis: Augsburg Publishing House, 1986], p. 157).

[9] Cf. the identical first person Qal imperfect form (with conjunction) in vv. 77, 116, and 144; also, note the Qal jussive form in v. 175 and the recurrent Piel imperative in vv. 25, 37, 40, 88, 107, 149, 154, 156, and 159. For further discussions on this syntactical preference (cf. above under "Translation and Notes"), see Delitzsch, *Psalms*, 3:246; and Cohen, *Psalms*, p. 396.

[10] BDB, p. 311.

[11] Cf. Anderson, *Psalms*, 2:814.

[12] Kidner, *Psalms 73–150*, p. 424; cf. Leupold, *Psalms*, p. 826; and Allen, *Psalms 101–150*, p. 142, who concludes by saying, "His life is threatened and weakened, and he craves that fullness of life which is one of the psalm's heartbeats of desire."

Progressive stages of intervention (i.e. v. 17a, b) will issue in a reciprocation on the part of the psalmist: "*then* I will keep Your Word" (v. 17c). The result (i.e. אֶחְיֶה) flowing out of God's well-doing (i.e. גְּמֹל עַל־עַבְדְּךָ) will generate a strong volitional response (i.e. וְאֶשְׁמְרָה דְבָרֶךָ [*wᵉ'ešmᵉrâ dᵉḇāreḵā*]) in the man of God. In other words, expecting a gracious fulfillment of his request which is aimed at personal vivification, he firmly commits himself to an energized obedience.

Verses 18 and 19 are basically two sides of the same coin. The psalmist is seeking an illumination of God's revelation, and he conveys this through the positively phrased imperative of verse 18 (i.e. reveal) and through the negatively phrased proscription of verse 19b (i.e. don't conceal).

"V. 18 is a clear example of an ever-present factor in Ps. 119: the psalmist approaches Torah in the context of his relationship with God, and is dependent on Yahweh to open his eyes and reveal his wonders out of Torah."[13] The leading Piel imperative directed towards God derives from the verb גָּלָה (*gālâ*) which in the Qal means "to uncover, remove."[14] It also means "to uncover" in the Piel stem; however, several nuances are possible in contexts such as the one under consideration: "to disclose, make known, show, reveal," etc.[15] When combined with עֵינַי (*'ênay*), "my eyes," there is an undergirding metaphor of uncovering or unveiling one's organs of visual perception.[16] He is beseeching the LORD for unveiled discernment, 20/20 spiritual acuity.

---

[13] Soll, "Psalm 119," p. 175.

[14] BDB, p. 162; Waltke well notes that "in the Qal the verb is used frequently with the organs of sense as the object: the ear (I Sam 9:15, *passim*) and the eye (Num 24:4) . . ." (*TWOT*, s.v. "גָּלָה (*gālâ*)," by B. Waltke, 1:160).

[15] BDB, p. 163; again, Waltke provides some helpful commentary: "Thus, though not a technical term for divine revelation, the verb *gālâ* frequently conveys this meaning. Likewise in the Piel it always denotes 'to uncover' something which otherwise is normally concealed. Thus it means 'to open' the eyes—to see an angel (Num 22:31 [also 24:4, 16]) or wonderful things in the law (Ps 119:18); . . ." (*TWOT*, 1:160–61).

[16] Cf. Kidner, *Psalms 73–150*, p. 424.

The goal or consequence[17] of God's assistance is communicated through yet another occurrence of the verb נָבַט (*nāḇaṭ*), "to look upon, behold, show regard."[18] This time the psalmist designates the object of his concentration as נִפְלָאוֹת מִתּוֹרָתֶךָ (*nip̱lā'ôt mittôrāṯeḵā*), "extraordinary things from Your law."[19] In the light of the immediate and larger circles of context it seems best not to perceive of these "wonders" as the man of God's preoccupation with the spectacular, but rather

> נִפְלָאוֹת is the expression for everything supernatural and mysterious which is incomprehensible to the ordinary understanding and is left to the perception of faith. The Tôra beneath the surface of its letter contains an abundance of such "wondrous things," into which only eyes from which God has removed the covering of natural short-sightedness penetrate; hence the prayer in ver. 18.[20]

---

[17] It seems that the syntax of the *waw* in this context would allow for either or both! Cf. the syntax of v. 17 which is similar (with the exception of its *three* sequenced verbals). If the verb form is regarded as a true cohortative, the consequential option may be the better rendering.

[18] BDB, p. 613; cf. vv. 6 and 15.

[19] The feminine plural Niphal participle used substantively comes from the root פלא (*pl'*): "Preponderantly both the verb and substantive refer to the acts of God, designating either cosmic wonders or historical achievements on behalf of Israel. That is, in the Bible the root *pl'* refers to things that are unusual, *beyond human capabilities*. . . . When *pl'* refers to man it means unsolvable, *suprarational*, incredible . . ." (*TWOT*, s.v. "פָּלָא (*pālā'*)," by V. Hamilton, 2:723 [emphasis added]).

[20] Delitzsch, *Psalms*, 3:246–47; Leupold's remarks are also insightful: "This faithful use of the Word involves ever new insights into the richness of God's revelation. It is for these prayer is made. Man is viewed as being afflicted by a natural blindness over against the Word, a shortcoming that God can remove by uncovering the eyes of a man. . . . The things that are disclosed by the enlightening effort of the Spirit of God are described as 'wondrous things.' This expression is apt to lead us to think of the deep and marvelous revelation that is disclosed in the divine Word. But in view of the practical slant of this psalm there is great likelihood that the psalmist has pri-

Presuppositions about authorship and location may affect one's interpretation of verse 19a. Both גֵּר (*gēr*)[21] and אֶרֶץ (*'ereṣ*)[22] may be viewed either comprehensively or restrictively: "I am a wayfarer on the earth," or "I am a foreigner in the land." Although the unrestricted view might be looked upon with favor in the light of a significant theological theme from progressive revelation (e.g. Heb 11:9ff.), the latter option may have an interpretive edge based upon the psalm's internal evidence.[23] However, no matter which view is preferred, "the point seems to be that wherever man lives, his existence is essentially transient, and dependent on the grace of God."[24] That our psalmist understood this truth in his heart of hearts is immediately verified through the entreaty which follows (v. 19b).

marily in mind 'simple practical truths of the law,' which man does not naturally discern unless the Spirit of God assists him" (*Psalms*, pp. 826–27). Requests for this practical illumination take various forms throughout the course of the psalm (e.g. the Hiphil imperatives from ירה (*yrh*) in v. 33 and בין (*byn*) in v. 34; cf. the allusion to illumination in v. 130).

21 גֵּר from גּוּר (*gûr*), to sojourn, refers to a "temporary dweller, new-comer (no inherited rights)" (BDB, pp. 157–58); cf. Gen 23:4; Exod 12:19; Lev 24:16; Num 15:30; Josh 8:23; etc. "According to Lev 25:23 Israel comprised a group of גרים permitted to live on Yahweh's property and dependent completely upon him" (Allen, *Psalms 101–150*, p. 135). The LXX employs the semantically parallel πάροικος (*paroikos*) which manifests itself in the NT in Eph 2:19 and 1 Pet 2:11, and the verb form is παροικέω (*paroikeō*) which appears at the outset of a significant theological discussion in Heb 11:9–16. In the Targum, we encounter דַּיּוֹר (*dayyôr*), an inhabitant, lodger, tenant; traveller, peddler (Jastrow, *Dictionary*, 1:297).

22 Two major usage spheres of אֶרֶץ are the "whole earth" and "land," i.e. "country, territory" (BDB, p. 76); cf. *TWOT*, s.v. "אֶרֶץ (*'ereṣ*)," by V. Hamilton, 1:74.

23 Cf., e.g., the cognate מָגוֹר (*māgôr*), "sojourning-place, dwelling-place" (BDB, p. 158) in v. 54 and some of the informing statements made in vv. 23, 46, 57, 111, 161, etc.

24 *TWOT*, s.v. "גּוּר (*gûr*)," by H. Stigers, 1:156.

The forcefulness of this negatively phrased request rivals the one previously encountered in verse 10b.[25] Desperation commendably yields to dependence as he cries out directly to God, "Do not hide/conceal Your commandments from me."[26] The direction of his request is adequately charted by Delitzsch when he comments: "Hence the poet prays in ver. 19 that God would keep His commandments, these rules of conduct for the journey of life, in living consciousness for him."[27]

One of several vivid metaphors with נַפְשִׁי (*napšî*)[28] emerges in verse 20.[29] The leading verb comes from the root גרס (*grs*) which occurs only here and in the causative Hiphil in Lamentations 3:16, respectively conveying to be crushed and to crush.[30] The same root in Aramaic גרס [*grs*]) means to crush, split, or grind,[31] and in

---

[25] Both are Hiphil jussives negated by אַל (*'al*), expressing a negative command that is usually adapted to a special situation. Herein, the activities of the זֵדִים (*zēḏîm*; v. 21), cf. שָׂרִים (*śārîm*; v. 23), provide some of the historical background of that situation.

[26] On the significance of the root סתר (*sṯr*) see *TWOT*, s.v. "סתר," by R. Patterson, 2:636. The Targum is somewhat paraphrastic but within the parameters of the nuanced context of v. 19 when it utilizes לָא תְסַלֵּק (*lā' ṯᵉsalēq*): "Don't remove!"

[27] Delitzsch, *Psalms*, 3:247; cf. Alexander, *Psalms*, 3:156.

[28] Usually translated as "my soul," it conveys "'I myself'" (Anderson, *Psalms*, 2:814); cf. vv. 25, 28, 81, 109, 129, 167, 175; cf. it with its parallel words in Ps 63:2 (v. 1, Eng). This term rarely, *if ever*, individuates as a reference to a separate immaterial part *of* man; "נֶפֶשׁ is the usual term for a man's total nature, for what he is and not just what he has" (*TDNT*, "The Anthropology of the OT," by E. Jacob, 9:620); cf. Wolff, "Man does not *have n.*, he *is n.*, he lives as *n.*" (*Anthopology of the OT*, p. 10). For a comprehensive usage survey with the important sub-categories of "Meaning person, individual man" and "With pronominal suffix [as here] it has the force of a reflexive or personal pronoun" see Ernest DeWitt Burton, *Spirit, Soul, and Flesh*, Historical and Linguistic Studies, 3 (Chicago: University of Chicago Press, 1918), pp. 62–68.

[29] Certainly in anticipation of the implicit contrast which will be drawn with the psalmist's enemies in v. 21.

[30] BDB, p. 176.

[31] Jastrow, *Dictionary*, 1:270 (cf. the Targum at Prov 8:28).

Arabic, its philological twin sister, גרשׂ (*grś*), connotes to bray, pound, or grind course.[32] It is this striking word-picture that the disciple enlists to characterize his longing for God's judgments.[33] Consequently, in verse 20, the psalmist is asserting that he is perpetually consumed or overwhelmed with a deep desire for the Word from which a disciple is able to understand more of the LORD's will and ways.[34]

Verse 21 takes an outward look at the psalmist's enemies. They are characterized as זֵדִים (*zēḏîm*), אֲרוּרִים (*'ărûrîm*), and הַשֹּׁגִים (*haššōgîm*). The masculine plural adjective זֵדִים is quite picturesque being derived from the root זוּד (*zûḏ*) or זִיד (*zîḏ*), "to be hot, boil,"[35] i.e. "to act proudly, presumptuously, rebelliously."[36] The true colors of these men whom the psalmist labels as presumptuous or insolent will take on a bolder resolution as he progressively calls more and more attention to their activities.[37]

---

[32] BDB, p. 176.

[33] I.e. לְתַאֲבָה אֶל־מִשְׁפָּטֶיךָ בְכָל־עֵת (*l^e^ta'ăbâ 'el-mišpāṭeykā b^e^kol-ʿēṯ*). תַּאֲבָה is being taken as a feminine singular noun occuring only here in the OT (cf. BDB, p. 1060); however, influenced by two occurrences of the verbal in vv. 40 and 174, Dahood renders it as a feminine singular verb with emphatic ל, i.e. "truly longs" (*Psalms*, 3:176).

[34] Cf. Kirkpatrick, *Psalms*, p. 708; Cohen, *Psalms*, p. 397; Delitzsch, *Psalms*, 3:247; and Anderson, *Psalms*, 2:814.

[35] *TDOT*, s. v. "זוּד (*zûdh*)," by J. Scharbert, 4:46; cf. p. 48 on the adjectival occurrences in Ps 119.

[36] BDB, p. 267; they suggest that the substantive adjective is used consistently as a technical term for "godless, rebellious men" (ibid.). The LXX's employment of the adjective ὑπερήφανος (*huperēphanos*), emphasizing pride and arrogance, not only captures the nature of these זֵדִים in Ps 119 but also provides a semantical/theological connection to the NT (cf., e.g. Luke 1:51; Rom 1:30; 2 Tim 3:2; Jas 4:6; 1 Pet 5:5).

[37] Cheyne's preliminary summary is noteworthy: "*The proud*. 'Boiling' or 'boiling over' suggested the idea of pride (see Gen. xlix.4, R.V. marg.) The word occurs six times in this psalm. Whether it refers to Jews (as Jer. xliii.2, Mal. iii.14) or to foreigners (as Isa. xiii.11), or to both, the context must decide. At any rate, opponents of the strict worship of Jehovah are meant—those who calumniate (vv. 69, 78) and (v. 122) oppress the speaker, and both transgress and mock at God's law (vv. 21, 51, 85)" (T. K. Cheyne, *The Book of Psalms*, vol. 2 [London: Kegan, Paul, Trench, Trubner and Company, Ltd., 1904], p. 326).

Frequently, a Qal passive participle of the verb אָרַר (*'ārar*), herein אֲרוּרִים, is used in OT curse formulas (e.g. Gen 3:14, 17; Deut 27:15ff.; 28:16ff.; Jer 11:3; 17:5; Mal 1:14; etc.).[38] Whether or not one accepts an immediate syntactical connection[39] between this "cursed" estate and "the ones who go astray, err" (i.e. הַשֹּׁגִים), there can be no denial of a conceptual one.[40] Although "the verb *š-g-h* may occasionally describe a sin of inadvertence (cf. Lev. 4:13; Num. 15:22), . . . the present context suggests a deliberate action, as in verse 118 and 1 Sam. 26:21."[41] It was personally and painfully obvious to the psalmist that these men had no regard for the commandments of God.[42]

Amidst all his pain, stemming from their pride and lawlessness, the man of God rests in the manner of God. He knows with absolute certainty that the LORD rebukes such men.[43] His confidence in God's imminent intervention against his enemies is indicated by his choice of words. After surveying the semantical data related to גָּעַר (*gā^c ar*),[44] Caquot summarizes the essence of this particular kind of *rebuke*, saying, "When the etymology and secular use of *gā'ar* ('to utter a cry') are taken into account, it seems that the central point in the religious use of *gā^c ar* and *ge^c arah* lies in the fearful and threatening voice of Yahweh, which he utters in the

[38] Cf. the broader ancient near eastern context (e.g. *TDOT*, s.v. "ארר (*'rr*)," by J. Scharbert, 1:408–12); on the ethical superiority of the OT occurrences, see *TWOT*, s.v. "אָרַר (*'ārar*)," by V.P. Hamilton, 1:75–76.

[39] Cf. the translation notes above on the major syntactical options for v. 21.

[40] This conceptual association also reaches backwards. In other words, the אֲרוּרִים (Qal *passive* participle, masculine plural) conveys the Divine estimation of such men, corroborated internally by their prideful insolence, and documented externally by their blatant apostasy.

[41] Anderson, *Psalms*, 2:815.

[42] Their negative example (i.e. the root שׁגה + מִן + a word for the Word), historically confirmed by a progressively intensifying antagonism against the psalmist, provides a black back-drop for one of his previous entreaties (i.e. v. 10b: the negative + the root שׁגה + מִן + the very same word for the Word).

[43] "The perfect tense (*hast rebuked*) states a general truth and is best translated by the present, *thou rebukest*" (Kirkpatrick, *Psalms*, pp. 708–09).

[44] The verb occurs 14 times in the OT, and various noun forms occur 16 times.

thunder, and which functions as a battle cry when he puts various enemies to flight."[45] Underneath all the pains of persecution the psalmist was moored to a Romans 8:31 type of anchorage.

Another impassioned prayer launches (i.e. v. 22a) the second stage of the disciple's lament in this stanza. Supported by the *Dead Sea Psalms Scroll* from Cave 11 and significant early versions, it seems best to regard the consonantal Hebrew text as reflecting an imperatival form from the root גלל (*gll*).[46] The verb "*gll* usually means 'to roll, turn' a stone, either to shut a well (Gen. 29:3, 8, 10) or a cave (Josh. 10:18), or to build an altar (1 S. 14:33)."[47] Joshua 5:9 provides special illumination for two reasons: (1) the town's name as it was derived from this root is explained, and (2) the accompanying verb form takes as its object חֶרְפָּה (*ḥerpâ*, i.e. the first of two objects that our psalmist mentions in v. 22): "Now the LORD said to Joshua, 'Today I have rolled off (גַּלּוֹתִי [*gallôṯî*]) from upon you the reproach (חֶרְפַּת [*ḥerpat*]) of Egypt,' so he named that place 'Gilgal' (גִּלְגָּל [*gilgāl*]) . . . ." In the light of these literal and metaphorical usages of גָּלַל, our psalmist is imploring the LORD "to roll away from upon him" (i.e. גַּל מֵעָלַי [*gōl mēʿālay*]) the heavy weights of "reproach" and "contempt."[48]

"Reproach" or "'scorn' (*ḥerpāh*) usually denotes the taunts and reproaches of the enemies ([Pss] 71:13, 79:12, 89:50), or the humiliating situation itself ([Pss] 69:19, 78:66, etc.) which is also the cause of the enemy's scorn. It can also describe the sufferer himself as the object of reproach ([Pss] 22:6 (M.T. 7), 31:11 (M.T. 12), 39:8 (M.T. 9), 79:4, 89:41 (M.T. 42), etc.)."[49] Concerning the second member of this couplet, בּוּז (*bûz*),

> Contempt is characteristic of the wicked (Prov 18:3) and is often directed at the righteous (Ps 31:18 [H 19]), who

---

[45] *TDOT*, s.v. "גָּעַר (*gaʿar*)," by A. Caquot, 3:53.

[46] Cf. the translation notes above on v. 22a; note also the LXX's περίελε (*periele*) which would support an imperative from גלל (*gll*).

[47] *TDOT*, s.v. "גלל (*gll*)," by G. Münderlein, 3:21.

[48] Anderson, *Psalms*, 2:815.

[49] Ibid.

> then cry for God's mercy and intervention (Ps 123:3–4; cf. Ps 119:22). To be regarded by others as unimportant or insignificant is the luxury of those who are secure (Job 12:5) but is irritable, if not hurtful, to those who are the objects of *bûz* and who understandably avoid it (Gen 38:23).[50]

As the remainder of these 176 verses unfolds it would seem that no other man in the course of human history[51] has suffered as much חֶרְפָּה וָבוּז (*ḥerpâ wābûz*). Understandably, his dependent cry comes forth with great intensity, "Roll away from me" these enormous burdens! Then to his poignant prayer he appends one of those interspersed affirmations of personal fidelity to God's special revelation (v. 22b).[52]

Verse 23 contains the first of several "unnatural" (i.e. supernaturally mediated) responses on the part of the psalmist in reference to his vicious antagonists.[53] Their malignant activities were undeniable realities as indicated by the concessive גַּם (*gam*) along with the verbs יָשַׁב (*yāšab*) and דָּבַר (*dābar*).[54] The second verb occurs in the Niphal which would suitably portray the concept of a conclave of conspiracy, and the accompanying preposition בְּ (*b*ᵉ) identifies the psalmist as the personal object of their hostility: "Al-

---

[50] *TWOT*, s.v. "בּוּז (*bûz*)," by E. Martens, 1:96.

[51] Except, of course, the God-Man Himself.

[52] In other places it will be seen that his own obedience seemed to operate as a catalyst for his enemies hatred and persecution; on an implicit connection of this phenomenon herein, see Leupold, *Psalms*, p. 827.

[53] Cf. the introduction on the force of these conceptually antithetical parallelisms which are usually strengthened by the asyndetonic relationship of the bicola. Herein the concessive גַּם (*gam*) of v. 23a prepares the way for the impacting response of the psalmist (i.e. v. 23b).

[54] Some translators combine the force of these two perfect verbs, e.g., "Even though the authorities have plotted in session against me . . ." (Allen, *Psalms 101–150*, p. 127), "Even though princes sit plotting against me . . ." (Soll, "Psalm 119," p. 173), etc., calling attention to the unified purpose of their actions.

though they have sat and *spoken with one another against me . . . .*"[55] Furthermore, he identifies these perpetrators as שָׂרִים (*śārîm*), chieftains, chiefs, rulers, officials, captains, or princes,[56] which makes his persecution all the more significant.

Yet their nefarious plottings did not prompt an immediate imprecation, but, on the contrary, this mature disciple turns upward and inward rather than outward as he persists in habitual meditation upon the ultimate Ruler's pronouncements (i.e. עַבְדְּךָ יָשִׂיחַ בְּחֻקֶּיךָ [*ᶜabdᵉkā yāśîaḥ bᵉḥuqqeykā*]). Kirkpatrick is probably correct in viewing verse 23b as "a further proof of his fidelity. Though those in authority sit in council and devise plans for his ruin, he continues to meditate on Jehovah's statutes."[57] In its theological setting this is yet another amazing testimony to the grace of God at work in the heart of the servant of God.[58]

---

[55] Cf. BDB, p. 180; also cf. similar experiences recorded in Jer 36:12 and Ezek 33:30.

[56] BDB, p. 978; cf. Anderson's helpful survey: "The Hebrew *śārim* (cf. the Akkadian *šarru*, 'king') is one of the most popular words for 'rulers' or 'leaders,' but it ought not to be confused with the 'sons of the King' (cf. Zeph. 1:8) although the latter might occupy an office designated by *śar*. The *śārîm* may be chieftans (Jg. 5:15), heads of families (Ezr. 8:29), elders (Job 29:9), or it may denote military officers (1 Kg. 9:22; 2 Kg. 1:14, etc.) and civil officials of the King (1 Kg. 4:2; Ps. 105:22; Jer. 26:10, etc.). It is also used of heads or chiefs of particular classes (Gen. 40:2; 1 Chr. 15:22) or, perhaps, as a term of dignity in general (cf. Isa. 23:8; Ps. 45:16 (M.T. 17), 82:7). . . . NEB 'the powers that be'" (*Psalms*, 2:816). This circumstance certainly fits the historical data we possess in reference to Daniel (cf. again Thrupp, *Introduction to the Study and Use of the Psalms*, 2:244–45, for internal evidence along with passages in Daniel such as 6:4ff.).

[57] Kirkpatrick, *Psalms*, p. 709.

[58] A reminder seems appropriate upon this second of 13 occurrences (cf. vv. 17, 23, 38, 49, 65, 76, 84, 122, 124, 125, 135, 140, 176) of עַבְדְּךָ (*ᶜabdᵉ kā*) as a self designation. The noun עֶבֶד (*ᶜebed*) coming from עָבַד (*ᶜābad*), "to work, serve," often designates a "servant" *or* "worshipper" (BDB, pp. 712–14). The concepts of *service* and *worship* are closely integrated throughout the OT (e.g., cf. the renderings of various translations for the root עבד in 2 Kgs 10:18ff.); consequently, עֶבֶד serves as another link in the descriptive chain of biblical discipleship. Not surprisingly, the LXX uniformly renders the Hebrew by ὁ δοῦλος σου (*ho doulos sou*), "Your *bond-slave*" (cf. the extremely significant employment of this substantive in the NT; e.g., Acts 16:17; Titus 1:1; 1 Pet 2:16; Rev 7:3; 15:3; etc.).

The second גַּם in as many verses stands at the head of verse 24; however, this time it is not functioning concessively. It is possible that it may bear either (or both?) of two nuances herein depending upon its syntactical allusion(s). In reference to v. 23b it would lend itself to correspondence (i.e. translating "also, moreover," or "yea"[59]); but, if it continues to build upon the antithesis with verse 23a, the emphasis upon contradiction (i.e. translating, "yet, but,"[60] or "nevertheless"[61]) is resumed. Irrespective of one's syntactical preference, the thinking of the psalmist is transparent. Even in the face of his powerful opponents who were practiced in subversion he finds comfort (v. 24a)[62] in the Divine resources.

He not only finds comfort but also *Divine* counsel (v. 24b). The last two words of this stanza in the Hebrew text stand in stark apposition to his affirmation of delight; without taking a breath, he goes on to affirm אַנְשֵׁי עֲצָתִי (*ʾanšê ʿăṣāṯî*), literally, "men of my counsel" (i.e. "[they are] 'my counsellors'"[63]). "He sought direction and advice from them [i.e. God's testimonies] as from a friend who would give him counsel. He looked to the revealed law of God to ascertain what was right; to know how he should act in the emergencies of life."[64] In the midst of his turmoil he clings to the LORD's own testimonies.

---

[59] BDB, pp. 168–69.

[60] Ibid., p. 169.

[61] Delitzsch's preference herein (*Psalms*, 3:247).

[62] I.e. "delight"; cf. the verb form from this same root in v. 16. It is noteworthy that both the *Bêṯ* and *Gimel* stanzas culminate with this transcendent consolation mediated through God's Word (also cf. Prov 8:30ff. which associates Wisdom and delight).

[63] BDB, p. 420; on the infinite superiority of the LORD's counsel, cf. Job 38:2; 42:3; Pss 1:1; 33:10ff.; Prov 12:15; 19:20–21; Isa 9:6; 11:2; etc.

[64] Barnes, *Psalms*, 3:155; Cohen suggests, "to foil their [i.e. the rulers of v. 23] schemes" (*Psalms*, p. 397); cf. Hengstenberg's connection of v. 24b with v. 23a (*Psalms*, 3:388).

ד

DALET STANZA
(vv. 25–32)

Translation and Notes

25 My soul[a] clings to the dust;
revive me according to Your word.

26 I have declared my ways[a] and You answered me;
teach me Your statutes.

27 Make me understand the way of Your precepts,[a]
then I will meditate[b] upon Your wonders.

28 My soul[a] weeps because of[b] grief;
establish me[c] according to Your word.

29 Remove from me[a] *the* way of deception,[b]
and be gracious unto me with Your law.[c]

30 I have chosen *the* way of faithfulness;[a]
I have agreed with[b] Your judgments.

31 I cling to Your testimonies;
O LORD, do not put me to shame.

32 I shall run the way of Your commandments,
because[a] You enlarge my heart.[b]

25:a Cf. v. 20 on the anthropological significance of נַפְשִׁי (*napšî*); e.g. the NAB renders, "*I* lie prostrate in the dust" [emphasis added]; the NIV, "*I am* laid low in the dust" [emphasis added]; and Allen translates, "The dust holds *me* prostrate" [emphasis added] (*Psalms 101–150*, p. 127).

26:a A few manuscripts of the LXX exhibit a second masculine singular pronominal suffix; however, the evidence for the first person suffix is compelling (cf. also the of דרכי DSS [Q11]).

27:a I.e., "Give me insight into the way taught in your charges" (Allen, *Psalms 101–150*, p. 127).

27:b Probably best taken as a "cohortative . . . the 1st pers. or plural of the imperfect lengthened by the ending ָה . . . . The cohortative lays stress on the determination underlying the action, and the personal interest in it" (GKC, ¶ 108a).

28:a Cf. vv. 20a and 25a above, i.e. "a circumlocution for the pronoun 'I'" (Anderson, *Psalms*, 2:817).

28:b I.e. the causal nuance of מִן (*min*); cf. BDB, pp. 579–80.

28:c Lit. "raise me" (Soll, "Psalm 119," p. 176).

29:a I.e. "away from me," the ablative force of מִן; cf. BDB, pp. 577–78.

29:b Or, "*the* false, deceptive way," i.e. a lying life-style, deceptive behavior.

29:c Note the double accusative, translating the personal object as an indirect object and the other object, "Your law," as an adverbial accusative.

30:a Or, "*the* steadfast, faithful way," i.e. a life characterized by fidelity, a life-style of integrity. For some comments on the subtle interrelationship between v. 29a and v. 30a, see: *TDOT*, s.v. "אָמַן *'āman*," by A. Jepsen, 1:317.

30:b Basing the translation upon שָׁוָה I (*šāwâ*), "agree with, be like, resemble . . . [Ps] 119:30 accounted suitable, meet" (BDB, pp. 1000–1001), i.e. to accept: "'accept'—RSV, NEB and BCP render this verb (*šwh*) as 'set,' but this requires the translator to provide the words 'before me,' present in Ps. 16:8 but not here. Kraus and others emend to *'wh* ('desire') which may receive support from the Syriac (see BHS note). There is, however, another root *šwh* with a basic meaning of 'agree with,' which can be rendered 'consent to' (Anderson), 'account suitable' (BDB), or, as here, 'accept.' This forms a good parallel with *bḥr* ('choose') in the first colon, and requires no emendation or added words" (Soll, "Psalm 119," p. 176); cf. the discussion in *TWOT*, s.v. "שׁוה (*shāwâ*) I" and "שׁוה (*shāwâ*) II," by V.P. Hamilton, 2:910–11.

32:a Either causal כִּי (*kî*) as translated above or temporal כִּי with the imperfect verb (cf. LXX: ὅταν ἐπλάτυνας [*hotan eplatunas*] . . .), i.e. "*when* You enlarge my heart," are possible in the context.

32:b The noetic dimension of לֵב (*lēḇ*) is especially in view, i.e. the psalmist's "understanding" is in the foreground (cf. Allen, *Psalms 101–150*, p. 127; Soll, "Psalm 119," p. 176; Anderson, *Psalms*, 2:818; etc.)

Synopsis and Outline

Discouragement and depression catalyze and accelerate the psalmist's lamentation in the *Dāleṯ* stanza. The נַפְשִׁי (*napšî*) lament introduced in verse 20 returns with amplified echoes in verses 25a and 28a. These painful complaints are immediately followed by two general requests for Divine assistance (i.e. vv. 25b and 28b). As a matter of fact, verses 25 and 28 correspond nearly beat for beat and thereby reveal the twofold division of this strophe—a complaint and request stand at the head of each major section.

Intricate developments of substructure flow from these respective captions of pain and plea. Professions and more specific requests alternate in a variety of patterns. However, the psalmist's preoccupation with his own character and conduct, especially in the light of the hostile occasion in which he found himself, binds all of these elements together. The five occurrences of דֶּרֶךְ (*dereḵ*) in construct are special confirmations of this stanza's thematic glue, the first of which is the explicit "my ways" of verse 26. Comparative parallelisms between "the way of Your precepts" (v. 27a), "*the* way of faithfulness" (v. 30a), and "the way of Your commandments" (v. 32a) illuminate the positive ethic desired by the man of God, and contrasting parallelisms between "*the* way of falsehood" (v. 29a) and all the previously mentioned "ways" spotlight the negative ethic demeaned by him.

Additional structural and thematic relationships are subtle, but they do provide more evidence for strophic integration. Verses 26–27 unfold chiastically: vv. 26a–b, professions; v. 26c, request; v. 27a, request; v. 27b, profession; and verses 29–31 exhibit a similar development with a thematic or theological orientation: vv. 29a–b, appeals for Divine enablement; vv. 30–31a, assertions of human responsibility; v. 31b, appeal for Divine enablement.

Pulling all of these variously colored threads together, in verses 25–32 the man of God voices two complaints which become the occasions for his requests and professions concerning character and conduct.

- 1A. (vv. 25–27) The first complaint takes in vv. 25–27 and may be paraphrased: "*I am utterly humiliated!*"
  - 1B. (v. 25a) His humiliation leads to the vocalization of this complaint.
  - 2B. (vv. 25b–27) His humiliation also leads into his requests and professions.
    - 1C. (v. 25b) His general request for spiritual revitalization.
    - 2C. (vv. 26–27) His specific requests and professions concerning edification.
      - 1D. (v. 26) They are based upon past edification.
      - 2D. (v. 27) They are based upon the hope for future edification.
- 2A. (vv. 28–32) The second complaint takes in vv. 28–32 and may be paraphrased: "*I am in great anguish!*"
  - 1B. (v. 28a) His great anguish leads to the vocalization of this complaint.
  - 2B. (vv. 28b–32) His great anguish also leads into his requests and professions.
    - 1C. (v. 28b) His general request for spiritual reinforcement.
    - 2C. (vv. 29–32) His specific requests and professions concerning integrity of life.

1D. (v. 29) Integrity of life is based upon God's continued intervention.
   1E. (v. 29a) The negative dimension of His intervention.
   2E. (v. 29b) The positive dimension of His intervention.
2D. (vv. 30–31a) Integrity of life is based upon an acute awareness of human responsibility:
   1E. (v. 30a) The psalmist has decided to follow the true course of life.
   2E. (v. 30b) The psalmist has personally ratified God's standards.
   3E. (v. 31a) The psalmist has adhered to God's revelation.
3D. (vv. 31b–32) Integrity of life is based upon determination being tapped into God's resources.
   1E. (v. 31b) The prerequisite for determination: dependence.
   2E. (v. 32a) The promise of determination: desire.
   3E. (v. 32b) The provision for determination: dynamic.

Commentary

"My soul clings to the dust" (v. 25a) is a striking metaphor for being utterly humiliated. The verb דָּבַק (*dāḇaq*) with basic meanings of "to cling, cleave, keep close,"[1] is appropriately rendered in the LXX by a verb which connotes "to glue to"[2] and in the Latin Vulgate by *adhesit* (cf. our English verb *adhere* and the noun *adhe-*

[1] BDB, p. 179; the parallel root in Aramaic (cf. the Targum herein) is generally rendered "to adhere" (Jastrow, *Dictionary*, 1:278).

[2] I.e. ἐκολλήθη (*ekollēthē*) from κολλάω (*kollaō*); for a general survey of usage, see Thayer, *Lexicon*, p. 353.

sive). That to which the person of the psalmist[3] is seemingly inextricably bonded is indicated by the articular preposition לְ (*le*), לֶעָפָר (*leʿāpār*). עָפָר (*ʿāpār*), "dry earth, dust," is often employed figuratively for humiliation.[4] The psalmist, so to speak, cries out to God as his total being lies prostrate upon the ground.[5]

Such a circumstantially prone position proved itself to be productive in the case of the psalmist. Verse 25 is a dramatic illustration of a precious paradox: whenever the "I" is thoroughly exasperated, the child of God is in a position to be completely dependent.[6] For the psalmist, that meant turning unreservedly to God for spiritual revitalization: חַיֵּנִי כִּדְבָרֶךָ (*ḥayyēnî kidbārekā*), "Enliven me according to Your word!" Once again, the parameters of restoration (as indicated by the strong Piel imperative from חָיָה [*ḥāyâ*]) extend beyond a mere survival to the scope of a meaningful "'abundant life.'"[7] This fullness of life in Divine favor[8] is unde-

[3] Remembering that "the נפשׁ as the essential of man stands for *the man himself* . . . [it is a] paraphrase for the pers[onal] pron[oun] esp[ecially] in poetry and ornate discourse" (BDB, p. 660). Kraus adds, "inadequate, dependent, and needy נֶפֶשׁ (*nepeš*) of the vulnerable individual. . ." (*Theology of the Psalms*, p. 145).

[4] BDB, pp. 779–80; "*ʿāpār* can be used in several senses; it may denote the dry, loose earth (2 Sam. 16:13), the substance of which our bodies are made (i.e. in popular speech) (Gen. 2:7; Ps. 103:14), or the place to which they return (104:29; Ec. 3:20). It may connote the whole earth (Job 19:25), or ground (Isa. 25:12, 26:5), and occasionally it stands for the netherworld (22:15, 29 (M.T. 16, 30), 44:25 (M.T. 26); Isa. 26:19), or the grave (Job 7:21; Ps. 30:9 (M.T. 10))" (Anderson, *Psalms*, 2:816). Anderson leans toward a brink-of-death imagery herein which is possible in view of the psalm's larger circles of context. The Targum's utilization of אַסִּי (*ʾăsî*) in v. 25b, "to make well," related to the noun "physician" (Jastrow, *Dictionary*, 1:92–93), may indicate a similar preference.

[5] Cf. the renderings of NIV; NAB; Allen, *Psalms 101–150*, p. 127; etc. The paraphrases of LB, "I am completely discouraged," and Cohen, "I am sunk to the ground under the crushing weight of trouble and grief" (*Psalms*, p. 397), capture other facets of this stark imagery.

[6] Cf., e.g., Isa 57:15, 2 Cor 12:9, Jas 4:10, 1 Pet 5:6, etc.

[7] Cf. v. 16 and the forthcoming occurrences of this root: vv. 37, 40, 77, 88, 107, 116, 144, 149, 154, 156, 159, 175; for discussion, see Hill, *Greek Words and Hebrew Meanings*, pp. 165, 168.

served although not unexpected in the light of the LORD's gracious promises. It has been noted that often in the Bible and especially in this psalm the preposition כְּ (*k*ᵉ) draws attention to Divine precedent.[9] One may indeed approach the "throne of grace" boldly (e.g. "Revive me!") since God's Word affirms that He is in the business of continually ratifying His precious promises. Our psalmist not only recognized this truth, he also lived by it!

At the outset of verse 26 the psalmist reminisces about a past bestowal of Divine grace. He had made known, i.e. "related, recounted, declared"[10] (the Piel of סָפַר [*sāpar*]) his ways,[11] and the LORD had graciously responded.[12] Based upon this personal precedent from his past reliance upon God,[13] the disciple issues forth

---

8 BDB, p. 311.

9 I.e. "as an accus[ative] of mode or limitation, in or with the like of (=like, as, according to, κατά) . . . expressing conformity to a standard or rule" (ibid., p. 454).

10 BDB, p. 708; cf. the LXX's ἐξαγγέλλω (*exangellō*), lit. to tell out, "to proclaim," as an appropriate term for general proclamation. The NIV's "confess" is too restrictive for ספר (one would expect a Hiphil or Hithpael form of the root יָדָה [*yādâ*] if confession only had been on the psalmist's mind): "The first clause is not to be restricted to a confession of sin, though that may be included, but extended to a statement of his cares, anxieties, and affairs in general" (Alexander, *Psalms*, 3:157); see also Leupold, *Psalms*, p. 829.

11 דְּרָכַי (*d*ᵉ*rākay*) generally refers to "the psalmist's own conduct and disposition" (Soll, "Psalm 119," p. 177), and specifically in its larger contextual setting it probably concentrates upon "'my troubles' (cf. 37:5) or 'my fate' (49:13 (M.T. 14), 139:3). This may be a reference to the past experience of the author. When he was in distress, he appealed to God (by means of a Psalm of lamentation or prayer) and Yahweh answered him by granting him the help needed. For similar expressions see 3:4 (M.T. 5), 18:41 (M.T. 42), 34:4 (M.T. 5), 118:5" (Anderson, *Psalms*, 2:817).

12 I.e. עָנָה I (*ᶜānâ*), "to answer, respond," is used some 77 times in the Pss for God's gracious answers (usually) to prayers (cf. BDB, p. 772). The Targum's paraphrase indicates how prevalent this conception was: אוֹרְחִי מְנִיתִי וְקַבֵּלְתָּא צְלוֹתִי (*'ôr*ᵉ*ḥî mānîṯî w*ᵉ*qabbēll*ᵉ*tā' ṣ*ᵉ*lôṯî*), "I committed my way and *You received my prayers*."

13 Cf. the relationship of the *propositional* precedent of v. 25b (i.e. "according to Your word") to the bold prayer request which immediately precedes it (i.e. "revive me").

a specific request for Divine instruction, "Teach me Your statutes!" (v. 26b).[14] Cohen offers a pleasing review of the psalmist's thought development in verse 26:

> I told my ways. The Psalmist affirms that he had laid bare before God all his vicissitudes, and the petitions addressed to Him had been answered. Accordingly he is emboldened to offer another prayer, viz. that God would enable him to gain a full knowledge of His statutes.[15]

The Hiphil imperative of בִּין (*bîn*)[16] not only launches verse 27 but it also introduces a chorus which resounds throughout this great psalm.[17] From studies in etymology,[18] other roots in parallel-

---

[14] Cf. v. 12; that he desires more than a mere impartation of cognitive data from the Master Teacher is understood through the parallelism with his next specific request for spiritual sensitivity in v. 27a. It was pointed out (above under "Synopsis and Outline") that vv. 26–27 are structurally related through a chiastic development (with vv. 26b–27a standing at the intersection), and such stylistic phenomena generally carry with them thematic integrations; for example, herein "he has rehearsed his walk in every detail to God [v. 26a], and has not been left without an answer [v. 26b], which has assured him of His good pleasure: may He then be pleased to advance him even further and further in the understanding of His word [v. 26c], in order that, though men are against him, he may nevertheless have God on his side, vers. 26, 27" (Delitzsch, *Psalms*, 3:247–48).

[15] Cohen, *Psalms*, p. 397; cf. Leupold's "deeper knowledge" (*Psalms*, p. 829), i.e. assimilation and internalization of God's statutes.

[16] "The understanding is most generally represented by *bin* (בִּין), to perceive, to be intelligent. This word, again, is used with many shades of meaning, such as to consider, discern, feel, know, look, mark, perceive, view" (Girdlestone, *Synonyms*, p. 74).

[17] Cf. the ensuing Hiphil imperatives in vv. 34, 73, 125, 144, and 169; other verbals based upon this important root occur in vv. 95, 100, 104, and 130. Concerning the issue of authorship, it is interesting how often the root בִּין appears in various forms in Daniel (i.e. 1:4; 2:21; 8:5, 15, 16, 17, 23, 27; 9:2, 22, 23; 10:1, 11).

[18] "The root *byn* is connected with the subst. *bayin*, 'interval, space between' (analogous to Arab. *bainun* or *baina*, Old South Arab. *byn*, Ugar. *bn*, and

isms,[19] and the general wisdom setting of בִּין,[20] "the verb refers to knowledge which is superior to the mere gathering of data."[21]

> From a number of instances, insight or moral understanding is a gift from God (Dan 2:21) and is not the fruit of empiricism. It is ethical discernment. A person prays for it (Ps 119:34) and since this insight is uniquely God's, he can reveal or conceal it (Isa 29:14).[22]

That this ethical enablement was exactly the desire of the psalmist's heart in verse 27 is confirmed by the object of content, דֶּרֶךְ־פִּקּוּדֶיךָ (*dereḵ–piqqûḏeyḵā*): "Cause me to understand *the way of Your precepts*!" "He wants to imbibe the whole of Torah in such a way that it transforms his whole mode of conduct."[23] Then, once the LORD graciously imparts deep ethical perception, the disciple will continue, with renewed motivation, to commit himself to a

---

Phoen.), used as a preposition (*ben*, 'between') [cf. both the verbal and preposition in 1 Kgs 3:9]. Consequently the original meaning of *byn* was '*to distinguish, separate*,' a meaning that also appears in different nuances in other Semitic languages: Arab. *bāna*, 'to be clear, understandable,' II 'to make clear, understandable,' *bayyinun*, 'clear, distinct,' Old South Arab. *byn*, 'to go away, carry off,' Ethiop. *bayyana*, 'to distinguish, separate, observe, perceive,' Ugar. *bn*, 'to understand,' . . ." (*TDOT* s.v. " בִּין, *bîn*" by H. Ringgren, 2:99). Even prior to the discovery and availability of some of the aforementioned cognates, Scroggie had concluded that "means to separate mentally, to discern, distinguish, and so to understand" (*Psalms*, p. 177). The LXX's preference of συνίημι (*syniēmi*) for בִּין is also corroborative: "to put (as it were) the perception with the thing perceived; to set or join together in the mind, i.e. *to understand*" (Thayer, *Lexicon*, p. 605).

19 Especially, the roots חכם (*ḥkm*) and שׂכל (*śkl*); cf. BDB, pp. 314–15; 968.

20 For a survey, see *TDOT*, 2:100–107.

21 *TWOT*, s.v. "בִּין (*bîn*)," by L. Goldberg, 1:103.

22 Ibid., pp. 103–104; cf. Anderson: "Yahweh is the real teacher of law and Wisdom, for he is the ultimate source of them both (Isa. 40:14)" (*Psalms*, 2:817).

23 Soll, "Psalm 119," p. 177 (cf. his whole paragraph of argumentation).

consistent meditation[24] upon God's "wonders" (v. 27b).[25] It is within this cycle of Divine initiative and dependent reciprocation that the disciple moves along a pathway of personal integrity and maturity.

Verses 25–27 proceeded from lament to liberation, now verses 28–32 follow suit.[26] In verse 28a, the verb דָּלַף (*dālap̱*)[27] plus the preposition מִן (*min*) attached to the noun תּוּגָה (*tûgâ*)[28] paint a powerful word-picture of great anguish. "דָּלַף refers to the soul, which is as it were melting away in the trickling down of tears."[29] From the psalmist's perspective he felt that he was dissolving in tears.[30]

---

[24] Cf. vv. 15, 23, 48, 78 and 148 for verbal occurrences, and vv. 97 and 99 for noun forms. Its essence throughout Ps 119 is a deep "silent reflection" (*TWOT*, s.v. "שִׂיחַ (*śîaḥ*)," by G. Cohen, 2:875) upon God's "wonders" (cf. בְּנִפְלְאוֹתֶיךָ [*bᵉnip̱lᵉ'ôṯeyḵā*], herein; see occurrences of this root in vv. 18 and 129) and/or His Word with a view toward spiritual growth and development.

[25] Once again, it seems best to regard the LORD's נִפְלָאוֹת (*nip̱lā'ôṯ*) as "the mysteries of God's Will revealed in His Law" (Kirkpatrick, *Psalms*, p. 710).

[26] For a structural review with an emphasis upon vv. 25 and 28 see Delitzsch, *Psalms*, 3:248.

[27] This verb occurs only here and in Job 16:20 (with "eye" as subject) and Eccl 10:18 (of a house leaking) indicating a common semantical denominator of "to drop, drip," and its related noun form דֶּלֶף (*delep̱*) occurs in Prov 19:13 and 27:15 (both referring to the *dropping* of rain); cf. BDB, p. 196. It should be pointed out that "the verb *dālap̱* ('to drip') is associated by some scholars with the Akkadian *dalāpu* . . . 'was restless' . . ." (Anderson, *Psalms*, 2:817). It is difficult to evaluate the significance of the Targum's paraphrase: "My soul is in grief from weariness" (אַגְמַת נַפְשִׁי מִדָּבוֹנָא [*'agmaṯ napšî midāḇônā'*]). The LXX's ἔσταξεν from στάζω (*stazō*) clearly means "to drop, fall in drops, trickle" (LSJ, p. 1632).

[28] תּוּגָה, from יָגָה I (*yāgâ*), "to suffer, grieve" (BDB, p. 387), means "grief, sorrow, heaviness" (*TWOT*, s.v. "יָגָה (*yāgâ*)," by R. Alexander, 1:361); cf. Prov 10:1; 14:13; and 17:21. "The Hebrew denotes grief and anxiety" (Cohen, *Psalms*, p. 398).

[29] Delitzsch, *Psalms*, 3:248; cf. Anderson: "The word-picture created by the *nepeš* ('soul') melting away is that of weeping" (*Psalms*, 2:817).

[30] Cf. Cohen, *Psalms*, p. 398.

There was, nevertheless, only one antidote for a collapsing soul (v. 28a),[31] and that was a supporting God (v. 28b).[32] Consequently, another bold imperative flows out of intense lamentation: קַיְּמֵנִי כִּדְבָרֶךָ (*qayyᵉmēnî kiḏḇāreḵā*). קַיְּמֵנִי, a Piel imperative with a first person singular suffix, means literally, "cause me to stand/stand up,"[33] i.e. "establish me."[34] The child of God was in desperate need of new strength,[35] spiritual reinforcement, and again, on account of the precedent of promise (i.e. כִּדְבָרֶךָ; cf. v. 25b), he was not hesitant to ask for it. So ask he did, both boldly and expectantly.

His general request for spiritual reinforcement is nuanced by the specific requests (e.g. vv. 29a–b, 31b) and responses (e.g. vv. 30–31a, 32) which follow. As he weaves his thoughts together a tapestry of desire for integrity of life emerges.

He first expresses the longing of his heart through a negative image: דֶּרֶךְ־שֶׁקֶר הָסֵר מִמֶּנִּי (*dereḵ - šeqer hāsēr mimmennî*), "Put far from me the way of deception" (v. 29a).[36] The disciple's pattern of issuing bold injunctions to God continues with this Hiphil imperative of the root סוּר (*sûr*).[37] סוּר was often employed in the OT in allegations of apostasy, and conversely, for affirmations of non-

---

[31] I.e. דָּלְפָה נַפְשִׁי (*dālᵉp̄â nap̄šî*).

[32] Cf. Scroggie's anecdote on v. 28: "The cause and cure of depression" (*Psalms*, p. 181).

[33] Cf. BDB, pp. 877–78; for a synopsis of this root's covenantal associations, see *TWOT*, s.v. "קוּם (qûm)," by L. Coppes, 2:793. On those opting for translations which reflect the subtle relationship between דָּלַף (v. 28a) and קוּם (v. 28b), see: Soll, "Psalm 119," p. 176, and Allen, *Psalms 101–150*, p. 127.

[34] BDB, p. 878; on the significance of the βεβαίωσόν με (*bebaiōson me*) in the LXX, cf. the NT occurrences of βεβαιόω (basically, *to make steadfast*) in 1 Cor 1:8 and 2 Cor 1:21.

[35] Cf. Anderson, *Psalms*, 2:817.

[36] Soll's appealing rendering ("Psalm 119," p. 176).

[37] The verb means "to turn aside, depart" (BDB, p. 693) in the Qal, and "to cause to depart, remove, take away" (ibid.) in the Hiphil, i.e. "make to depart" (Alexander, *Psalms*, 3:158); cf. the root's recurrences in vv. 102, 115.

departure.[38] Herein, his forthright plea for removal is complemented by the preposition מִן (*min*, i.e. stressing separation) with a first person singular suffix (i.e. the psalmist), clearly indicating that what he wanted God to make him by-pass was a way of lying or deceit, i.e. "the way of falsehood which leads away from, instead of to God."[39] The man of God is therefore petitioning his Master to bring about a severance of anything and everything profane from his character and conduct.[40]

Correspondingly, in a positive vein, the disciple longs for God to overwhelm him with His word: וְתוֹרָתְךָ חָנֵּנִי (*wᵉtôrāṯeḵā ḥonnēnî*), "Graciously grant me Thy law" (v. 29b).[41]

> The verb *ḥānan* depicts a heartfelt response by someone who has something to give to one who has a need. . . . The overwhelming number of uses in the Qal stem, some forty-one instances, have Yahweh as the subject. The plea *ḥonnēnî*, "be gracious to me," appears nineteen times in the Psalms.[42]

---

[38] "The root is often used of Israel's apostasy. In many cases it is translated 'turn aside/away' (e.g. Ex 32:8; Deut 9:12; 11:16). Conversely, 'not to turn aside' was a way of affirming a man's steadfastness before the Lord (I Kgs 22:43 [2 Kgs 18:5–6]). Such a course of following strictly the will of God is frequently depicted by wedding the root to the familiar right hand—left hand motif. Thus, it was said of Josiah that he 'did not turn aside to the right hand, nor to the left' (II Kgs 22:2; cf. Deut 2:27; 5:32 [H 29]; Josh 1:7)" (*TWOT*, s.v. "סוּר (*sûr*)," by R. Patterson, 2:621). It should be noted that post-Fall men are universally characterized by spiritual departure (e.g. Ps 14:3; cf. Jer 17:5); only God's gracious intervention is capable of turning around their disastrous direction (e.g. Jer 32:40).

[39] Cohen, *Psalms*, p. 398; based upon an assumed context of covenant (and obviously viewing it in an antithetically parallel relationship with "the way of faithfulness" in v. 30a), Allen translates it "the way of faithlessness" (*Psalms 101–150*, p. 127).

[40] The burden of his request is captured by the rendering of the LXX: ὁδὸν ἀδικίας ἀπόστησον ἀπ᾽ ἐμοῦ (*hodon adikias apostēson ap emou*), "Separate away from me *the* unrighteous way!"

[41] NASB; cf. the use of חָנַן (*ḥānan*) in Gen 33:5.

[42] *TWOT*, s.v. "חָנַן (*ḥānan*) I," by E. Yamauchi, 1:302.

Our psalmist contributes three of those nineteen pleas for Divine mercy (vv. 29, 58, 132),[43] and the implication of his request in this context is that the Master Teacher not only graciously illumine[44] His heavenly Guidebook for human direction[45] but also mercifully impart the needed resources for conforming to it.[46]

Three rapid-fire affirmations of fidelity ensue (vv. 30–31a)[47] implicitly bolstering the surrounding injunctions (i.e. vv. 28b–29, 31b). The first of these is foundational in that the man of God had volitionally devoted himself to a life characterized by trustworthiness. His assertion, בָּחַרְתִּי (*bāḥartî*), "I have chosen" or "I have selected," appropriates theologically significant terminology.[48] בָּחַר (*bāḥar*) usually "involves a careful, well thought-out choice."[49] Herein, "the worshipper emphasizes that he has chosen the way of faithfulness, the way of Yahweh's precepts."[50]

---

[43] Cf. the aorist impv. from ἐλεέω (*eleeō*) in the LXX, and the Pael impv. from חוס (the root *ḥûs* connotes "to bend over, have affection for, to protect, spare, have consideration for" [Jastrow, *Dictionary*, 1:436–37]) in the Targum.

[44] Cf. Alexander, *Psalms*, 3:158.

[45] Calling to mind once again the basic facet of תּוֹרָה (from יָרָה) as a bibliological term; it is God's "law" which points out, shows the *way* (cf. the 5 occurrences of דֶּרֶךְ in this stanza).

[46] Cf. Kidner, *Psalms 73–150*, p. 424, on these two emphases.

[47] Concerning two of these historical testimonies and the forthcoming future affirmation (i.e. v. 32a), Kidner argues, "The three opening verbs, of choosing, cleaving and running, make a fine summary of godliness: cf., e.g., Hebrews 11:25; Acts 11:23 (AV); Philippians 3:12–14" (*Psalms 73–150*, pp. 424–25).

[48] For an adequate survey of "Human Choices as Acts of Religious Confession," see *TDOT*, s.v. "בָּחַר (*bāchar*)," by J. Bergman, H. Ringgren, and H. Seebass, 2:86–87; and "בחר as an act of Religious Confession" in *TDNT*, s.v. "ἐκλέγομαι," by G. Quell, 4:149–52, cf. larger discussion within pp. 145–68; note Deut 30:19; Josh 24:15, 22; Ps 25:12; and also, Ps 119:173; and for a brief survey of בָּחַר as a primary term for Divine election, see: *TWOT*, s.v. "בָּחַר (*bāḥar*)," by J. Oswalt, 1:100.

[49] *TWOT*, 1:100; cf. *TDOT*, 2:74–75.

[50] *TDOT*, 2:87.

That way of אֱמוּנָה (*'ĕmûnâ*), i.e., a feminine noun meaning "firmness, steadfastness, fidelity,"[51] also focuses attention upon a great reservoir of theologically significant terminology derived from the root אמן (*'mn*).[52] This root never stands far away from the concept of reliability,[53] a reliability which comes out of a Divine mold.[54] As a matter of fact, God Himself is the personification of all fidelity and reliability as dramatically illustrated in Christ being called the "Amen" (i.e. אָמֵן [*'āmēn*]; cf. Rev 3:14).[55] God's children should therefore bear the impress of such a mold:

> *'ĕmûnâ* is . . . used to refer to those whose lives God establishes. He expects to see faithfulness in them (Prov 12:22; II Chr 19:9). Indeed, such faithfulness or a life of

---

[51] BDB, p. 53.

[52] Inflected "אָמַן (*'āman*) to confirm, support, uphold (Qal); to be established, be faithful (Niphal); to be certain, i.e. to believe in (Hiphil). . . . אֹמֶן (*'ōmen*) faithfulness. אָמֵן (*'āmēn*) verily, truly, amen. . . . אֵמֻן (*'ēmun*) faithful, trusting. אֱמוּנָה (*'ĕmûnâ*) firmness, fidelity, steadiness . . . ," etc. (*TWOT*, s.v. "אָמַן (*'āman*)," by J. Scott, 1:51).

[53] "When a Hebrew heard the various words derived from the root *'mn*, the basic idea that came to his mind was apparently 'constancy.' When they were used of things, they meant 'continual'; and when they were connected with persons, 'reliability'" (*TDOT*, s.v. "אָמַן ('āman)," by A. Jepsen, 1:322–23; cf. his survey, pp. 292–323; also cf. Girdlestone, *Synonyms*, pp. 102–03; *TWOT*, 1:51–53; Walter Eichrodt, *Theology of the Old Testament*, trans. by J. A. Baker (Philadelphia: Westminster Press, 1967), 2:284–85; *NIDNTT*, s.v. "πίστις," by O. Michel, 1:597; the excursus "The words denoting 'Faith'" in J. B. Lightfoot, *The Epistle of St. Paul to the Galatians* (Grand Rapids: Zondervan, 1957), pp. 154–58; Dodd, *The Bible and the Greeks*, p. 66; and for some cautions, James Barr, *The Semantics of Biblical Language* (London: Oxford, 1961), pp. 161–205.

[54] E.g., "The Niphal participle means 'to be faithful, sure, dependable' and describes believers (Num 12:7; I Sam 2:35; Neh 9:8). This form is also used to describe that upon which all certainty rests: God himself (Deut 7:9), and his covenant (Ps 89:28 [H 29])" (*TWOT*, 1:51–52).

[55] Also, note 2 Cor 1:20; obviously, our word "amen" has come to us through a channel of transliteration: אָמֵן to the Greek ἀμήν to "amen." Also, cf. His designation "faithful and true," πιστός καὶ ἀληθινός (*pistos kai alēthinos*) which directly relates to the Hebrew root אמן (Rev 19:11; 21:5; 22:6).

> faith is characteristic of those justified in God's sight (Hab 2:4). God's word of truth establishes man's way of truth or faithfulness (Ps 119:30).
>
> From this we can also see the concept of a duty being entrusted to a believer which becomes his trust (faithful responsibility, I Chr 9:22; II Chr 31:15, etc.) or office.[56]

Our psalmist's testimony in verse 30a exemplifies a disciple's basic understanding of commitment and constancy.

A corollary to commitment is conformity. Consequently, the man of God also says, "'I consent to your ordinances'" (v. 30b).[57] In this testimony he asserts that he fully *agrees with* the LORD's "rules of righteous administration."[58] Submission ever remains as a primary attribute of the Master's disciples.

Another attribute of a disciple is dependent adherence: "I hold fast to your statutes" (v. 31a, NIV). It is not merely a coincidence that the psalmist has returned to the verb דָּבַק (*dāḇaq*; cf. and contra v. 25a). When personal resources are thoroughly depleted (v. 25a) it is time to cling like "bone to skin"[59] to the Divine resources.[60] Additionally,

> *I cleave to thy testimonies* . . . is reminiscent of Deuteronomy, where cleaving to God is usually associated with obeying his voice (Dt. 30:20), serving him (Dt. 10:20, 13:4), and walking in his ways (Dt. 11:22). The verb *dāḇaq*

---

56 *TWOT*, 1:52; for a discussion of the relationship of הֶאֱמִין (*he'ĕmîn*), "to believe" (e.g. Gen 15:6) and "faith" and "faithfulness" (אֱמוּנָה), see my article "Interpretive Challenges Relating to Habakkuk 2:4b," *GTJ*, 1:1 (Spring 1980): 43–69.

57 Anderson's suggested rendering for שָׁוָה I (*Psalms*, 2:818); on the preference of שָׁוָה (*šāwâ*) I over שָׁוָה II, see the translation notes above on v. 30b.

58 Scroggie's synopsis of the bibliological nuance of מִשְׁפָּטִים (*mišpāṭîm*).

59 Cf. BDB, p. 179, on the significance of דָּבַק complemented by the preposition בְּ (*bᵉ*).

60 In this case, the LORD's "testimonies": "He cleaves to the testimonies of God; may Jahve not disappoint the hope which to him springs up out of them, according to the promise" (Delitzsch, *Psalms*, 3:248).

("to cleave") may also suggest oneness. Just as a man "cleaves to his wife and they become one flesh" (Gen. 2:24) so the will of the Psalmist becomes one with that of God.[61]

The vocative employment of the Divine name par excellence, יהוה (*YHWH*), provides a meaningful transition from the attributes of the disciple to the overwhelmingly pure attributes of his LORD.[62] Therefore, based upon both his circumstances and confessions,[63] and his God's documented covenantal consistencies, he cries out: יהוה אַל־תְּבִישֵׁנִי (*YHWH 'al-tᵉḇîšēnî*), "O LORD, do not put me to shame!"[64] His aversion to shame has been and will continue to be evidenced throughout the development of this psalm (vv. 6, 31, 46, 80 [contra v. 78], 116).

With confidence in a gracious response on the part of his LORD, our disciple regains his spiritual second wind and concentrates on the "race set before him."[65] Previous occurrences of the metaphor of *walking* (e.g. vv. 1, 3, etc.) now accelerate to *running*.[66] He is deter-

---

[61] Anderson, *Psalms*, 2:818.

[62] Of יהוה, Girdlestone has observed that this special name "sums up the merciful and the judicial aspects of the Divine character. . . . [It] sets forth His essential and unswerving principles of mercy and judgment" (*Synonyms*, p. 40). Seemingly, ever since God gave His self-ascription to Moses in Exod 3:14 there have been conjectures on the derivation and significance of יהוה. "Most take it as Qal of (הוה=היה); *the one who is*: i.e. *the absolute and unchangeable one*, Ri [E. Riehm]; *the existing, ever-living*, as self-consistent and unchangeable, Di [A. Dillmann] . . ." (BDB, p. 218). Based upon this suggestion, the first person "I am" (אֶהְיֶה [*'ehyeh*]) of Exod 3:14 was presumably taken by Moses and placed into the appropriate third person form, "He is" (i.e. יִהְיֶה [*yihyeh*]=יהוה). For a brief survey of the issues and problems, see the comments of both J.B. Payne and R.L. Harris in *TWOT*, s.v. "הָוָה (*hāwâ*) II," 1:210–12.

[63] "*Put me not to shame*. By failing to show me Thy favour, in consequence of which I am taunted in a time of distress by evil-doers on the futility of obeying the commandments" (Cohen, *Psalms*, p. 398).

[64] Cf. his bold requests with the conditional negative אַל (*'al*) in vv. 8b, 10b, 19b.

[65] Cf. the NT's extensive employment of this metaphor of *running* (τρέχω [*trechō*]) the race of life (e.g. Rom 9:16; Gal 5:7; Phil 2:16; *Heb 12:1*; etc.).

[66] Note the juxtaposition of both metaphors in Prov 4:12 (cf. vv. 10–12); it should also be noted that our psalmist associates the roots רוּץ (*rûṣ*) and רחב (*rḥḇ*) in v. 32 and returns to הלך (*hlḵ*) plus רחב in v. 45.

mined to run the course of God's injunctions: דֶּרֶךְ־מִצְוֹתֶיךָ אָרוּץ (*derek-miṣwôṯeykā 'ārûṣ*), "I shall run the way of Your commandments."[67] His determination, however, is predicated upon a divinely mediated stamina: "when" or "because You enlarge my heart" כִּי תַרְחִיב לִבִּי ([*kî tarḥîḇ libbî*]). This causative imperfect from רָחַב (*rāḥaḇ*), "*to be*, or *grow, wide, large*,"[68] likely refers to the LORD's customary *enlargement*[69] of His disciple's mind and will (i.e. לֵב [*lēḇ*]).[70] The root רחב also carries with it the concept of liberty; consequently, "when his heart is set free from the cramping constraint of trouble and anxiety [i.e. v. 32b], the Psalmist will use his liberty for more energetic service" [i.e. v. 32a].[71] In the light of this intricate association, another principle of discipleship emerges: "The feet should follow the heart. A dilated heart and dilatory feet do not belong to the same person."[72]

---

[67] Certainly, "the vigorous 'run' implies more than an apathetic following" (Leupold, *Psalms*, p. 830).

[68] BDB, p. 931.

[69] The Targum renders the תַרְחִיב with an appropriate form of the root פתי (*pṯy*), cf. the Heb פתה (*pṯh*), which conveys several strong actions, e.g. "to influence, persuade, win, conquer, entice, seduce," etc. (Jastrow, *Dictionary*, 2:1253–54).

[70] For the root רָחַב (*rāḥaḇ*) plus לֵב (*lēḇ*), cf. 1 Kgs 5:9 (4:29, Eng) and Isa 60:5. On the noetic and volitional emphasis, see Soll, "Psalm 119," p. 176.

[71] Kirkpatrick, *Psalms*, p. 710; cf. Delitzsch, *Psalms*, 3:248. Also, cf. Kidner's informative excursus on our psalmist's view of "liberation": "The paradox that where God is master, 'service is perfect freedom', is found not only in verse 96, . . . (a *commandment*—note the word—which is broader than anything on earth) but equally in verse 45, where 'liberty' is found in God's precepts, not in release from them. Two elements of this freedom are, first, the breaking of sin's 'dominion' as one's steps are steadied by the Word (133), and secondly the mind-stretching encounter with a greater wisdom and vision than one's own. 'At liberty' (45) means 'at large': it is like the 'broad place' that David found in Psalm 18:19 (20, Heb.); but in verse 32 it recalls the 'largeness of mind' which Solomon was given. Moffatt's paraphrase of the verse captures both aspects of this breadth: 'I will obey thee eagerly, as thou dost open up my life'" (*Psalms 73–150*, p. 421). Soll has appropriately wondered if James (2:12) had these great truths in mind when he spoke of the "law of liberty" ("Psalm 119," pp. 177–78).

[72] Scroggie, *Psalms*, p. 181.

ה

HE STANZA *(vv. 33–40)*

Translation and Notes

33 Teach me,[a] O LORD, the way of Your statutes,
so that[b] I may observe it *to the* end.[c]

34 Grant me understanding,[a] so that[b] I may observe Your law
and keep it wholeheartedly.[c]

35 Cause me to march in the pathway of Your commandments,
for[a] I delight in it.

36 Incline my heart unto Your testimonies,
and not[a] unto profit-making.[b]

37 Turn away my eyes from looking at vanity;
revive me in Your way.[a]

38 Establish Your word[a] to Your servant,
which *is* for the fear of You.[b]

39 Take away my reproach[a] which I dread,
for Your judgments are good.

40 Behold,[a] I long for Your precepts;
revive[b] me in[c] Your righteousness.

33:a The LXX's νομοθέτησον from νομοθετέω (*nomotheteō*), lit., "to law-give," probably reflects a Hellenistic eccentricity in view of its perspective on תּוֹרָה (*tôrâ*); cf. the discussion on תּוֹרָה in the "Theological Overview."

33:b Either a voluntative *waw* expressing intention (BDB, p. 254), or possibly, an inferential usage stressing consequence (i.e. "then . . .").

33:c The translation of עֵקֶב (ᶜēqeḇ) is disputed: "*To the end* is one sense of a word which also means 'consequence' or 'reward,' as in Psalm 19:11 (12, Heb.). Hence NEB here has 'I shall find my reward'; and in verse 112 'they are a reward that never fails.' Either sense is possible, and as each has its counterparts elsewhere in the psalm (e.g. 44 for constancy, 72 for enrichment) it remains an open question" (Kidner, *Psalms 73–150*, p. 425).

34:a Lit. "Make me understand"; i.e. "Give me insight" (Allen, *Psalms 101–150*, p. 127); or, "Give me discernment" (NAB); cf. v. 27.

34:b Cf. 33:a above (i.e. either a volitional or inferential *wāw*); the only difference herein is the involvement of *compound* subordinate clauses.

34:c Another occurrence of בְּכָל־לֵב, "with a whole heart."

35:a Remembering that "the causal relation expressed by כִּי is sometimes subtle, esp[ecially] in poetry. . . . Thus s[ome]t[ime]s it justifies a statement or description by pointing to a pregnant fact which involves it" (BDB, p. 473).

36:a An obvious ellipsis: "(and let) not (my heart be inclined) unto . . . ."

36:b [Utilizing] D. Kellermann's appealing suggestion for a neutral translation of בֶּצַע (*beṣa*ᶜ) (*TDOT*, s.v. "בצע (*ḇṣ*ᶜ)," 2:207).

37:a Several minor variants relate to the MT's בִּדְרָכֶךָ (*biḏrāḵeḵā*): some construe it as a defective plural, "in Your ways" (Delitzsch, *Psalms*, 3:249); cf. Anderson, "*thy ways*: so many MSS., as well as S and V, while some Hebrew MSS. and LXX read the singular: 'thy way'" (*Psalms*, 2:820). Another deviation is דרך (*drḵ*) to דבר (*dḇr*), i.e. "way" to "word"; Soll opts for this: "emendation from *drk* to *dbr* has the support of 11QPsᵃ, 2 Heb. mss., and the Targum" ("Psalm 119," p. 178). It should be pointed out that the DSS (Q11) manuscript also has a different preposition, כ (*k*) for ב (*b*) , "according to" for "in." None of these minor differences would lead to any major theological problem; however, there seems to be no compelling reason to depart from the MT's reading which is upheld by the LXX. The continued emphasis on "way" (be it

דרך, ארח, נתיב, etc.) fits well into the immediate context, and this setting would adequately explain דרך, by synecdoche, standing in the place of a possibly expected דבר.

38:a Or, "Confirm Your promise."

38:b Obviously, an objective genitive: "'to thy fear,' the abstract being put for the concrete term; or it might be rendered 'for thy fear' that thou mayest be feared" (Alexander, *Psalms*, 3:160).

39:a The Targum's "pardon my shame" obviously interprets the MT's somewhat ambivalent statement in a negative sense.

40:a The הִנֵּה (*hinnēh*) may color its clause (i.e. v. 40a) with a light causal relationship in reference to v. 40b: "*Since* I long for . . . revive me . . . ." There may be some additional support for this syntactical nuance from the apparent chiastic arrangement of vv. 39–40, with the הִנֵּה clause of v. 40a paralleling the כִּי (*kî*) clause of v. 39b.

40:b Herein, one of those occurrences of חנן (*ḥnn*) in DSS (Q11) in comparison with the MT's חיה (*ḥyh*).

40:c Or, instrumentally, "with, through, by means of."

Synopsis and Outline

Following up the five occurrences of the root דרך (*dr<u>k</u>*) in the *Dāle<u>t</u>* stanza, *Hē'* continues with three more plus the introduction of a new synonym for the pathway of life in verse 35 (i.e. נָתִיב [*nā<u>t</u>î<u>b</u>*]). Therefore, the psalmist's major theme of applied Bibliology is also quite conspicuous in *Hē'*; his "earnest desire is to make God's law the governing principle of his conduct."[1] At least

[1] Dahood, *Psalms*, 3:172. Needless to say, our psalmist is never satisfied with a merely external conformity, but also, and especially, he remains convicted of the overarching need for internal conformity as his life is being evaluated by the omniscient Judge (cf., e.g., the imperative plus a reference to his "heart" in v. 36): "We, therefore, need not merely instruction through God's word but also to have our hearts guided and inclined towards what is right and pleasing to God" (Moll, *Psalms*, p. 595).

two sub-themes interact with this major emphasis. Neither of these dovetailing sub-themes is a newcomer; each, however, surfaces with more frequency and with a greater amplification in verses 33–40. One of them, indicated by the nine imperatives functioning as channels for passionate pleas,[2] spotlights the disciple's acute awareness of his total dependence. The other one, indicated by the directional nature of the verbs and prepositions involved,[3] identifies his consuming burden—he is in desperate need of Divine guidance.

There also seems to be a slight theological shift between the requests of verses 33–35 and those contained in verses 36–40. The former group appears to be more direct; they are solicitations for an immediate exercise of Divine intervention. The general nature of the latter group is more providential; these injunctions invite a mediate exercise of Divine influence or control.

Consequently, in the *Hē'* stanza the disciple's dependent requests enlist two levels of Divine guidance.

1A. (vv. 33–35) The first level of immediate guidance is reflected by:
- 1B. (v. 33) His request for spiritual education.
  - 1C. (v. 33a) Its demand.
  - 2C. (v. 33b) Its design.
- 2B. (v. 34) His request for spiritual illumination.
  - 1C. (v. 34a) Its burden.
  - 2C. (v. 34b–c) Its bearing.
- 3B. (v. 35) His request for spiritual conformity.
  - 1C. (v. 35a) Its sanction.
  - 2C. (v. 35b) Its satisfaction.

---

[2] "The *he* strophe lends itself naturally to a series of prayers beginning with the causative *he* and so relating to divine working in the human life" (Allen, *Psalms 101–150*, p. 142).

[3] Note the directional actions (*or inferences*) of the roots ירה (*yrh*: v. 33), דרך (*drk̲*: v. 35), נטה (*nṭh*: v. 36), עבר (*ᶜb̲r*: vv. 37, 39), and קום (*gwm*: v. 38) along with the orientation of the prepositions בְּ (*bᵉ*: v. 35), אֶל (*'el* [2x]: v. 36), and מִן (*min*: v. 37).

2A. (vv. 36–40) The second level of mediate guidance is reflected by:
- 1B. (vv. 36–37) His specific requests:
  - 1C. (v. 36) His request for an affinity to God's Word instead of greediness.
  - 2C. (v. 37) His request for godliness instead of emptiness.
- 2B. (vv. 38–40) His general requests:
  - 1C. (v. 38) His request for ratification.
  - 2C. (v. 39) His request for relief.
  - 3C. (v. 40) His request for revival.

Commentary

A causative imperative from the root ירה (*yrh*, i.e. the same root from which תּוֹרָה [*tôrâ*], "law, direction, instruction," derives[4]) launches the first of nine bold prayer requests in this stanza. "The three most frequent uses of this root deal with shooting arrows, sending rain and teaching."[5] The element of direction is seen more or less conspicuously in each of these semantical fields. Consequently, a very natural object for the psalmist's plea that the LORD "direct, teach, instruct"[6] him is דֶּרֶךְ חֻקֶּיךָ (*derek ḥuqqeykā*), "*the way of* Your statutes."[7] Dependently, the disciple approaches the Master Teacher[8] for personal ethical direction through all the vicissitudes of life.

---

4 Cf. the introduction on words for the Word.

5 *TWOT*, s.v. "יָרָה (*yārâ*)," by J. Hartley, 1:403.

6 BDB, p. 435.

7 For a brief review of the metaphorical impact of דֶּרֶךְ, see *ISBE* (1939) s.v. "Way," by Morro, 5:3075–76. Also, cf. דֶּרֶךְ in construct in v. 27 as the content object of the causative imperative הֲבִינֵנִי (*hᵃbînēnî*), "give me understanding," then note the very same imperatival form which leads off the parallel request of v. 33a in v. 34a; such subtle structural and conceptual ties pervade this magnificent psalm.

8 Cf., e.g., Job 36:22; Pss 25:9; 86:11; Matt 23:8; the two verses from Pss 25 and 86 are especially significant in the light of vocabulary recurrences in Ps 119.

The immediate issue of the LORD's positive response[9] would be a renewed commitment to obedience along that "way" of life.[10] He further qualifies his obedience with עֵקֶב (ēqeb), "*consequence,* usu[ally] as ***adv[erbial] acc[usative]*** *as a consequence of, because* (that), also *reward, end.*"[11] Translations and commentators seem to be divided on the rendering herein. It seems best, however, in the light of the LXX,[12] the Targum,[13] and the apparently appositional parallelism in verse 112,[14] to construe it temporally, "to the end" (i.e. of my life).[15] Additional support may come from a parallelism with the prepositional phrase, בְּכָל־לֵב (b^e^kol lēb), which also functions adverbially (i.e. "wholeheartedly") at the end of verse 34. In other words, in verse 33 the man of God *quantifies* his obedience, and in verse 34, he puts an emphasis upon the *quality* of his promised compliance.

הֲבִינֵנִי (h^ă^bînēnî), lit. "cause me to understand, perceive, discern" (cf. v. 27), "seems to be a variation of verse 33."[16] The disciple's need for transcendent tutoring (v. 33a) includes with it a need for Divine discernment (v. 34a). Once such moral perception is graciously imparted, it prompts obedience[17] to God's directional revelation.[18]

---

[9] Cf. v. 102 as an indication of the psalmist's optimistic expectation herein.

[10] The obvious antecedent of the third feminine singular suffix attached to the first person imperfect verb from נָצַר (*nāṣar*) is דֶּרֶךְ which in certain contexts is construed as a feminine noun (cf. BDB, pp. 202–04).

[11] BDB, p. 784.

[12] I.e. δὶα παντός (*dia pantos*), "through all."

[13] I.e. עַד גְמִירָא (*ᶜad g^e^mîrā'*), "until finished."

[14] I.e. לְעוֹלָם עֵקֶב (*l^eᶜ^ôlām ᶜēqeb*), "to the very end" (NIV).

[15] Cf. BDB, p. 784.

[16] Anderson, *Psalms*, 2:819.

[17] Both נָצַר (*nāṣar*; cf. v. 32) and שָׁמַר (*šāmar*) occur as terms for obedience here; cf. these terms in the *Ālep* stanza (vv. 1–8). Another indication that these are synonymous terms for obedience comes from the Targum herein which renders both of them by the root נטר (*nṭr*).

[18] Note how תּוֹרָה (*tôrâ*) also contributes to the integration of vv. 33–34 by reaching back through the root ירה (*yrh*) to הוֹרֵנִי (*hôrēnî*); therefore, His instruction (verb; v. 33a) and His insight (v. 34a) are necessary prerequisites for living according to (i.e. vv. 33b; 34b–c) His *I*nstruction (noun; v. 34b).

The third Hiphil (i.e. causal) imperative in as many verses turns the familiar noun דֶּרֶךְ (*dereḵ*), "way," into a verbal:

> When the verb [i.e. דָּרַךְ (*dāraḵ*)] occurs in the Hiphil stem, it consistently refers to God as he leads the righteous in straight paths. This can mean the road from the wilderness or from Babylon (Ps 107:7; Isa 42:16; cf. Isa 11:15) or, more commonly, the metaphorical path of uprightness or truth (Prov 4:11, Ps 25:5, 9).[19]

The impact of this verbal metaphor of הַדְרִיכֵנִי (*haḏrîḵēnî*), "cause me to march" (i.e. lead me) is multiplied by its complementing prepositional phrase, בִּנְתִיב מִצְוֹתֶיךָ (*binṯîḇ miṣwôṯeyḵā*), "in the *pathway of* Your commandments." נָתִיב (*nāṯîḇ*), being a synonym of the noun דֶּרֶךְ,[20] also refers to "a course or manner of life" with stress upon "men's conduct or inward life-purpose."[21] In its present context, "the 'path of thy commandments' . . . is the conduct characterized by obedience to the revealed divine will."[22]

For such Divine leadership our disciple diligently prays, not merely out of duty but especially out of desire. In reference to that biblically charted "pathway," he affirms, כִּי־בוֹ חָפָצְתִּי (*kî-ḇô ḥāp̄āṣtî*), "for I delight *in it*" (v. 35b). The "true meaning" of חָפֵץ (*ḥāp̄ēṣ*), "to delight in, take pleasure,"[23] "is not so much an intense pleasurable emotion, as a favorable disposition."[24] This commendable attitude was obviously fueled by a deep desire to

---

[19] *TWOT*, s.v. "דָּרַךְ (*dāraḵ*)," by H. Wolf, 1:196; Wolf well adds, "The best path is to follow God's commandments (Ps 119:35)" (ibid.). For a quite comprehensive survey of the root דרך and its synonyms, see *TDOT*, s.v. "דֶּרֶךְ (*derekh*), *et al.*," by J. Bergman, A. Haldar, H. Ringgren, and K. Koch, 3:270–93; see esp. "In the Psalms," pp. 284–86.

[20] Cf. *TDOT*, 3:280.

[21] *ISBE* (1939) s.v. "Path," by Edwards, 4:2263.

[22] Anderson, *Psalms*, 2:819.

[23] BDB, p. 342; Soll appropriately comments, "What one delights in both reveals and determines character" ("Psalm 119," p. 179). For the opposite attitude, see Jer 6:10.

[24] Girdlestone, *Synonyms*, p. 69.

please his LORD.[25] Consequently, "man's delight and God's dynamic"[26] is a fitting summary of his testimony in verse 35.

The theological significance of the causative imperative at the outset of verse 36, i.e. from נָטָה (*nāṭâ*), "to bend, turn, incline," etc.,[27] plus לֵב (*lēḇ*) as object, plus a directional preposition (in this case אֶל ['*el*]) is introduced by Wilson when he observes that

> . . . most usages [of נָטָה] are figurative. One's heart may "turn away" (i.e. shift its loyalty, apostatize; cf. I Kgs 11:2–4, 9) or "be swayed" (II Sam 19:14 [H 15]). On the other hand, one's heart may be "inclined" to God and his commands (Josh 24:23; I Kgs 8:58; Ps 119:36). Also common is the expression "to incline the ear" (i.e. listen obediently) in reference to men paying heed to God (Jer 7:24, 26; 11:8; 17:23 et al.), God toward men (II Kgs 19:16; Isa 37:17; Dan 9:18), and men to the words of a sage (Prov 4:20; 5:1, 13; 22:17).[28]

---

25 Cf. Ps 37:23: "The steps of a man are established by the LORD; and He delights in his way" (NASB).

26 Scroggie, *Psalms*, p. 181.

27 *TWOT*, s.v. "נָטָה (*nāṭâ*)," by M. Wilson, 2:573; cf. the verb κλίνω (*klinō*) in the LXX and צְלֵי (*ṣᵉlê*) in the Targum, both reinforcing the directional orientation of the psalmist's "heart."

28 Ibid., p. 574; these observations pertain not only to נָטָה but also to several other Hebrew verbs used to portray heart orientation; e.g., הָלַךְ (*hālaḵ*: Ezek 20:16; *et al.*), רָחַב (*rāḥaḇ*: Isa 29:13; *et al.*), שִׂים (*śîm*: Exod 9:21; Dan 1:8; Mal 2:2; *et al.*), שִׁית (*šîṯ*: Ps 62:11 [v. 10, Eng]), סוּר (*sûr*: Jer 5:23; 17:5; *et al.*), פָּנָה (*pānâ*: Deut 30:15–18; *et al.*), שָׂטָה (*śāṭâ*: Prov 7:25), כּוּן (*kûn*: Ezra 7:10; 2 Chr 12:14; *et al.*), נָתַן (*nāṯan*: Dan 11:11–12; 1 Chr 22:19; *et al.*), etc.

The disciple knew that his natural inclination would be toward (i.e. אֶל [*'el*]) "profit"[29] or "material gain,"[30] so he implores his LORD to take the initiative[31] in directing his "heart" (i.e. the comprehensive anthropological term emphasizing rationality and volitionality) toward His testimonies rather than an innate pull to profit.[32] "This is" truly "a confession of man's utter dependence upon God."[33]

Several subtle phenomena draw the requests of verses 36 and 37 closely together.[34] First, both pleas pertain to vital issues of per-

---

[29] I.e. the neutral signification of בֶּצַע (*beṣaᶜ*) (cf. BDB, p. 130). The LXX's πλεονεξία (*pleonexia*), "greed," besides being an adequate rendering of this OT term, opens the door to several prominent NT warnings against this natural propensity (e.g. Rom 1:29; Eph 5:3; Col 3:5; 2 Pet 2:3; etc.); cf. the words αἰσχροκερδής (*aischrokerdēs*, adj., e.g. 1 Tim 3:3) and αἰσχροκερδῶς (*aischrokerdōs*, adv., e.g. 1 Pet 5:2). On the strictly negative coloring of the Hebrew terminology, "gain made by violence, unjust gain" (BDB, p. 130), note its appearance as both a verbal and noun in Hab 2:9.

[30] Allen's commendable rendering (*Psalms 101–150*, p. 127).

[31] The LORD *must* take the initiative in both initial heart orientation (e.g. שׁוּב [*šûḇ*], μετανοέω [*metanoeō*], i.e. "repentance" [change of mind/mind-set]) and progressive heart inclination because of man's "heart 'trouble' or 'condition'" (i.e. Gen 6:5; 8:21; Jer 17:5, 9; Mark 7:20–23; Eph 4:17–19; etc.); cf. God as Heart-Knower (1 Kgs 8:39; Pss 44:22 [v. 21, Eng]; 139:23; Jer 17:10; Acts 1:24; 15:8), Heart-Transplanter (Jer 24:7; 32:40; Ezek 36:26; Acts 11:18), and Heart-Director (1 Kgs 8:57–58; Neh 2:12; Pss 119:36; 141:4; etc.). Our psalmist understood the profound truth of such *seemingly* paradoxical passages as Lam 5:21, "Turn us that we may turn!" Cf. his dependent request herein and his devoted response in v. 112. For a quite thorough treatment of the centrality of the mindset (i.e. heart-direction) in salvation and sanctification, see my article "Aiming the Mind: A Key to Godly Living," *GTJ*, 5:2 (Fall 1984): 205–27.

[32] The ellipsis with the conditional negation אַל (*'al*), "and (do) not (incline it) towards profit," also provides internal evidence that fits well into the historical circumstances of Daniel's opportunities for great personal gain.

[33] Anderson, *Psalms*, 2:819.

[34] As a matter of fact, there is a theological interrelationship of vv. 35–37: the psalmist makes his way from an external perspective on his behavior (v. 35) to the deep internal perspective on his mindset (v. 36) and then he mentions an important sensual bridge, the eyes as a vehicle from the external to the internal.

sonal sanctification; however, the plea of verse 36a is framed positively while the one of verse 37a exhibits a preventative emphasis.[35] Secondly, the psalmist's "heart" is the focal point of verse 36, and in verse 37, it is his "eyes" which are of concern to him. The disciple's concern regarding his eyes should not be regarded as superficial, since those organs constitute "one of the chief channels of information for man."[36] Furthermore, much attention is given in the Bible to "the eye of the heart or mind, the organ of spiritual perception."[37] A third factor of note is his desire that God enable him to avert[38] the potential distractions of both "greediness" (i.e. בֶּצַע [*beṣaᶜ*], v. 36) and "emptiness" (i.e. שָׁוְא [*šāwᵉʾ*], v. 37).[39]

There is an implicit urgency to the psalmist's request that his LORD turn his eyes away *from looking at* (i.e. מֵרְאוֹת [*mērᵉʾôṯ*]) anything that is morally "valueless,"[40] in that the prepositional infinitive מֵרְאוֹת, lit. "from seeing," ultimately includes the hazard of

---

[35] This is brought about largely through the correlation of the directional imperatives with their respective targeting prepositions: הַט (*haṭ*; turn, incline, direct) plus אֶל (*'el*; to, unto) in v. 36, and הַעֲבֵר (*haᶜᵃḇēr*; turn away) plus מִן (*min*; from, away from) in v. 37.

[36] *ISBE* (1939) s.v. "Eye," by Luering, 2:1069.

[37] Ibid.; cf., e.g., Matt 5:27–28; 6:22–23.

[38] I.e. the basic thrust of the causative imperative from עָבַר (*ᶜāḇar*); cf. הָסֵר (*hāsēr*) from סוּר (*sûr*) in v. 29.

[39] שָׁוְא, "m.n. emptiness, nothingness, vanity" (BDB, p. 996), "is part of the OT vocabulary for moral evil" (Allen, *Psalms 101–150*, p. 136). This term "implies all that is hollow, worthless, and trivial" (Leupold, *Psalms*, p. 831). "It designates anything that is unsubstantial, unreal, worthless, either materially or morally" (*TWOT*, s.v. "שׁוא (shw') I," by V.P. Hamilton, 2:908). Anderson subcategorizes שָׁוְא when he concludes that it "has two shades of meaning. It can denote either what is materially unsubstantial (i.e. unreal, empty), or what is morally unsound (i.e. false, frivolous, insincere)" (*Psalms*, 2:819). Note the LXX's ματαιότητα (*mataiotēta*); cf. Eph 4:17 and 2 Pet 2:18 on the seriousness of the distraction of vanity, and also note the Vulgate's *vanitatem* (cf. our "vanity"). For a more strictly negative connotation, see Soll, "Psalm 119," p. 178.

[40] Allen's rendering of שָׁוְא (*Psalms 101–150*, p. 128).

"being attracted by, and so finding pleasure in."[41] "So this prayer specifies that the eyes may be turned away from trivialities by the grace of Him who alone can shape the deeper destinies of life."[42] With an acute awareness of those "deeper destinies of life," the man of God immediately follows with the request: "Cause me to live in Your way."[43] This positive emphasis on God's *way* (דֶּרֶךְ) in the latter half of the verse dovetails into the former request for aversion so that the total impact is one of "perilous distraction [i.e. v. 37a] and true direction [i.e. v. 37b],"[44] or phrased differently, "vitality [i.e. v. 37b] is the cure for vanity" [i.e. v. 37a].[45]

An overall impression of theocentricity in verse 38 comes from three second person singular pronominal suffixes: "*Your* servant," "*Your* word," and "*Your* fear" (i.e. the fear of You). These references also serve to strengthen the impression of the disciple's dependency. The Hiphil imperative הָקֵם (*hāqēm*) from קוּם (*qûm*), "establish,"[46] occurs quite frequently in contexts referring to the establishing *or* the *confirming* of God's covenant.[47] It seems likely that the latter case of confirmation is in view here[48] even though there is no explicit mention of בְּרִית (*b^e^rîṯ*), "covenant" in the immediate context. The most common rendering for the preposition לְ (*l^e^*; i.e. "to" or "for"), the "humble self-designation"[49] עַבְדְּךָ (*^c^aḇd^e^ḵā*; i.e. "Your servant") and the nuanced אִמְרָתֶךָ (*'imrāṯeḵā*; i.e. "Your *promise*") apparently all combine to suggest that the psalmist's request was colored by considerations of covenant remembrance and renewal; consequently, he prays, "Confirm Your promise to Your servant."

---

[41] Perowne, *Psalms*, p. 353.
[42] Leupold, *Psalms*, p. 831.
[43] I.e. בִּדְרָכֶךָ חַיֵּנִי (*biḏrāḵeḵā ḥayyēnî*). On the acceptance of the text as it stands see the notes on the translation.
[44] Scroggie, *Psalms*, p. 181.
[45] Spurgeon, *Treasury of David*, 6:95.
[46] Cf. the Piel occurrence also functioning causatively in v. 28.
[47] Cf. *TWOT*, s.v. "קוּם (*qûm*)," by L. Coppes, 2:793.
[48] Cf., e.g., Weiser, *Psalms*, p. 731; Soll, "Psalm 119," p. 178; and cf. the translations of NIV; Allen, *Psalms 101–150*, p. 128; etc.
[49] Anderson, *Psalms*, 2:820.

"The strict sense of the second line," אֲשֶׁר לְיִרְאָתֶךָ (*'ăšer lᵉyir'āṯeḵā*), "is 'which is for the fear of thee,'" conveying "a statement about the practical purpose of God's word."[50] The LORD's word was intended to be a funnel for fear,[51] never an instigator of self-effort.[52] That God's word is designed to induce an initial "fear" that leads to salvation is generally accepted. However, the scriptural fact that the same "fear"[53] of God should play a significant role in the motivation of believers has often been challenged. Notwithstanding these challenges, be they well-intentioned or not, "the fear of God is the soul of godliness."[54] Our psalmist fully grasped the truth that the *fear* of the LORD, conveyed by the total impression of the word of the LORD, was to be retained as an ever-present warning against every and any shred of self-reliance.[55]

The psalmist returns to a request for removal utilizing the same imperative which stood at the head of verse 37, הַעֲבֵר

---

[50] Kidner, *Psalms 73–150*, p. 425.

[51] Note the insertion of יִרְאַת יהוה (*yir'aṯ YHWH*), "the fear of the LORD" (Ps 19:10a [v. 9a, Eng]) into a whole series of terms for God's special revelation (i.e. vv. 8–10b [vv. 7–9b, Eng]). Remembering that "the fear of the LORD" is the *beginning* of "wisdom" (e.g. Ps 111:10) and "knowledge" (e.g. Prov 1:7) is essential to a correct understanding of the fear of God in its total biblical context.

[52] Cf. the testimony of Paul in Rom 7:7ff.; contra. the NT Pharisees.

[53] I.e. using both יָרֵא / יִרְאָה (*yārē'/yir'â*; respectively, "to fear" and "fear") and φοβέω/φόβος (*phobeō/phobos*; respectively, "to fear" and "fear") in their primary senses. In the context of Scripture this primary sense never fully evaporates into some sort of warm respect or subdued reverence.

[54] John Murray, *Principles of Conduct* (Grand Rapids: Eerdmans, 1957), p. 229; his whole argument should be carefully followed (pp. 229–42). Cf. Lev 25:17; Deut 10:12; 17:19; 31:12; etc.; in the NT, cf. Matt 10:28; Acts 9:31; Rom 11:20–21; 2 Cor 7:1; Phil 2:12; Heb 4:1; 10:27, 31; 1 Pet 1:17; 2:17; etc.

[55] "The appropriate φόβος ["fear"] is simply awareness that man does not stand on his own feet. It is the concern not to fall from χάρις ["grace"], whether in frivolity or the pride of supposed security" (*TDNT*, s.v. "πιστεύω, *et al.*," by R. Bultmann, 6:221).

(*ha*ᶜᵃ̆*ḇēr*), "take away, avert, remove."[56] This particular removal in verse 39 is directed towards his "reproach" (i.e. חֶרְפָּה [*ḥerpâ*]). The suffix "*my* reproach" חֶרְפָּתִי ([*ḥerpāṯî*]) technically could be interpreted as subjective (i.e. the "reproach" or "scorn" coming from him[57]) or objective (i.e. that which was coming at him). However, חֶרְפָּתִי "must refer to the troubles of the Psalmist which he is already experiencing (see on verse 22), and which are the cause of the ridicule of his enemies. Kirkpatrick . . . takes 'reproach' as the scorn which the Psalmist 'has to bear for his loyalty to God's law.'"[58] That this was scorn coming at him is also supported by a verbal occurrence from this same root in verse 42 (i.e. he was being *taunted*[59]). It is no wonder that he adds concerning this relentless ridicule אֲשֶׁר יָגֹרְתִּי (*'ăšer yāḡōrᵉtî*), "which I dread."[60]

But with the acuity of twenty-twenty theological vision, he testifies, "for Your judgments are good" (v. 39b). For the mature man of God derision does not automatically yield to deep depression, because God's decisions have proven themselves to be appropriate. Therefore, he rests expectantly in his LORD's sovereign sway.

---

[56] Cf. BDB, p. 719.

[57] Cf. the Targum's "pardon my shame."

[58] Anderson, *Psalms*, 2:820.

[59] Cf. *TWOT*, s.v. "חָרַף (*ḥārap̄*) I," by T. McComiskey, 1:326.

[60] This word for fear generally connotes great dread (cf. Deut 9:19; 28:60; Job 3:25; 9:28; Jer 22:25; 39:17). Also note the subtle parallelism between the relative clause of v. 38 ("which is for the fear of You") and this one in v. 39 ("which I fear, dread"). This possibly uncovers an implicit yearning that his dread of men (v. 39) be subdued by his fear of God (v. 38).

Verse 40a surprisingly breaks the rhythm of the imperatives.[61] The initial demonstrative particle הִנֵּה (*hinnēh*), normally rendered "lo" or "behold," quite often "points generally to some truth either newly asserted, or newly recognised."[62] "Indeed,"[63] says the psalmist, in the light of my fears and frustrations, "I long for Your precepts."[64]

It is this strong affirmation of desire which bolsters the last plea of this stanza: "Revive me in Your righteousness!" The man of God has requested revival so far in conjunction with three different prepositional-phrase qualifiers: "according to Your word" (v. 25), "in Your way" (v. 37), and now "in Your righteousness."[65] The latter two are associated not only by proximity but also by encompassing intent (cf. v. 37b). Concerning this "helping righteousness of God,"[66] Cohen has rightly remarked that "from this source he prays to be refreshed to meet the troubles of life."[67]

---

[61] The *Hē'* stanza "is almost entirely devoted to petition. The first seven lines all begin with Hiphil imperatives. This is, of course, very repetitive, but the repetition makes the last line's departure from the pattern all the more effective" (Soll, "Psalm 119," p. 179).

[62] BDB, p. 244.

[63] Allen's rendering of הִנֵּה in this context (*Psalms 101–150*, p. 128).

[64] Cf. the other occurrence of the verb תָּאַב (*tā'aḇ*) in v. 174 and the noun in v. 20. This root occurs in Aramaic with the same meaning; however, the Targum employs a different synonym, רְגַג (*r^{e}gag*), "to desire, long, covet" (Jastrow, *Dictionary*, 2:1447), herein. This root is probably related to the more frequently occurring אבה (*'ḇh*). Based upon a suggested parallelism of "precepts" (v. 40a) with "judgments" (v. 39b), Anderson argues, "In the situation envisaged by the Psalm, the poet is waiting for divine help, and therefore 'precepts' (*piqqûḏîm*, cf. verse 4) may refer not so much to divine commands as to divine acts of judgment which bring help to the afflicted" (*Psalms*, 2:820).

[65] As the psalm advances the most prevalent will be the preposition כְּ (*k^{e}*), "according to," attached to a word for the Word (cf. vv. 149, 154, 156); however, it will also be associated with an attribute of God in v. 88 (i.e. His חֶסֶד [*ḥeseḏ*]).

[66] Anderson, *Psalms*, 2:820.

[67] Cohen, *Psalms*, p. 399; cf. Delitzsch, *Psalms*, 3:249.

ו

WAW STANZA
(vv. 41–48)

Translation and Notes

41 And let Your[a] grace[b] come[c] to me, O LORD,
Your salvation according to Your Word.

42 Then I shall answer *the* one who reproaches[a] me *with* a word,[b]
for I trust in Your Word.[c]

43 And do not snatch[a] *the* word of truth utterly[b] from my mouth,
for I wait for Your judgments.[c]

44 Then I will keep Your law continually,
forever and ever.[a]

45 And I will walk about freely,[a]
for I seek Your precepts.

46 And I will speak of Your testimonies before kings,
and I shall not be ashamed.

47 And I shall delight myself in Your commandments
which I love.

48 And I shall lift up my hands[a] to Your commandments which I love,[b]
and I will meditate[c] on Your statutes

41:a Only the DSS (Q11) omits the 2 m s suffix here.

41:b The MT *points* as a plural; however, the DSS (Q11) and the major versions (except the Syriac) uniformly render חסד (*ḥsḏ*) as singular. On the rendering "grace" for חסד (*ḥsḏ*) see the forthcoming discussion under "Commentary."

41:c The MT and DSS (Q11) construe the verb as a plural; this would infer that both חֶסֶד (*ḥeseḏ*) and תְּשׁוּעָה (*tᵉšûᶜâ*), although appositionally related, should be regarded as its subjects (cf. Soll, "Psalm 119," p. 180).

42:a The LXX and Syriac interpret as a plural. Apparently in the light of this, the vocalization options, and the psalm's internal evidence, Allen suggests that "the singular [of the MT] is probably collective" (*Psalms 101–150*, p. 136).

42:b Construing דָּבָר (*dāḇār*) as an adverbial accusative alongside of the personal accusative, חֹרְפִי (*ḥōrᵉpî*).

42:c The singular of the MT is corroborated by the DSS (Q11), while the LXX, Syriac and Targum render this second דָּבָר (*dāḇār*) as a plural.

43:a The suggestion to emend to אָצַל (*'āṣal*) with a *seemingly* weaker semantical connotation (cf., e.g., Allen, *Psalms 101–150*, p. 136) is inadvisable, lacking textual support and precedent. The more graphic נָצַל (*nāṣal*) in such contexts as this one could also be rendered by "to withhold" (cf. Anderson, *Psalms*, 2:821).

43:b The עַד־מְאֹד (*ᶜaḏ-mᵉ'ōḏ*) of the MT is supported by the DSS (Q11) and the early versions (except the Syriac); therefore, any suggestion, whether based upon metrical and/or contextual preferences, to delete it (e.g. Soll, "Psalm 119," p. 180; Allen, *Psalms 101–150*, p. 136) should be resisted.

43:c Most likely a defective plural (cf. Delitzsch, *Psalms*, 3:249).

44:a The early versions support this compounded phrase after תָּמִיד (*tāmîḏ*), while the DSS (Q11) has only ועד (*wᶜḏ*).

45:a Lit. "in a wide, roomy, space (fig.)" (BDB, p. 932), i.e. without restriction. Interestingly, the DSS (Q11) shows a plural rendering, i.e. "in its broadways" (cf. Sanders, *Dead Sea Psalms Scroll*, p. 49), and the Targum has a paraphrastic addition: "'in the highway of the Law'" (Jastrow, *Dictionary*, 2:1253).

48:a Lit. "palms."

48:b Even Delitzsch entertains the possibility of dittography (cf. v. 47) concerning this phrase (*Psalms*, 3:250; cf. Allen, *Psalms 101–150*, p. 136). Soll consequently argues for the deletion of אֲשֶׁר אָהָבְתִּי (*'ᵃšer 'āhāḇtî*) but commendably resists emending אֶל־מִצְוֹתֶיךָ (*'el-miṣwōṯeyḵā*) to אֵלֶיךָ (*'ēleyḵā*) ("Psalm 119," p.

181). However, neither of these emendations is supported by any textual data.

48:c The DSS (Q11) alone reads ואשׂישׂה (*w'šyšh*) (i.e. to rejoice, exult) herein.

Synopsis And Outline

The thematic common denominator of the *wāw* stanza is the psalmist's "testimony among men."[1] Subtle thematic threads are also evident as pointed out by Kidner: "The prayer of Acts 4:29, 'to speak thy word with all boldness', is not only anticipated here (42f., 46) but put in context; for the word spoken is first of all the word appropriated (41), trusted (42b, 43b), obeyed (44), sought (45) and loved (47f.)."[2]

Structurally, however, the stanza is far more sophisticated and challenging, largely due to the acrostical employment of the initial *wāw*.[3] For some, this means that little or no consideration is paid to the *wāw* conjunctions which expectedly lead off each verse of this stanza.[4] Several translations therefore treat these conjunctions as pleonastic[5] occurrences (e.g. NIV). However, it is better to evaluate each occurrence independently paying close attention to form, other syntactical indicators, and the progression of the psalmist's argument.

Obviously, the first *wāw* could be translated "and," simply indicating the continuation of the psalm, or it could be treated pleo-

---

1 Allen, *Psalms 101–150*, p. 142. Delitzsch well characterizes this as a "true and fearlessly joyous confession" (*Psalms*, 3:249).

2 Kidner, *Psalms 73–150*, p. 425.

3 For a satisfying discussion, see Soll, "Psalm 119," pp. 181–82; e.g., "the letter *waw* poses a problem to the acrostic poet. . . . This dilemma may account for the omission of *waw* lines in Pss. 25 and 34. Ps. 119 resolves the problem as only a stanzaic acrostic could: by employing the same letter (*aleph*) [in six of seven cases a 1 c s imperfect verb form] after the *waw* in each line. Only the first line does not conform to this scheme: an instance of theological considerations taking precedence over pattern" (ibid., p. 181).

4 Cf., e.g., Moll, *Psalms*, p. 590.

5 See Williams, *Hebrew Syntax*, ¶ 435.

nastically, placing an emphasis upon the introductory supplication of this new stanza. The *wāw* at the head of the next verse (i.e. v. 42) strongly suggests inference or consequence (e.g. "so," or "then")[6] reflecting the psalmist's anticipation of the LORD's positive response to his previous request (i.e. v. 41). It is not coincidental that the consequence of verse 42a is immediately followed by a כִּי (*kî*) clause which calls attention to the psalmist's commitment especially in the face of his trials (i.e., v. 43b). So the pattern of verses 41–42 is request, response, resolve; i.e., supplication, anticipated consequence, accompanying commitment.

This pattern, although augmented and extended, is also observable in verses 43–48. Verse 43 commences with the issuance of another request related to the psalmist's desire for a bold testimony. This supplication is immediately followed by a declaration of the psalmist's resolve (i.e. v. 43b) and then by the responses (e.g. vv. 44a, 45a, 46a, 47a, 48a) anticipated. Interspersed among these divinely initiated consequences is yet one more affirmation of commitment (cf. v. 45b).[7]

Based upon these variegated phenomena, the child of God, being burdened by a desire for a bold testimony in Psalm 119:41–48, documents two supplications for Divine intervention with consequences and commitments.

1A. (vv. 41–42) A positively expressed supplication for grace for communication.
  1B. (v. 41) His desire.
  2B. (v. 42) His documentation:
    1C.(v. 42a) The anticipated consequence.
    2C.(v. 42b) The accompanying commitment.
2A. (vv. 43–48) A negatively expressed supplication for grace for credibility.
  1B. (v. 43a) His desire.
  2B. (vv. 43b–48) His documentation:

---

[6] Cf. BDB, p. 254.

[7] I.e. another כִּי (*kî*) clause; there may be two *implicit* indications of resolve in the אֲשֶׁר אָהָבְתִּי (*ʾăšer ʾāhābtî*) clauses of vv. 47b and 48b.

1C. (vv. 44, 45a, 46–48) The anticipated consequences:
  1D. (v. 44) Obedience.
  2D. (v. 45a) Freedom.
  3D. (v. 46) Boldness.
  4D. (vv. 47–48) Satisfaction:
    1E. (v. 47) Its emotional manifestation.
    2E. (v. 48a) Its volitional manifestation.
    3E. (v. 48b) Its rational manifestation.
2C. (vv. 43b, 45b) The accompanying commitments:
  1D. (v. 43b) His expectation of God's Word.
  2D. (v. 45b) His exploration in God's Word.

Commentary

The opening וִיבֹאֻנִי (*wîḇō'unî*) bears the psalmist's personal supplication. This Qal jussive from בּוֹא (*bô'*) is a serviceable vehicle for the conveyance of Divine blessing.[8] In this case, the man of God earnestly seeks the LORD's חֶסֶד (*ḥeseḏ*) and תְּשׁוּעָה (*tᵉšûᶜâ*).

It is universally recognized that חֶסֶד is one of the most theologically significant words in the Bible. Treatises on this term abound,[9] but its depths are unfathomable, and its multifaceted connotations seem to be irreducible. Early versions[10] and translations, ancient and modern, have struggled with single or multiple-term renderings, all of which have failed to capture the theological breadth of it. Important associations have been explored (e.g. חֶסֶד with בְּרִית [*bᵉrîṯ*], "covenant"; חֶסֶד with אֱמֶת [*'emeṯ*], "truth," i.e. fidelity; etc.) often issuing in dogmatic assertions about the term's basic meaning, e.g. "covenant loyalty," "loyal

---

8 See BDB, p. 98; cf. Preuss' discussion of "The Coming and Fulfilled Salvation" in *TDOT*, s.v. "בּוֹא *bo'*," by H. Preuss, 2:38–41.

9 Cf. a sampling of this bibliography in *TDOT*, s.v. "חֶסֶד *ḥesed*," by H. Zobel, 5:44; and *TWOT*, s.v. "חסד (*ḥsd*) I," by R. Harris, 1:305–07.

10 The usual rendering of חֶסֶד in the LXX is ἔλεος (*eleos*), "mercy," which is far too restrictive.

11 Brief but excellent is Harris' survey: *TWOT*, 1:305–07.

love," etc.[11] However, when a high percentage of the contexts surrounding this noun's 245 occurrences are examined, the best one can do is to observe that "it is a kind of love, including mercy, *ḥannûn,* when the object is in a pitiful state."[12] In the light of this credible assessment, what better term than "grace" is suitable?[13] It is therefore חֶסֶד, not necessarily חֵן (*ḥēn*),[14] which is the conceptual and theological forbearer of NT χάρις (*charis*).[15]

The parallelism of תְּשׁוּעָה (*tᵉšûᶜâ,* i.e. "deliverance, salvation"[16]) dovetails, and, in conjunction with the intention of verse 42a, the fragile child of God is pleading for the sustaining grace of *rescue* which alone will make available to him the *Divine* resources[17] that he desperately needs to respond properly to reproach.[18] He once again perceives his request to be in accord with the nature of his LORD, as indicated by the climactic כְּאִמְרָתֶךָ (*kᵉ'imrāṯeḵā*). God's bestowal of "grace" and "salvation" is not surprising but characteristic, because His "word" or "promise" assures us of His beneficent inclinations.

In verse 42 the previous generalizations about his "reproach"

---

[12] Ibid., p. 307.

[13] Cf. *TDOT,* 5:51.

[14] I.e. the OT word normally rendered "grace" or "favor" (cf. BDB, p. 336).

[15] For a brief summary of this important association, see Charles C. Ryrie, *The Grace of God* (Chicago: Moody Press, 1963), p. 15.

[16] BDB, p. 448. Anderson, *Psalms,* 2:821, correctly points to the synonymity of תְּשׁוּעָה (cf. also v. 81) with יְשׁוּעָה (*yᵉšûᶜâ*; cf. vv. 123, 155, 166, 174), both deriving from the impacting root ישׁע (*yšᶜ*); also, cf. his balanced statements on salvation in the OT (*Psalms,* 2:277).

[17] The repetition of the second person singular suffix, not only on חֶסֶד and תְּשׁוּעָה, but also on אִמְרָה (*'imrâ*), heightens the theocentric focus of v. 41.

[18] It is important to remember that "there is nothing in the word *yasha'* which indicates the mode or which limits the extent of salvation. It evidently includes divinely bestowed deliverance from every class of spiritual and temporal evil to which mortal man is subjected" (Girdlestone, *Synonyms,* p. 125). Statistically, there is a higher percentage of temporal contexts in the OT, while the reciprocal is true in the NT. Cf. ibid., pp. 124–26; and Geoffrey W. Grogan, "The Experience of Salvation in the Old and New Testaments," *Vox Evangelica* 5 (1967): 4–26.

[19] Allen, *Psalms 101–150,* p. 128.

[20] Soll, "Psalm 119," p. 180.

(cf. חֶרְפָּה [*ḥerpâ*] in vv. 22, 39) are personalized in a direct reference to חֹרְפִי (*ḥōrᵉp̱î*), "one who reproaches me," i.e. "the one who insults me,"[19] "my slanderer."[20] As the whole of the psalm bears witness, our psalmist was painfully acquainted with verbal *abuse*;[21] his enemies[22] "scoffed" at him,[23] "defamed" him,[24] and ultimately conspired to exterminate him.[25] It is no wonder that he was in desperate need of Divine enablement when his time of answering or *response* came.[26] This dependent attitude of the psalmist modeled what Peter had in mind in 1 Peter 3:15.

Answering or responding "a word" or "*with* a word"[27] seems to be more than pleonasm, since דָּבָר (*dāḇār*) recurs in verse 42b. From the psalmist's perspective there may have been a subtle association between his "word" and the Divine "Word" in which he had the utmost *confidence*.[28] His commitment to (i.e. reliance upon[29]) the Word of God and the God who stands behind that Word served as a mainstay in the face of misery.[30]

---

[21] Kutsch considers "abuse" to be the basic semantical force of חרף (*ḥrp̄*) II (*TDOT*, s.v. "חרף *ḥrp̱* I," by E. Kutsch, 5:204–205).

[22] As noted above (cf. the translation notes on v. 42) this singular substantive participle is best understood as a collective; his enemies were many.

[23] Cf. *TDOT*, s.v. "חרף *ḥrp̱* II," by E. Kutsch, 5:211–12.

[24] I.e. "impute blame or guilt to someone in order to harm his character" (*TWOT*, s.v. "חָרַף (*ḥārap̱*) I," by T. McComiskey, 1:325).

[25] As previously mentioned, this scenario aptly fits Daniel.

[26] On עָנָה (*ʿānâ*) I, "to respond, answer," see BDB, pp. 772–73; cf. *TWOT*, s.v. "עָנָה (*ʿānâ*) I," by R. Allen, 2:679–80. Anderson notes, in the light of the immediate and larger circles of context, that his "answer" was "not necessarily a reply to a question, but rather a refutation of the affirmation [i.e. allegations] of the enemies" (*Psalms*, 2:821).

[27] Taking דָּבָר (*dāḇār*) as an adverbial accusative.

[28] On this emphasis of בָּטַח (*bāṭaḥ*), esp. as complemented by the preposition בְּ (*bᵉ*), "to trust in, believe in, put confidence in," see BDB, p. 105; *TWOT*, s.v. "בָּטַח (*bāṭaḥ*) I," by J. Oswalt, 1:101–02; and *TDOT*, s.v. "בָּטַח *bātach*," by A. Jepsen, 2:88–94.

[29] בָּטַח as *reliance upon* someone or something is predominant in the OT (cf. *TDOT*, 2:89; and *NIDNTT*, s.v. "πίστις," by O. Michel, 1:596).

[30] Concerning the significance of this כִּי (*kî*) clause (i.e. v. 43b), Anderson paraphrases "I trust in thy word" with "'I am confident that you are both able and willing to fulfil your promises'" (*Psalms*, 2:821).

The supplication of verse 43 perpetrates the theme of the *Wāw* stanza: "Do not snatch the word of truth utterly from my mouth."[31] Some have stumbled at the occurrence of the graphic אַל־תַּצֵּל (*'al-taṣṣēl*);[32] however, the intention of verse 43a is clear: "The meaning of the prayer is, that God may not suffer him to come to such a pass that he will be utterly unable to witness for the truth."[33] He bolsters his impassioned plea with an affirmation of commitment relating to his "waiting" or "hoping for"[34] the LORD's "commandments." The verb he utilizes, יָחַל (*yāḥal*), is an important term indicating confident expectation (cf. vv. 49, 74, 81, 114, 147).[35] In this context the anchorage of his hope is לְמִשְׁפָּטֶךָ (*lᵉmišpāṭeḵā*), "God's ordinances," likely referring to "the righteous judgments of Yahweh, which will bring relief to the Psalmist."[36]

Another string of first person imperfect verbs indicating the consequences of a positive response to his supplication (i.e. v. 43a) follows (i.e. vv. 44–48). Consequently, these manifestations of responsibility constitute not only a syntactical, but also a theological, apodosis as they look back dependently to the theocentric protasis in verse 43a. Once again, clearly evident is the truth that the psalmist's resolve and response are totally dependent upon the LORD's rescue.

Obedience is the first anticipated consequence to surface as indicated by the introductory וְאֶשְׁמְרָה (*wᵉ'ešmᵉrâ*) of verse 44. The priority of obedience has been and will continue to be conspicuous throughout the psalm, but herein the man of God is especially bold, qualifying his commitment not only with תָּמִיד (*tāmîḏ*), i.e. "continuously,"[37]

---

[31] Soll appropriately makes the connection, noting, "Vv. 42 and 43 both relate to the psalmist's verbal response to slander and his capacity to bear witness to divine faithfulness" ("Psalm 119," p. 182; cf. Delitzsch, *Psalms*, 3:249).

[32] Cf. the brief remarks above (i.e. the translation notes on v. 43).

[33] Delitzsch, *Psalms*, 3:249.

[34] Cf. יָחַל (*yāḥal*) plus לְ (*lᵉ*) in BDB, p. 404.

[35] On this basic thrust, see *TWOT*, s.v. "יָחַל (*yāḥal*)," by P. Gilchrist, 1:373. "*Yāḥal* is used of 'expectation, hope' which for the believer is closely linked with 'faith, trust' [cf. v. 42b] and results in 'patient waiting'" (ibid.).

[36] Anderson, *Psalms*, 2:821.

[37] BDB, p. 556.

[38] On לְעוֹלָם (*lᵉ*ᶜ*ôlām*) cf., e.g., vv. 93, 98, 111, 112; the stress is upon "emotions and activities continuous through life" (BDB, p. 762).

but also with לְעוֹלָם וָעֶד (*le*c*ôlām wā*c*ed*), "forever and ever." His sights are set high; *perpetual fidelity* is the bull's-eye of his target.[38]

Freedom occupies his thoughts next (i.e. v. 45a). The Hithpael of הָלַךְ (*hālak*) is a vivid metaphor which depicts the living of life in all of its dimensions, and the qualifying prepositional phrase בָרְחָבָה (*bār*e*ḥābâ*)[39] idiomatically delineates the nature of that desired life. He longs to walk about "'unconstrainedly,'"[40] i.e. freely. Indeed, the persecuted one was acutely aware of his need for elbow room both to walk (v. 45) and to witness (v. 46).

Verse 45b interjects a testimony which rehearses his commitment to pursue God's Word. As observed previously, the verb דָּרַשׁ (*dāraš*) is frequently employed to indicate the seeking of God and/or the studying of His revelation (see internally, vv. 2, 10, 94, 155; cf. Ezra 7:10).[41] "Here the verb portrays the Psalmist as preoccupied with God's precepts. . . . This would involve both their study and their application to life."[42]

An earlier semantical and conceptual thread (cf. v. 42) is picked up by the leading verb וַאֲדַבְּרָה (*wa'ădabb*e*râ*, "and I will *speak*") in verse 46.[43] This man of God anticipates a divinely mediated boldness in order that he might proclaim God's testimonies before kings,[44] and to do so *unashamedly*, i.e. וְלֹא אֵבוֹשׁ (*w*e*lō' 'ēbôš*).[45] That

---

[39] Lit., "in a wide, roomy, space" (BDB, p. 932).

[40] Delitzsch, *Psalms*, 3:250. Delitzsch interprets this as an "inward freedom which makes itself known outwardly" (ibid.). The immediate context would support this, and there may be some distant corroboration from the important occurrence of the root רחב (*rḥb*) as a verb in v. 32.

[41] Cf. Kirkpatrick, *Psalms*, p. 712.

[42] Anderson, *Psalms*, 2:822.

[43] The Vulgate reads at v. 46 *et loquar in testimoniis tuis coram regibus et non confundar*, and this rendering has gained some historical significance: "Ver. 46 is the motto of the Augsburg Confession according to the historical view of the verbs in the Vulgate, which, however, does not correspond with the Heb. text" (Moll, *Psalms*), p. 590).

[44] It is possible to take נֶגֶד מְלָכִים (*neged m*e*lākîm*) *literally*, esp. if someone like Daniel had been the source of these words. Therefore, Anderson's statement seems to be a premature rationalization: "The term *kings* is probably a poetical exaggeration for the sake of emphasis" (*Psalms*, 2:822).

[45] Lit. "and I will not be ashamed"; on his passion for not being ashamed before God and/or men, remember vv. 6, 31, 80. Cf. the examples of Nehemiah, Paul, etc.

for which he was praying had no *explicit* precedent, but one day it would have in the promise of Christ (i.e. Matt 10:18–19).

The orientation of verses 47–48 is more inward focusing upon personal satisfaction. These particular consequences would not be received as new experiences but as continuing fortifications flowing from the LORD through the conduit of the Word[46] to the inner man. For example, when the psalmist says, "I will delight myself in Your commandments which I love" (v. 47), he looks forward to the continuing blessing of a deep-seated, and in this context, a transcendent, joy[47] adhering to his LORD's commands.[48]

Volitional and rational consequences are cited by the man of God in verse 48. The first part of this verse contains "a bold expression of yearning for God's revelation in Scripture."[49] "The lifting up of the hands . . . does not refer to the observance of the commandments, . . . still less to the worship of the law in the later Jewish manner . . . , but to the longing desire expressed by stretching out the hands after the commandments . . . , often parallel to the lifting up of the heart to the highest good."[50] Then an emphasis upon the activity of שִׂיחַ (*śîaḥ*), the contemplative internalization of God's Word for character and conduct,[51] secures the intricate movements of this stanza to a familiar mooring.

---

[46] Soll has therefore observed: "Torah appears in this strophe not so much as motivation for prayer but as part of its answer; the salvation of Yahweh will enable the psalmist to participate in Torah more fully" ("Psalm 119," p. 182).

[47] Cf. noun and verbal occurrences of the root שׁעע (š^cc^) II in vv. 16, 24, 70, 77, 92, 143, 174; and note the discussion above at v. 16 and in Part II: Overview under the heading "Dependent Appropriation, Internalization, and Application."

[48] As will be documented by subsequent occurrences of the root אהב (*'hb̲*), his affirmation of love (i.e. v. 47b; cf. v. 48b) "has not only an emotional content, but it also suggests a love which is manifested in the doing of God's will as expressed in his law. Cf. Dt. 5:10, 7:9, 10:12f., etc." (Anderson, *Psalms*, 2:822).

[49] Kidner, *Psalms 73–150*, p. 425; cf. Delitzsch, *Psalms*, 3:250

[50] Moll, *Psalms*, p. 590.

[51] Cf. occurrences of the root שׂיח (*śyḥ*) in vv. 15, 23, 27, 78, 97, 99, 148; and see the discussion in Part II: Overview under the heading "Dependent Appropriation, Internalization, and Application."

ז

ZAYIN STANZA
(vv. 49–56)

Translation and Notes

49 Remember *Your*[a] word[b] to Your servant,
upon which[c] You have made me hope.[d]

50 This is my comfort[a] in my affliction,
that Your promise revives me.

51 Insolent men utterly deride me;
nevertheless,[a] I have not turned aside from Your law.

52 I remember Your judgments from of old,[a]
O LORD, and I take comfort.[b]

53 Burning anger[a] seizes me because of[b] wicked men,
who forsake Your law.

54 Your statutes are my songs
in the place[a] of my sojourning.[b]

55 I remember Your name in the night, O LORD,
and I will keep Your law.[a]

56 This is mine,[a]
that[b] I keep Your precepts.

49:a The DSS (Q11) contains both the 2 m s suffix and a plural form (i.e. "Your words"), while original LXX and the Syriac have the 2 m s suffix with a singular form of the noun (i.e. "Your word"). Stylistically, an appeal could be made for a balance between the two 2 m s suffixes of v. 49a with the two 1 c s suffixes of v. 50a. Notwithstanding these observations, the translation above does not necessarily support an emendation of the MT, since, by sense, דָּבָר (*dābār*) as juxtaposed with לְעַבְדֶּךָ (*le^cabdekā*) would imply that the psalmist has in mind a personal application of *God's* Word to him.

49:b Or the sense of "promise" herein, (cf. אִמְרָה [*'imrâ*] in v. 50b).

49:c עַל אֲשֶׁר (*^cal 'ăšer*) is quite frequently used pleonastically to indicate cause, i.e. "because" (cf. BDB, p. 758); however, the more literal rendering, "upon" or "on which" seems to be more suitable in this context. Cf. Allen's rendering of v. 49b: "which you have made the basis of my hope" (*Psalms 101–150*, p. 128).

49:d There is no textual evidence for emending this 2 m s verb with 1 c s suffix to merely a 1 c s verb form.

50:a The LXX and Syriac read as verbals instead of this f s noun with 1 c s suffix.

51:a One of the several impacting asyndetonic antithetical parallelisms which capture the reader's attention. Another way to render this striking feature in translation is to construe the first clause concessively; e.g.: "Though the proud scoff bitterly at me, I turn not away from your law" (NAB).

52:a The מֵעוֹלָם (cf. *mē^côlām*; BDB, p. 761) most likely qualifies מִשְׁפָּטֶיךָ (*mišpāṭeykā*); cf. Allen, *Psalms 101–150*, p. 136.

52:b Lit. "and I comfort myself" (Hithpael imperfect 1 c s).

53:a Lit. "raging heat," fig. of zeal (BDB, p. 273).

53:b Causal מִן (*min*), i.e. "on account of, in consequence of" (GKC, ¶ 119z).

54:a I.e. בַּיִת (*bayit*); usually, but not always, rendered "house."

54:b Cf. NAB on v. 54b: "in the place of my exile."

55:a Construing אֶשְׁמְרָה (*'ešm^erâ*) as a cohortative.

56:a The Targum adds לִזְכוּתָא (*lizkûtā'*), "for acquittal" (Jastrow, *Dictionary*, 1:398). On some translational interpretive options regarding v. 56a, see Soll, "Psalm 119," pp. 182–83.

56:b The above translation reflects a nominalizing interpretation of כִּי (*kî*), cf. v. 50 (cf. Williams, *Hebrew Syntax*, ¶ 451). A causal function could also be supported from the immediate and larger contextual settings (i.e. "This has belonged to me, because I have kept Your precepts").

Synopsis and Outline

Parallels and paradoxes are the earmarks of the *Zayin* stanza. A primary semantical parallel based upon the root זכר (*zk̲r*) is immediately observable (cf. vv. 49, 52, 55), and indeed, it is this emphasis upon remembrance which supplies the thematic cohesion to these eight verses.[1] Woven into this fabric of reminiscence are sub-themes of the psalmist's comfort (i.e. vv. 50, 52) amidst affliction (i.e. v. 50; cf. vv. 51, 53) and alienation (i.e. v. 54), his providential possessions (i.e. vv. 50, 54, 56),[2] and his characteristic preoccupations with trust and obedience (e.g. vv. 49a, 51b, 52, 55).

When one steps back and gazes upon the panorama of these various affirmations which have issued from the mouth of this man of God, the impression is that he, by God's great grace, was progressively realizing in his heart of hearts the strategic balance between dependence and duty. Without such a biblical perspective real life becomes not only inexplicable but also intolerable. Consequently, the following proposition and outline should help us recapture his findings and thereby learn and grow with him: Amidst life's tough realities three cycles of remembrance provide spiritual perspective for the child of God.

1A. Cycle 1 (vv. 49–50): amidst his affliction he anticipates God's remembrance and obtains comfort.
 1B. (v. 49) The remembrance: his future expectation is grounded upon a past assurance.
 2B. (v. 50) The result: his present consolation is grounded upon a past precedent.

---

[1] Allen has well observed that "memory . . . plays a dominant role, both God's and man's" (*Psalms 101–150*, p. 143).

[2] Vv. 54a and 56a are structured as normal possessive idioms, while v. 50a expresses the psalmist's spiritual advantage without any verbal complemented by possessive לְ (*lᵉ*). It should be noted that vv. 50b and 56b are כִּי (*kî*) clauses which throw more light on their respective leading affirmations, while v. 54a is quite self-contained being followed simply by a prepositional phrase.

2A. Cycle 2 (vv. 51–53): amidst his adversity he remembers the Word of God and feels righteous indignation (i.e. towards the apostates).
   1B. (v. 51) The reality: their hostility contrasts with his integrity.
   2B. (v. 52) The remembrance: the Word's fidelity supplies his consolation.
   3B. (v. 53) The result: his indignation stems from their apostasy.
3A. Cycle 3 (vv. 54–56): amidst his alienation he remembers the God of the Word and matures in obedience.
   1B. (v. 54) The reality: God's Word pre-empts his loneliness.
   2B. (v. 55) The remembrance: God's Person prompts his commitment.
   3B. (v. 56) The result: God's providence pilots his sanctification.

Commentary

The only prayer of this stanza is the psalmist's introductory plea for his Master's remembrance in the form of the imperative זְכֹר (*z^e^k̲ōr*).[3] This leading invocation, especially as complemented by לְעַבְדֶּךָ (*l^ec^ab̲dek̲ā*; "to Your servant"), "serves primarily to express an . . . activity that is relational and personal."[4] Furthermore, such "activity" would not only include God's "remembering," i.e. "paying attention to" the psalmist but would also anticipate the LORD's beneficent intervention into the circumstances of his re-

[3] It has been previously intimated that his own remembrances (i.e. vv. 52, 55) form the semantical and logical backdrop for this particular request. For a thorough work which explores the remembrance of both God and man, see Brevard S. Childs, *Memory and Tradition in Israel* (London: SCM, 1962), esp. chs. 3–4, "God Remembers" and "Israel Remembers."

[4] *TDOT*, s.v. "זָכַר (*zākhar*)," by H. Eising, 4:65.

quest.[5] Needless to say, when this kind of remembrance is sought, it in no way assumes any forgetfulness on the part of the LORD.[6]

The object that the psalmist holds up to be the target of God's remembrance is דָּבָר (*dāḇār*), "a word," or better, "promise."[7] Often God's remembrance is directly associated with His covenant,[8] and although explicit covenantal terminology does not accompany this request, the psalmist's employment of דָּבָר should be regarded as an implicit reference to God's commitments to covenant.[9] Once again, this man of God is quick to personalize His LORD's promises.

That he was expecting God's fulfillment of that promise is indicated by verse 49b, עַל אֲשֶׁר יִחַלְתָּנִי (*ʿal ʾăšer yiḥaltānî*), "upon which (promise) You have caused me to hope."[10] Normally, the Piel of יחל (*yḥl*) is rendered actively, "to wait for" or "to hope,"[11] but in this context it takes on a causative function with God as the agent of expectation and the psalmist as the recipient of it. Concerning the basic nature of such a trusting expectation within its larger biblical framework, Gilchrist has well observed that "this *yāḥal* 'hope' is not a pacifying wish of the imagination which

---

[5] For an excellent discussion of a prevalent fusion between the primary fields of usage "for completely inward mental acts such as 'remembering' or 'paying attention to,'" and "for such inward mental acts accompanied by appropriate external acts," see *TWOT*, s.v. "זָכַר (*zākar*)," by T. McComiskey, 1:241.

[6] "When God is challenged to 'remember' the meaning is better taken as 'pay attention to' since nothing ever escapes God's omniscience" (ibid.).

[7] The proximity of דָּבָר (*dāḇār*) in v. 49a with אִמְרָתְךָ (*'imrāṯᵉkā*), "Your promise," in v. 50b provides some justification that these terms should be looked upon as denotative parallels herein.

[8] Cf. *TDOT*, 4:69–71, and *TWOT*, 1:241.

[9] Cf. Anderson's association of v. 49a with the parallelism of Ps 105:8 (*Psalms*, 2:823). In addition, the ensuing subordinate clause (i.e. v. 49b) lends credence to this conclusion.

[10] Cf. Allen again, "which you have made the basis of my hope" (*Psalms 101–150*, p. 128), i.e. "Thou . . . hast directed my expectation thereunto" (Delitzsch, *Psalms*, 3:250).

[11] BDB, pp. 403–04; cf. the comments on this root above at v. 43 (note also vv. 74, 81, 114, 147, and cf. Pss 42:5 [v. 6, Heb], 11 [v. 12, Heb]; 43:5; 130:7; Job 13:15; Mic 7:7; etc.).

drowns out troubles, nor is it uncertain (as in the Greek concept), but rather *yāḥal* 'hope' is the solid ground of expectation for the righteous."[12]

The efficacy of the God of the Word (i.e. v. 49) picks up an echo in verse 50 in the form of the efficacy of the Word of God. In this verse, the testimony of the man of God commences with a striking paradox. In the midst of acute personal affliction[13] (i.e. בְעָנְיִי [*ḇeʿonyî*]), he found personal consolation (i.e. נֶחָמָתִי [*neḥāmāṯî*][14]).[15] Then, he briefly sketches out the nature[16] of such comfort in the latter portion of the verse by continuing to testify that God's promise had preserved and was preserving him (i.e. כִּי אִמְרָתְךָ חִיָּתְנִי [*kî 'imrāṯekā ḥîyyāṯenî*]). As Delitzsch notes, "this is his comfort in his dejected condition, that God's promissory declaration has quickened him and proved its reviving power in his case."[17]

The psalmist's reference to his affliction in general (i.e. v. 50a) is partially specified in verse 51a: זֵדִים הֱלִיצֻנִי עַד־מְאֹד (*zēḏîm hĕlîṣunî ʿaḏ-meʾōḏ*), "Insolent men have utterly derided me."[18] These scoundrels were regarded as "godless, rebellious men,"[19] and herein attention is drawn to their relentless derision. Substantives

---

[12] *TWOT*, 1:373.

[13] It must be remembered that "the psalmist was not only scorned and taunted by his enemies (verses 22, 39, 42, 51, etc.), but his very life was in danger (verses 87, 109)" (Anderson, *Psalms*, 2:823).

[14] The only other occurrence of this feminine noun for "comfort" is found in Job 6:10 (cf. its context).

[15] Cf. Allen, *Psalms 101–150*, p. 142; he also calls attention to vv. 52, 54, 55a.

[16] Some opt for a resultative interpretation of the כִּי (*kî*) clause rather than a recitative or nominalizing function (e.g. Moll, *Psalms*, p. 590); however, the introductory demonstrative זֹאת (*zō'ṯ*) in this setting would quite naturally anticipate a further delineation of his seemingly paradoxical comfort.

[17] Delitzsch, *Psalms*, 3:250.

[18] It is interesting that the Hebrew roots of the first two words in this verse also appear respectively in the first and third words of Prov 21:24. Additionally, the second root which occurs as a finite verb in Ps 119:51 appears as a substantival participle (i.e., לֵצִים [*lēṣîm*], "scorners," "mockers," "scoffers," etc.) in Ps 1:1.

[19] BDB, p. 267; on the antagonistic nature of these זֵדִים (*zēḏîm*), cf. the previous discussion of them within the commentary at v. 21.

of the verb לִיץ (*lîṣ*), "to scorn, deride," occur throughout the Book of Proverbs providing a profile on such prideful mocking.[20] As a matter of fact, the biblically pervasive truth of Proverbs 3:34, "though He scoffs at the scoffers, yet He gives grace to the afflicted" (NASB), may have constrained our psalmist, especially as he penned verses 49–51.

From a merely human perspective, his response (i.e. v. 51b) to their heinous actions is totally inexplicable. In the pressure cooker of all such persecution, he maintained that he had not detoured from the LORD's road map for life (cf. v. 157). The verb נָטָה (*nāṭâ*) was often used figuratively in reference to "deviating from [the] path of loyalty,"[21] e.g. to apostatize. When this man of God emphatically denied any such declension from God's preceptive instruction: מִתּוֹרָתְךָ לֹא נָטִיתִי (*mitôrāṯᵉḵā lō' nāṭîṯî*), "from Your law I have not turned aside," he was not engaging in pharisaical braggadocio. On the contrary, his ethical conformity was ever and always dependent upon God's grace operating within and through him.[22]

His explicit reminiscences commence with the testimony of verse 52, and they are "of a bittersweet nature."[23] At the outset, however, he accentuates their transcendent sweetness. In the midst of persisting pain the psalmist opened the doors of his memory to the reality of our LORD's eternal[24] מִשְׁפָּטֶיךָ (*mišpāṭeyḵā*). Normally translated "Your judgments" or "Your ordinances," here the emphasis seems to be upon the inscripturated

[20] For a brief survey, see *TWOT*, s.v. "לִיץ (*lîṣ*)," by W. Kaiser, 1:479.

[21] BDB, p. 640; cf. *TWOT*, s.v. "נָטָה (*nāṭâ*)," M. Wilson, 2:574.

[22] E.g., cf. his prior use of the root נָטָה (*nāṭâ*) in the dependent prayer request of v. 36. The only basis for his not declining in habit was his LORD's inclining him in heart.

[23] Soll, "Psalm 119," p. 184.

[24] Construing מֵעוֹלָם (*mēʿôlām*), "from of old," with the noun instead of the verb. If it were taken with the verb זָכַרְתִּי (*zāḵartî*), "I have remembered," the emphasis would be upon the longevity of this particular remembrance. The former syntactical option seems to have an edge of preference due to the placement of מֵעוֹלָם between the noun and the Tetragrammaton employed as a vocative.

"salvation-history of Israel, . . . the saving judgments of God in the past, whereby the righteous have been delivered."[25] As the man of God reflects upon these historic verifications of his Lord's mercy, he personalizes their precedent.[26]

The consequence of his remembrance is comfort (וָאֶתְנֶחָם [*wā'etneḥām*]); indeed, such a reminiscence (i.e. v. 52a) brings relief (i.e. v. 52b).[27] This particular semantical field of usage (i.e. consolation or comfort) for the root נחם (*nḥm*) often carries with it the attendant features of support and encouragement.[28] In addition, the rendering παρεκλήθην (*pareklēthēn*) in the LXX not only reflects a quite consistent translational pattern for נחם within the OT, but it also comes to its ultimate fulfillment in the NT.[29] Occurrences of the παρακαλέω (*parakaleō*) word-group[30] throughout the NT confirm that God is *the* Source of the disciple's comfort (e.g. 2 Cor 1:3–4) which is mediated through the instrumentality of the Scriptures (e.g. Rom 15:4–5).[31]

Vivid personification launches verse 53: זַלְעָפָה אֲחָזַתְנִי (*zalʿāpâ 'ăḥāzatnî*), lit., "raging heat grasps me." Psalm 11:6 and Lamentations 5:10 provide examples of literal usages of the noun זַלְעָפָה (*zal'āpâ*), but in its present setting it is obviously being used figuratively for the psalmist's inflamed zeal.[32] As such, the word is appropriately rendered by "hot indignation"[33] or "passionate

---

[25] Anderson, *Psalms*, 2:824.

[26] For some appropriate commentary, see Delitzsch, *Psalms*, 3:250.

[27] On the Hithpael of נחם (*nḥm*), "comfort oneself, be relieved," see BDB, p. 637; cf. the Piel occurrences in vv. 76 and 82.

[28] For a handy survey of some crucial passages, see *TWOT*, s.v. "נָחַם (*nāḥam*)," by M. Wilson, 2:571; and for argumentation on this point, see Girdlestone, *Synonyms*, p. 91.

[29] Cf. Thayer's helpful survey (*Lexicon*, p. 483).

[30] Esp. παρακαλέω and παράκλησις (*parakaleō* and *paraklēsis*).

[31] See Girdlestone, *Synonyms*, p. 92. Beyond this, the more technically nuanced παράκλητος (*paraklētos*) as an appellation for both Christ (1 John 2:1) and the Spirit (John 14:16, 26; 15:26; 16:7) certainly includes among its rich denotations a connotation of comfort.

[32] Cf. BDB, p. 273.

[33] Anderson, *Psalms*, 2:824.

[34] Allen, *Psalms 101–150*, p. 128.

fury."[34] Such burning anger seized[35] the man of God because of the nature and actions of the רְשָׁעִים (*rešāʿîm*; cf. vv. 61, 95, 110, 119, 155).

"*Rešaʿîm*[i.e. 'wicked men'] is a characteristic designation of the enemies of the Psalmists .... They are men who are guilty before God, because of their neglect of the divine law and revelation (verse 53b)."[36] Although these men were his formidable enemies (cf. again vv. 61, 95, and 110), the primary reason that he cites for his revulsion of them is their apostasy (cf. v. 155). Characteristically, they forsake God's will for man's way (i.e. עֹזְבֵי תּוֹרָתֶךָ [*ʿōzeḇê tôrāṯeḵā*]);[37] therefore, he is unable to tolerate this rejection of his LORD's law.

Between verses 53 and 54 the pendulum swings from the treachery of the godless to the tranquility of the godly.[38] In an alien context (i.e. בְּבֵית מְגוּרָי [*bebêṯ megûrāy*], lit. "in the house of my sojourning"[39]), the psalmist clutched a precious possession, God's "statutes," and they had become his "songs" (i.e. זְמִרוֹת [*zemirôṯ*]).[40]

---

[35] Concerning אָחַז (*'āḥaz*), "a common idiom is to be seized by pain, sorrow or fear, often as a women in childbirth . . ." (*TWOT*, s.v. "אָחַז (*'āḥaz*)," by H. Wolf, 1:32). The LXX's κατέχω (*katechō*) herein most likely leans towards the "take-possession-of" dimension of אָחַז.

[36] Anderson, *Psalms*, 2:824. Girdlestone notes that "in the Psalms they are represented as busily occupied in disturbing the peace of others, and as trying to destroy them" (*Synonyms*, pp. 81–82). For a commendable survey of this important word group with a special emphasis upon "words semantically parallel," see *TWOT* s.v. "רָשַׁע (*rāshaʿ*)," by G. Livingston, 2:863–64.

[37] Contrast the psalmist in vv. 55 (a parallel with תּוֹרָה [*tôrâ*]), 87 (a לֹא־עָזַבְתִּי [*lō ʿāzaḇtî*], "I-have-*not*-abandoned" pattern), etc.

[38] It should be noted that all the declarations of this stanza seem to alternate between promise or privilege and pressure.

[39] On the noun מָגוֹר (*māgôr*), see BDB, p. 158; and *TWOT*, s.v. " גּוּר (gûr) I," by H. Stigers, 1:156. For arguments opting for a literal interpretation of the root גּוּר (*gûr*) in Ps 119, see the commentary above at v. 19; cf. the rendering of the NAB: "in the place of my exile" (v. 54b).

[40] On this masculine noun, see BDB, p. 274.

That these were not dirges or a repertoire of the blues is confirmed by a survey of the biblical occurrences of the root זמר (*zmr*)[41] which suggests that they were "songs of rejoicing."[42] The child of God has at his disposal the Divine resources which allow him to praise even from the pits of persecution and peril.

The psalmist's nocturnal reminiscence[43] in verse 55 entailed a pondering of his LORD's name (i.e. שֵׁם [*šēm*]). This activity likely included deep reflections upon His "existence, character, and reputation."[44] It is not surprising, therefore, that such contemplations of the Person of the Word (i.e. v. 55a) would consequently lead to[45] a rekindled commitment[46] to the precepts of the Word (i.e. v. 55b).

A variety of translations and interpretations have been offered for verse 56.[47] It seems best to view the possessive affirmation of verse 56a as a bridge between the truth of verse 55b (*in its larger contextual setting*)[48] and that truth's climactic recapitulation in verse 56b.[49] In other words, he testifies that his obedience, even under oppression, is God's providence for his life.[50] Yet to come,

---

[41] Cf. *TDOT*, s.v. "זמר (*zmr*)," by C. Barth, 4:91–98; and *TWOT*, s.v. "זָמַר (*zāmar*) I," by H. Wolf, 1:245.

[42] *TDOT*, 4:94, cf. p. 98.

[43] I.e. בַּלַּיְלָה (*ballayᵉlâ*), "at, in," or "during the night"; night time brought opportunity for a contemplative reflection upon the God who is and does.

[44] These are significant aspects of the term שֵׁם (*šēm*) as it surfaces throughout the OT (*TWOT*, s.v. "שֵׁם (*shēm*)," by W. Kaiser, 2:934). Kaiser also commendably emphasizes the fact that "the name of God also signifies the whole self-disclosure of God in his holiness and truth" (ibid.).

[45] Above (cf. "Translation and Notes"), it was suggested that ואשׁמרה (*w'šmrh*) be rendered as a (volitional) cohortative which would call only for a repointing of the conjunction. As such, this would follow the *consequential* precedent of the form in v. 44a.

[46] Even, and yet, especially in the face of great trial. This brings greater resolution to the antithesis of their departure from (v. 53b) and his dependence upon God's תּוֹרָה (*tôrâ*), "Law" (v. 55b).

[47] Cf. Soll's review of and interaction with the major options ("Psalm 119," p. 183).

[48] Cf. ibid.; and Kidner, *Psalms 73–150*, p. 425.

[49] Cf. Anderson's emphasis (*Psalms*, 2:825).

[50] Cf. Delitzsch, *Psalms*, 3:251.

we shall observe more explicit recognitions (e.g. vv. 65ff.) of God's sovereign providence over all the circumstances of his life, both past and present. Therefore, armed with this conviction, the man of God could face the uncertainty of the future with a greater degree of confidence.

ח

HETH STANZA (vv. 57–64)

Translation and Notes

57 The LORD *is* my portion;[a]
I have promised to keep Your words.[b]

58 I entreat Your[a] favor wholeheartedly;[b]
be gracious to me according to Your promise.[c]

59 I thought[a] about my[b] ways,[c]
and turned[a] my feet toward Your testimonies.

60 I hurried and did not delay[a]
to keep Your commandments.

61 *The* cords[a] of wicked *men* have surrounded me;[b]
but, I have not forgotten Your law.

62 *At* midnight[a] I rise to praise You
because of Your righteous judgments.

63 I *am* a friend[a] of all who fear You
and keep Your precepts.

64 The earth is full of Your grace,[a] O LORD;
teach me Your statutes.[b]

57:a There are three basic translational options for v. 57 (cf. commentary below). The options construing יהוה (*YHWH*) as a vocative have likely been influenced by the LXX and Vulgate.

57:b The LXX reads τόν νόμον σου (*ton nomon sou*), "Your Law."

58:a Lit., "Your face" (פָּנֶיךָ [*pāneyk̲ā*]), another circumlocution for the LORD's person and/or presence (cf. BDB, pp. 815–16).

58:b בְּכָל־לֵב (b^ekol-lēḇ), lit. "with a whole heart."
58:c I.e. כְּאִמְרָתֶךָ (k^e'imrāṯeḵā), "according to Your Word."
59:a Construing both verbs according to the retrospective mood of the previous and subsequent stanzas.
59:b I.e. first person singular pronominal suffix, MT; cf. DSS (Q11), Targum, Vulgate, Syriac; contra LXX (i.e. τὰς ὁδούς σου [tas hodous sou], "Your ways").
59:c The Targum adds לְאוֹטָבָה (l^e'ôṭāḇâ), "to do good."
60:a V. 60a could be translated idiomatically; e.g., "Without any delay I hasten..." (Allen, *Psalms 101–150*, p. 129).
61:a The Targum has סִיעָא (sî^ca'), "company, troop, band, party" (Jastrow, *Dictionary*, 2:984).
61:b DSS (Q11) corroborates both the root and the pointing of the verb in the MT (i.e. עִוְּדֻנִי [^ciww^eḏunî]).
62:a Lit. the "middle of night."
63:a I.e. associate, close companion, comrade. The LXX has μέτοχος (metochos), "partner," etc.; cf. Paul's usage of συμμέτοχος (symmetochos; e.g. Eph 3:6).
64:a I.e. חֶסֶד (heseḏ).
64:b DSS (Q11) only has a singular herein (חוקכה [hwqkh], "Your statute").

Synopsis and Outline

This eighth strophe is basically continuative, and yet there are some subtle hints of transition imbedded within it. Concerning continuance, the thread of obedience with which the previous stanza concluded (v. 56) is immediately picked up in Ḥêṯ (i.e. v. 57b). Furthermore, "remembrances" continue to play a significant role in the development of the psalm even though the root זכר (zkr) is left behind. This is true not only for verses 57–64 but also, and especially, for verses 65–80.

However, those stanzas which follow Ḥêṯ demonstrate a growing emotive element as they draw closer to the impassioned laments of Kap̄ (i.e. vv. 81–88). This crescendo of emotion by no means negates the psalmist's theological discernment, but the tone of his meditations heightens as we follow his testimony from the *Ḥêṯ* stanza through the *Ṭêṯ* and *Yôḏ* stanzas on the way to *Kap̱*. Transitionally, verses 57–64 introduce certain moods which were spawned by his interactions with the circumstances into which he had been immersed. Although indications of these moods will resurface, his contemplations in the stanza before us seem to be more rational than reactionary. These moods also have relational roots in reference to his LORD, his enemies, and his "friends" (i.e. the fellowship of the faithful). In view of these features, three moods surface from the various contexts of the psalmist's promises and petitions in verses 57–64:

1A. (vv. 57–60) A mood of compensation surfaces out of a context of providence.
  1B. (v. 57a) His recognition of this compensation.
  2B. (v. 58) His reaction to this compensation.
  3B. (vv. 57b, 59–60) His responsibilities in view of this compensation:
    1C. (v. 57b) Commitment.
    2C. (v. 59a) Contemplation.
    3C. (vv. 59b–60) Commencement.
2A. (vv. 61–62) A mood of consternation surfaces out of a context of persecution.
  1B. (v. 61a) His recognition of this consternation.
  2B. (v. 61b) His reaction to this consternation.
  3B. (v. 62) His responsibility in spite of this consternation.
3A. (vv. 63–64) A mood of continuation surfaces out of a context of privilege.
  1B. (vv. 63–64a) His reasoning leading to the recognition of this continuation:[1]

---

1 This assumes, based upon larger contextual considerations, that he extrapolated from companionship to continuance. The fellowship of the faithful has historically provided a model for perseverance (note the implications of vv. 1–3, 74, 79, etc.; cf. more explicitly the argument which undergirds Heb 11:1–12:1).

1C. (v. 63) In its micro setting of true community.
2C. (v. 64a) In its macro setting of all creation.
2B. (v. 64b) His responsibility commensurate with this continuation.

Commentary

Three basic syntactical interpretations of verse 57[2] are represented respectively by the translations of the NIV, NAB, and NASB. The first view construes the Tetragrammaton as a vocative (cf. LXX) supplying, based upon an assumed omission, the independent pronoun אַתָּה (*'attâ*): "You are my portion, O LORD; I have promised to obey your words" (NIV). Acceptance of this interpretation is frequently bolstered by the argument that a radical shift from the third person (v. 57a) to the second (v. 57b) is conveniently avoided. The second view is similar in its construing of יהוה (*YHWH*) as a vocative; however, it conflates the bicolon into a single affirmation predicating that the *whole* verse stands in conceptual parallelism with verse 56:[3] "I have said, O LORD, that my part is to keep your words" (NAB). The third, and preferred, option is reflected in the following translation: "The LORD is my portion; I have promised to keep Thy words" (NASB). It has the advantage of taking the Hebrew text just as it stands. Furthermore, shifts from the third to the second person and vice versa are not at all uncommon especially in animated poetry.[4] In addition, the predication חֶלְקִי יהוה (*ḥelqî YHWH*) seems to have become a stereotyped formula (cf. Num 18:20; Pss 16:5; 73:26; 142:6 [v. 5, Eng]; Lam 3:24).[5]

---

[2] For discussions, see Moll, *Psalms*, p. 591; Anderson, *Psalms*, 2:825; and Soll, "Psalm 119," pp. 184–85.

[3] This conceptual parallelism has been acknowledged, but the association, based upon the normal parallelisms within this psalm's bicola, is better drawn between vv. 56 and 57*b*.

[4] Cf. GKC, § 144 p.

[5] Cf. Allen, *Psalms 101–150*, p. 136.

The significance of that "old levitical formula" apparently conveyed "dependence upon Yahweh for material support rather than upon tribal land."[6] Indeed, the term חֵלֶק (*ḥēleq*) "commonly . . . refers to a share in an inheritance. Early in the OT the word is used with a technical nuance of share of land given to all the tribes when they entered the land. In this use the term is parallel with 'inheritance' (*naḥălâ*)."[7] Consequently, this affirmation, "the LORD is my portion," becomes, in the context of *not* possessing a share in the land because of one's tribal status (i.e. the Levites) or because of exile, an astounding testimony to God's sufficiency.[8] Even an Israelite whose attention was glued to the land promises of the covenant could, at least in his present circumstances of alienation, rejoice in the Divine compensation of spiritual resources in lieu of spatial real estate.

Verse 57b then picks up the recurrent theme of obedience. The psalmist's employment of אָמַר (*'āmar*), "to say," in the sense of "to promise" is confirmed not only by the complementary infinitive which follows[9] but also by a forthcoming occurrence of the cognate noun אִמְרָה (*'imrâ*), "promise," in verse 58b. This man of God had unconditionally pledged fidelity to the "words" (i.e. דְּבָרֶיךָ [*dᵉḇāreyḵā*]), the particularized precepts, from His Master's Word.

Verse 58 commences with an idiomatic usage of the root חלה (*ḥlh*).[10] Of its sixteen usages in the Piel, all complemented by פָּנִים

---

6 Ibid. Note that this may be another evidence of the psalmist's condition of exile (see vv. 19 and 54); God Himself more than compensated for his deportation (cf. Daniel again).

7 *TWOT*, s.v. "חָלַק (*ḥālaq*) I," by D. Wiseman, 1:293. For etymological and cognate considerations, see *TDOT*, s.v. "חָלַק *chālaq* II," by M. Tsevat, 4:447–448, 450.

8 Cf. *TWOT*, 1:293.

9 Cf. BDB, p. 56.

10 Most frequently this root conveys, both in Hebrew and cognate languages, the concepts of sickness and weakness (cf. *TDOT*, s.v. "חָלָה *chālāh*," by K. Seybold, 4:400, 402). However, its Piel occurrences with פָּנִים (*panîm*) do not readily fit into this etymological setting (cf. ibid., pp. 402, 407–09; *TWOT*, s.v. "חָלָה [*ḥālâ*] II," by C. Weber, 1:287; etc.).

(*pānîm*), "thirteen . . . refer to . . . favor being sought of the Lord";[11] therefore, BDB suggest renderings of "mollify, appease," and especially, as here, to "entreat the favor of."[12] The complementary פָּנִים (*pānîm*) often stands for the Person and/or the presence of the LORD.[13] This combination "sets the stage for prayer to Yahweh, and lends to this prayer special weight."[14] It also appropriately conveys the disciple's vulnerability and his commensurate dependence upon a sovereign God.[15]

And to that sovereign God he immediately flees with one of his recurring petitions (cf. vv. 29 and 132):[16] חָנֵּנִי (*ḥonnēnî*), "Show favor to me" or "Be gracious to me!"[17] The recurrences of this prayer request, as rendered by the LXX, emphasize an urgent need for the LORD's *mercy*.[18] A sublime optimism accompanies this particular request for mercy as documented by an appearance of the precedent-bearing prepositional phrase כְּאִמְרָתֶךָ (*ke'imrāṯekā*), "according to Your promise" (cf. vv. 41, 76, 116, 170). This man of God had confidence in "Yahweh's faithful discharge

---

[11] *TWOT*, 1:287; Weber well adds that this usually "involves a prayer for mercy or help in the threat of danger" (ibid.).

[12] BDB, p. 318; cf., e.g., 2 Chr 33:12; Job 11:19; Ps 45:13 (v. 12, Eng).

[13] Some therefore take it as a circumlocution for the LORD Himself (cf. the translation in NAB). For the interesting idiom of God's intimate communication with Moses פָּנִים אֶל־פָּנִים (*pānîm 'el-pānîm*), "face to face," see Exod 33:11.

[14] *TDOT*, 4:409; Seybold, however, presses the cultic background a little too hard as he continues, "Even in Ps. 119:58, which clearly emphasizes the inward attitude ('with all my heart'), *ritual actions* are still involved . . . . The expression designates *a gesture* of respect, of worship, and of submission, *performed* with the purpose of seeking favor" [emphasis added] (ibid.).

[15] Such a mindset and mood is further enhanced by the quantitative and qualitative בְּכָל־לֵב (*bekol-lēḇ*), "with a whole heart."

[16] Contrast the attitude of Malachi's audience by comparing the context of corresponding appearances of the roots חלה (*ḥlh*) and חנן (*ḥnn*) in Mal 1:9a.

[17] Cf. BDB, p. 336; the Targum herein has חוּס (*ḥûs*) plus עַל (*ᶜal*): "to protect, spare, have consideration for" (Jastrow, *Dictionary*, 1:437).

[18] Cf. *again* vv. 29 and 132 in the LXX, and also, Matt 9:27; 15:22; 20:30; *et al.*, in the NT.

of his relational commitment"[19] even amidst circumstances which would normally lead other men to believe the contrary.

Verses 59–60 develop in accord with the biblical paradigm of human responsibility in sanctification: pondering followed by performance.[20] Indeed, there may be three stages in the process reflected herein: the rational, the volitional, and the behavioral. The seedbed of the psalmist's commitment, commencement, and continuance (i.e. vv. 59b–60) was his contemplation: חִשַּׁבְתִּי דְרָכָי (*hiššaḇtî dᵉrāḵay*),[21] "I have thought about, considered[22] my ways" (v. 59a). Although this is the only occurrence of the root חשׁב (*ḥšḇ*) in Psalm 119, it musters with a number of crucial noetic terms and truths.[23] "The piel of *ḥšḇ*," as here, "shifts the semantic emphasis to the result of the thought process. Attention is directed to planning that issues in action . . . ."[24] That is precisely the significance of the testimony which immediately follows: וָאָשִׁיבָה רַגְלַי אֶל־עֵדֹתֶיךָ (*wā'āšîḇâ raglay 'el ᶜēḏōṯeyḵā*), "then I turned my feet to Your testimonies" (v. 59b).

An over-arching understanding of the psalmist's affirmations in verse 59 should not be restricted to confession.[25] There is another dimension which is quite positive: "our Psalmist plans *his* life, but he maps out his path in constant reference to the law of God, or his testimonies."[26] Consequently, personal praxis should not become tardy, and in the case of this true disciple it certainly was not (v. 60). As a matter of fact, a confirmation of haste and a

---

[19] Allen, *Psalms 101–150*, p. 136; cf. Allen's translation of v. 58b: "treat me dutifully as your sayings promise" (ibid., p. 129).

[20] Another form of this paradigm will occur shortly in v. 63: attitude (i.e. "fear") followed by action (i.e. fidelity: "keep").

[21] Cf. the collocation of the roots חשׁב (*ḥšḇ*) and דרך (*drk*) in Prov 16:9.

[22] BDB, p. 363. Wood notes that "the basic idea of the word is the employment of the mind in thinking activity" (*TWOT*, s.v. "חָשַׁב (*hāshab*)," by L. Wood, 1:330).

[23] Cf. previous occurrences of בִּין (*bîn*) and לֵב (*lēḇ*); e.g., vv. 34, 36, etc.

[24] *TDOT*, s.v. "חָשַׁב *hāšaḇ*," by K. Seybold, 5:234.

[25] Although that emphasis is coming in the *Ṭeth* stanza, v. 59 seems to be more generic (cf. Anderson, *Psalms*, 2:825).

[26] Ibid.

denial of procrastination are juxtaposed (i.e. v. 60a) with great impact as he focuses upon the fruition of all his Word-guided ponderings and plannings, obedience (i.e. v. 60b).

With a change of context comes a change in mood (i.e. vv. 61–62). The realities of an experience of relentless persecution quite naturally kindled consternation in the disciple (v. 61a).[27] However, that consternation did not cancel his commitment (vv. 61b–62). One of several vivid metaphors is employed herein to depict the mean-spirited activity of his persecutors: חֶבְלֵי רְשָׁעִים עִוְּדֻנִי (*ḥeblê rešāʿîm ʿiwweḏunî*), "Cords of wicked men have surrounded me." Although חֶבְלֵי (*ḥeblê*) has been variously interpreted,[28] its meaning should be "determined according to ver. 110"[29] along with the explanatory parallelisms of passages such as Psalm 140:6 (v. 5, Eng). These "cords" were the "snares" which godless men had placed all around him. The psalmist's enemies were the crafty fowlers; he was the endangered prey.[30] Nevertheless, the man of God did not resort to retaliation but to revelation: "Yet (i.e. however, but, etc.) I have not forgotten Your law" (v. 61b).[31]

Furthermore, when the unrighteous deeds of unholy men (v. 61a) are contrasted with the righteous dealings[32] of the Holy One (v. 62b), a pattern of praise[33] should be evident: חֲצוֹת־לַיְלָה אָקוּם לְהוֹדוֹת לָךְ (*ḥăṣôṯ-layelâ 'āqûm lehôḏôṯ lāḵ*), "At midnight[34] I rise to praise You" (v.

[27] For a brief review of the negative circumstances of our psalmist's context of life, see Kidner, *Psalms 73–150*, pp. 422–23.

[28] Cf. usages in BDB, p. 286, and discussion in Moll, *Psalms*, p. 591.

[29] Delitzsch, *Psalms*, 3:251.

[30] Anderson well concludes that "these adversaries are portrayed as hunters setting their snares to entrap their victim" (*Psalms*, 2:826).

[31] Note yet another eye-catching instance of asyndetonic antithetical parallelism.

[32] For מִשְׁפְּטֵי צִדְקֶךָ (*mišpeṭê ṣiḏqeḵā*), lit. "the judgments of Your righteousness," i.e. "Your righteous judgments," "your just ordinances" (NAB), "the justice of your rulings" (Allen, *Psalms 101–150*, p. 129), etc.; cf. v. 7 (note a similar association with the psalmist's praise).

[33] The switch to an imperfect verb followed by the infinitive denoting intention stresses customary and characteristic activity.

[34] On the accusative of time, see Davidson, *Hebrew Syntax*, § 68. For a survey of the variety of its interpretations, see Anderson, *Psalms*, 2:826. Cf. the psalmist's more generalized reference in v. 55a.

62a).[35] Our model pilgrim understood that the weight of Divine rectitude far exceeded that of human recalcitrance; therefore, the only fitting response for him was a customary expression of genuine thanksgiving.

In verses 63–64 his contemplations regarding companionship and communion become an impetus for another mood, a mood of continuation (i.e. perseverance). Like the great cloud of witnesses in Hebrews 12:1, this fellowship of the faithful provided for him a measure of encouragement to keep on keeping on.

He chose the word חָבֵר (*ḥāḇēr*), an "associate" or "fellow,"[36] which "is used as an adjective and noun to refer to the very close bond that can exist between persons,"[37] as a descriptive term for spiritual fellowship. The particular semantical field of the verb from which this substantive is derived includes the ideas of "to be joined, coupled, league, . . . have fellowship with . . . ."[38] Some sort of common bond is always in view, and, in this case, that

---

[35] On יָדָה (*yādâ*), "to give thanks, laud, praise" (BDB, p. 392), within individual laments, see *TDOT*, s.v. "ידה *ydh*," by G. Mayer, 5:432. The grounds of thanksgiving are usually indicated by כִּי (*kî*) clauses (see ibid., pp. 433–34); cf. the use of עַל (*ʿal*) herein. Consequently, both the *when* (i.e. חֲצוֹת־לַיְלָה) and the *why* (i.e. עַל) provide more definition to this, his personal pattern of praise.

[36] BDB, p. 288. Incidentally, the LXX utilizes μέτοχος [*metochos*] which is the basal form of Paul's συμμέτοχος [*symmetochos*] in Eph 3:6.

[37] *TWOT*, s.v. "חָבַר (*ḥābar*)," by G. Van Groningen, 1:260. This terminological choice could also be another piece of evidence concerning the hand of Daniel: "In Aramaic the term indicates the close relationship between Daniel and his three friends because of their common faith and loyalty to God (Dan 2:13–18). The Psalmist expressly states that the fear of God is the common bond between 'companions' (Ps 119:63)" (ibid.).

[38] Ibid., p. 259. For a survey of the variety of this root's semantical fields within cognate languages, see *TDOT*, s.v. "חָבַר *chābhar*," by H. Cazelles, 4:193–94.

[39] There is apparently no interpretive difference between the relative clause with the *perfect tense* of יָרֵא (*yārēʾ*) and the substantive *participle* of שָׁמַר (*šāmar*); both respectively convey the characteristic mindset and manner of these people (cf. the participles of יָרֵא [*yārēʾ*] in vv. 74, 79; and note the participial renderings of both roots in v. 63 in the LXX and Targum). Kraus well notes that "those who fear Yahweh live in obedience to God's will, in permanent attentiveness and submission" (*Theology of the Psalms*, p. 157).

common bond is his spiritual affinity to all men who are responsive to the Person of God and the precepts of God. Consequently, when this man of God says that he is a companion with, a friend of "all who fear You and keep Your precepts" (לְכָל־אֲשֶׁר יְרֵאוּךָ וּלְשֹׁמְרֵי פִּקּוּדֶיךָ [*l^e^kol-'^ă^šer y^e^rē'ûkā ûl^e^šōm^e^rê piqqûdeykā*]),[39] he is affirming that the criteria of his horizontal communion are determined by common vertical orientations, "fear"[40] and fidelity.[41]

Lifting up his eyes to an even wider horizon of motivation, the psalmist moves from his consideration of communal grace (v. 63) to common grace (v. 64a). חֶסֶד (*ḥesed*), God's "lovingkindness" (i.e. grace), "is here widened, as in [Psalms 33:5;] 136:1–9; 145:8–9; Jonah 4:11, to Yahweh's care for all his creatures."[42] As Anderson notes, "It embraces the whole 'universe,' although not in the same manner as it surrounds Israel. In its universal application the relationship is not based upon a Covenant, but upon creation."[43] With this meditation on God's awesome mercy the psalmist makes a transition to another request for Divine instruction (v. 64b). Fittingly, the Creator and Benefactor of the whole earth is the only Resource of the practical pedagogy needed for facing the thoroughly challenging vicissitudes of real life.

---

40 Cf. v. 120 and the discussion on the noun form in v. 38.

41 As always, attitude (herein "fear") precedes action (herein obedience), and yet, action is often looked upon as a factor in evaluating the genuineness of attitude.

42 Allen, *Psalms 101–150*, p. 137.

43 Anderson, *Psalms*, 2:826; cf. Kidner, *Psalms 73–150*, p. 426.

ט

TETH STANZA
(vv. 65–72)

Translation and Notes

65 You have dealt well[a] with Your servant,
O LORD, according to Your word.

66 Teach me good[a] judgment and knowledge,
for I believe in Your commandments.

67 Before I was afflicted,[a] I was straying,
but now I keep Your word.

68 You *are* good[a] and do good;
teach me Your statutes.

69 Insolent *men* have plastered falsehood over me;[a]
nevertheless,[b] I shall wholeheartedly[c] keep Your precepts.

70 Their heart[a] is gross like fat;
however,[b] I take delight in Your law.

71 It was good for me that I was afflicted,[a]
in order that[b] I might learn Your statutes.

72 The law of Your mouth is better to me
than thousands *of pieces of*[a] gold and silver.[b]

65:a Lit. "You have done good" (cf. NAB), i.e. "You have treated your servant well" (Allen, *Psalms 101–150*, p. 129).

66:a Dahood (*Psalms*, 3:181) has argued that this occurrence of טוֹב(*tûḇ*) not be taken as the initial word of v. 66 (i.e. "*good* judgment") but as the final word of v. 65 (i.e. "Your *good* word"), thereby forming an inclusio for v. 65 and also balancing the meter of vv. 65, 66. Some look upon his rearrangement with favor (e.g. Allen, *Psalms 101–150*, p. 137; Soll, "Psalm 119," p. 186) while others look upon the טוֹב at the outset of v. 66 as a dittograph and suggest its deletion (e.g. Anderson, *Psalms*, 2:827); however, there is no compelling reason to reject the MT just as it reads herein. Although the LXX does not construe טוּב as an adjective in v. 66, it does render it as *one* of the three things sought by the psalmist ("*goodness* and instruction and knowledge"). Furthermore, the Targum uses a synonym of טוּב (i.e. שַׁפִּיר [*šappîr*]) at the outset of v. 66 indicating its rendering of a text in the masoretic tradition. Also, the lines and words of DSS (Q11) support the MT beat for beat.

67:a The pointing of the MT (i.e. אֲעַנֶּה [*'eᶜĕneh*]) obviously needs to be changed to that of the Niphal imperfect (i.e. אֵעָנֶה [*'ēᶜāneh*]) as confirmed by the LXX (cf. πρὸ τοῦ με ταπεινωθῆναι [*pro tou me tapeinōthēnai*]), other ancient versions, and nearly all modern versions and translations. For some commentary, see Soll, "Psalm 119," p. 186.

68:a Interestingly, the DSS (Q11) adds not יהוה (*YHWH*) but the vocative אדוני (*'d̲wny*); also note the κύριε (*kyrie*) of the LXX (however, the rest of v. 68a [obviously to be taken as v. 68b in LXX] deviates with a subordinate prepositional phrase which is related to δίδαξον [*didaxon*] adverbially). The evidence is mixed and not substantial enough to suggest the addition of a vocative occurrence of יהוה (*YHWH*) to the MT.

69:a Cf. BDB, p. 381, for this quite literal rendering. Acceptable renderings of this vivid imagery are: "the arrogant have forged a lie against me" (NASB), or they "have smeared me with lies" (NIV), etc.

69:b Once again the strong contrast in behavior is conveyed through asyndetonic antithetical parallelism. In the present case the emphatic אֲנִי (*'ănî*) adds even more weight (cf. Soll's "as for me" addition both here and in v. 70 ["Psalm 119," p. 185]). In this verse and the next (i.e. v. 70) the LXX appropriately translates this phenomenon with adversative δέ (*de*).

69:c Lit. "with a whole heart."

70:a The Targum adds יִצְרָא (*yiṣrā'*), i.e. "the inclination of their heart . . ."; for a biblical emphasis (without Rabbinic accretions) upon man's noetic culpability see יֵצֶר (*yēṣer*) plus לֵב (*lēḇ*) in Gen 6:5.

70:b The second occurrence of asyndetonic antithetical parallelism in as many verses. Note that the orientation of these contrasts deepens, proceeding from contrasting actions (v. 69) to contrasting attitudes(v. 70).

71:a The LXX and DSS (Q11) render the verb עָנָה (*ʿānâ*) actively with God as the subject and the psalmist as the object. However, these renderings were likely influenced by the psalmist's forthcoming active phraseology in v. 75 (cf. Allen, *Psalms 101–150*, p. 137) and by, in the case of the DSS (Q11), a consuming interest in *direct* Divine involvement (cf. the comments in Part I: "Textual Assessment" on DSS). Conceptually, the NT textual variations at Rom 8:28 provide an illustrative parallel; the passive renderings in both instances (i.e. Ps 119:71 and Rom 8:28) are not watered-down theological statements but rather strong affirmations, on the part of their respective authors, of God's sovereign providence.

71:b The fully telic force of לְמַעַן (*lemaʿan*) is secondarily confirmed by the Targum's rendering (i.e. מִן [*min*] + בִּגְלַל [*biglal*] + the particle דְּ [*de*] + the verb; very lit., "because on account of that . . .").

72:a "M.T. omits the monetary unit after the numeral *thousands* and probably we should assume the word 'shekels,' or simply 'pieces,' since the expression was intended to suggest a very large but indefinite amount; cf. NEB: 'a fortune in gold and silver'" (Anderson, *Psalms*, 2:828). The Targum, from its orientation, adds כַּכְּרִין (*kikkerîn*), "talents."

72:b Instead of כֶּסֶף (*kesep*), the Targum interestingly reads סִימָא (*sîmāʾ*), a general word for "treasure." Cf. Jesus' emphasis upon one's personal θησαυρός (*thēsauros*), "treasure," in the Gospels.

Synopsis and Outline

Seemingly paradoxical concepts interface in the *Ṭêṯ* stanza. Affliction[1] is referred to directly in verses 67 and 71 and indirectly in verses 69 and 70. On the other hand, some facet of God's goodness (i.e. the root טוב [*ṭwḇ*]) occurs at the outset of verses 65, 66, 68, 71 and 72. Both statistically and practically in these verses the psalmist's acute affliction is definitely over-powered by his LORD's goodness.[2] Furthermore, the divinely mediated and spiritually illuminated perception of our man of God allows him to see his persecution as definitely providential and therefore part and parcel of his God's beneficent dealings with him; consequently, "God's goodness, manifested also in the affliction which He permits His servant to suffer, drives him closer to the Word."[3] Delitzsch synthesizes the impact of the stanza as follows:

> The good word of the gracious God is the fountain of all good; and it is learned in the way of lowliness. He reviews his life, and sees in everything that has befallen him the good and well-meaning appointment of the God of salvation in accordance with the plan and order of salvation of His word.[4]

Our disciple is assuredly singing another chorus of the ever-expanding song of Joseph (retrospectively, cf. Gen 45:1–8; 50:19–21, and prospectively, cf. Rom 8:28; *et al.*).

By combining the semantic, stylistic and systematic characteristics of verses 65–72, we find the child of God painting three pictures of Divine goodness on a dark canvas of human distress:

1A. (vv. 65–67) The first picture is one of a past restoration to fellowship by means of distress.

---

1 This theme will maturate in the next stanza (i.e. vv. 73–80).

2 Cf. Spurgeon, *Treasury of David*, 6:162, 166.

3 Leupold, *Psalms*, p. 837.

4 Delitzsch, *Psalms*, 3:251–52.

- 1B. (v. 65) The man of God's appraisal of his restoration to fellowship.
- 2B. (v. 66) The man of God's prayer since his restoration to fellowship.
- 3B. (v. 67) The man of God's confession about his restoration to fellowship.[5]
  - 1C. (v. 67a) His confession about the past.
  - 2C. (v. 67b) His confession about the present.

2A. (vv. 68–70) The second picture is one of a present preservation in the midst of distress.

- 1B. (v. 68) The man of God's preservation depends upon God's Person and provision.
- 2B. (vv. 69–70) The man of God's preservation depends upon his reliance upon God's Word.
  - 1C. (v. 69) He must rely on the Word because of the action of wicked men.
  - 2C. (v. 70) He must rely on the Word because of the nature of wicked men.[6]

3A. (vv. 71–72) The third picture is one of continued edification as the product of distress.

- 1B. (v. 71) God uses the man of God's distress to catalyze spiritual progress.
- 2B. (v. 72) God uses the man of God's distress to cultivate spiritual priorities.

---

[5] It is the time antithesis of this verse which establishes the *general* occasion of vv. 65–67. It should be noted, however, that there are no further data which might provide more detail to this vague historical sketch.

[6] There is probably an implicit double comparison being drawn between his great God (i.e. v. 68a: God's attribute of goodness; God's activity of goodness) and his enemies (i.e. v. 69a: their activity of wickedness; v. 70a: their attribute of wickedness). Also note that this comparison is unveiled chiastically adding to its impact.

Commentary

Our psalmist's testimony in this particular stanza qualifies as a proleptic illustration of the seemingly paradoxical truths conveyed so starkly through Paul and James in Romans 5:3–5 and James 1:2–4 respectively. Our good and gracious God skillfully but lovingly (cf. Heb 12:3–13) employs affliction and adversity, pressure and pain, trials and tribulations, as crucial instruments in His process of maturing those who belong to Him. Such contexts of life are crucibles for discipleship (note the three occurrences of the root למד [*lmd̲*], i.e. vv. 66, 68, 71, in this stanza); discipleship and discipline frequently join hand-in-hand in the outworking of His good providence. This theological reality served as the hub of the man of God's reflections in these verses.[7]

As he reminisces about a past restoration to fellowship by means of distress, he prefaces his direct reference to it (i.e. v. 67) with praise (i.e. v. 65) and a prayer (i.e. v. 66). Significantly, his preface of praise brims with allusions to his LORD's covenantal fidelity.[8] He immediately labels that Divine loyalty as טוֹב (*ṭôb*), "good."[9] Herein it seems best to render this word adverbially in conjunction with the verb עָשָׂה (*ʿāśâ*), i.e. "You have dealt *well* . . . ." The combination of the verb עָשָׂה (*ʿāśâ*) and the noun טוֹב (*ṭôb̲*) serves as a conceptual double for the verb יָטַב (*yāṭab̲*)[10] which is a close semantical relative of טוב (*twb*).[11] The precedent of God's well-doing *is* extremely well-founded as indicated by the prepositional phrase כִּדְבָרֶךָ (*kid̲b̲āreḵā*), "according to Your Word."[12] Our

---

[7] As Soll appropriately points out, "the retrospective mood is continued in this strophe (see esp. vv. 65, 67 and 71)" ("Psalm 119," p. 186).

[8] Cf. Anderson's brief synopsis (*Psalms*, 2:826–27). For several semantical illustrations of the vocabulary of v. 65 couched in a secular covenantal context, cf. Gen 26:28–29.

[9] For a general survey of the verb, noun, and adjective built upon the root טוב (*ṭwb̲*), scan *TWOT*, s.v. "טוֹב (*ṭôb*)," by A. Bowling, 1:345–46.

[10] Cf. *TWOT*, s.v. "יָטַב (*yāṭab*)," by P. Gilchrist, 1:375.

[11] Cf. BDB, pp. 373–75 with 405–06.

[12] Leupold rightly contends that "the point . . . is that, when the Lord deals thus with His servants, that is in conformity with what His Word or promises toward them had led them to anticipate" (*Psalms*, p. 837).

psalmist obviously had a river of affirmations flowing through his mind. For example, "God's 'doing good' to his people pervades the book of Deut in the frequently repeated formula 'that it may go well with you' (4:40; 5:16, 29 [H 26]; 6:3, 18; 12:25, 28; 22:7) and often in Jer (7:23; 38:20; 40:9; 42:6)."[13] That he was quick to personalize these promises is indicated not only by his employment of the preposition עִם (*ᶜim*), "with," which is used to convey an intimate association (cf. the μετά [*meta*] of the LXX)[14] but also by the striking juxtaposition of עַבְדְּךָ (*ᶜab̲dᵉk̲ā*), "Your servant" (i.e. the psalmist), with the vocative יהוה (*YHWH*), "O LORD."[15]

A prayer for the impartation of spiritual discernment immediately follows (i.e. v. 66a) the psalmist's appraisal of his LORD's past goodness to him (i.e. v. 65). The Piel imperative with the pronominal suffix of the first person, לַמְּדֵנִי (*lammᵉd̲ēnî*), "teach me," is not a new petition (cf. vv. 12, 26, 64);[16] however, the content of his desired instruction is herein defined more applicationally. Rather than saying, "teach me Your statutes," etc., he prays that the LORD impart to him טוּב טַעַם וָדַעַת (*ṭûb̲ ṭaᶜam wād̲aᶜat̲*), lit. "good taste and knowledge." Concerning טַעַם (*ṭaᶜam*), it "can mean 'taste' (Exod. 16:31; Jer. 48:11), or it can be used figuratively of 'judgment, discernment' (34:1 (M.T. 2); Prov. 11:22). . . ."[17] Contextually, its figurative dimension, good "discernment" or "judgment," is obviously in view; he desires from his LORD "spiritual

---

[13] *TWOT*, 1:375. Gilchrist appropriately continues, "Conversely, the covenanted servant's response is ever to be well pleasing to his Lord" (ibid.). It is quite likely that the recognition of an appropriate reciprocation prompted the disciple's affirmations of dependence and obedience in this particular context.

[14] Cf. *TWOT*, s.v. "עִם (*ᶜim*)," by G. Van Groningen, 2:676–77. Illustratively, this preposition is the leading member of the compound "*Immanuel*," "God *with* us." Furthermore, עִם (*ᶜim*) combines adverbially with the verb עָשָׂה (*ᶜāśâ*) to indicate *advantage* (cf. Williams, *Hebrew Syntax*, ¶ 331).

[15] It should be remembered that the 24 occurrences of the Tetragrammaton in Ps 119 are placed strategically and exhibit various degrees of emphasis upon God's fidelity, especially to covenant.

[16] Note its forthcoming occurrences in vv. 108, 124, and 135.

[17] Anderson, *Psalms*, 2:827; the figurative connotation of the cognate word in the Targum signifies among other things "sense" (Jastrow, *Dictionary*, 2:543).

discrimination."[18] Coupled with this ethical discernment is דַּעַת (*da*ᶜ*at*), "knowledge" or "perception";[19] therefore, "here it [i.e. דַּעַת] is not merely information, but also, if not more so, responsibility and it carries a religious overtone (cf. Hos. 4:1, 6, 6:6)."[20]

Just as the Divine fidelity (i.e. v. 65) implicationally provides the primary precedent for the psalmist's voicing of the request of verse 66a, so the evidence of human responsibility (i.e. v. 66b) optimistically anticipates a gracious response to his request. This כִּי (*kî*) clause[21] is designed to draw the LORD's attention to His disciple's unwavering confidence in the Word of God. In so doing, he uses the Hiphil of אָמַן (*'āman*) complemented by the preposition בְּ (*b*ᵉ), a combination which normally conveys one's personal *trust* (i.e. faith) *in* the God of the Word (cf., e.g. Gen 15:6).[22] The phraseology is both striking and pregnant. It also implies that the LORD's answer to our psalmist's prayer request for practical moral discernment would very likely be mediated through a deeper understanding of His "commandments" (i.e. מִצְוֹתֶיךָ [*miṣwōṯeykā*]). Cook's paraphrase is a fitting rehearsal of the thrust of verse 66: "'Instruct me in true knowledge to discern the right and the wrong: for I have believed in Thy commandments, the only sources of wisdom and of divine instruction.'"[23]

---

18 Kidner, *Psalms 73–150*, p. 426; Kidner also appropriately cites Job 34:3 as an illustration and compares the psalmist's request with the ultimate goal of Heb 5:14. In corroboration, Delitzsch says of טַעַם (*ṭa*ᶜ*am*) that it "is ethically the capacity of distinguishing between good and evil" (*Psalms*, 3:252). Rotherham labels it a "quick moral perception" (*Psalms*, p. 506), and Girdlestone characterizes it as "a keen moral and spiritual perception" (*Synonyms*, p. 251). The παδείαν (*padeian*) of the LXX also helps to focus attention on the desire of the man of God in v. 66a.

19 BDB, p. 395.

20 Anderson, *Psalms*, 2:827; cf. Anderson's subsequent remarks and references (ibid.).

21 I.e. "for, since, because," etc.; כִּי (*kî*) would generally supply a motive for any previous imperative.

22 For a brief synopsis, see the "Summary" on הֶאֱמִין (*he'*ᵉ*mîn*) in *TDOT*, s.v. "אָמַן *'āman*," by A. Jepsen, 1:307–08.

23 F. C. Cook, *Psalms*, p. 447.

At the head of each member of the bicolon of verse 67 stands a term for time orientation: "*before*" (i.e. then, v. 67a) . . . "but[24] *now*" (v. 67b) . . . , dividing our pilgrim's confession into two eras, the past and the present. His confession about the past is succinct and somewhat surprising in light of the biographical data noted thus far. Prior to his having been afflicted by God[25] he describes himself[26] as שֹׁגֵג (*šōggēg*), "erring, straying, wandering," etc.[27] The participial form would suggest that he viewed his prior experience of wandering as quite characteristic,[28] but more importantly this evaluative reminiscence indicated the arrival of a major monument of maturity, an acute sensitivity to sin.[29] The nuance of sin viewed as שָׁגַג (*šāgag*) is normally looked upon as inadvertence or ignorance (cf. Lev 5:18; Num 15:28).[30] Excluding all "high-handed," premeditated sins, it encompasses "all sins done not in a spirit of rebellion against the law or ordinance of Jehovah—sins committed through human imperfection, or human ignorance, or human passion; sins done when the mind was directed to some end connected with human weakness or selfishness, but not formally opposed to the authority of the Lawgiver."[31] Notwithstand-

24 The antithetical parallelism calls for a contrastive rendering of the *waw* conjunction (cf. Alexander, *Psalms*, 3:170). It should also be remembered that the imperfect tense following the particle טֶרֶם (*ṭerem*) regularly signifies past time, i.e. "*before* I *was* afflicted . . ." (cf. GKC, ¶ 107 c).

25 Cf. the translation note on v. 67 (above) indicating the need for a Niphal pointing of אענה (*ʾᶜnh*).

26 Note the independent pronoun אֲנִי (*ʾănî*), "I," as the subject of the participle.

27 Cf. BDB, p. 992, and *TWOT*, s.v. "שָׁגַג (*shāgag*)," by V. Hamilton, 2:903–04. Non-hamartiological occurrences of this root describe the wandering of sheep and the staggering of drunken men.

28 Cf. Alexander, *Psalms*, 3:170.

29 That he would evaluate his *current* walk from the vantage point of the same hamartiological monument is documented by several forthcoming allusions among which his testimony in v. 176a will stand as a fitting climax (the תָּעָה [*taᶜâ*] of v. 176a is a near synonym of שָׁגַג [*šāgag*] in v. 67a).

30 Cf. the Targum's employment of שְׁלָה (*šᵉlâ*), "to be unaware, err, make a mistake" (Jastrow, *Dictionary*, 2:1582), at Ps 119:67.

31 A. B. Davidson, *The Theology of the Old Testament*, ed. by S. D. F. Salmond (NY: Charles Scribner's Sons, 1907), p. 315.

ing, all sin is serious as documented generally by the sacrificial provisions for sins of inadvertence and specifically by God's heavy hand of chastisement upon the psalmist.

What the LORD used to break the pattern of his wandering was affliction (cf. also vv. 71, 75, 107). Most Semitic cognates of עָנָה (*ᶜānâ*) III, "to afflict, oppress, humble,"[32] place a strong emphasis upon humiliation,[33] and persistent occurrences of the ταπεινός (*tapeinos*) word group for עָנָה (*ᶜānâ*) in the LXX corroborate this phenomenon.[34] God has always been in the business of humbling men in order to drive them to repentance and dependence.[35] In the case at hand the confirmation of God's time-tested method comes through the child of God's subsequent attestation of personal obedience (i.e. v. 67b).

In verses 68–70 the psalmist's meditations on past providence are replaced by his scrutiny of present providence. Although being avalanched by persecution he realizes in these verses that the God who is and does good would preserve him. In order to gain such an accurate perspective on one's personal circumstances it is imperative to begin with God (cf. the second person personal pronoun as subject in v. 68a, i.e. אַתָּה [*'attâ*]) prior to becoming preoccupied with the secondary actors of oneself (cf. the first person pronominal suffixes and pronouns, esp. אֲנִי [*'ănî*], in vv. 68b, 69b, 70b) and others, especially when they are personal enemies (cf.

[32] *TWOT*, s.v. "עָנָה (*ᶜānâ*) III," by L. Coppes, 2:682.

[33] For example, "Ugaritic attests this root with the meaning 'cowed, humbled' (active) and 'was humbled, punished' (passive)" (ibid.); for a survey of other Semitic cognates with a similar emphasis, see BDB, p. 776.

[34] Cf. *TDNT*, s.v. "ταπεινός ," by W. Grundmann, 8:6–12.

[35] Coppes appropriately places the experience of the psalmist into its larger theological context when he writes, "God uses affliction to prompt repentance; for example, the purpose of the wilderness wanderings was to humble Israel (Deut 8:23). This is a recurrent theme in Scripture. The Exile is similarly viewed as to nature and end (Ps 102:23 [H 24]; Isa 64:12 [H 11]; Zech 10:2). God is therefore thanked for affliction (Ps 88:7 [H 8]; 90:15; 119:75; Lam 3:33)" (*TWOT*, 2:682). It may be well to point out that the service of suffering exhibits various facets; it is not only corrective but also spiritually formulative (cf. v. 71; Rom 5:3–5; Jas 1:2–4; etc.), preventative (e.g. 2 Cor 12:7–10), and even doxological (e.g. John 9:1–3).

the third person references in vv. 69a, 70a). Therefore, the man of God commences his analysis of adversity with "You are good[36] and are doing good"[37] (v. 68a). Once again, a biblical construct surfaces: the actions of God flow from the attributes of God.[38] In this context, "God is called טוֹב [*ṭôḇ*, i.e. "good"] as He who is graciously disposed towards man, and מֵטִיב [*mēṭîḇ*, i.e. "doing good"] as He who acts out of this disposition."[39] God's documented character and active concern (v. 68a) consequently serve as a logical grounds herein for the disciple's acute request for Divine instruction (i.e. v. 68b),[40] just as his LORD's care (v. 65) had served previously as the foundation of a similar request in verse 66a.

Now if God's nature and nurture supply the logically positive precedent for Divine assistance, his enemies' invectives (i.e. v. 69a) and insensitivity (i.e. v. 70a)[41] add the logically negative precedent for such assistance. Therefore, of these insolent men[42] he cries out that they "have plastered falsehood over me."[43] The verb טָפַל (*ṭāpal*)

---

[36] Cf. Pss 25:8; 100:5; etc.; for God's Word sharing this quality, cf. Ps 119:39.

[37] I.e. the "dynamic quality" (Anderson, *Psalms*, 2:827).

[38] At this juncture, Scroggie aptly generalizes: "What God does is determined by what He is" (*Psalms*, p. 182).

[39] Delitzsch, *Psalms*, 3:252; cf. Alexander: "Good, both essentially and actively or practically; good in thyself and good to others. The participle, as in v. 67, denotes habitual constant action, (ever) doing good" (*Psalms*, 3:171).

[40] For commentary on v. 68a being the logical grounds for v. 68b, note Alexander, *Psalms*, 3:171, and Cohen, *Psalms*, p. 403. The logical development of Ps 86:10–11a should also be noted. It is interesting that the interpretive wording and syntax of the LXX makes this association direct rather than merely logical.

[41] Note the parallelisms between the goodness of God's attributes and actions and the wickedness of the actions and attributes of the psalmist's enemies. These comparisons and contrasts even unfold chiastically: his God's good character and good conduct, v. 68a; his enemies' wicked conduct (v. 69a) and wicked character (v. 70a).

[42] Again the זֵדִים (*zēḏîm*) are encountered: "*The Proud*. The same overbearing, tyrannical oppression already mentioned" (Perowne, *Psalms*, p. 357).

[43] BDB's literal rendering of טָפַל (*ṭāpal*) plus שֶׁקֶר (*šeqer*) and the preposition עַל (*ʿal*) with 1 c s pronominal suffix (BDB, p. 381).

which substantially contributes to this striking word-picture means to smear, stick, glue, plaster, etc.,[44] and with שֶׁקֶר (*šeqer*), a "lie" (cf. Job 13:4), the combination idiomatically signifies that "by their slanderous allegations" (cf. vv. 78, 86) his enemies had given "him a character utterly different from what was his."[45] They had fabricated an ugly façade over an essentially blameless framework. Interestingly, in an attitude which would characterize NT ethics (cf., e.g., Matt 5:11; 1 Pet 2:20; 4:14–16; etc.), the man of God did not sue for defamation of character but rather sanctified himself unreservedly for obedience to God's Word and will (i.e. v. 69b).[46]

The dramatic imagery of verse 70a exposes the sub-surface attitude of his enemies' actions: "Their heart is gross like fat."[47] The leading verb טָפַשׁ (*ṭāp̱aš*) occurs only here in the OT; however, its Aramaic cognate, occurring in various contexts such as the Targum of Isaiah 6:10, means to be fat. Consequently, when this verb is complemented, as here, by חֵלֶב (*ḥēleḇ*), "fat," the two conceptual cognates reinforce each other. Their heart being literally "fat like fat" or "fat with fat"[48] is viewed as *exceedingly* fat, i.e. "a figure of insensibility and obduracy."[49] The psalmist's enemies were absolutely impervious to God's Word and ways. However, in his case,[50] the law of his LORD provided for him the utmost satisfaction (i.e. v. 70b).

---

44 Ibid. The Targum employs a similar word meaning to fasten, join; cf. חַבַּרוּ(*ḥabbarû*) in Jastrow, *Dictionary*, 2:421.

45 Cohen, *Psalms*, p. 403. As Delitzsch argues, these men made his "true nature unrecognisable as it were by means of false plaster or whitewash," "by slander" they made "him into a caricature of himself" (*Psalms*, 3:252). Cf. the experience of Daniel.

46 Notice how starkly the asyndetonic antithetical parallelism of v. 69 contrasts the psalmist's activity with that of his enemies (cf. v. 70).

47 BDB's quite literal rendering (p. 382); of the complementary כַּחֵלֶב (*kaḥēleḇ*) they suggest that "their heart is as unresponsive as the midriff-fat near it" (ibid., p. 316).

48 Anderson, *Psalms*, 2:828 (cf. his whole development on pp. 827–28).

49 Delitzsch, *Psalms*, 3:252; cf. Moll, *Psalms*, p. 591. The note in NAB reads: "Their heart has become gross and fat: a Hebrew idiom for, 'Their mind has become dull and insensitive.' But it may also be understood to signify a 'cruel heart.' Cf. Ps 17, 10."

Having pondered the providential product of his past affliction (vv. 65–67) and God's current preservation of him in the midst of continuing distress (vv. 68–70), the man of God now bears personal witness to the truth that the sovereign LORD initiates adversity for spiritual advancement (vv. 71–72). Since he knows that God is in the business of using personal affliction as a catalyst for spiritual growth (cf. v. 71) and also as a cultivator of right attitudes and proper priorities (cf. v. 72), he could face the uncertain circumstances of both today and tomorrow from a proper vantage point. However, his testimonies in these verses are deeper and richer than merely some sort of theological acquiescence. The atmosphere of these affirmations is one of transcendent joy;[51] in his case, he experienced a heavenly relaxation amidst that human rage which was directed at him by his enemies.

In view of this, his first words are both concise and captivating: טוֹב־לִי (*tôḇ lî*), lit. "good for me"! The combination may be rendered, "It *is* good for me" or "It *was* good for me." What was good for him is clearly indicated by the nominalizing clause כִּי עֻנֵּיתִי (*kî ᶜunnêṯî*):[52] "that I have been afflicted." Obviously, "this is a striking affirmation of faith in the providence of God, in which even affliction is seen as a mark of divine favour, and as a fatherly correction."[53]

One more powerful link remains in the syntactical-theological chain of verse 71, the purpose clause which targets God's good

---

[50] Allen appropriately renders the pronoun אֲנִי (*'ănî*) in this context as "in my case" (*Psalms 101–150*, p. 129). Not only did his action differ from that of his enemies (cf. v. 69 above), but even more significantly, the asyndetonic antithetical parallelism of v. 70 reveals that his attitude was radically different from theirs.

[51] Again, this disciple exemplifies the truth delineated in Job 5:17; Ps 94:12; Prov 3:11–12; Rom 5:3–5; Heb 12:5–11; Jas 1:2–4; etc.

[52] Cf. the syntactical remarks of BDB on pp. 374, 471.

[53] Anderson, *Psalms*, 2:828. Kidner well speaks of "the psalmist's gratitude for bitter medicine" (*Psalms 73–150*, p. 426). On the Pual verb (i.e. a Divine passive in this context) Alexander argues, "The idea of compulsory subjection to this salutary process is suggested by the passive causative form of the verb used in v. 67" (*Psalms*, 3:172); cf. v. 75 for the active verb with God as the subject.

goal. Therefore, when the disciple says לְמַעַן אֶלְמַד חֻקֶּיךָ (*l^e^ma^c^an 'elmad ḥuqqeykā*), "in order that I should learn Your statutes,"[54] he personally embraces the Divine intention of his LORD's mysterious workings. Consequently, he "accepts his suffering as a divine education which spurs him on to learn more of God's statutes (see verse 5)."[55] "How beneficial has the school of affliction through which he has attained to this, been to him!"[56]

The balance of priorities exhibited in verse 72 is not new.[57] The psalmist wanted his treasury filled with the right kind of stuff (cf. v. 11). He affirms this in an eye-catching manner, i.e. through another occurrence of טוֹב לִי (*tôb lî*; lit. "good to/for me") with תּוֹרַת־פִּיךָ (*tôrat-pîkā*; "the law of/from Your mouth") as the focal point of his attention in a stark comparison[58] with "thousands of *pieces* of gold and silver."[59] In the realms of "riches transient and eternal,"[60] like this child of God, every disciple needs to be thoroughly convinced of the fact that the practical instruction for life which emanates from God Himself through His word[61] is inestimably precious both in this life and that to come.

---

[54] This is the third occurrence of the root למד (*lmd*) in this strophe; however, herein it is not in the familiar Piel imperative (i.e. a request to be taught; cf. vv. 12, 26, 64, 66, 68, 108, 124, 135) but in the Qal (cf. vv. 7, 73) *imperfect* which stresses the *life-long preoccupation* of a disciple (cf. a תַּלְמִיד [*talmîd*] and esp. the NT μαθητής [*mathētēs*]). For brief synopses of this word's strategic significance in reference to the essence of discipleship, see: Girdlestone, *Synonyms*, p. 225; and *TWOT*, s.v. "לָמַד (*lāmad*)," by W. Kaiser, 1:480.

[55] Anderson, *Psalms*, 2:828. Leupold recognizes how the psalmist ties his recent contemplations together in v. 71: "Even as in v. 67 the writer pointed out how affliction had been beneficial, he feels impelled again to stress this thought, for this experience rightly met, gives a man deeper insight into God's statutes" (*Psalms*, p. 838).

[56] Delitzsch, *Psalms*, 3:252.

[57] Cf. v. 14 and look ahead to vv. 103, 127; outside this psalm, see Ps 19:10; Prov 3:13ff.; 8:10ff.; Matt 6:19ff.; etc.

[58] Obviously, the preposition מִן (*min*) is employed for comparison here.

[59] See the "Translation and Notes" above.

[60] Scroggie's synopsis of v. 72 (*Psalms*, p. 182).

[61] Allen appropriately comments as follows on the significance of תּוֹרַת־פִּיךָ (*tôrat-pîkā*) in this context: "The dynamic quality of the Torah is graphically expressed in v 72a: it enables the psalmist to hear the very voice of the living God speaking directly to him" (*Psalms 101–150*, p. 143).

י

YODH STANZA (vv. 73–80)

Translation and Notes

73 Your hands have made me and constituted[a] me;
give me understanding that[b] I may learn Your commandments.

74 Let those who fear You see me and rejoice,[a]
because I wait for[b] Your word.

75 I know, O LORD, that Your judgments are right[a]
and *that in* faithfulness[b] You have afflicted me.

76 Please let Your grace[a] become my comfort[b]
according to Your promise[c] to Your servant.

77 Let Your compassion[a] come to me that[b] I may live,
for Your law is my delight.

78 Let *the* insolent[a] be ashamed because they have wrongfully subverted me;[b]
however,[c] I meditate[d] upon Your precepts.

79 Let those who fear You turn[a] to me,[b]
that they may know[c] Your testimonies.

80 Let my heart be blameless[a] in Your statutes,
that[b] I may not be ashamed.

73:a BDB's construing the Polel of כּוּן (*kûn*) herein as "constitute, make" (p. 466) is preferable to the majority of the renderings in the versions (e.g. "form, mold, fashion," etc.) which apparently follow the lead of the LXX (i.e. πλάσσω [*plassō*]).

73:b I.e. purpose of request; or anticipated consequence: "then I will learn. . . ."

74:a I.e. "be glad."
74:b Or, "hope for" (BDB, p. 404); cf. vv. 43, 81, 114, 147.
75:a Lit. "righteousness," the concrete noun from צדק (*ṣdq*) instead of the adjective.
75:b Obviously, אֱמוּנָה (*'^{e}mûnâ*) functions as an adverbial accusative herein; cf. the dative form in the LXX and the Targum's addition of the preposition בְּ (*b^{e}*); cf. Davidson, *Hebrew Syntax*, ¶ 71.
76:a I.e. חֶסֶד (*ḥesed*).
76:b Lit. "Please let Your grace be to comfort me," or ". . . be for my comforting"; i.e. the jussive יְהִי (*y^{e}hî*) followed by a dynamic occurrence of an infinitive construct with first person singular suffix. Or some take the הָיָה in its rarer sense of come (cf. the parallel jussive from בּוֹא [*bô'*] at the outset of v. 77), i.e. "Let Your grace come to comfort me."
76:c I.e. אִמְרָה (*'imrâ*), "word."
77:a The noun of the root רחם (*rḥm*), characteristically in the plural intensive (cf. BDB, p. 933).
77:b I.e. purpose of request; or anticipated consequence: "then I will live."
78:a Lit. "insolent (men)."
78:b שֶׁקֶר (*šeqer*), used adverbially, magnifies the thrust of עָוַּת (*^{c}āwaṯ*) in the Piel, to bend, make crooked, i.e. to subvert (cf. BDB, p. 736); the implication is that they "twisted the truth about me (cf. La. 3:36)" (Kidner, *Psalms 73–150*, p. 426).
78:c Another occurrence of asyndetonic antithetical parallelism; in this case the emphatic אֲנִי (*'^{a}nî*) adds intensification.
78:d This imperfect should be interpreted as customary or habitual.
79:a Or, "return" (i.e. שׁוּב [*šûḇ*]).
79:b The Targum adds לְאוּלְפָנִי (*l^{e}'ûl^{e}p̄ānî*), "to my instruction" which provides some interpretive (and textual, re v. 79b in the MT) insight.
79:c This rendering accepts the consonantal text as it stands (וְיֵדְעוּ [*w^{e}yēḏ^{ec}û*]) rejecting many versions (cf. LXX and modern) which accept the Qere (וְיֹדְעֵי [*w^{e}yōḏ^{ec}ê*]), i.e. "even those

who know. . . ." For arguments supporting the retention of the text as it stands, see Alexander, *Psalms*, 3:174; Delitzsch, *Psalms*, 3:253; Soll, "Psalm 119," pp. 187–88; and Anderson, *Psalms*, 2:830.

80:a Cf. the ἄμωμος (*amōmos*) of the LXX and the דְּלָא מוּת (*d͟elā' mûṯ*) of the Targum, i.e. "without blemish." It should be remembered, however, that תָּמִים (*tāmîm*) leans in an essentially positive direction (cf. comments on v. 1), i.e. "complete, sound" (BDB, p. 1071).

80:b Here the telic לְמַעַן (*lᵉmaᶜan*) reveals the intention of this prayer.

Synopsis and Outline

In this stanza the misery and the maturity of the psalmist continue to thirst for the mercy of God. What the psalmist stated implicitly in verses 65–72 about the hand of the LORD in his own affliction is now voiced explicitly. Deliverance has not yet been experienced; however, the avalanche of prayer requests (cf. vv. 73b, 74a, 76a, 77a, 78a, 79a, 80a), preponderantly jussives, would indicate that this afflicted child of God soon anticipated abundant manifestations of God's grace. His dependency without denial serves as a model of biblical response in reference to the many scriptural exhortations given to those who suffer persecution. As a matter of fact, his would have been a proleptic fulfillment of the response that Peter was eliciting when he urged, "Therefore, let those also who suffer according to the will of God entrust their souls to a faithful Creator in doing what is right" (1 Pet 4:19, NASB).

Structurally, this *Yôd* stanza is quite complex, since it unfolds in an introverted pattern. This phenomenon is most readily observable by noting literary and/or conceptual parallelisms from the core of the strophe outwardly. In verse 76 and 77 not only do the leading jussives correspond, but also the near synonyms for the grace of God mirror one another. Moving outward, verses 75 and 78 both deal conceptionally with the psalmist's affliction. Then in verses 74 and 79, third person plural jussives, each with the substantive יְרֵאֶיךָ (*y*^{e}*rē'ey<u>k</u>ā*; "the ones who fear You") as its subject, antiphonally respond to one another across verses 75–78. Finally, an interest in the psalmist's own spiritual rectitude relates verse 73 to verse 80 conceptionally. Consequently, in verses 73–80, the man of God echoes four concentric circles of prayer requests based upon his chronic experience with affliction:

1A. (vv. 73, 80) The largest circle encompasses the man of God's desire for deep maturity.
  - 1B. (v. 73) His desire leads him to pray for more discernment of the Word of God.
    - 1C. (v. 73a) The predication of his prayer.
    - 2C. (v. 73b) The proposal of his prayer.
    - 3C. (v. 73c) The purpose of his prayer.
  - 2B. (v. 80) His desire leads him to pray for total conformity to the Word of God.
    - 1C. (v. 80a) The request for conformity.
    - 2C. (v. 80b) The reason for conformity.

2A. (vv. 74, 79) The second largest circle encompasses the man of God's concern for other believers.
  - 1B. (v. 74) He prays to be a visual testimony to other believers.
  - 2B. (v. 79) He prays to be a vocal testimony to other believers.

3A. (vv. 75, 78) The third largest circle encompasses the man of God's exposure to trials.
  - 1B. (v. 75) The man of God's acknowledgement of the Divine Source of trials.
  - 2B. (v. 78) The man of God's petition concerning the human instruments of trials.

4A. (vv. 76, 77) The innermost circle encompasses the man of God's deepest needs.
  - 1B. (v. 76) His need for Divine consolation.
  - 2B. (v. 77) His need for Divine compassion.

Commentary

A prayer for more discernment of God's special revelation resides at the heart of the introductory verse to this stanza. Its proposal is phrased in the oft-repeated הֲבִינֵנִי (*h^{a}ḇînēnî*), "give me understanding" (cf. vv. 27, 34, 125, 144, 169), i.e. grant me practical perception for real life (esp., amidst its many pressures). This man of God apparently never seemed to be in need of constant reminders about the timeless truths so well summarized by James when he urged, "But if any of you lacks wisdom, let him ask of God, who gives to all men generously and without reproach, and it will be given to him" (Jas 1:5, NASB). His life exemplified this kind of prayerful dependence.

The preface of the afflicted disciple's prayer contains a significant affirmation about the One who answers such prayers.[1] In this predication he affirms that God's sovereign power had full sway over his being (i.e. יָדֶיךָ עָשׂוּנִי וַיְכוֹנְנוּנִי [*yāḏeykā ᶜāśûnî way^{e}ḵôn^{e}nûnî*]). The imagery of his LORD's "hands" speaks not only of power in general,[2] but also, and especially in this context, of the creative and constituting dimensions of Divine omnipotence. Concerning "the verb *ᶜāśāh*," it "is often used in the Psalter of divine creation e.g. of heavens (96:5), moon (104:19), heaven and earth (146:6), sea (95:5), and all that is in it (146:6); also of the creation of man (95:6, 100:3, 138:8)."[3] But, even more importantly, he indicates that God's hands "gave me my constitution."[4] It must

---

1 There may also have been a secondary apologetical dimension to this preface (e.g., cf. Ps 138:8).

2 For a good synopsis of the theological implication of יָד (*yāḏ*), see *TDOT*, s.v. "יָד (*yāḏ*)," by J. Bergman, W. von Soden, and P. Ackroyd, 5:418–22; note the wide cultural distribution of this imagery (i.e. pp. 393ff.); cf. *TWOT*, s.v. "יָד (*yād*)," by R. Alexander, 1:362–64.

3 Anderson, *Psalms*, 2:828.

4 Allen's (*Psalms 101–150*, p. 129) preferred translation of כּוּן (*kûn*); contra the many versions, as if the original contained a form of the root יצר (*yṣr*). As Kidner notes, כּוּן is "not the potter's word of, e.g., 33:15; 139:16" (*Psalms 73–150*, p. 426).

be stressed that the emphasis of the verb כּוּן (*kûn*) is "on giving a thing its firm constitution (cf. 'established', or 'constituted', in verse 90 or in Ps. 8:3 (4, Heb.); . . . also Jb. 10:8). Hence NEB, 'made me what I am'; and cf. JB, TEV."[5] Indeed, this man of God understood that to which many have born testimony,[6] that God knows us infinitely better than we know ourselves, since He has sovereignly overseen the framing of our personalities and potentialities. Consequently, these affirmations fittingly constitute the predication of any prayer request.

On the telic side of this disciple's entreaty lay the words וְאֶלְמְדָה מִצְוֹתֶיךָ (*we'elmedâ miṣwōṯeykā*), "that I may learn Your commandments." His purpose was in alignment with his LORD's, that he would be continually maturing in his conformity with the standards of God's lessons for life. Implicationally, such breadth and depth in application of the Divine curriculum would provide the stability he longed for, especially in view of his trying circumstances.

"He wishes in ver. 74 that all who fear God may see in him with joy an example of the way in which trust in the word of God is rewarded."[7] In view of the psalmist's affirmation in verse 63, it is not surprising to see his interest in the covenant community, designated as יְרֵאֶיךָ (*yerē'eykā*; cf. v. 79), "those who fear You," resurface.[8] His request to be a visual testimony (i.e. יִרְאוּנִי [*yir'ûnî*]; "let them see me") to other believers along with its attendant affect of joy upon them (i.e. וְיִשְׂמָחוּ [*weyiśmāḥû*]; "and let them be glad, rejoice") is another indication of his basic maturity. This disciple was not so utterly preoccupied with his personal problems that he thought of no one else but himself.

---

[5] Kidner, *Psalms 73–150*, p. 426.

[6] Cf., e.g., Jeremiah and Paul, respectively in Jer 1:5 and Gal 1:15.

[7] Delitzsch, *Psalms*, 3:253; cf. Leupold, *Psalms*, p. 839; and Cohen, *Psalms*, p. 404.

[8] Allen well ties these verses together when he says, "A concern for the God-fearing community, vv 74, 79, takes the motif of v 63 further" (*Psalms 101–150*, p. 143.

The final causal clause, כִּי לִדְבָרְךָ יִחָלְתִּי (*kî liḏḇārᵉḵā yiḥāltî*), "because I wait for (or hope for) Your word," indicates the particular testimony he wished to visualize for the benefit of those believers who were acquainted with his plight. His burden was that the open book of his life would be read by others[9] in the family of faith as a volume about *the Book* and patience under pressure. Concerning his original audience of God-fearers and subsequent generations of believers who have "watched" this disciple, his example of trusting God's Truth in tribulation remains worthy of emulation.

The pastel thread of affliction in the fabric of verses 67 and 71 radiates a bold and bright color in the cloth of verse 75. What has been affirmed implicitly is now acknowledged explicitly, the LORD is the Divine Source of the psalmist's trials.[10] The man of God herein personally recognizes (i.e. יָדַעְתִּי [*yāḏaʿtî*]; "I know")[11] two seemingly paradoxical truths[12] about his LORD. The first of these flows rather easily from his lips: צֶדֶק מִשְׁפָּטֶיךָ (*ṣeḏeq mišpāṭeyḵā*), "Your rulings are just."[13] In such contexts as this, God's מִשְׁפָּטִים (*mišpāṭîm*) "seem to point to rules of righteous administration."[14] Alexander's literal rendering of this affirmation as accompanied by a periphrastic elucidation of its main point help to reconstruct the deep conviction of the man of God: "*Thy judgments*, thy sovereign decisions and their execution, *are righteousness* itself, i.e., perfectly righteous."[15]

---

9 Cf. the implications of 2 Cor 3:2–3.

10 The vocative יהוה (*YHWH*) is especially significant in this regard.

11 Cf. *TWOT*, s.v. "יָדַע (*yāḏaʿ*)," by J. Lewis, 1:366–67, and *TDOT*, s.v. "יָדַע *yāḏaʿ*," by J. Bergman and G. Botterweck, 5:448–81; on the ἔγνων (*egnōn*) of the LXX, i.e. on γινώσκω (*ginōskō*) for יָדַע see Thayer, pp. 117–18, *passim*, for a review.

12 As indicated by the compound elements of the nominalizing כִּי (*kî*).

13 Allen's acceptable rendering (*Psalms 101–150*, p. 129).

14 Girdlestone, *Synonyms*, p. 209; cf. Scroggie, *Psalms*, p. 171. Also, note the basis of Abraham's argumentation in Gen 18:25.

15 Alexander, *Psalms*, 3:173.

By itself, such an acknowledgement might be looked upon as a polite theological concession paralleling those generic and, far too frequently, superficial references to Romans 8:28 by modern-day NT believers. However, the psalmist refuses to allow the issue to remain somewhat nebulous and stranded in the more public domain. He, therefore, as a genuine child of God, immediately brings the aforementioned reality into his private domain by adding with a burst of transparent testimony וֶאֱמוּנָה עִנִּיתָנִי (*we'ĕmûnâ ʿinnîṯānî*), "and in faithfulness You have afflicted me."[16] "This means not only that there was justice in Yahweh's action, but an ultimate good purpose behind it."[17]

The reference to God's אֱמוּנָה (*'ĕmûnâ*), "firmness, steadfastness, fidelity, faithfulness," etc.[18] speaks of His perpetual trustworthiness as outlined in His word. In this context it apparently refers to the LORD's "faithfulness to the Covenant, or to his word in general, God must chastise the disobedient or the negligent, and bless the loyal servants (cf. [Ps] 89:28–37 (M.T. 29–38))."[19] Consequently, "the Psalmist acknowledges that his punishment has been just and deserved (cf. verses 67 and 71), for God does not capriciously afflict his people (Lam. 3:33)."[20] Furthermore, there are intimations that the psalmist does not dwell merely on the punitive significance of his tribulations, but more importantly, he focuses his faculties upon the pedagogical potential of these divinely issued sufferings. As Delitzsch has well said, "He knows that God has humbled him אֱמוּנָה . . . , being faithful in His intentions towards him; for it is just in the school of affliction that one first learns rightly to estimate the worth of His word, and comes to feel its power."[21]

---

[16] Cf. Allen's dynamic rendering: "you have made me suffer out of faithfulness" (*Psalms 101–150*, p. 129).

[17] Soll, "Psalm 119," p. 188.

[18] Cf. BDB, p. 53.

[19] Anderson, *Psalms*, 2:829; he appropriately continues with the illustration of 2 Sam 7:14ff.

[20] Ibid.; Anderson also notes that "Dt. 8:16 summarizes the general OT attitude on this point" (ibid.). It should be remembered, however, that God has other purposes for affliction besides the corrective (e.g. preventative, cf. 2 Cor 12:7–10; and doxological, cf. John 9:1–3).

[21] Delitzsch, *Psalms*, 3:253.

Although structurally verse 75 relates to verse 78 due to introverted strophic development,[22] it also evidences a sequential and conceptual relationship with verses 76 and 77. Scroggie succinctly sketches this progression as follows: "the afflicter . . . is the comforter."[23] In these verses (i.e. vv. 76–77) hope rises out of hurt, because amidst the tempestuous seas of this man of God's life his anchor gripped that great grace of God which was so appropriately outlined by Jeremiah when he cried out, "For men are not cast off by the Lord forever. Though he brings grief, he will show compassion, so great is his unfailing love" (Lam 3:31–32, NIV).[24]

Intense is the intimacy constituting the bull's-eye (i.e. vv. 76–77) of this stanza. Not only are there a total of eight second and first person suffixes juxtaposed in the brief confines of these two verses, but also two synonyms for God's all-sufficient grace each stand forward in their respective verses. Herein their complementary nuances seem to highlight a fatherly type of consolation (i.e. חֶסֶד [*ḥeseḏ*] in v. 76)[25] and a motherly type of compassion (i.e. רַחֲמִים [*raḥᵃmîm*] in v. 77).[26]

---

[22] Cf. the previous discussion.

[23] Scroggie, *Psalms*, p. 182. In a similar vein Delitzsch notes, "But trouble, though sweetened by an insight into God's salutary design, is nevertheless always bitter; hence the well-justified prayer of ver. 76, that God's mercy may notwithstanding be bestowed upon him for his consolation . . ." (Delitzsch, *Psalms*, 3:253).

[24] This is the second *seeming* allusion to the truths of Lam 3 in as many verses (cf. Lam 3:33 and v. 75b above). However, this may be more than a seeming allusion if Daniel indeed be the author of this psalm, since it is known that Daniel was drawn to the writings of his older contemporary (cf. Dan 9:2).

[25] Cf. previous observations about חֶסֶד (e.g. vv. 41, 64) and the term's biblical distribution in predominantly cognitive contexts. This entreaty for "loyal love" (Allen's nuanced meaning herein, *Psalms 101–150*, p. 129) seems to point to that essentially rational and volitional dimension of his LORD's great grace which he anticipated would be manifested in a fatherly form of firm (i.e. unfaltering) consolation.

[26] Cf. the possible etymology of the root רחם (*rḥm*), i.e. be soft, along with the relationship of the nouns רַחֲמִים (*raḥᵃmîm*; "compassion") and רֶחֶם or רַחַם (*reḥem/raḥam*; "womb") in BDB, p. 933. If indeed חֶסֶד (v. 76) is more rationally and volitionally oriented, רַחֲמִים (v. 77) adds an emotional dimension to God's multifaceted grace, thereby suggesting that this disciple also yearned for a motherly form of tender loving care.

Verse 76 opens with the third of seven jussive requests ("may . . ." or "let . . .") which characterize this stanza. Here the יְהִי (*yᵉhî*), in the sense of "may it come"[27] (i.e. be present[28]), is complemented by the emphatic particle of entreaty, i.e. "*Please* let Your grace (i.e. חֶסֶד [*ḥesed*]) come, be present. . . ." Furthermore the compensation of God's good grace is not left unexpressed, since the man of God recognized its potential for consolation as evidenced by the complementary Piel infinitive construct לְנַחֲמֵנִי (*lᵉnaḥᵃmēnî*), lit. "to comfort me" (i.e. for my comfort).[29] That this disciple personally anticipated such a manifestation of Divine "support and encouragement"[30] is corroborated by the closing words of verse 76: כְּאִמְרָתְךָ לְעַבְדֶּךָ (*kᵉ'imraṯᵉḵā lᵉʿaḇdeḵā*), "according to Your promise to Your servant."[31] Applicationally, Leupold well summarizes the thrust of verse 76 by concluding, "The one important fact that can always serve as a substantial comfort to those who suffer affliction is that God's 'steadfast love' is the supreme comfort as God has promised that it will be."[32]

A picturesque usage of the verb בּוֹא (*bô'*), to "come (approach, arrive),"[33] is introduced by the initial jussive of verse 77. What our dependent disciple is soliciting is his LORD's T. L. C., i.e. רַחֲמֶיךָ (*raḥᵃmeyḵā*), "Your 'tender mercy.'"[34]

---

[27] Cf. BDB, p. 224, and its obvious parallelism with the more explicit יְבֹאוּנִי (*yᵉḇō'ûnî*) cf. v. 77.

[28] Cf. *TDOT*, s.v. "הָיָה *hāyāh*," by K.-H. Bernhardt, 3:373.

[29] Cf. the analogous Aramaic form in the Targum, and the infinitive παρακλέσαι (*parakalesai*) of the LXX. It has been suggested previously that the presence of the infinitive rather than one of the noun forms (e.g. נֶחָמָה [*neḥāmâ*], v. 50) of נחם (*nḥm*) emphasizes the *dynamic* of God's consoling ministry.

[30] See Girdlestone's excursus on נָחַם / παρακαλέω (*nāḥam/parakaleō*) (*Synonyms*, p. 91).

[31] Anderson comments that "the basis of his plea was probably a previous experience of the goodness of God" (*Psalms*, 2:829).

[32] Leupold, *Psalms*, p. 839.

[33] BDB, p. 98; see also Preuss' discussion on "*bô'* in Prayers" in *TDOT*, s.v. "בּוֹא *bô'*," by H. Preuss, 2:33.

[34] Cf. *TWOT*, s.v. "רָחַם (*rāḥam*)," by L. Coppes, 2:841.

> This root refers to deep love (usually of a "superior" for an "inferior") rooted in some "natural" bond. In the Piel it is used for the deep inward feeling we know variously as compassion, pity, mercy. . . . The depth of this love is shown by the connection of this word with *reḥem/raḥam* [i.e. "womb"]. Compare, Jeremiah (21:7) who uses it of a mother's love toward her nursing baby. It can also refer to a father's love (Ps 103:13). Apparently, this verb connotes the feeling of mercy which . . . is most easily prompted by small babies (Isa 13:18) or other helpless people. . . . This root is frequently used of God. It incorporates . . . the strong tie God has with those whom he has called as his children (Ps 103:13). God looks upon his own as a father looks upon his children; he has pity on them (cf. Mic 7:17).[35]

Later on (v. 156a), the man of God will acknowledge the existence of a bottomless reservoir of God's רַחֲמִים (*raḥămîm*),[36] but for the present, out of the anguish of his emotionally parched being, he deeply desires a cup of "water" from that unfathomable well. Upon arrival, he is convinced that it will quench his desiccated spirit and thereby revitalize him (i.e. וְאֶחְיֶה [*wᵉ'eḥyeh*]).[37] According to pattern "the reason . . . generally follows a prayer,"[38] and that precedent is once again strengthened by the ensuing noun clause

---

[35] Ibid., pp. 840–841; note in Coppes' subsequent discussion that he commendably links רָחַם to God's unconditional election and His "continuing mercy and grace" (ibid.). Note that the LXX's οἰκτιρμοί (*oiktirmoi*) builds a semantical and theological bridge to a host of significant NT usages which further develop the tender mercies of our gracious God (e.g. the synopsis of Rom 12:1).

[36] It is interesting that the root רחם (*rḥm*) is also vitally associated with the person of Daniel (cf. Dan 1:9; 9:9, 18).

[37] I.e. "that [or, then] I may enjoy life in all its fullness" (Anderson, *Psalms*, 2:829).

[38] Scroggie, *Psalms*, p. 178.

with causal conjunction: כִּי־תוֹרָתְךָ שַׁעֲשֻׁעָי (*kî-tôrāṯᵉḵā šaᶜăšuᶜāy*), "because Your instruction is my delight."[39]

A touch of imprecation rises in verse 78 with a return appearance of the זֵדִים (*zēḏîm*), those arrogant agitators of the psalmist. Although this man of God recognized his LORD's sovereign sway over all things, especially including his own affliction (e.g. v. 75), he also understood that these malignant servants of trial were nonetheless morally responsible and therefore deserving of retributive justice.[40] And it is just for that he boldly prays יֵבֹשׁוּ זֵדִים (*yēḇošû zēḏîm*), "Let the insolent be ashamed."[41]

Explicit (i.e. v. 78b) and implicit documentation (i.e. v. 78c) for the propriety of Divine vengeance follows. First, the persecuted one throws a spotlight on their unjust[42] subversion of him. Literally, כִּי־שֶׁקֶר עִוְּתוּנִי (*kî-šeqer ᶜiwwᵉṯûni*) translates as "because they made me crooked (i.e. twisted me) with a lie." Interestingly, the same verb occurs in Lamentations 3:36: "To subvert a man in his cause, the Lord approveth not."[43] Consequently, "for oppressing me unjustly,"[44] "for wronging me without cause,"[45] he reasons,

---

[39] Alexander conjectures about the masculine plural intensive noun of the root שׁעע II: "The plural (*delights*) expresses fulness and completeness, or perhaps implies that this joy is equal or superior to all others, or includes them all. The Hebrew noun is derived from the verb in vs. 16, 47, 70" (*Psalms*, 3:174).

[40] Cf. the roles of Assyria (Isa 10:5–19), the Chaldeans in Hab (1:5ff.), Haman in Esther (ch. 3ff.), etc. Each actor on the stage of human history is responsible for every scene of his role, and yet, the Divine Director standing backstage is determining every detail of the production (cf. the theology of Peter in Acts 2:23; 4:27–28).

[41] Contrast what he has prayed and will yet pray for himself in vv. 5–6, 80. On this particular imprecation Anderson (*Psalms*, 2:829) notes, "The prayer for the godless (see verse 21) to be put to shame is a well-known theme in the Psalms of Lamentation (6:10 (M.T. 11), 31:17 (M.T. 18), 35:4, 26, 83:17 (M.T. 18), etc.)."

[42] The adverbial force of שֶׁקֶר (*šeqer*) herein is appropriately rendered as ἀδίκως (*adikōs*), "unjustly," in the LXX.

[43] Cohen, *Psalms*, p. 404; note that the allusions to Lam 3 continue.

[44] NAB.

[45] NIV.

these slanderers deserve shame. Finally, this mature disciple emphatically contrasts their profane perversion with his pure preoccupation, adding the positive grounds for Divine intervention: אֲנִי אָשִׂיחַ בְּפִקּוּדֶיךָ (*'ănî 'āśîaḥ bᵉpiqqûdeykā*), i.e. "'As for me'[46] I (characteristically, customarily) meditate[47] on Your precepts."

Attention is once again drawn in verse 79 to those who fear the LORD (i.e. יְרֵאֶיךָ [*yᵉrē'eykā*]; cf. v. 74). The psalmist's desire for them here is that they would "turn" or "return" to him (i.e. יָשׁוּבוּ לִי [*yāšûbû lî*]).[48] If the Hebrew text is not emended,[49] what follows is the pedagogical purpose for their return,[50] וְיֵדְעוּ עֵדֹתֶיךָ (*wᵉyēdᵉcû cēdōteykā*), "that they may know Your testimonies." By both life and lip this disciple wanted to convey to the covenant community the sustaining power of God's sufficient revelation for real life.

In some ways this stanza has been a review of the primary personalities in the psalmist's life: his God (e.g., vv. 73a–b, 75–77), his spiritual community (vv. 74, 79), and his adversaries (v. 78). Now, in verse 80, he returns to himself (cf. v. 73c) and to his consuming longing for spiritual rectitude. Once again, his focus is not merely on external compliance but especially on internal conformity. This is first documented by the disciple's request (i.e. v. 80a) and then by his reasoning (i.e. v. 80b).

His request emphasizes the governing impetus which stands

---

[46] Allen's proper emphasis upon אֲנִי (*'ᵃnî*) at the head of this antithetical bicolon (*Psalms 101–150*, p. 130).

[47] Stressing the *imperfect* Qal. On שִׂיחַ (*śîaḥ*), it should be remembered that "the word means to commune, to muse, to contemplate, to ponder, to pray, and it implies a spirit of devotion" (Scroggie, *Psalms*, p. 175).

[48] Allen's interpretive choice which is reflected in his rendering "come back to me" is appealing (*Psalms 101–150*, p. 130). For one possible scenario regarding their departure from the psalmist, see Anderson, *Psalms*, 2:829.

[49] See above under "Translation and Notes."

[50] "If instead of וְיֹדְעֵי . . . , we read according to the *Chethîb* וְיֵדְעוּ (cf. ver. 125), then what is meant by יָשׁוּבוּ לִי is a turning towards him for the purpose of learning: may their knowledge be enriched from his experience" (Delitzsch, *Psalms*, 3:253). Cf. Anderson's argument (*Psalms*, 2:830).

behind an "unreserved, faultless, unwavering adherence to God's word":[51] יְהִי־לִבִּי תָמִים בְּחֻקֶּיךָ (*y^e^hî-libbî tāmîm b^e^ḥuqqeyḵā*), "Let my heart (i.e. my rational, volitional, and emotional nucleus of personality and responsibility) be blameless (i.e. sound or complete) in Your statutes." He well knew that integrity of life-style (cf. תָמִים [*tāmîm*] in v. 1) only comes from integrity of heart. And furthermore, this child of God understood that the Divine mediation of such a deep-seated rectitude (i.e. v. 80a) could supply the exclusive antidote for shame (i.e. v. 80b).[52] As so often, once again we are confronted with a significant measure of maturity.

---

[51] Delitzsch, *Psalms*, 3:253.

[52] Cf. this occurrence of לֹא אֵבוֹשׁ (*lō' 'ēḇôš*) with v. 6 and contra the deserved shame of the ungodly in v. 78.

כ

KAPH STANZA
(vv. 81–88)

Translation and Notes

81 My soul[a] languishes[b] for Your salvation;
I wait for[c] Your word.

82 My eyes[a] are strained[b] *looking* for Your promise,[c]
saying,[d] "When will You comfort me?"

83 Although[a] I have become[b] like a skin-bottle[c] in thick smoke,[d]
I do not forget Your statutes.[e]

84 How many *are* the days of Your servant?
When will You execute judgment on[a] those who are persecuting me?

85 Insolent *men* have dug pits[a] for me
which *is* not according to Your law.[b]

86 All Your commandments *are* reliable;[a]
they have persecuted me *with* lies;[b] help me!

87 They almost[a] exterminated me[b] in[c] the land,
but I[d] have not abandoned Your precepts.

88 Revive me[a] according to Your grace,[b]
then[c] I will keep the testimonies[d] of Your mouth.

81:a On נַפְשִׁי (*napšî*) as a periphrasis for "I," cf. its parallelism with the 1 c s verb in v. 81b and its previous occurrences in vv. 25, 28; note also the picturesque עֵינַי (*ʿênay*) in the next verse.

81:b I.e. Kidner's pleasing rendering of כָּלָה (*kālâ*) (*Psalms 73–150*, p. 426); he appropriately notes that "it is the same verb, but intransitive, as that of 87a" (ibid.).

81:c Or, "hope for."
82:a Only the DSS (Q11) would read עיני (*ᶜyny*) as a singular ("my eye") due to its collocation with the singular form of the verb (i.e. כלתה [*klṯh*]) therein.
82:b "Strained" renders the same verbal root translated "to languish" in the previous verse (note the LXX's employment of the verb ἐκλείπω [*ekleipō*] in both instances). BDB documents the nuanced meaning of "strained" noting: "esp[ecially] of eyes exhausted by weeping La 2:11, strained by looking (fig[urative]) for relief or refreshment, *fail, languish,* 4:17, Ps 69:4, Jb 11:20, 17:5, Je 14:6 . . . in spiritual sense 119:82, 123" (BDB, p. 477).
82:c Or, "word" אִמְרָה (['*imrâ*]).
82:d Some suggest the deletion of לֵאמֹר (*lē'mōr*) based upon an alleged dittography from the previous word (i.e. לְאִמְרָתֶךָ [*le'imrāṯeḵā*]) and/or its very low frequency in the Psalms (cf. Soll, "Psalm 119," p. 190). However, its textual documentation is pervasive, and its function (i.e. the introduction of a dramatic direct quotation) is obvious. Herein, others prefer to ease the stark and somewhat awkward personification which arises through the association of עֵינַי with לֵאמֹר by translating the latter as "I ask" (cf. Allen, *Psalms 101–150,* p. 130, and Sanders, *Dead Sea Psalms Scroll,* p. 53).
83:a Although some take this כִּי (*kî*) as explanatory (cf. Soll, "Psalm 119," p. 189), it seems best, in the light of the syntax and parallelism of v. 83, to construe it concessively (cf. Delitzsch, *Psalms,* 3:253).
83:b The unique rendering of DSS (Q11), עשיתני [*ᶜśyṯny*], "You have made me," is most likely interpretive, stemming from their previously documented preoccupations with Divine sovereignty.
83:c BDB, p. 609; i.e. "a leathern flask: tanned hides were used for holding water or wine; such containers, if kept in the dry heat next to the fireplace, gradually became brittle and useless" (NAB note, p. 685).
83:d The Targum's rendering of v. 83a, "if I am like a leather bag which is hung in the smoke," aids our conceptualization of this graphic simile.

83:e DSS (Q11) alone reads חסדכה (*ḥsdkh*) instead of חֻקֶּיךָ (*ḥuqqeykā*).
84:a The common verb, עָשָׂה (*ʿāśâ*) with מִשְׁפָּט (*mišpāṭ*) and the בְּ (*bᵉ*) which indicates the direction of the Divine justice (cf. BDB, p. 794).
85:a DSS (Q11) apparently renders as a singular, i.e. "a pit."
85:b Versions and translations construe the antecedent of the relative clause differently; e.g., the godless men (i.e. "*men* who . . ."), the pits (i.e. "[pits] which *are* . . ."), or the act of digging such pits (i.e. "which *is* . . ."). The last option, as Soll argues, is most credible: "To translate, as KJV does, '[pits] which do not conform to thy law' makes it sound as though the pits might conform if they were, say, a cubit less wide. But neither does it seem felicitous to apply the phrase *lōʾ kᵉtôrāteka* to persons. It seems best to see this clause as referring to the malicious act of digging pits (so also JB)" ("Psalm 119," p. 190). Also, as a reference to a lawless act, see the paraphrase of the Targum. Consequently, v. 85b could be translated, "this is against your law" (NAB).
86:a I.e. אֱמוּנָה (*ʾĕmûnâ*), lit. a noun meaning "firmness, steadfastness, fidelity" (BDB, p. 53). Herein, its antithetical juxtaposition with שֶׁקֶר (*šeqer*) is eye-catching and significant (cf. *TDOT*, s.v. "אָמַן *ʾāman*," by A. Jepsen, 1:318).
86:b Lit. "a lie"; or, as an adverbial accusative it might be rendered "wrongfully" (cf. v. 78).
87:a I.e. כִּמְעַט [*kimʿaṭ*], lit. "like a little," is an adverbial idiom meaning "almost" (BDB, p. 590) or "nearly."
87:b Another occurrence of כָּלָה (*kālâ*); cf. vv. 81, 82.
87:c Or, "on earth," etc.; note that DSS (Q11) has the preposition מִן (*min*), "from earth," instead of בְּ (*bᵉ*).
87:d Another occurrence of emphatic אֲנִי (*ʾănî*) standing in stark antithesis: "but as for me . . ." (cf. Soll's ["Psalm 119," p. 189] rendering).
88:a Cf. the previously discussed variant throughout DSS (Q11), i.e. חנן (*ḥnn*) for חיה (*ḥyh*).
88:b I.e. חֶסֶד (*ḥesed*).
88:c This syntactical option seems best if וְאֶשְׁמְרָה (*wᵉešmᵉrâ*) is viewed as a cohortative. Other possible renderings are "and I shall keep," "that I may keep," etc.

88:d "Lit. 'the testimony of . . . ,' meaning perhaps the sum total of the divine law (cf. 19:7 (M.T. 8))" (Anderson, *Psalms*, 2:831).

Synopsis and Outline

Indications of intense lament abound in this stanza. Not only the strophe's phraseology but also its pulsating interrogatives (e.g., vv. 82b, 84a, 84b) and staccato outbursts (cf. v. 86) draw attention to this reality. As Soll affirms, "We are given a lament of great intensity and urgency."[1]

Sprinkled into the psalmist's emotional and tearful yearnings[2] are summations of his own fidelity (vv. 81, 82a, 83b, 87b) alongside of the contrasting infidelity of his enemies (vv. 85–87a). This admixture helps to identify the mood of the man of God, which may be described as a frantic dependence upon the God of the Word and the Word of God (reviewing his implicit longings in vv. 81, 82, 84, and noting his explicit ejaculations in vv. 86c, 88a). Therefore, in Psalm 119:81–88, two crescendos of lament drive the desperate disciple to an unreserved dependence upon God and His resources:

1A. (vv. 81–84) The first crescendo issues primarily from a theological context (i.e. God and the psalmist).
  1B. (vv. 81–82) He voices his personal predicament:

---

1 Soll, "Psalm 119," p. 190; his surrounding comments are also noteworthy: "The breaks which precede and follow this strophe are sharpest in Ps. 119. . . . The hopeful stance of the *Yod* strophe is simply dropped, and we plunge headlong into an abyss of fear and isolation. . . . The deeper lament of this strophe (for this is truly the nadir of the psalm) prepares the way for the greater consolation of the *Lamed* strophe and the overflow of rapture in the *Mem* strophe" (ibid.).

2 Cf. Allen, *Psalms 101–150*, p. 143, and note the Targum's employment of the root רגג (*rgg*), to desire, long, covet (Jastrow, *Dictionary*, 2:1447), etc. for כלה (*klh*) in v. 81a.

1C. (vv. 81–82a) By exposing his feelings.
2C. (v. 82b) By expressing his frustration.
2B. (v. 83) He voices his precarious perseverance by employing a vivid metaphor of contrast.
3B. (v. 84) He voices his dependent pleas by surfacing the depths of his exasperation.
1C. (v. 84a) His transparent plea.
2C. (v. 84b) His transitional plea.
2A. (vv. 85–88) The second crescendo issues primarily from a sociological context (i.e. God, the psalmist, *and his enemies*).
1B. (vv. 85–86) He voices his painful predicament:
1C. (v. 85) By exposing their tactics.
2C. (v. 86a) By extolling God's truth.
3C. (v. 86b) By expressing his turmoil.
2B. (v. 87) He voices his precarious perseverance by contrasting their determination and his dedication.
3B. (v. 88) He voices his dependent plea:
1C. (v. 88a) By appealing to precedent.
2C. (v. 88b) By adding a promise.

Commentary

The emotional intensity of this stanza is personally enhanced by the immediate appearance of two anthropological synecdoches.[3] Rather than hearing the psalmist cry "I . . . I . . . I . . . ," we encounter more arresting, but yet spontaneous designations of *himself* as נַפְשִׁי (*nap̱šî*), "my soul" (v. 81; cf. vv. 25, 28) and עֵינַי (*ᶜēynay*), "my eyes" (v. 82). Furthermore, both of these colorful terms with wholistic emphases stand as the subjects of two nu-

[3] The phenomenon of parts being utilized in parallelisms for the whole man is a characteristic of OT (and sometimes NT) anthropology, esp. in poetry; for a classic example, see Ps 63:2 (v. 1, Eng).

anced occurrences of the verb כָּלָה (*kālâ*), literally to be finished, at an end, spent, etc.[4] Consequently, the hurting disciple embarks on his consuming lament with some very graphic expressions of personal exhaustion.

In verse 81 an exhaustion of "soul" wells up: "My soul pines for your salvation" (NAB), cries the child of God. Allen idiomatically renders כָּלְתָה לִתְשׁוּעָתְךָ נַפְשִׁי (*kālᵉṯâ liṯšûᶜāṯᵉḵā nap̱šî*) by "I feel exhausted, waiting for your salvation."[5] This affirmation colors the one which comes after it, לִדְבָרְךָ יִחָלְתִּי (*liḏbārᵉḵā yiḥāltî*), "I wait for Your word."[6] Or, in reverse order, his deep longing for satiation from God's Book (v. 81b) comes on the heels of his draining desire for salvation by its Author (v. 81a). Then, at the outset of verse 82, an exhaustion of "eyes" comes alongside to complete his picture of desperation: כָּלוּ עֵינַי לְאִמְרָתֶךָ (*kālû ᶜênay lᵉʾimrāṯeḵā*), "My eyes fail, looking for your promise" (NIV). In combination, verses 81–82a expose the unsettled feelings of the child of God, thereby providing a backdrop for his rhetorical expressions of frustration which immediately follow.

The first question that he asks his God is מָתַי תְּנַחֲמֵנִי (*māṯay tᵉnaḥᵃmēnî*), "When will You comfort me?" The מָתַי (*māṯay*; i.e. "when?" or "how long?"), as a pointed interrogative directed towards God, seems to be in bounds theologically when an urgent appeal is made on the basis of Divine justice or covenant care. The precedent of justice attends its appearance in verse 84b, while herein in verse 82b, the implicit basis for its occurrence seems to be sovereign grace, since "Yahweh is the comforter of his people (cf. Isa. 12:1, 49:13, 51:3, 12, 52:9; Jer. 31:13; Zech. 1:17) and the Psalmists see him also as the consoler of the individual (71:21, 86:17, 119:76)."[7]

---

[4] BDB, p. 477; for an adequate synopsis of כָּלָה (*kālâ*) in both positive and negative contexts, see *TWOT*, s.v. "כָּלָה (*kālâ*)," by J. Oswalt, 1:439.

[5] Allen, *Psalms 101–150*, p. 130.

[6] In this context the parallelisms are better interpreted as synthetical rather than antithetical: נַפְשִׁי . . . כָּלְתָה (*kālᵉtâ . . . nap̱šî*) is mirrored in יִחָלְתִּי (*yiḥālṯî*), and the directional prepositional phrase לִתְשׁוּעָתְךָ (*liṯšûᶜāṯᵉḵā*) picks up an echo in its counterpart, לִדְבָרְךָ (*liḏbārᵉḵā*).

Prior to the resumption of his bold statements of interrogation (cf. v. 84) the disciple submits his personal example of precarious perseverance as a kind of secondary documentation for the propriety of Divine intervention (i.e. v. 83). His perseverance (v. 83b) indeed stands in bold relief when compared with the picture he paints of his plight (v. 83a). The simile is captivating: כִּי־הָיִיתִי כְּנֹאד בְּקִיטוֹר (*kî-hāyîṯî kenō'ḏ beqîṭôr*), "Although I have become like a skin-bottle in thick smoke. . . ." Similar to a wine-skin which had been hung too close to a smoky fireplace, the man of God looks upon himself as having become "shriveled and charred."[8] He felt that the thick smoke of his fiery trials was "destroying and rendering [him] useless."[9] Nevertheless, he conscientiously clung to his LORD's resources, since he testified in the same breath: "I do not forget Your statutes."[10]

More vulnerability arrives with the first question of verse 84: כַּמָּה יְמֵי־עַבְדֶּךָ (*kammâ yemê-ʿaḇdeḵā*), "How many are the days of Your servant?"[11] "The expression . . . how many . . . occurs here in the sense: how few, Ps. xxxix.5. The entreaty of an immediate interference of God is evoked and supported by the thought of the brevity of human life."[12] "Therefore God must hasten the vindication of his servant . . . before the latter passes away"[13] (i.e. v. 84b): "When will You execute judgment on those who are persecuting me?" As much as his own vulnerability pre-documents this priority request for Divine justice, the villainous behavior of his enemies post-documents it: כָּרוּ־לִי זֵדִים שִׁיחוֹת (*kārû-lî zēḏîm šîḥôṯ*), "Insolent *men* have dug pits

---

[7] Anderson, *Psalms*, 2:830.

[8] Soll, "Psalm 119," p. 191; i.e. "black and unsightly (cf. Job 30:30; Lam. 4:8)" (Anderson, *Psalms*, 2:830).

[9] Moll, *Psalms*, p. 591.

[10] On the volitional emphasis of שָׁכַח (*šāḵaḥ*), "to forget," cf. vv. 16, 61, 93, 109, 141, 153, 176; contra. his enemies' deliberate forgetting in v. 139.

[11] I.e. "How much longer does your servant have?" (Soll, "Psalm 119," p. 189).

[12] Moll, *Psalms*, p. 591; cf. Delitzsch, *Psalms*, 3:254. For other biblical affirmations of the important truth of man's transitoriness, note Ps 89:47 (v. 48, Heb); Isa 40:6–8 and Jas 4:14.

[13] Anderson, *Psalms*, 2:830–31.

for me" (v. 85a). The man of God depicts his enemies as crafty trappers of animals. In verse 110 he will similarly characterize them as layers of snares. In both cases he was targeted as their innocent victim. So whether by pit שִׁיחָה ([šîḥâ]), snare (פַּח [paḥ]),[14] or net (רֶשֶׁת [rešeṯ]),[15] their tactics stood in marked opposition to God's revelation (i.e. v. 85b). Frustratingly, "he and his foes" were "not playing the game by the same rules."[16]

The man of God surfaces for a breath of fresh spiritual air in verse 86a only to return by way of contrast to the depths of his mistreatment in verse 86b. Both extremes then serve as bases for his plea of panic which climaxes this verse. No matter how wrong the surrounding realities of his life seemed to be, he could still lean on the rightness of revelation.[17] The acute infidelity of men's actions[18] could not extinguish the abounding fidelity of God as conveyed through His word.[19] Appropriately, therefore, he bursts forth with his plea: עָזְרֵנִי (*ᶜozrēnî*), "Help me!"[20] Although this is the only imperatival occurrence of the root עזר (*ᶜzr*) in Psalm 119,[21] infinitive and imperfect (i.e. jussive) recurrences serve strategically as a part of its climax (cf. respectively vv. 173 and 175). Outside of the Psalms this word often carries with it connotations of military assistance;[22] however, within the Psalter it is employed

---

14 For שִׁיחָה in parallelism with פַּח note Jer 18:22.

15 For שִׁיחָה in parallelism with רֶשֶׁת note Ps 57:7 (v. 6, Eng).

16 Soll, "Psalm 119," p. 191.

17 For a good discussion of the significance of the constituents of v. 86, see Delitzsch, *Psalms*, 3:254.

18 I.e. שֶׁקֶר רְדָפוּנִי (*šeqer rᵉḏāpûnî*), "they have persecuted me with a lie" (NASB), or "men persecute me without cause" (NIV [cf. v. 161]).

19 I.e. כָּל־מִצְוֹתֶיךָ אֱמוּנָה (*kol-miṣwōṯeykā ʾᵉmûnâ*), "all your commandments are steadfast" (NAB), i.e. reliable.

20 This seems to be a variation on his normal emergency entreaty חַיֵּנִי (*ḥayyēnî*), "Revive me!"

21 Herein the Targum renders עזר appropriately with a synonym, סְעַד (*sᵉᶜaḏ*), to assist, help (Jastrow, *Dictionary*, 2:1009); and the LXX utilizes a semantical equivalent, βοηθέω (*boētheō*), etymologically "to run to the cry," i.e. "to help, succor, bring aid" (Thayer, *Lexicon*, p. 104); for two illuminating contexts of the latter's occurrences in the NT, see Mark 9:22, 24, and Heb 2:18.

more generally by individual psalmists seeking Divine help.[23] Indeed, herein the distraught disciple begs the assistance of the Holy Helper.[24]

Thoughts of his precarious perseverance return in verse 87.[25] Here he contrasts the malicious determination of his persecutors (i.e. v. 87a) with his own mature dedication (i.e. v. 87b). Drawing once again upon the verb כָּלָה (*kālâ*),[26] the psalmist asserts that his enemies have nearly destroyed, or even more graphically, have almost *exterminated* him on earth.[27] Nevertheless, he[28] did not vacillate spiritually in the presence of those ruthless villains: לֹא־עָזַבְתִּי פִקֻּודֶיךָ (*lō' ᶜazabtî piqquwdeykā*), "I have not forsaken Your precepts." This bold affirmation not only reflected the gracious enablement of his LORD[29] but also evidenced a contrasting scenario with the apostasy which surrounded the disciple.[30]

In view of these positive and negative realities, he concludes the *Kap* strophe with his prevalent petition for life: חַיֵּנִי (*ḥayyēnî*), "Revive me!"[31] Sometimes, in voicing this bold plea, the man of God calls attention to the precedent of God's Word, promise, etc. (cf. vv. 25, 154, 156), but here and in verse 159 he appeals directly to the precedent of personal Divine grace (i.e. כְּחַסְדְּךָ [*kᵉḥasdᵉkā*]). That he was convinced of its sufficiency even in the context of his great suf-

---

22 *TWOT*, s.v. "עָזַר (*ᶜazar*) I," by C. Schultz, 2:660–61.

23 Ibid., p. 661; e.g., "Yahweh is the helper of the fatherless (10:14), or of the afflicted in general (30:10 (M.T. 11), 37:40, 54:4, (M.T. 6))" (Anderson, *Psalms*, 2:831).

24 Conceptually, God as עֵזֶר (*ᶜēzer*), helper, in the OT is closely paralleled by God as παράκλητος (*paraklētos*), helper, advocate, etc., in the NT.

25 Cf. v. 83.

26 Cf. vv. 81, 82.

27 Or, "in the land."

28 Note the emphatic וַאֲנִי (*wa'ănî*), "but I," at the juncture of this antithetical couplet.

29 Cf. עָזַב (*ᶜāzab*) in v. 8.

30 Cf. עָזַב (*ᶜāzab*) in v. 53.

31 As Kidner argues, "*Spare my life* is too restricted a translation. Better, 'give me life' (cf. 93, 107, etc.), which is a prayer for more than bare survival" (*Psalms 73–150*, p. 426).

fering[32] is indicated by his closing words: וְאֶשְׁמְרָה עֵדוּת פִּיךָ (*wᵉ'ešmᵉrâ ᶜēḏûṯ pîḵā*), "then I will keep the testimony of Your mouth."[33] His LORD's grace would be received with gratitude and would affect him volitionally, generating further obedience. Herein Deuteronomy 8:3 is exemplified: "Man shall *live*[34] on everything that comes forth from[35] *the mouth of the LORD*" (emphases added).[36]

---

[32] Cf. the truth of 2 Cor 12:9 in its context.

[33] The telic option would be rendered "*that* I may keep the testimony of Your mouth." Although עֵדוּת פִּיךָ (*ᶜēḏûṯ pîḵā*) could be regarded as "a roundabout expression for 'you' (i.e. 'your testimony' . . .)" (Anderson, *Psalms*, 2:831), it is better to take it as an expression which emphasizes the ultimate *Source* of God's revelation.

[34] I.e. יִחְיֶה (*yiḥyeh*), the Qal imperfect of the root חיה (*ḥyh*); cf. the Piel imperative in Ps 119:88a.

[35] I.e. עַל־כָּל־מוֹצָא (*ᶜal-kol-môṣā'*).

[36] I.e. פִּי־יְהוָה (*pî-YHWH*); cf. פִּיךָ (*pîḵā*) in Ps 119:88b.

ל

LAMEDH STANZA
(vv. 89–96)

Translation and Notes

89 Forever, O LORD,[a]
Your word stands firm[b] in heaven.

90 Your faithfulness[a] *continues*[b] from generation to generation;[c]
You established the earth and it stands.

91 They stand[a] at present[b] according to Your judgments,
because all things[c] are Your servants.

92 Unless Your law had been my delight,
I would have[a] perished in my affliction.[b]

93 I will never forget[a] Your precepts,
because You gave me life[b] by means of them.[c]

94 I am Yours;[a] save me,
because I have sought Your precepts.

95 Wicked men[a] have lain in wait for me to destroy me;
however,[b] I diligently consider[c] Your testimonies.

96 I have seen a limit[a] to all perfection,[b]
but,[c] Your commandment is exceedingly broad.

89:a Some translate as two complementary (i.e. appositional) clauses, the first of which is treated as an adverbial affirmation about God and the second as a participial confirmation (cf. Syriac, NIV, NAB, etc.).

89:b Lit. "is standing firm," the participle stresses continuity which is further reinforced by the introductory לְעוֹלָם (*le*ᶜ*ôlām*).

90:a Some emend from אֱמוּנָתְךָ (*'ᵉmûnāṯeḵā*) to אִמְרָתֶךָ (*'imrāṯeḵā*) not on the basis of any textual evidence but upon a subjective desire for a parallel (cf. דָּבָר in v. 89) word for the Word in v. 90 (e.g. Soll, "Psalm 119," p. 192; cf. Allen's note [*Psalms 101–150*, p. 137]).
90:b A verbal expressing continuity needs to be supplied, e.g., *is, continues, remains, extends.*
90:c Lit. "to generation and generation," i.e. permanently.
91:a LXX reads as a singular; contra DSS (Q11) and other early versions which agree with the plural of the MT.
91:b Lit. "the day," i.e. the prevalent adverbial-temporal idiom "today," or "presently."
91:c I.e. the comprehensive הַכֹּל (*hakkōl*); cf. the LXX's τὰ σύμπαντα (*ta sympanta*) herein and the NT's conceptual parallel τὰ πάντα (*ta panta*).
92:a Or, translating the לוּלֵי . . . אָז (*lûlê . . . 'āz*) protasis/apodosis with its negative emphasis: "*If* Your law *had not been* my delight, *then* I would have . . ." (emphasis added).
92:b DSS (Q11) reads בעווני (*ḇᶜwwhy*), i.e. "in my iniquity"; contra. LXX, Targum, Vulgate, etc. which all agree with the MT.
93:a I.e. an objective negation (i.e. לֹא [*lō'*]) amplified by לְעוֹלָם (*lᵉᶜôlām*).
93:b The Piel perfect of חיה (*ḥyh*) is taken historically herein, and correspondingly its semantical field of *to give life* is preferred over *to restore life* (cf. commentary below). It should also be noted that the DSS (Q11) reads חייתני (*ḥyytny*) along with the MT, i.e. there is no characteristic substitution in the *Psalms Scroll* of חונני (*ḥwnny*) for the MT's חייתני herein.
93:c I.e. instrumental בְּ (*bᵉ*).
94:a Lit. "I belong to You" (לְךָ־אָנִי [*lᵉḵā-'ᵃnî*]).
95:a LXX follows its own precedent (cf. vv. 53, 61) by rendering רְשָׁעִים (*rᵉšāᶜîm*) ἁμαρτωλοί (*hamartōloi*), "sinners."
95:b I.e. once again, asyndetonic antithetical parallelism.
95:c I.e. the intensive-reflexive, a Hithpolel of בִּין (*bîn*).
96:a Lit. "end" (קֵץ [*qeṣ*]).
96:b I.e. human completeness or perfection in this context; see Girdlestone, *Synonyms*, p. 95, and note the paraphrase of the

Targum which reads, "Of all 'that which was begun and has been finished' I have observed an end" (Jastrow, *Dictionary*, 2:1574).

96:c Obviously, yet another occurrence of asyndetonic antithetical parallelism.

Synopsis and Outline

After climbing up steeply through some very forbidding terrain the spiritually cramping muscles of the man of God have been pushed seemingly beyond their limit and are in desperate need of the kind of rest that only stable ground can provide. Some sure-footed territory is discovered by our psalmist on the firm high plateau of the *Lāmed̠* and *Mêm* stanzas. There he finds respectively both rest and refreshment prior to his taxing descent which will take him through yet more of life's crags, caves, and crevices.

From his lofty vantage point in *Lāmed̠* he feasts the eyes of his heart upon "the great certainties."[1] First, by meditating upon the attributes of the Word of God and the God of the Word, additionally illustrated by the handiwork of God, he feeds upon Divine *stabilities* in verses 89–91. Then in verses 92–96 he drinks deeply from the vessel of special revelation which brims with its supernatural *sufficiency*.

These Divine consistencies are surfaced and interrelated throughout the development of this refreshing stanza by semantical, theological, and stylistic means. Semantically, a rapid-fire burst of words which denote stability launches these eight verses. The roots נצב (*nṣb̠*), אמן (*'mn*), כון (*kwn*) and עמד (*ᶜmd̠*) find their common denominator in the concepts of permanence,[2] immutability, consistency, reliability, etc. In application, these

[1] Kidner's fitting caption for this strophe (*Psalms 73–150*, p. 426).

[2] It is interesting that the LXX renders both נצב (in v. 89b) and עמד (in vv. 90b and 91a) with διαμένω (*diamenō*), "to stay permanently, remain permanently, continue" (Thayer, *Lexicon*, p. 140).

affirmations of Divine *dependability* bolster the child of God. Furthermore, through theological development, the fidelity of God (v. 90a) guarantees the dependability of His special revelation (v. 89) as confirmed by His general revelation (vv. 90b–91).[3] Then verses 92–96 leave the illustration of general revelation behind and return to the introductory verity of special revelation; however, with a new applicational focus, the sufficiency of God's Word in a fallen (cf. esp. v. 95) and finite (cf. esp. v. 96) world. These stylistic contrasts bring a great deal of resolution to this new focus of sufficiency.

The following outline is an attempt at mapping out the subtle integration of these major themes in *Lāmeḏ* (i.e. the Person of God, the permanence of His Word, the preservation of His universe, and the consequent perseverance of His children).

There are two consistencies upon which the child of God may always depend.

1A. (vv. 89–91) The stability of God and revelation.
  1B. (v. 89) His special revelation is stable.
    1C. (v. 89a) The focal-point of this stability.
    2C. (v. 89b) The firmness of this stability.
  2B. (v. 90a) His personal revelation is stable.
  3B. (vv. 90b–91) His general revelation is stable:
    1C. (v. 90b) Via creation.
    2C. (v. 90c–91) Via preservation.
2A. (vv. 92–96) The sufficiency of God's special revelation (i.e. His Word).
  1B. (vv. 92–94) This sufficiency includes all areas of faith and practice.
    1C. (v. 92) The Word's sufficiency in testimony.
    2C. (vv. 93–94) The Word's sufficiency in salvation:
      1D. (v. 93) Considered historically.
      2D. (v. 94) Considered progressively.

[3] Allen well argues that "the stable universe is a visible token of Yahweh's faithfulness" (*Psalms 101–150*, p. 143).

2B. (v. 95) This sufficiency meets attacks from the world.
 1C. (v. 95a) The reality of them.
 2C. (v. 95b) The relief from them.
3B. (v. 96) This sufficiency transcends human limitations.
 1C. (v. 96a) The limitation of the finite.
 2C. (v. 96b) The liberation of the infinite.

Commentary

It has been observed generally that "the *lamed* strophe contrasts what stands with what perishes."[4] Verse 89 emphasizes the positive side of a prevalent biblical contrast[5] when it affirms that the Word of the LORD continually stands firm. The introductory לְעוֹלָם (*l^ecôlām*), whether taken unrestrictively as "forever" or "always"[6] or restrictively as "from old,"[7] adverbially amplifies the concept of duration[8] which is not only semantically present in the root נצב (*nṣb*)[9] but also is syntactically enhanced by its participial form (i.e. נִצָּב [*niṣṣāb*]). Here the Niphal participle signifies something which is "standing firm,"[10] i.e. "firmly"[11] or "unalterably fixed."[12] As modified by בַּשָּׁמָיִם (*baššāmāyim*), lit. "in heaven," the

---

4 Ibid.

5 E.g. Isa 40:6–8; cf. 1 Pet 1:24–25 in its motivational context.

6 BDB, p. 762; notice that they categorize its occurrence in Ps 119:89 under "continuous existence . . . of God's laws" (ibid.).

7 Cf. Dahood, *Psalms*, 3:153.

8 Cf. Girdlestone, *Synonyms*, pp. 316–17, on לְעוֹלָם and its Greek counterpart εἰς τὸν αἰῶνα (*eis ton aiōna*).

9 It should be mentioned that the vocative יהוה, with its theological associations of eternality and immutability, also significantly contributes to this verse's particular emphasis on stability.

10 BDB, p. 662; cf. the Targum's קָיָם (*qayām*) with emphases upon existing, lasting, enduring, etc. (Jastrow, *Dictionary*, 2:1359).

11 Anderson, *Psalms*, 2:831.

12 Alexander, *Psalms*, 3:177.

reference seems to portray a "heaven-like stability."[13] Obviously, in verse 89, the focal-point of such a portrait of firmness is the LORD's Word, i.e. דְּבָרְךָ (*d^e^bār^e^kā*). Furthermore, in this particular setting (cf. vv. 89–91), דָּבָר (*dābār*) encompasses not only "the written word" but also "the expression of God's all-embracing purpose and will."[14]

The invested stability of special revelation (i.e. v. 89) and of general revelation (cf. vv. 90b–91) is derived from the inherent stability of God's Person (i.e. v. 90a).[15] Therefore, recognizing that all manifestations of reliability[16] flow out of this Personal Well-Spring, the child of God extols his LORD's absolute fidelity at the outset of verse 90: "Your faithfulness (i.e. אֱמוּנָה [*'ĕmûnâ*]) *continues* throughout all generations" (i.e. לְדֹר וָדֹר [*l^e^dōr wādōr*]).[17] Jepsen respectively outlines the generalized thrust of אֱמוּנָה, its association with God (as herein), and that association's commensurate significance for the believer when he comments:

---

[13] I.e. "It has heaven as its standing place, and therefore it also has the qualities of heaven" (Delitzsch, *Psalms*, 3:254). Contra. Soll, "Psalm 119," p. 192, who renders בְּ + נָצַב (*nāṣab* + *b^e^*) "stationed over," i.e. as a reference to "the word's authority over the heavens." Although (as Soll argues) a precedent for this translation and interpretation may be noted in the creation theology of certain psalms, a slightly stronger philological precedent seems to support the traditionally accepted locative interpretation of נִצָּב בַּשָּׁמָיִם. From the root also comes the feminine noun מַצֵּבָה (*maṣṣēbâ*), a monument or pillar, esp. a personal monument (cf. BDB, p. 663, for renderings and scriptural references; also recall the extra-biblical significance of such *stela*). It is quite possible that the terminology of Ps 119:89b alludes to the Word pictured as God's eternal monument firmly foundationed in His own heavenly presence.

[14] Anderson, *Psalms*, 2:831; cf. Allen, *Psalms 101–150*, p. 137, and Soll, "Psalm 119," pp. 77, 194–95.

[15] The preliminary discussion (*see* Overview) which related the attributes of the Word to their Source in its Author should be recalled. Various parallelisms have and will continue to confirm this phenomenon as the examination of the psalm's 176 verses continues.

[16] Cf. אֱמוּנָה (*'ĕmûnâ*) in vv. 30, 75, 86, 138.

[17] לְדֹר וָדֹר is one of the biblical idioms "used to indicate endless time" (*TWOT*, s.v. "דּוּר (*dûr*)," by R. Culver, 1:186–87). For a near parallel to Ps 119:90a, cf. and contra. Ps 100:5c.

> *'emunah* denotes the conduct of a person corresponding to his own inner being. . . . [It] is used of God's conduct, which corresponds to the nature of his deity. . . . It is God's stability, which is a true reflection of his deity, that is motivation for calling on him in time of distress and for praising him.[18]

Indeed, God's "total dependability"[19] is an indispensable ingredient for the survival and service of His disciples throughout all ages.

In verses 90b–91 another (cf. v. 89) theological tangent spins off the nuclear truth just capsulized in verse 90a. Concerning the relationship of verses 90b–91 to their immediately preceding context Kidner's brief comments serve as an adequate introduction: "A striking feature of these verses is the coupling of God's creative, world-sustaining word with His law for man. Both are the product of the same ordering mind."[20] With the words כּוֹנַנְתָּ אֶרֶץ (*kônantā 'ereṣ*), "You established the earth," the illustration of God's creation comes to mind first. The Polel perfect of כּוּן (*kûn*) exhibits various meanings, e.g. to "make firm, set up, establish,"[21] but herein its setting suggests an inceptive nuance, i.e. bringing "the totality of land"[22] into existence.[23] Such an acknowledgment carries with it a measure of assurance for the child of God: "As God's

[18] *TDOT*, s.v. "אָמַן *'āman*," by A. Jepsen, 1:320; cf. his helpful treatment of other attributes in parallelism with אֱמוּנָה (ibid., p. 319).

[19] Scott's general synopsis of God's אֱמוּנָה (*TWOT*, s.v. "אָמַן (*'āman*)," by J. Scott, 1:52).

[20] Kidner, *Psalms 73–150*, p. 426.

[21] BDB, p. 466.

[22] Holladay's most inclusive rendering for אֶרֶץ (William L. Holladay, *A Concise Hebrew and Aramaic Lexicon of the Old Testament* [Grand Rapids: William B. Eerdmans Publishing Company, 1971], p. 28).

[23] On interpreting כּוּן as a verb of creation note the LXX's ἐθεμελίωσας (*ethemeliōsas*), "You have 'foundationed'" the earth. For theological parallels, Ps 33:6–9; Heb 11:3; etc. should be compared, and for an explicit Christological connection, see Col 1:16.

work in the creation of the universe is constant, it testifies to the permanence of His attributes of faithfulness which governs His relationship with man."[24]

Immediately, the psalmist's mind turns to a corollary illustration which functions similarly, the phenomenon of God's preservation of that which He originally created (i.e. vv. 90c–91).[25] The two occurrences of עָמַד (*ᶜāmad*) in verses 90c and 91a serve "as a practical proof and as a scene of His infinite, unchangeable faithfulness."[26] The first verb is feminine singular, standing obviously in contextual concord with the preceding אֶרֶץ (*'ereṣ*); however, the second form is third common plural. Consequently, a host of potential subjects have been proposed by interpreters; for example:[27] (1) God's "judgments" (מִשְׁפָּטִים [*mišpāṭîm*]);[28] (2) "the day (הַיּוֹם [*hayyôm*]) and the night" [subjectively supplying the latter member of the alleged couplet]; (3) the ensuing "all things" (הַכֹּל [*hakkōl*]) of verse 91b;[29] and (4) "the heavens [by semantical suggestion from v. 89] and the earth" (v. 90b). The last interpretation seems to be the most plausible and also carries with it the greatest number of supporters historically.[30]

The first portion of the *Lāmed* stanza closes with a vivid personification: כִּי הַכֹּל עֲבָדֶיךָ (*kî hakkōl ᶜᵃbādeykā*), "for all things are

[24] Cohen, *Psalms*, p. 406.

[25] Cf. Heb 1:3 in the NT along with Col 1:17 for the explicitly Christological connection.

[26] Delitzsch, *Psalms*, 3:254–55.

[27] For examples and interactions, see Moll, *Psalms*, pp. 591–92; Delitzsch, *Psalms*, 3:255; and Anderson, *Psalms*, 2:832.

[28] The מִשְׁפָּטִים in this context should not be restricted merely to the written word (cf. the LXX's first departure from κρίματα [*krimata*] or κρίσιν [*krisin*, v. 84] here at v. 91 with its τῇ διατάξει [*tē diataxei*]). This prepositional idiom at the outset of v. 91 could be rendered quite generally as "by Your appointment" (cf. Anderson, *Psalms*, p. 832; Kidner, *Psalms 73–150*, p. 426; Delitzsch, *Psalms*, 3:255; Moll, *Psalms*, p. 591; etc.).

[29] For support see Delitzsch, *Psalms*, 3:255.

[30] Note the conclusions of Soll, "Psalm 119," p. 192; and Allen, *Psalms 101–150*, p. 137.

Your servants" (v. 91b).[31] This affirmation is literally as inclusive as the universe;[32] "the [whole] ordered world" in view herein pays "homage to its Master."[33] In retrospect, the psalmist's thinking has followed discernible theological trails: his God is stable (applicationally, cf. Hab 1:12); his God's Word is stable (applicationally, cf. 1 Kgs 8:56); his God's created and preserved world is stable (applicationally, cf. Jer 33:25–26); therefore, he, being a child of God, is secure (applicationally, cf. Ps 102:25–28).[34] "Because of who God is, the survival of God's people is assured."[35]

A conditional hypothetical contemplation[36] functioning as a testimony (v. 92) pivots the psalmist's thoughts in the direction of the sufficiency of his LORD's special revelation (vv. 92–96). In the protasis of his contemplation (v. 92a) the man of God returns to a recurrent testimony, that God's inscripturated direction for living[37] has been his[38] delight.[39] He understood that "devotion to God's Torah is the only means of sustenance: it is the divinely intended channel of true life."[40] The depth of his understanding of

---

[31] Interestingly, after citing Ps 119:91, Erickson makes the following systematic-theological observation: "While all ends are part of God's plan, all means are as well" (Erickson, *Christian Theology*, p. 353).

[32] On this synecdochical employment of articular כֹּל (*kōl*), i.e. the universe with everyone and everything in it, see BDB, pp. 482–83; cf. Ps 103:19b.

[33] Allen, *Psalms 101–150*, p. 143.

[34] Or, more theocentrically expressed: all exhibitions of stability flow from the unfathomable reservoir of God's personal fidelity through His Word and created world unto His children.

[35] Soll, "Psalm 119," p. 194; for his expanded treatment, see pp. 193–94.

[36] See Davidson, *Hebrew Syntax*, § 131; cf. Williams, *Hebrew Syntax*, § 459 and note his example of Judg 14:18 as a syntactical parallel. Also, see the εἰ μὴ ὅτι . . . τότε (*ei mē hoti . . . tote*) syntactical correlation of the LXX.

[37] I.e. תּוֹרָה (*tôrâ*).

[38] Once again the intimate fellowship between the psalmist and his God is detected through the juxtaposition of the 2ms suffix with תּוֹרָה and the 1cs suffix with שַׁעֲשֻׁעִים (*ša*$^{c\breve{a}}$*šu*^{c}*îm*).

[39] I.e., שַׁעֲשֻׁעִים deriving from the root שעע (*š*^{cc}), to "treat fondly, caress" (Holladay, *Concise Lexicon*, p. 380); cf. the plural intensive noun form in vv. 24, 77, 143, 174.

[40] Allen, *Psalms 101–150*, p. 143.

this verity is conveyed in the apodosis of this testimony (v. 92b) wherein he affirms that without God's sufficient Word he would have died[41] in his affliction[42] "because he would have been without any force to encourage him to persist."[43] By stripping off the hypothetical vehicle of verse 92 and by phrasing the psalmist's affirmations more positively within their contextual setting, Delitzsch has appropriately condensed the disciple's testimony: "Joy in this ever sure, all-conditioning word has upheld the poet in his affliction."[44] Didactically, God's sufficiency is more than a match for our suffering.

From sufficiency and suffering, the man of God moves on quite naturally to sufficiency and salvation, first considering it historically (v. 93) then progressively (v. 94).[45] The basis[46] of his introductory reminiscence about never forgetting his LORD's precepts (v. 93a) seems to encompass not only God's present ministry of revitalization[47] but also His initial granting of life to the psalmist.[48] The disciple's respect for the Word of God and his reverence for the God of the Word, although closely related, are not identical. That is crystal clear since he affirmed that his life came to him

---

[41] I.e. אָבַד (*'āḇaḏ*), in the Qal, "to perish"; cf. the apparently intentional connection with the Piel occurrence (to cause to perish, i.e. to destroy) in v. 95.

[42] An occurrence of the explicit עָנְיִ (*ᶜŏnî*), i.e. affliction, suffering, misery, frustration, etc. (cf. vv. 50, 153); note the Vulgate's *pressura* herein.

[43] Cohen, *Psalms*, p. 406; i.e. "without Torah as his delight the psalmist would have given up hope" (Soll, "Psalm 119," p. 195).

[44] Delitzsch, *Psalms*, 3:255.

[45] Structurally, respective occurrences of פִּקּוּדֶיךָ (*piqqûdeyḵā*), כִּי (*kî*) clauses launching the second members of the bicola, and a conceptual development with לְךָ־אָנִי (*lᵉḵā-'ᵃnî*) standing at the nexus, contribute to the coherence of vv. 93–94. Thematic unity is supplied largely through the soteriological denotations of the roots חיה (*ḥyh*) and ישׁע (*yšᶜ*).

[46] I.e. the כִּי (*kî*) clause of v. 93b.

[47] I.e. חיה (*ḥyh*) as *to sustain alive*, its widest field of usage; cf. Girdlestone, *Synonyms*, pp. 123, 125.

[48] I.e. חיה as *to make alive*, its narrowest field of usage; cf. ibid., p. 123.

from God[49] through the instrumentality of His precepts.[50] Since "he traces the life from the channel to the source and places the glory where it is due,"[51] he may not be accused of bibliolatry.

Because God had graciously granted him life he could proclaim "I'm Yours"![52] This highly compacted possessive idiom, לְךָ־אֲנִי (*lᵉkā-'ănî*), lit. "I belong to You," is deeply profound and exceedingly significant. Positionally, he is God's "possession and property,"[53] and therefore, propositionally,[54] he comes boldly to the 'throne of grace' with his plea for deliverance: הוֹשִׁיעֵנִי (*hôšîᶜēnî*), "save me!"[55] Although progressive manifestations of Divine deliverance (i.e. his plea, v. 94b) are looked upon as anticipated because of his personal relationship with God (i.e. his position, v. 94a), they are also regarded by him as appropriate in accordance with a secondary factor, his persistent pursuit of God's precepts (i.e. his practice, v. 94c).[56] Indeed, "consecration is a good plea for preservation."[57]

---

49 Note the 2 m s verb with 1 c s suffix, i.e. חִיִּיתָנִי (*ḥiyîṯānî*).

50 The preposition בְּ (*bᵉ*) herein connotes means or instrumentality, and its 3 m pl pronominal suffix refers back to פִּקּוּדֶיךָ (*piqqûdeykā*), "*God's* precepts." For a close conceptual parallel in the NT, cf. Rom 1:16 with 10:17.

51 Spurgeon, *Treasury of David*, 7:215.

52 Cf. the "boast" of Jer 9:24.

53 Delitzsch, *Psalms*, 3:255.

54 As Anderson well notes, the לְךָ־אֲנִי "forms the basis for his appeal for help" (*Psalms*, 2:832).

55 The force of יָשַׁע (*yāšaᶜ*), to save, deliver, rescue, help, etc., herein refers to the LORD's "saving care over individuals, especially over those who in their helplessness and trouble need and claim His protection" (Girdlestone, *Synonyms*, p. 124). Concerning this acute invocation, Allen rightly notes that it is not intended to demean the previously documented "steady infusion of truth and grace" mediated through the Word of God, but "there may be need of direct and dramatic intervention in the believer's life. It is for this that the staccato prayer . . . craves" (*Psalms 101–150*, p. 143).

56 Cf. דָּרַשׁ (*dāraš*) in vv. 2, 10 (pursuing God; cf. v. 2), 45.

57 Spurgeon, *Treasury of David*, 7:215.

Perched upon his high plateau of stability and sufficiency, the man of God looks back down upon his malevolent persecutors in verse 95. His transcendent perspective, assuring and comforting as it is, does not erase the reality of their commitment to his demise.[58] The vivid terminology he employs confirms his awareness of their intentions and his own precarious situation. First,he labels them "wicked men" (רְשָׁעִים [*rᵉšāᶜîm*]), calling attention to their documented criminality.[59] Then he portrays them as being poised like predators through his selection of a Piel verb form from קָוָה (*qāwâ*), "to wait for" or "to lie in wait for."[60] The root of this word exhibits a connection to the concepts of twisting or stretching with a resultant significance of "tenseness" or "eagerness."[61] And finally, as part of his personal experience with attacks from the world,[62] the persecuted pilgrim exposes their unwavering intention which just happens to be his personal extermination.[63]

It would seem that the time was ripe for a justifiable burst of outrage issuing in an imprecation;[64] however, once again, this dedicated disciple shunned outcries of victimization and focused his attention upon those internal resolves which issue in appro-

---

[58] As Soll points out the previously noted consolation "does not remove the psalmist's need or danger . . . , but it does put them in perspective" ("Psalm 119," p. 195).

[59] Cf. BDB, p. 957. Girdlestone tries to characterize them as agitators (*Synonyms*, p. 81). He may be on shaky ground etymologically, but conceptionally this certainly is one descriptive facet of the רְשָׁעִים in the OT.

[60] BDB, p. 875; note the cited cognate words and the poetic parallels in Ps 56:7 (v. 6, Eng).

[61] Holladay, *Concise Lexicon*, p. 315. One could envision the spring-like tension of a big cat ready to pounce upon its prey; however, it probably depicts the straining anticipation of a hunter in the light of the other images he employs for his enemies (cf. vv. 61, 85, 110).

[62] This psalmist, had he lived in the NT era when Paul penned 2 Tim 3:12 and Peter wrote 1 Pet 4:12, etc., could have participated in a deeply sincere and resounding response of "Amen."

[63] The purpose infinitive in the causative Piel (remembering the preparatory occurrence of the Qal of אָבַד [*'ābad*] in v. 92), i.e. לְאַבְּדֵנִי (*lᵉ'abbᵉdēnî*), to cause to perish, destroy, kill, exterminate, etc.

[64] E.g., cf. David in 2 Sam 12:5–6.

priate responses.[65] According to custom,[66] he was showing himself attentive and diligently considering[67] the testimonies of his LORD (v. 95b). Both in perspective and in practice he faced attacks from the world according to this Divine precedent.[68]

An exceedingly comprehensive statement about the sufficiency of Scripture closes the *Lāmeḏ* stanza, and it comes characteristically packaged in a poignant contrast.[69] The key verb רָאִיתִי (*rāʾîṯî*), "I have seen," reveals the empirical nature of the psalmist's observations.[70] In his first observation (i.e. v. 96a) he has seen, throughout the course of his life, the dead end (קֵץ [*qēṣ*])[71] of[72] *all* (human or earthly) *perfection*,[73] i.e. after thoroughly examining the utmost limits of all things human,[74] everything falls short.[75]

---

[65] E.g., cf. Daniel in Dan 6:10ff.

[66] Taking the imperfect tense habitually or customarily.

[67] Cf. BDB, p. 107, on the significance of this reflexive form of בִּין (*bîn*).

[68] It is as if he were a proleptic example of Jesus' teaching in John 17:14–17.

[69] Scroggie's anecdote well capsulizes the members of this antithetical couplet: "The finite and the infinite" (*Psalms*, p. 183).

[70] For this reason, Kidner is correct in arguing that "this verse could well be a summary of Ecclesiastes, where every earthly enterprise has its day and comes to nothing, and where only in God and His commandments do we get beyond these frustrating limits" (*Psalms 73–150*, pp. 426–27).

[71] A noun form based upon the verb קָצַץ (*qāṣaṣ*), to cut off (BDB, p. 893). In this context the noun could well be translated "limit."

[72] Cf. the introductory preposition לְ (*lᵉ*), i.e. *in reference* or *as applied to*, etc.

[73] It is interesting that both כָּל (*kol*) and תִּכְלָה (*tiḵlâ*) come from כָּלָה (*kālâ*), mutually reinforcing the idea of "to be finished" or "completed" (cf. Anderson, *Psalms*, 2:833), i.e. "he knows from experience that all (earthly) perfection . . . has an end (inasmuch as, having reached its height, it changes into its opposite) . . ." (Delitzsch, *Psalms*, 3:255).

[74] A modification of Girdlestone's paraphrase of v. 96a (*Synonyms*, p. 95).

[75] Cf. Allen's paraphrase of v. 96a (*Psalms 101–150*, p. 130).

God's Word, however, stands in stark contrast in that it is "the one thing in the world with a window on eternity."[76] It bears the impress of the Infinite rather than the finite.[77] By experience, the LORD's commandment (מִצְוָתְךָ [*miṣwōṯ^e^kā*]) has proven itself to be to the man of God רְחָבָה . . . מְאֹד (*r^e^ḥāḇâ . . . m^e^'ōḏ*), "very broad" or "so wide in its scope,"[78] i.e. immeasurable[79] or limitless,[80] and also by contextual implication, *liberating*.[81] What fresh air this disciple has discovered on his high plateau of stability and sufficiency!

---

[76] Soll, "Psalm 119," p. 195.

[77] For an interesting parallel employment of the adjective רְחָבָה (*r^e^ḥāḇâ*), cf. Job 11:7–9. Therein (in Job) it is applied to the God of the Word, while herein (in Ps 119:96) it is applied to the Word of God. The significance of the verb form of this root, utilized back in 119:32b, also needs to be brought to mind.

[78] Allen's rendering (*Psalms 101–150*, p. 130).

[79] Moll, *Psalms*, p. 592.

[80] Soll, "Psalm 119," p. 195; Delitzsch adds "unlimited in its duration and verification" (*Psalms*, 3:255).

[81] Cf. Soll, "Psalm 119," p. 195. Were our psalmist alive today he would not have any problem understanding and practicing the truth of 1 John 5:2–3.

מ

MEM STANZA
(vv. 97–104)

Translation and Notes

97 O how[a] I love Your law!
It *is* my meditation[b] continually.[c]

98 Your commandment[a] makes me wiser[b] than[c] my enemies,
because it[a] *is* mine forever.

99 I have had more insight[a] than all[b] my teachers,
because Your testimonies *are* my meditation.

100 I show myself to have[a] more understanding[b] than *the* aged,[c]
because I have kept[d] Your precepts.

101 I have withheld[a] my feet from every evil way,[b]
in order that I might keep[c] Your word.[d]

102 I have not turned aside[a] from Your judgments,
for You Yourself[b] have[a] instructed[c] me.

103 O how[a] smooth[b] Your words *are*[c] to my palate,
more than honey to my mouth!

104 I get understanding[a] from Your precepts;
therefore,[b] I hate every deceptive way.[c]

97:a "The originally interrogative מָה [*mâ*] is used to introduce exclamations of wonder or indignation=*O how!* . . ." (GKC, ¶ 148; cf. Williams, *Hebrew Syntax,* ¶ 127).

97:b The feminine noun שִׂיחָה (*śîḥâ*), "musing, study," i.e. meditation, with 1cs pronominal suffix; cf. its occurrence in v. 99 with possessive *Lāmed̲* and 1 c s suffix. The verbal occurrences of this root (שׂיח [*śyḥ*]) in vv. 15, 23, 27, 48, 78, 148 should also be compared.

97:c כָּל־הַיּוֹם (*kol-hayyōm*) is lit. "all the day"; cf. BDB, p. 481, on its adverbial impact.
98:a The consonantal text מצותך (*mṣwtk*) should be regarded as a singular; cf. the following (v. 98b) feminine singular pronoun (הִיא [*hîʾ*]) and the singular reading in the LXX.
98:b The wisdom root here is חכם (*ḥkm*).
98:c The first of three consecutive usages (i.e. v. 98a, v. 99a, v. 100a) of comparative מִן (*min*).
99:a The wisdom root here is שׂכל (*śkl*).
99:b The combination of comparative מִן (*min*) with כֹּל (*kōl*) is one of the ways to express the superlative degree in Hebrew (cf. GKC, § 133b).
100:a Stressing the reflexive stem (cf. BDB, p. 107).
100:b The wisdom root is בין (*byn*).
100:c Or, "elders" (זְקֵנִים [*zeqēnîm*]).
100:d Taking the perfect tense historically; or, taking it as a freeze-frame picture of customary or habitual behavior, it could be rendered "I keep."
101:a Cf. note 100:d on the perfect tense.
101:b Or, "path" for אֹרַח (*ʾōraḥ*).
101:c Once again, נָצַר (*nāṣar*; v. 100b) and שָׁמַר (*šāmar*; v. 101b) appear in consecutive verses as primary terms for obedience.
101:d The LXX reads as a plural.
102:a Again, cf. note 100:d.
102:b The verb plus emphatic אַתָּה (*ʾatâ*).
102:c This Hiphil perfect meaning to direct, teach, instruct (BDB, p. 435) comes from the root ירה (*yrh*) as does תּוֹרָה (*tôrâ*); it was the LORD Himself, who so-to-speak, "torahed" the psalmist. The Vulgate reads *inluminasti me*, looking upon this Divine ministry as one of illumination.
103:a Cf. note 97:a.
103:b מלץ (*mlṣ*) is a *hapax legomenon*; the LXX and Targum assume its connotation to be sweetness, apparently because of the illustration of דְּבַשׁ (*debaš*), "honey," which follows it in v. 103b.

103:c Early versions read אמרתך (*'mrtḵ*) as a plural, i.e. אמרתיך (*'mrtyḵ*), in concord with the 3 c pl verb. For commentary, see BDB, p. 57; Dahood, *Psalms*, 3:184; Davidson, *Hebrew Syntax*, § 115; and Delitzsch, *Psalms* 3:256.
104:a The wisdom root is בין (*byn*).
104:b The עַל־כֵּן (*ʿal-kēn*) emphasizes the reality of the results (cf. BDB, p. 487).
104:c Lit., "every path of falsehood." Cf. and contra. the כָּל־אֹרַח־שָׁקֶר (*kol-'ōraḥ-šāqer*) of v. 104b with the מִכָּל־אֹרַח רָע (*mikkol-'ōraḥ-rāʿ*) of v. 101a. The Targum's paraphrase of v. 104b is striking: "I hate every human being who lies."

Synopsis and Outline

In *Mêm*, testimony continues regarding the Divine sufficiencies, and sufficiency is these eight verses is characterized generally as that *wisdom* which comes *from* the God of the Word *through* the Word of God *to* the child of God (cf. Deut 4:5–6). Semantically, this theme is conveyed explicitly through occurrences of the roots חכם (*ḥḵm*; cf. v. 98), שׂכל (*śḵl*; cf. v. 99), בין (*byn*; cf. vv. 100, 104), and ירה (*yrh*; cf. v. 102). It also comes across implicitly and applicationally via references to the psalmist's preoccupation (cf. the noun שִׂיחָה [*śîḥâ*], "meditation," in vv. 97, 99) and pleasure (cf. the illustration of smoothness and/or possibly sweetness in v. 103).

The strophe's seemingly lopsided structure stems from the two exclamatory appearances of מָה (*mâ*, i.e. "O how!") which come at the outset of verses 97 and 103.[1] The remaining verses commence with the preposition מִן (*min*) which originally signified separation.[2] This basic signification is functionally discernible in verses 101 and 102, while comparative usages (cf. vv. 98, 99, 100;

[1] In these verses, cf. the ὡς (*hōs*) of the LXX and the *quam* of the Vulgate.
[2] See GKC, § 119 v–z; § 133 a–e.

also note v. 103b)[3] and one indication of source (or possibly cause; cf. v. 104) launch the affirmations of the other four verses.[4] Considered consecutively, these various uses of the preposition מִן (*min*) emphasize the compensation (vv. 98–100), the protection (vv. 101–102), and the illumination (v. 104) which are available to the man of God through the Divine sufficiencies (cf. 2 Tim 3:16–17). Obviously, all of these prepositional appearances combine to magnify the stanza's major message, the psalmist's gratitude for God's wisdom.

Strikingly, there are no requests in *Mêm*, and although his testimony moves on from one bold affirmation to another, the overall flow of it is doxological. What that disciple breathes out has unquestionably been affected by the sustaining atmosphere he breathes in at the top of that high plateau upon which he has temporarily settled.

In the light of these observations, two exclamations form the framework of the disciple's gratitude for Divine wisdom in verses 97–104.

- 1A. (vv. 97–102) The introductory exclamation concerning Divine wisdom.
  - 1B. (v. 97) The special adoration of this Divine wisdom.
    - 1C. (v. 97a) The confession of it.
    - 2C. (v. 97b) The confirmation of it.
  - 2B. (vv. 98–102) The special advantages of this Divine wisdom.
    - 1C. (v. 98) It gives prudence in the presence of antagonists.
    - 2C. (v. 99) It multiplies insight in the presence of intellectuals.
    - 3C. (v. 100) It increases discernment in the presence of the more experienced.

---

[3] Cf. the four corresponding occurrences of ὑπέρ (*hyper*) and *super* in the LXX and Vulgate respectively.

[4] For a survey of the primary functions of מִן, see Williams, *Hebrew Syntax*, §§ 315–327.

4C. (vv. 101–102) It grants direction in the presence of alternatives.
  1D. (v. 101) This direction is viewed from the positive (i.e., preventative) perspective.
  2D. (v. 102) This direction is viewed from the negative (i.e., prohibitive) perspective.

2A. (vv. 103–104) The summary exclamation concerning Divine wisdom.
  1B. (v. 103) The summary association of this Divine wisdom: the satisfaction of honey.
  2B. (v. 104) The summary advantage of this Divine wisdom: the suppression of sin.

Commentary

Energized by his meditations upon the stability and sufficiency of the Word of God in *Lāmeḏ*, the man of God explodes with his exclamation at the outset of *Mēm*: "O how I love Your law!" (v. 97a). That the confession of his love (v. 97a) immediately issues in a confirmation of it (v. 97b) is in keeping with the *biblical* essence of love. When the disciple speaks of love using the verb אָהֵב (*'āhēḇ*),[5] emotionality stands in the shadows backstage.[6] Biblically—through the Divine paradigm, covenantal connections, semantical parallelisms, and the word's prevalent situation in contexts of obedience[7]—the spotlight is upon *commitment* to someone or something.[8] In its present context that something is תּוֹרָה (*tôrâ*), the "revelation of the will of God for the life of man."[9]

---

[5] Cf. the appropriate usage of ἠγάπησα (*ēgapēsa*) in the LXX for the אָהַבְתִּי (*'āhaḇtî*) of the MT; contra. the off-semantical-center usage of רְחִימֵית (*rᵉḥîmêt*) in the Targum.

[6] On the word's secondary connotations of desire and affection, see Girdlestone, *Synonyms*, p. 110.

[7] Cf., e.g. Exod 20:6; Deut 7:6–8; 10:12; 11:13, 22; 19:9; 30:19–20; Josh 22:5; 1 Sam 18:1–3; Jer 31:3; etc. for a mosaic of the settings of אָהֵב in the OT.

[8] For a good synopsis of the root אהב (*'hḇ*) and its significance, see TDNT, "Love in the OT," by G. Quell, 1:21–35.

[9] Scroggie, *Psalms*, p. 171.

Nothing changes in the NT through its frequent employment of the ἀγαπάω (*agapaō*) word group,[10] except that the biblical spotlight is intensified.[11] Consequently, both אָהֵב / אַהֲבָה (*'āhēb* / *'ahᵃbâ*) and ἀγαπάω / ἀγάπη (*agapaō* / *agapē*) are utilized most frequently when there is a need for an emphasis upon obedience to God's special revelation. Wallis' synopsis and especially his applicational conclusion are noteworthy:

> Not only does love presuppose a concrete inner disposition . . . but it includes a conscious act in behalf of the person who is loved or the thing that is preferred. . . . He serves God actively who loves his commandments, precepts, and instructions (Ps. 119 *passim*).[12]

The first step towards outward obedience must be internal compliance, and so the documentation of the psalmist's love for the law begins with his thorough internalization of it (v. 97b).[13] Or, in the words of Leupold, "Evidence of this love is the fact that the writer meditates on this subject all the day."[14] It is because he "unceasingly occupies himself" with his LORD's *tôrâ* that he is privileged with the precious benefits which follow.[15]

In verses 98–100 the Word of God is seen as compensating the child of God with its transcendent wisdom in three sociological contexts of real life, respectively: adversity, 'academics', and age. Then in verses 101 and 102 its personal advantage is summarized when the disciple extols its indispensable help in the context of ethical alternatives. Not only is there a progression of profitability

---

10 Remembering that the LXX at v. 97 reads ἠγάπησα (*ēgapēsa*) providing a natural bridge to the NT's teaching on this vital issue of love.

11 Cf., e.g., John 3:16; 14:15, 21, 23–24; 15:9–10; 1 John 2:4–6; 5:1–3; 2 John 6a; etc. In the NT love is inextricably welded to discipleship and obedience.

12 *TDOT*, s.v. "אָהַב *'ahabh*," by G. Wallis, 1:105, 107.

13 I.e. שִׂיחָה (*śîḥâ*) + כָּל־הַיּוֹם (*kol-hayyôm*).

14 Leupold, *Psalms*, p. 844.

15 On the transitional significance of v. 97b, see Delitzsch, *Psalms*, 3:255; cf. Leupold, *Psalms*, p. 844.

in reference to God's Word in these verses, there is also a progression of responsibility in reference to God's child. The advantage that is the psalmist's in verse 98a is related to his *possession* of God's Word in verse 98b; the compensation he enjoys in verse 99a is tied to his *preoccupation* with God's Word (i.e. study, meditation) in verse 99b; and finally, his benefit from inscripturated wisdom praised in verse 100a is complemented by his *practice* (i.e. obedience) in verse 100b.[16] This progression of responsibility is then subsequently illustrated in verses 101 and 102.

In his first bold affirmation[17] the disciple revels in the reality that his LORD's commandment characteristically makes him wiser[18] than his crafty opponents.[19] When it comes to characterizing and illustrating divinely mediated wisdom, this causative (Piel) imperfect of the verb חָכַם (*ḥākam*),[20] to "make wise, teach wisdom,"[21] is especially suitable. Consistently in the OT the source of חכם (*ḥkm*) is God, and that which He imparts is wholly practical and ethical. "The essential idea of *ḥākam* represents a manner of thinking and attitude concerning life's experiences; including matters of general interest and basic morality."[22] Applicationally, "it is that adaptation of what we know to what

---

[16] For a similar progression of responsibility see Ezra 7:10.

[17] The first halves of vv. 98–102, phrased as stark indicatives, need to be received as facts, but they should not be looked upon as indications of pharisaical arrogance. What the psalmist had experienced was graciously mediated to him from God through His Word, as confirmed by the immediate and larger contexts of his affirmations.

[18] On this dynamic of the word of God, see Ps 19:8 (v. 7, Eng) and cf. 2 Tim 3:15–17 for an illustration.

[19] It is interesting that herein the Targum intensifies the comparative מִן (*min*) with the adverb יַתִּיר (*yattîr*), "more" (Jastrow, *Dictionary*, 1:604), lit. "'more wiser than' my enemies."

[20] Cf. the ἐσόφισας (*esophisas*) in the LXX which opens the door to the important σοφία (*sophia*) word group in the NT (cf. *TDNT*, s.v. "σοφία, σοφός, σοφίζω" by U. Wilckens and G. Fohrer, 7:489–96; 514–25).

[21] BDB, p. 314.

[22] *TWOT*, s.v. "חָכָם (*ḥākam*)," by L. Goldberg, 1:282.

we have to do."[23] This sustaining benefit belongs to the man of God because he is in possession of the Word of God (v. 98b).[24] Indeed, his ever-present[25] well of wisdom will never dry up.

The boast of verse 99a[26] is grounded upon the "because" (i.e. the כִּי [*kî*]) of verse 99b: "No conceit is implied in the claim. He had received instruction from many teachers, but he maintains that by constant meditation upon God's testimonies, he has obtained the truest discernment of Torah as the best guide of living."[27] That "discernment" which he had experienced in the presence of the intelligentsia[28] is fittingly conveyed through the root שׂכל (*śkl*).[29] Essentially a synonym of חכם (*ḥkm*) and בין (*byn*), שׂכל (*śkl*)[30] emphasizes

[23] Girdlestone, *Synonyms*, p. 74; cf. "cleverness and skill for the purpose of practical action" (*TDNT*, 7:476). For a few helpful comments on its ANE context, semantical parallels, etc., see *TDOT*, s.v. "חָכָם *chākham*," by H. Müller and M. Krause, 4:364–85; however, its thrust is best grasped in the context of the biblical wisdom writings (esp. those coming through the hand of Solomon) wherein it is explicitly and implicitly connected with the fear of the LORD.

[24] The possessive idiom הִיא־לִי (*hî'-lî*), although terse, is not lacking in impact; he *owns* God's commandment.

[25] I.e. לְעוֹלָם (*leʿôlām*); cf. v. 111a.

[26] For its ultimate setting, again cf. Jer 9:23–24.

[27] Cohen, *Psalms*, p. 407; cf. Alexander, *Psalms*, 3:179; and Anderson, *Psalms*, 2:833.

[28] Conjectures that he was engaging in a polemic directed at some *specific* (i.e. hellenizing) group of "teachers" (cf. the brief interactions of Moll, *Psalms*, p. 592; and Delitzsch, *Psalms*, 3:255) are just that. His opposition is better taken as general, i.e. "an opposition is indicated to a worldly wisdom whose source is not the word of revelation" (Moll, *Psalms*, p. 592). On some connections to the worldly wisdom nakedly exposed in the NT, note Kidner, *Psalms 73–150*, p. 427.

[29] The Aramaic's סכל (*skl*; cf. the Targum), e.g., "to become wise" (Jastrow, *Dictionary*, 2:990), is phonetically and semantically parallel. Interestingly, the LXX renders both the הִשְׂכַּלְתִּי (*hiśkaltî*) herein and the אֶתְבּוֹנָן (*'eṯbônān*) of v. 100 by συνῆκα (*synēka*), the aorist indicative of συνίημι (*syniēmi*) which implies "to put (as it were) the perception with the thing perceived; to set or join together in the mind, i.e. *to understand*" (Thayer, *Lexicon*, p. 605).

[30] For a helpful catalog of citations and parallelisms involving these three crucial wisdom words, see *NIDNTT*, s.v. "σοφία," by J. Goetzmann, 3:1027–28; and *TDOT*, s.v. "בִּין *bîn*," by H. Ringgren, 2:100–02. Note the association of these terms with Daniel in Dan 1:4, 17, 20; etc.

prudence, insight, wisdom, understanding, etc.[31] The nuance of the Hiphil[32] verb herein is to "have insight, comprehension."[33] Psalm 14:2–3 makes it absolutely clear that fallen man does not possess such sagacity innately. It must come to him, as it did to this man of God, by grace from above.[34]

The compensation that God's Word brings in verse 100 is conveyed through בִּין (*byn*).[35] In the Hithpolel stem[36] the term's most frequent connotation is to show "oneself attentive, consider diligently."[37] However, "this 'giving heed' or 'considering' leads to comprehending and understanding: . . . Ps. 119:104, 'Through thy precepts "I get understanding"' (cf. v. 100, 'I "understand more" than the aged, for I keep [*natsar*] thy precepts')."[38]

This bold affirmation is particularly striking when it is placed within its cultural context, since "among primitive peoples authority seems naturally to be invested in those who by virtue of greater age and, consequently, experience [i.e. the זְקֵנִים (*zeqēnîm*)] are best fitted to govern"[39] and teach. But this man of God solemnly affirms that "the source of his understanding of life is superior" to those "whose knowledge is obtained from long experience."[40] Accordingly, "true wisdom does not depend upon a lifelong experience but rather upon obedience to God's *precepts*."[41]

---

[31] Cf. its noun form שֶׂכֶל (*śeḵel*) in BDB, p. 968; and in *TWOT*, s.v. "שָׂכַל (*śākal*)," by L. Goldberg, 2:877.

[32] Of this root's verbal occurrences, 72 of 74 are in the Hiphil stem.

[33] BDB, p. 968.

[34] Cf. Jas 1:17; 3:13–18.

[35] For a general semantical survey, see Girdlestone, *Synonyms*, p. 74.

[36] Cf. here and vv. 95 and 104.

[37] BDB, p. 107.

[38] *TDOT*, 2:104. It should also be noted that בִּין (*bîn*) is not an innate possession of man in general nor the man of God in particular. These affirmations in the Hithpolel need to be placed alongside of his passionate pleas for בִּין; cf. the Hiphil imperatives in vv. 27, 34, 73, 125, 144 and 169.

[39] *ISBE* (1939), s.v. "Elder," by Stearns, 2:924; he goes on to note that "from the first, the Hebrews held this view . . ." (ibid.). For an explicit OT illustration, cf. Job 32:4 in its context, and for an implicit NT illustration, cf. 1 Tim 4:12.

[40] Cohen, *Psalms*, p. 407. Again, the scenario of Daniel comes to mind.

[41] Anderson, *Psalms*, 2:833.

The remaining verses of this stanza major on, largely through life-style illustrations, concrete ethical applications of this divinely imparted wisdom.[42] Verses 101 and 102 are conceptionally parallel, both stressing the disciple's active avoidance of apostasy.[43] In compliance with the solemn truths of Proverbs 4:14 and 4:18, his first testimony is that he had "restrained" or "withheld"[44] his feet from every evil way[45] for the purpose of keeping God's word.[46] "This verse teaches clearly that the keeping of God's word is something incompatible with treading any evil path."[47] "One cannot be lax about evil and expect to profit in the use of the Word."[48]

In the OT, the combination of the verb סוּר (*sûr*), "to turn aside,"[49] and an ablative usage of the preposition מִן (*min*) is a tandem vehicle for expressing apostasy.[50] As Patterson briefly sum-

---

[42] Figures for the pathway of life (e.g. אֹרַח [*'ōraḥ*], vv. 101, 104; רֶגֶל [*regel*], v. 101), a reference to Divine direction along that pathway (cf. יָרָה [*yārâ*], v. 102b), and the psalmist's obedience (e.g. v. 101b) exemplified in his restraints (cf. vv. 101a, 102a) and reactions (e.g. vv. 103, 104b) integrate this mosaic.

[43] By semantical illustration (i.e. כָּלָא [*kālā'*], v. 101) and syntactical illustration (i.e. לֹא [*lō'*], v. 102) the negative side of responsibilities relating to sanctification surfaces; cf., e.g., Ps 1:1.

[44] Cf. BDB, p. 476, on כָּלָא (*kālā'*); also note the Targum's utilization of מְנַע (*m^e na^c*), "to withhold" (Jastrow, *Dictionary*, 1:802); the LXX's choice of κωλύω (*kōlyō*), "to cut off, cut short, hinder, prevent, forbid, restrain," etc. (Thayer, *Lexicon*, p. 367); and the Vulgate's *prohibui*.

[45] מִכָּל־אֹרַח רָע (*mikkol- 'ōraḥ rā^c*) is a comprehensive phrase for *all bad behavior* (for a brief synopsis, see Anderson, *Psalms*, 2:833–34); cf. כָּל־אֹרַח שָׁקֶר (*kol-'ōraḥ šāqer*) in v. 104, i.e. *all deceptive behavior*.

[46] This bold assertion is anticipatory of and balanced by the enablement he will shortly acknowledge in v. 105; note how רֶגֶל (*regel*) and yet another metaphor for the highways and byways of life (i.e. נָתִיב [*nāṯîḇ*]) bind vv. 101 and 105 together. V. 101 is also conceptually reminiscent of v. 9.

[47] Alexander, *Psalms*, 3:180; cf. Cohen, *Psalms*, p. 407.

[48] Leupold, *Psalms*, p. 845; he also appropriately argued that "this verse presents a searching test of true wisdom: Does it enable a man to shun evil?" (ibid., p. 844).

[49] BDB, p. 693; cf. some cognates which amplify this concept with the attendant idea of rebellion (ibid.).

[50] Cf. Exod 32:8; Deut 9:12; Judg 2:17; Jer 17:5; etc.; cf. סוּר (*sûr*) without מִן (*min*) in Ps 14:3. "To turn aside from God's ordinances means to neglect and to disobey them (Mal. 3:7)" (Anderson, *Psalms*, 2:834).

marizes, "the root [i.e. סוּר] is often used of Israel's apostasy. In many cases it is translated 'turn aside/away'. . . . Conversely, 'not to turn aside' was a way of affirming a man's steadfastness before the Lord. . . ."[51] The latter case is precisely what this man of God is objectively[52] affirming in verse 102a.[53] His boast however is grounded upon God's blessing (v. 102b).[54] God *Himself*[55] had responded to His child's earnest solicitation for Divine direction.[56] In the light of this, Allen skillfully distills the pedagogical implications of our psalmist-pilgrim's testimony when he asserts:

> Yahweh is acclaimed as wisdom teacher via his Torah. V 102b makes clear that it is no do-it-yourself manual which God has handed over to man to use as best he can. It is the written part of a life long teach-in.[57]

---

[51] *TWOT*, s.v. "סוּר (*sûr*)," by R. Patterson, 2:621. Note how this combination also perpetuates the metaphors for the journey of life.

[52] On the objective negation לֹא (*lōʾ*) cf. its force in v. 3. Barnes well clarifies the issue herein: "This cannot mean that he had *never* done this, but that as a great rule of life he had not done it. The character and aim of his life had been obedience, not disobedience" (*Psalms*, 3:207).

[53] He was following the precedent of Joshua's charge (1:7) and the examples of Hezekiah and Josiah (2 Kgs 18:5–6; 22:2).

[54] As Perowne argues, "This is the secret of all the previous boast, this is the source of all his wisdom" (*Psalms*, 2:360). Cf. Alexander, *Psalms*, 3:180.

[55] Again, stressing the emphatic אַתָּה (*ʾattâ*): "The word *thou* is emphatic. Here is the guarantor of biblical truth, and the One who alone opens the disciple's eyes to see it" (Kidner, *Psalms 73–150*, p. 427). "Following such an Instructor, he could not go astray" (Cohen, *Psalms*, p. 407).

[56] This Hiphil *perfect* (v. 102), i.e. הוֹרֵתָנִי (*hôrēṯānî*) from יָרָה (*yārâ*), "to direct, teach, instruct" (BDB, p. 435), pointing to the fact of the LORD's direction down the highway of the psalmist's life, needs to be compared with the disciple's earnest plea which he previously expressed in v. 33, i.e. הוֹרֵנִי (*hôrēnî*), the Hiphil *imperative* built upon the same root. On the metaphorical continuity maintained through the appearance of this root ירה (*yrh*), see Alexander, *Psalms*, 3:180.

[57] Allen, *Psalms 101–150*, p. 143.

As previously noted, this stanza's final exclamation contains both a summary association and a summary advantage of Divine wisdom.[58] The main verb standing near the head of verse 103 only occurs here in the OT. Some early translators and interpreters assumed that it connoted sweetness, basically because of the illustration of honey which follows.[59] However, Delitzsch's argument and final preference seem to be more credible semantically:

> נִמְלְצוּ [*nimlᵉṣû*], ver. 103*a*, is not equivalent to נִמְרְצוּ [*nimrᵉṣû*], Job vi.25 . . . , but signifies, in consequence of the dative of the object לְחִכִּי [*lᵉḥikkî*], that which easily enters, or that which tastes good (LXX. ὡς γλυκέα [*hōs glykea*]; therefore surely from מָלַץ [*mālaṣ*]= מָלַט [*mālaṭ*], to be smooth: how smooth, entering easily (Prov. xxiii.31), are Thy words (promises) to my palate or taste![60]

So when the exclamation, the verb מָלַץ (*mālaṣ*),[61] its object חֵךְ (*ḥēḵ*),[62] and דְּבַשׁ (*dᵉḇaš*), "honey,"[63] as an illustration are combined, the total package is well rendered: "How palatable I find your sayings, more so than honey to my mouth!"[64] Here is the disciple's unambivalent confirmation; human satiation truly comes from the Divine sufficiencies.[65]

---

[58] Conceptionally integrating the two, Kidner extrapolates, "Attraction to the true [i.e. v. 103] and revulsion against the false [i.e. v. 104] are, for us, acquired tastes" (*Psalms 73–150*, p. 427).

[59] This tradition persists; cf., e.g., Anderson, *Psalms*, 2:834. His conclusion is true, however, no matter what connotation for the leading verb is preferred: "in other words, the law of God is more enjoyable than the most delicious food (cf. [Ps] 19:10 (M.T. 11); Prov. 16:24; Ezek. 3:3)" (ibid.).

[60] Delitzsch, *Psalms*, 3:256.

[61] I.e., in combination, "*how smooth* (agreeable, pleasant) . . . ," based upon the meaning "to be smooth" or "slippery" for מָלַץ (BDB, p. 576).

[62] I.e. "palate, roof of mouth, gums" (BDB, p. 335).

[63] "*Honey* (*dᵉḇaš*) is usually the honey of wild or 'domesticated' bees (2 Chr. 31:5), but it may also denote grape syrup (cf. the Arabic *dibs*) which was used for sweetening purposes . . ." (Anderson, *Psalms*, 2:834).

[64] Allen's rendering (*Psalms 101–150*, p. 131).

[65] Cf. Job's testimony in 23:12 and implicationally Jesus' in John 4:32, 34.

From *"all* that God had communicated by revelation,"[66] the psalmist had gained understanding or insight,[67] i.e. that divinely mediated facility "to distinguish between right and wrong and give preference to the former."[68] One of the results[69] of genuine ethical discernment is the personal revulsion[70] of all deception[71] whether manifested in oneself or in others. Since the disciple derived his norms or values from the written repository of God's wisdom for real life,[72] he was equipped to recognize both truth and error, and by his LORD's attendant grace, to shun the latter.[73] That indeed constitutes one of his testimonies of gratitude upon the high plateau of Divine sufficiencies.

---

66 Barnes' synopsis of מִפִּקּוּדֶיךָ (*mippiqqûḏeyḵā*) (*Psalms*, 3:208).

67 I.e. the same Hithpolel form of בִּין (*byn*) encountered in v. 100.

68 Cohen, *Psalms*, p. 407.

69 Again the עַל־כֵּן (*ᶜal-kēn*) indicates the fact of the results which follow it (cf. BDB, p. 487).

70 I.e. hatred (שָׂנֵאתִי [*śānē'ṯî*]); cf. those usages of "hate" which indicate a settled righteous disposition against any and all forms of evil; e.g., Exod 18:21; Pss 5:6 (v. 5, Eng); 31:7 (v. 6, Eng); 45:8 (v. 7, Eng); 97:10; Prov 6:16ff.; Amos 5:15; Mal 2:16; etc. Therefore, the man of God in Ps 119 hated "every false way" (vv. 104, 128), duplicity (v. 113), and lying (v. 163).

71 Delitzsch more formally dubs כָּל־אֹרַח שָׁקֶר (*kol-'ōraḥ šāqer*) "all the heterodox tendencies which agree with the spirit of the age" (*Psalms*, 3:256).

72 In this context, it is likely that Prov 8:13 was explicitly in his mind.

73 Cf. Heb 5:14.

נ

NUN STANZA
(vv. 105–112)

Translation and Notes

105 Your word[a] *is* a lamp for my feet,[b]
and[c] a light for my pathway.[d]

106 I swear[a] and I will fulfill *it*,[b]
to keep[c] Your righteous judgments.[d]

107 I am exceedingly[a] afflicted;[b]
O LORD, revive me[c] according to Your word.[d]

108 Please[a] accept the freewill offerings of my mouth,
and teach me Your judgments.[b]

109 My life *is* continually in my[a] hand,[b]
but[c] I do not forget Your law.

110 Wicked *men* have laid a bird-trap for me,
but[a] I have not wandered from Your precepts.

111 I have taken possession of Your testimonies forever;
indeed,[a] they *are* the joy of my heart.

112 I have inclined my heart to practice[a] Your statutes
forever, *even to the* end.[b]

105:a DSS (Q11) reads plural (דבריכה [*dḇryḵh*]); however, the LXX agrees with the singular reading in the MT.
105:b The *pointing* of the MT interprets as a singular, but the consonantal text should be regarded as plural; cf. the plural in LXX and the sense of the passage.
105:c DSS (Q11) reads as a simple apposition (no conjunction); contra. the MT and early versions with conjunctions.

105:d Although the early versions (including LXX) and the DSS (Q11) render as a plural (לנתיבותי [*lntybwty*]), the singular of the MT has been retained for translation purposes. On the whole verse, note that the expanded paraphrase of the Targum translates basically as follows: "Your revelation *is* like the lamplight of the morning star to my feet, even the light for my path." It is interesting to compare the truths of the Hebrew text and this paraphrase with the language of 2 Pet 1:17–*19*, wherein the reference is to the Living Word (cf. John 8:12 generally).

106:a Translating the Niphal *perfect* of שָׁבַע (*šābaᶜ*) by "instantaneous action" (cf. Williams, *Hebrew Syntax*, ¶ 164).

106:b The Piel imperfect (or *cohortative*) from קוּם (*qûm*), to fulfill, confirm, etc., combines forces with the previous declaration of swearing. Some would treat the two virtually as a hendiadys; e.g. "this and the preceding verb may be coordinated: 'I have undertaken a solemn oath'" (Anderson, *Psalms*, 2:835).

106:c DSS (Q11) exhibits a near synonym for obedience, i.e. an infinitive of עָשָׂה (*ᶜāsâ*), "to do," instead of שָׁמַר (*šāmar*), "to keep."

106:d Differing from the MT and early versions, DSS (Q11) reads singular, משפט צדקכה (*mšpṭ ṣdqkh*), i.e. "Your righteous judgment."

107:a I.e. עַד־מְאֹד (*ᶜad meʾōd*), lit. "unto muchness," i.e. very much, exceedingly, etc.; cf. the ἕως σφόδρα (*heōs sphodra*) in the LXX.

107:b The MT with a Niphal perfect of the root ענה (*ᶜnh*) III unequivocally puts the emphasis upon *affliction* (cf. also the early versions), whereas DSS (Q11) using a more ambivalent verb, i.e. a Niphal perfect of עוה (*ᶜwh*), allows for the antithetical emphases of persecution (i.e. affliction) or perversion.

107:c Once again DSS (Q11) has חונני (*ḥwnny*), "be gracious to me," instead of חיני (*ḥyny*), "revive me" (i.e. the MT and most early versions).

107:d The word for the Word in the MT is דָּבָר (*dābār*), but it is אִמְרָה (*ʾimrâ*) in DSS (Q11).

108:a The emphatic נָא (*nā'*) particle (cf. δή [*dē*] in the LXX); missing in DSS (Q11).
108:b A simple accusative in the MT and early versions. It appears that the DSS (Q11) affixes the preposition מִן (*min*), i.e. "from Your judgments," but this is probably a case of dittography.
109:a A few manuscripts of the LXX and very few early versions read 2 m s (i.e. a reference to God); however, the 1 c s pronominal suffix of the MT is supported by DSS (Q11), original LXX, Targum, etc.
109:b The LXX reads as a plural, "hands."
109:c In DSS (Q11) the *waw* conjunction is missing, whereas it is retained in the MT and early versions.
110:a The *waw* conjunction is again missing in DSS (Q11); cf. note 109:c.
111:a Rendering the כִּי (*kî*) emphatically, i.e., e.g., "*Truly*. Recognizing in *ki* the emphatic particle" (Dahood, *Psalms*, 3:185). Other treatments leave the conjunction untranslated or render it as a light causal, e.g., "for." The conjunction of the MT is well attested in the early versions; however, it is missing in DSS (Q11).
112:a I.e. לַעֲשׂוֹת (*laᶜăśôṯ*), lit. "to do."
112:b Or, possibly "reward" for עֵקֶב (*ᶜēqeḇ*); cf. v. 33.

Synopsis and Outline

The time has arrived for the psalmist's descent back into a dark and dangerous world. As he does so, however, he goes with a renewed perspective on the sufficiencies of God (cf. *Lāmeḏ* and *Mēm*) and with the assurance that they will accompany him on his journey. For this reason, the returning laments are bathed in continuing gratitude. As Allen notes, this "strophe too contains much praise of the Torah, but it is interwoven now with complaint motifs."[1]

[1] Allen, *Psalms 101–150*, p. 143.

In this *Nûn* stanza the comforting excellencies of the Word of God are also complemented by the reactions and resolutions of the man of God.[2] An acute awareness of *personal* responsibility pulsates through these eight verses. This is partially conveyed through such references as "my feet" (v. 105), "my mouth" (v. 108), "my 'soul,'" "my hand" (v. 109), and "my heart" (vv. 111, 112), and it is substantively conveyed through his bold affirmations (e.g., vv. 106, 108a, 109b, 110b, 111, 112).

His resolutions of obedience seem to group around three situations, contexts, or settings, the first and last being quite positive (i.e. vv. 105–106 and 111–112) while the middle one is obviously quite negative (i.e. vv. 107–110). Therefore, based upon the shifts of nuance between verses 106 and 107 and between verses 110 and 111, three settings form the background for the man of God's resolutions to obedience in the *Nûn* stanza:

- 1A. (vv. 105–106) A positive setting of guidance is the basis for this resolution to obedience.
  - 1B. (v. 105) The man of God's testimony concerning the guidance of the Word of God.
    - 1C. (v. 105a) It guides in the next immediate step of life.
    - 2C. (v. 105b) It guides throughout the whole journey of life.
  - 2B. (v. 106) The man of God's resolution in view of this guidance from the Word of God.
- 2A. (vv. 107–110) A negative setting of distress is the basis for these resolutions to obedience.
  - 1B. (vv. 107–108) The man of God's distress encourages him to depend upon his LORD.
    - 1C. (v. 107) He depends upon his LORD to enliven him.
    - 2C. (v. 108) He depends upon his LORD to enlighten him.

[2] Allen well integrates the disciple's laments into this context when he argues that "the complaint motifs are introduced only to enhance this devotion: come wind, come weather, his determination is all the stronger" (ibid.).

2B. (vv. 109–110) The man of God's distress emboldens him to make resolutions.
1C. (v. 109) He resolves fidelity to God's Word in the face of his ever-present dangers.
2C. (v. 110) He resolves conformity to God's Word in the face of his seemingly eventual demise.

3A. (vv. 111–112) A positive setting of contentment is the basis for this resolution to obedience.
1B. (v. 111) The man of God's contentment is a motivational reality.
1C. (v. 111a) He is content because the Word of God is his eternal inheritance.
2C. (v. 111b) He is content because the Word of God is his present satisfaction.
2B. (v. 112) The man of God's contentment leads him to a faithful practice of God's Word.

Commentary

As already noted, major motifs both continue and return in the *Nûn* stanza. In addition to those previously mentioned, the ethical emphasis conveyed so graphically in *Mēm* through "road" and "way" metaphors is resumed with נְתִיבָה (*n*^{e}*tîḇâ*) in verse 105, a term which pictures the psalmist's "pathway" of life.[3] That that pathway makes its way through pitch-black terrain[4] is assumed by the illuminating provisions of "God's torch for a dark world."[5] Consequently, as a transition, verse 105 is especially qualified. It is

[3] For added discussion on these metaphorical continuities, see Alexander, *Psalms*, 3:181.

[4] Cf., e.g., vv. 109–110 which follow.

[5] Allen, *Psalms 101–150*, p. 143; as Delitzsch appropriately stresses, "The way here below is a way through darkness, and leads close past abysses: in this danger of falling and of going astray the word of God is a lamp to his feet, i.e. to his course, and a light to his path . . . his lamp or torch and his sun" (*Psalms*, 3:256).

like a grappling hook that is securely anchored on that high plateau of stability and sufficiency (i.e. vv. 89–104), but at the same time, attached to it is the first length of fragile cord for the disciple's dangerous descent downwards.

In verse 105 God's Word (i.e. דְּבָרֶךָ [*d*^e^*ḇārekā*])[6] is regarded as both a focused (v. 105a) and a diffused light source (v. 105b). As a נֵר (*nēr*), "lamp,"[7] it is like a flashlight's beam aimed at the next step of one's feet on life's dark path.[8] As אוֹר (*'ôr*), "light,"[9] it is like a floodlight which penetrates the murky shadows surrounding the meandering highway ahead.[10] Both nuances are doxological affirmations and practical applications of the truths about Divine guidance summarized in Proverbs 6:23. It must be reiterated however that "this is not convenient guidance for one's career, but truth for moral choices."[11] For the disciple, this "heavenly light on the earthly path"[12] is a most precious commodity which graciously comes to him from God through His word.

In the light of such Light, a rush of resolution immediately follows. To express his great resolution the man of God respectively

---

6 It is interesting to note that דָּבָר (*dāḇār*) and מִשְׁפָּט (*mišpāṭ*) alternate as terms for God's Word in the first four verses of the *Nûn* stanza.

7 BDB, p. 632; cf. the λύχνος (*lychnos*) of the LXX and the שְׁרָגָא (*š*^e^*rāgā'*), "lamp, lantern," etc. (Jastrow, *Dictionary*, 2:1628), of the Targum. Throughout Bible times, the reference was to small earthenware bowls, usually lipped or necked, some open and some more or less closed, designed to hold (olive) oil and a wick which could be lit when light was needed. Interestingly, God Himself is called "Lamp" in 2 Sam 22:29.

8 As such it can detect camouflaged snares (cf. v. 110a).

9 BDB, p. 21; cf. the φῶς (*phōs*) of the LXX and the נְהוֹרָא (*n*^e^*hôrā'*) of the Targum. For a satisfying treatment of its figurative usages, esp. אוֹר (*'ôr*) with "Walking and Way," with "The Light of the Law and of Wisdom," and with "Light and Darkness in Ethical Contexts," see *TDOT*, s.v. "אוֹר (*'ôr*)," by S. Aalen, 1:160–63.

10 As such it prevents disciples from veering off course (cf. v. 110b).

11 Kidner, *Psalms 73–150*, p. 426.

12 Scroggie, *Psalms*, p. 184.

amalgamates perfect and imperfect[13] verbal forms of the roots שׁבע (*šb*ᶜ), to swear, i.e. "to bind oneself by an oath,"[14] and קום (*qwm*), to fulfill (in the Piel stem), i.e. to resolve, confirm, promise, pledge, etc.[15] Then the momentum of this packaged combination carries it directly into the infinitive phrase which follows (i.e. 106b).[16] Soll pleasingly captures the overall thrust of the disciple's resolve in verse 106 with a contemporary rendering: "I am bound and determined to keep your righteous judgments."[17]

Reality (i.e. v. 107a; cf. vv. 109–110) immediately confronts and tests the resolve of the man of God.[18] Although this is his sixth *explicit* reference to affliction,[19] it is the first modified by עַד־מְאֹד (ᶜ*ad* *m*ᵉ*'ōd*), i.e. he was "sorely," "greatly," "exceedingly," etc. "bowed

---

[13] Possibly cohortative because of the options of pointing for the *wāw* conjunction on the leading edge of this form and the ָה (â) on the trailing edge of it; this option would catalyze all the more the psalmist's volitional commitment (i.e. "and I *will* fulfill . . .").

[14] *TWOT*, s.v. "שָׁבַע (*šhāba*ᶜ)," by V. Hamilton, 2:899. For a generally profitable scriptural survey of the controls, warnings, and prohibitions concerning oath-taking, see *TDNT*, s.v. "ὀμνύω," by J. Schneider, 5:176–185.

[15] Cf. Barnes, *Psalms*, 3:208; Cohen, *Psalms*, p. 408; Anderson, *Psalms*, 2:835; Alexander, *Psalms*, 3:182; Allen, *Psalms 101–150*, p. 131; etc.

[16] Whether the leading infinitive לִשְׁמֹר (*lišmōr*), the psalmist's most frequently occurring term for *obedience* (cf. the discussion near the end of Part II), is construed telically (stressing purpose), ecbatically (stressing result), complementally, etc., the *total* impact of v. 106 remains essentially the same. Scroggie expresses that impact briefly and didactically with one of his clever anecdotes: "Solemn promises should be speedily performed" (*Psalms*, p. 184).

[17] Soll, "Psalm 119," p. 197. Concerning the מִשְׁפָּטִים (*mišpāṭîm*) as qualified by the LORD's צֶדֶק (*ṣedeq*), Anderson has well observed that "these ordinances are not arbitrary, but they are an expression of what is right" or just (*Psalms*, 2:835); cf. Girdlestone, *Synonyms*, p. 209.

[18] The close association of vv. 107 and 106 along with other implicational associations scattered throughout the psalm may indicate that the growing resistance he faced may have been fueled to a significant degree by his own resolve to live a godly life (cf. Kirkpatrick, *Psalms*, p. 722; and Spurgeon, *Treasury of David*, 6:244).

[19] I.e. employing either verb or noun forms of ענה (ᶜ*nh*) III; note the Vulgate's *adflictus* herein.

down under heavy afflictions."[20] Therefore, he must depend upon God to enliven him in accordance with His own promise (v. 107b). This pilgrim's context of persecution and cry for preservation are aptly conveyed through Allen's rendering of verse 107: "I am undergoing acute suffering: Yahweh, give me the life promised by your word."[21]

In the next verse human praise (i.e. v. 108a) antiphonally responds to hostile pressure (i.e. v. 107a), and a plea for Divine instruction (i.e. v. 108b) forms a duet with the previous one for Divine infusion (i.e. v. 107b). Sacrificial terminology pervades the psalmist's initial request; however, he obviously was not using the terms in a literal sense. In the OT the נְדָבָה (*n^e^d̲āḇâ*) was a "freewill" or "voluntary offering,"[22] referring to "that which is given willingly, bountifully, liberally," etc.[23] When he stresses that the source of his own נִדְבוֹת (*nid̲bôt*), "freewill offerings," was his mouth (i.e. פִּי [*pî*]), he was obviously referring to his own "prayers of praise."[24] Concerning these offerings of thanksgiving he reverently[25] invokes their acceptance by his LORD. The imperative

---

[20] Delitzsch, *Psalms*, 3:256.

[21] Allen, *Psalms 101–150*, p. 131.

[22] BDB, p. 621. The wording of Deut 23:23 may have been in the psalmist's mind when his own words in vv. 106 and 108a are compared.

[23] Girdlestone, *Synonyms*, p. 203; an attendant feature was its reference "to the motive and spirit of the offerer" (ibid.).

[24] Allen, *Psalms 101–150*, p. 137; or possibly, "prayer and praise" (Cohen, *Psalms*, p. 408). As Soll correctly notes, "Prayer and praise are elsewhere depicted as sacrifice in the psalms" ("Psalm 119," p. 198); note, e.g., Pss 19:15 (v. 14, Eng); 50:14; 51:19 (v. 17, Eng); 100; etc.; and cf. also Heb 13:15 and the implications of 1 Sam 15:22; the ironical statement of Jer 7:21–23; Hos 6:6; etc. The psalmist's "spiritualized" (Allen, *Psalms*, p. 137) references herein may also be considered as part of the evidence that he was in exile, out of the land and deprived of the cultic means through which literal sacrifices could have been made.

[25] When the emphatic נָא (*nā'*) particle is appended to an imperative coming from an inferior to a superior it has a softening affect, i.e. it puts the request "in a more courteous form" (GKC, § 110d). The combination herein could be translated literally via the tautologism "Please be pleased!"

that the man of God employs comes from the verb רָצָה (*rāṣâ*), meaning "to accept" or "to be pleased," which in other places is "used as a technical term for accepting one's sacrifice (Lev. 7:18, 19:7, 22:25, etc.)."[26] Long before the NT episode at Sychar happened this disciple keenly understood the priority of worshipping God in spirit and in truth.

A major prerequisite for true worship is a dependent attitude, and that is once again, exemplified through this child of God in verse 108b. "The recurrence of the prayer, *thy judgments teach me*, shows that the writer's object was to make everything tend to this conclusion, and that however a sentence may begin, it cannot be complete without a repetition of this favorite idea."[27] Indeed, no matter how a *section* begins, it will eventually return here! As Kirkpatrick points out, "Vows of obedience [cf. v. 106] are vain without Divine instruction and grace."[28] All high flights of human responsibility depart from and return to the refuge of Divine resource.

Another highly integrated couplet of verses follows. Generalized (i.e. v. 109a) and particularized (i.e. v. 110a) affirmations of affliction are strikingly balanced[29] by the victim's personal testimonies regarding both his attitude (i.e. v. 109b) and his action (i.e. v. 110b) in response to that affliction. An emphatic idiom[30] characterizes the jeopardy of the child of God in verse 109a:

---

[26] The LXX's εὐδόκησαν (*eudokēsan*) from εὐδοκέω (*eudokeō*), "to be well pleased with, take pleasure in" (Thayer, *Lexicon*, p. 258), opens several passageways from the רָצָה / רָצוֹן (*rāṣâ / rāṣôn*) word group in the OT to the εὐδοκέω / εὐδοκία (*eudokeō / eudokia*) word group in the NT (for a data survey, see *TDNT*, s.v. "εὐδοκέω, εὐδοκία," by G. Schrenk, 2:738–51). Cf., e.g., Matt 3:17; 12:18 (a messianic quote of Isa 42:1); 1 Cor 10:5; Heb 10:6, 8 (quoting Ps 40:6).

[27] Alexander, *Psalms*, 3:182–83.

[28] Kirkpatrick, *Psalms*, p. 722.

[29] On these eye-catching occurrences of antithetical parallelism, cf. Scroggie, *Psalms*, p. 177.

[30] The Targum's paraphrastic expansion, "I am constantly exposed to danger" (Jastrow, *Dictionary*, 1:203), well expresses the idiom of the Hebrew text.

> To have one's soul in his hand . . . signifies, according to context, to remain consciously in danger of death. To *take* one's soul in his hand (Judges xii.3; 1 Samuel xix.5; xxvii.21; Job xiii.14) means: to be prepared to give up one's life. Delitzsch cites the Talmudical saying: Man's prayer is not heard unless he takes his life in his hand; i.e. unless he is ready to sacrifice his life.[31]

Although he was consciously and continually aware of his precarious situation, this dedicated disciple would never allow anything to fade out the focus of his faculties,[32] i.e. his LORD's law. His response of transcendent surrender in the face of temporal suffering[33] has generated an educational legacy of the highest order. The motto emblazoned on its coat of arms is: "The man who carries his life in his hand, should carry the law in his heart."[34]

The hunting metaphor which launches verse 110 exposes the nature of his enemies. These men, whom he again labels as "wicked,"[35] are pictured as crafty fowlers.[36] Their preoccupation was the arrangement (i.e. placing, setting, etc.)[37] of snares or traps for him.[38] In the ancient world a פַּח (*paḥ*) was "primarily a bird-

---

[31] Moll, *Psalms*, p. 592; cf. Delitzsch, *Psalms*, 3:256–57; Cohen, *Psalms*, p. 408; Allen, *Psalms 101–150*, p. 137; Anderson, *Psalms*, 2:835; and the note in NAB which similarly interprets it but goes on to assign such jeopardy to the psalmist's enemies who are aggravated by his fidelity.

[32] On שָׁכַח (*šākaḥ*) plus the objective negation לֹא (*lōʾ*) in reference to the psalmist's conscious commitment not to allow his mindset to drift off course, see this refrain in vv. 16, 61, 83, 93, 141, 153, 176. In this crucial area he remained "faithful even in constant peril of death" (Perowne, *Psalms*, p. 361).

[33] Paul's observations (e.g. 2 Cor 4:16–18) in the context of his own pressures (e.g. 2:12ff.) constitute a similar spiritual paradigm.

[34] Scroggie, *Psalms*, p. 184.

[35] Cf. רְשָׁעִים (*rᵉšāʿîm*) in vv. 53, 61, 95, 119, 155.

[36] What was implicit in v. 61 now becomes very explicit.

[37] The wide-spectrum Hebrew verb נָתַן (*nāṯan*) is narrowed by this context and appropriately picked up by the τίθημι (*tithēmi*) of the LXX and the סְדַר (*sᵉḏar*) of the Targum.

[38] The לִי (*lî*), "for me," indicates that they had one particular species in mind, i.e. the psalmist.

trap or a snare of the fowler, composed of a base and two nets which could spring up and trap the victim (cf. ANEP, pl. 189)."[39] These were usually camouflaged and baited. Then the hunter would wait for his prey beyond the range of its senses. In this case these man-hunters eagerly anticipated the apostasy of their victim.[40] But "the devices and temptations of the wicked were as powerless as all the other causes previously mentioned, in leading him away from the path of truth and safety."[41] By the great grace and good gifts of his God, among which was a brilliantly illuminated pathway (i.e. v. 105), the wary child of God was able to skirt those potentially fatal obstacles strewn along the pathway of life by the emissaries of the evil one.[42]

Strong attestations of contentment (v. 111) followed by a comprehensive affirmation of continuance (v. 112) draw the psalmist's meditations in *Nûn* to a close. One cannot properly assess the impact of the disciple's attestations in verse 111 without being aware of how important the land promises have always been to Israelites. The word chosen for this particular attestation is נחל (*nḥl*),[43] a

---

[39] Anderson, *Psalms*, 2:835. This imagery is widespread in the OT; cf. Pss 9:16 (v. 15, Eng); 35:7; 38:13 (v. 12, Eng); 69:23 (v. 22, Eng); Isa 8:14; 24:17; Jer 18:22; Hos 9:8; Amos 3:5. Note how many of these verses place in parallelism our psalmist's references in vv. 85 and 110.

[40] Note the force of תָּעָה (*tāʿâ*) plus מִן (*min*) in v. 110b; on this combination as a reference to culpable apostasy, cf. Prov 21:16; Ezek 14:11; 44:10, 15; etc. Based upon v. 110b Kirkpatrick argued that the goal of the wicked in v. 110a was to lure the psalmist into "indifference or apostasy" (*Psalms*, p. 722).

[41] Alexander, *Psalms*, 3:183.

[42] Cf. our ultimate Example, the God-Man, as He encountered the master trapper in Matt 4:1–11.

[43] The noun form occurs 224 times as "possession, property, inheritance" and the verb (as here) built from it (i.e. denominative) indicates "to get" or "take as a possession" (BDB, p. 635). Cf. the root *nḥlt* in Ugaritic, *naḥala* in Arabic, the Aramaic's חֲסַן (*ḥăsan*), "to take possession (for one's self and heirs)" (Jastrow, *Dictionary*, 1:488; cf. the Targum of 119:111), the LXX's preferred rendering of κληρονομία / κληρονομέω (*klēronomia / klēronomeō*; cf. Eph 1:14; 1 Pet 1:4; etc. in the NT), and the Vulgate's *hereditas* herein. For a data survey see "נַחֲלָה and נָחַל in the OT" in *TDNT*, s.v. "κλῆρος, κτλ.," by J. Herrmann, 3:769–76; for LXX and NT observations note W. Foerster's contribution (ibid., pp. 776–85).

term which bears covenantal freight.[44] It is especially associated with the LORD's inalienable promise to give the "Holy Land" to Israel (cf., e.g., Exod 32:13). Consequently, when the man of God says, "I have taken possession of Your testimonies forever" (v. 111a), he was magnifying his timeless inheritance in the law beyond any territorial possession of the land. He was *not* depreciating the land promise but was elevating his law possession,[45] especially since it appears that the persecuted child of God was very likely in exile.[46] Therefore, just as he had previously confessed that the LORD Himself was his חלק (*ḥlq*; v. 57), "portion," so he now testifies that God's word was his everlasting inheritance, i.e. נחל (*nḥl*; v. 111a).[47] That he was enjoying his precious possession is indisputably clear from verse 111b. Those very testimonies were truly the "exultation" or "joy" (i.e. שָׂשׂוֹן [*śāśôn*])[48] of his heart. His everlasting inheritance (v. 111a) always brought him present satisfaction (v. 111b).

As regularly observed, the disciple's privilege of possession often triggers his responsibility of practice. So it is again in verse 112. Furthermore, his former prayer for God to direct his mindset toward obedience (v. 36a) is now manifested in his rational and

---

[44] Note the brief but accurate summations of Anderson (*Psalms*, 2:836) and Soll ("Psalm 119," p. 198).

[45] Cf., e.g., Perowne, *Psalms*, p. 361.

[46] As Cohen credibly conjectures: "Instead of Canaan, an inheritance now under foreign domination, the pious Israelite boasted of an eternal, inalienable inheritance in the law of God" (*Psalms*, p. 408).

[47] Cf. the psalmist's language with Daniel's balanced perspective on land (e.g., 9:2) and law (*passim*).

[48] BDB, p. 965; from שׂוּשׂ (*śûś*) "to exult, rejoice" (cf. vv. 14, 162). This lower frequency word for joy in the OT often stands in parallelism with the significant root שׂמח (*śmḥ*).

volitional commitment toward that very end.[49] Concerning this affirmation of resolve and purpose along with a brief notation of its biblical significance, Anderson has observed: "*I incline my heart*: i.e. I have determined to obey your statutes. . . . The heart . . . , as the centre of the will, can determine one's actions: it can turn one away from the Lord (I Kg. 11:9), or it can incline or be directed 'to the Lord' (Jos. 24:23)."[50] And the ultimate proof of the latter mindset is a persistent performance of God's revealed will even "to the end of [one's] life."[51] The child of God, convicted by the "observe to do" challenges of the Word of God and upheld by the "help to do" comforts of the God of the Word, walked his pathway with significant measures of integrity and faithfulness.

---

[49] Cf. the Hiphil imperative of נָטָה (*nāṭâ*) + לֵב (*lēḇ*) + 1 c s pronominal suffix + the directional preposition אֶל (*'el*) in v. 36 with the 1cs Qal form of נָטָה + לֵב + 1cs pronominal suffix + the orientation of the infinitive construct לַעֲשׂוֹת (*la*ᶜ*ᵃśôṯ*) here in v. 112 (cf. also the parallel renderings in the LXX and Targum in reference to both vv. 36 and 112). For semantical and syntactical commentary see v. 36.

[50] Anderson, *Psalms*, 2:836. Cf. the somewhat paraphrastic but conceptionally accurate rendering of NIV: "My heart is set on keeping your decrees to the very end."

[51] On עֵקֶב (*ᶜēqeb*; cf. v. 33) plus לְעוֹלָם (*l*ᵉᶜ*ôlām*) as a reference to a consistent and persistent obedience throughout life, see Barnes, *Psalms*, 2:210; Kidner, *Psalms 73–150*, p. 427; and Delitzsch, *Psalms*, 3:257, who mentions not a fully semantical parallel but the syntactical analogy of v. 44.

ס

SAMEKH STANZA
(vv. 113–120)

Translation and Notes

113 I hate[a] half-hearted *men,*[b]
but[c] I love[a] Your law.

114 You are my hiding-place and my shield;
I hope in[a] Your word.[b]

115 Depart from me, evildoers,
and[a] I will keep the commandments of my God.

116 Sustain me according to[a] Your word and[b] I shall live,
and do not put me to shame because of[c] my hope.

117 Support me and[a] I shall be saved,
then[a] I will continually regard[b] Your statutes.

118 You reject[a] all who stray from Your statutes,
for[b] their deceitfulness *is* vain.[c]

119 You[a] remove[b] all *the* wicked of *the* earth *as* dross;
therefore,[c] I love Your testimonies.

120 My flesh[a] bristles[b] from dread of You,
and I am afraid of Your judgments.

113:a Note the sharp love-hate (i.e. אָהֵב / שָׂנֵא [*'āhēḇ/śānē'*]; cf. LXX: ἀγαπάω / μισέω [*agapaō /miseō*]) antithesis.

113:b סֵעֲפִים (*sē*$^{c\breve{a}}$*p̱îm*), supposedly from סעף (*s*^{c}*p̱* II), is an adjectival *hapax legomenon*. It is assumed that this root shows up in one noun occurrence in 1 Kgs 18:21, סְעִפִּים (*s*^{ec}*ippîm*), i.e. divided *opinions* (cf. BDB, p.704). Its occurrence in 119:113 is rendered by παρανόμους (*paranomous*) in the LXX; by the periphrastic combination דְחָשְׁבִין מַחְשְׁבָן סְרִיקִין (*d^eḥāš^ebîn maḥš^ebān s^erîqîn*), lit. "those who think empty thoughts," in the Targum; and by *tumultuosos* in the Vulgate (for other historical treatments and interpretations, see Moll, *Psalms*, p. 592; and Anderson, *Psalms*, 2:836).

113:c The MT exhibits the *waw* conjunction herein (cf. most early versions); contra. DSS (Qll) where it is absent.

114:a Or, "wait for" (i.e. יִחָלְתִּי [*yiḥāltî*]).

114:b The MT and early versions support the singular, while DSS(Qll) reads plural (i.e. לדבריכה [*ldbrykh*]).

115:a Or, "that I may keep . . ." for this *wāw* conjunction.

116:a Although some versions would support the preposition בְּ (b^e) herein, the כְּ (*k^e*) of the MT is well attested (cf. also DSS [Qll]).

116:b Or, the *wāw* conjunction may be construed appropriately as "that" or "then."

116:c Note the pleonastic ממשברי (*mmšbry*) in DSS (Qll).

117:a There are several legitimate syntactical options, e.g. "and . . . and," "and . . . then," "that . . . and," "that I may be . . . then," etc.

117:b I.e. from שָׁעָה, "to gaze at, regard" (BDB, p. 1043). Some early versions read as if the text had been "delight, enjoy" (e.g. Targum) or "practice, exercise" (e.g. LXX) while the DSS (Qll), omitting both the final ה (*h*) on אשאה and the initial ב (*b*) on בחקיך, might be viewed as signifying "lift up" (cf. Sanders, *Dead Sea Psalms Scroll*, p. 55). In support of the MT note the alliteration of ואשעה with ואושעה (cf. Allen, *Psalms 101–150*, p. 138).

118:a BDB, p. 699, apparently reliant upon Assyrian and Arabic parallels, suggest that סָלָה (*sālâ*) I be rendered *make light of, toss aside*; however, based upon parallel roots in Aramaic and Syriac (ibid.), most contemporary translators prefer renderings of "to despise" or "to reject." Anderson suggests that "the verb *s-l-h* is probably an Aramaism" (*Psalms*, 2:837).

118:b Or, emphatic , i.e. כִּי "*indeed*, their deceitfulness (leads to) disappointment."

118:c I.e. שֶׁקֶר (*šeqer*) as that which "deceives, disappoints and betrays one" (BDB, p. 1055). On the juxtaposition of שֶׁקֶר with תַּרְמִית (*tarmîṯ*) and interactions with some proposed emendations of the latter term, see Allen, *Psalms 101–150*, p. 138.

119:a Contra. the 1 c s inflection of DSS (Q11) and LXX.

119:b Or, "destroy," i.e. cause to *cease* or *desist* (BDB, p. 991); cf. the NIV's "discard," apparently based upon the "dross" imagery. However, some manuscripts and early versions support חשׁב (*ḥšḇ*) instead of the Hiphil of שׁבת (*šḇṯ*). For textual discussions and preferences, see Anderson, *Psalms*, 2:837; and Soll, "Psalm 119," p. 199.

119:c The MT has לָכֵן (*lāḵēn*), whereas DSS (Qll) exhibits the variation על כן (*ʿl ḵn*). The latter also adds כון (*kwn*) before the word for the Word.

120:a Or בְשָׂרִי (*ḇeśārî*) may be taken as a personal paraphrasis (i.e. "*I* bristle") in parallelism with the 1 c s verb of v. 120b.

120:b I.e. to shudder, tremble, creep, etc. (cf. NAB; Allen, *Psalms 101–150*, p. 131; Anderson, *Psalms*, 2:838; etc.). The Targum, utilizing צַלְהֵב (*ṣalhēḇ*), to redden, etc. (Jastrow, *Dictionary*, 2:1282) conveys different imagery from the MT and most of the early versions.

Synopsis and Outline

Sāmeḵ contains a variety of terms and expressions semantically,[1] a number of parallelisms stylistically, different relationships personally, but one integrated argument polemically. Also, emotionally it flows with the currents and eddies of a great river. Its headwaters are immediately discovered in verse 113 where the psalmist expresses his hatred for the lawless (v. 113a) and his love for the law (v. 113b; cf. v. 119b). From there, the stanza quickly branches out into two tributaries. The one runs deeply develop-

[1] As an example, "like the *Het* strophe, the lines in this strophe all begin with a different word" (Soll, "Psalm 119," p. 199).

ing the amorous relationship between the child of God and his LORD or his LORD's Word (i.e., vv. 113b, 114, 115b, 116, 117, 120), and the other runs the rapids caused by the adversarial relationship between the wicked and himself, his God, and his God's revelation (i.e. vv. 113a, 115a, 118, 119). Consequently, these flowing channels clearly demarcate the psalmist's fidelity, his enemies' infidelity,[2] and his God's justice.

Trying to map this river system is not an easy task, because its meanderings are especially convoluted. The structural development of verses 113–120 is similar to the eight verses of the *Yôd* stanza (i.e. vv. 73–80), except in *Yôd* a four-staged chiastic arrangement surfaces whereas here in *Sāmek̲* a three-staged introversion is discernible. Consequently, verses 113 and 120 correspond as do verses 114–115 with 118–119, and finally, verses 116–117 reside at the core of this strophe. This three-staged introversion is employed as a literary vehicle which conveys respectively the psalmist's critical emotions, critical relationships, and critical needs.[3] Therefore, in Psalm 119:113–120 the child of God deals with three critical areas in his life.

- 1A. (vv. 113, 120) He deals with his critical emotions.
  - 1B. (v. 113a) He reveals his aggravation towards the hypocritical.
  - 2B. (v. 113b) He reacts with his ardor for the Bible.
  - 3B. (v. 120) He reflects upon his awe of:
    - 1C. (v. 120a) The God of the Word.
    - 2C. (v. 120b) The Word of God.
- 2A. (vv. 114–115; 118–119) He deals with his critical relationships.
  - 1B. (v. 114) The relationship between God and himself provides security in life.
  - 2B. (v. 115) The relationship between his enemies and himself provokes resolution for life.

---

[2] They are graphically labeled as "double-minded" (v. 113), "evildoers" (v. 115), apostates (v. 118), and malignant men who are undesirable (i.e. v. 119).

[3] Note how this nucleus of needs which only God can meet constitutes the heart of both *Yôd* (cf. vv. 76–77) and *Sāmek̲* (cf. vv. 116–117).

3B. (vv. 118–119) The relationship between God, his enemies, and himself promotes perspective on life:
1C. (v. 118) God *is* in control of apostates.
2C. (v. 119) God *is* in control of autocrats.
3A. (vv. 116–117) He deals with his critical needs.
1B (v. 116) He is desperately in need of God's assurance.
1C. (v. 116a, c) The declarations of this need of assurance.
2C. (v. 116b) The design of this need of assurance.
2B. (v. 117) He is desperately in need of God's assistance.
1C. (v. 117a) The declaration of this need of assistance.
2C. (v. 117b, c) The designs of this need of assistance.

Commentary

Love and hate show themselves regularly throughout the progress of this psalm's 176 verses.[4] These antonyms, grouped in such a compact bicolon as verse 113, make the antithesis all the more dramatic.[5] In contrast with love, the שָׂנֵא *(śānē')* word group in the OT often "expresses an emotional attitude toward persons and things which are opposed, detested, despised and with which one wishes to have no contact or relationship."[6] Such hatred when coming from saved sinners should be predicated upon Divine patterns and purposes.[7] Consequently,

---

4 Note the root אהב (*'hb̲*) for love in vv. 47, 48, 97, 113, 119, 127, 132, 140, 159, 163, 165, 167. V. 132 refers to loving the name of God and the others, employing different words for the Word as objects, emphasize loving the law of God. Hate is mentioned in vv. 104, 113, 128, 163. In vv. 104, 128, and 163 the psalmist's hatred is aimed at deviant behavior, whereas in v. 113 it is directed at the deviants themselves.

5 As Michel notes, "μισεῖν and ἀγαπᾶν are always antonyms in the Wisdom literature" (*TDNT*, s.v. "μισέω," by O. Michel, 4:687).

6 *TWOT*, s.v. "שָׂנֵא (*śānē'*)," by G. Van Groningen, 2:880.

7 Cf., e.g., Pss 5:6 (v. 5, Eng); 31:7 (v. 6, Eng); 45:8 (v. 7, Eng); 97:10; 139:21; Prov 6:16f.; 8:13; 14:17; Amos 5:15; 2 Chr 19:2; etc. For some discussion, cf. ibid. As Michel also notes, "As God hates evil, so do the righteous" (*TDNT*, 4:687).

> when the righteous of the old covenant hate evil, this is not primarily an emotion of the human heart. It is a passionate disowning in faith of the evil or the evil person whom God Himself has rejected. In his hatred the wise man is on the side of the divine judgment.[8]

Vindication of this disciple's attitude comes via his designation of those persons hated as half-hearted or double-minded.[9] In this context these men had obviously shown themselves to have been vacillating syncretists and/or hypocrites.[10]

In the light of the enormous instability of those who surrounded him (i.e. v. 113) the man of God submitted himself to the One who kept him safe (i.e. v. 114). He claimed the LORD (herein אַתָּה ['attâ], i.e., "You") as both his shelter and his shield. The former noun, סֵתֶר (*sēṯer*), meaning covering, hiding-place, secret place, etc.,[11] most frequently pictures God Himself as "a place of refuge and protection from all dangers for the believer."[12] The second noun, מָגֵן (*māgēn*), a shield, from גָּנַן (*gānan*), to cover, surround, defend (with the LORD always subject),[13] is also a graphic metaphor for God's protection of His people.[14] With this compounded recognition of his personal security in God, the disciple

---

[8] *TDNT*, 4:687; cf. some of Michel's credible syntheses of the NT data (ibid., pp. 690–92).

[9] Conceptually, compare the סֵעֲפִים (*sēcăpîm*) men of Ps 119:113 with the δίψυχος (*dipsychos*) man of Jas 1:8.

[10] For some of their probable characteristics, cf. Delitzsch, *Psalms*, 3:257; Kidner, *Psalms 73–150*, p. 427; and Moll, *Psalms*, p. 592; for further commentary, see v. 163.

[11] BDB, p. 712.

[12] *TWOT*, s.v. "סָתַר (*sātar*)," by R. Patterson, 2:636; he appropriately cites Pss 17:8; 27:5; 31:21 (v. 20, Eng); 32:7; 64:3 (v. 2, Eng); 91:1; 119:114. Concerning background, it is possible that the asylum once provided by special *places* is now epitomized in the special *Person* (cf., e.g., Anderson, *Psalms*, 2:836).

[13] BDB, pp. 170–71.

[14] As Smith notes, "In view of the fact that God is always the one who protects (*gānan*) his people, it is no surprise that he is so often called the shield (*māgēn*) of Israel" (*TWOT*, s.v. " (*gānan*)," by J. Smith, 1:169).

moves on to another affirmation of his confidence in propositional security (i.e. v. 114b; cf. vv. 43, 49, 74, 81, 147). Truly there is hope in the message (v. 114b) of the Defender and Protector (v. 114a).

With such renewed assurance the man of God briefly but boldly addresses his enemies in verse 115.[15] His vocative of choice for them is "evildoers."[16] He who had not departed from his God nor from his God's ordinances (cf. סוּר [*sûr*] in v. 102) now commands his enemies to depart[17] from him. As the last half of the verse indicates his desire for their departure[18] was not merely to procure for him an opportunity for personal relief, but to provide for him an occasion for the free exercise of personal responsibility, i.e. "I intend to observe my God's commands."[19]

"He, however, stands in need of grace in order to persevere and to conquer. For this he prays in vers. 116, 117."[20] Without Divine assurance (v. 116a) and assistance (v. 117a) surely his life would become listless (vv. 116b, 117b) and his dedication would dwindle (v. 117c). Furthermore, it might even seem to appear that his hope might turn into a hoax (v. 116c).

---

[15] Soll has noted that "this is the only verse in the psalm, after v. 3, which does not address God directly. It is an apostrophe to the wicked, and seems to be an allusion to Ps 6:9 [v. 8, Eng.]. There, the statement was an assurance of being heard ('Depart from me . . . for the LORD *has heard*')" (Soll, "Psalm 119," p. 199).

[16] A substantive Hiphil participle from רָעַע, to be evil, bad (BDB, p. 949); cf. the exact form in Job 8:20; Pss 22:17 (v. 16, Eng); 26:5; 27:2; 37:1; 37:9; 64:3 (v. 2, Eng); 92:12 (v. 11, Eng); 94:16; Prov 24:19; Isa 1:4; 14:20; 31:2; Jer 20:13; 23:14.

[17] Because of its dramatic setting, Delitzsch labels סוּרוּ, the m. pl. imperative, "an indignant 'depart'" (*Psalms*, 3:257).

[18] Cf. the "Translation and Notes" on v. 115:a above concerning the *waw* which introduces v. 115b. For other syntactical commentary, see Moll, *Psalms*, p. 592.

[19] Allen's suitable rendering (*Psalms 101–150*, p. 131) of v. 115b. Note the continued polemic in the psalmist's reference to "the commandments of *my* God."

[20] Delitzsch, *Psalms*, 3:257.

Consequently, in verse 116 the earnest disciple immediately asks his LORD to "support, uphold, sustain" him.[21] Characteristically, he bolsters his request with another revelational precedent כְּאִמְרָתְךָ (*k*e*'imrāṯ*e*kā*), indicating that his prayer is totally *in accord with* God's Word, or better, His personalized promise. Based upon his confident expectation of a soon-coming answer from heaven, the man of God anticipates personal revival, i.e. a fresh influx of genuine life with its "spiritual roots and goals."[22] Nevertheless, he bookends his transcendent optimism (v. 116b) with another request; now a negatively phrased prayer (v. 116c) follows his positively phrased plea (v. 116a). His consuming desire is that the Author of sovereign providence would not allow his hope to turn into disappointment.[23] This disciple's recurrent concern to avoid shame (cf. vv. 6, 31, 46, 80) is herein associated explicitly with his hope (i.e. שֵׂבֶר [*śēḇer*][24]): LORD, "do not put me to shame because of my hope."[25]

Further Divine support is sought at the outset of verse 117. The imperative which is addressed to God and is intended to re-

---

[21] Cf. סָמַךְ (*sāmaḵ*) in BDB, p. 701; note occurrences of this root in Gen 27:37; Pss 3:6 (v. 5, Eng); 37:17, 24; 51:14 (v. 12, Eng); 145:14; Isa 59:16. Anderson appropriately concludes that "the verb *s-m-k* is often used of divine help in general" (*Psalms*, 2:837).

[22] Kaiser's synopsis of the biblical nature of חָיָה (*ḥāyâ*) (Walter C. Kaiser, Jr., *Toward an Old Testament Theology* [Grand Rapids: Zondervan, 1978], p. 172). Cf. the root חיה in. vv. 17, 25, 37, 40, 50, 77, 88, 93, 107, 144, 149, 154, 156, 159, 175, remembering the theological significance of passages like Deut 8:3; 30:20; 32:47; etc.

[23] Besides the existence of a conceptual parallel of v. 116c with Rom 5:5a, the LXX reflects a semantical parallel on the verbal level (cf. καταισχύνω [*kataischunō*] in both).

[24] Although this root is used in extra-biblical Aramaic, its only other occurrence in the OT is found in Ps 146:5 (see Anderson, *Psalms*, 2:837). However, it is a conceptual parallel of the יחל (*yḥl*) word group in Hebrew (note the proximity of יחל in v. 114).

[25] Cf. Delitzsch on בּוֹשׁ מִן (*bôš min*) (*Psalms*, 3:257); or another legitimate rendering is "and do not let me find disappointment resulting from my hope" (Allen, *Psalms 101–150*, p. 131; cf. his note, p. 137, on בּוֹשׁ מִן).

bound to the psalmist himself as beneficiary comes from the verb סָעַד (*sāʿad*), variously rendered to sustain, support, establish, strengthen, comfort.[26] Often a synonym of סָמַךְ (*sāmak*; cf. verse 116a[27]), סָעַד is frequently employed in solicitations of Divine help under a variety of circumstances.[28] Here the progressive goal of such Divine aid[29] is heavenly deliverance (v. 117b) for human dedication (v. 117c). The Niphal imperfect, וְאִוָּשֵׁעָה (*weʾiwwāšēʿâ*), to "be liberated, saved,"[30] in this context speaks of a liberation from circumstantial restraints (cf. those imposed upon the psalmist by his enemies).[31] Once he has experienced God's assistance of rescue from restriction (cf. v. 115) then the dedicated disciple will be enabled to occupy himself volitionally[32] with the internalization and actualization of his LORD's statutes, and to do so far more consistently.[33] The man of God knew that his pathway must proceed along the lines of Divine rescue from debilitating resistance to dependent resolve.

Another meditation on God's perfect justice refreshes the persecuted pilgrim in verses 118–119. His LORD's control and ulti-

---

[26] *TWOT*, s.v. "סָעַד (*sāʿad*)," by R. Patterson, 2:629; note that the Targum employs the same root at v. 117a.

[27] Ibid.

[28] Even the two different verbals in the LXX, ἀντιλαμβάνομαι (*antilambanomai*) in v. 116a and βοηθέω (*boētheō*) in v. 117a, exhibit substantial synonymity (cf. *TDNT*, s.v. "ἀντιλαμβάνομαι," by G. Delling, 1:375–76; and s.v. "βοηθέω," by E. Stauffer, 1:628–29).

[29] On the syntactical options, see the "Translation and Notes" above. One of the best options is the one which regards the *waw* standing at the head of v. 117b as reflecting intentionality followed by a consequential usage at the outset of v. 117c thereby preparing the way for this exercise of the psalmist's volitionality.

[30] BDB, p. 446; cf. the future passive of σώζω (*sōzō*) in the LXX.

[31] For brief but helpful reviews of יָשַׁע (*yāšaʿ*), see Girdlestone, *Synonyms*, pp. 124–25; and *TDNT*, s.v. "σώζω, κτλ." by G. Fohrer, 7:970–978.

[32] It is appropriate to construe the ָה (*â*) ending on שָׁעָה, to "*gaze* at, *regard* (with favour)" (BDB, p. 1043), as a true (volitional) cohortative (cf. Delitzsch, *Psalms*, 3:257; cf. GKC, § 75 ¶ l).

[33] I.e. תָּמִיד (*tāmîd*).

mate retribution of apostates and autocrats alike gives him a better perspective on perseverance. Furthermore, his awe of the God of the Word (vv. 118a, 119a) intensifies his adoration of the Word of God (v. 119b).

Although the verb סָלָה (*salâ*), with which verse 118 opens, has been variously rendered in the light of different Semitic cognates,[34] it is obviously intended to convey a very strong response on the part of God towards the wicked.[35] His fixed[36] reaction in reference to those who stray from His special revelation, i.e. those who are characterized by apostasy,[37] is to despise, spurn, reject, or to repudiate them. As verse 118 continues one is reminded of the conceptual and semantical parallel of Jeremiah 8:5 wherein apostasy is also associated with deceit. It is best not to emend the תַּרְמִיתָם (*tarmîṯām*) of the MT,[38] but to render it as "their deceitfulness." Such deceit will ultimately result in disappointment; vanity is its destination.

---

[34] Its only other verbal occurrence in the OT is Lam 1:15. Concerning various Semitic parallels, e.g. to throw off, shake off, be forgetful, neglectful, to despise, reject, see BDB, p. 699.

[35] The Targum utilizes a form of כְּבַשׁ (*kᵉḇaš*), i.e. to tread upon, stamp out, to suppress, oppress, to conquer, withhold, detain, etc. (Jastrow, *Dictionary*, 1:610–11), and the LXX employs a form of ἐξουδενέω (*exoudeneō*), to hold and treat as of no account, utterly to despise, to set at nought, etc. (Thayer, *Lexicon*, p. 224).

[36] Note the perfect both here and in v. 119.

[37] A second occurrence of the participle of שָׁגָה (*šāgâ*) complemented with the preposition מִן (*min*) attached to a word for the Word (cf. v. 21); also, recall the psalmist's prayer for himself to avoid any such apostasy in v. 10.

[38] As Delitzsch well commented, "the LXX. and Syriac read תַּרְעִיתָם [*tarʿîṯām*], 'their sentiment' [or, planning, cunning]; but this is an Aramaic word that is unintelligible in Hebrew, which the old translators have conjured into the text only on account of an apparent tautology" (*Psalms*, 3:257). Note that the Targum was not inhibited by any problem with tautology, since it juxtaposed שִׁקְרָא (*šiqrāʾ*) with נִכְלָא (*niḵlāʾ*), i.e. deceit (Jastrow, *Dictionary*, 2:911).

God's rejection of the wicked (v. 118) is followed by His removal (i.e. שָׁבַת [*šāḇaṯ*]) of them as dross (v. 119a). "The basic thrust of the verb is . . . 'to sever, put an end to'"[39] something or someone, and by employing סִגִים (*sigîm*) alongside of it as a "technical metallurgical term"[40] (cf. Prov 25:4; 26:23; Isa 1:22, 25; Ezek 22:18, 19), the resultant metaphor for God's judgment is especially impacting (cf. Jer 6:27–30; Mal 3:2; etc.). In view of this awesome portrayal of God's justice,[41] the disciple is driven to a deeper devotion regarding His decrees.

Interestingly, this stanza opened with an antithesis of hate and love (v. 113a, b); now it closes with an intricate association between love (v. 119b) and fear (v. 120a, b). Throughout the Bible fear and love are presented as corollaries,[42] and the fruit of this combination is obedience.[43]

The imagery pertaining to the psalmist in verse 120a is just as arresting as that which pertained to the wicked in verse 119a. To paint his fear in iridescent colors the disciple speaks of "his flesh" *bristling up*.[44] Several nuances are possible; for example, his flesh may be pictured as creeping;[45] his hair may be envisioned as standing on end;[46] or, his person might be viewed as trembling or

---

[39] *TWOT*, s.v. "שָׁבַת (*shābat*)," by V. Hamilton, 2:902. On some of the proposed emendations of v. 119a, see Anderson, *Psalms*, 2:837; Soll, "Psalm 119," p. 199; and Delitzsch, *Psalms*, 3:257–58.

[40] Anderson, *Psalms*, 2:837; סִגִים (*sigîm*) refers to "the residuum of smelted metal" (Moll, *Psalms*, p. 592).

[41] I.e. as a consequence or result of it (לָכֵן [*lākēn*]).

[42] Cf. Leon Morris, *Testaments of Love: A Study of Love in the Bible* (Grand Rapids: Eerdmans, 1981), pp. 58–59; and Eichrodt, *Theology of the OT*, 2:268–77, 290–301. Cf. also comments above at v. 97.

[43] Cf. Eichrodt, *Theology of the OT*, 2:299.

[44] See BDB, p. 702, on סָמַר (*sāmar*).

[45] Cf. Allen's translation (*Psalms 101–150*, p. 131).

[46] Delitzsch, *Psalms*, 3:258. Although the LXX does not exhibit the same terminology, the concept of hair bristling up is found in Jas 2:19.

shuddering.[47] No matter how the imagery is cast, the psalmist's characteristic experience[48] was precipitated by פַּחְדְּךָ (*paḥdᵉḵā*), i.e. "the terror of God."[49] An echo of the dread of the LORD (v. 120a) is his fear[50] of the law (v. 120b). In other words, fearing these judgments constitutes an important dimension of fearing the Judge; therefore, both assertions evidence the genuine wisdom and true knowledge of a child of God.[51]

---

[47] Cf. Anderson, *Psalms*, 2:838; he adds that "the reference may be to goose-flesh" and cites Job 4:15 as a parallel (ibid.).

[48] Construing the perfect tense as an overview of his life with the LORD.

[49] See Moll, *Psalms*, p. 592. For a brief usage survey, see *TWOT*, s.v. "פַּחַד (*paḥad*) I," by A. Bowling, 2:720–21; note especially Deut 2:25; 28:67; 1 Sam 11:7; 1 Chr 14:17; 2 Chr 20:29; Job 13:11; Ps 14:5. Also, note the verbal occurrence of this root in Ps 119:161.

[50] I.e. יָרֵאתִי (*yārēʾtî*) from the more commonly attested root ירא (*yrʾ*), to fear.

[51] For a good theological synopsis of the fear of the Lord, esp. as true wisdom, see W. C. Kaiser, Jr., *Toward an Old Testament Theology*, pp. 168–71.

ע

AYIN STANZA
(vv. 121–128)

Translation and Notes

121 I have done[a] *what is* just and right;[b]
do not[c] abandon me to my oppressors.[d]

122 Be Your servant's[a] surety for *his* welfare;[b]
do not[c] let insolent men oppress me.

123 My eyes fail for Your salvation,[a]
and[b] for Your righteous word.[c]

124 Deal with Your servant according to Your grace,[a]
and teach me Your statutes.

125 I *am* Your servant; give me understanding,
that[a] I may know Your testimonies.

126 It is time for the LORD[a] to act;[b]
they have broken Your law.

127 Therefore,[a] I love Your commandments
more than gold, even more than pure gold.

128 Therefore, I reckon as right[a] all precepts *about* all *things;*[b]
I hate every false way.[c]

121:a A few manuscripts support a second person reading, i.e. "You have done"; nevertheless, the early versions corroborate the 1 c s verb of the MT.

121:b Lit., "I have done justice and righteousness." Another appealing translational option is to construe both מִשְׁפָּט (*mišpāṭ*) and צֶדֶק (*ṣedeq*) adverbially in the light of an obviously ethical context: "I have dealt justly and rightly."

121:c בַּל (*bal*) is a poetic negation. Most older grammarians took it strictly or nearly strictly as an objective negation (Davidson, *Hebrew Syntax*, § 128, Rem. 5; GKC, § 152t); however, today a wider function (i.e. either objective or subjective negation) with verbs is generally recognized (cf. Williams, *Hebrew Syntax*, §§ 412, 413, 415; and Waltke and O'Connor, *Biblical Hebrew Syntax*, 34, n. 6).

121:d This is the first designation of the psalmist's enemies as "oppressors," i.e. from the root עשׁק (*ᶜšq*); cf. the substantive participle herein (v. 121b) with the jussive occurrence of this root in the next verse (v. 122b). In cognate languages the root often suggests roughness or injustice; however, in Aramaic and Syriac it also carries nuances of accusation and slander (BDB, p. 798), i.e. those particular varieties of *oppression* often experienced by the human author of Ps 119.

122:a Some have emended עַבְדְּךָ (*ᶜabdᵉkā*) to דְּבָרְךָ (*dᵉbārᵉkā*) for various reasons (i.e. conjectures; e.g., the desire to find a word for the Word herein), none of which have textual or versional support.

122:b The abbreviated syntax of v. 122a allows for several translational options; e.g., cf. "Be surety for Thy servant for good" (NASB); "Ensure your servant's well-being" (NIV); "Be surety for the welfare of your servant" (NAB); "Stand surety for your servant's welfare" (Allen, *Psalms 101–150*, p. 132); etc.

122:c Here the subjective negation אַל (*'al*) stands parallel with the previous prohibition (i.e. v. 121b) except its force is more indirect since it stands with a jussive.

123:a Note the parallels with v. 82. Although the focal point therein is אִמְרָה (*'imrâ*), here the *immediate* focus is upon יְשׁוּעָה (*yᵉšûᶜâ*), "salvation"; nevertheless, in v. 123b אִמְרָה occurs as a secondary focal point.

123:b Or, render the conjunction "even," i.e. taking God's "righteous promise" appositionally with His "salvation."

123:c Recalling that אִמְרָה (literally a "*word*" for the Word) is often well rendered more explicitly as "promise."

124:a Another significant occurrence of חֶסֶד (*ḥesed*); cf. vv. 41, 64, 76, 88.

125:a Or, possibly, "then I shall know. . . ."

126:a The prepositional prefix (i.e. לְ [l^e]) on יהוה (*YHWH*), attested in all Hebrew manuscripts except one, has been largely responsible for some different translations and interpretive renderings. For example, Delitzsch takes the psalmist rather than the LORD as the subject of this taking action: "It is time to interpose for Jahve" (*Psalms*, 3:239; cf. his comments on p. 258; note the Targum's paraphrastic "*it is* time to do the good will of the LORD"). Most early versions and modern translations, however, regard v. 126a as a request for the LORD to take action in the light of the psalmist's straits. Furthermore, it is possible to construe the preposition which is attached to יהוה either as a vocative particle (cf. Dahood, *Psalms*, 3:187) or to take it a little less directly and more inferentially. The last option seems to be preferred contextually; cf. Soll: "the *lamed* here may have been deferential in its intent, to make the statement sound more like an assertion of faith than a command to the deity" ("Psalm 119," p. 201).

126:b I.e. an infinitive of עָשָׂה (*ᶜāśâ*; to do, perform, act, etc.), a root that contributes to this stanza's emphasis on ethics in motion (cf. vv. 121 and 124).

127:a Manuscript evidence and the early versions attest that both vv. 127 and 128 begin with עַל־כֵּן (*ᶜal-kēn*), "*upon ground of such conditions, therefore*" (BDB, p. 487). However, many, having problems logically with v. 126 providing a grounds for the psalmist's affirmation of love in v. 127, emend the כֵּן to כֹּל (*kōl*) by conjecture so that the resultant prepositional phrase, "above all," is utilized adverbially to intensify the declaration of the psalmist's love for God's Word. However, it is better to be faithful to the textual and versional evidence even though it is difficult to interpret the relationship of v. 127 to the immediately preceding context. Some logical scenarios have been offered in reference to the initial עַל־כֵּן of v. 127; e.g., "But a deduction is not unfitting. The anticipated intervention of Yahweh is a double stimulus (vv 127–28), both to devotion to his revelation (cf. v 119) and to renouncing behavior alien to it" (Allen, *Psalms 101–150*, p.

138); or secondarily, consider Kidner's connection: "at first sight the *therefore* of verse 127 may seem out of place, . . . but it is the logic of loyalty, to be the more devoted the more the pressure grows" (*Psalms 73–150*, pp. 427–28).

128:a Cf. "esteem right, approve" (BDB, p. 448). It is possible, however that this Piel of the root ישׁר (*yšr*) may be taken not merely as an ethical declaration but as an ethical demonstration; cf., e.g., "'I have lived uprightly'" (*TWOT*, s.v. "יָשַׁר (*yāshar*)," by D. Wiseman, 1:417); "I go forward" (NAB); "I direct my steps" (Sanders, *Dead Sea Psalms Scroll*, p. 57); "I follow" (Soll, "Psalm 119," p. 201); etc. However, many of those who construe it in this manner do so on the basis of their rejection of that part of the Hebrew text which precedes the verb (cf. note 128:b below) along with their corresponding acceptance of the renderings found in LXX and Vulgate.

128:b The text behind this rendering, כָּל־פִּקּוּדֵי כֹל (*kol-piqqûḏê ḵōl*), has given rise to a complex textual debate (for an example of someone caught between the poles of this debate, cf. Moll, *Psalms*, p. 592). Several transpositional emendations have been suggested. The conjecture with the longest history is לְכָל־פִּקּוּדֶיךָ (*lᵉḵol-piqqûḏeyḵā*); for a survey of a few of the more recent modifications, see Allen, *Psalms 101–150*, p. 138; and Soll, "Psalm 119," pp. 128–29. It is argued that some early versions (e.g. LXX) justify these kinds of emendation; however, DSS (Q11) reads על כן פקודי כול (*ʿl ḵn pqwḏy ḵwl*), and the Targum reduplicates with Aramaic equivalents all the "awkward" features of the MT. Consequently, Delitzsch's defense of the Hebrew text as it stands remains undaunted: "Therefore he [the psalmist] is as strict as he possibly can be with God's word, inasmuch as he acknowledges and observes all precepts of all things (כָּל־פִּקּוּדֵי כֹל), *i.e.* all divine precepts, let them have reference to whatsoever they will, as יְשָׁרִים, right. . . . On כָּל־פִּקּוּדֵי כֹל, 'all commandments of every purport,' cf. Isa. xxix. ll, and more as to form, Num. viii. 16, Ezek. xliv. 30. The expression is purposely thus heightened" (*Psalms*, 3:258–59).

128:c A prevalent ethical idiom (cf. similar expressions internally manifested at vv. 29 and 104) alluding to all forms of deception and deviant behavior.

Synopsis and Outline

Several thematic threads are interwoven in this stanza. First and most pervasive is an emphasis upon ethics. The psalmist begins and ends with references to his own ethical integrity (vv. 121a, 127, 128) which stand in contrast with the unethical exhibitions of his enemies (vv. 121b, 122b, and 128b by implication). Even in sharper contrast stand his allusions to the ultimate ethical norms, the personal God of the Word and the propositional Word of God.[1] It is obvious, however, that he is not engaging in meditations on theoretical ethics, but contrastingly, he is longing for practical exhibitions of Divine rectitude, i.e. ethics in motion.[2]

All of this is heightened by an atmosphere of personal intimacy largely sustained by recurrences of עַבְדְּךָ (*ᶜabdᵉkā*), "Your servant," in verses 122, 124, and 125.[3] It has well been pointed out

[1] Besides conceptual interfacings and logical associations thematic glue also comes from semantical parallelisms. For example, the psalmist's *reflections* of מִשְׁפָּט (*mišpāṭ*) and צֶדֶק (*ṣedeq*) in his life-style (cf. v. 121a) emanate *innately* from the corresponding attributes of God's word (e.g., cf. the roots [*ṣdq*] and ישׁר [*yšr*] respectively in vv. 123b and 128a). Furthermore, this propositional source issues from the Personal source to Whom the child of God makes bold appeal upon these very grounds. This stanza is an ethical harbinger of *Ṣādê*, vv. 137–144.

[2] This is also documented both inferentially and semantically. Of special notation are the occurrences of the root עשׂה (*ᶜśh*) in this stanza, beginning with the psalmist's personal affirmation and proceeding to his direct and indirect appeals for the LORD to act (cf. respectively, vv. 121a, 124a, 126a). For Divine ethics in action also cf. vv. 65 and 68, and for applicational derivations in reference to human responsibility, cf. 112 and 166.

[3] Allen goes so far as to say עַבְדְּךָ (*ᶜabdᵉka*) is the key term of this stanza (*Psalms 101–150*, p. 144).

that this term, often viewed as a polite self-designation,[4] indicates "not only the writer's dependence upon God, but also the more personal relationship based on a Covenant."[5] The contextual settings of the term in verses 122 and 124 are quite compatible with covenantal language. However, its abbreviated form and setting in verse 125 make it more directly personal.[6] From this personal position of grace the oppressed disciple conveys his expectations and delivers his petitions for Divine intervention.

From within this complex matrix key affirmations surface providing the pivots around which his overall burden is developed (cf. vv. 121a, 123a, 125a). In the light of this stylistic phenomenon, three personal affirmations provide the framework for the disciple's bold requests for Divine attention in Psalm 119:121–128.

- 1A. (vv. 121–122) His ethical affirmation.
  - 1B. (v. 121a) Its expression.
  - 2B. (vv. 121b–122) Its expectations:
    - 1C. (vv. 121b, 122b) Prevention.
    - 2C. (v. 122a) Protection.
- 2A. (vv. 123–124) His devotional affirmation.
  - 1B. (v. 123) Its expression.
  - 2B. (v. 124) Its expectations:
    - 1C. (v. 124a) Grace.
    - 2C. (v. 124b) Guidance.
- 3A. (vv. 125–128) His relational affirmation.
  - 1B. (v. 125a) Its expression.
  - 2B. (vv. 125b–128) Its expectations:
    - 1C. (vv. 125b–126a) These expectations are voiced:
      - 1D. (v. 125b, c) Illumination.
      - 2D. (v. 126a) Intervention.
    - 2C. (vv. 126b–128) These expectations are verified:

---

[4] Cf. *TWOT*, s.v. "עָבַד (*ᶜābad*)," by W. Kaiser, 2:639.

[5] Anderson, *Psalms*, 2:838.

[6] Concerning intimacy, cf. the עַבְדְּךָ־אָנִי (*ᶜab̠dᵉk̠ā-'ānî*) of v. 125a with the לְךָ־אֲנִי (*lᵉk̠ā-'ănî*) of v. 94a.

1D. (v. 126b) Negatively, by the actions of the oppressors.
2D. (vv. 127–128) Positively, by the attitudes of the oppressed; e.g.:
  1E. (vv. 127–128a) Loving what is right.
  2E. (v. 128b) Loathing what is wrong.

Commentary

The child of God begins this stanza with an assertion about his ethical integrity. This and the other references to personal piety in *Ayin* (cf. 127a, 128a) provide a secondary, but significant, basis for his expectation of Divine intervention.[7] Concerning the specific focus of verse 121a in its immediate context, Delitzsch has noted that "in the consciousness of his godly behaviour . . . the poet hopes that God will surely not . . . leave him to the arbitrary disposal of his oppressors."[8]

Indeed, the collocation of the roots שׁפט (*špṭ*; i.e. *justice*) and צדק (*ṣdq*; i.e. *righteousness*), along with the dynamic verb from the root עשׂה (*ᶜśh*, i.e. to make, do, deal, perform, practice, etc.), unequivocally introduce the biblically strategic issue of ethics in action. The key nouns or qualities explicitly mentioned herein inform one another throughout biblical revelation. Concerning מִשְׁפָּט, "justice,"[9] Herntrich, based upon background studies and usage surveys, has credibly argued that it

---

[7] By setting the assertion of v. 121a into a probable background of covenant stipulations and commitment, Allen notes that "the poet ventures to plead that he has done his part in the divine-human relationship" (*Psalms 101–150*, p. 144).

[8] Delitzsch, *Psalms*, 3:258.

[9] Note Culver's disclaimers and warnings of associating מִשְׁפָּט with the narrower semantical scope of "justice" in English (*TWOT*, s.v. "שָׁפַט (*shāpaṭ*)," by R. Culver, 2:948; cf. his whole survey of the richness of the word group in Hebrew, pp. 947–49).

> is a term which expresses relationship. It regulates the relationships in a specific society. It can be understood only in the light of its validity in this society. The idea is that of a Judge who, on the basis of His ownership as the Lord, regulates the social relationships within His tribe. It is that of the God who in the covenant has bound Himself to the people as its Lord and Judge. It is that of the God who has revealed His will and who is just as concerned about the observance of this revealed will as He is about keeping the promise given in the covenant. . . . The מִשְׁפָּטִים [*mišpāṭim*, "judgments, ordinances," etc.[10]]. . . present in detail the revelation of the will of Yahweh given at the conclusion of the covenant. They are thus a binding norm for the people. On the revelation of God's will, i.e., on His מִשְׁפָּט, there rests the obligation of the whole people and of each individual. . . .[11]

"An ethicising of law"[12] is also a primary emphasis relating to the development of the צדק (*ṣdq*) word group (cf. צֶדֶק [*ṣeḏeq*], herein).[13] Concerning the end of that process, Girdlestone has summarized the impact of צֶדֶק (*ṣeḏeq*, i.e. "righteousness, justice") as follows: "This quality indeed may be viewed, according to Scripture, in two lights. In its relative aspect it implies conformity with the line or rule of God's law; in its absolute aspect it is the exhibition of love to God and to one's neighbor. . . ."[14] Therefore,

---

[10] I.e. one of the key words for the Word used throughout this psalm (cf. vv. 7, 13, 20, 30, 39, 43, 52, 62, 75, 84, 91, 102, 106, 108, 120, 137, 149, 156, 160, 164, 175).

[11] *TDNT*, s.v. "κρίνω, κτλ.," by F. Büchsel and V. Herntrich, 3:926–27; most of Herntrich's survey is valuable, cf. "The OT Terms מִשְׁפָּט," pp. 923–33.

[12] *TDNT*, s.v. "δίκη, κτλ.," by G. Quell and G. Schrenk, 2:174; cf. Quell's "The Concept of Law in the OT," pp. 174–78.

[13] At this juncture, cf. *TWOT*, s.v. "צֶדֶק (*ṣedeq*)," by H. Stigers, 2:752–55, for a survey of this word group; more commentary relating to its significance will surface in the eighteenth stanza of this psalm, esp. vv. 137–38. Also, review noun occurrences in vv. 7, 62, 75, 106 (and notice those forthcoming in vv. 123, 142, 144, 160, 164, 172).

[14] Girdlestone, *Synonyms*, p. 101.

these attributes of מִשְׁפָּט and צֶדֶק, which reside innately and perfectly in the person and precepts of God, must also be increasingly manifesting themselves through the people of God. The ethical conduct enjoined by Moses (e.g. Deut 10:12–13) and exhorted by the prophets (e.g. Isa 1:17; 56:1; 61:8; Jer 22:3; Mic 6:8), must be exhibited through the life-styles of true disciples. That the psalmist took these challenges very seriously is confirmed by his dynamic conformity to these ethical norms (עָשִׂיתִי [*ᶜāśîṯî*], i.e. "*I have dealt* justly and equitably [i.e. with others]").

Immediately flowing out of his right conduct issues his request for rescue (v. 121b). Phrasing the plea negatively, he prays that his LORD will not abandon him to his oppressors. The word he employs for abandonment is not the commonly attested עָזַב (*ᶜāzaḇ*),[15] but a Hiphil verb from the root נוּחַ (*nûaḥ*). In this stem the term literally denotes "to cause to rest"; however, it exhibits a wide variety of connotations in its various contextual settings. Examples of meaning in some negative settings could be to lay down forcibly, leave (in present condition), leave behind, abandon, let alone, etc.[16] It is difficult to determine whether this form is functioning more literally or more metaphorically (and ironically) in verse 121b, since

> in the Hiphil the root moves in two directions, the causative and the permissive. First, in the sense of "deposit," i.e. cause something (someone) to *nûaḥ*. . . . The second use is "to allow something (someone) to be at rest," i.e. leave alone.[17]

---

[15] Internally, cf. its occurrence at v. 8. It is interesting to note that the Targum uses שְׁבַק (*šᵉḇaq*), an Aramaic equivalent for the Hebrew עָזַב (*ᶜāzaḇ*), in its rendering of the Hiphil of נוּחַ (*nûaḥ*) herein; however, whereas the LXX regularly employs ἐγκαταλείπω (*egkataleipō*) for עָזַב, it turns to the more graphic παραδίδωμι (*paradidōmi*), i.e. *to deliver over* (cf., e.g., its occurrences in Rom 1:24, 26, 28; it is even the word of choice for the concept of *betrayal* in the NT) for capturing the nuance of נוּחַ herein.

[16] BDB, pp. 628–29. They also mention "bequeath" when complemented by the preposition לְ (*l*) as here (p. 629); if it is used in this manner in v. 121b it is obviously an ironic, eye-catching metaphor.

[17] *TWOT*, s.v. "נוּחַ (*nûaḥ*)," by L. Coppes, 2:562.

His impassioned prayer that God *not* cause him to נוּחַ could legitimately be looked upon as going in either of the aforementioned directions.

Nevertheless, irrespective of what subtle nuances the child of God may have had in mind when he delivered this plea of prohibition to the LORD, his realm of rescue is clearly delineated by the substantive participle with first person singular suffix from עָשַׁק (*ᶜāšaq*, to oppress, wrong, etc.),[18] i.e. deliverance from "*my oppressors.*"[19] Often in the OT it is this root which characterizes a life-style which is conceptionally antithetical to that exemplified in verse 121a,[20] since "*ᶜāšaq* is concerned with acts of abuse of power or authority, the burdening, trampling, and crushing of those lower in station."[21] With such acts of hostility this suffering servant was intimately acquainted; therefore, he urgently implores his LORD's intervention.

Before reiterating a similar plea for the prevention of oppression in verse 122b, he breathes a positive prayer for protection in verse 122a: "Stand surety for your servant's welfare."[22] The imagery that carries this petition heavenward is extremely rich. The

---

[18] BDB, p. 798; for an enlightening survey of Semitic cognates, see *TWOT*, s.v. "עָשַׁק (*ᶜāshaq*)," by R. Allen, 2:705.

[19] The LXX says in v. 121b that these people were doing wrong to him, i.e. they were treating him unjustly (from ἀδικέω [*adikeō*]; contra his behavior in v. 121a); however, in v. 122b where an imperfect form of the same Hebrew root occurs, the Greek employs a form of the verb συκοφαντέω (*sykophanteō*), meaning to slander, accuse falsely (cf. previous affirmations of the psalmist along these lines), to extort, etc. The Latin Vulgate, however, utilizes the same term in both verses in correspondence with the recurrence of the same root in Hebrew (cf. also the Targum), and interestingly, the Latin terminology comes into English as "calumniators" and "to calumniate" respectively in vv. 121b and 122b.

[20] E.g. note Jer 21:12; 22:3; Pss 72:4; 103:6; 105:14; 146:7; Prov 14:31; etc. In the light of the total impact of Ps 119:121 it is likely that the persecuted psalmist had these and/or similar texts and truths in his mind.

[21] *TWOT*, 2:705.

[22] Allen's pleasing rendering (*Psalms 101–150*, p. 132); he appends the following note to his translation: "Heb. ערב [*ᶜrḇ*] means to take over responsibility for another" (p. 138).

verb עָרַב (*ᶜārab*), from which the leading imperative of verse 122a derives, means "to be/become surety, mortgage, engage, occupy, undertake for; . . . to be/become bail for," etc.[23] It "signifies to stand in any one's place as furnishing a guarantee."[24] "In legal terminology this would mean that a person is held legally responsible for the debt of another man (see Gen. 43:9, 44:9; Prov. 6:1, 11:15, 17:18, 20:16, etc.)."[25] Herein the intention is that God would boldly interpose as a "mediator," placing "Himself between" the disciple "and his enemies."[26] Therefore, the basic thrust of his prayer is: "'Be my protector and helper.'"[27] It is possible that similar pleas having come from the lips of Job (17:3) and Hezekiah (Isa 38:14) were echoing in the ears of this tormented saint's burdened heart.

His appeal for *direct* Divine intervention conveyed through the imperative addressed to God in verse 122a is now recast more *indirectly* (i.e. providentially) through a negated jussive of which the זֵדִים (i.e. "impetuous men"[28]) is subject: "Do not allow insolent men to oppress me" (v. 122b). Also, with the negative, the dimension of prevention (cf. v. 121b) once again comes to the forefront. This time the substantive changes from "my oppressors" to the "proud ones";[29] however, the key verb once again focuses on oppression. Consequently, in the light of the prayers of vv. 121b, 122a, and 122b the dependent disciple fully recognizes that the

---

[23] *TWOT*, s.v. "עָרַב (*ᶜārab*) II," by R. Allen, 2:693; his survey of Semitic cognates, discussion of background, and theological observations pertaining to both Testaments is worthy of study (pp. 693–94). Concerning the noun form of this Hebrew root having become a loan word with rich associations, esp. as strategically employed in the NT, see the brief summary in *TDNT*, s.v. "ἀρραβών [*arrabōn*]," by J. Behm, 1:475 (note esp. 2 Cor 5:5 and Eph 1:14).

[24] Delitzsch, *Psalms*, 3:258; cf. Moll, *Psalms*, p. 592.

[25] Anderson, *Psalms*, 2:838.

[26] Delitzsch, *Psalms*, 3:258.

[27] Anderson, *Psalms*, 2:838.

[28] Cf. this appellation in vv. 21, 51, 69, 78, 85.

[29] Many translations prefer this rendering for זֵדִים (*zēḏîm*); it should be noted that with the exception of v. 85 the LXX employs ὑπερήφανοι (*huperēphanoi*), "arrogant ones," throughout the psalm for זֵדִים.

primary basis for his expectation of deliverance resides with God, Who is the ultimate source of all rectitude.[30]

An assertion (v. 123) breaks the string of petitions, thereby introducing a new focus. The hurting child of God resurrects and reassembles the language of longing from verses 81a and 82a[31] at this juncture in order to state his personal devotion. His *expression* of expectation here also seems (cf. v. 121a) to function as a kind of secondary basis for Divine attention. However, in the phrasing of those things which constitute the *objects* of his expectation, i.e. God's "salvation" and God's "word of righteousness," he unveils his transcendent basis of hope. Amidst all sorts of dark circumstances a flame of real confidence in God's word burned within him. His hope of Divine deliverance was fanned by the personalizing of his God's righteous promise along with the anticipation of its fulfillment.[32]

The request for Divine concern and care in verse 124a resides in a covenantal context. Besides referring to himself again as עַבְדְּךָ (*ᶜa<u>b</u>dᵉ<u>k</u>ā*), "Your servant," this needy worshipper predicates his bold request upon the precedent of his LORD's loyalty, i.e. "in accord with Your 'covenant grace.'"[33] The combination of God's *doing* (i.e. עשׂה [*ᶜśh*]) חֶסֶד (*ḥese<u>d</u>*), i.e. of His dealing faithfully and loyally, is found in a host of passages throughout the Scriptures.[34] In addition, this bold prayer request is personalized by the preposi-

---

[30] Cf. the secondary basis of his own ethical conduct in v. 121a.

[31] Note the significance of the verb כָּלָה (*kālâ*) in those verses, especially in combination with "my eyes." The first two words of v. 82 are identical to the first two of v. 123 except the order is reversed (obviously in order to integrate them into their respective acrostic patterns).

[32] Cf. Anderson, *Psalms*, 2:838.

[33] I.e. Zimmerli's appealing rendering of חֶסֶד (*ḥese<u>d</u>*) in such contexts as this one; see *TDNT*, s.v. "χάρις, κτλ.," by H. Conzelmann and W. Zimmerli, 9:383. His whole treatment should be surveyed for its many excellent observations and because of its recognition of the balance of the term's major theological contributions (ibid., pp. 381–87).

[34] Cf. the explicit combination of עשׂה (*ᶜśh*) plus חסד (*ḥs<u>d</u>*) in the following strategic contexts: Exod 20:6; Deut 5:10; Jer 9:23 [v. 24, Eng]; 32:18; etc. Besides עשׂה many other dynamic verbals are used with חסד to guarantee His promise, thereby giving to His people assurance of eventual action.

tion עִם (*ᶜim*) which "in particular stresses a close relationship."[35] The disciple therefore awaits Divine "conduct in relation, and in demonstration of this relation, . . . grace shown, or ready to show itself, in relation."[36]

The first phase of God's grace personally mediated will undoubtedly come through Divine guidance (v. 124b). Amidst the pressures of his persecutors a recurrent plea[37] for transcendent insight emerges. As Delitzsch notes, "The one chief petition of the poet . . . to which he comes back in vers. 124 sq., has reference to the ever deeper knowledge of the word of God; for this knowledge is in itself at once life and blessedness, and the present calls most urgently for it."[38] Irrespective of conditions, however, to be taught the Word of God by the God of the Word should be every disciple's perennial desire.[39]

The pattern of affirmation (cf. vv. 121a; 123) followed by expectation (cf. vv. 121b–122; 124) continues, but now in an extended form. A third affirmation of the primary variety is found in verse 125a, and it is followed by explicit and implicit expectations (i.e. vv. 125b–126) which are secondarily grounded upon the essential fidelity of the child of God (cf. vv. 127–128). One must circle back, however, to discover the primary basis of all his expectations, a vital relationship with God: עַבְדְּךָ־אָנִי (*ᶜabdᵉkā 'ānî*), "I *am* Your servant" (v. 125a). This statement picks up the previous contextual associations of covenant and personal relationship; however, now that vital intimacy established by the sovereign grace of God shines even more brightly.[40] As to the significance of this af-

---

[35] *TWOT*, s.v. "עמם (*ᶜmm*)," by G. Van Groningen, 2:677. On the corresponding significance of μετά (*meta*; cf. the LXX at Ps 119:124a), see *TDNT*, s.v. "σύν-μετά," by W. Grundmann, 7:766–97.

[36] *TDNT*, 9:382.

[37] See vv. 12, 26, 64, 68, 135; cf. vv. 66, 108.

[38] Delitzsch, *Psalms*, 3:258.

[39] This is *true discipleship* (i.e. again note the significance of the root למד [*lmd*]), being personally and very practically instructed by God.

[40] Cf. Anderson's appropriate note herein: "The term 'servant' . . . may suggest, not only the writer's dependence upon God, but also the more personal relationship based on a Covenant" (*Psalms*, 2:838).

firmation in its immediate context it would be advantageous to compare the pronouncement of verse 94a (i.e. לְךָ־אֲנִי [*lᵉkā ʾănî*]; "I *am* Yours") in its respective setting.

Verse 125a is pivotal in another way. On each side of it, like bookends, stand two of the disciple's primary prayer requests: "Teach me!" (v. 124b)[41] and "Give me understanding!" (v. 125b; cf. vv. 27, 34, 73, 144, 169).[42] Although both requests are intimately related in a conceptual manner, the former is more succinct in that it is followed by a simple direct object, "Your precepts," i.e. one of the terms for God's preceptive declarations for life's demands. However, the full directional orientation of the persecuted poet's plea for a transcendent understanding (i.e. v. 125b) is manifested through the intentional clause which follows it: "that" (or, "then") "I may (or, "shall") know Your testimonies" (v. 125c). Consequently, his prayer for *Divine discernment* (the essence of בין [*byn*]) is made all the more clear through its focus on *practical perception* (the essence of ידע [*ydᶜ*]).[43] Concerning ידע in such contexts as this, Schmitz has well observed:

> Experience becomes a reality in a relationship based on familiarity with the person or thing known. The use of *yādaᶜ* in the wisdom literature is an example of this. It speaks of a knowledge which is empirical and living. . . . While the Gks. were concerned with detached knowledge and a speculative interest in the metaphysical nature of things, the OT regards knowledge as something which continually arises from personal encounter.[44]

---

[41] Cf. v. 124 above for the data spread.

[42] Also cf. the non-imperatival occurrences of בִּין (*bîn*) in vv. 95, 100, 104, 130.

[43] For a few helpful observations based upon ידע (*ydᶜ*) in the OT, see: *TDNT*, s.v. "γινώσκω, κτλ.," by F. Büchsel, 1:696–703.

[44] *NIDNTT*, s.v. "Knowledge," by E. D. Schmitz, 2:395, 396; for some general background on the Hebrew conception of wisdom, cf. *NIDNTT*, s.v. "Wisdom, Folly, Philosophy," by J. Goetzmann, C. Brown, and H. Weigelt, 3:1023–38.

It is only that kind of personal knowledge of the God of the Word mediated through the Word of God[45] that can provide sufficient resources for the pressures and pains, and in the case of this psalmist, the persecutions of life in the real world.

Divine intervention[46] in the presence of human infidelity is the heart's desire of the suffering sojourner in the last portion of this stanza. The implicit imprecation of verse 126a is first justified negatively in light of the actions of the enemies of God and His disciple (i.e. v. 126b), then, in a positive vein, its appropriateness is confirmed by the contrasting attitudes of the child of God (i.e. vv. 127–28).

Concerning the negative dimension of his evidence for the propriety of Divine intervention, he summarizes the whole gamut of their malignant behavior by affirming that "they have broken Your law." The key verb is a Hiphil perfect of פָּרַר (*pārar*) I, to break or frustrate.[47] The significance and seriousness of such an accusation is illuminated by this verb's Semitic cognates (e.g. to shatter, destroy[48]), by some of the renderings of the early versions (e.g. to break or desecrate [Aramaic Targum],[49] to disband [LXX]),[50] and by the fact that in nearly one-half of the term's occurrences in the OT the object of such breakings is the covenant.[51] In an ethical context such as this there is an unmistakable reference to the violation of revealed truth.[52] Concrete examples of violation have surfaced and will continue to surface throughout the psalmist's cycles of lament.

---

45 Appropriately His "testimonies" (i.e. that which bears witness to Him) herein.

46 Cf. the translation notes on the viability of this interpretive option.

47 BDB, p. 830.

48 Ibid.

49 I.e. פִּיס (*pîs*); cf. Jastrow, *Dictionary*, 2:1166.

50 I.e. an aorist of διασκεδάννυμι (*diaskedannymi*).

51 See *TWOT*, s.v. "פָּרַר (*pārar*) I," by V. Hamilton, 2:738.

52 Ibid.

However, in reference to the faithful child of God, he reveres (v. 127) and respects (v. 128a) whatever is right but repulses whatever is wrong (v. 128b). Love for the word of God is again prioritized in verse 127 (cf. esp. v.72).[53] Anderson briefly but adequately sets the comparison that the psalmist draws into its biblical background: "The idea that wisdom is superior to gold and silver is quite a common concept in the Sapiential literature (cf. Job 22:25, 28:15f.; Prov. 3:14, 8:10, 19, 16:16, etc.). Here the comparison is between the commandments of God and gold."[54] However, the child of God accentuates his affirmation of love even further by adding the appositional statement "even more than pure gold." By referring to פָּז (*paz*), fine gold or unalloyed gold,[55] he unequivocally confesses that his commitment to God's revelation is more intense than man's infatuation with the purest form of earth's most precious metal.

Between statements of his love (v. 127) and of his hate (v. 128b) stands an affirmation (v. 128a) which has historically precipitated significant textual conjectures and hermeneutical opinions.[56] Often those who emend the Hebrew construct chain of "all precepts *concerning* all *things*" (כל פקודי כל [*kl pqwdy kl*]) to "by all Your precepts" (i.e. the traditional conjecture: לכל פקודיך [*lcl pqwdyk*]),[57] do

---

[53] Cf. also אָהֵב (*'āhēb*) in vv. 47, 48, 97, 113, 119, 132, 140, 159, 163, 165, 167; and on the comparative force of the preposition מִין (*min*), see BDB, pp. 582–83.

[54] Anderson, *Psalms*, 2:839.

[55] Cf. Ps 19:11 (v. 10, Eng). Note the Targum's אוֹבְרִיזָא (*'ôbᵉrîzā'*) at v. 127b; cf. Jastrow, *Dictionary*, 1:21. As Anderson has observed, "'Fine gold' (*paz*) is one of the several words used to denote gold in the OT, and the main difference between the various types of gold was probably in the degree of purity" (*Psalms*, 2:839).

[56] For a synopsis of the textual emendations and their tangential interpretive options see the translation notes above.

[57] Other more recent options proposed have been כל פקודיך לישרתי (*kl pqwdyk lysrty*; cf. J. H. Eaton, *VT* 18 [1968]: 557–58) and כל פקודיך לי (*kl pqwdyk ly*; cf. Soll "Psalm 119," p. 202).

so in order to align their interpretation of the leading verb from ישׁר (*yšr*) with the renderings of the LXX and Vulgate which they feel are more in line with what the psalmist was intending to express. The assumption is that what he wanted to say was: "I *make* (my steps) *straight* by means of Your precepts." However, Semitic tradition (e.g. DSS [Q11] and the Aramaic Targum) substantively supports the allegedly awkward phraseology of the MT. For example, the Targum uses a verbal of תְּרַץ (*tᵉraṣ*), meaning "set aright (mentally), settle, harmonize,"[58] to render the Hebrew verb from יָשַׁר (*yāšar*).

Consequently, the text as it stands would suggest that it is best to conclude that the verb puts more emphasis on the psalmist's attitude than upon his actions,[59] i.e. the disciple reckons all the stipulations of God's Word to be right about everything. This understanding may also be supported by the verb's placement between the two strongly attitudinal verbs for love and hate. Nevertheless, as already noted, in Hebrew ethics the emphasis is never merely upon contemplation. Always in the background are the assumptions of internalization and realization.

A significant by-product of such reckonings based upon the Word's universally applicable infallible standards is a hatred of all expressions and exhibitions of falsity (v. 128b).[60] An important facet of biblical ethics, as well exemplified herein by the man of God, is a consistently negative attitude toward, and recoil from, anything and everything the norms of Scripture expose as unethical.

---

[58] Jastrow, *Dictionary*, 2:1702.

[59] Cf. BDB's suggestion for this occurrence: "esteem right, approve" (p. 448).

[60] Cf. שֶׁקֶר in vv. 29, 69, 78, 86, 104, 118, 163.

פ

PE STANZA (vv. 129–136)

Translation and Notes

129 Your testimonies are wonderful;[a]
therefore,[b] my soul[c] keeps[d] them.[e]

130 The unfolding[a] of Your words[b] gives light,[c]
giving understanding to *the* simple.

131 I open[a] my mouth and pant,[a]
because[b] I long for[a, c] Your commandants.

132 Turn to me and be gracious to me
according to *Your* custom[a] with those who love Your name.

133 Establish[a] my footsteps by means of[b] Your word,[c]
and do not let any iniquity have dominion[d] over me.

134 Redeem me from mankind's[a] oppression,
and I will[b] keep[c] Your precepts.

135 Make Your face shine[a] on Your servant,
and teach me Your precepts.

136 My eyes shed streams of tears,[a]
because[b] *people*[c] do not[d] keep Your law.

129:a Lit., "Your testimonies are wonders" (fpl noun). Note that DSS (Q11) has פלגי נפת (*plgy npṯ*), "streams of honey" herein; however, no other textual or versional evidence differs in this way from the MT.
129:b The third occurrence of עַל־כֵּן (*ʿal-kēn*) in as many verses.
129:c Or, נַפְשִׁי (*napšî*) standing pleonastically for "I."

129:d נָצַר (*nāṣar*) as the term for obedience here (cf. vv. 2, 33, 34, 69, 115, 145).

129:e Note the rare discord of gender between the pronominal suffix on נְצָר (i.e. mpl) and its obvious antecedent עֵדְוֹתֶיךָ (*ᶜēdwōṯeykā*); i.e. fpl).

130:a Taking פתח (*pṯḥ*) as the masculine noun פֵּתַח (*pēṯaḥ*), meaning "opening, unfolding," from פָּתַח I (*pāṯaḥ* I), "to open" (cf. BDB, pp. 834–836). Some take as the masculine noun פֶּתַח (*peṯaḥ*), "doorway, entrance," from the same root (ibid., p. 835; cf. the Vulgate and also Symmachus). The LXX renders ἡ δήλωσις (*hē dēlōsis*), "manifestation, explanation," etc.; cf. Allen's preference of "revelation" (*Psalms 101–150*, pp. 132, 138). It is suggested by others that the form should be re-pointed as an imperative (i.e. "unfold . . . !" cf. Sanders, *Dead Sea Psalms Scroll*, p. 57). Another option may be noted in the Targum; its rendering גְּלִיפָא (*gᵉlîp̱āʾ*), "shaping (of writing), impress," etc. (cf. Jastrow, *Dictionary*, 1:249) obviously looked upon the Hebrew word as having come from פָּתַח (*pāṯaḥ*) II, to "engrave" (cf. BDB, p.836).

130:b Some manuscripts exhibit a singular, דברך (*dḇrḵ*) i.e. "Your word," but note DSS (Qll), LXX, Targum, etc. stand in agreement with the plural of the MT.

130:c DSS (Qll) reads as an imperative, והאר (*wh'r*), i.e. "and enlighten . . . !"

131:a The three verbs respectively are perfect, imperfect consecutive, and perfect. Although in narrative this would normally require "I opened . . . I panted . . . I desired. . . ," they are better construed as linear or characteristic herein (cf. the comments made about tense or aspect in vv. 2ff.).

131:b DSS (Qll) omits causal כִּי (*kî*).

131:c The verb יָאַב (*yā'aḇ*) represents a *hapax legomenon*. It is very likely an Aramaism, but not necessarily "late" as BDB (p. 383) always assume. Note that DSS (Qll) reads תאב (*t'ḇ*) herein (cf. this root for *desire* in vv. 40 and 174). Based upon an alignment of two out of three consonants, it is likely that both יאב and תאב derive from אבה (*'ḇh*; cf. Delitzsch, *Psalms*, 3:259).

132:a Taking the prepositional phrase with מִשְׁפָּט (*mišpāṭ*) idiomatically (cf. BDB, p. 1049); cf. the use of הִלְכְתָא (*hilkᵉtā'*), "custom, habit" (Jastrow, *Dictionary*, 1:353) in the Targum and note an English conceptualization of this idiom in NIV: "as you always do to those who love your name." However, there are some acceptable options for connecting the prepositional phrase's meaning with a more literal usage of מִשְׁפָּט (cf., e.g., Anderson, *Psalms*, 2:840; and Soll, "Psalm 119," pp. 202–03).

133:a Or, "make firm"; BDB, p. 466, suggest "direct" or "order aright" with an ethical metaphor such as "steps."

133:b Taking the preposition בְּ (*bᵉ*) of MT instrumentally. DSS (Qll) has ל (*l*), while the LXX reads as if the text had been כְּ (*kᵉ*). Concerning a trend herein among several modern translations Kidner has appropriately commented: "'By (or, in) thy word' is the meaning of the Hebrew, which makes very good sense. But *bᵉ* ('by' or 'in') and *kᵉ* ('according to') are easily confused, and some early evidence favours the latter, which is followed, perhaps unnecessarily, by most modern versions" (*Psalms 73–150*, p. 428).

133:c Or, once again, more specifically as "Your *promise*."

133:d Concerning the minor variant relating to gender herein Allen has noted: "*Pace BHS* LXX *S* do not imply ישלט [*yšlṭ*] 'he will master' but wrongly construed און [*'wn*] as feminine" (*Psalms 101–150*, p. 138).

134:a I.e. אָדָם (*'āḏām*).

134:b I.e. with a cohortative emphasis (cf. Alexander, *Psalms*, 3:189). Other options are "that" or "then I may . . ." (cf. Dahood, *Psalms*, 3:188).

134:c שָׁמַר (*šāmar*) as the term for obedience here (cf. vv. 4, 5, 8, 9, 17, 34, 44, 55, 57, 60, 63, 67, 88, 101, 106, 136, 146, 158, 167, 168); cf. its synonym נָצַר (*nāṣar*) in v. 129.

135:a As one of the "standard expressions for the restoration of a relationship of favour between God and man," see Eichrodt, *Theology of the OT*, 2:36–37.

136:a Lit., "My eyes run down *with* channels of waters" (cf. Davidson, *Hebrew Syntax*, § 73, Rem. 2).

136:b The syntax of the MT is abbreviated having only עַל (*ᶜal*). DSS (QII) reads על כי (*ᶜl ky*), and the versions generally support a causal rendering. Therefore, Anderson's conclusion is credible: "The preposition *ᶜal* is apparently used for *ᶜal ʾᵃšer*, or it has the force of a conjunction (cf. BDB, p. 758a)" (*Psalms*, 2:840–41). For notations, see GKC § 155n; and Williams, *Hebrew Syntax*, § 534.
136:c I.e. "they" (3 c pl verb); herein, *ad sensum* (cf., e.g. the אָדָם [*ʾāḏām*] of v. 134).
136:d I.e. the objective negation לֹא (*lōʾ*); likely for polemical emphasis, "they *never* keep . . . ."

Synopsis and Outline

The *Pē* stanza is a mosaic of thematic and stylistic constituents. For example, verses 129–131 are affirmations about the Word of God, while verses 132–135 contain petitions delivered to the God of the Word. This leaves verse 136 which summarizes the psalmist's reaction to the enemies of both God and His Word.

Building explicitly upon the truth of verse 18 and implicitly upon requests such as those recorded in verses 33–34, *et al.*, this stanza further develops the priority of illumination (cf., esp., v. 130).[1] This emphasis fits very well into the larger context of the disciple's preoccupation with and longing for a sustained Divine guidance.[2]

---

[1] There also may be *within* this stanza both explicit and implicit evidence relating to illumination. When the total impact of v. 135 is contemplated (esp. the recurrence of the root אור [*ʾwr*] in v. 135a followed by a request to be taught in v. 135b), it is possible to regard the psalmist as being concerned about his need for both propositional (i.e. v. 130) and personal (i.e. v. 135) illumination.

[2] Note that a new metaphor, פְּעָמַי (*pᵉᶜāmay*), "my footsteps," is added to a stockpile of word-pictures relating to the rigorous road of life. Incidentally, there are no repetitions of initially occurring words in this stanza for the maintenance of the פ (*p*) acrostic.

More subtly, the child of God places himself within two contrasting contexts. His personal affirmations and requests (vv. 129b, 131, 132a, 133, 134, 135, 136a) stand among some third person generalizations (vv. 129a, 130, 132b, 134a, 136b). In the first four verses of *Pē* he stands as a member of the people of God,[3] while in the last four verses he stands opposed by the enemies of God.[4] Adding this insight to the previous observations, in this seventeenth stanza of Psalm 119 the child of God contemplates Divine direction from the context of two different associations.

1A. (vv. 129–132) The child of God contemplates Divine direction through a positive association with the obedient.
    1B. (vv. 129–131) The statements of the child of God in association with the obedient.
        1C. (v. 129) His statement on the extraordinary nature of revelation.
        2C. (v. 130) His statement on the value of illumination.
        3C. (v. 131) His statement on strong desire for spiritual refreshment.
    2B. (v. 132) The privileges available to the child of God in association with the obedient.
2A. (vv. 133–136) The child of God contemplates Divine direction through a negative association with the disobedient.
    1B. (vv. 133–135) The needs of the child of God in association with the disobedient.
        1C. (v. 133) His need for stability.
        2C. (v. 134) His need for rescue.
        3C. (v. 135) His need for communion.
    2B. (v. 136) The burden of the child of God in association with the disobedient.
        1C. (v. 136a) The effect of his burden.
        2C. (v. 136b) The reason for his burden.

---

[3] Especially noteworthy are his references to "giving the simple insight" (v. 130b), and to "the ones who love Your name" (v. 132b).

[4] Of special import are his references to "all iniquity" (v. 133b), "the oppression of man" (v. 134a), and "they do not keep Your law" (v. 136b).

Commentary

A noun form built upon the root פלא (*pl'*) puts this stanza into motion.[5] The same root occurred as a Niphal participle (i.e. נִפְלָאוֹת [*niplā'ôt*]; "wonderful things") back in verse 18b.[6] Significantly, its context of usage therein (cf. v. 18a) parallels its proximate association herein with illumination (cf. v. 130). Since God's "testimonies are 'extraordinary, hard to be understood,'"[7] i.e. since both His word and His works[8] reveal "things that are unusual, beyond human capabilities,"[9] or, as expressed in the words of Delitzsch, "things, exalted above every-day life and the common understanding,"[10] a divinely assisted "contemplation of them" is essential "in order to understand them."[11] Prior to his summary of that transcendent enablement in verse 130, the dedicated disciple again affirms his obedience to his LORD's testimonies (v. 129b). Furthermore, such unwavering fidelity to God's Word is viewed logically[12] as being commensurate with the very essence or nature of that word.

The structure of verse 130 closely parallels verses 8a, 8b, 9a, and 9b (in Eng: vv. 7a, 7b, 8a, 8b) in the Nineteenth Psalm—an affirmation followed by a demonstration. In the case of Psalm 19

---

5 It is noteworthy that this root is used in conjunction with both the written and the Living Word of God (cf. Judg 13:18; Isa 9:6).

6 As Hamilton has aptly concluded "there appears to be no significant difference here between *pele'* and *niplā'ōt*, both referring to God's wonders, either in a general sense, or in a specific historical antecedent" (*TWOT*, s.v. "פָּלָא [*pālā'*]," by V. Hamilton, 2:723).

7 BDB, p. 810.

8 Cf. Anderson: "'wonders' (*pᵉlā'ôt*) may refer to God's revelation both in word and deed" (*Psalms*, 2:839). At this juncture, it may be helpful to survey the LXX's utilization of the θαῦμα word group esp. for פלא; for a synopsis see *TDNT*, s.v. "θαῦμα, κτλ.," by G. Bertram, 3:29–36.

9 *TWOT*, 2:723.

10 Delitzsch, *Psalms*, 3:259.

11 Moll, *Psalms*, p. 592.

12 Cf. the עַל כֵּן (*ʿal kēn*), and note Scroggie's comment on v. 129: "Because God's Word is wonderful it should be believed and obeyed" (*Psalms*, p. 184).

the affirmations relate to what God's Word *is*, and the demonstrations[13] exemplify what it *does*. This verse pertains to *the illumination of* the Word of God and what *it* accomplishes. It is first described through picture (v. 130a), then through process and power (v. 130b).

The picture painted is one of the Word being opened[14] thereby resulting in a characteristic emanation[15] of brilliantly diffused light (cf. אוֹר [*'ôr*] in v. 105). God's opening up the Scriptures provides spiritually *necessary* illumination because of man's finite and fallen faculties.[16] Both innate darkness and lingering shadows are dispelled by His incandescent intervention.[17]

---

[13] In both psalms these characteristic demonstrations are conveyed powerfully through causal participles. Semantical and conceptual parallelisms are also detectable; for example, the root אור (*'wr*) occurs in Pss 119:130a and 19:9b, the word פֶּתִי (*peṯî*) in 119:130b and 19:8b, and the participle from בִּין (*bîn*) in 119:130b corresponds conceptually with the participle from the root חכם (*ḥkm*) in 19:8b.

[14] Although the LXX employs δήλωσις (*dēlōsis*; cf. the translation notes above), the action noun of the Hebrew (i.e. פֵּתַח [*pēṯaḥ*]) is conceptually analogous with the Greek verb διανοίγω (*dianoigō*); cf. NT usage at Luke 24:32, 45; Acts 16:14; 17:3. Those who prefer the alternate pointing פֶּתַח (*peṯaḥ*), "doorway, entrance" (BDB, p. 835), apparently do so based upon the imagery they felt the psalmist was desiring to convey; for example, cf. Cohen: "lit. 'doorway'. In Palestine houses are mostly windowless, the light entering through the doorway. Light comes through God's word as the sun's light through an eastern door" (*Psalms*, p. 411).

[15] Stressing the causative *imperfect* form of the root אור (*'wr*), i.e. יָאִיר (*yā'îr*): "it [habitually] gives light."

[16] Concerning the root אור (*'wr*) in this and similar contexts, Pratt notes that it "refer[s] to the light that comes chiefly to the *intellect* or *mind* through Divine instruction" (*ISBE* [1939], s.v. "Light," by Pratt, 3:1891). Through the gracious process of opening up the richness of revelation God transmits spiritual "insight" (cf. Dahood, *Psalms*, 3:188) to needy recipients. Only in His light do we see light (cf. Ps 36:9).

[17] For further theological commentary predicated upon this text, see Alexander, *Psalms*, 3:188.

The subordinate participial phrase of verse 130b, well rendered "giving understanding unto the simple,"[18] illustrates the powerful process of illumination. בִּין (*bîn*), a primary term in this psalm for perception and insight, again surfaces,[19] but this time in the form of a causative participle (i.e. מֵבִין [*mēḇîn*]). Its thrust in this context is that God's opening up the words from His Word brings illumination by characteristically imparting understanding (i.e. spiritual perception and discernment) to those who are open-minded. In reference to people designated as פְּתָיִים (*peṯāyîm*),[20] "simple" or "open-minded" (ones),[21] usage in context must determine whether the term is being used in a derogatory or a commendable way.[22] In Psalms 19:8 (v.7, Eng); 116:6; and especially in 119:130, these "simple ones" are characterized by a humble dependence upon God and His resources. They stand diametrically opposed to haughty and double-minded people in Scripture.[23] In 119:130 they are obviously noted for their teachability;[24] they

[18] Cf., e.g., Delitzsch, *Psalms*, 3:240.

[19] Cf. this root in vv. 27, 34, 73, 95, 100, 104, 125, 144, 169. For a brief but adequate survey of this term in the OT the reader is once again directed to Girdlestone's *Synonyms*, p. 74. As Scroggie notes: "The Psalmist recognizes the importance of right thinking. Ten times he speaks of understanding. . . . *Biyn* means to separate mentally, to discern, distinguish and so to *understand*" (*Psalms*, p. 177).

[20] In Hebrew, both ends of v. 130 are related through paronomasia: פְּתָיִים . . . פֵּתַח (*pēṯaḥ* . . . *peṯāyîm*). Also, it is likely that both derive from the same Hebrew root (i.e. to open; cf. BDB, pp. 834–36).

[21] BDB, p. 834.

[22] A fairly consistent differentiation is detected in the LXX. In positive contexts, as here, the term of choice for the Hebrew פֶּתִי (*peṯî*) is νήπιος (*nēpios*), a child or infant (in the NT, cf. esp. Matt 11:25 [para. Luke 10:21] and 21:16). For a good summary paragraph relating to the positive usage of νήπιος in the Psalms, see *TDNT*, s.v. "νήπιος," by G. Bertram, 4:917. In pejorative contexts, the term ἄφρων occurs quite regularly as indicating a senseless, foolish, or witless one. Such an one is "open to all kinds of enticement, not having developed a discriminating judgment as to what is right or wrong" (*TWOT*, s.v. "פֶּתִי (*peṯî*)," by L. Goldberg, 2:742).

[23] Recall esp. the סֵעֲפִים (*sēcăp̄îm*) of v. 113.

[24] Cf. Scroggie, *Psalms*, p. 185.

"keep their heart open to [the Word's] beneficial influences."[25] Delitzsch's review of verse 130 also uncovers a conceptual transition to the next verse:

> The opening, disclosure . . . of God's word giveth light, inasmuch as it makes the simple . . . wise or sagacious; in connection with which it is assumed that it is God Himself who unfolds the mysteries of His word to those who are anxious to learn. Such an one, anxious to learn, is the poet: . . .[26]

Graphic metaphors[27] expose his deep desire for spiritual refreshment in verse 131. These first two verbs "are figurative expressions of the idea conveyed directly by the third verb, which occurs nowhere else, but differs only in a single letter from the verb of the same meaning used in vs. 40, 174."[28] Consequently, the disciple's *longing* or *desire*[29] for his LORD's commandments (v. 131b) is illustrated by a parched and panting animal (v. 131a).[30] He stands before his Creator like an antelope doggedly pursued by hunters, i.e. "with gaping mouth."[31] The verb פָּעַר (*pā^{c}ar*) with its object פִּי (*pî*) denotes literally, "I opened wide my mouth," obviously a statement "of eager desire."[32] As Dahood notes, the term's

---

[25] Leupold, *Psalms*, p. 852. Anderson cites "I Qp Hab xii:4: 'the simple ones of Judah who keep the law'" (*Psalms*, 2:840).

[26] Delitzsch, *Psalms*, 3:259.

[27] Some would take the two assertions as a hendiadys; e.g. "I gasp with open mouth" (NAB), or "I pant open-mouthed" (Allen, *Psalms 101–150*, p. 132).

[28] Alexander, *Psalms*, 3:188; on that third verb as a *hapax legomenon* see the translation notes above.

[29] Cf. BDB, p. 383. It has been mentioned that both יָאַב (*yā'aḇ*) here and תָּאַב (*tā'aḇ*) in vv. 40, 174 (cf. also the noun form in v. 20) are related to אָבָה (*'ābâ*) to be willing, etc. (BDB, p. 2)—or possibly אָוָה (*'āwâ*) II—often connoting "the inclination which leads towards action" (Girdlestone, *Synonyms*, p. 67).

[30] A similar illustration but employing different vocabulary occurs in Ps 42:2 (v. 1, Eng).

[31] Dahood, *Psalms*, 3:188.

[32] BDB, p. 822.

occurrence in Job 29:23, "'they opened wide their mouths as for the springs rains,'" provides "a fitting commentary on our text since it describes the attention with which Job's listeners absorbed his words."[33] The connected verb שָׁאַף (*šā'ap̱*), to gasp, pant, pant after, long for,[34] also speaks of an "eager longing."[35] When packaged together all the terms of verse 131 express his "devotion and earnestness"[36] in the presence of the only One who can meet such acute needs.

Panting gives way to his pursuit of privileges in verse 132. The first imperative that he uses to solicit benefits is from פָּנָה (*pānâ*), "to turn," and when it is used in combination with the directional preposition אֶל (*'el*), "to" or "unto," the result is a quite common idiomatic package which most frequently connotes personal attention (cf. the metaphor which stands at the head of v. 135).[37] From this plea for God's undivided attention, the child of God moves on immediately to a request for his LORD's gracious affection.[38] The root חנן (*ḥnn*)[39] stands as a member of an important trilogy (cf. חסד [*ḥsḏ*] and רחם [*rḥm*]) used to extol or beseech the

---

[33] Dahood, *Psalms*, 3:188.

[34] BDB, p. 983.

[35] Cohen, *Psalms*, p. 411.

[36] Scroggie, *Psalms*, p. 185.

[37] Cf. BDB, p. 815; in cases such as this they suggest the translation "regard" (ibid.). It should be noted that the LXX uses ἐπιβλέπω + ἐπί (*epiblepō* + *epi*), "contextually, to look upon in pity for the sake of giving aid" (Thayer, *Lexicon*, p. 236). Also, the connection with v. 135 seems to be more than logical; it is theological. From the root פנה also comes the Hebrew word for face, פָּנִים (*pānîm*). In Num 6:25ff. פָּנִים stands in parallelism with the root חנן (*ḥnn*, i.e. the *next* imperative of Ps 119:132). Therefore, referring to 119:132 and a few other passages, Freedman and Lundbom comment, "Indeed, the other Hebrew word most often translated 'favor' is פנים *pānîm*, 'face'. . . . Yahweh is frequently asked to 'turn'. . . and show favor . . . , i.e. turn and show his face (in mercy or kindness). To show one's face then means to be favorably disposed toward a person" (*TDOT*, s.v. "חָנַן *ḥānan*," by D. Freedman and J. Lundbom, 5:24).

[38] It is profitable to note the same combination of פָּנָה (*pānâ*) and חָנַן (*ḥānan*) in Pss 25:16 and 86:16.

[39] Cf. vv. 29 and 58 for verbal occurrences.

grace, favor, pity, compassion, etc., of God.[40] Yamauchi's brief synopsis of the Qal imperative with first person pronominal suffix in the Psalter is informative:

> The verb *ḥānan* depicts a heartfelt response by someone who has something to give to one who has a need. . . . The plea *ḥonnēnî*, "be gracious to me," appears nineteen times in the Psalms. The Psalmist asks Yahweh to show him favor in view of his loneliness . . . , his distress . . . , his transgressions . . . , etc.[41]

This psalmist's bold requests for favor are not immediately followed by the particulars of his predicament but by a general precedent for God's beneficent intervention.

The prepositional phrase כְּמִשְׁפָּט (*kᵉmišpāṭ*), "after the manner, custom, fashion,"[42] indicates that it is customary for the LORD to bestow such personal attention and affection.[43] However, the psalmist wishes to qualify his understanding of Divine beneficence somewhat by restricting it[44] to "those who love Your name."

---

[40] For a survey of Divine favor in the OT, see *TDOT*, 5:30–36.

[41] *TWOT*, s.v. "חָנַן (*ḥānan*) I," by E. Yamauchi, 1:302; his whole article on the חנן word group is excellent.

[42] BDB, p. 1049; cf. also their notes on כְּ (*kᵉ*) on pp. 453–54.

[43] That Leupold has grasped the significance of this phrase is indicated by the following comment: "What makes the psalmist bold to pray thus is the fact that God's gracious attitude toward men is His customary procedure in dealing with [H]is own" (*Psalms*, p. 852); cf. Dahood, *Psalms*, 3:188.

[44] The preposition לְ (*lᵉ*) is best construed herein as one of reference, e.g., "defining those in reference to whom a predicate is affirmed, hence oft[en]=belonging to, of" (BDB, p. 512). An interesting and informative NT comparison would be the dative substantive participle in Rom 8:28: τοῖς ἀγαπῶσιν τὸν θεόν (*tois agapōsin ton theon*), "(in reference) to those who love God."

God's special and most personalized privileges are reserved for those who are committed[45] to Him,[46] i.e. to those who are noted for their obedience to precept and Person.[47]

The precedent capsulized in verse 132b relates not only to the requests which precede it but also, by implication, to the avalanche of prayers which comes after it (i.e. vv. 133–135). Such an avalanche is triggered by a shift in context. The disciple is more distraught since he now logically views himself through the lens of his negative association with the disobedient.

In such a trying context he is liable to stagger and stumble. Consequently, his first request, a Hiphil imperative from כּוּן (*kûn*), implores stability.[48] With פְּעָמַי (*pe‘āmay*), "my steps," i.e. another metaphor for "conduct and life,"[49] the basic intent of his plea is "stabilize my steps!" Once again, such Divine direction[50] is expected to come to the troubled and teetering child of God through the channel of his LORD's reliable word.[51]

A negatively phrased request quickly follows: "Do not allow any iniquity to domineer me" (v. 133b). Only the supremely Sovereign One could restrain the tyrannical reign of iniquity or wick-

---

45 Cf. אָהֵב (*'āhēḇ*), "love," in vv. 47, 48, 97, 113, 119, 127, 140, 159, 163, 165 (substantive participle also), and 167, wherein some dimension of commitment is always discernible. Interestingly, the Vulgate herein employs a word which comes over into English as "to be diligent."

46 Cf. v. 55 for the other occurrence of שִׁמְךָ (*šimeḵā*), "Your name," in this psalm. God's "name" frequently stands for the totality of His "(revealed) character" (BDB, p. 1028); therefore, Briggs' comment on v. 132b is eminently germane: "Love for the name of God is another phase of the love of God Himself and of his Law so characteristic of this Ps." (*Psalms*, p. 433).

47 Recalling esp. the demands paralleled with אָהֵב (*'āhēb*) in covenant contexts (e.g. Deut 10:12; 11:13, 22; 19:9; 30:6; Josh 22:5; 23:11; etc.).

48 I.e. a primary significance of the root כּוּן (cf., e.g., Girdlestone, *Synonyms*, p. 102).

49 Barnes, *Psalms*, 2:216.

50 On this connotation of כּוּן plus פַּעַם see BDB, p. 466; Anderson, *Psalms*, 2:840; Allen, *Psalms 101–150*, p. 132; etc.

51 Cf. the translation notes above on a preference for an instrumental usage of the preposition בְּ (*be*) attached to אִמְרָתֶךָ (*'imrāṯeḵā*), i.e. "by," "with," or "by means of Your word" or "promise."

edness.[52] Concerning such אָוֶן (*'āwen*), "the primary meaning of the word seems to have two facets: a stress on trouble which moves on to wickedness, and an emphasis on emptiness which moves on to idolatry."[53] In the light of the immediate (cf. the root עשק [*ᶜšq*] in v. 134) and larger circles of context in Psalm 119, the former connotation seems to be paramount.[54] This term frequently "stresses the planning and expression of deception and points to the painful aftermath of sin."[55] But whose iniquity does the psalmist have in mind? His or that of others? In view of verses 134a and 136b, Anderson's suggestion is appealing: "It is possible that the Psalmist was not thinking of his own possible disobedience, but rather of the mischief caused by his opponents."[56]

The comprehensiveness of his request is conveyed through the association of כֹּל (*kōl*), "all," with the negative אַל (*'al*),[57] i.e. his heart's desire was that not one shred of iniquity would rule over

---

[52] Cf. Girdlestone, *Synonyms*, p. 83, on these primary renderings of אָוֶן (*'āwen*). The Semitic background of this explicit term used for sin manifests the concept of *power* (cf. *TDOT*, s.v. "אָוֶן *'āven*," by K. Bernhardt, 1:140–41), a concept eminently suitable in view of the graphic verb of prohibition utilized herein. For a good synopsis of this term's employment in the Psalter, see ibid., pp. 144–47.

[53] *TWOT*, s.v. "און (*'wn*)," by G. Livingston, 1:23. Girdlestone, probably wrongly, assumes that the latter stress on vanity is always dominant (*Synonyms*, p. 83).

[54] On a larger scale Livingston has well observed that "this trend of meaning in *'āwen* is reinforced by its proximity to standard Hebrew words for deception, fraud, and falseness . . ." (*TWOT*, 1:23; cf. *TDOT*, 1:142).

[55] *TWOT*, 1:23. It is interesting that the Targum employs שְׁקָר (*šᵉqār*) for אָוֶן here.

[56] Anderson, *Psalms*, 2:840. Nevertheless, as already observed, he himself was never arrogant or complacent. A true disciple is always aware of the potentiality of his own declension apart from a consistent dependence upon the gracious resources of God. Therefore, Delitzsch's observation is not outside the scope of theological reality: "כָּל־אָוֶן refers pre-eminently to all sin of disavowal (denying God), into which he might fall under outward and inward pressure" (*Psalms*, 3:259–60).

[57] Cf. GKC, § 152b, on a parallel usage of כֹּל plus לֹא (*lō'*).

him. The most eye-catching feature of verse 133b, however, is the choice of verbs on the part of the child of God. The verb שָׁלַט (*šālaṭ*) may be rendered "exercise power (over), dominate, have mastery."[58] Austel's comments on שָׁלַט, including his reference to Psalm 119:133, are very helpful:

> The essential idea of this root is "to exercise autocratic control over," "to have one's own way with" anyone. It appears with its derivatives fifteen times in the Hebrew and thirty-two times in the Aramaic, where the meaning is similar to the Hebrew. Akkadian and Arabic use the root in similar fashion. (The Arabic word "Sultan" is formed from the same root.) . . . In Ps 119:133, the psalmist prays that iniquity shall not have dominion over him. He wants to be firmly established in the Word of God so that he can be free from the terrible tyranny of sin.[59]

In verse 134 the lingering reality of the oppression that he was suffering at the hands of sinful men[60] again nearly consumes him. Therefore, his prayer to God for relief is especially graphic; he begs his LORD to release him from the bondage of his enemies. The background of the verb פָּדָה (*pādâ*), "to deliver, redeem, ransom, rescue," etc.,[61] illumines the nature of his request:

---

[58] *TWOT*, s.v. "שָׁלַט (*shālaṭ*) I," by H. Austel, 2:928.

[59] Ibid., p. 929. When the verb is complemented by the preposition בְּ (*b*ᵉ), as here, it indicates what or whom is overpowered or domineered (cf. BDB, p. 1020, for a survey of this combination). This psalmist wanted no form of iniquity lording it over him. For some conceptual (not directly semantical) parallels on sin mastering someone, see Ps 19:14 (v. 13, Eng) in the OT and Paul's use of κυριεύω (*kurieuō*) in Rom 6:14 in the NT.

[60] Cf. the occurrence of the root עשק (*ᶜšq*) here with those in vv. 121–122. Interestingly, the more specific renderings of the LXX and the Vulgate would convey that these sinful men were *slanderers*.

[61] Cf. the brief synopsis in Girdlestone, *Synonyms*, p. 120; note esp. his comparison and contrast with the root גאל (*g'l*), i.e. the kinsman redeemer concept (ibid.; cf. *TDNT*, s.v. "λύω, κτλ.," by O. Procksch, 4:331–35).

> the Hebrew *p-d-h* can denote the redemption of a slave or captive (cf. Exod. 21:8), as well as the ransom of a person (or an animal) from death, either by a substitute or by payment of money (cf. Exod. 13:13, 15; Num. 18:15f.). It can also be used figuratively to describe deliverance from any sort of trouble or from death. . . .[62]

Indeed, the experience of this disciple was not unique, for "the Psalms often speak of God's deliverance or redemption of life from some danger (Ps 26:11; 31:5; 34:22 [H 23]; 44:26 [H 27]; 71:23), or from the hand of human oppression (Ps 55:18 [H 19]; 69:18 [H 19]; cf. also Job 6:23)."[63]

When God does deliver, the man of God will have greater freedom for obedience, as the latter part of the verse implies. His intention[64] regarding Divine intervention, as so often has been the case, is oriented in the direction of practical worship. Such grateful obedience is here pledged through the strong volitional assertion "I *will* keep (אֶשְׁמְרָה [*'ešmᵉrâ*]) Your mandates."

In the context of his negative association with the disobedient, the child of God senses an acute need for personal communion with his God.[65] Therefore, he solicits both His personal blessing (v. 135a) and His personal instruction (v. 135b).[66] By returning to the root אוֹר (*'ôr*; cf. the noun in v. 105 and the verb in v. 130), "to

---

62 Anderson, *Psalms*, 2:840; for a fuller treatment, see *TWOT*, s.v. "פָּדָה (*pādâ*)," by W. Coker, 2:716–17. The statistically prevalent rendering in the LXX (i.e. λυτρόω [*lytroō*]) provides a bridge to both general (e.g. Luke 24:21) and soteriological usages in the NT (e.g. Titus 2:14).

63 *TWOT*, 2:716.

64 Cf. the translation notes on a purpose function for this subordinate *waw* clause.

65 Grammatically, note the three occurrences of 2 m s suffixes referring to God: "*Your* face," "*Your* servant," "*Your* statutes."

66 Scroggie's anecdote interestingly relates the two halves of the verse in the following manner: "The light in which we can best learn our lessons" (*Psalms*, p. 185). Once again, Ps 36:9 comes to mind.

be bright,"[67] or in Hiphil occurrences, such as here, "to disseminate light,"[68] "to cause to shine,"[69] the shadow-darkened disciple seeks illumination, not only the propositional illumination which comes through the Word of God but also the personal illumination which comes from the presence of the God of the Word. He wants to be the beneficiary of[70] the very countenance of God (פָּנֶיךָ [*pāneykā*], i.e. "Your face"),[71] i.e. he wants to experience His personal favor and grace.[72] Such language is obviously reminiscent of the Aaronic benediction of Numbers 6:25–26 (cf. Pss 4:6; 31:16; 67:1; 80:3, 7, 19; etc.).[73] After this request (v. 135a), he comes "back . . . to the one chief prayer 'teach me'" (v. 135b).[74] As Scroggie notes, "The Psalmist is resolved to learn, and he repeatedly calls upon the Lord to *teach* him."[75]

Verses 134b–135 are related to verse 136 by a conceptual antithesis, a stark contrast between the obedient and the disobedient.[76] The mood of the psalmist in verse 136 is not so much one of righteous indignation (cf. vv. 53, 158) as it is one of broken-hearted pity.[77] Scroggie captures that mood in his one-liner:

---

[67] *TDOT*, s.v. "אוֹר *ôr*," by S. Aalen, 1:148.

[68] Ibid.

[69] Cf. BDB, p. 21.

[70] The preposition בְּ (*bᵉ*) attached to עַבְדֶּךָ (*ʿabdekā*), "Your servant," is best rendered "on" or "upon" in the context of this metaphorical package.

[71] In keeping with the intent of the Hebrew metaphor, the Targum interprets with "Shine *the countenance of* (זִיוָא [*zîwā'*]) Your face. . . ."

[72] Cf. *TDOT*, 1:161; cf. *TWOT*, s.v. "אוֹר (*'ôr*)," by H. Wolf, 1:25.

[73] The metaphor persists in NT times, e.g., cf. Zacharias' benediction (Luke 1:68–79) wherein it is once again associated with salvation, deliverance, redemption, etc.

[74] Delitzsch, *Psalms*, 3:259. Cf. לַמְּדֵנִי (*lammᵉdēnî*) in vv. 12, 26, 64, 66, 68, 108, 124 and differently inflected forms from the same root in vv. 7, 71, 73, 99, 171. It must be stressed again that this is the language of discipleship.

[75] Scroggie, *Psalms*, p. 176.

[76] Cf. Leupold's comments (*Psalms*, p. 852).

[77] Cf. Delitzsch, *Psalms*, 3:260.

"Abundant sorrow for abounding sin."[78] The effect of the psalmist's burden is vividly pictured by his eyes running down copiously with rivulets of tears (v. 136a). Several times in Scripture eyes are mentioned as weeping (e.g. Jer 8:23 [9:1, Eng]; 31:16; Lam 3:49; Job 16:20; Ps 116:8; etc.); however, only here and in Lamentations 3:48 are the "eyes" found in combination with the picturesque verb יָרַד (*yāraḏ*), literally, "to descend," and its graphic complement פַּלְגֵי־מַיִם (*palgê-mayim*), literally "channels of water."[79] The total impact points to his burden being so great that floods of tears poured forth from his eyes.[80]

The reason for this stirring reaction on the part of the psalmist immediately follows (i.e. v. 136b).[81] It is not because "they" had relentlessly victimized him (although they indeed had). Nor is his deep sorrow grounded upon any other self-oriented standard, but it is an expression of grief over their blatant disregard of his LORD's law. He views these people as having absolutely no concern for God's will and way, and it is for that reason that he is heart-broken. In application, Barnes has argued that "there is nothing for which we should be excited to deeper emotion in respect to our fellow-men than for the fact that they are violators of the law of God, and exposed to its fearful penalty."[82]

---

[78] Scroggie, *Psalms*, p. 185. One should also call to mind Jeremiah's grief (e.g. Lam 3:48), or Paul's (e.g. Acts 17:16), but most supremely, Christ's (e.g. Luke 19:41–44).

[79] For nearly conceptual parallels, however, lacking one or more of the metaphorical constituents of Ps 119:136 and Lam 3:48, cf. Jer 9:17; 13:17; 14:17; Lam 1:16; and Isa 15:3.

[80] Cf., e.g., Cohen, *Psalms*, p. 411; and Barnes, *Psalms*, 2:216.

[81] See the translation notes which opt for עַל (*ᶜal*) as functioning herein as a causal conjunction; cf. Williams, *Hebrew Syntax*, § 534.

[82] Barnes, *Psalms*, 2:216–217.

צ

TSADHE STANZA
(vv. 137–144)

Translation and Notes

137 You *are* righteous, O LORD,
and Your judgments *are* upright.[a]

138 You have commanded Your testimonies
in[a] righteousness and exceeding faithfulness.

139 My zeal[a] consumes[b] me,
because my adversaries forget[b] Your words.

140 Your word[a] *is* exceedingly refined,
therefore,[b] Your servant loves it.

141 I *am* insignificant and despised,
but[a] I do not forget[b] Your precepts.

142 Your righteousness *is* an everlasting righteousness,
and Your law is truth.

143 Distress and constraint have come upon me,[a]
but[b] Your commandments *are* my delight.

144 Your testimonies *are* eternally righteous;[a]
give me understanding that[b] I may live.

137:a In the MT the adjective reads as a singular and the noun as a plural (cf. DSS [Q11] wherein both are plural and the LXX for singular renderings). On the MT's disagreement in number, note GKC, § 145r; Davidson, *Hebrew Syntax*, § 116 R. 3; and Williams, *Hebrew Syntax*, § 75. On the syntax of predicate adjectives in verbless clauses, see Waltke and O'Connor, *Biblical Hebrew Syntax*, 14.3.2.

138:a Translating both nouns, צֶדֶק (*ṣeḏeq*) and אֱמוּנָה (*'ĕmûnâ*), as adverbial accusatives. However, some prefer to render these words appositionally, i.e. "as righteousness, as truth, or: as justice, as fidelity" (e.g., cf. Moll, *Psalms*, p. 592).
139:a The LXX reads ὁ ζῆλος τοῦ οἴκου σου (*ho zēlos tou oikou sou*; "the zeal of your house"), an obvious incorporation from Ps 69:10 (v. 9, Eng).
139:b The perfect tense again rendered comprehensively and characteristically (cf., e.g., the following perfect of אָהֵב in v. 140).
140:a Or, "promise."
140:b The *waw* clause (i.e. v. 140:b) is best taken as a consequence or result (cf. v. 140:a). The conjunction, attested in the MT and early versions, is absent from DSS (Q11).
141:a No conjunction is present; however, the parallelism of this asyndetic bicolon follows a frequently documented precedent in this psalm (e.g. vv. 51, 61, 69, 78, 95, etc.). The intent of such antithetical assertions may be conveyed in translation by placing a contrasting conjunction at the head of the second member of the bicolon (as here) or by affixing a concessive particle to the first member (e.g. "Although . . .").
141:b Cf. the note on the perfect tense above (i.e. 139:b).
143:a Lit., "have found me."
143:b Cf. note 141:a above.
144:a Lit., "righteousness." Also, note the disconcord of gender and number between צֶדֶק (*ṣeḏeq*) and עֵדְוֹתֶיךָ (*ᶜēḏwōṯeyḵa*).
144:b Or, "then I shall live."

Synopsis and Outline

The rectitude of God and His special revelation is especially emphasized in the *Ṣādê* strophe of Psalm 119. This stabilizing reality of Divine fidelity is conveyed largely through occurrences of the root צדק (*ṣdq*; cf. vv. 137a, 138a, 142a, 144a) along with some of its most important theological parallels (e.g. ישר [*yšr*] in v. 137b and אמן [*'mn*] in vv. 138b and 142b). Enhancing this impact is the fact that most of the psalmist's assertions are cast in noun or adjectival clauses (e.g. vv. 137a, 137b, 140a, 142a, 142b, 144a). Such syntax is a suitable vehicle for conveying these key attributes of the LORD and His law. For further accentuation the devoted disciple sprinkles in a few adverbial idioms for qualitative and quantitative intensification (cf., e.g., מְאֹד [*m*ᵉ*'ōḏ*] in vv. 138b and 140a, and לְעוֹלָם [*l*ᵉᶜ*ôlām*] in vv. 142a and 144a).

Different kinds of assertions in this same eight-verse portion bring up the negative situation of the psalmist. He rehearses his plight by testifying how he feels (cf. v. 139a), how others regard him (cf. v. 141a), and how providence has pressured him (cf. v. 143a). Amidst all of this adversity not only had he not defected (cf. v. 141b), but he also had continued to delight in the written expressions of God's will (cf. v. 143b). If these assertions of human anxiety are interfaced with the ones pertaining to Divine rectitude, verses 137–144 deal with three adverse situations from which the child of God extols the fidelity of God and His Word.

- 1A. (vv. 137–139) The first adverse situation is that he is surrounded by infidels.
  - 1B. (vv. 137–138) The resources of Divine fidelity.
    - 1C. (v. 137a) The fidelity of God's Person.
    - 2C. (vv. 137b–138) The fidelity of God's Propositions.
  - 2B. (v. 139) The reality of human infidelity.
- 2A. (vv. 140–141) The second adverse situation is that he is rejected by others.
  - 1B. (v. 140) His rejection is compensated for by God's refined revelation.
  - 2B. (v. 141) His rejection does not affect his obedience.
- 3A. (vv. 142–144) The third adverse situation is that he is besieged by pressure and stress.
  - 1B. (v. 142) The weapons enabling him to withstand pressure and stress.
  - 2B. (vv. 143–144) The warfare against pressure and stress.
    - 1C. (v. 143) He knows how to experience joy in the midst of pressure and stress.
    - 2C. (v. 144) He prays for Divine enablement in the face of pressure and stress.

Commentary

Attributes of fidelity abound in verses 137–138. However, before associating qualities of integrity with the Word of God (i.e. vv. 137b–38), the grateful disciple extols the personal Source of all rectitude in verse 137a when he exclaims, "You *are* righteous, O LORD."[1] The adjective צַדִּיק (*ṣaddîq*), meaning "just" or "righteous,"[2] is derived from the significant Hebrew root צדק (*ṣdq*), which comprehensively includes "the ideas of *righteousness, justification,* and *acquittal.*"[3] Concerning the development of this word group, Hill's comments are not only informing but also theologically preparatory:

> The צדק-words do not appear in biblical Hebrew as *new* words. . . . Although the biblical Hebrew use of the צדק-words was founded on the earlier usage which it inherited, the words were given a characteristic content by their particular association with the terminology of the covenant-relation. . . . The suggested threefold development in the history of the צדק-words may be of guidance in the understanding and interpretation of other religious and theological terms. This development takes the word from an association with man and his life . . . to an association with Yahweh, and back again to man, with a richer content and colour drawn from its relation to deity. . . . The idea of conformity to a norm seems to be the basic significance of the root צדק which most satisfactorily accounts for its various developments.[4]

---

1 All the great attributes of the Word of God are derived innately from the God of the Word. Concerning the root צדק (*ṣdq*) herein, Kirkpatrick has well argued that "this fundamental attribute of the Author of the law necessarily determines its character in all its aspects" (*Psalms*, p. 726).

2 BDB, p. 843. Stigers would add "lawful" (see *TWOT*, s.v. "צָדֵק (*ṣādēq*)," by H. Stigers, 2:752).

3 Girdlestone, *Synonyms*, p. 159. For other occurrences of this root in Ps 119, cf. vv. 7, 40, 62, 75, 106, 121, 123, 138, 142 (x2), 144, 160, 164, 172.

4 Hill, *Greek Words and Hebrew Meanings*, pp. 96–97. For an outline of this root's ethical application to man, i.e. "human righteousness in relationship to God," see Gerhard von Rad, *Old Testament Theology*, trans. by D. M. G. Stalker (NY: Harper and Row, 1962), 1: 380–83.

Picking up on the concept of conformity to a norm in the context of covenant, Cranfield advances the term's biblical significance by noting:

> Where *ṣeḏeḳ* is used in connexion with the conduct of persons, it refers to the fulfillment of the obligations arising from a particular situation, the demands of a particular relationship. . . . The adjective *saddîk* is used to describe those whose conduct and character, whether specifically in relation to the administration of justice or quite generally, are characterized by *ṣeḏek*.[5]

Statistically, this word group "is frequently used in the Old Testament to denote the quality of righteousness or justice and is preeminently predicated of God. As applied to God it refers to his attribute of righteousness or justice."[6] Now bringing these observations full circle and applying them to verse 137 and similar contextual parallels, Anderson appropriately concludes:

> Righteousness is one of God's fundamental attributes, and it can express itself in the rewarding of the faithful and in the punishing of the wicked (cf. Neh. 9:33; Ps. 11:6f.). It can also be seen in the help given to the needy and oppressed (116:5f., 145:17f.). In a legal sense it means that God is beyond reproach, and that no accusation can be brought against him (Jer. 12:1; cf. also Job 34:10–30; *I QH* xiv:15).[7]

Quite fittingly, the psalmist capstones this affirmation of God's impeccable character with one of the twenty-four occurrences of the ineffable Tetragrammaton, "O LORD."[8]

---

5 Cranfield, *Romans*, 1:94.

6 John Murray, *The Epistle to the Romans*, NICNT (Grand Rapids: Wm. B. Eerdmans Publishing Co., 1965), 1: 336.

7 Anderson, *Psalms*, 2:841; for a more comprehensive ethical summation, cf. the many excellent observations by Stigers in *TWOT*, 2:752–55.

8 Of these 24 occurrences of יהוה (*YHWH*) only three of them are not cast as vocatives (cf. vv. 1, 57, 126).

A conceptual parallel of צדק is the root ישר (*yšr*) which follows in verse 137b.[9] Here the adjective יָשָׁר (*yāšār*), variously rendered as straight, straightforward, level, right, upright, just, etc.,[10] qualifies God's judgments (cf. Neh 9:13). The child of God briefly but boldly affirms the rectitude of revelation.

Revelation's fidelity (e.g. v. 137b), as pointed out previously, has been implicitly associated with the rectitude of its Author (e.g. v. 137a).[11] Now it is more explicitly associated with Him in reference to its bestowal (i.e. v. 138). That bestowal is depicted as a Divine imposition of His will-revealing testimonies. It is interesting to note that the leading Piel verb from the root צוה (*ṣwh*), meaning to "lay charge (upon), give charge (to), charge, command, order,"[12] is directly related to one of the frequently occurring terms for the Word in this Psalm (i.e. מִצְוָה [*miṣwâ*], "a commandment"). However, the spotlight of verse 138 shines more intensely on the nouns צֶדֶק (*ṣedeq*), "righteousness" or "justice," and אֱמוּנָה (*'ĕmûnâ*), "firmness, steadfastness, fidelity" or "faithfulness."[13] Consequently, that which the disciple wishes to emphasize most strongly is admirably conveyed through Allen's translation: "The terms you have imposed *are marked by*[14] justice and by complete

---

[9] E.g. both צדק and ישר are collocated as attributes for the fidelity of God in Deut 32:4. Some have argued that a basic idea of straightness seems to have been in the background of both terms and that this connotation bloomed into the extended concept of moral or ethical straightness (cf. *TWOT*, 2:752; Girdlestone, *Synonyms*, p. 159; and *TWOT*, s.v. "יָשַׁר (*yāshar*)," by D. Wiseman, 1:417). On an occurrence of a verb form from this root see v. 128.

[10] BDB, p. 449.

[11] The logical association of the nature of propositional revelation (vv. 137b–38) with that of its personal Source (v. 137a) is analogous to a previous association of the dependability of general revelation (cf. vv. 90b–91) with the unwavering stability of its Creator (cf. v. 90a).

[12] BDB, p. 845; in such contexts as this there may be a denotation of appointing or setting up (cf. Girdlestone, *Synonyms*, p. 207). Also, cf. this verb's usage with פִּקֻּדֶיךָ (*piqqudeykā*), "Your precepts," in v. 4.

[13] BDB, p. 53. Related terms derived from the two roots of these words in v. 138 (i.e. צדק [*ṣdq*] and אמן [*'mn*]) will surface again in v. 142.

[14] My emphasis of his way of rendering the subordinate relationship of צֶדֶק (*ṣedeq*) and אֱמוּנָה (*'ĕmûnâ*) to צִוִּיתָ (*ṣiwwîtā*) and עֵדֹתֶיךָ (*ᶜēdōteykā*). Cf. Anderson's "distinguished by" rendering (*Psalms*, 2:841).

faithfulness."[15] The inference of the man of God is that "the requirements of the revealed law proceed from a disposition towards and mode of dealing with men which is strictly determined by His holiness (צדק), and beyond measure faithfully and honestly designs the well-being of men (אמונה מאד)."[16]

In verse 139 the focus shifts from the transcendent realities of Divine fidelity (vv. 137–38) to the tormenting realities of human infidelity. He characterizes his "antagonists"[17] or "adversaries"[18] as having forgotten God's "words" (v. 139b). It must be remembered that שָׁכַח (*šāḵaḥ*), "to forget," very rarely refers to a loss of memory in the OT, but almost always points to a culpable disregard of someone or something.[19] He looks upon these people as apostates who have ignored God's special revelation.[20]

Their declension is the explicitly voiced reason[21] for his passionate response described in verse 139a. With a seeming outburst he vents: "My zeal consumes me."[22]

> "My zeal" (*ḳin'ātî*) denotes an enthusiastic, exclusive devotion (I Kg. 19:14) which at times may border on fanaticism, as in the case of Jehu (2 Kg. 10:16f.). The same

---

[15] Allen, *Psalms 101–150*, p. 132.

[16] Delitzsch, *Psalms*, 3:260.

[17] Cf. Dahood, *Psalms*, 3:189.

[18] The noun for "adversary," "foe," or "enemy" comes from צרר (*ṣrr*) III, a graphic verb meaning to show "hostility toward, treat with enmity, vex, harass," etc. (BDB, p. 865). As Hartley concludes, "This root deals with the harassment and torment engendered by an enemy" (*TWOT*, s.v. "צָרַר (*ṣārar*) II," by J. Hartley, 2:779). Concerning the noun צַר (*ṣar*), Anderson has observed that it "is a frequent term in the Psalter, to denote the enemies of the Psalmists" (*Psalms*, 2:841).

[19] Cf. Hamilton's survey in *TWOT*, s.v. "שָׁכַח (*shākaḥ*)," by V. Hamilton, 2:922–23. For this nuance in Ps 119, see vv. 16, 61, 83, 109, 139, 141, 153, 176.

[20] Cf. Dahood, *Psalms*, 3:190; and contra. his own commitment to special revelation in v. 141b.

[21] Note the כִּי (*kî*) which stands at the head of v. 139b.

[22] Or, cf. Allen's rendering: "My passion overwhelms me" (*Psalms 101–150*, p. 132).

> noun (*kin'āh*) can also describe Yahweh's zeal, or His exclusive character. . . . In some texts *ḳin'āh* has become a synonym of "anger" (e.g. in 79:5; Isa. 42:13, 59:17; cf. Ps. 78:58).[23]

The term itself is apparently neutral in the sense that specific contextual considerations must be used in order to determine whether its connotation is one of ardor[24] or of anger.[25] Is his קִנְאָה (*qin'â*) a "jealousy for the Law and its observance," which "has brought upon him persecution from his adversaries who violate it,"[26] or is it a more direct expression of his anger towards apostates?[27] It may be the better part of wisdom in this present context to avoid dogmaticism in either direction since there is an explicit reason for anger (v. 139b) along with an implicit basis for devoted zeal (vv. 137–38). One thing, however, is certain, and that is the fact that his ardor and/or anger is intensified by the verb of which it is subject. The verb צָמַת (*ṣāmaṯ*) is hyperbolic; it literally means to "put an end to, exterminate, annihilate."[28] Most modern versions render it by "consumes"; however, the NIV preserves some of its hyperbolic force with its "wears me out." Indeed it was an exhausting קִנְאָה (*qin'â*) that he was experiencing.

Prior to expressing his painful situation of being rejected by others (v. 141) he once again climbs to the heights where he gets a panoramic view of the purity of God's promise (v. 140). From there he revels in the refinement of revelation as he speaks of the Word being exceedingly fire-tried, i.e. it is "'thoroughly refined' . . . very

[23] Anderson, *Psalms*, 2:841.

[24] Cf., e.g., the implications of his previous statements in vv. 137–38.

[25] Cf., e.g., the use of Ps 69:10 (v. 9, Eng) in John 2:17.

[26] Briggs, *Psalms*, p. 434; cf. the principle of 2 Tim 3:12.

[27] Cf. his attitude in vv. 53 and 158.

[28] BDB, p. 856. Note that the LXX employs a word which conveys a melting away, the Targum uses one that connotes being destroyed or diminished, and the Vulgate reads *consumpsit*.

pure like a precious metal smelted in the furnace."[29] Applicationally, this guarantees its truthfulness and reliability.[30]

Herein, the disciple's committed devotion to that promise is based upon its purity not upon some pragmatic benefit that he might obtain from it. His affirmation in verse 140, however, is part of a larger pool of evidence which points to the maturity of this man of God. Barnes has keenly picked up on this phenomenon when he springboards from verse 140b to similar testimonies scattered throughout the psalm:

> Therefore *I* love it. I love it *because* it is pure, holy, true; not merely because it will save *me*. Apart from all references to myself, I *love* thy truth *as* truth; I love purity *as* purity; I love law *as* law; I love holiness *as* holiness.[31]

Admirably attempting a compression of the psalmist's good response into a maxim for emulation, Scroggie outlines the ethical gist of verse 140 as follows: "The unadulterated Word has a right to the undivided heart."[32]

Personal pain once again interrupts the psalmist's praises (i.e. v. 141a). The couplet of the adjective צָעִיר (*ṣāʿîr*), "little, insignificant, young,"[33] and the descriptive Niphal participle נִבְזֶה (*nibzeh*), "despised,"[34] would suggest that this particular pain was his re-

---

[29] Leupold, *Psalms*, p. 853. Cf. other occurrences of passive participles from the root צרף (*ṣrp*), to smelt, refine, test (BDB, p. 864) modifying אִמְרָה (the LORD's Word or promise) in Pss 12:7 (v. 6, Eng; through a parallelism with the root טהר [*ṭhr*]); 18:31 (v. 30, Eng); and Prov 30:5. Furthermore, the imagery of v. 127 was probably still fresh in his mind (note also there that the refinement of revelation is connected with the psalmist's love for it, as here).

[30] Cf., e.g., Allen, *Psalms 101–150*, pp. 132, 138; the note on v. 140 in NAB; and Anderson, *Psalms*, 2:841.

[31] Barnes, *Psalms*, 3:218.

[32] Scroggie, *Psalms*, p. 185.

[33] BDB, p. 859.

[34] BDB, p. 102.

jection by others. Concerning the former word some would opt for its more literal connotation (i.e. "small, little" or "young") based largely upon the psalmist's statement of youthfulness in verse 9 in conjunction with the rendering of the LXX (i.e. νεώτερος [*neōteros*]) here.[35] However, based upon the parallelism of צָעִיר with נִבְזֶה, the emphasis seems to be one of "insignificance in the esteem of his fellows."[36] By referring to himself also as נִבְזֶה (i.e. as being looked upon with contempt[37]), he "may have had in mind [Ps] 22:7 (M.T. 8) and Isa. 53:3, which depict the sufferer as despised by others. In a small way he is a reflection of the suffering servant of the Lord."[38]

Another one of those surprising reactions (i.e. from a merely human or humanistic perspective) follows in verse 141b. Degradation and defamation, although they may have kindled some flashes of dejection in the disciple, did not produce any kind of deep depression. Rather, they seemed to serve as yet another impetus which drove this feeble child of God to a greater dependence upon the resources of His LORD's precepts. Others may have deliberately resisted and rejected God's will for man's way (e.g. v. 139b), but he would not. Furthermore, he was obviously aware of the fact that among those precepts were a significant number of encouragements lovingly directed by God towards His pilgrims who might be undergoing various kinds of persecution.

There is a slight shift in verses 142–144. The adverse situation from which the child of God extols the Divine sureties is phrased generally (cf. v. 143a) rather than specifically and illustratively (cf. vv. 139b, 141a). In the last portion of this eighteenth strophe he personifies the pressure and stress that he was facing daily.

---

35 Cf., e.g., Dahood, *Psalms*, 3:190.

36 Cohen, *Psalms*, p. 412. Furthermore, based upon usages of צָעִיר in other contexts, Anderson has suggested that the term "may be a sort of proverbial expression describing a person chosen in spite of his insignificance (cf. Jg. 6:15; I Sam. 9:21; Ps. 68:27 (M.T. 28); Isa. 60:22; Mic. 5:2)" (*Psalms*, 2:841).

37 For a survey of the בָּזָה word group, see *TDOT*, s.v. "בָּזָה *bāzāh*," by M. Börg, 2:60–65.

38 Anderson, *Psalms*, 2:842.

Prior to that personification of persecution, however, according to the precedent of this stanza, the grateful child of God first accentuates the positive in verse 142. As a matter of fact, the temporal reality of his suffering (v. 143a) pales in the presence of the eternal[39] reality of Divine rectitude expressed both in its Personal (v. 142a) and propositional (v. 144a) forms.[40] Verse 142a is not a vain tautology. When the psalmist affirms that "Your righteousness (i.e. צְדָקָה [*ṣ^e^d̲āqâ*][41]) *is* an everlasting righteousness (i.e. צֶדֶק [*ṣed̲eq*]), "צדקה is . . . the name of the attribute and of the action that is conditioned in accordance with it; צדק is . . . the name of the state that thoroughly accords with the idea of that which is right."[42] God is inherently righteous; therefore, He always rules righteously.

Furthermore, His law *is* truth (v. 142b).[43] Informative parallelisms are observable. "Your *law*" (v. 142b) corresponds to "*Your* righteousness" (v. 142a) on the subject side of the bicolon, and "truth" (אֱמֶת [*'emet̲*]) corresponds with "righteousness" on the predicate side. As already observed,[44] ascriptions of rightness (the root צדק) and reliability (the root אמן [*'mn*]) are fully applicable to either the LORD or His law. Concerning "truth" (אֱמֶת) as it derives from the root אמן, the term itself retains the

39 Certainly the occurrences of לְעוֹלָם (*l^ec^ôlām*) in vv. 142a, 144a help to provide a transcendent vantage point from which to view life's personal tribulations (cf., e.g., that same perspective coming from God through Paul in 2 Cor 4:16–18).

40 I.e., the God of the Word (v. 142a) is forever צדק (*ṣd̲q*) and so is the Word of God (v. 144a).

41 For a helpful usage survey of the feminine noun צְדָקָה (*ṣ^e^d̲āqâ*), see Cranfield, *Romans*, 1:94.

42 Delitzsch, *Psalms*, 3:260. He continues: "So too in ver. 144: צדק are Jahve's testimonies for ever, so that all creatures must give glory to their harmony with that which is absolutely right" (ibid., pp. 260–61).

43 Note similar affirmations in vv. 151, 160; cf. Jesus' appeal to this reality in John 17:17.

44 Cf. esp. v. 138.

> primary idea of "firmness," "stability," . . . "constancy," "faithfulness". . . . In the Bible the known will of God is final for man as a standard of truth, not as arbitrary, but as expressive of God's nature. . . . The term "truth" is sometimes, therefore, nearly equivalent to the revealed will of God.[45]

In this context God's revealed will is explicitly identified as תּוֹרָה (*tôrâ*)[46] which in turn is identified as truth itself.

The alternating pattern of the last half of the *Ṣadê* stanza continues to unfold: human suffering (v. 141a), Divine sufficiencies (v. 142a, b), and now again, human suffering (v. 143a) followed by Divine sufficiency (v. 144a). In response to these positive and negative realities the child of God may be looked upon as both a dedicated (vv. 141b, 143b) and a dependent disciple (v. 144b).

What verse 143a lacks in specificity it makes up in literary vitality. Two closely bonded nouns and their corresponding verb come forth in bold personification.[47] In reference to the nouns, they are very close synonyms. The first word, צַר (*ṣar*), normally translated as "straits" or "distress,"[48] derives from the root צרר (*ṣrr*), which "may refer to anything . . . narrow or confining."[49] It "describes the personal anguish one encounters in adverse circumstances."[50] The second noun מָצוֹק (*māṣôq*), rendered in the OT

[45] *ISBE* (1939), s.v. "Truth," by Carver, 5:3025.

[46] Remembering esp. תּוֹרָה from ירה (*yrh*) as "instruction, teaching, direction," etc., i.e. God's inscripturated means for showing man His way.

[47] This bold personification is like the dark, reverse side of that shining, obverse reality which David depicts vividly in Ps 23:6 when he speaks of God's *goodness* (טוֹב [*ṭôḇ*]) and *grace* (חֶסֶד [*ḥeseḏ*]) as being in hot *pursuit* (רָדַף [*rādap̱*]) of him "all the days of his life."

[48] BDB, p. 865.

[49] *TWOT*, s.v. "צָרַר (*ṣārar*) I," by J. Hartley, 2:778. This root gives birth to both an adjective which exhibits a more literal lineage, i.e. צַר (*ṣar*) I, "narrow, tight," and to a noun with extended meaning, i.e. צַר II, "distress, trouble" (ibid., p. 779; cf. the noun herein).

[50] Ibid., p. 779. Interestingly, the LXX utilizes the noun θλίψις (*thlipsis*), meaning "oppression, tribulation, distress, straits, pressure" (Thayer, *Lexicon*, p. 291; cf., e.g., NT occurrences in John 16:33; Rom 5:3; 2 Cor 4:17; etc.) for צַר. The Vulgate employs the self-explanatory *tribulatio* (cf. tribulation in Eng).

as "straightness, straits" or "stress,"[51] comes from the verb צוק (*ṣûq*) I, which occurs in the Hiphil stem with the meanings of to "constrain, bring into straits, press upon."[52] Some Semitic cognates[53] of this root convey the concepts of narrowness and restriction which were also associated with the former noun.[54] However, מָצוֹק (*māṣôq*) in contexts such as this "refers to . . . great external pressure,"[55] and quite often such pressures were recognized to have come into one's experience through the avenue of God's sovereign providence.[56]

That the latter notion was also part of this psalmist's conception is intimated by his choice of verbs. The verb מָצָא (*māṣāʾ*) literally means "to find" in the active Qal, and in the Niphal passive it frequently bears the strong meanings of to be "overpowered, captured, apprehended."[57] However, in settings similar to the one exhibited in verse 143a it is normally rendered to "come upon, light upon . . . befall."[58] In view of the many explicit documentations of the various persecutions that this man of God had been enduring, he legitimately looked upon himself as being *besieged* by pressure and stress.

---

[51] BDB, p. 848.

[52] Ibid., p. 847.

[53] Cf., e.g., the Arabic (ibid.).

[54] Cf. Barnes on מָצוֹק (*māṣôq*) in Ps 119:143, "It properly refers to a situation where there is no room to move, and where we are pent up in a narrow place" (*Psalms*, 3:218).

[55] *TWOT*, s.v. "צוק (*ṣûq*) I," by J. Hartley, 2:760. Illustratively, cf. the related noun, מְצוּקָה (*m^eṣûqâ*), also deriving from the same root, in Zeph 1:15 where it describes the Day of the LORD. Additionally, the LXX employs ἀνάγκη (*anagkē*; "calamity, distress, straits" [Thayer, *Lexicon*, p. 36]) for מָצוֹק in Ps 119:143 (cf. NT occurrences with these nuances in Luke 21:23; 2 Cor 6:4; 12:10; 1 Thess 3:7; etc.).

[56] Cf., e.g., Grundmann's comments on ἀνάγκη as it was historically used to relate Jewish thinking on various kinds of tribulation (*TDNT*, s.v. "ἀναγκάζω, ἀναγκαῖος, ἀνάγκη" by W. Grundmann, 1:345–46).

[57] See *TWOT*, s.v. "מָצָא (*māṣāʾ*)," by V. Hamilton, 1:521; he also says, "Note that in the LXX the translation of *māsāʾ* is often not *euriskō* [it is, however, in v. 143] but something like *haliskomai* 'be caught, held'" (ibid.).

[58] BDB, p. 593. For an enlightening parallel, see Ps 116:3 where multiple occurrences of both the verb מָצָא and nouns built upon the root צרר surface all in the context of the psalmist's suffering.

Nevertheless,[59] although his pain was very real, the disciple was not utterly consumed by his circumstances, but was lifted above them through the consolation of God's commandments. As a matter of fact, these Divine resources are not viewed by him as merely balancing out, or even neutralizing, his trials, but they are quite positively perceived as the gracious means of his deep-seated stability and confidence. By stylistic juxtaposition and logical development it is evident that *God's* commandments were truly *his* delight.[60] Looking back over the testimony of the whole verse, Leupold has well argued: "In this verse he comes back to the subject so regularly touched on in the psalm, that the writer's position has involved him in 'trouble and anguish.' But that does not drive him away from the divine commandments but has moved him all the more to find his delight in them. They are a real solace at such time."[61]

Like the eternal righteousness of God (v. 142) is the enduring righteousness of His testimonies (v. 144).[62] The unwavering rectitude sourced in his LORD flowed through and adhered to his LORD's inscripturated decrees. Therefore, what he needed was not more revelation but greater insight[63] into that sufficient, deep

---

[59] Another case of asyndetonic antithetical parallelism, and again the disciple's reaction, by the grace of God, transcends all the innate inclinations of fallen, egocentric humanity.

[60] Note the brevity and beauty of v. 143b: מִצְוֺתֶיךָ שַׁעֲשֻׁעָי (*miṣwōṯeykā šaʿăšuʿāy*).

[61] Leupold, *Psalms*, p. 854; cf. Alexander, *Psalms*, 3:191–92, and Barnes, *Psalms*, 3:218.

[62] The word for the Word herein is appropriately עֵדוּת (*ʿēḏûṯ*), i.e. as attestations which bear witness to their Author. For comments on the analogy of their rectitude (v. 144) with God's (vv. 137, 142), see Kirkpatrick, *Psalms*, p. 727; Cohen, *Psalms*, p. 412; Delitzsch, *Psalms*, 3:260–61; Leupold, *Psalms*, p. 854; Yates, "Psalms," p. 541; *et al.* On their lasting rightness, cf. Anderson, *Psalms*, 2:842, who illustrates with Matt 5:17f.

[63] The causative imperative of בִּין (*bîn*) returns in v. 144b (cf. vv. 27, 34, 73, 125, and forthcoming in 169).

reservoir of God's declarations for His disciples (v. 144b). When the LORD would answer his prayer for a transcendent perception, then he would be able to live more as God had intended man to live (v. 144c).[64] As Delitzsch has said, "To look ever deeper and deeper into this their [i.e. God's testimonies] perfection is the growing life of the spirit. The poet prays for this vivifying insight."[65] Along similar lines, Allen sets the plea and purpose contained in verse 144b–c first into its thematic setting within this stanza[66] and then into the larger context of that preeminent need which had arisen due to the psalmist's suffering: "It prompts a prayer for deeper insight as the basis for a meaningful life. Uniquely life, elsewhere in the psalm contrasted with the stress of persecution, is associated with growth of understanding of the Torah."[67] The child of God knew that this particular grace, not necessarily deliverance from his enemies, opened up the door to *genuine* life as defined by God in His Word.

---

[64] On the syntactical breadth of וְאֶחְיֶה (*wᵉ'eḥyeh*), Alexander notes: "*And (then) I shall live*, which includes *let me live* and *that I may live*" (*Psalms*, 3:192).

[65] Delitzsch, *Psalms*, 3:261.

[66] As Allen recognized earlier in his treatment, "the *ṣade* strophe . . . is shot through with references to Yahweh's 'righteousness'" (*Psalms 101–150*, p. 144).

[67] Ibid.; cf. Cohen, *Psalms*, p. 412.

ק

QOPH STANZA
(vv. 145–152)

Translation and Notes

145 I cry out[a] wholeheartedly;[b]
answer me, O LORD!
I will[c] keep Your statutes.

146 I cry out *to* You;
save me!
Then I will keep[a] Your testimonies.

147 I come before morning twilight and cry for help;[a]
I wait for[b] Your word.[c]

148 My eyes anticipate[a] *the* night watches[b]
to meditate on Your word.[c]

149 Hear[a] my voice according to Your grace![b]
O LORD, revive me according to Your judgments.[c]

150 Those who pursue an evil purpose draw near;[a]
they are far from Your law.

151 [a]You *are* near, O LORD,
and all Your commandments are truth.[b]

152 Long ago[a] I came to know[b] from[c] Your testimonies[d]
that You have established them[e] forever.

145:a Intensifying קָרָא (*qārā'*), normally "to call" or "cry" (e.g. BDB, p. 895), a bit because of the context of an apparently intense lament; cf. the LXX's choice of κράζω (*krazō*) here rather than καλέω (*kaleō*). Taking the perfect tense again (both here and in the verses which follow), as "a class of actions which, being of frequent occurrence, have been proved by experience" (Davidson, *Hebrew Syntax*, § 40c). For an updated discussion on the exceedingly difficult issue of Hebrew tense and aspect, see Waltke and O'Connor, *Biblical Hebrew Syntax*, 29.1–29.6.

145:b Lit. "with a whole heart" (cf. esp. vv. 2, 10, 34, 58, 69).

145:c I.e. the longer form אֶצֹּרָה (*'eṣṣōrâ*) translated here intensively: "I *will*"; cf. in vv. 34, 115; contra in v. 69 (i.e. the shorter form). For traditional discussion, see GKC, § 48a–e.

146:a I.e. also a longer form, וְאֶשְׁמְרָה (*we'ešmerâ*), translated intensively; cf. in vv. 17, 44, 55, 88, 134; contra in vv. 8, 34, 101 (i.e. the shorter form). Other syntactical options are: "And I will/shall keep . . . ," "that I may keep. . . ."

147:a Interestingly, the Targum reads "and I pray"; however, there is no textual reason to doubt the שָׁוַע (*šāwaᶜ*) in the MT. It is obviously a near synonym of the two previous occurrences of קָרָא (*qārā'*); cf. the three consecutive occurrences of ἐκέκραξα (*ekekraxa*), in as many verses, in the LXX.

147:b Or, "I hope for/in," for יָחַל (*yāḥal*).

147:c The translation reflects the *qerê*, the *ketîḇ* being לדבריך, "Your words." There is manuscript and versional evidence for the singular plus a seeming precedent, i.e. "the psalmist's use of *yḥl*, which elsewhere has the singular *dābār* for its object (vv. 49, 74, 81, 114)" (Soll, "Psalm 119," p. 205).

148:a Note that this is the same verb which led off v. 147: there translated, "I come before"; here, "I anticipate." Cf. προέφθασα (*proephthasa* from προφθάνω [*prophthanō*], to anticipate) at the head of vv. 147, 148 in the LXX.

148:b BDB, p. 1038, suggest "watch" for אַשְׁמוּרָה (*'ašmûrâ*); however, cf. *TWOT*, s.v. "שָׁמַר (*shāmar*)," by J. Hartley, 2:939, for "night watch." The context (cf. the נֶשֶׁף [*nešep̱*] of v. 147) would also suggest that the psalmist wanted to stress a time past sunset in v. 148. Interestingly, the Targum's expansion reads "the watch of morning and evening."

148:c Or more explicitly, "Your promise." Only a few manuscripts and the LXX read as a plural here.

149:a Most modern grammars do not accept a difference in emphasis between longer (cf. the שִׁמְעָה [*šimᶜâ*] herein) and shorter forms of the imperative (see Waltke and O'Connor, *Biblical Hebrew Syntax*, 34.2.2, 34.4). The longer form expressed here is quite characteristic in the Psalms (note BDB, p. 1033).

149:b I.e. חֶסֶד (*ḥesed*).

149:c A few minor variants are noted in the apparatus of *BHS*; e.g., the position of the vocative, "LORD," is different in the LXX (i.e. it comes before both prepositional phrases), a few manuscripts along with the Syriac version (not LXX, Targum, etc.) read בְּ (*bᵉ*) instead of כְּ (*kᵉ*) as the preposition of the two phrases, and a plural form of מִשְׁפָּט (*mišpāṭ*) is conjectured. The last option (cf. Targum; contra LXX) is accepted in the above translation due to precedent (cf. vv. 7, 13, 20, 30, 39, 52, 62, 75, 91, 102, 106, 108, 120, 137, esp. 156, 164). Most of the singular forms are easily explained by usage and/or idiom (e.g., vv. 84, 121, 132, 160); therefore, the occurrences in vv. 43, 149 and 175 may be construed as defective plurals (i.e. singular in the consonantal text of the MT but to be translated as plurals).

150:a Or possibly, "My persecutors are coming close with malicious intent" (Allen, *Psalms 101–150*, p. 133). Soll offers the rationale for this alternative rendering: "Repointing MT *rod'pê* to *rōd'pay* with support of some Heb. mss, LXX, Symmachus, Syriac, and Jerome, and reading *zimmāh* as an adverbial accusative. The MT phrase 'pursuers of malice' is possible, but draws attention away from the fact that they are, at the moment, pursuing the psalmist" ("Psalm 119," p. 205).

151:a In view of the logical antithesis between vv. 150 and 151 some supply in translation a contrasting conjunction at the outset of this verse; e.g., "*But . . .* ," "*However . . .* ," "*Nevertheless . . .* ," "*Yet . . .* ," etc.

151:b I.e. אֱמֶת (*'emeṯ*). Some translations, though not quite as literal, acceptably render the noun in this syntactical setting as an adjective, i.e. "true."

152:a I.e. קֶדֶם (*qedem*), a masculine noun translated as "ancient time, aforetime" in temporal contexts (BDB, p. 869), and here taken as functioning adverbially, quite similarly to מִקֶּדֶם (*miqqedem*), "from of old . . . anciently, of old" (ibid.). From the perspective of the psalmist the sense is "for a long time" (cf. Delitzsch's translation, *Psalms*, 3:241).

152:b I.e. the perfect יָדַעְתִּי (*yāda*^{c}*tî*); the sense seems to be long ago "I realized" this truth and this recognition effectively remains with me (again, on some of the possibilities of the perfect inflectional pattern in Hebrew, see Davidson, *Hebrew Syntax*, §§ 39–40).

152:c Taking the preposition מִן (*min*) most naturally as source. Soll, however, having a different view of קֶדֶם takes the preposition's usage as one of specification; note his translation and argumentation pertaining to v. 152a: "'I know that your decrees are from of old'—a difficult phrase. Most translators and commentaries understand *qedem* as having an adverbial relation to *yāda*^{c}*tî*, and translate 'Long have I known' (or similarly). But *qedem*, when it refers to time, is everywhere else a primeval term, reaching far beyond personal experience. The present translation [i.e. Soll's] understands the preposition *min* not as one of source, but of specification ('I know concerning your testimonies . . .'; cf. 1 Sa. 23:23 for similar use of *min* with *yd*^{c}). That the phrase is awkward I readily grant; the awkwardness may stem from the fact that the psalmist had to use *qedem* instead of *miqqedem* in the acrostic format" ("Psalm 119," p. 205). The *immediate* context and phraseology of the Hebrew text, however, seems to align more readily with the traditional interpretation of v. 152a.

152:d Interestingly, without other versional parallels, DSS (Q11) reads מדעתכה (*md*^{c}*tkh*), "from knowledge *of You*."

152:e Again, without a textual parallel, DSS (Q11) reads יסדתני (*ysdtny*), "You founded *me*." On the disagreement in gender regarding the suffix in the MT, Delitzsch appropriately, notes: "יְסַדְתָּם [*y*^{e}*sadtām*] for יְסַדְתָּן [*y*^{e}*sadtān*], like הֵמָּה [*hēmmâ*] in v. 111" (*Psalms*, 3:261).

Synopsis and Outline

A mood of relative tranquility (cf. *Ṣāḏê*, esp. vv. 137–38, 140, 142, 144) is displaced by one of significant turmoil in *Qôp̱*. Furthermore, that mood, with minimal interruption, will continue through the *Rêš* Stanza. Indeed, these two strophes are not only characterized by intense lament, but each also unfolds in a markedly similar fashion, i.e. from agitation to adoration. Beyond thematic and developmental similarities, logical[1] and semantical[2] binders contribute to this intra-strophic cohesion.

In the *Ṣāḏê* stanza there was only one petition, and that came in the last verse (cf. v. 144b). Within *Qôp̱* the first six verses are saturated with pleas and complaints. Only at its end come praises for the presence of God (v. 151a) and the perfections of His Word (vv. 151b–152). As one therefore moves through Psalm 119:145–152 it should become obvious that the disciple's two choruses of lamentation gradually ebb in the light of Divine sufficiencies.

1A. (vv. 145–148) The disciple's cries for protection result in his being drawn to the Word of God.
- 1B. (vv. 145–146) His cries for protection express his need for dependency.
  - 1C. (v. 145) God needs to respond in order for him to live obediently.
  - 2C. (v. 146) God needs to rescue in order for him to live obediently.

---

1 Generally, note how vv. 145, 146, 147, 149, 153, 154, 156, and 159 contain explicit and implicit pleas for Divine intervention.

2 Specifically, note the four imperatives of חיה (*ḥyh*) in vv. 149, 154, 156, 159, and the occurrences of the root רחק (*rḥq*) in vv. 150 and 155. As the lament, so characteristic of these two stanzas, subsides the psalmist returns to those transcendent truths which preoccupied him in *Ṣāḏê* (cf. the roots אמן [*'mn*] and צדק [*ṣḏq*] in v. 160 with vv. 137, 138, 142, 144). Furthermore, as each of these three stanzas (*Ṣāḏê*, *Qôp̱*, and *Rêš*) culminates, the child of God experiences a degree of respite predicated upon some everlasting (cf. לְעוֹלָם [*l*^{ec}*ôlām*] in vv. 144, 152, 160) quality of God's Word.

- 2B. (vv. 147–148) His acknowledged dependency leads to an anticipation of God's sufficiencies.
  - 1C. (v. 147) Early in the morning he anticipates God's good response through His Word.
  - 2C. (v. 148) Late at night he appropriates God's good response through His Word.

2A. (vv. 149–152) The disciple's cries for attention rest in his being drawn to the God of the Word.

- 1B. (v. 149) His cries for attention express his need for a sustaining relationship.
- 2B. (vv. 150–152) His need for a sustaining relationship is satisfied through a renewed appreciation of God's sufficiencies.
  - 1C. (v. 150) This appreciation is intensified by contrast.
  - 2C. (v. 151) This appreciation is implemented by contact.
  - 3C. (v. 152) This appreciation is integrated by confidence.

Commentary

Verses 145 and 146 both begin with first person verbal occurrences of קָרָא (*qārā'*), which means to *call on* or *to cry (out)* in invocational contexts such as this.[3] Although this term is not perpetuated in verses 147ff., its concept surely is.[4] As indicated quite explicitly by the imperative and vocative following it in verse 145 (i.e. עֲנֵנִי יהוה [*ᶜănēnî YHWH*], "answer me, O LORD!"), קָרָא "is customarily addressed to a specific recipient and is intended to elicit a specific response."[5] The child of God also personalizes and in-

---

[3] Cf. *TDNT*, s.v. "κράζω, ἀνακράζω, κραυγή, κραυγάζω" by W. Grundmann, 3:899. Statistically, he notes that קָרָא (*qārā'*) "occurs predominantly in the Psalms in the context of crying or calling on God in some individual or national emergency" (ibid.; cf. Anderson, *Psalms*, 2:842).

[4] Cf. a similar verb, שָׁוַע (*šāwaᶜ*), in v. 147 and the noun קוֹל (*qôl*) in v. 149.

[5] *TWOT*, s.v. "קָרָא (*qārā'*) I," by L. Coppes, 2:810.

tensifies his cry for protection with a favorite prepositional idiom used adverbially,[6] בְּכָל־לֵב (*b^e^kol-lēḇ*), lit., "with a whole heart," i.e. I am crying out to You, LORD, "with all my being."[7]

The disciple's pledge which brings the first verse of the *Qôp* stanza to a close also implicitly places a purpose before God as to why He should respond favorably to the request of His servant.[8] As so often is the case, that purpose focuses upon obedience (here נָצַר [*nāṣar*]; cf. שָׁמַר [*šāmar*] in v. 146). Filling in between the lines of his request the child of God is saying, 'In the light of my precarious situation, I am crying out to You wholeheartedly. Please answer me, LORD! *Then* I shall be able to keep on obeying Your declarations for disciples.'

His solicitation of a general response from God in verse 145 (i.e. "answer me") becomes more specific in verse 146. By his crying out to the LORD in this context he longs for personal rescue, i.e. הוֹשִׁיעֵנִי (*hôšîᶜēnî*), "save me!"[9] As in the previous verse, here the disciple's diligence (v. 146c) is causally and consequentially related to his deliverance (v. 146b). If his LORD would graciously intervene, the man of God would be able to conform more consistently to his Master's Word.

---

6 Cf. vv. 2, 10, 34, 58, 69.

7 Anderson, *Psalms*, 2:842; i.e. he was holding nothing back; nothing was kept in reserves.

8 Although this last clause is asyndetic, logically it conveys an apologetic of purpose, a phenomenon previously encountered in this psalm. It should also be pointed out that along with those previously mentioned semantical and logical parallels between vv. 145 and 146, there seems to be a syntactical parallelism between v. 145a, b, c and v. 146a, b, c (taking the הוֹשִׁיעֵנִי [*hôšîᶜēnî*] of v. 146 more independently—cf. the עֲנֵנִי יהוה of v. 145—rather than as merely the object of content after קְרָאתִיךָ [*q^e^rā'tîḵā*]). Consequently, the parallel of v. 145c would be v. 146c, and the latter exhibits the *wāw* conjunction which is normally interpreted as indicating intentionality.

9 On the significance of (*yāšaᶜ*) in such contexts, cf. vv. 94, 117.

In verses 147 and 148 forms of the verb קָדַם (*qāḏam*) launch two logically interdependent testimonies of the child of God.[10] In the first instance the verb קִדַּמְתִּי (*qiddamtî*) is modified by the prepositional phrase בַנֶּשֶׁף (*ḇannešep̱*), lit. "in the morning twilight."[11] Therefore, the sense of the verb in that context is "I come before dawn"[12] or "Before morning twilight I rise. . . ."[13] In verse 148 the verb קִדְּמוּ (*qiddᵉmû*), of which עֵינַי (*ᶜênay*), "my eyes," is subject[14] and אַשְׁמֻרוֹת (*'ašmurôṯ*), "watches," is object, bears the contextual nuance of *anticipation.*[15] By further comparisons and contrasts between these verses, it seems that the second clause of verse 147, i.e. וָאֲשַׁוֵּעָה (*wā'ᵃšawwēᶜâ*), literally "and I cry for help,"[16] carries with it a degree of intentionality as does its infinitival counterpart, לָשִׂיחַ בְּ (*lāśîaḥ bᵉ*), "to meditate upon," in verse 148.[17] The psalmist's intention, therefore, in verse 147 seems to be that he came to his LORD very early in the morning once again to pray for Divine intervention. Similarly, but on the extreme end of this temporal continuum of a disciple's dependence (i.e. far into the dark hours of the night[18]), he came to contemplate deeply the inscripturated source (i.e. the "word" or "promise") of God's answers to life's difficult and most painful questions. The additional affirmation with which verse 147 concludes, "I wait for" or "hope

[10] I.e. from pre-dawn to post-dark he dependently seeks the sufficiencies of God.

[11] Cf. BDB, p. 676.

[12] Cf. BDB, p. 870, for the rendering "to be beforehand."

[13] Allen, *Psalms 101–150*, p. 133.

[14] The anthropological paraphrasis עֵינַי (*ᶜênay*), although it does carry on the "I" (1 c s) affirmations, is eminently suitable to the vivid imagery of its immediate context.

[15] Cf. BDB, p. 870.

[16] On this petitionary verb, cf. Pss 5:3; 18:42 (v. 41, Eng); Job 36:13; Isa 58:9; Jonah 2:3 (v. 2, Eng); Hab 1:2; Lam 3:8.

[17] For profitable discussions of the semantical and syntactical interrelationships of vv. 147–148, see Delitzsch, *Psalms*, 3:261; and Moll, *Psalms*, pp. 592–93.

[18] Cf. v. 62. In the Hebrew reckoning of evening (v. 148) and morning (v. 147), "earnest early prayer is matched by an even earlier study of the written Torah" (Allen, *Psalms 101–150*, p. 144).

in Your words,"[19] introduces a positive element of expectation and may also serve as a logical reason for the disciple's continued expenditure outlined in verse 148.

Verse 149 seems to be both a recapitulation of the psalmist's mounting requests and a transition to a brief period of relaxation in the resources of God. With its two imperatives addressed directly to the LORD and its two prepositional phrases which acknowledge crucial Divine precedents, the impression is that the child of God is enabled to look beyond the proximity of his persecutors (cf. v. 150) to the protective presence of his Sovereign (cf. v. 151a).

The first imperative of verse 149 is from the exceedingly common verb שָׁמַע (*šāmaᶜ*), generally meaning to hear.[20] Some of its extended meanings are "listen to, pay attention, obey," and to hear in the sense of answering prayer.[21] The last semantical nuance is obviously its meaning here especially since קוֹל (*qôl*) stands as the object of שִׁמְעָה (*šimᶜâ*). In this context, by mutual influence, the noun קוֹל, normally translated "sound" or "voice,"[22] denotes the "petition" put forth by the man of God.[23] When the psalmist grounds his plea for Divine attention upon his LORD's personal fidelity of love (i.e. כְּחַסְדֶּךָ [*kᵉḥasdekā*], "according to Your grace"), the total impact of his initial prayer becomes: "Hear my appeal in accord with your loyal love!"[24]

The second half of the verse commences with a highly appropriate occurrence of the vocative יהוה (*YHWH*), "LORD." As the weakened child of God voices his second prayer in verse 149

---

[19] If the plural, דְּבָרֶיךָ (*dᵉbāreykā*), i.e. the *kᵉtîb* in the MT, is retained, this may signal an occurrence of דָּבָר (*dābār*) functioning similarly in a semantical way with its logical parallel אִמְרָה (*'imrâ*) in v. 148, i.e. I hope in Your *promises*.

[20] BDB, p. 1033.

[21] *TWOT*, s.v. "שָׁמַע (*shāmaᶜ*)," by H. Austel, 2:938.

[22] BDB, p. 876.

[23] *TDNT*, s.v. "φωνή, κτλ.," by O. Betz, 9:281; besides Ps 119:149, he exemplifies with Deut 1:45; 26:7; 33:7; Judg 13:9; 2 Sam 22:7; 1 Kgs 17:22; Isa 58:4; Pss 55:17; 130:2; Jonah 2:3 (v. 2, Eng); etc. (cf. ibid., pp. 281–82).

[24] Allen, *Psalms 101–150*, p. 133.

specificity is added. He moves on from asking God to pay attention to him (v. 149a) to imploring Him to energize him (v. 149b).[25] Also, propositional grounds (כְּמִשְׁפָּטֶךָ [*kᵉmišpāṭekā*], "according to Your judgment[s]") are coupled to his request for revival.[26] He was obviously expecting his LORD's help based upon the many promises and precedents contained in His reliable Word.

In verse 150a the disciple returns to his difficult situation with a dramatic flare. He depicts his antagonists as (once again) approaching him with wickedly mischievous intentions.[27] The introduction of the root קרב (*qrḇ*), here inflected as a verb, "to come near" or "approach,"[28] is pivotal in that it will be followed by its primary antonym, the root רחק (*rḥq*), i.e. to be or become far or distant,[29] in verse 150b, and then in verse 151a it will return as a predicate adjective describing the presence of God.[30]

The child of God identifies those who draw near as ones who are consistently characterized by their pursuit of malevolence. The substantive participle from רָדַף (*rāḏap̄*), a common word with two general meanings, to chase, pursue or to persecute,[31] exhibits the former sense in this context, i.e. to follow after or to pursue something with the implication of aiming to secure it.[32] What

---

25 Cf. the prevalent חַיֵּנִי (*ḥayyēnî*) in vv. 25, 37, 40, 88, 107, 154, 156, 159.

26 Quite apparently, corresponding to the personal precedent which bolstered his former request.

27 The generalization of v. 150a is given definitude illustratively in verses such as 23, 61, 69, 78, 95, 110, 161.

28 BDB, p. 897.

29 Ibid., p. 934.

30 As Delitzsch notes, "The correlative relation of vers. 150 and 151 is rendered natural by the position of the words" (*Psalms*, 3:261).

31 BDB, p. 922.

32 Ibid. Note that רָדַף (*rāḏap̄*) is also used in Ps 119 as a reference to his adversaries as *persecutors*; cf. vv. 84 (subst. ptc.), 86, 157 (subst. ptc.), 161. It is interesting that the LXX uses less-common, intensified forms of διώκω (*diōkō*) throughout this particular psalm apparently to emphasize the tenacity of the disciple's tormentors. Herein, it utilizes a corresponding participial form of καταδιώκω (*katadiōkō* ; cf. vv. 84, 86, 161), a term well-suited for their close (i.e. hot) pursuit.

these men are hotly pursuing is evaluated by the psalmist[33] as זִמָּה (*zimmâ*), an (evil) "device" or "plan."[34] Often in the OT the term is associated with harlotry and adultery, in both its literal and metaphorical expressions;[35] therefore, it suitably depicts the faithlessness[36] and the lawlessness[37] of his enemies. Indeed, such men are "far from Your law" (v. 150b). Rather than pursuing after righteousness, peace, and other character qualities enjoined in God's Word,[38] these men had alienated themselves from the Word of God, and by implication, from its Author[39] not only because of such omissions but most flagrantly because of their commissions of unethical atrocities. Their dedication to wicked devices had resulted in a chasm which seemingly could not be bridged.

By God's grace, that was not true of the psalmist, for his LORD was very near to him (v. 151a). Concerning the impact of the semantical and logical interrelationships of verses 150 and 151, Kidner has provided valuable assistance for the interpreter: "Note the realism of the double statement, *They draw near . . . but thou art near*. The threat is not glossed over; it is put in perspective by a bigger fact."[40] That infinitely "bigger fact" of the presence of

---

[33] His evaluation, however, is ultimately based upon the Divine standard of all conduct, i.e. the LORD's law (cf. v. 150b). He is not responding merely by reflex or reaction, although he *has* been persecuted and feels thoroughly victimized.

[34] *TDOT*, s.v. "זמם *zmm*," by S. Steingrimsson, 4:89; he renders the participial phrase in v. 150a as "pursuers of deceit" (ibid.).

[35] Cf. BDB, p. 273.

[36] The parallel term in Aramaic, lit. "prostitution, unchastity, voluptuousness," is utilized in the Targum at v. 150, and Jastrow suggests that it figuratively connotes faithlessness (*Dictionary*, 1:406).

[37] Note here the ἀνομία (*anomia*) of the LXX.

[38] For a brief survey of various ethical characteristics presented as the good objects of רָדַף (*rāḏap̄*) in the OT, see *TDNT*, s.v. "διώκω," by A. Oepke, 2:230.

[39] The combination of רָחַק (*rāḥaq*) plus מִן (*min*) is poignant (cf. BDB, pp. 934–35). For a brief consideration of the hamartiological significance of רָחַק, see *TWOT*, s.v. "רָחַק (*rāḥaq*)," by W. White, 2:844.

[40] Kidner, *Psalms 73–150*, p. 428.

the omnipotent One certainly "gives comfort to the affected man."[41] Furthermore, he was sustained not only by the assurance that his Protector was at hand but also by the conviction that his LORD's commandments were "altogether self-verifying truth" (v. 151b; cf. the root אמן ['mn] in vv. 138b, 142b).[42]

The refreshing change of mood reflected by the psalmist in verse 151 persists in the last verse of the *Qoph* stanza. In verse 152a he bears witness to the fact that a particular realization that he had obtained long ago from the Word of God[43] about the Word of God applies to all situations under all circumstances, including, by contextual implication, his current plight. What he had specifically come to know was that the LORD had established, founded, or firmly fixed[44] His testimonies *forever* (v. 152b). Therefore, since "the testimonies of God . . . are eternally valid . . . no vicissitudes of life can call in question the faithfulness of the divine lawgiver (cf. [Ps] 111:7f.)."[45] In an even tighter application, "God's decrees . . . represent a more enduring dimension of reality than the psalmist's present experience."[46] Deeply internalized recognitions of the presence of God (v. 151a) and the purity (v. 151b) and perpetuity (v. 152) of His Word are very practical sufficiencies in the face of all kinds of suffering.

---

[41] Anderson, *Psalms*, 2:843; he goes on, suggesting that "the nearness of *God* means deliverance and protection (cf. [Pss] 69:18 (M.T. 19), 73:28; Isa. 50:8)" (ibid.).

[42] Delitzsch, *Psalms*, 3:261.

[43] I.e. מֵעֵדֹתֶיךָ (*mēʿēḏōṯeykā*), "Your testimonies."

[44] *TWOT*, s.v. "יָסַד (*yāsad*)," by P. Gilchrist, 1:384. On the term's architectural background, note Jacob, *Theology of the OT*, p. 142. Cf. a conceptual parallelism with v. 89.

[45] Anderson, *Psalms*, 2:843.

[46] Soll, "Psalm 119," p. 206.

ר

RESH STANZA
(vv. 153–160)

Translation and Notes

153 Look upon my affliction and rescue me,
for[a] I have not forgotten[b] Your law.

154 Conduct my case[a] and redeem me;[b]
revive[c] me according to[d] Your word.[e]

155 Salvation *is* far[a] from *the* wicked,[b]
for they do not seek Your statutes.

156 Many *are* Your mercies,[a] O LORD;
revive me according to Your judgments.[b]

157 Many *are* my persecutors and my adversaries;
nevertheless,[a] I have not turned aside[b] from Your testimonies.

158 I look upon[a] *the* treacherous[b] and feel[a] a loathing,[c]
because[d] they do not keep Your word.[e]

159 Take notice[a] that I love Your precepts;
O LORD, revive me according to Your grace.[b]

160 The sum of Your word[a] is truth,
and every one of Your righteous judgments[b] *endures* forever.[c]

153:a I.e. the causal conjunction כִּי (*kî*); although DSS (Qll) omits it, the resultant asyndetic relationship of v. 153b to 153a maintains it even there by implication.
153:b Or, "I do not forget" for the Qal perfect here.

154:a The root ריב (*ryb*), here manifested in both an imperative and a cognate accusative, often conveys an important legal motif (cf. the psalmist's desire in a contemporary expression: 'Be my defense attorney').
154:b The root גאל (*g'l*) also manifests an important Semitic motif (cf. 'Act as my kinsman').
154:c Interestingly, the DSS (Qll) does read חיני (*ḥyny*) here along with the MT; however, its prevalent variant of חונני (*ḥwnny*) returns in vv. 156b, 159b, etc.
154:d The preposition here is לְ (*l*[e]); it should be taken as denoting reference to a norm or standard (cf. BDB, p. 516) much like כְּ (*k*[e]) is taken in parallel contexts (e.g. vv. 149, 156, 159, etc.).
154:e Or, more explicitly, "Your promise."
155:a Technically speaking, the noun and adjective exhibit disconcord in gender (cf. disconcord in number at v. 137, noting the comments of GKC § 145r on both verses). Practically speaking, Alexander construes the noun יְשׁוּעָה (*y*[e]šû[c]â) "as a neuter" (*Psalms*, 3:194). However, Dahood, *Psalms*, 3:191, takes רָחוֹק (*rāḥôq*) as an infinitive absolute functioning as an imperative; therefore, he renders v. 155a as an imprecation: "Keep distant . . . your salvation."
155:b Lit., "from wicked *ones*" or "wicked *people*."
156:a Or, "Your compassion is abundant," i.e. "Your compassion is so multiplied" (Allen, *Psalms 101–150*, p. 133). The plurals were retained in the above translation of v. 156a in order to highlight the obviously intended parallelisms with v. 157a.
156:b DSS (Qll) also supports the plural of the MT.
157:a Another asyndetic bicolon amplifying the psalmist's perseverance under pressure. His intention is best conveyed through a supplied conjunction at the head of the second member of the bicolon (cf. the translation above) or by appending a concessive statement to the first member (e.g. "Notwithstanding the fact that my persecutors and antagonists are multiplied, I do not . . .").
157:b Or, "I do not turn aside."
158:a Or, "I looked upon (or "beheld") . . . and felt. . . ."

158:b Lit., "ones," "men," or "people who act/deal treacherously."
158:c The two main verbs of v. 158a may be syntactically combined in various ways. In addition to the quite literal rendering above, cf. "I look on the faithless with loathing" (NIV), "When I see deceitful people I loath *them*," "the sight of the faithless fills me with disgust" (Allen, *Psalms 101–150*, p. 133), etc.
158:d An apparently causal usage of אֲשֶׁר (*'ăšer*), "for as much as, in that, since, because," etc. (cf. BDB, p. 83).
158:e DSS (Qll) supports the singular reading of the MT.
159:a Or, "consider that" (cf. Delitzsch, *Psalms*, 3:241), i.e. another way of rendering רְאֵה כִּי (*rᵉ'ēh kî*) quite literally. More conceptually, cf. the "See how I love . . ." of the NIV.
159:b I.e. God's חֶסֶד (*ḥeseḏ*).
160:a Some manuscripts, texts, and versions read as a plural (e.g. DSS [Qll], LXX), "Your words."
160:b The last two nouns (standing obviously in a bound relationship) are singular in the MT (cf. DSS [Qll]); however, several manuscripts, and versions support the plural reading (e.g. LXX, Targum, etc.).
160:c Or, ". . . *is* everlasting."

Synopsis and Outline

As previously noted,[1] the intense cries for help in verses 145–152 continue to echo with renewed amplification in the *Rêš* Stanza. In this vein, Delitzsch quite generally has noted that "the nearer it draws towards its end the more importunate does the psalm become."[2] More specifically in application to *Rêš*, Soll has observed that "there is a sense of urgency in this strophe."[3] To a

1 Cf. the "Synopsis and Outline" discussion of the *Qôp* Stanza (esp. notes 1, 2).
2 Delitzsch, *Psalms*, 3:262.
3 Soll, "Psalm 119," pp. 206–207.

significant degree the intensity of verses 153–160 is borne along by eight imperatives which the fragile child of faith directs to his LORD.

As in the case of the previous stanza, the disturbed disciple does not become utterly distraught. By the sovereign mercy of his LORD, he is enabled to gaze beyond his acute circumstances and to focus upon the perfections,[4] promises,[5] and protection[6] of his good and great God. His faith, being ultimately grounded upon the right foundations of God and His Word, therefore does not flounder.

It should be noted that the child of God is much more emotional at the outset of the stanza. Statistically, five of the eight imperatives occur in the first two verses. Then statements about the wicked bracket (cf. vv. 155 and 158) the middle portion of *Rêš*. However, these are tempered by an even greater reality, the great grace of God (cf. v. 156a). Finally, in verses 159–160, the tempest further subsides subjectively through trust and objectively through Truth. Based upon the aforementioned mood swings, the disciple's three cycles of cries for deliverance in verses 153–160 progressively subside in the presence of the comforting attributes and assurances of God and His Word.

1A. (vv. 153–54) The emotional cycle of cries is related to the psalmist's affliction.
    1B. (v. 153) This emotional cycle comes through cries which refer to his affliction explicitly.
    2B. (v. 154) This emotional cycle also comes through cries which refer to his affliction implicitly.

---

[4] Cf., e.g., God's רחם (*rḥm*) in v. 156 and His חסד (*ḥsd*) in v. 159.

[5] Cf., e.g., the prepositions לְ (*l*[e]) and כְּ (*k*[e]) with אִמְרָה (*'imrâ*) and מִשְׁפָּטִים (*mišpāṭîm*) respectively in vv. 154 and 156. Also note the qualities of those inscripturated promises in v. 160.

[6] Cf., e.g., the significance of the roots חלץ (*ḥlṣ*), ריב (*ryḇ*), גאל (*g'l*), and חיה (*ḥyh*) respectively in vv. 153a, 154a, 154b, 156b, 159b. In addition, occurrences of the root ראה (*r'h*) in its sense of *paying careful attention to* point to the LORD's benevolent inclinations both to care (e.g. v. 159a) and to cure (e.g. v. 153a).

- 2A. (vv. 155–58) The theological cycle of cries is related to the psalmist's afflicters.
  - 1B. (v. 155) The comprehensive theological assertion about his afflicters (i.e. a soteriological assertion).
  - 2B. (vv. 156–57) The comparative theological assertion about his afflicters (i.e. a providential assertion):
    - 1C. (v. 156) The light side of this comparison: abounding grace.
    - 2C. (v. 157) The dark side of this comparison: abounding grief.
  - 3B. (v. 158) The critical theological assertion about his afflicters (i.e. a hamartiological assertion).
- 3A. (vv. 159–60) The tranquil cycle of cries is related to the psalmist's affection.
  - 1B. (v. 159) This tranquil cycle is reflected in the statement of his affection.
  - 2B. (v. 160) This tranquil cycle is also reflected in the substructure of his affection.

Commentary

The first imperative in this plea-packed section derives from the exceedingly common verb רָאָה (*rā'â*) which often simply means "to see." However, in this context the psalmist obviously has more in mind than a request for God to glance casually upon him in his "affliction."[7] "Behold!" comes closer; however, the disturbed disciple's heart was likely recalling the rich historical testimony of the LORD who had often looked intensely upon the troubles of His people *so as to intervene and care for them* (i.e. a freighted use of ראה [*r'h*]).[8] For example, in Genesis 22, by faith

[7] I.e. from the root ענה (*ᶜnh*) III; cf. noun occurrences in vv. 50 and 92 and verbal occurrences in vv. 67, 71, 75, 107. For the same combination of רְאֵה (*rᵉ'ēh*) + עָנְיִי (*ᶜonyî*) see Pss 9:14 (v. 13, Eng); 25:18; etc.

[8] Cf. to "look at with kindness, helpfulness" (BDB, p. 908); also cf. metaphorical sub-categories (3) and (4) in *TWOT*, s.v. "רָאָה (*rā'â*)," by W. White, 2:823.

Abraham recognized this great grace. In verse 8 he told Isaac literally "God will see" (יִרְאֶה [*yir'eh*]), i.e. He will *take care of* the matter of the sacrificial means. After the substitute for Isaac's life had been mercifully provided by the LORD, it is noted that Abraham called that place יהוה יִרְאֶה (*YHWH yireh*), "the LORD will provide," or better, taking this imperfect verb from ראה (*r'h*) as customary and thereby thoroughly establishing the precedent, "the LORD provides," i.e. He quite characteristically *looks upon to care for* His people in their plight. Similarly in Exodus 3, God Himself tells Moses about this tendency for intervention. He associates both His descent to deliver (v. 8) and His sending of a deliverer (v. 10) with an antecedent *observation* (i.e. ראה [*r'h*]) of His people's oppression (v. 9). Based upon these and other testimonies, the man of God realized that God's surveillance of suffering normally prompted the salvation of His servants; therefore, his prayers in this stanza commence with "Look upon (i.e. take care of) my affliction!"

That salvation from suffering was uppermost in his mind is indicated by the roots of the next four imperatives which quickly follow. The first is a Piel imperative[9] from חָלַץ (*ḥālaṣ*) I. Although this word in the OT is statistically the least prevalent of the soteriological terms in this string of imperatives, it is no less graphic. In certain contexts it literally denotes to draw off or out.[10] Some have therefore postulated a movement from the more literal to the figurative sphere of meaning along the lines of physical *removal* to spiritual *rescue*.[11] Other soteriological synonyms exhibit

---

[9] Cf. the imperative forms in Pss 6:5 (v. 4, Eng) and 140:2 (v. 1, Eng).

[10] BDB, p. 322.

[11] Cf. Barth's review of etymological conjectures in *TDOT*, s.v. "חָלַץ *chalats*," by C. Barth, 4:437. He, however, is more restrained in his conjectures opting for the attested active meanings of "escape, withdraw" as the background for the causative Piel meanings of "deliver, save" (ibid., pp. 436, 438). On the 15 occurrences bearing these latter senses in the OT, see ibid., p. 438; and BDB, p. 322.

a similar background of *extrication*.[12] No matter how the term may have developed, the child of God was obviously requesting Divine *deliverance*.

An interlude of personal affirmation (i.e. v. 153b) briefly interrupts the five staccato-like imperatives of verses 153–154. Between their second and third soundings a causal (i.e. כִּי [*kî*]) clause intrudes providing a secondary basis for the LORD's intervention.[13] Since the child of God, as a pattern of life,[14] had not "forgotten," i.e. *ignored*,[15] the demands of God's law for life, he views his requests for Divine visitation and extrication (v. 153a) as reasonable. On a larger scale, this reasonability for rescue is amplified all the more when his own obedience is viewed in contrast with his enemies' flagrant disobedience (cf. vv. 155b, 158b).

Verse 154 launches forth with a Qal imperative[16] of the significant root ריב (*ryḇ*) followed by its noun object from the very same semantical root.[17] This word group exhibits a usage field ranging from physically contending with someone to striving legally *against* (i.e. in a judicial sense), and sometimes even *for*, some-

---

[12] Cf., e.g., נצל (*nṣl*), משׁה (*mšh*), מלט (*mlṭ*), פּלט (*plṭ*), לקח (*lqḥ*) (cf. *TDOT*, 4:438 for brief notations). It is interesting that the LXX reads ἐξελοῦ (*exelou*) at Ps 119:153, and Barth concedes [but not without subsequent qualification] that "*exairein* . . . in the sense of 'deliver' may have been motivated by an etymology of 'taking out'" (ibid., p. 439).

[13] As in the case of previous mentionings of the psalmist's own piety contextually employed to document the appropriateness of Divine intervention, they must be regarded as secondary bases for prompting the actions of God. The fidelity of the promises of God (e.g. v. 154b) and the integrity of the grace and Person of God Himself (e.g. v. 156) always overshadow (but yet never obliterate) factors of finite, though faithful, obedience.

[14] I.e. another occurrence of the perfect tense with the objective negation לֹא (*lō'*); cf., e.g., v. 2.

[15] Cf. שָׁכַח (*šāḵaḥ*) in vv. 16, 61, 83, 93, 109, 139, 141, 176.

[16] The ָה (â) ending may indicate that this is an emphatic imperative. If so, this would lend even more intensity to the request.

[17] רִיבָה רִיב (*rîḇâ rîḇ*), "conduct my case, preside over my cause," i.e. a cognate accusative (cf. 1 Sam 24:16 [v. 15, Eng]; Jer 50:34; 51:36; Lam 3:58; Mic 7:9; Pss 43:1; 74:22; Prov 22:23). Cf. the Greek mirroring of this Semitic phenomenon in the rendering of the LXX here (i.e. κρῖνον τὴν κρίσιν [*krinon tēn krisin*]).

one.[18] In its latter sense the advocacy motif is dictated by context, as it is here.[19] Therefore, when the victimized child of God boldly approaches his LORD saying, "Plead Thou my cause,"[20] he is most certainly inviting Him to act as his personal and powerful Advocate.[21] He thirsts for that vindication which only God can secure.[22]

His intention is completely confirmed in the voicing of his next plea: (As one of Your very own) "redeem me!"[23] The imperative used here is from the root גאל (*g'l*) I, which quite often stands in a parallel relationship with other important soteriological terms.[24] Although etymological considerations are highly speculative and therefore of questionable value concerning גאל, the cultural or social background of the term in the OT amply elucidates its theological impact.[25] In this connection the participle "*go'el* is

---

[18] Cf. BDB, pp. 936–37; and esp., *TWOT*, s.v. "רִיב (*rîb*)," by R. Culver, 2:845–46.

[19] E.g., the overall comparison of the psalmist with his enemies, the parallelism of ריב (*ryb̲*) with גאל (*g'l*), the force of the cognate accusative, etc.

[20] *TWOT*, 2:845. One of the ways to translate the Targum's rendition here would be "Wrangle my quarrel" (cf. Jastrow, *Dictionary*, 2:824, 928).

[21] As BDB, p. 936, note, the structure of the words carries with it the connotation of taking one's part. Cf. the Christological significance of 1 John 2:1.

[22] Scroggie's anecdote on v. 154 flows from this particular request of the psalmist: "The clients of the LORD have a mighty Advocate" (*Psalms*, p. 186).

[23] That God was noted for both His advocacy and the protection of those that are His may be noted in the axioms of Prov 23:11 wherein גאל (*g'l*) and ריב (*ryb̲*) are also conspicuously juxtaposed. Paying particular attention to this proverb, Girdlestone has noted that "God takes the place of kinsman and also of avenger to the poor and helpless" (*Synonyms*, p. 119).

[24] Concerning these "verbs of delivering (rescuing)" Ringgren has observed that "the main word that stands in parallelism with and is almost synonymous to *ga'al* is פדה *pādhāh*, 'to ransom' (Hos. 13:14; Isa. 35:10; Jer. 31:11; Ps. 69:19 [Eng. v. 18]), but *hoshia*^{c} (ישׁע *yāsha*^{c}), 'to save, deliver' (Isa. 60:16; Ps. 106:10), *hitstsil* (נצל *nātsal*), 'to save, rescue' (Mic. 4:10), and עזר ^{c}*āzar*, 'to help' (Isa. 41:14), also occur in parallel" (*TDOT*, s.v. "גָּאַל *gā'al*," by H. Ringgren, 2:351).

[25] Ibid., pp. 350–53. However, some do postulate cautiously about original meaning; e.g., cf. Girdlestone: "Perhaps the original meaning of the word is to 'demand back,' hence to extricate" (*Synonyms*, p. 117). Apart from this conjecture, the rest of Girdlestone's treatment objectively develops the occurrences of גאל in the OT (ibid., pp. 118–120).

used of a man's nearest relative at a particular time. In Lev. 25:48f., it refers to a man's brother, uncle, cousin, or some other kinsman who is responsible for standing up for him and maintaining his rights."[26] The most extensive illustration of this responsibility/privilege is found in the Book of Ruth (cf. esp. 2:20; 3:12; 4:4–6, 9ff.).[27] The duty of such a person is "to do the part of a kinsman and thus to redeem his kin from difficulty or danger."[28] Consequently, the psalmist's wish, like Job's hope (cf. Job 19:25), graphically pictures "the work of God who as friend and kinsman through faith will ultimately redeem,"[29] i.e. rescue or deliver His own from humanly helpless situations.

The third appeal of verse 154 is a familiar one: "Revive me!"[30] Its concentrated occurrences, i.e. here and in verses 156 and 159, suggest that these are acute appeals "for life amidst an aura of death."[31] So exceedingly precarious is the plight of this pilgrim that he once again bolsters his prayer with the precedent of God's promise.[32] Upon the basis of his LORD's integrity as guaranteed by His word, deliverance should be forthcoming. With this brief flash of hope the tense emotional cycle of cries about his affliction climaxes providing a transition to the theological cycle which immediately follows.

As the child of God speaks of his enemies in verses 155–158, he does not merely emote because of their presence, but rather he evaluates them in their various relationships concluding that they

---

26 *TDOT*, 2:351.

27 There are actually two social precedents exemplified in Ruth, i.e. "kinsman redemption and levirate marriage" (cf. *TWOT*, s.v. "גָּאַל (*gā'al*)," by R. Harris, 1:144, for a good discussion of both).

28 Ibid.

29 Ibid., pp. 144–145.

30 Cf. the Piel imperative of חיה (*ḥyh*) in vv. 25, 37, 40, 88, 107, 149 and its related intentional occurrences in vv. 17, 77, 116, 144, 175.

31 Allen, *Psalms 101–150*, p. 144.

32 I.e. לְאִמְרָתֶךָ (*le'imrāṯekā*), lit. "in reference to Your word," i.e. "according to Your promise."

33 Note his subsequent reaction bound up in the Hithpolel form of the verb קוּט (*qûṭ*), i.e. וָאֶתְקוֹטָטָה (*wā'eṯqôṭāṭṭâ*), lit. "I loath (them)."

are utterly wanting on the basis of God's standards (cf. esp. vv. 155b, 158b). He first comes to a soteriological conclusion based upon their lack of pursuing God's Word in verse 155. Correspondingly, in verse 158 he very personally comes[33] to a hamartiological conclusion[34] grounded upon their disobedience of the Word of God. Contrastingly, their infidelity is all the more conspicuous when it is compared implicitly with the persistent fidelity of the psalmist (v. 157b) and the perfect fidelity of his LORD (v. 156a).[35] A further contrast within verses 156–157, i.e. between the coexisting realities of the overflowing mercies of God and the inundating meanness of his afflicters,[36] leads him to a providential conclusion. Although he asserts that the number of his afflicters might seem limitless (v. 157), God's supply of compassion (v. 156) will never fail.

Salvation, יְשׁוּעָה (*yᵉšûᶜâ*),[37] is the express subject of verse 155. As previously indicated, "deliverance or salvation (Heb. *yᵉšûᶜâh* and cognates) is the work of God, but its precise content varies according to context and circumstances."[38] That the ישׁע (*yšᶜ*) word group is nuanced temporally in the majority of its occurrences in the OT is granted; however, in some places it does seem to carry eschatological overtones.[39] Although most of the psalmist's requests in this psalm pertain to deliverance or rescue from the predicament of his situation, this particular affirmation about salva-

---

[34] His appellation בֹּגְדִים (*bōgᵉḏîm*), "treacherous ones," is poignant.

[35] Vv. 155 and 158 seem to relate to vv. 156–57 by a contextual contrast.

[36] Both realities are qualified by רַבִּים (*rabbîm*), "much, many," indicating the great abundance of each.

[37] On this same noun form, see vv. 123, 166, 174. For a synonymous noun, תְּשׁוּעָה (*tᵉšûᶜâ*), cf. vv. 41, 81, and for verbal occurrences of the root ישׁע (*yšᶜ*) see vv. 94, 117, 146.

[38] *NIDNTT*, s.v. "σῴζω," by C. Brown, 3:207; cf. Anderson, *Psalms*, 1:277; and Driver's famous synopsis: "The words seldom . . . express a spiritual state *exclusively*: their common theological sense in Hebrew is that of *a material deliverance attended by spiritual blessings* . . ." (S. R. Driver, *Notes on the Hebrew Text and the Topography of the Books of Samuel* [Reprinted; Winona Lake, IN: Alpha Publications, 1984], p. 119).

[39] Cf. this minority report in the OT with the majority report of the NT references (i.e. most of the latter are non-temportal in nature).

tion in reference to his enemies seems to be generic and quite comprehensive. Consequently, it is best to look upon his predication about their state as an axiomatic generalization: "Salvation," יְשׁוּעָה (*yᵉšûᶜâ*) without qualification (i.e. allowing for its full range of semantical applicability including, and possibly even emphasizing, the eternal status of his persecutors) "is far from the wicked." The combination of the predicate adjective רָחוֹק (*rāḥôq*) plus the preposition מִן (*min*) functioning separatively[40] is very arresting.[41] God's precious salvation is "lacking" in reference to or "absent from"[42] רְשָׁעִים (*rᵉšāᶜîm*), "wicked ones."[43]

Since the servant's statement recorded in verse 155a possibly might seem too sensationalistic, he offers a reason for its credibility in verse 155b. Having probably taken a quick mental inventory of his painfully personal experiences of such wicked men's attitudes and actions,[44] the man of God characterizes them as not having any concern for God's statutes.[45] Just as the faithful are generally characterized by pursuing God and His word,[46] these infidels are characterized by their lack of any such pursuit.[47]

---

[40] Cf., e.g., Williams, *Hebrew Syntax*, § 315.

[41] Contrast the nearness of God's salvation to 'fearers of Him' in Ps 85:10 (v. 9, Eng).

[42] Suggested renderings for מִן + רָחוֹק (*rāḥôq* + *min*) by BDB, p. 935. Cf. the parallel Aramaic renderings in the Targum, the μακρὰν ἀπό (*makran apo*) of the LXX, and the *longe ab* of the Vulgate.

[43] Cf. this plural adjective functioning substantively in vv. 53, 61, 95, 110, 119.

[44] What is said about them in the verses mentioned in the previous note would suffice as a point of embarkation in reference to the data base relating to their heinous exploitations.

[45] Anderson suggests the following significance for v. 155b: "they do not apply God's law to practical life" (*Psalms*, 2:844).

[46] Cf. the seeking (i.e. דרשׁ [*drš*]) on the part of all the faithful in v. 2 generally (remembering esp. the parallelism of obeying God's word with seeking Him), and in particular, the psalmist's own responses of pursuit in vv. 10, 45, 94. Internally to the stanza, their disobedience (לֹא דָרָשׁוּ [*lō' dārāšû*], v. 155b) stands opposed to his obedience (לֹא שָׁכָחְתִּי [*lo' šākāḥtî*], v. 153b); here the contrast between these כִּי (*kî*) clauses is drawn conceptionally rather than semantically.

[47] One should recall the use of the root דרשׁ (*drš*) in Pss 14:2 and 53:3 (v. 2, Eng). This was of course one of the powerful indictments levelled by Paul against all classes of fallen humanity in Rom 3:11.

In between the negative realities of verses 155b and 157a the child of God takes refuge in the transcendent bastion extolled in verse 156a. He recognized that God's people, including himself, were surrounded by tender expressions of their sovereign Protector's compassionate care. That these "'many' mercies"[48] indeed signified not merely "a sentiment, but a concrete manifestation of pity to the weak and afflicted"[49] is borne out by an observable pattern to the occurrences of the root רחם (*rḥm*) throughout the OT. Fittingly, this saint's personal recognition of such grace is capstoned with a doxological occurrence of the vocative יהוה (*YHWH*), "O LORD!" Also, and by now,[50] quite expectedly, the bold man of faith does not hesitate to implore the bestowal of such *attested*[51] benefits immediately as he again cries out: "Revive me!"[52]

The earthly dimension of reality returns as verse 157 commences. Allen's translations of verses 156a and 157a capture both the intended parallelism and the disciple's re-entry and descent back into the context of his consternation: "Your compassion is so multiplied, Yahweh. . . . My persecutors and foes are multiplied too. . . ."[53] His conceptual movement from the transcendent to the terrestrial was very painful but not personally overwhelming. Although those who were relentlessly persecuting him[54] and ha-

[48] Cf. Alexander's insistence on "many" rather than "great" (*Psalms*, 3:194).

[49] Anderson, *Psalms*, 2:844.

[50] I.e. in the course of walking through these many verses with the child of God.

[51] In addition to the history of help that the reference to רחם (*rḥm*) in v. 156a brings to mind, the prepositional phrase כְּמִשְׁפָּטֶיךָ (*kᵉmišpāṭeykā*) in v. 156b is another reminder of the inscripturated precedent of God's personal availability to dependent ones.

[52] It many be of some interest to note that 7 out of the 9 occurrences of the Piel imperative of חיה (*ḥyh*) in the Hebrew text of Ps 119 are rendered by imperatives of the Aramaic root אֱסִי (*'ᵃsî*), "to cure, heal," in the Targum (cf. vv. 25, 37, 40, 107, 154, 156, 159; contra vv. 88, and 149 where forms of the root קום [*qwm*], "to establish," are found). The exact nature of the metaphorical impact of אֱסִי in these Targum occurrences is not obvious.

[53] Allen, *Psalms 101–150*, p. 133. In view of larger theological (e.g., cf. the larger principle mentioned by Paul in Rom 5:20b) and contextual (e.g., cf. the psalmist's response which immediately follows in v. 157b) qualifiers the respective parallelism between abounding grace and abounding grief should *not* be viewed merely as a conceptual wash out (cf. also Ps 3:1–3).

[54] Cf. the root רדף (*rdp*) in vv. 84, 86, 150, 161.

bitually harassing and oppressing him[55] were multitudinous, they did not deter him from his pathway of obedience. To affirm his non-apostasy he uses a particularly emphatic chain of terms: the verb נָטָה (*nāṭâ*), "to incline, bend, turn aside,"[56] denied by the objective negative לֹא (*lō'*) and complemented by a prepositional phrase with partitive מִן, "away from."[57] No matter what, he had not deviated from his LORD's testimonies. The precedent to which this child of God had contributed is phrased by Scroggie as follows: "When we suffer we should not swerve."[58]

In the spirit of David in Psalm 139:21 the man of God revulses in verse 158 upon his observation and contemplation[59] of disobedient people.[60] Here he calls his afflicters בֹּגְדִים (*bōgᵉḏîm*), "treacherous ones."[61] "The verb" בָּגַד (*bāgaḏ*) "expresses the unstable relationship of a man to an existing established regulation."[62] In this context[63] his designation mirrors their covenant infidelity.[64] A reflexive form of the verb קוּט (*qûṭ*) reveals how he spontaneously

---

55 Cf. the root צרר (*ṣrr*) in vv. 139, 143.

56 BDB, pp. 639–40; cf. respectively, invoked, negated, and affirmed occurrences of נטה (*nṭh*) in vv. 36, 51, 112.

57 The metaphor of a path or way delineated by God obviously stands behind this chain of words.

58 Scroggie, *Psalms*, p. 186.

59 רָאָה (*rā'â*) in this context likely bears both of these nuances.

60 Cf. the reaction of this man of God in v. 53.

61 I.e. "ones who act/deal treacherously, faithlessly, deceitfully" (cf. BDB, p. 93).

62 *TDOT*, s.v. "בָּגַד *baghadh*," by S. Erlandsson, 1:470; he continues, noting that the term "is used when the OT writer wants to say that a man does not honor an agreement, or commits adultery, or breaks a covenant or some other ordinance given by God. . . . Thus *baghadh* . . . has primarily a religious function. . . . The *boghedim* are contrasted with those who live in harmony with the divine order" (ibid., pp. 470, 472).

63 Cf. esp. the immediate context of v. 158b.

64 Anderson, *Psalms*, 2: 844. Note the appropriate rendering of the LXX. The corresponding substantive participle in the Greek text ἀσυνθετοῦντας (*asynthetountas*), i.e. the negating alpha privative plus συντίθεμαι (*syntithemai*), emphasizes covenant breaking; cf. the adjective ἀσύνθετος (*asynthetos*), "covenant-breaking, faithless" (Thayer, *Lexicon*, p. 82), which Paul employs similarly as a derogatory plural in Rom 1:31. The rendering of the Targum, בָּזוֹזֵי (*bāzôzê*), "robbers, plunderers" (Jastrow, *Dictionary*, 1:152), is too focused.

and deeply felt about such derelicts. Apart from a fairly wide range of semantical possibilities,[65] the "root [קוט] denotes the deep emotional reaction of the subject issuing in a desired repulsion . . . of the object."[66] In this instance the disciple's "profound disgust"[67] regarding them is directly documented by their disobedience (v. 158b),[68] i.e. they had not kept God's word.

The pendulum swings in a different direction in verse 159a, this time away from their infidelity towards his own integrity. By employing the verb רָאָה (*rā'â*) a third time in this stanza as a lead-off word (cf. vv. 153a, 158a), the child of God begs the undivided attention of his LORD. In verse 153 he used an identical Qal imperative imploring his Sovereign to take deep personal interest in his affliction. There his focus was upon Divine deliverance in the form of an immediate extrication from persecution. Here he urges the Divine Examiner of all men to pay special attention[69] to His disciple's care for and commitment to (cf. אָהֵב [*'āhēb*], esp. in v. 97) the preceptive declarations of God's will and ways. Anticipating a favorable verdict from above regarding this evidence,[70] the needy devotee immediately places a consequential request for personal sustenance before his supreme Benefactor.[71] This third request for

---

[65] E.g. "felt a loathing" (BDB, p. 876), "sickened" (Alexander, *Psalms*, 3:194; possibly influenced by the ἐκτήκω [*ektēkō*] of the LXX, i.e. to pine, waste away), "mightily indignant" (Cook, *Psalms*, p. 454), etc.

[66] *TWOT*, s.v. "קוּט (*qûṭ*)," by L. Coppes, 2:792.

[67] Delitzsch, *Psalms*, 3:262; cf. Allen's rendering "fills me with disgust" (*Psalms 101–150*, p. 133).

[68] The אֲשֶׁר (*'ăšer*) here is obviously functioning causally (cf. BDB, p. 83) and should be rendered as "because" or "since," thereby providing the grounds for his intense loathing.

[69] The רְאֵה כִּי (*rᵉ'ēh kî*) may be rendered "Take (careful) notice that"; cf. also, "Consider how" (NASB), "See how" (NIV), etc.

[70] Such positive perspectives on the equitable justice of God are part of an extensive historical lineage which even antedated Abraham's axiomatic statement of the precedent (cf. Gen 18:25).

[71] Again, the vocative יהוה (*YHWH*) is placed strategically between the *secondary* (cf. note 73 below) support for and substance of the request.

preservation of life[72] in *Rêš* is somewhat subdued when compared with the contextual settings of the other two (i.e. vv. 154b, 156b). In the former settings he was occupied with the temporal realities of his enemies' breathing down his neck. But, in this setting, the disciple seems to be more tranquil due to the fact that he becomes preoccupied with the unfathomable grace of God (v. 159b)[73] and the inestimable gift of God, His all-sufficient word (i.e. v. 160). It would seem that tranquility progressively dispels the shadows of trepidation as one's focus shifts from the more temporal to the more transcendent.

Indeed, a primary means for bridging the gap between the realities of heaven above and earth beneath is the Book of God. In verse 160, the psalmist looks at that Divine revelation first wholistically then atomistically.[74] By juxtaposing the word רֹאשׁ (*rō'š*), literally "head," with דְּבָרְךָ (*dᵉḇārᵉḵā*), "Your word," he draws attention to the "sum"[75] of God's written communications to mankind, that is, the "totality" of the word.[76] He associates with the "sum-total"[77] of his LORD's inscripturated directives for life a primary attribute of אֱמֶת (*'ĕmeṯ*), "truth" (v. 160a; cf. v. 142 and John 17:17 again). Then as he shifts his perspective slightly, moving to the various parts of the whole with the phrase כָּל־מִשְׁפַּט צִדְקֶךָ (*kol-*

---

[72] Once again, the Piel imperative of חָיָה (*ḥāyâ*) likely bears a significant qualitative dimension in addition to its more obvious reference to continuance of physical existence (cf. BDB, p. 311).

[73] I.e. חַסְדְּךָ (*ḥasdᵉḵā*); note the attached preposition כְּ (*kᵉ*) which indicates that his bold request for Divine intervention is *ultimately* grounded upon (cf. and contra. the secondary basis just mentioned by implication in v. 159a) the inexplicable precedent of the sovereign grace of God.

[74] I.e. ". . . Torah, both in its entirety and in its parts" (Soll, "Psalm 119," p. 207).

[75] Cf. BDB, p. 911.

[76] Cohen, *Psalms*, p. 414; cf. "the essence" (Dahood, *Psalms*, 3:192). On the early versions, esp. the LXX (ἀρχή [*archē*]) and Targum (שֵׁירוּי [*šēyrûy*]), Moll has well noted that "רֹאשׁ, according to the context, does not mean: the beginning . . . , but the sum, the total number of all the items in the reckoning" (*Psalms*, p. 593).

[77] Delitzsch, *Psalms*, 3:262.

mišpaṭ ṣiḏqeḵā), "(each and) every one of Your righteous judgments,"[78] the grateful child of God spotlights the Word's attribute of permanence (v. 160b; cf. Isa 40:6–8). Consequently, whether surveyed as one piece or as parts of a unit, God's Book has proven itself to be both dependable and imperishable. For needy pilgrims it exudes its never-failing reliability which enables them through a transcendent perspective to endure and persevere amidst the tempestuous tribulations of life in a hostile world.

[78] The plural translation is supported by several Hebrew manuscripts, the LXX, Targum, and Syriac versions, along with the occurrence of the phrase מִשְׁפְּטֵי צִדְקֶךָ (*mišp^{e}ṭê ṣiḏqeḵā*), "Your righteous judgments" in vv. 7, 62, 106, 164.

ש

SHIN STANZA
(vv. 161–168)

Translation and Notes

161 Princes persecute[a] me undeservedly,[b]
but my heart[c] dreads[d] Your words.[e]

162 I rejoice[a] over[b] Your word[c]
like[d] someone who finds much booty.

163 I hate and detest[a] falsehood;
however,[b] I love[a] Your law.

164 I praise You[a] seven times a day
because of[b] Your righteous judgments.

165 The ones who love Your law have[a] great peace,
and they do not experience[b] stumbling.[c]

166 I hope for[a] Your salvation, O LORD,
and[b] I practice[a] Your commandments.

167 My soul[a] keeps[b] Your testimonies,
and[c] I love[b] them exceedingly.

168 I keep[a] Your precepts and testimonies,
because all my ways *are* before You.

161:a Or, "have persecuted" for the Qal perfect of רָדַף (*rāḏap̱*).

161:b Lit. "out of favor." The lengthened form (cf. Waltke and O'Connor, *Biblical Hebrew Syntax*, 5.7e) found here often functions adverbially in the sense of "gratuitously, without cause, undeservedly" (BDB, p. 336); cf. the δωρεάν (*dōrean*) of the LXX and the מַגָּן (*magān*) of the Targum.

161:c לִבִּי (*libbî*), much like נַפְשִׁי (*napšî*; e.g. v. 167), is an anthropological circumlocution connoting "I."

161:d Or, "has been in dread" or "awe," i.e. the Qal perfect of פָּחַד (*pāḥad*).

161:e The *k^etîb* is well supported textually (cf. also DSS [Q11], LXX, etc.); therefore, the evidence for the suggested *q^erê* is not compelling.

162:a The form שָׂשׂ (*śāś*) is somewhat puzzling in view of the pronoun אָנֹכִי (*'ānōkî*) which follows (cf. the note to 35.5.2d in Waltke and O'Connor's *Biblical Hebrew Syntax*).

162:b Cf. BDB p. 965, for שִׂישׂ (*śîś*) plus עַל (*ᶜal*), i.e. "over" or "at"; Soll, in contrast with most versions and translations, construes the עַל as a causative ("Psalm 119," p. 207).

162:c Or, more specifically, "Your promise"; note that the singular אִמְרָתֶךָ (*'imrāṯeḵā*) is well attested (cf. DSS [Q11], Targum, etc.).

162:d The preposition כְּ (cf. LXX, Targum, etc.) attached to the participle introduces the simile of v. 162b; DSS (Q11), however, exhibits a comparative מִן (*min*), i.e. "more than. . . ." In either case, v. 162b *illustrates* the great joy confessed by the psalmist in v. 162a.

163:a Or respectively, "I have hated," "I have detested," "I have loved." On the pointing of the second verb, Allen has well suggested that "the alternative pointing וָאתעבה [*wa'tᶜbh*] 'I detest' (cf. *BHS*) is preferable" (*Psalms 101–150*, p. 138).

163:b The MT exhibits another instance of asyndetic antithetical parallelism; however, DSS (Q11) shows an explicit *wāw* conjunction attached to the lead-off תּוֹרָתְךָ (*tôrāṯ^eḵā*) of v. 163b (cf. the postpositive δέ [*de*] of the LXX).

164:a Or, "I have praised You."

164:b Here the עַל (*ᶜal*) is probably causal; another option would be "concerning."

165:a I.e. possessive לְ (*l^e*).

165:b I.e. the particle of non-existence with possessive לְ (*l^e*).

165:c Interestingly, the Targum has added interpretive phrases to the ends of the bicolon (cf. the italicized portions): "To the ones who love Your instruction there is great peace *in this world*, and they do not have a stumbling block *in the world to come*."

166:a Or respectively, "I have hoped for," "I have done."

166:b This *waw* conjunction could possibly be regarded as connoting a light causal relationship, e.g., "I hope for Your salvation, *since* I have . . . ," or be viewed consequentially, e.g., ". . . therefore. . . ."

167:a נַפְשִׁי (*napšî*) again stands as a periphrasis for the person, i.e. "I"; cf. the simple first person verb of v. 168a.

167:b Or respectively, "has kept," "and I have loved them."

167:c As in the previous verse, this conjunction could possibly be construed causally, i.e. "*since* I love them . . ." (in addition to possibly internal contextual indicators for a light causal rendering in vv. 166b, 167b, note the explicitly causal statement of v. 168b).

168:a Or, "I have kept."

Synopsis and Outline

Śîn/Šîn (vv. 161–168) is different from the other stanzas, not only by what it contains but also by what it does not contain, i.e. acute prayer requests. Furthermore, although the rest of this psalm's 21 strophes and 168 verses regularly exhibit sprinkles of the author's personal declarations of integrity, this eight-verse segment is characterized by a deluge of them. Interestingly, these affirmations of fidelity are sandwiched in between brief synopses of the two great (and often, motivational) realities in the psalmist's life, human pressure (v. 161a) and Divine penetration (v. 168b). As the psalm draws to a close, the disciple documents both his past pleas and his forthcoming finale of requests in *Tāw* (vv. 169–176) with a great flourish of evidences of personal piety (i.e. vv. 161b, 162, 163, 164, 165 [by implication], 166, 167, 168a).[1]

---

[1] Note similarly the comments of Soll ("Psalm 119," p. 207) and Allen (*Psalms 101–150*, p. 144).

Generally, there seems to be a progressive development in the articulation of his statements about basic integrity. Throughout the psalm (and the rest of the Scriptures) one observes an obvious interplay between attitudes and actions, and logically (i.e. theologically), the assumption is that the former should always constitute the basis of the latter. Here, in this next to the last strophe of Psalm 119, there is movement from fear (v. 161b), joy (v. 162a), hate (v. 163a), love (vv. 163b, 165a, 167b), gratitude (v. 164), peace (v. 165), and hope (v. 166a)[2] to obedience (vv. 166b, 167a, 168a). In other words, concrete "doing" (עָשָׂה [*ʿāśâ*], v. 166b) and "keeping" (שָׁמַר [*šāmar*], vv. 167a, 168a) flow out of attitudinal orientations of the heart. Stylistic phenomena also complement the logical coherence of verses 161–168. Semantical and syntactical parallelisms, usually formulated antithetically, help to bind the flow of thought together. For example, the psalmist's awe of the Divine (v. 161b) overwhelms his concerns about human hostility (v. 161a), exultation (v. 162a) responds antiphonally to fear (v. 161b), and his hatred (v. 163a) is counter-balanced by his love (v. 163b, *et al.*).

In putting the pieces of Psalm 119:161–168 together, the reader observes the child of God verbally laying out before the LORD six indications of basic integrity for the purpose of documenting his previous and forthcoming requests.

1A. (v. 161) His godly fear prevails over human pressure.
2A. (v. 162) His godly contentment rivals human materialism.
3A. (v. 163) His godly commitment provides perspective on human injustice.
4A. (v. 164) His godly praise is the product of Divine justice.
5A. (v. 165) His godly peace (i.e. as a member of the community of the faithful) promises a reassuring stability.
6A. (vv. 166–168) His godly obedience is prompted by:
    1B. (v. 166) A confident expectation.
    2B. (v. 167) A consuming adoration.
    3B. (v. 168) A complete penetration.

---

[2] Several of these affirmations on the part of the psalmist obviously correspond to some of the fruit of the Spirit representatively enumerated in Gal 5:22–23.

Commentary

Verse 161 reintroduces the psalmist's enemies through a familiar form, an antithetical couplet; he contrasts their wickedness with his own worship.[3] The thrust of his testimony is apparent: "his fear of God's words is greater than that of any earthly ruler."[4] Only in one other place does he refer to his enemies as (*śārîm*), i.e. as "formidable foes."[5] His reference to them as such in verse 23 unveiled the planning stage of their hostile preoccupations, while here in verse 161 attention is drawn to their actual pursuit and persecution of him. What made their relentless campaigns especially abominable was the fact that they had no grounds for their attacks upon the child of God.[6]

In the light of such unjust treatment one might expect an imprecation against them; however, the disciple is once again overwhelmed by his own responsibilities before God and His word. As he adjusts his attention from the horizontal to the heavenly plane, ultimate reality grips him as he emotes: "but it is your [i.e. God's] words that fill my heart with dread" (v. 161b).[7] What his

---

[3] As a reminder, the verse may be translated by connecting the two clauses with a contrasting conjunction, e.g. "but," "however," "nevertheless," etc.; or v. 161a could well be rendered into English as a concessive clause, e.g. "though," "although," etc., paving the way for the psalmist's statement of unwavering piety in v. 161b.

[4] Soll, "Psalm 119," p. 207.

[5] As a "term of rank" or "dignity" in the ancient Near East these men were indeed looked upon by the psalmist as "formidable foes" in v. 161 (BDB, p. 161); cf. the ἄρχοντες (*archontes*) of the LXX (for a brief survey, see *TDNT*, s.v. "ἄρχων," by G. Delling, 1:488–89), the usage of רַבְרְבִין (*rabrebîn*) in the Targum, and Allen's more generic rendering of "the authorities" (*Psalms 101–150*, p. 133).

[6] Cf. this collocation of רָדַף (*rādap*) and חִנָּם (*ḥinnām*), "without cause," with רָדַף plus שֶׁקֶר (*šeqer*) in v. 86, i.e. therein a reference to *fraudulent* or *wrongful* persecution (cf. BDB, p. 1055).

[7] Allen's dynamic rendering of the psalmist's testimony (*Psalms 101–150*, p. 133).

enemies lacked, a healthy fear of the person and the precepts of God, the psalmist possessed in full measure.

A profound and trembling respect for Divine revelation is complemented by a habitual joy over it in verse 162.[8] The exultation that the promise of God generates in the psalmist resembles that which is experienced by a man when he rakes in an abundance of spoil.[9] The imagery of שָׁלָל (*šālāl*) within its ancient Near Eastern context[10] would have been especially captivating, since "the Hebrew *šālāl* is usually the booty of war" and "the division of the spoils of war was an occasion of great rejoicing . . . (Isa. 9:3; cf. Jg. 5:30)."[11] So the child of God once again understands and bears witness to the ultimate priorities (cf. vv. 14, 36, 57, 72, 111, 127, etc. with Matt 6:19–33).

The conceptual antithesis between fear (v. 161) and joy (v. 162) is followed by another which is internally manifested through the antithetical parallelism of verse 163. In this case a thoroughgoing revulsion from wrong (v. 163a) is juxtaposed with a deep-seated regard for the word (v. 163b). The disciple fastens together two unambivalent verbs, שָׂנֵא (*śānē'*, "to hate"; cf. vv. 104, 113, 128)[12]

---

8 At this juncture Anderson suggests the possible backdrop for this conceptual antithesis: "the tension between awe (verse 161) and joy (verse 162) . . . may be a reflection of the two opposites implicit in the Covenant law: blessing and curse (cf. Dt. 27:11–28:68)" (*Psalms*, 2:844).

9 On שָׁלָל רָב (*šālāl rāḇ*; e.g., "much plunder," "great booty"; "a lot of spoil" [Allen, *Psalms 101–150*, p. 133], etc.) cf. also the σκῦλα πολλά (*skyla polla*) of the LXX, the עֲדִי סַגִּי (*cădî sagî*) of the Targum, and the *spolia multa* of the Vulgate.

10 For a helpful survey of the שׁלל (*šll*) word group, its synonymous word group, בזז (*bzz*), and their ancient Near Eastern cognates, see *TDOT*, s.v. "בזז *bzz;* שׁלל *šll*," by H. Ringgren, 2:68.

11 Anderson, *Psalms*, 2:845. For other helpful commentary on the שׁלל word group, see *TWOT*, s.v. "שָׁלָל (*shālal*) II," by H. Austel, 2:930, noting sample occurrences in 1 Sam 15:19, 21; 1 Chr 20:2; 2 Chr 14:12 (v.13, Eng); Ps 68:13 (v. 12, Eng); Isa 10:6; etc. The historical practice of plundering made שׁלל a prime metaphorical candidate, especially in contexts of ancient Hebrew poetry (e.g. Gen 49:27; Exod 15:9; Judg 5:30), prophetic or eschatological revelations (e.g. Isa 53:12; Zech 14:1), and wisdom affirmations (e.g. Ps 119:162; Prov 1:13; 16:19; 31:11).

12 Note the linguistic equivalents in the Targum (i.e. סְנֵי [*sᵉnê*]) and LXX (i.e. μισέω [*miseō*]).

and תָּעַב (*tā*c*aḇ*, "to abhor, loathe, detest"),[13] in order to express the negative dimension of his commitment to the Divine ethic. Several times in the OT the second term "denotes God's hostility to evil";[14] therefore, it expressively indicates that the child of God stands diametrically opposed to any and all manifestations of שֶׁקֶר (*šeqer*), "falsehood, deception, deceit, fraud, wrong," etc.[15]

The positive dimension of his ethical commitment quickly follows as he affirms his love for God's law. Such an intricate, divinely-mediated balance between love and hatred is a prerequisite for right living. Although Morris' comments are precipitated by the imperative of Psalm 97:10, his conclusions are also confirmed by the illustration of Psalm 119:163:

> Those who love God also develop a fierce hatred of what is wrong: "You who love the Lord hate evil" (Ps 97:10, RSV mg.). There is no room for half-measures in loving God. Because God is totally opposed to everything evil, the man who loves him must likewise be implacably opposed to evil. Love for God cannot co-exist with a love for evil. The very fact of the believer's love for God means that he is dedicated to stamping out evil.[16]

The psalmist's piety manifests itself as praise in verse 164. Interestingly, this is the first occurrence of the root הלל (*hll*), "to praise," in the psalm, but the verb will return for an encore in

---

[13] Note the Vulgate's *detestatus*. For a survey of the denominative Piel verb and its parent noun תּוֹעֵבָה (*tô*c*ēḇâ*), see *TWOT*, s.v. "תָּעַב (*tā*c*ab*)," by R. Youngblood, 2:976–77.

[14] *TDNT*, s.v. "βδελύσσομαι," by W. Foerster, 1:598; he also cites from the LXX places where βδέλυγμα (*bdelygma*) stands in a parallel relationship with ἀνομία (*anomia*), i.e. Jer 4:1; Ezek 11:18; 20:30; Amos 6:8; Pss 5:7; 13:1; 52:1; 118:163 [i.e. 119:163, MT]; Job 15:16, thereby enhancing its ethical impact (ibid.).

[15] BDB, p. 1055. It must not be forgotten that he personally experienced a wide variety of such painful manifestations of שֶׁקֶר (*šeqer*).

[16] Morris, *Testaments of Love*, p. 53. Unfortunately, the reciprocal of the psalmist's attitude is often observed (cf., e.g., Amos 5:10 for a blatant perversion of the Divine standard).

verse 175.[17] These seemingly late arrivals of this significant root[18] may be one of the indications (i.e. a doxological one) that the psalmist's *magnum opus* is drawing to a close. Semantically, this "most general"[19] OT word for praise is partially understood in its sacred settings (such as here) by comparing it with its occurrences in secular contexts.[20] Both in its secular and sacred settings "this root connotes being sincerely and deeply thankful for and/or satisfied in lauding a superior quality(ies) or great . . . act(s) of the object."[21] In the OT, quite obviously, its utilization in doxological contexts predominates[22] with the focus being upon gratitude for the Person or performance of God.

Here the fact of his praising God is not as surprising as the frequency of his laudatory expressions. "Not merely morning and evening, not merely three times a day . . . , but seven times . . . he gives thanks to God. . . ."[23] שֶׁבַע בַּיּוֹם (*šeḇaᶜ bayyôm*) "is to be under-

---

[17] In both verses the Targum uses the near synonym שְׁבַח (*šᵉḇaḥ*), the LXX αἰνέω (*aineō*), and the Vulgate the verb from which the English form "to laud" derives.

[18] "The same verb is also used in the cultic exclamation 'Hallelujah,' or 'Praise Yahweh'" (Anderson, *Psalms*, 2:845), and a plural noun form of the root, i.e. תהלים (*ṯhlym*), "praises," is the Hebrew title for the Book of Psalms.

[19] Girdlestone, *Synonyms*, p. 220; his etymological speculations, however, should not be accepted without significant qualifications since they are based upon older cognate studies relating to הלל I, not הלל II. For more relevant conjectures, see *TDOT*, s.v. "הלל *hll* I and II," by H. Ringgren, 3:404–05; based upon the cognates of הלל II seemingly connoting a common denominator of excitability, Ringgren suggests that "we are probably dealing with an onomatopoetic word" (ibid., p. 404).

[20] Among which Ringgren cites Gen 12:15; 2 Sam 14:25; Ezek 26:17; Prov 12:8; 31:31; Cant 6:9; 2 Chr 23:12f.; *et al.* (*TDOT*, 3:405–06). Interestingly, the LXX reserves αἰνέω (*aineō*) for the praise of God alone; for the aforementioned secular occurrences of הלל it draws upon other terms (cf. *NIDNTT*, s.v. "αἰνέω," by H. Schultz, 3:816–17).

[21] *TWOT*, s.v. "הָלַל (*hālal*) II," by L. Coppes, 1:217.

[22] "The most frequent use of our root relates to praising the God of Israel" (ibid.).

[23] Delitzsch, *Psalms*, 3:262; on *seven* times, cf. Gen 4:24; Lev 26:18; Ps 12:7 (v. 6, Eng); Prov 24:16; Matt 18:21ff.; Luke 17:4; etc. Allen suggests that seven in comparison with three times (e.g. Ps 55:18 [v. 17, Eng]; Dan 6:10–11) indicates "piety beyond the norm" (*Psalms 101–150*, p. 138).

stood here . . . not arithmetically, but symbolically, representing a continued course of devotional exercises, complete in itself, and surrounding and pervading, with its sacred influences, all the duties of the day";[24] therefore, acceptable connotations of this adverbial prepositional phrase would be "many times" or "constantly."[25] "Ever and ever again" the dependent disciple availed "himself of every prayerful impulse."[26] And the grounds for his gratitude were compelling.[27] When he says in verse 164b, "because of Your righteous judgments" or "for your righteous laws" (NIV),[28] the child of God confesses that he is especially thankful for all indications of Divine rectitude. Once again, a primary attribute, in this case צֶדֶק (*ṣeḏeq*), "righteousness," describes what God does, summarizes what He has revealed, and characterizes who He is.

Periodically the psalmist has looked upon himself as part of the community of true disciples. He does so again in verse 165 with his reference to אֹהֲבֵי תוֹרָתֶךָ (*'ohᵃḇê tôrāṯeḵā*), "those that love Your law."[29] As previously stressed,[30] the root אהב (*'hḇ*) in contexts such as the present one emphasizes *commitment* to covenant and/or the God of the covenant. Not surprisingly, the psalmist here specifies as the object of love his LORD's covenant "law," i.e. His gracious gift of revealed "instruction" or "direction" for life. The

---

24 Moll, *Psalms*, p. 593.

25 Anderson, *Psalms*, 2:845.

26 Delitzsch, *Psalms*, 3:262; cf. in the NT the dependent attitudes of incessant (note ἀδιαλείπτως [*adialeiptōs*] in 1 Thess 5:17) prayer and perpetual (note ἐν παντί [*en panti*] in 1 Thess 5:18; πάντοτε [*pantote*] in Eph 5:20; Phlm 4; *et al.*) praise.

27 For a helpful survey of some scripturally expressed reasons for praise, see *TDOT*, 3:408–09.

28 Cf. Allen's "for your just rulings" (*Psalms 101–150*, p. 133). It should be noted that the introductory עַל (*ʿal*) of v. 164b, whether construed causally or more generally in the sense of specification, refers to a significant impetus for the psalmist's praise.

29 Cf. the substantive usage of the plural Qal active participle from אָהַב (*'āhaḇ*) in v. 132.

30 Cf. also the forthcoming reference in v. 167b.

children of God, being characterized by their love-commitment,[31] possess[32] "great peace."[33] Due to the situation of the persecuted psalmist, applicationally שָׁלוֹם (*šālôm*) herein refers "primarily to internal, rather than external, well-being."[34] In addition to a positive possession of peace, the psalmist, as numbered among the faithful, is protected from a "cause of disaster."[35] Verse 165b rendered literally reads, "and 'for them there is no stumbling block,'"[36] i.e. "nothing can make them stumble" (NIV). Indeed, a very strategic by-product of love for the "law" is the protection that God grants through it so that His children might not stumble and fall along "the path of life."[37]

Straightforward assertions of a godly obedience, as especially indicated by the עָשָׂה (*ᶜāśâ*) of verse 166b and the שָׁמַר (*šāmar*) of verses 167a and 168a, characterize the poet's testimony in the final three verses of this next to the last strophe of Psalm 119. How his other assertions, especially those of verses 166a and 167b, relate syntactically to these explicit affirmations will be a factor of interpretive interest. Some translations,[38] however, make no at-

---

[31] Although every form of human initiative comes from the ultimate impetus of God's grace, the Scriptures sometimes nevertheless speak of antecedent exhibitions of human fidelity, esp. love for the Lord, as prerequisites for the blessings of God (cf., e.g., Deut 5:10; 7:9; etc.).

[32] Note the possession by idiom with the preposition לְ (*lᵉ*) attached to the substantive participle (i.e. לְאֹהֲבֵי [*lᵉʾōhᵃbê*].

[33] In the light of the overall context and the conceptual parallelism within this bicolar unit, Allen renders שָׁלוֹם רָב (*šālôm rāḇ*) more dynamically as "ample security" (*Psalms 101–150*, p. 133). For a brief synopsis of שָׁלוֹם note Anderson, *Psalms*, 2:845; and for a more thorough survey, see *TDNT*, s.v. "שָׁלוֹם in the OT," by G. von Rad, 2:402–06.

[34] Soll, "Psalm 119," p. 208.

[35] Stählin's suggestion for מִכְשׁוֹל (*mikšôl*) at v. 165 (*TDNT*, s.v. "σκάνδαλον, κτλ.," by G. Stählin, 7:341). Cf. and contrast the occurrence of σκάνδαλον (*skandalon*) in 1 John 2:10 with the LXX's use of it for מִכְשׁוֹל (*mikšôl*) throughout the OT.

[36] Soll, "Psalm 119," p. 207.

[37] Cf. *TWOT*, s.v. "כָּשַׁל (*kashal*)," by R. Harris, 1:458.

[38] E.g. NASB; cf. also the non-interpretive renderings under "Translation and Notes."

tempt to construe the significance of the syntax of the *waw* conjunctions standing at the mid-points of verses 166 and 167; they merely render them as simple copulas, i.e. "and." Needless to say, other syntactical options need to be considered with a view towards clarifying the overall intention or intentions of the psalmist's words.

Verse 166 presents the greatest number of syntactical options. In addition to viewing the verse merely as conveying independent pieces of information, i.e. an affirmation of hope (v. 166a) "and" an affirmation of obedience (v. 166b), it is possible to construe the conjunction causally, translating it "because" or "since." Anderson leans towards this option when he suggests that "the reason for his confidence is, partly, his loyalty to the commandments. . . ."[39] This view, being compatible with immediate[40] and larger circles of context,[41] has much to commend it, but Anderson's little adverb "partly" astutely keeps the door open to other options. An especially appealing syntactical option looks upon the disciple's godly obedience (v. 166b) as being the logical consequence of his expectation of Divine deliverance (v. 166a). In other words, his "confident expression of hope and waiting for God's salvation"[42] seemingly functions motivationally and thereby stimulates compliance with his LORD's commandments.

---

[39] Anderson, *Psalms,* 2:845.

[40] E.g., it is a logical option for the parallelism within the verse, and it could possibly be looked upon as patterning the explicit causal development of v. 168 and also the implicit causal relationship within v. 167.

[41] It should be remembered that the psalmist has previously employed evidences of his own faithfulness to point out how appropriate Divine intervention on his behalf would be.

[42] Cohen's synopsis of the Piel of שׂבר (*śḇr*) with special application to Ps 119:166 (*TWOT*, s.v. "שָׂבַר (*śābar*)," by G. Cohen, 2:870); cf. the noun form of this root is v. 116.

As transition is made from verse 166 to verse 167 there is a slight semantical shift from *doing* (עשה [ᶜśh]) to *keeping* (שמר [šmr]), but the concept of obedience is quite obviously being perpetuated. נַפְשִׁי (*napšî*), literally, "my soul," once again, stands for the person of the psalmist.[43] Therefore, as he, so to speak, steps back for perspective, the child of God associates the keeping of God's testimonies with his *whole being*.[44] Furthermore, the impetus for his fidelity immediately follows: "since I love them exceedingly" (v. 167b).[45] The disciple's consuming adoration of God's Word produced in him a consistent pattern of walking in God's ways. Such a love-commitment certainly exemplifies "a disposition tempered by divine tutelage,"[46] i.e. an attitude which stands in need of much contemporary emulation:

> Christians today often think of the law as a burdensome restriction, but that was not the way the psalmist responded to it. To him the law was God's loving gift meant to guide his people in the right way, and the psalmist welcomed it, exulted in it, and loved it.[47]

---

[43] Cf. vv. 20, 25, 28, 81, 109, 175, "i.e. I myself" (Anderson, *Psalms*, 2:845). The parallelism of נַפְשִׁי (*napšî*) with the first person verbs וָאֹהֲבֵם (*wā'ōhᵃḇēm*), "and *I* love them" (v. 167b), and שָׁמַרְתִּי (*šāmartî*), "I keep" (v. 168a), documents this anthropological phenomenon.

[44] Interestingly, whether designed or not, there are three semantical parallels with the great שְׁמַע (*šᵉmaᶜ*) passage: נֶפֶשׁ (*nep̄eš*; v. 167a, Deut 6:5b), אָהַב (*'āhaḇ*; v. 167b, Deut 6:5a), and מְאֹד (*mᵉ'ōḏ*; v. 167b, Deut 6:5b).

[45] Cf. the causal rendering in the NIV: "for I love them greatly." Note that the adverb מְאֹד (*mᵉ'ōḏ*) in this setting could also be rendered "dearly" (Allen, *Psalms 101–150*, p. 134) or "passionately."

[46] Soll, "Psalm 119," p. 208.

[47] Morris, *Testaments of Love*, p. 49; most of the rest of the paragraph which precedes this excerpt constitutes a brief applicational synopsis of "love" in the 119th Psalm. Scripturally, recall 1 John 5:2–3 in the light of its epistolary and Christological background (e.g. John 14:15, 21–24; 15:10; 2 John 6; etc.).

The שָׁמַרְתִּי (*šāmartî*), "I keep," which leads off verse 168 is a conceptual equivalent of the circumlocutory rendition which stood at the head of verse 167.[48] Here, however, the psalmist cites two terms for the Word as the joint objects of this godly obedience;[49] he has committed himself to keeping God's "precepts" (i.e. פִּקּוּדֶיךָ [*piqqûḏeyḵā*]) and His "testimonies" (i.e. עֵדֹתֶיךָ [*ᶜēḏōṯeyḵā*]; cf. v. 167a). The *ultimate* reason for the disciple's dedication now surfaces with great clarity as he cries out: "because (i.e. כִּי [*kî*]) all my ways are before You," or more dynamically, "because every way I take is open to your gaze."[50] The pilgrim's preoccupation with obedience was directly connected with his understanding of the LORD's omniscience.[51] His testimony, therefore, once again speaks of "reverence for God Himself, not for Scripture in isolation."[52]

There is a timeless lesson to be learned from his recognition (v. 168b) and response (v. 168a), and that lesson is transparent: since all "daily conduct is known to God"[53] those who belong to Him should be thoroughly committed to walking "as children of light."[54] Towards this end contemporary disciples need great grace, the same grace which God Himself evidenced in the life of the psalmist whereby He turned potentially terrorizing penetrations of His omniscience into transforming impulses which issued in a godly pilgrimage.

---

48 I.e. שָׁמְרָה נַפְשִׁי (*šāmᵉrâ napšî*), "my soul keeps."

49 As Anderson appropriately notes "the metre, as well as the ancient versions, support M.T." (*Psalms*, 2:846).

50 Allen, *Psalms 101–150*, p. 134.

51 Or, in Allen's words, "a sense of Yahweh's omniscience is one motive for obedience: cf. Job 31:4; Prov 5:20, 21" (ibid., p. 138).

52 Kidner, *Psalms 73–150*, p. 429.

53 Anderson, *Psalms*, 2:846; he cites Job 31:4 as an example to which it would be wise to add David's assertions in Ps 139.

54 Cf. Eph 5:8 in its context.

ת

TAW STANZA
(vv. 169–176)

Translation and Notes

169 Let[a] my resounding cry[b] approach You,[c] O LORD;
give me understanding according to Your word.[d]

170 Let my supplication for favor[a] come before You;
deliver me according to Your word.[b]

171 May[a] my lips pour forth praise,[b]
because[c] You teach me Your statutes.

172 May[a] my tongue sing *of* Your word,[b]
because all Your commandments are righteous.[c]

173 Let Your hand be *present*[a] to help me,[b]
because I have chosen[c] Your precepts.

174 I long for[a] Your salvation, O LORD,
and[b] Your law is my delight.

175 Allow my soul[a] to live[b] that[c] it may praise You,
and let Your judgments[d] help me.

176 I have wandered about[a] like a lost sheep;[b]
seek Your servant,
for I have not forgotten[c] Your commandments.[d]

169:a "Let," "may," "allow," etc. are English vehicles for rendering Hebrew jussives.
169:b I.e. רִנָּה (*rinnâ*), "ringing cry" (BDB, p. 943).
169:c Very lit., "come near . . . *to Your presence.*"
169:d I.e. דָּבָר (*dāḇār*), a recurrent general word for the Word.

170:a BDB's suggested rendering for תְּחִנָּה (*tᵉḥinnâ*) (BDB, p. 337).
170:b Or, more specifically, "Your promise" for אִמְרָתְךָ (*'imrāṯᵉḵā*).
171:a The above translation construes תַּבַּעְנָה (*tabbaᶜnâ*) also as a jussive, not by form but by function; cf. NASB, NIV, and note Allen's comment: "v 171a is probably a wish in view of the clear jussive form in the parallel v 172a" (*Psalms 101–150*, p. 139). Other translations (RSV, NAB, etc.) and commentaries (e.g. Delitzsch, *Psalms*, 3:242; Soll, "Psalm 119," p. 208; etc.), however, prefer translating it as a simple imperfect.
171:b Interestingly, DSS (Q11) adds לכה (*lḵh*), "to You," to the end of this line; however, its addition is not supported by other textual witnesses.
171:c Rendering the כִּי (*kî*) herein causally; the LXX construes it conditionally (cf. the ὅταν [*hotan*], "whenever"), and some translations, probably based upon their rendering of תַּבַּעְנָה (*tabbaᶜnâ*) as a simple imperfect, translate is as "that" (cf. RSV).
172:a The same observations (cf. v. 171a) pertaining to rendering the verb as a jussive or a simple imperfect generally apply to v. 172a, except some employ a jussive rendering for v. 172a but not for v. 171a (cf., e.g., NAB).
172:b אִמְרָה (*'imrâ*) returns and probably bears its specialized nuance of "promise." "Gunkel, Kraus, *et al.* read *'ᵉmûnateḵā* ('of your faithfulness'), but there is no real reason for this emendation; 11 Q Psᵃ=M.T." (Anderson, *Psalms*, 2:846).
172:c I.e. צֶדֶק (*ṣeḏeq*), lit. "righteousness."
173:a An additional word such as "present," "there" (Soll, "Psalm 119," p. 208), "ready" (NASB, NIV, RSV, etc.), or the like, helps to make the combination of the jussive with the infinitive more fluid in translation.
173:b Note how literally the LXX reflects the syntax of the Hebrew text: γενέσθω ἡ χείρ σου τοῦ σῶσαί με (*genesthō hē cheir sou tou sōsai me*).
173:c Interestingly, the Targum, unlike other versions which are semantically equivalent to the MT, renders the בָּחַר (*bāḥar*) of v. 173b as רְעֵי (*rᵉᶜê*), "to desire, take delight in" (Jastrow, *Dictionary*, 2:1486).
174:a Or, "I have longed for," for the Qal perfect. תָּאַבְתִּי (*tā'aḇtî*).

174:b DSS (Q11) is asyndetonic; contra. other early versions which verify the *wāw* conjunction of the MT.

175:a A final anthropological periphrasis for "I," i.e. herein, "me."

175:b Another way of rendering the jussive, in this case the 3 f s form תְּחִי (*t*[e]*ḥî*) from חָיָה (*ḥāyâ*) with נֶפֶשׁ (*nepeš*) as subject; the intent of this word unit may be "let my life be spared" (Anderson, *Psalms*, 2:847).

175:c Lit. "and"; however, the *wāw* conjunction very likely connotes the psalmist's intention.

175:d I.e. ". . . defective plural, as in vers. 43, 149 . . ." (Delitzsch, *Psalms*, 3:263).

176:a Or, "I wander."

176:b Or, "like a sheep which strays." Note: although "the verse is longer than any of the preceding ones in this psalm" (Soll, "Psalm 119," p. 210), this phrase is not to be held in suspect: "Duhm, Gunkel, *et al.* delete this phrase as a gloss which overloads the metre, but M.T. has the support of the ancient versions and 11 Q Ps[a]" (Anderson, *Psalms*, 2:847).

176:c Or, "I do not forget."

176:d DSS (Q11) surprisingly deviates from the MT and early versions regarding its word for the Word herein; it reads עדוותיכה (*[c]dwwtykh*), "Your testimonies" instead of מִצְוֹתֶיךָ (*miṣwōteykā*), "Your commands."

Synopsis and Outline

The twenty-first stanza of Psalm 119 drew to a close with an emphasis on the presence of God (cf. נֶגְדֶּךָ [*negdekā*], lit. "in front of You," i.e. "in Your sight" or "presence," v. 168b), and so, the twenty-second opens similarly with two occurrences of לְפָנֶיךָ (*l*[e]*pāneykā*), "before You" (cf. vv. 169a and 170a). The stress upon "His presence" at the outset of this last strophe, however, does not merely serve as a contextual vehicle to reveal an ultimate motive for the psalmist's obedience (cf. the thrust of the previous stanza), but rather, it functions as a transitional buttonhook in that it reintroduces an appropriate setting for his petitions.

Although *Tāw* (vv. 169–176) is characterized by a flurry of personal pleas, it also displays many of the other salient features which have regularly manifested themselves throughout the development of this great psalm. For this reason, these concluding eight verses may be regarded as offering a microcosm which skillfully images the macrocosm of the whole work. As Soll aptly remarks, "the strophe serves as a recapitulation for the entire psalm,"[1] and in a similar vein, Allen posits that "in the *taw* strophe the gamut of the psalm's concerns are reflected, a double prayer, an avowal of piety and a reference to the situation of complaint."[2] Indeed, this high flight of inscripturated poetry touches down with a most magnificent landing.

The unit is obviously doxological. Several indications point to this reality. For example, there are *two* occurrences of the Tetragrammaton functioning as a noun of direct address (cf. יהוה [*YHWH*] in vv. 169, 174). However, it is an abundance of jussives that particularly sets the doxological tone. Although three requests in imperative form (cf. vv. 169b, 170b, 176b) directly solicit God's attention, six to eight jussive forms[3] ascend more delicately into the LORD's presence. These circumlocutory phrasings with third person castings do not minimize the psalmist's dire need. They too orient themselves to the supreme Benefactor.

In the first half of this last stanza a heavenward movement is detected as conveyed by the meanings of the leading jussives along with their respective "subjects," i.e. "my cry" (v. 169), "my supplication" (v. 170), "my lips" (v. 171), and "my tongue" (v. 172). Then in verses 173ff., with the introduction of God's "hand," there is a shift in point of emanation resulting in an earthward movement of the subsequent jussives. At the same time, throughout *Tāw* the personal intimacy between the disciple and his LORD is borne along to new heights. First person references by the

1 Soll, "Psalm 119," p. 209.

2 Allen, *Psalms 101–150*, p. 144.

3 Cf. the options above (i.e. translations recognize either 6, 7, or 8 jussive functions): "Translation and Notes," esp. notes 171:a, 172:a.

psalmist to himself abound[4] along with personal suffixes which refer to God,[5] and regularly they are juxtaposed through striking parallelisms which magnify that close relationship.[6] Drawing these bits and pieces together, two tides of petition in the final stanza of Psalm 119 recapitulate the disciple's dependence upon God and His Word.

1A. (vv. 169–172) The swelling tide rises heavenward in anticipation of communication with God.
  1B. (vv. 169–170) The acute communication of his burdens.
    1C. (v. 169) His burden for scriptural insight.
    2C. (v. 170) His burden for supernatural intervention.
  2B. (vv. 171–172) The accompanying communication of his blessings:
    1C. (v. 171) Personal instruction.
    2C. (v. 172) Propositional integrity.
2A. (vv. 173–176) The ebbing tide returns earthward in anticipation of compassion from God.
  1B. (vv. 173–174) The anticipated compassion of Divine protection.
    1C. (v. 173a) The disciple's desire.
    2C. (vv. 173b–174) The disciple's documentation (positive).

---

4 Cf. vv. 169a, b; 170a, b; 171a, b; 172a; 173a, b; 174a, b; 175a, b; 176a, c [plus a third person circumlocution in 176b].

5 Cf. the 2 m s pronominal suffixes in vv. 169a, b; 170a, b; 171b; 172a, b; 173a, b; 174a, b; 175a, b; 176b, c; other more subtle vehicles of reference to the LORD are also contained in these eight verses.

6 Synthesizing the data through translation, note the following patterns, their order, and the resultant mood conveyed: v. 169: "*my* cry"—"*Your* presence"—"*Your* word"—"grant *me* understanding"; v. 170: "*my* supplication"—"*Your* presence"—"*Your* word"—"rescue *me*"; v. 171: "*my* lips"—"*You* teach *me*"—"*Your* statutes"; v. 172: "*my* tongue"—"*Your* word"—"*Your* commandments"; v. 173: "*Your* hand"—"to help *me*"—"*Your* precepts"; v. 174: "*Your* salvation"—"*Your* law"—"*my* delight"; v. 175: "*my* soul"—"praise *You*"—"*Your* judgments"—"help *me*"; v. 176: "*Your* servant"—"*Your* commandments."

2B. (vv. 175–176) The anticipated compassion of Divine preservation.
   1C. (v. 175) The disciple's desire.
   2C. (v. 176) The disciple's documentation (negative and positive).

Commentary

The parallelisms between verses 169 and 170 are striking. Apart from the vocative occurrence of יהוה (*YHWH*), "O LORD," in the middle of verse 169, one-for-one correspondences answer each other synonymously and in sequence. Note the leading jussive verbs (v. 169: תִּקְרַב [*tiqrab̲*], "come near"; v. 170: תָּבוֹא [*tāb̲ô'*], "enter"); the subjects of those verbs each with a first person pronominal suffix (v. 169: רִנָּתִי [*rinnāt̲î*], "my ringing cry"; v. 170: תְּחִנָּתִי [*teḥinnāt̲î*], "my supplication"); the same prepositional idiom with second person pronominal suffix (vv. 169, 170: לְפָנֶיךָ [*lepāneyk̲ā*], "Your presence"); the phrases which follow, each with the same preposition and suffix but with a different, but yet near, synonym for the Word of God (v. 169: כִּדְבָרְךָ [*kid̲b̲āre k̲ā*], "according to Your word"; v. 170: כְּאִמְרָתְךָ [*ke'imrāt̲ek̲ā*], "according to Your promise"); and finally, the second person singular imperatives with first person singular object suffixes (v. 169: הֲבִינֵנִי [*hăb̲înēnî*], "give me understanding"; v. 170: הַצִּילֵנִי [*haṣṣîlēnî*], "deliver me"). Obviously, these introductory verses will inform one another as to the total impact of the psalmist's burden at the outset of this final strophe.

Returning to verse 169, his desire is that his "ringing cry"[7] might enter the very presence of God. Normally, a רִנָּה (*rinnâ*) is an expression of joy or exuberance, being related to its verb which often connotes a "shout of jubilation";[8] however, sometimes it is

---

[7] BDB, p. 943.
[8] *TWOT*, s.v. "רָנַן (*rānan*)," by W. White, 2:851.

couched in a context of petition and/or lament.[9] In the light of its correspondence to תְּחִנָּה (*teḥinnâ*), a "supplication for favor,"[10] i.e. an urgent request for grace (v. 170),[11] along with the implication of the two imperative requests of verses 169b and 170b, רִנָּתִי (*rinnāṯî*) herein refers to the needy disciple's petition for Divine intervention, i.e. to his "cry for help,"[12] not to a joyous expression of his praise.[13] What he is therefore delivering heavenward at the very outset of *Tāw* is an echoing or resounding cry of entreaty.[14]

His hope is that his personal plea would come very close to God. The verb he employs to catapult his cry into the immediate presence[15] of the LORD[16] "in its causative form, is practically a technical term for the presenting of an offering to God."[17] More basically, קָרַב (*qāraḇ*)I conveys "a way of approach and acceptance

---

[9] Ibid. In the *general* category of *entreaty* or *supplication*, BDB list, along with Ps 119:169; 1 Kgs 8:28 (cf. 2 Chr 6:19); Jer 7:16; 11:14; 14:12; Pss 17:1; 61:2 [v. 1, Eng]; 88:3 [v. 2, Eng]; 106:44; 142:7 [v. 6, Eng].

[10] BDB, p. 337.

[11] In this vein it should be noted that Delitzsch's generalization regarding the two terms for prayer in vv. 169 and 170, although possibly helpful contextually, is too sweeping and therefore not universally applicable: "רִנָּה is a shrill audible prayer; תְּחִנָּה, a fervent and urgent prayer" (*Psalms*, 3:263).

[12] Allen, *Psalms 101–150*, p. 139; he also points out that רִנָּתִי (*rinnāṯî*) "is poetically personified" in this context (ibid.).

[13] The next doublet of verses (i.e. vv. 171 and 172), however, will shift to the praise mode.

[14] Note that the LXX picks up on the general sense of רִנָּתִי with its ἡ δέησίς μου (*hē deēsis mou*), "my prayer, petition, entreaty," etc.

[15] Again, note the first of two occurrences of לְפָנֶיךָ (*lepāneyḵā*) in these opening verses, i.e. "before You," "into Your presence," etc.

[16] Again, note the vocative occurrence of יהוה (*YHWH*), "LORD," in v. 169.

[17] Anderson, *Psalms*, 2:846; he continues: "it is possible that the Psalmist thought of his cry (i.e. prayer) as an offering to God . . ." (ibid.). The likelihood of such a possibility would increase if one were to consider that the place for literal offerings might have been inaccessible due to exile, etc. However, such figurative language normally pertains to "offerings" of *praise* or *thanksgiving* from the "mouth" or "lips" (e.g. Ps 100:4; Heb 13:15; etc.).

. . . *a way of access.*"[18] The "root denotes being or coming into the most near and intimate proximity of the object . . ." and sometimes "entails actual contact with the object."[19] Although verse 169a is phrased with a high degree of poetic delicacy, there can be no doubt that the man of God comes to the throne of grace very boldly with these words.

The substance of his cry for help, or at least a significant portion of it, is revealed in verse 169b. This is the sixth and final occurrence of the verb בִּין (*bîn*) as a Hiphil (causative) imperative.[20] In each case the disciple urges his Master to impart personally to him the practical insight that he desperately needs for real life in the real world. The mature man of God also understands that his request is in harmony with the whole tenor of the Word of God, so he again speaks very boldly.[21] In view of this, Allen's paraphrase of this prepositional modifier is acceptable: "Give me the insight *promised by your word*" (i.e. כִּדְבָרְךָ [*kidbārekā*]).[22] Furthermore, he had also come to learn that such practical perception is normally conveyed by God to a humble recipient through the instrumentality (v. 104)[23] and illumination (v. 130)[24] of the Divine

---

[18] Girdlestone, *Synonyms*, p. 186. He also illustrates the word group's semantical commonality of *nearness*; however, his extended association with קרב II through the concept of *intimacy* is tenuous (ibid.). Cf. Allen's translation of קָרַב as a way of approach: "May my cry have access to you, Yahweh" (*Psalms 101–150*, p. 134).

[19] *TWOT*, s.v. "קָרַב (*qārab*) I," by L. Coppes, 2:811; his survey of sub-categories of usage is valuable (ibid., pp. 811–12). The LXX employs an appropriate form of ἐγγίζω (*engizō*) at Ps 119:169, and its usage patterns throughout the Greek OT are nearly identical to קָרַב I in the Hebrew text (cf. *TDNT*, s.v. "ἐγγύς, ἐγγίζω, προσεγγίζω," by H. Preisker, 2:330–331).

[20] Cf. vv. 27, 34, 73, 125, 144, and here in v. 169.

[21] In a stanza containing so many indicators of the psalm's grand finale, it is not surprising to encounter these two occurrences of the preposition כְּ (*ke*) stressing precedent in vv. 169b and 170b.

[22] Allen, *Psalms 101–150*, p. 134 (with my emphasis). Cf. NAB's "in keeping with your word."

[23] Cf. the Hithpolel imperfect of בִּין (*bîn*) in v. 104.

[24] Cf. the Hiphil (causative) participle of בִּין (*bîn*) in v. 130, the implied subject of which is the Divine illumination of the Scriptures.

Word.

Concerning the puzzling interrelationship of the imperatives which stand in parallelism with one another, respectively relating to his burden for spiritual insight (v. 169b) and to his burden for supernatural intervention (v. 170b), it should be pointed out that he needed fortification along with (or possibly, until) extrication. As Delitzsch puts it, "the petitions 'give me understanding' and 'deliver me' go hand-in-hand, because the poet is one who is persecuted for the sake of his faith, and is just as much in need of the fortifying of his faith as of deliverance from the outward restraint that is put upon him."[25]

The jussive request of verse 170a antiphonally responds to the one that stood at the head of verse 169. In this verse the disciple dubs his prayer a תְּחִנָּה (*tᵉḥinnâ*), a "cry for favor" or "supplication."[26] In the OT "the word occurs twenty-four times and means a prayer for grace on all but two occasions. . . ."[27] It derives from the root חָנַן (*ḥānan*) I, which "depicts a heartfelt response by someone who has something to give to one who has a need."[28] Obviously, the vulnerable child of God had previously recognized his great need and had run to his LORD for grace (cf. the Qal imperatives of חָנַן in vv. 29, 58, 132), and now he does so again through

---

[25] Delitzsch, *Psalms*, 3:263.

[26] *TDOT*, s.v. "חָנַן *ḥānan*," by D. Freedman and J. Lundbom, 5:25.

[27] *TWOT*, s.v. "חָנַן (*ḥānan*) I," by E. Yamauchi, 1:304; interestingly, he also notes that "half of all the occurrences appear in Solomon's prayer at the dedication of the temple (I Kgs 8–9; II Chr 6)" (ibid.).

[28] Ibid., p. 302; Semitic cognates provide an illuminating background, e.g., Akkadian, "to grant a favor"; Ugaritic, "to be gracious, to favor"; Arabic, "to feel sympathy, compassion" (ibid.).

[29] Cf. Anderson, *Psalms*, 2:846. Concerning the parallelism of תְּחִנָּתִי (*tᵉḥinnāṯî*) here with רִנָּתִי (*rinnāṯî*) in v. 169a, 1 Kgs 8:28 provides a similar association: "the chiastic ordering of terms in 1 K. 8:28, *tᵉp̄illaṯ/tᵉḥinnāṯô—hārinnâ/hattᵉp̄illâ*, argues for linking *rinnâ*, 'ringing cry,' with *tᵉḥinnâ*, 'cry of supplication'" (*TDOT*, 5:26).

[30] Since בּוֹא (*bô'*) is used "for the most part with everyday meanings of 'go, arrive, enter a house,'" etc. (*TWOT*, s.v. "בּוֹא (*bô'*)," by E. Martens, 1:93).

his "prayer for favor."[29]

He hopes that his solicitation of grace will enter the presence of God. Although his use of the verb תָּבוֹא (*tāḇô'*), of which his "supplication" stands as its subject in verse 170a, seems to be more straightforward than his employment of קָרַב (*qāraḇ*) in verse 169a,[30] this exceedingly common verb[31] may also denote the bringing of an offering and/or prayers to God.[32] Most basically, בּוֹא (*bô'*) relates to "a movement directed toward a certain goal in space and time."[33] An approach, arrival, or even an entry may be indicated by the context. As the term takes its first steps into theological settings it may convey God's movement toward man or man's movement toward God.[34] In the case of the latter, this could involve a man's physical coming to the tabernacle or temple as the designated place for presents and prayers to God.[35] Less cultically oriented, these "comings" may also include the movement of all communications to the LORD in heaven apart from a specific point of earthly embarkation. As such, one's prayer could be viewed from the perspective of ascent *as here*, or from the vantage point of answered prayer descending upon the recipient as the related usages of בּוֹא (*bô'*) in verses 41 and 77 would show.

When the prepositional phrase לְפָנֶיךָ (*l^e^pāneyḵā*)[36] is brought alongside of the verb בּוֹא (*bô'*), it becomes apparent that the disciple's earnest wish was that his "petition for favor" would "reach"[37] or "be admitted to"[38] the immediate presence of God. Uppermost in his mind was his Master's personal acceptance[39] of

---

[31] BDB, p. 97, tabulate 2569 occurrences, and Martens notes that it is "the fourth most frequently occurring verb in the OT" (*TWOT*, 1:93).

[32] Cf., e.g., BDB, p. 99.

[33] *TDOT*, s.v. "בּוֹא *bô'*," by H. Preuss, 2:21.

[34] Ibid., p. 22.

[35] Ibid., pp. 22–23; cf. also "*bô'* in Laments" (p. 32) plus "*bô'* in Prayers" (p. 33).

[36] Cf. its occurrence and force in v. 169a; also, note that in both places the LXX appropriately renders it ἐνώπιόν σου (*enōpion sou*).

[37] Cf. NAB.

[38] Cf. Allen, *Psalms 101–150*, p. 134.

[39] Cf. Anderson, *Psalms*, 2:846.

this plea for grace.

A significant particular of that grace is spelled out via the imperative request of verse 170b, הַצִּילֵנִי (*haṣṣîlēnî*), "deliver me!"[40] נָצַל (*nāṣal*) stands among the primary soteriological terms of the OT. Through cognate analysis the root's basic physical concept seems to be one "of drawing out or pulling out,"[41] that is, an extrication. Occurrences in the Hiphil stem preponderate,[42] ranging from a few with the more physical connotation of "take away" or "snatch away"[43] to the many which convey *deliverance* or *rescue* from precarious situations, be they of temporal or eternal consequence.[44] Here the whole backdrop of the psalmist's persecution furnishes insight into the intent of his plea for extrication. Once again, he states his petition very strongly by personalizing the precedent of the Word's promise (i.e. כְּאִמְרָתְךָ [*kᵉ'imrātᵉkā*], "according to Your word" or "promise").[45]

Almost imperceptibly, the poetic couplet of pleas (vv. 169–70) gives way to one which focuses on praise in verses 171 and 172. The parallelisms between these two verses are almost as precise as those which bound the former poetic doublet together. However, in the terminal part of each verse of this second pair stands a כִּי (*kî*) clause which identifies the grounds of the desire which launches each verse. Or, in sequential development, the pattern

---

40 Cf. the Hiphil imperatives of the near synonym יָשַׁע (*yāšaᶜ*), also with 1cs pronominal suffixes, in vv. 94 and 146.

41 *TWOT*, s.v. "נָצַל (*nāṣal*)," by M. Fisher, 2:594.

42 BDB, p. 664, note that 190 of the verb's 212 occurrences are in the Hiphil.

43 Ibid.; cf. this sense in v. 43, the only other occurrence of this root in Ps 119.

44 Cf. ibid., pp. 664–665, and *TWOT*, 2:594. Note that the LXX appropriately utilizes an aorist imperative from ῥύομαι (*hruomai*) at Ps 119:170. Not only is this in keeping with a conspicuous translation precedent in the Greek OT (cf. *TDNT*, s.v. "ῥύομαι," by W. Kasch, 6:999, 1001–02), but it also provides significant background for the NT occurrences of this important soteriological concept.

45 Allen's paraphrase captures the impact of the prepositional phrase: "deliver me, *as your sayings promise*" (*Psalms 101–150*, p. 134 [emphasis added]).

is: verse 170a, desire to praise the God of the Word; verse 170b, documentation of the blessing of Personal instruction; verse 171a, desire to praise the Word of God; verse 171b, documentation of the blessing of propositional integrity. It should also be noticed that the first person singular pronominal suffixes which characterized the leading subjects of the first doublet continue on into the second pair of verses. Later a major shift in orientation, that is from the psalmist to God to one from God to the psalmist, will commence with the opening words of verse 173.

The disciple enlists a picturesque verb to indicate the desired activity of his lips in verse 171. The background imagery of נָבַע (*nāḇaᶜ*) suggests "the bubbling up of a spring."[46] However, figurative usages for speech, e.g. to "pour forth, emit, belch forth,"[47] "utter,"[48] "assert,"[49] etc., predominate in the OT.[50] Such references may be found in a negative setting or in a *positive* one (cf. Pss 19:3 [v. 2, Eng]; 145:7).[51] Obviously, here the heart's intention of the child of God was that his lips might become a gushing vehicle for

---

[46] Kidner, *Psalms 73–150*, p. 429; cf. the NIV's "overflow."

[47] BDB, p. 615.

[48] Cf. NASB.

[49] Note the verb בְּעֵי (*bᵉᶜê*) in the Targum with a likely meaning of "assert" (cf. Jastrow, *Dictionary*, 1:181).

[50] Also, some would associate the root נבע (*nbᶜ*) with the root נבא (*nb'*), i.e. "prophet" and "to prophesy," in its history of development (cf. Culver's mention of this view [among others] in *TWOT*, s.v. "נָבִיא [*nāḇî'*]," by R. Culver, 2:544, and also note the cognate notations of BDB, pp. 611, 615).

[51] For one scenario on the interrelationship of such usages see *TWOT*, s.v. "נָבַע (*nāḇāᶜ*)," by L. Coppes, 2:548.

[52] Cf. the primary meanings of תְּהִלָּה (*tᵉhillâ*) in BDB, pp. 239–40 and *TDOT*, s.v. "הלל *hll* I and II," by H. Ringgren, 3:410. Note also our psalmist's employment of the verb from which this feminine noun derives in vv. 164, 175. The ὕμνον (*hymnon*) of the LXX, i.e. "a hymn" or "song," probably construed the Hebrew תְּהִלָּה (*tᵉhillâ*) herein as among its liturgical occurrences, i.e. a "praise-song" (cf. BDB, p. 240). The parallel verb of v. 172 may have also affected their translational nuance.

praise, adoration, and thanksgiving[52] to God.

Such a vibrant expression of gratitude is eminently fitting in the light of the LORD being his personal Tutor in the Divine Word (i.e. v. 171b).[53] Out of the thirteen occurrences in Psalm 119 of the verb לָמַד (*lāmad*; i.e. "to learn"), an OT root explicitly related to discipleship, eight of them have been *direct* solicitations of Divine instruction (cf. vv. 12, 26, 64, 66, 68, 108, 124, 135).[54] Now in verse 171b the man of God bears witness to the fact that his LORD *does* personally and regularly tutor him in life's ultimate survival Manual. The pilgrim's praise based upon this personal instruction, among other things, is a fulfillment of the pledge he voiced back in verse 7.

As previously mentioned, the pattern of verse 171 is nearly identically cloned in verse 172; mostly generally, his expressions of gratitude (i.e. vv. 171a, 172a) are built upon obvious grounds for gratitude (i.e. vv. 171b, 172b). The instrument for conveying praise in verse 172 now becomes לְשׁוֹנִי (*lᵉšônî*), "my tongue" (cf. שְׂפָתַי [*śᵉpāṯay*], "my lips," in v. 171a).[55] Furthermore, the imagery for the actual expression of his thanksgiving moves from "bub-

---

53 The syntax, though simple, is quite profound. The personal beneficiary of the LORD's teaching is the psalmist himself (cf. the 1 c s pronominal suffix attached to the 2 m s verb) and the propositional subject matter, or exclusive curriculum, is indicated by the direct object, i.e. God's "statutes." Cf. and contrast the allusion to human "teachers" in v. 99.

54 In each case the psalmist directs a Piel second person singular imperative to God.

55 It is possible to regard both terms, i.e. "my lips" in v. 171 and "my tongue" in v. 172, as anthropological periphrases for the total man (cf. Anderson, *Psalms*, 2:846).

56 The element of contingency comes from the fact that the root ענה (*ᶜnh*) exhibits four semantical fields of usage out of which there might arise some instances of confusion between the first and fourth of them (cf. *TWOT*, s.v. "עָנָה [*ᶜānâ*] IV," by R. Harris, 2:684; cf. also, Kidner, *Psalms 73–150*, p. 429). Some early versions and modern translations (e.g. LXX; Targum; Delitzsch, *Psalms*, 3:242; Soll, "Psalm 119," p. 208; etc.) would seem to support עָנָה I, i.e. "to answer, respond, speak, testify," etc. (cf. BDB, pp. 772–73) while others would lean towards the more specific semantical field of עָנָה IV, i.e. "to sing" (cf. NASB; NIV; NAB; Allen, *Psalms 101–150*, p. 134; etc.). Parallels with v. 171a seem to give an interpretive edge to *singing out* (cf. BDB, p. 777).

bling up" (v. 171) to probably one of "singing out" (v. 172).[56] Not surprisingly, the object "of" or "about which"[57] the disciple sings is God's *word* or more definitely construed, His *promise* (i.e. the nineteenth and final occurrence of אִמְרָה [*'imrâ*] in Ps 119).

As the child of God makes a subtle transition through the subordinating כִּי (*kî*) clause from his voiced gratitude to its immediately documented basis, he focuses upon the rectitude of all the Divine "commands" (v. 172b). This is in keeping with his previous assumptions about *propositional* integrity.[58] However, some of the words for the Word of God, e.g. מִצְוֹת (*miṣwōṯ*), "commandments" (as here), seem to move quite fluidly from the propositional arena into the providential arena, i.e. as God's commands *applied* and *implemented*. Allen suggests that this indeed is one of those occasions:

> The double prayer of vv 169–70 and the appeal to Yahweh's "rulings"[59] or judicial intervention illustrate the two poles of the psalm. At one end stands the revealed Torah, and it is for insight into this that the psalmist prays so that he may fulfill Yahweh's moral will in his life. At the other stands the hope of divine providential intervention, and for this too he prays out of his distress. The dual manifestation of God is itself bridged by the Torah's examples and promises of aid to the faithful. The psalmist is in the center, communing with God through the fellowship of prayer and looking this way with the

---

[57] The jussive of עָנָה (*ʿānâ*) IV, i.e. תַּעַן (*taʿan*), calls for some translational ease (e.g. "of" or "about") with its direct object, i.e. אִמְרָתֶךָ (*'imrāṯeḵā*; "Your word" or "promise").

[58] In this case the attribute predicated of the word is צֶדֶק (*ṣeḏeq*), "righteousness."

[59] He is obviously referring to the כָּל־מִצְוֹתֶיךָ (*ḵol-miṣwōteyḵā*), "all Your commands" or "rulings" in v. 172b.

> eyes of faith and that way with the eyes of hope. From this double stance the same living God both manifests himself through the written revelation and can be expected to manifest himself through the providential overruling of adversity in the believer's life.[60]

Therefore, being accompanied by these overtones and undertones of Divine reality he directs his melodious solo of praise heavenward in verse 172.

Now that the swelling tide of his burdens and blessings has reached heaven's shore, the ebbing tide of Divine responses begins its hoped-for earthward movement with the statement of his desire in verse 173a. The subject of this jussive request is God's hand. Like "arm" (i.e. זְרֹעַ [*zᵉrōaᶜ*]) in the OT, the "hand" (i.e. יָד [*yā*d̲]) sometimes stands symbolically for a person's power or strength,[61] and the psalmist's mention of the Divine hand would most likely have been prompted by biblical images of "Yahweh in action, either helping the needy ([Pss] 80:17 (M.T. 18), 139:10) or punishing the wicked ([Ps] 32:4; Isa. 5:25)."[62] The awe-struck disciple employed a plural form back in verse 73 (i.e. יָדֶיךָ [*yād̲eyk̲ā*], "Your hands") to extol God's creative power; now he employs the singular form in conjunction with a jussive of the verb *to be* to evoke his LORD's powerful intervention via a manifestation of personal aid.

Indeed, it is the infinitive לְעָזְרֵנִי (*lᵉᶜozrēnî*], "to help me," that directs the volitional intent of the leading verb to its definite target. The total syntactical package of verse 173a *more delicately* con-

---

[60] Allen, *Psalms 101–150*, pp. 144–45.

[61] Cf. BDB, p. 390; in reference to God's *"hand=display of strength, action* of" the LORD, they cite Exod 14:31; Deut 34:12; Job 27:11; and Ps 78:42 as representative occurrences (ibid.). For more extensive observations, see *TDOT*, s.v. "יָד *yād*," by J. Bergman, W. von Soden, and P. Ackroyd, esp. 5:395, 409–10, 418–20.

[62] Anderson, *Psalms*, 2:846.

veys the disciple's desire than the occurrence of the direct imperative from עֲזָר (*ᶜāzar*) in verse 86.[63] However, in both cases, his obvious vulnerability and commensurate need for Divine help were just as acute. As noted several times throughout the unfolding of this great psalm, the dependent disciple often anticipates the probable vehicle of Divine intervention or enablement. It is no different as the termination of his literary journey draws near, since this particular solicitation of help in verse 173a will shortly be followed by the believer's assumption that the LORD's "judgments" will be the avenue for his aid (i.e. v. 175b).[64]

The third כִּי (*kî*) clause in as many verses now introduces affirmations by the psalmist intended to amass evidences for the justifiability of Divine intervention. He documents the 'reasonability' of his expressed desire (v. 173a)[65] respectively with his volitional commitment to his LORD's *word* (v. 173b), his dependent reliance upon his LORD's *work* (v. 174a), and his deep-seated sat-

[63] Cf. v. 86 on the verb עָזַר (*ᶜāzar*). For a summary of the word's background and usage, see *TWOT*, s.v. "עָזַר (*ᶜāzar*) I," by C. Schultz, 2:660–61, esp. his brief paragraph about its occurrences in the Psalms (ibid., p. 661). Since it is used quite frequently in the Psalms to plead for Divine assistance, עָזַר could well be classified, at least secondarily, as a soteriological term (cf., e.g., the loose parallelism between the term's occurrences in 119:173a and 175b with God's "salvation" in v. 174a). Interestingly, here in v. 173 the LXX uses a corresponding infinitive of the more semantically specific σώζω (*sōzō*), "to save"; however, in both vv. 86 and 175 it utilizes a general counterpart of the Hebrew term, i.e. forms of the verb βοηθέω (*boētheō*; cf. in the NT, e.g., Matt 15:25; Mark 9:22, 24; 2 Cor 6:2 [Q: Isa 49:8]; Heb 2:18) "to assist, come to the rescue." Note that the general Aramaic term סַיַּע (*sîaᶜ*), "to aid, assist" (Jastrow, *Dictionary*, 2:984) occurs at all three places in the Targum.

[64] Therein (i.e. v. 175b) God's מִשְׁפָּטִים (*mišpāṭîm*) stand as the subject of the Qal imperfect (jussive) of the verb עָזַר (*ᶜāzar*).

[65] It must be remembered that such bases for Divine action must not be taken out of context. Time and time again, the psalmist understood that any indications of his own maturity were fully circumscribed by God's grace and goodness. To this reality he will once more bear witness (although more implicitly than in other settings) in vv. 175–76.

isfaction with his LORD's *way* (i.e. תּוֹרָה [*tôrâ*], v. 174b). The "choosing" on the part of the man of God in verse 173b (cf. v. 30), raises again the issue of the responsibilities of covenant commitment. As Seebass discusses the בָּחַר (*bāḥar*) word-field within the parameters of "*Human Choices As Acts of Religious Confession*," he asserts that

> it is from Deuteronomy on that *bḥr* first appears as an act of religious confession. Dt. 30:19 admonishes the hearers of the law to choose life. . . . The classical expression of this is found in Josh. 24:15, 22. . . .
>
> Now a later use of the word *bḥr* agrees with this use of the word. It is more concerned with the aspect of deciding, so that *bḥr* is not so much the carefully weighed choice as the careful activity of choosing itself. . . . In Ps. 25:12 we almost have an ambiguous teaching. This poem says that anyone who wishes to be instructed by Yahweh will be instructed by him concerning the way he should choose, i.e., in favor of which he should decide. The choice is and remains an action of the godly. Life and death will be set before him, and tacitly he is made aware of the risk that is involved in choosing life. Here one would do well to compare Ps. 119:30, 173, where the worshipper emphasizes that he has chosen the way of faithfulness, the way of Yahweh's precepts.[66]

Anderson appropriately applies the covenantal significance of the pilgrim's profession in verse 173b to his preceding plea when he notes that "the Psalmist has chosen to obey God's commandments by loving him and by walking in his ways (see Dt. 30:15f.), and therefore he can claim the promises of God."[67]

---

[66] *TDOT*, s.v. "בָּחַר *bāchar*," by J. Bergman, H. Ringgren, and H. Seebass, 2:86–87. Note that my ellipses were employed both to excerpt and to edit (e.g., some of his invalid "Deuteronomistic" assumptions).

[67] Anderson, *Psalms*, 2:846–47.

His assertion of yearning picks up a pattern woven into the psalm's fabric largely through the threads of the תָּאַב (*tā'aḇ*) word group (cf. the noun in v. 20 and the verb in v. 40).[68] In this context that for which he longs is God's יְשׁוּעָה (*yᵉšûᶜâ*),[69] i.e. His "salvation." Such a deep desire for Divine deliverance is fittingly punctuated by the psalm's twenty-fourth and final occurrence of the ineffable Tetragrammaton as a noun of direct address.

In the last part of verse 174 the juxtaposition of תּוֹרָתְךָ (*tôrāṯᵉḵā*), "Your law" and שַׁעֲשֻׁעָי (*šaᶜăšuᶜāy*), "my delight" brings back memories of verses 77 and 92. Furthermore, other words for the Word (e.g. God's "testimonies" in v. 24 and God's "commandments" in v. 143) have also been utilized to express the inextricable association between the psalmist's transcendent joy and God's special revelation.[70] Although his distress was exceedingly acute and although he had no guarantee in hand on how or when his LORD might act on his behalf, the man of God was still drawing refreshment out of the unfathomable well of the Word of God.

Generally speaking, the last two verses of this great psalm relate to each other in the following manner: the child of God expresses his desire for compassion via Divine preservation in verse 175, then in verse 176 he supports that solicitation first negatively through his need (i.e. v. 176a) and second positively through his commitment (i.e. v. 176c).[71] According to the pattern of this last stanza he enlists the service of two more jussive verbs in verse 175. In the Hebrew text these two expressions of wish book-end the whole line.

---

[68] Conceptionally, it is also a reflection of v. 81a.

[69] Cf. vv. 123, 155, 166; and for its nearly identical twin, תְּשׁוּעָה (*tᵉšûᶜâ*), cf. vv. 41, 81.

[70] The verbal affirmations built upon שָׁעַע (*šāᶜaᶜ*) II, "to delight in" (cf. vv. 16, 47, 70) complete this picture of the psalmist's deep-seated delight being associated with God's Word.

[71] V. 176b also expresses his desire (cf. v. 175) through the final direct imperative addressed to God; however, this petition should be regarded as an *immediate reaction* to his propensity to stray (i.e. v. 176a).

The disciple's first desire is that the God of the Word might mediate sustaining life to him (v. 175a), then as he subtly but significantly shifts his focus to the Word of God, he prays that it will administer spiritual first aid to him (v. 175b). The jussive תְּחִי (*tᵉḥî*; i.e. "allow, let, permit," etc. . . . "live")[72] in relation to which the circumlocutory נַפְשִׁי (*napšî*; lit. "my soul") stands as its subject (v. 175a), expresses in a round-about but delicate way (i.e. "let my soul live") essentially the same request that the disciple has persistently directed to his LORD through recurrences of the Piel imperative of חָיָה (*ḥāyâ*) with a pronominal suffix (i.e. חַיֵּנִי [*ḥayyēnî*], "revive me"; cf. vv. 25, 37, 40, 88, 107, 149, 154, 156, 159). Also, via precedent, the child of God tacks on a reason why his Master should infuse him with sustaining life.[73] In this instance the documentation for intervention is doxological, וּתְהַלְלֶךָּ (*ûtᵉhallekā*), "that I may praise You." Inferentially, he may have been bringing into the picture the fact that "the dead do not praise the LORD" (Ps 115:17a, NASB).[74]

As suggested previously, the association of God's "judgments"[75] with His "hand" comes through their parallel connections with the verb עָזַר (*ᶜāzar*), "to help": "May your hand be ready to help me" (v. 173a, NIV) and "let Your judgments help me" (v. 175b). The apparent connection is that "the word is the medium of His hand."[76] Furthermore, it is also possible that God's inscripturated precepts, i.e. His "judgments," may have been looked upon not only as the instruments of God's wisdom and/or the vehicles of His compassion towards the psalmist, but also as His "rulings,"[77] His "due administration of judgment."[78] The per-

---

72 For other Qal imperfect occurrences of חָיָה (*ḥāyâ*) cf. vv. 17, 77, 116, 144.

73 Most translations correctly interpret the *waw* conjunction as voluntative.

74 Cf. Anderson, *Psalms*, 2:847.

75 Taking וּמִשְׁפָּטֶךָ (*ûmišpāṭekā*) as a defective plural; again, see Delitzsch, *Psalms*, 3:263.

76 Ibid.

77 Cf. Allen's rendering herein (*Psalms 101–150*, p. 134).

78 Cf. Girdlestone, *Synonyms*, p. 101, for this overarching concept of מִשְׁפָּט (*mišpāṭ*).

secuted pilgrim may have been mentally nuancing these מִשְׁפָּטִים (*mišpāṭîm*) in the *fully* applicational sense of the LORD's providential administrations of Divine justice.

Many commentators have been puzzled and some of them have become quite critical of the psalm due to the seeming contradiction which launches its last verse: תָּעִיתִי כְּשֶׂה אֹבֵד (*tāʿîṯî keśeh 'ōḇēḏ*), "I have strayed like a lost sheep." After all, has not the psalmist time and time again pointed to his own basic integrity and faithfulness, even as a secondary basis for God's intervention on his behalf? Even beyond that, did he not say back in verse 110, "I have not strayed (i.e. לֹא תָעִיתִי [*lō' ṯāʿîṯî*], no less!) from Your precepts"? The respective contexts in general and these two verses in particular, however, are not outright contradictions but another biblical and theological instance of an apparent "antinomy."[79] This particular manifestation of a scriptural antinomy is one that surfaces here and there throughout the Psalms, but has been most frequently spotted in Psalm 119. The tension precipitated by verse 176a belongs to a sub-set of the truism that has bridged these twenty-two stanzas, i.e. the child of God may be seen exerting himself but is never observed trusting himself.[80]

Remembering that the school days of a disciple are never over in this life, that moral perfection is not consummated in this world, the child of God is to keep on growing in the grace and knowledge of his LORD. As he indeed does mature and evidence real growth verified by measurable patterns of consistency (e.g. v. 110), at the same time, he keeps on rising to new vistas provided by the Word of God from which he gains progressively even more insight into the sufficiencies of God, and correspondingly, the insufficiencies of self. In verse 176a, the child of God chooses to fo-

---

[79] Employing Packer's term for apparently conflicting (i.e. to the mind of man) truths in the Bible (J. I. Packer, *Evangelism and The Sovereignty of God* [Downers Grove, IL: Inter-Varsity Press, 1961], esp. pp. 18–25).

[80] Again, note Spurgeon's *Treasury of David*, 6:33.

cus on his innate bankruptcy as he employs this blanket statement with its vivid simile (cf. the word-picture of Isa 53:6).[81] Allis appropriately contends that

> this may seem a feeble ending, an anticlimax. But should we not rather think of it as a most fitting conclusion for this great poem in praise of the law of God? For it shows us how deeply conscious the writer was of the perfection of the law and of his utter inability to fulfill its demands in his own strength. Only God the giver of the law can enable his servant to keep it.[82]

In a similar vein, Soll argues that

> the final verse forms a touching conclusion to the poem. The verse is longer than any of the preceding ones in this psalm, yet in it the psalmist "makes himself small." The psalmist states that he has "wandered off like a lost sheep" (at once a lament and a confession) and prays for God to seek him, since he has not forgotten God's commandments. But if he has not forgotten God's commandments, how is it that he has wandered off like a lost sheep? The answer lies in the dilemma posed at the very beginning of the psalm: the psalmist's "ways" are not yet in line with the way of the Torah, and much learning remains even for the faithful. Neither the composition nor the reading of the psalm has resolved the

---

[81] Although Isa 53:6 uses a different word for "sheep" (i.e. צֹאן [*ṣō'n*]; cf. the corporate emphasis on the whole *flock*) with the verb תָּעָה (*tāᶜâ*), the concept is the same in Ps 119:176a (contra. Delitzsch, *Psalms*, 3:263, who tries to get around the psalmist's words by making them hypothetical). For an excellent response to and refutation of Delitzsch's conclusion regarding this point, see O. T. Allis, *The Old Testament: Its Claims and Its Critics* (Nutley, NJ: Presbyterian and Reformed, 1972), p. 95.

[82] Allis, *Old Testament: Claims and Critics*, p. 95.

> problem, but it has provided both psalmist and reader with opportunities to open themselves to God and his law at a number of levels. The psalm, therefore, concludes on a note of humility and hope. The humility resides, not in breast beating, but in the knowledge that God's ways are not our ways, and that before him we can make no pretence to greatness of any kind. The hope lies in the affirmation that God can and must take the initiative with his servants, not only in the beginning, but all along the way of Torah.[83]

So, with biblical prescription lenses, the child of God sees himself as an "isolated and . . . sorely imperilled sheep,"[84] and being confronted with this accurate self-portrait he comes face to face with his own vulnerability. This phenomenon needs to recur in progressive stages wherein his own sin becomes more exceedingly sinful.[85] Axiomatically, a preeminent indication of significant spiritual growth and development is one's increasing sensitivity to personal sin (cf., e.g., Paul in Rom 7:14ff.).

However, retrospective and introspective analyses are spiritually legitimate only when the person responds appropriately to them, and that is when the sense of despair that these self-portraits paint generates dependence rather than depression. Characteristically, the child of God in Psalm 119 has responded in the right way, and it is no different here at the end. Unwavering dependence is the immediate response to his own finiteness and

---

[83] Soll, "Psalm 119," pp. 209–10. The thrust of Soll's comments, although basically on target, is somewhat anemic in reference to its *full* penetration into the psalmist's confession.

[84] Delitzsch, *Psalms*, 3:244. On the "sheep" metaphor as it depicts "defenselessness," see Anderson, *Psalms*, 2:847; and on the ethical implications of the attributive participle אֹבֵד (*'ōḇēḏ*), cf. Girdlestone, *Synonyms*, p. 275.

[85] As intimated previously, these episodes will normally coincide with one's progressive insight into the holiness of the LORD and the derived perfection of the way of the LORD's Word.

fallenness: בַּקֵּשׁ עַבְדֶּךָ (*baqqēš ᶜabdekā*), "Seek Your servant!"[86] Self-examination is truly effectual when complacency has been rooted out and displaced by dependency.

Coming full circle, the psalmist's statement in verse 176c, "*because* I have not forgotten Your commandments," supplies the final arc to his sanctification cycle.[87] Again, his previous confession (v. 176a) is not "necessarily inconsistent" with this "affirmation of loyalty."[88] His model throughout has been one of commendable balance, and its pattern is once more exhibited in verse 176. Kidner, looking at both ends of this verse together and also framing it in its total context, has aptly concluded that "the love of Scripture, which has motivated the scribes of every age, need not harden into academic pride. This man would have taken his stance not with the self-congratulating Pharisee of the parable, but with the publican who stood afar off, but went home justified".[89]

This is truly how the Word of God in the child of God is to operate.

---

[86] It is more than merely interesting that this psalm gets underway with the responsibility of believers seeking God (v. 2b) and docks with the reality of God seeking believers. The LORD necessarily continues to take the initiative.

[87] I.e. on this particular 360° circuit, since the circle is really an ascending spiral of sanctification.

[88] Anderson, *Psalms*, 2:847; cf. Moll, *Psalms*, p. 593.

[89] Kidner, *Psalms 73–150*, p. 429.

Appendix

Diagrammatical Analyses

א
Stanza

Psalm 119 : 1–8

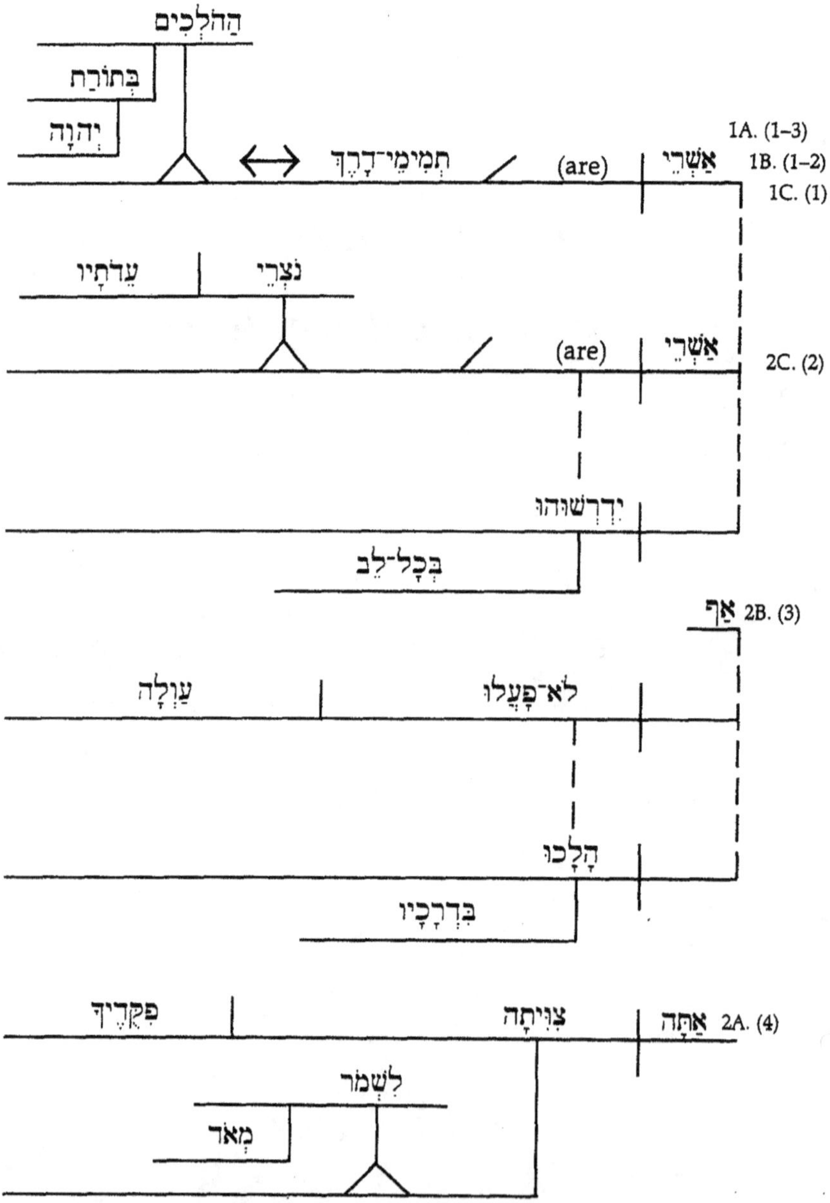

Psalm 119 : 5–8

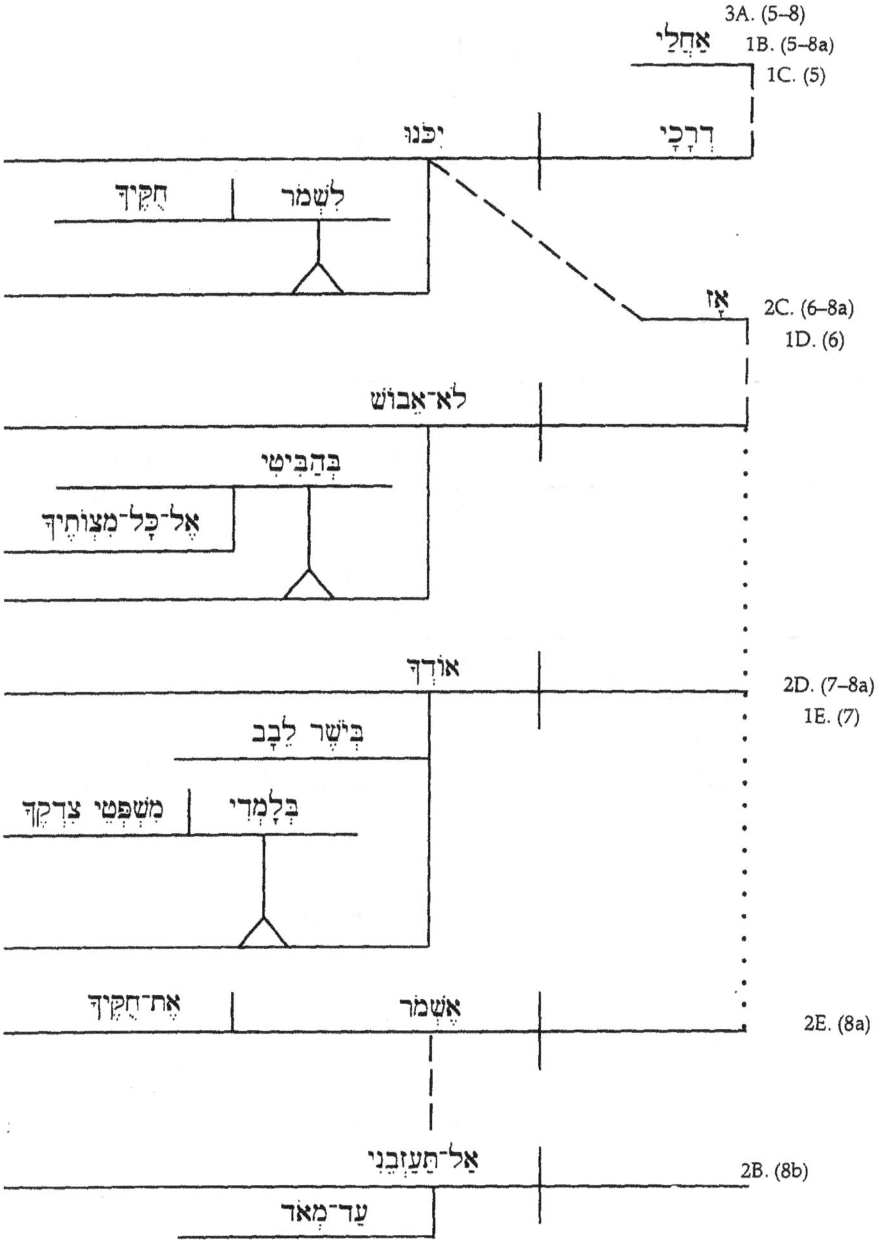
3A. (5–8)
אַחֲלַי
1B. (5–8a)
1C. (5)
דְרָכָי
יִכֹּנוּ
לִשְׁמֹר
חֻקֶּיךָ
אָז
2C. (6–8a)
1D. (6)
לֹא־אֵבוֹשׁ
בְּהַבִּיטִי
אֶל־כָּל־מִצְוֹתֶיךָ
אוֹדְךָ
2D. (7–8a)
1E. (7)
בְּיֹשֶׁר לֵבָב
בְּלָמְדִי
מִשְׁפְּטֵי צִדְקֶךָ
אֶשְׁמֹר
אֶת־חֻקֶּיךָ
2E. (8a)
אַל־תַּעַזְבֵנִי
2B. (8b)
עַד־מְאֹד

ב Stanza

Psalm 119 : 9–16

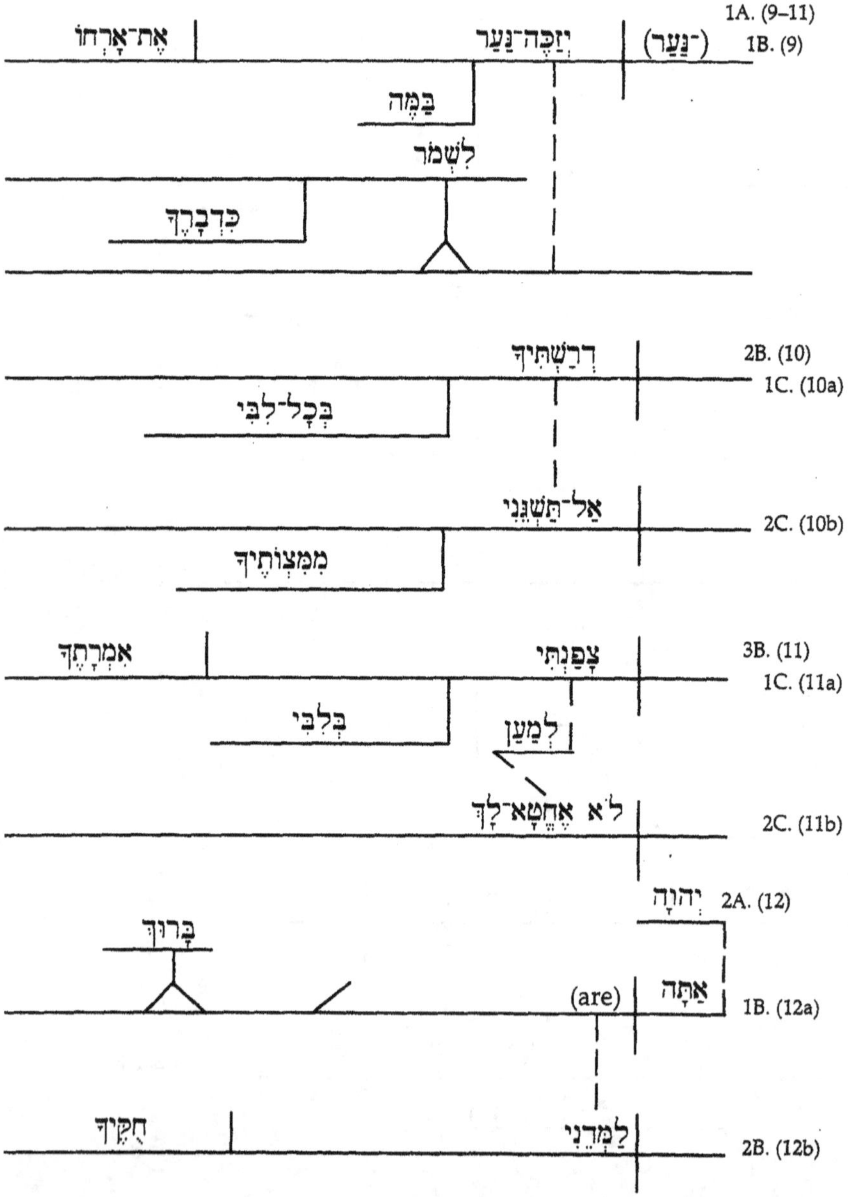

Psalm 119 : 13–16

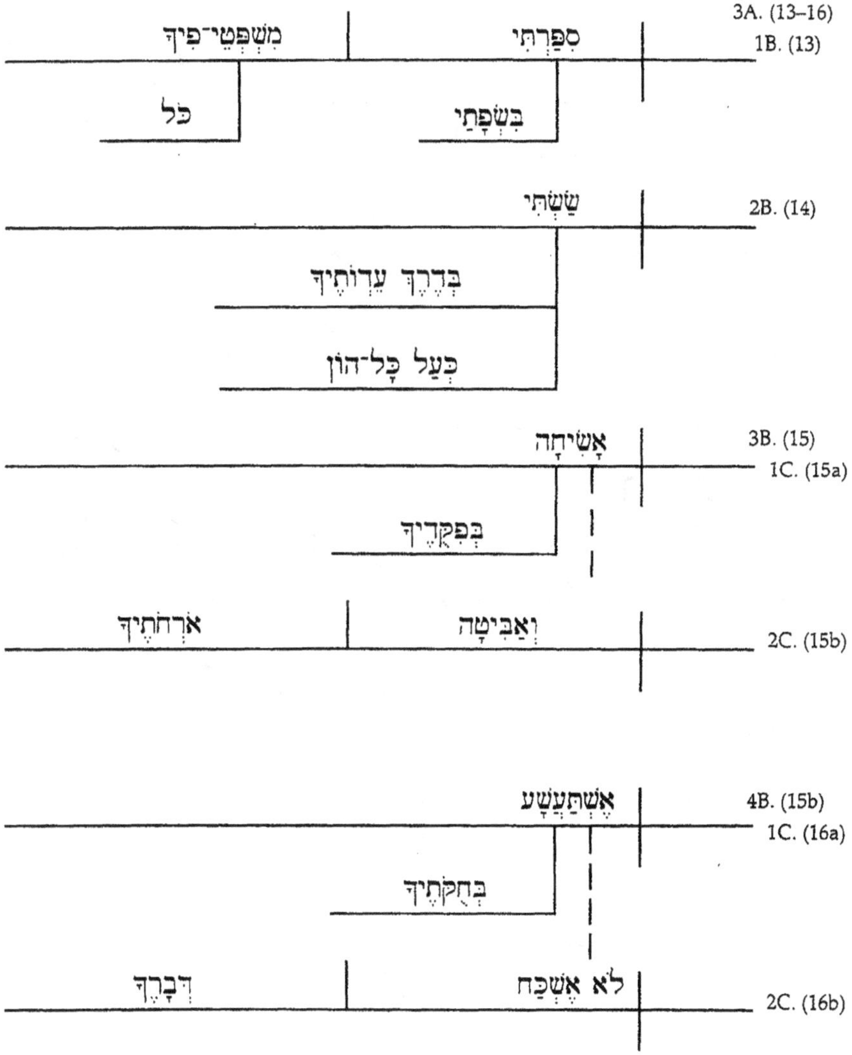

ג
Stanza

Psalm 119 : 17–24

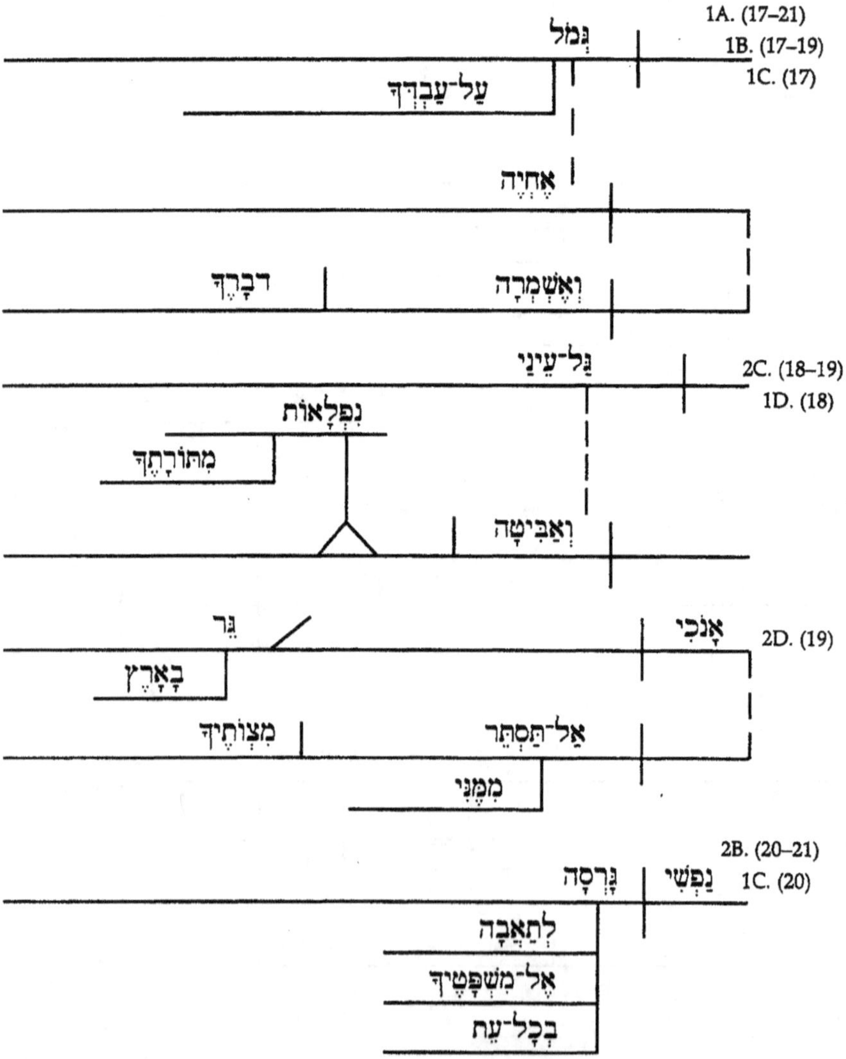

Psalm 119 : 21–24

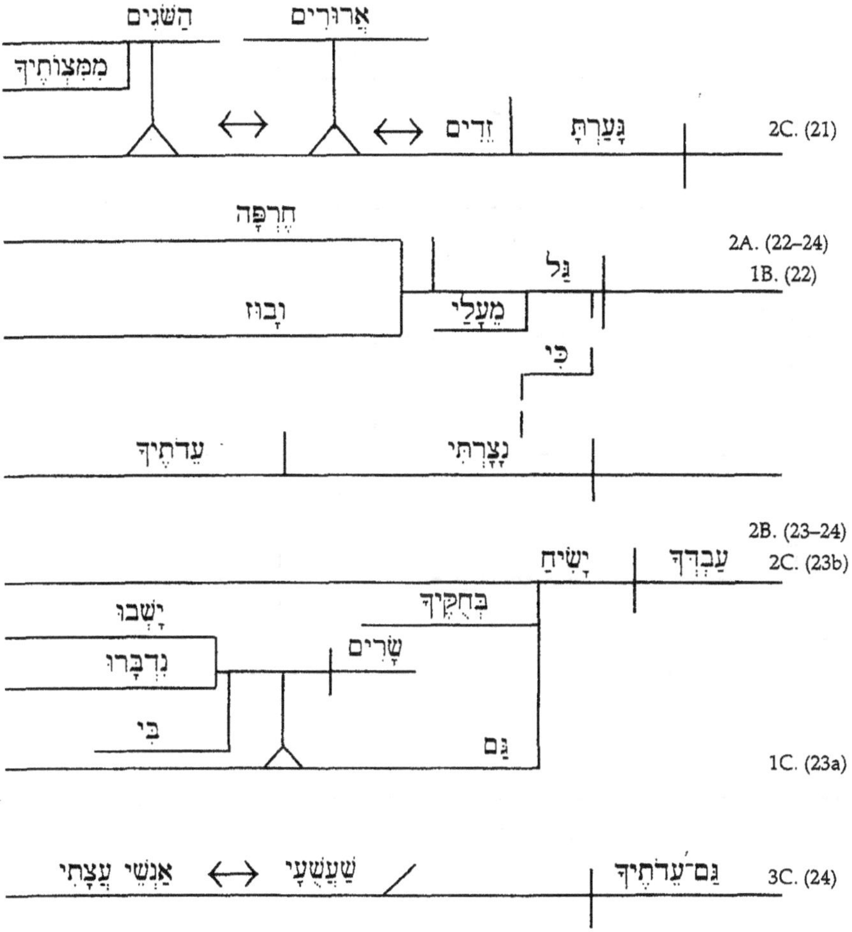

ד Stanza

Psalm 119 : 25–32

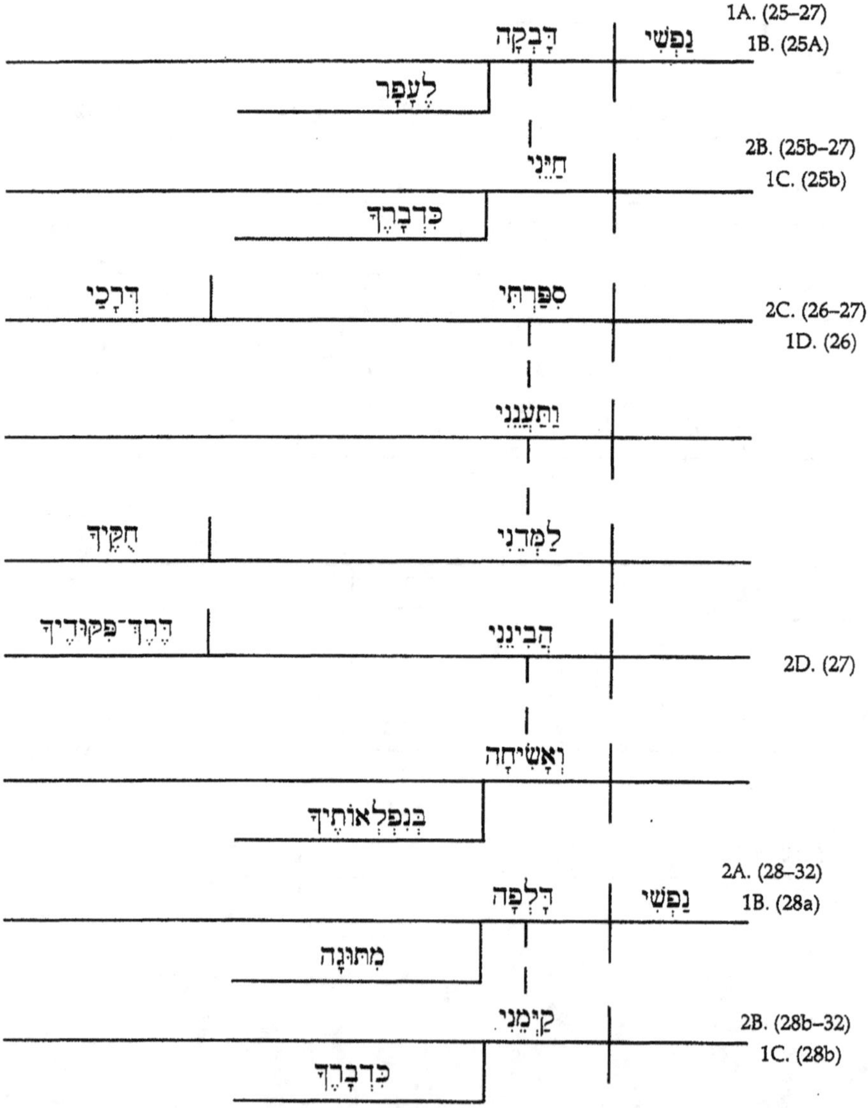

Psalm 119 : 29–32

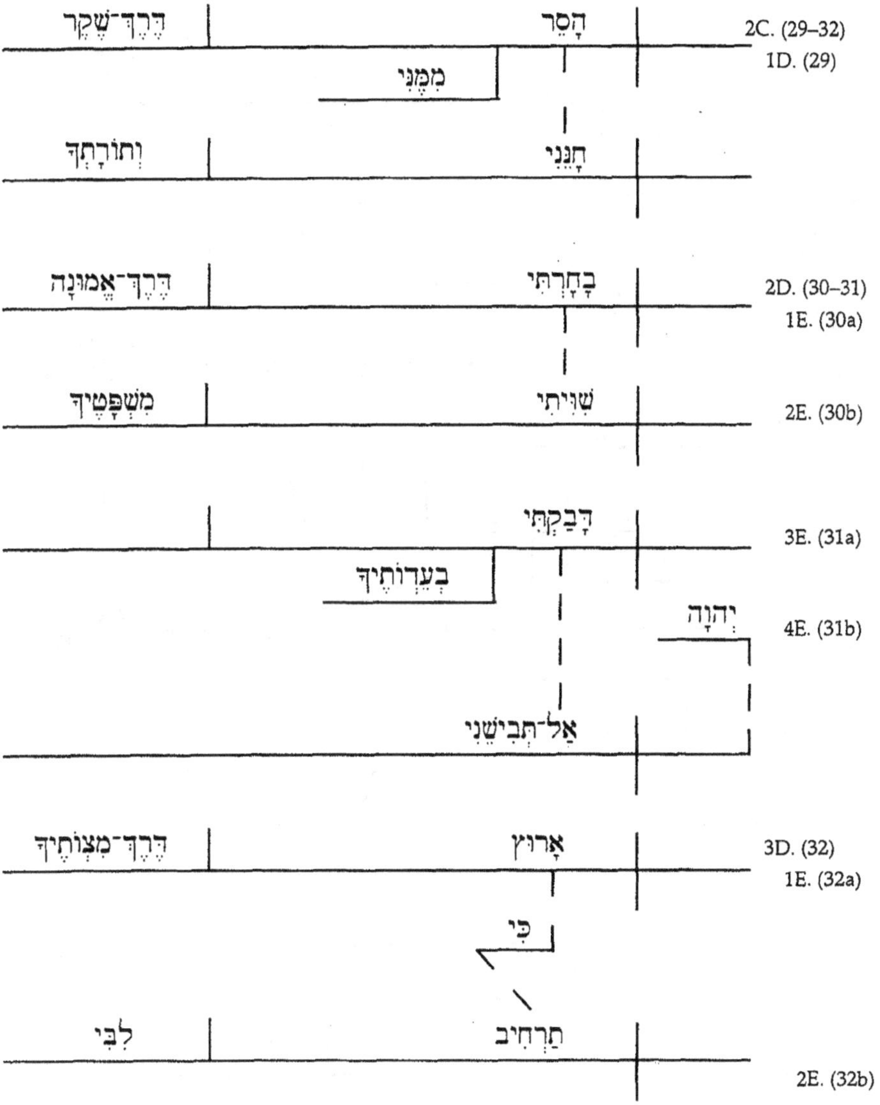

ה
Stanza

Psalm 119 : 33–40

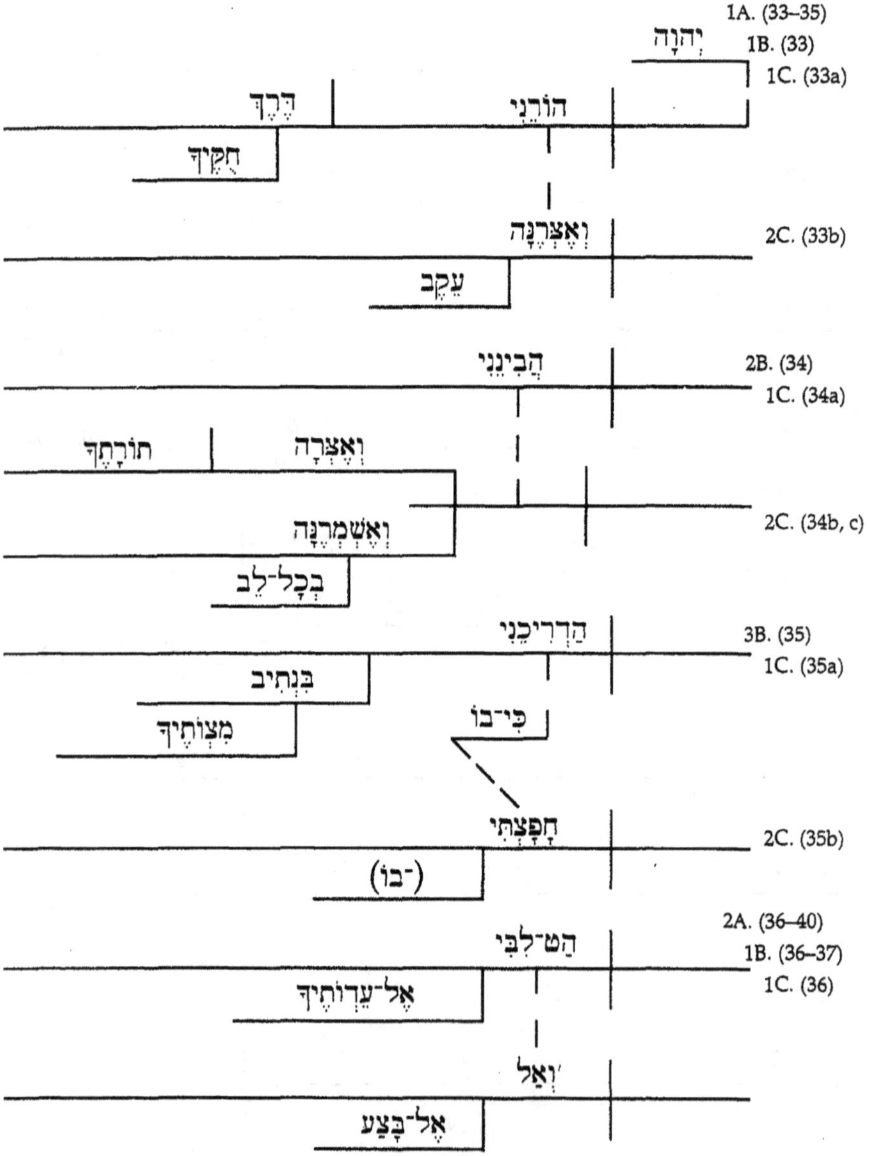

Psalm 119 : 37–40

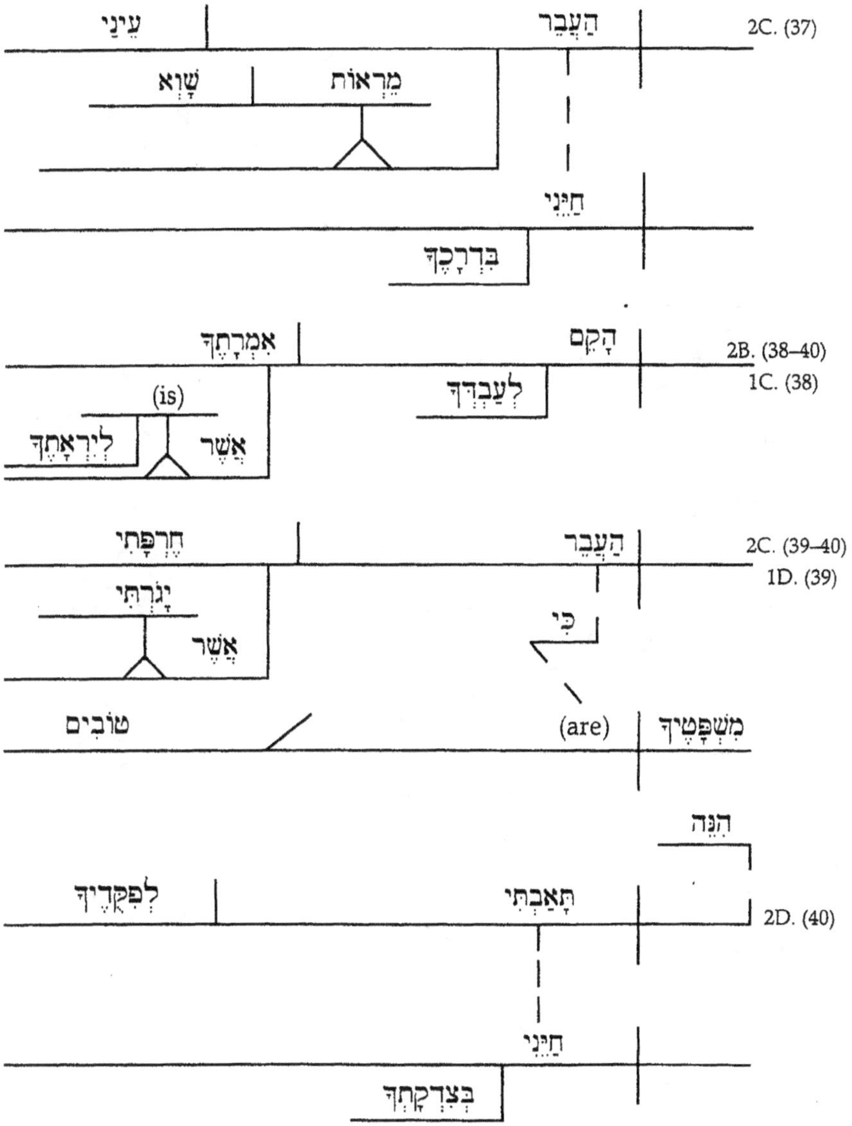

ו
Stanza

Psalm 119 : 41–48

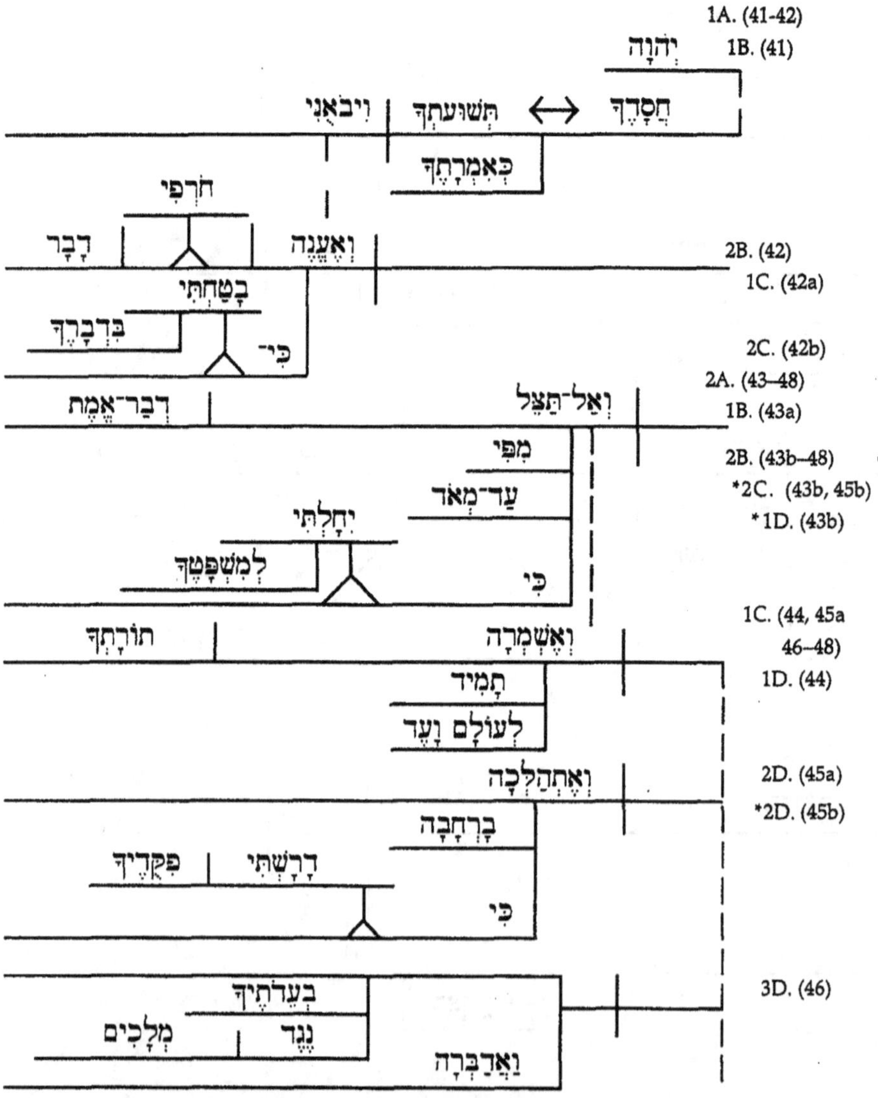

Psalm 119 : 47–48

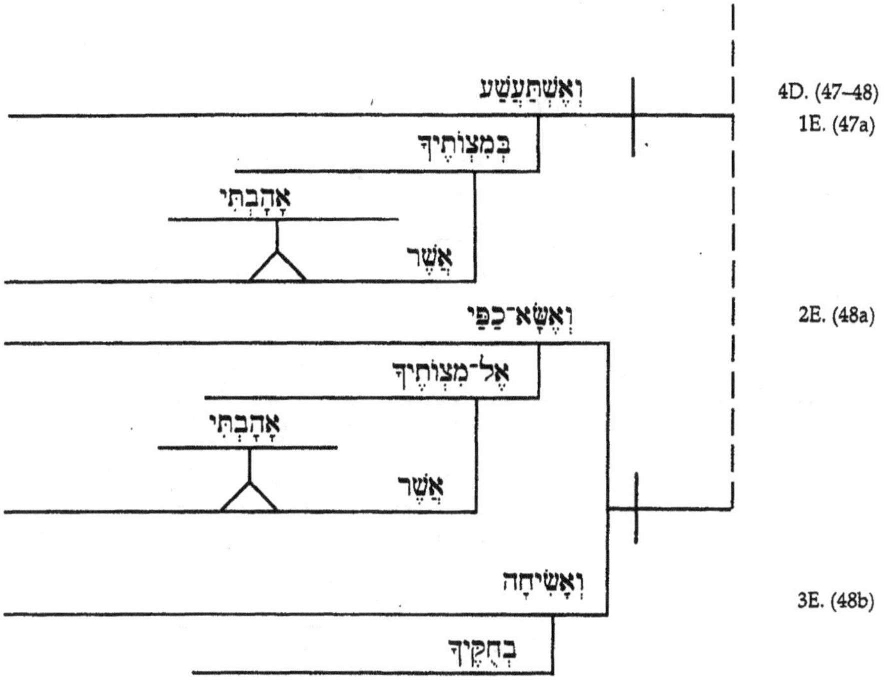

ז
Stanza

Psalm 119 : 49–56

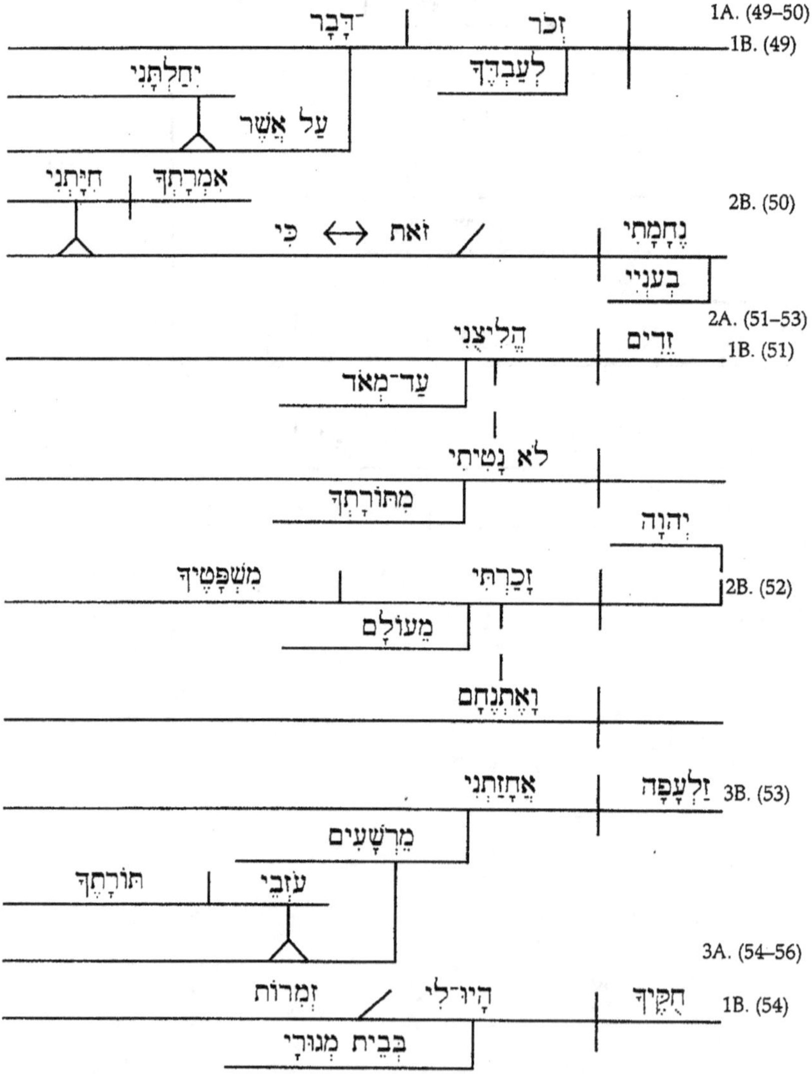

Psalm 119 : 55–56

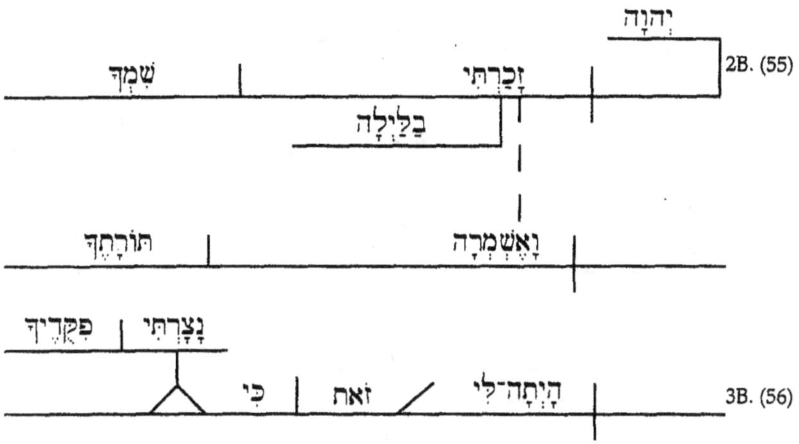

ח Stanza

Psalm 119 : 57–64

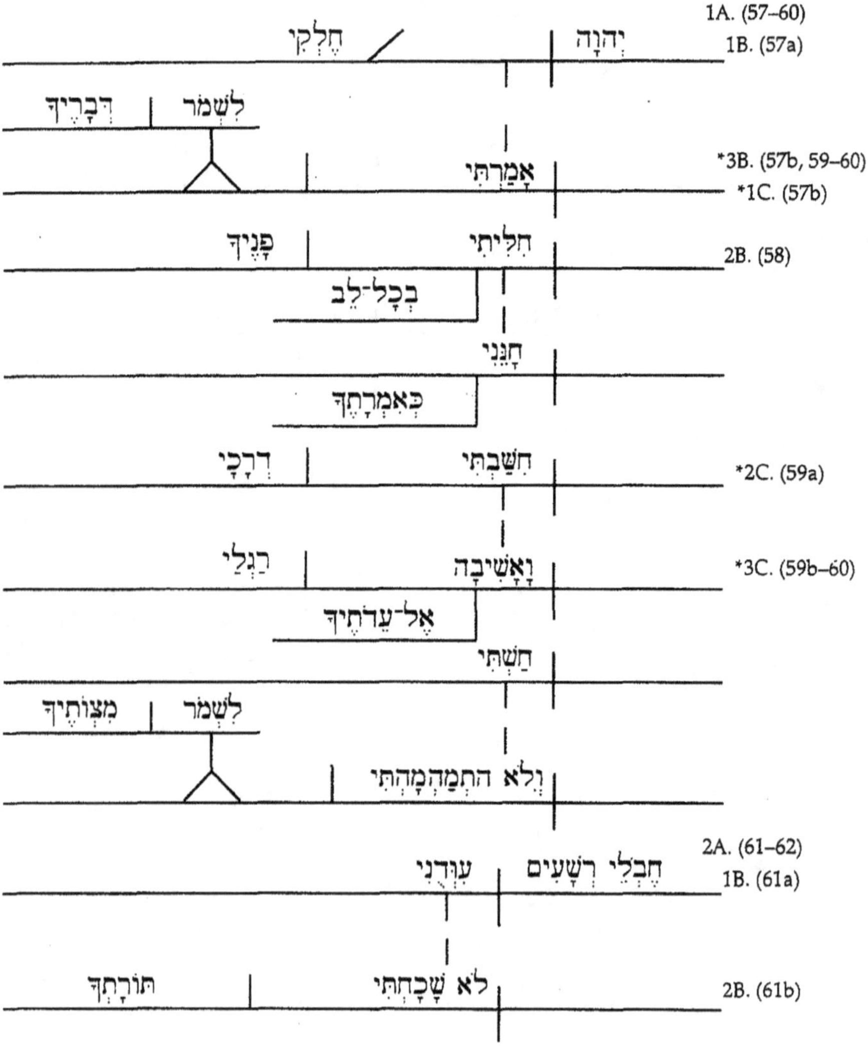

Psalm 119 : 62–64

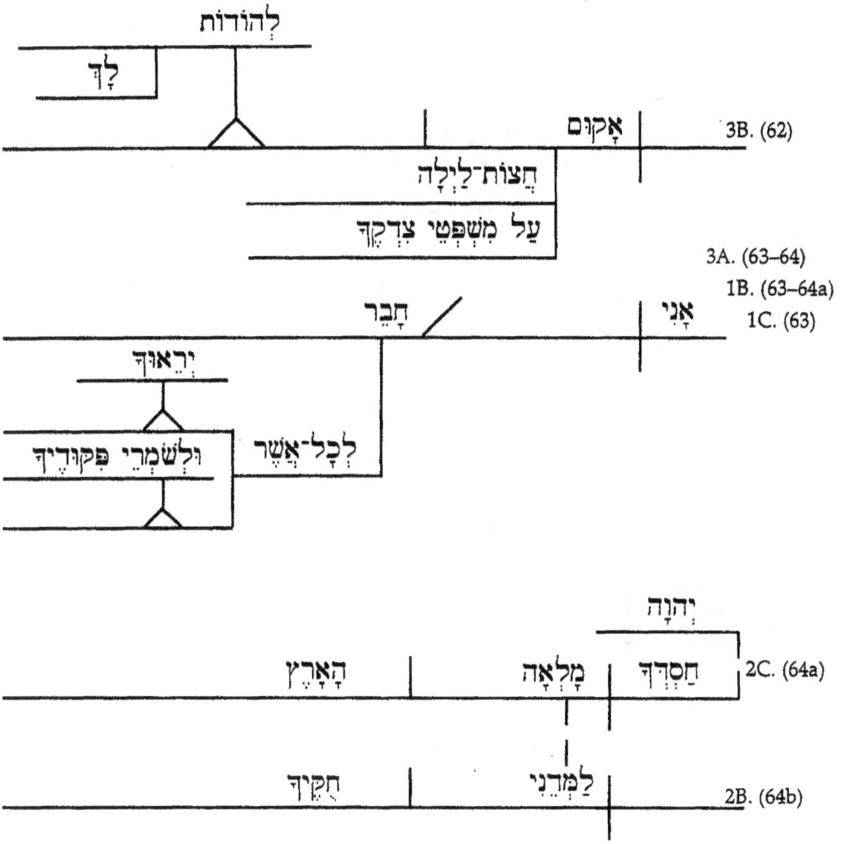

ט Stanza

Psalm 119 : 65–72

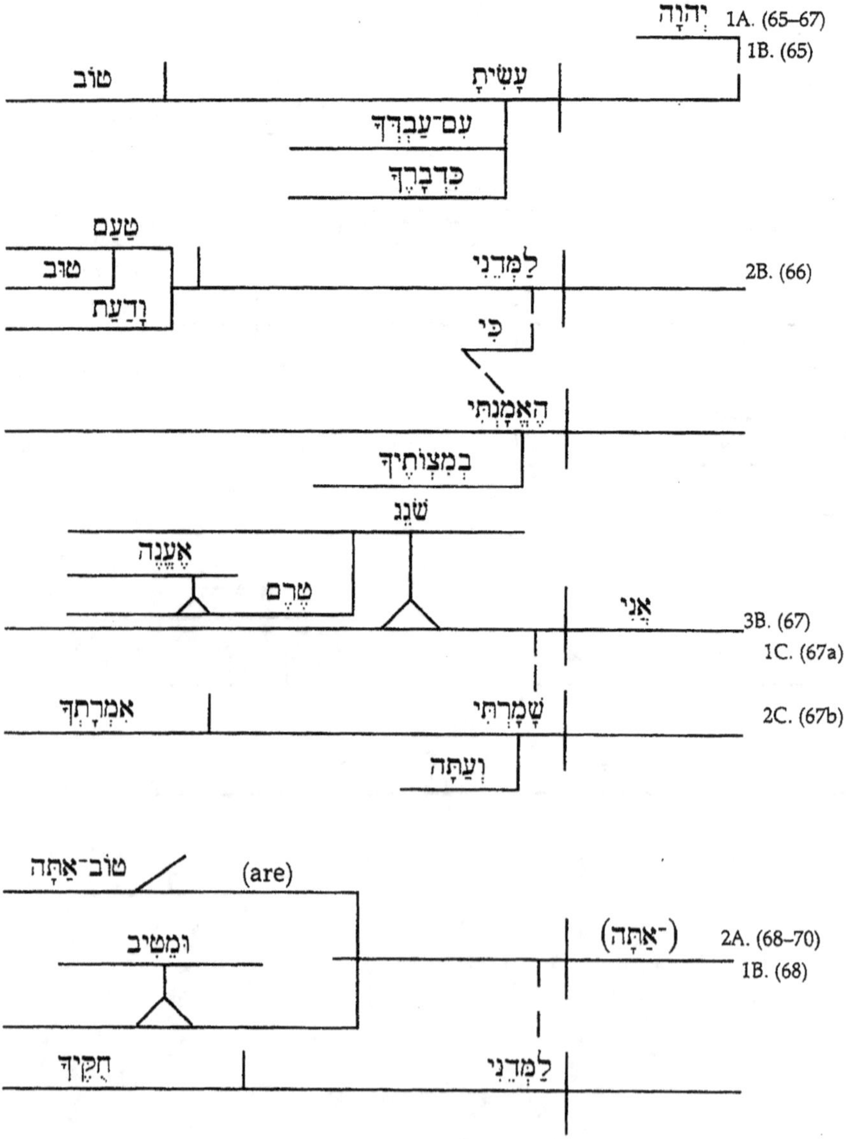

Psalm 119 : 69–72

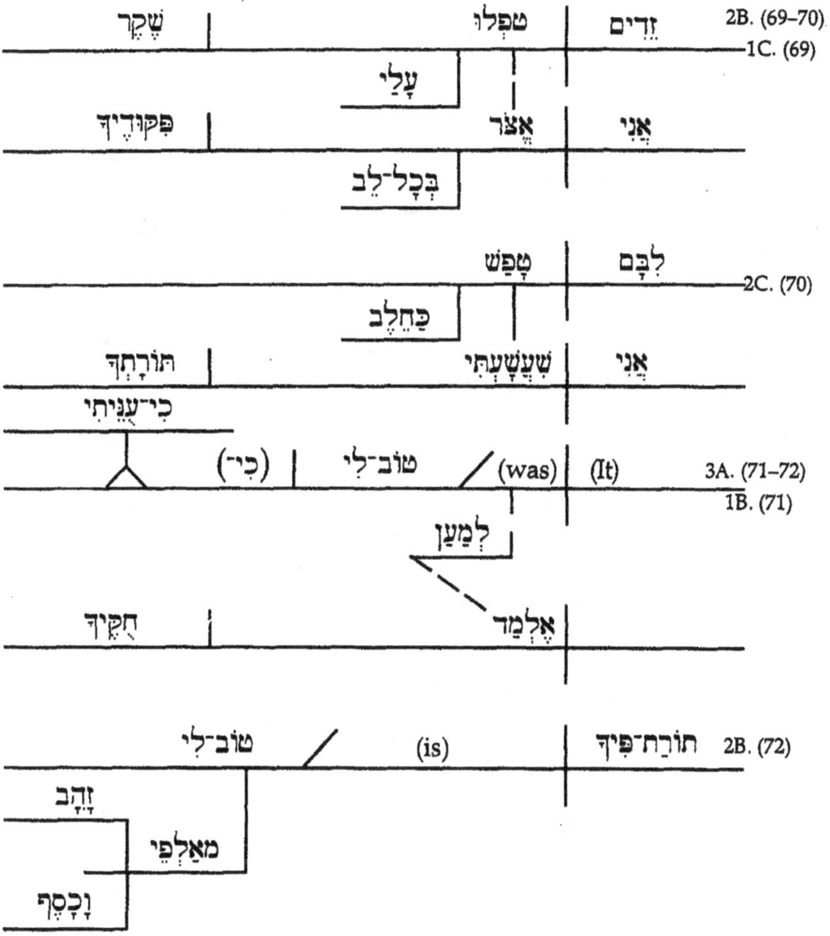

י
Stanza
Psalm 119 : 73–80

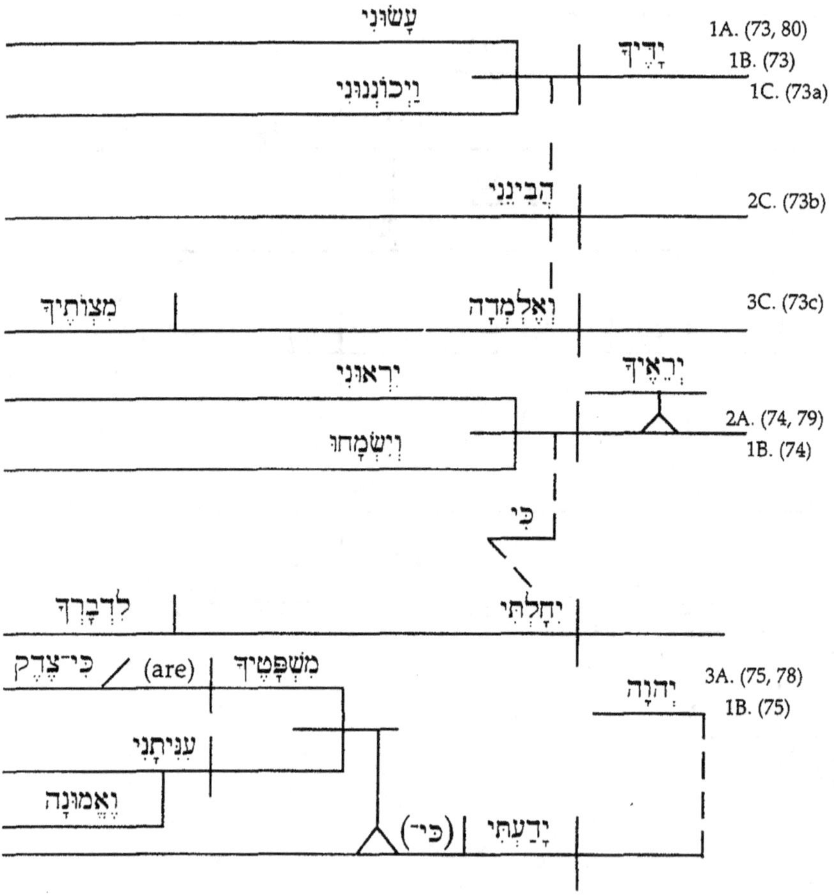

Psalm 119 : 76–80

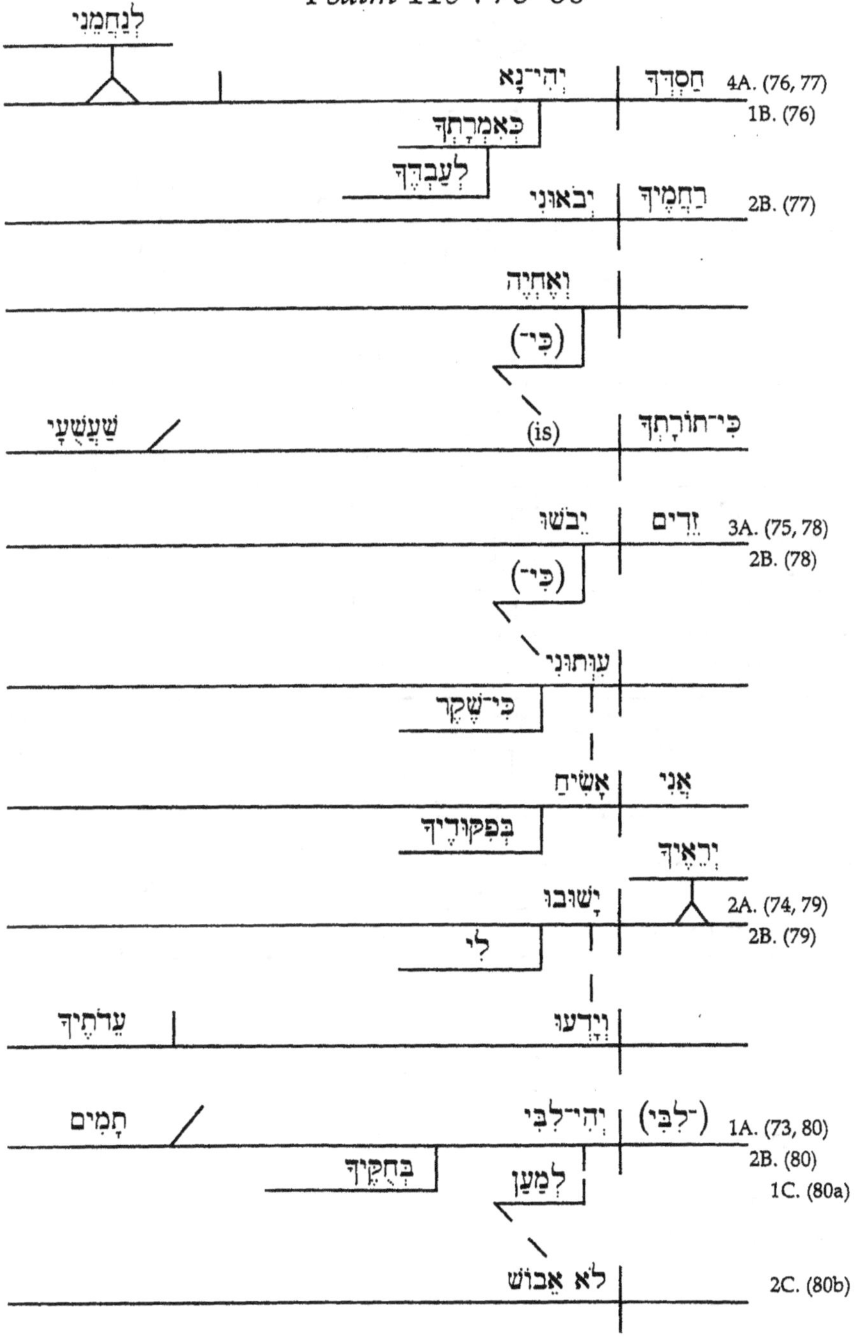

כ
Stanza

Psalm 119 : 81–88

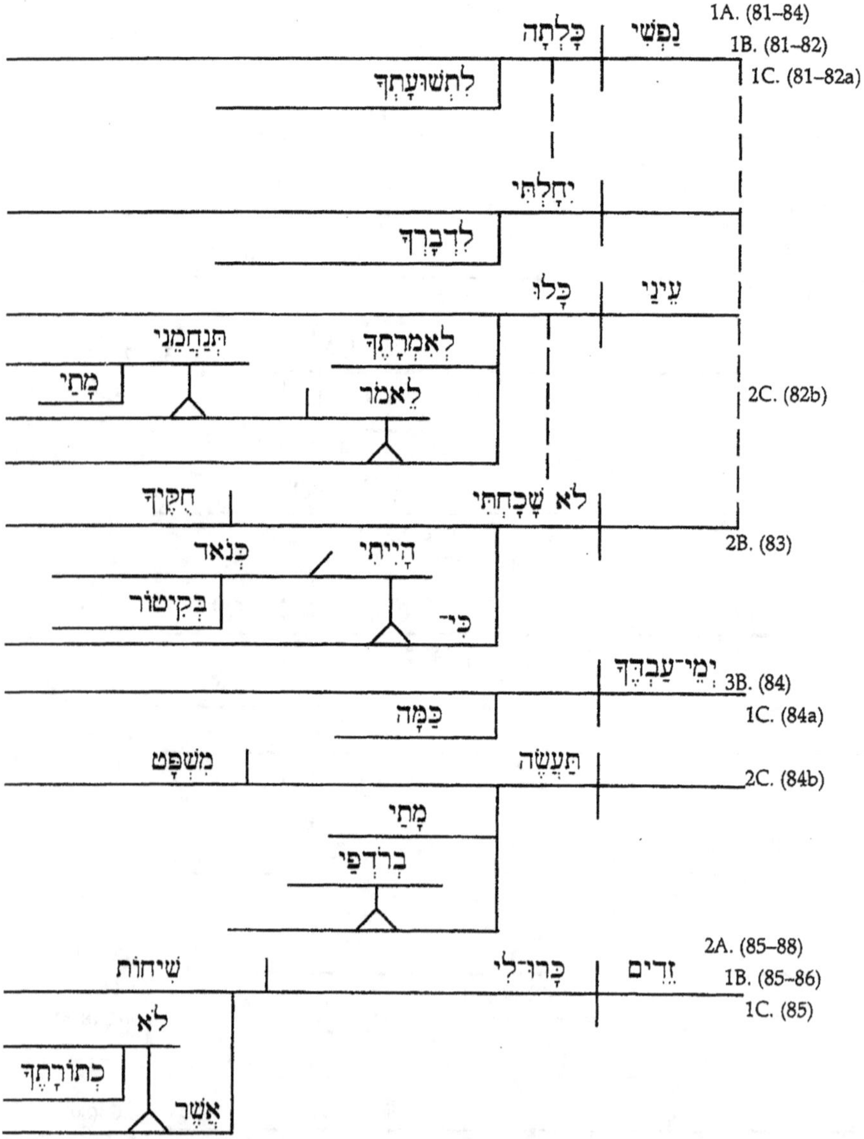

Psalm 119 : 86–88

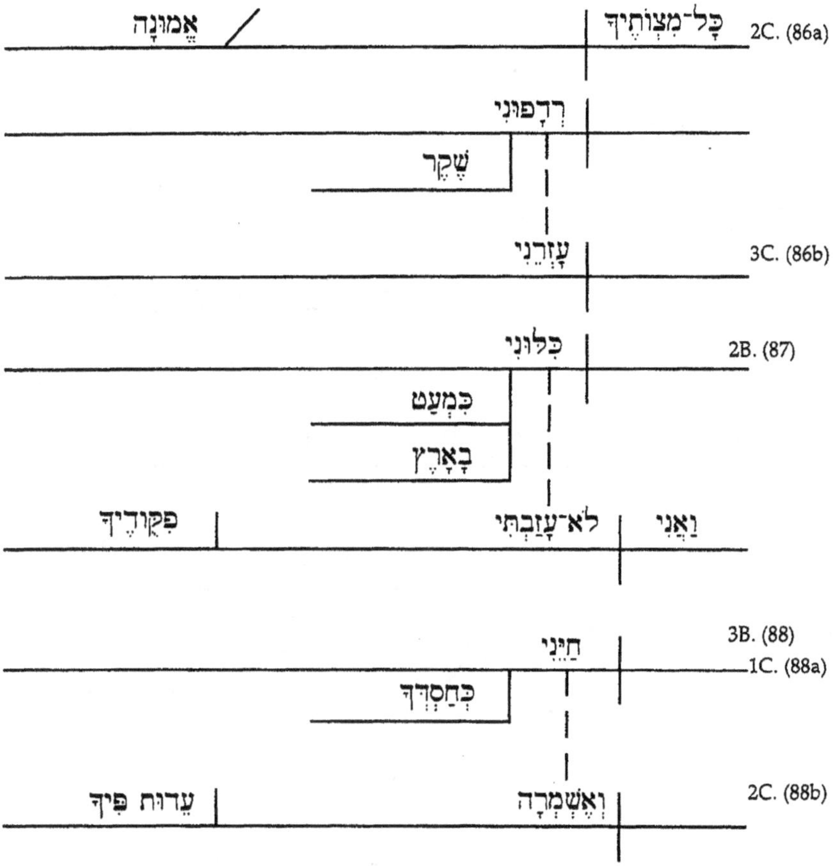

ל Stanza

Psalm 119 : 89–96

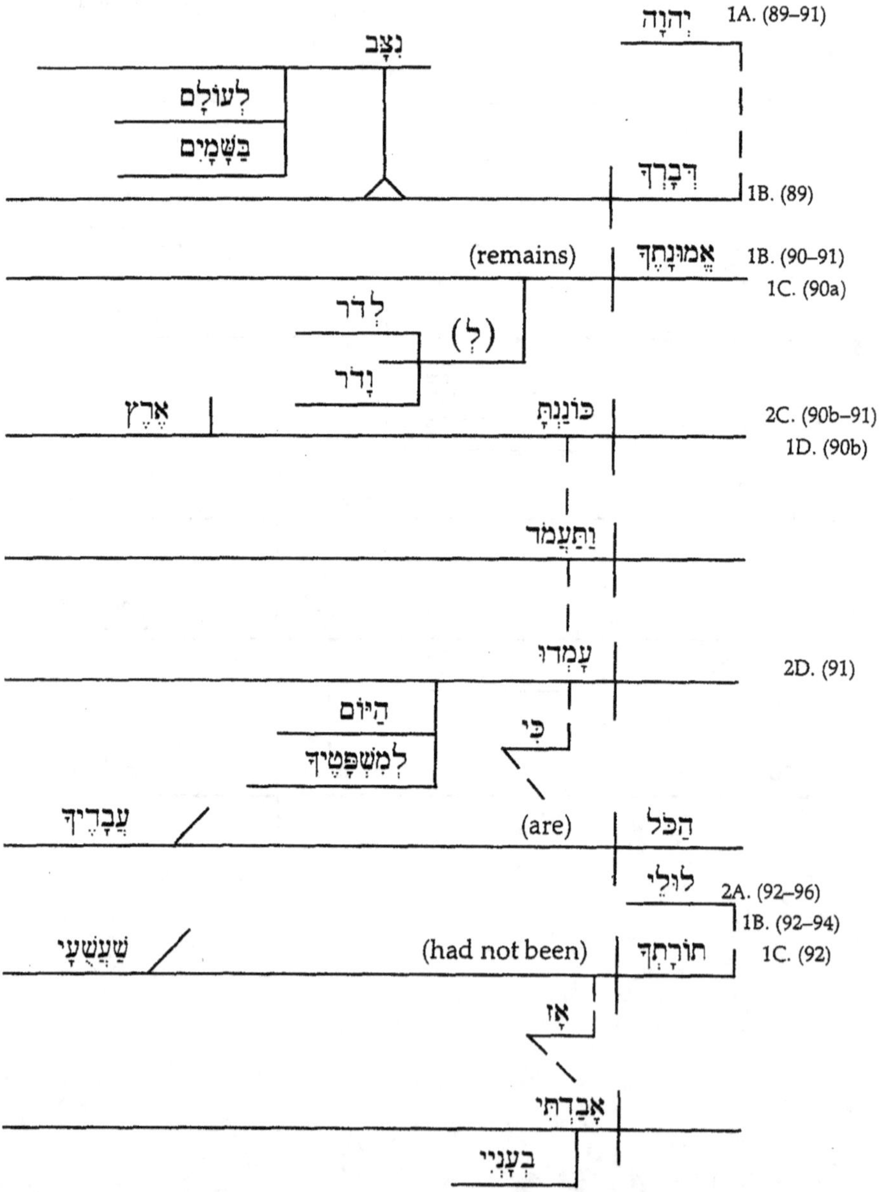

Psalm 119 : 93–96

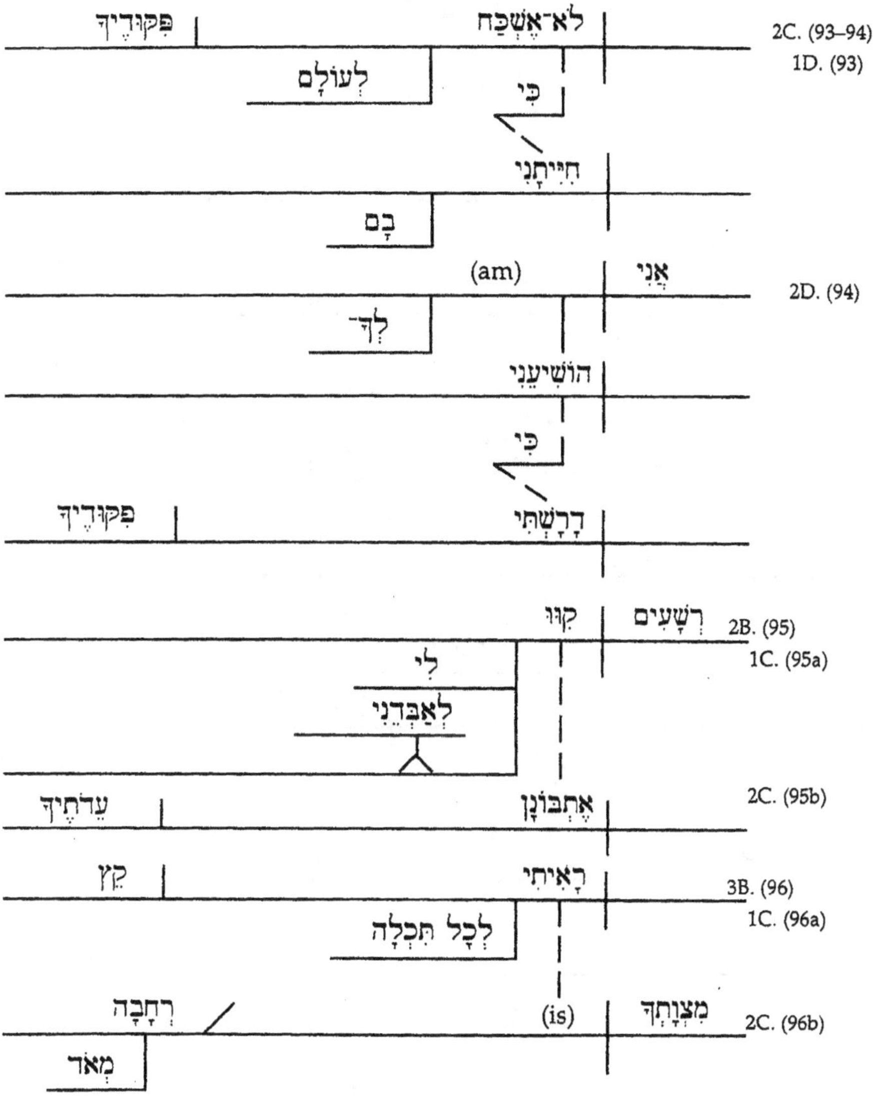

מ
Stanza

Psalm 119 : 97–104

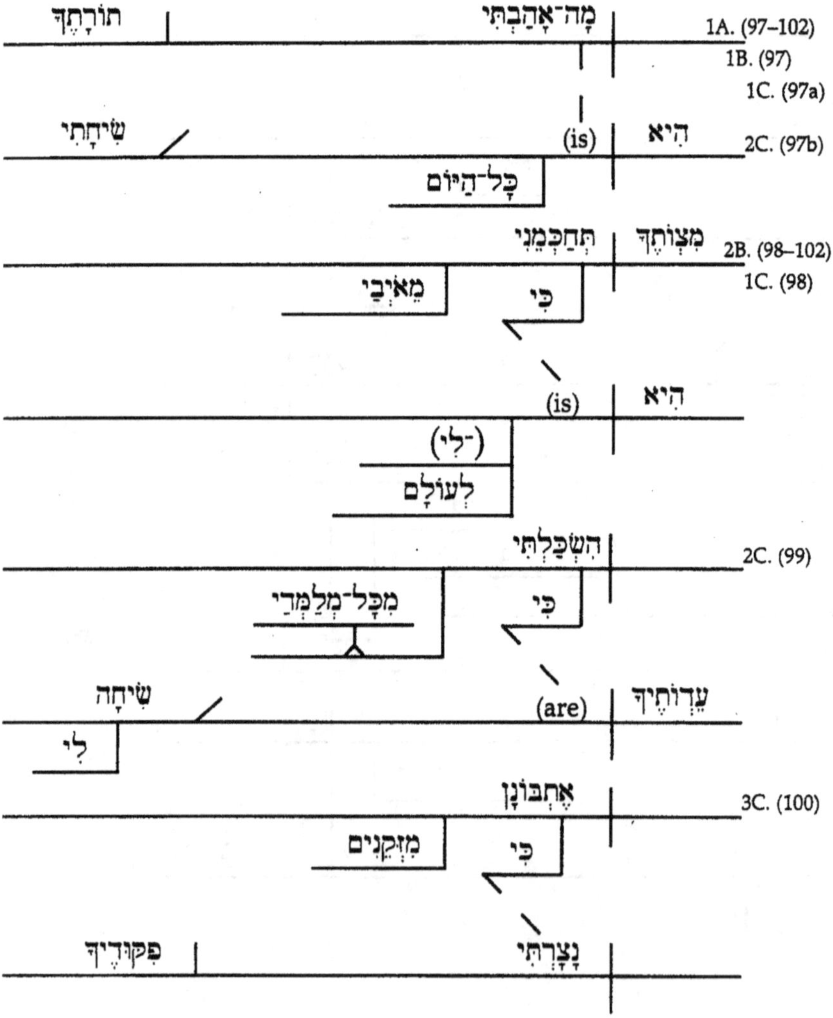

Psalm 119 : 101–104

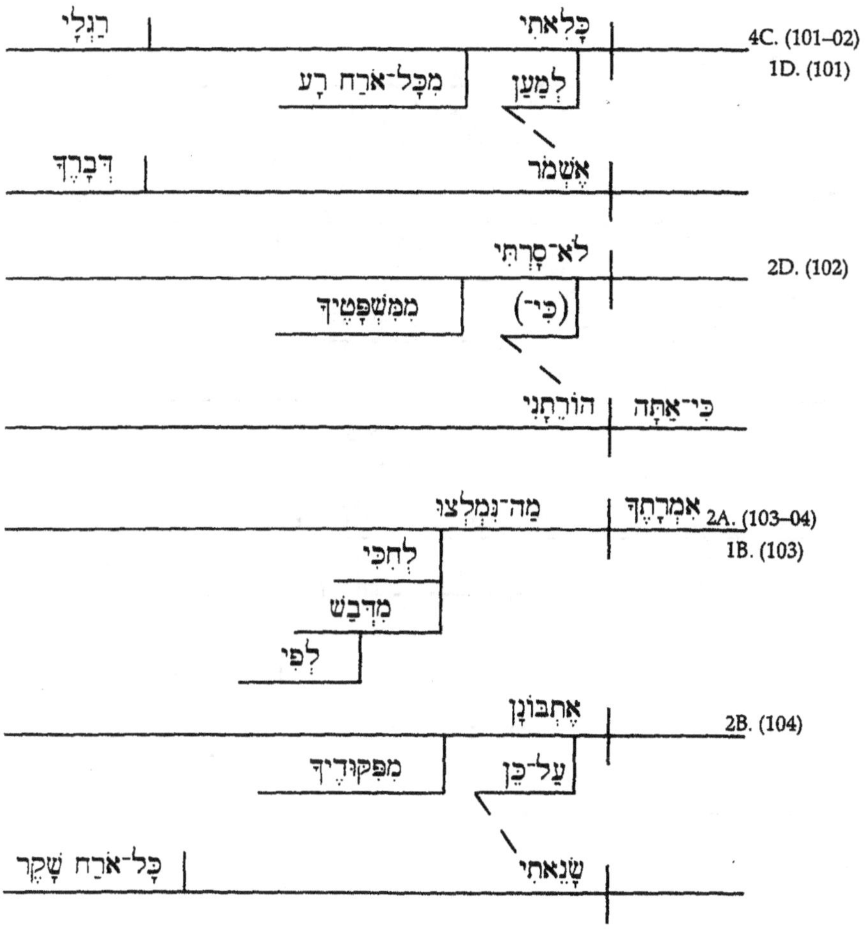

נ
Stanza

Psalm 119 : 105–112

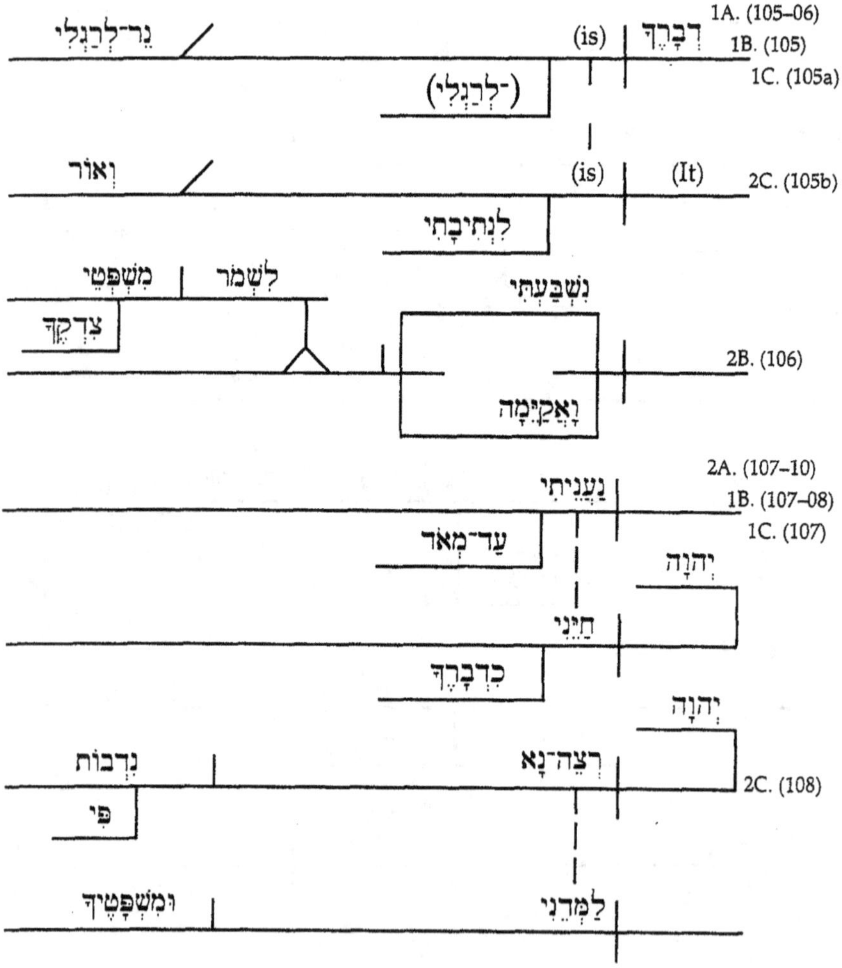

Psalm 119 : 109–112

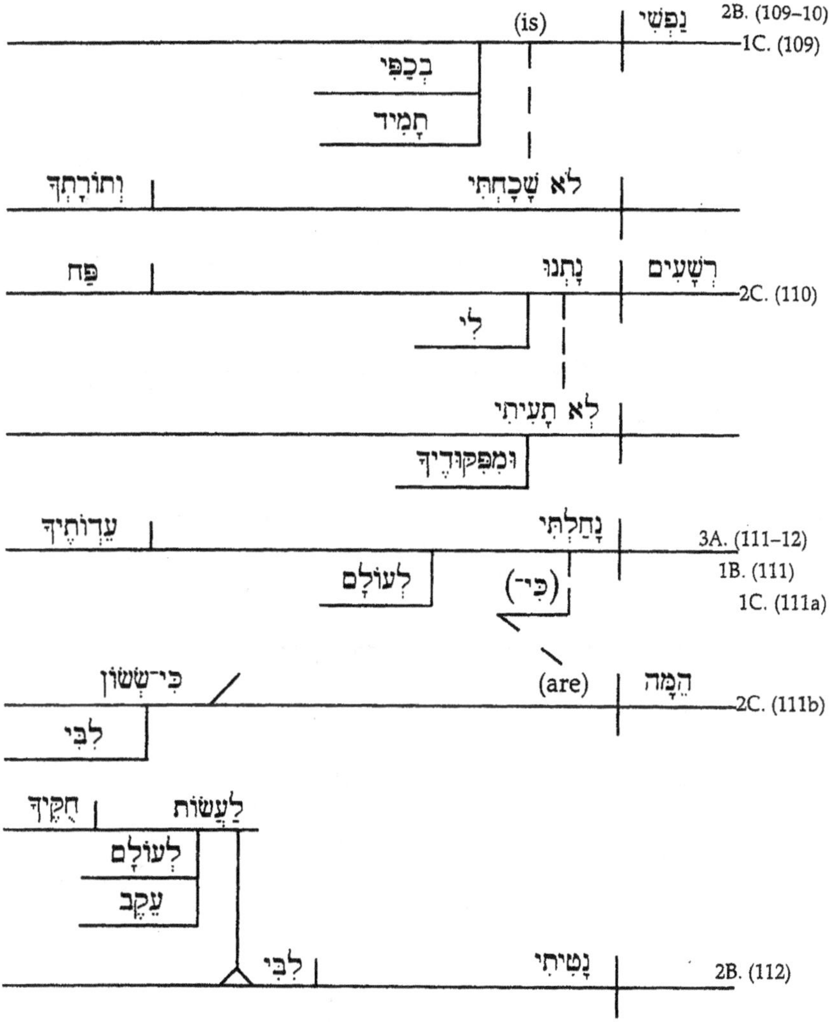

ס
Stanza

Psalm 119 : 113–120

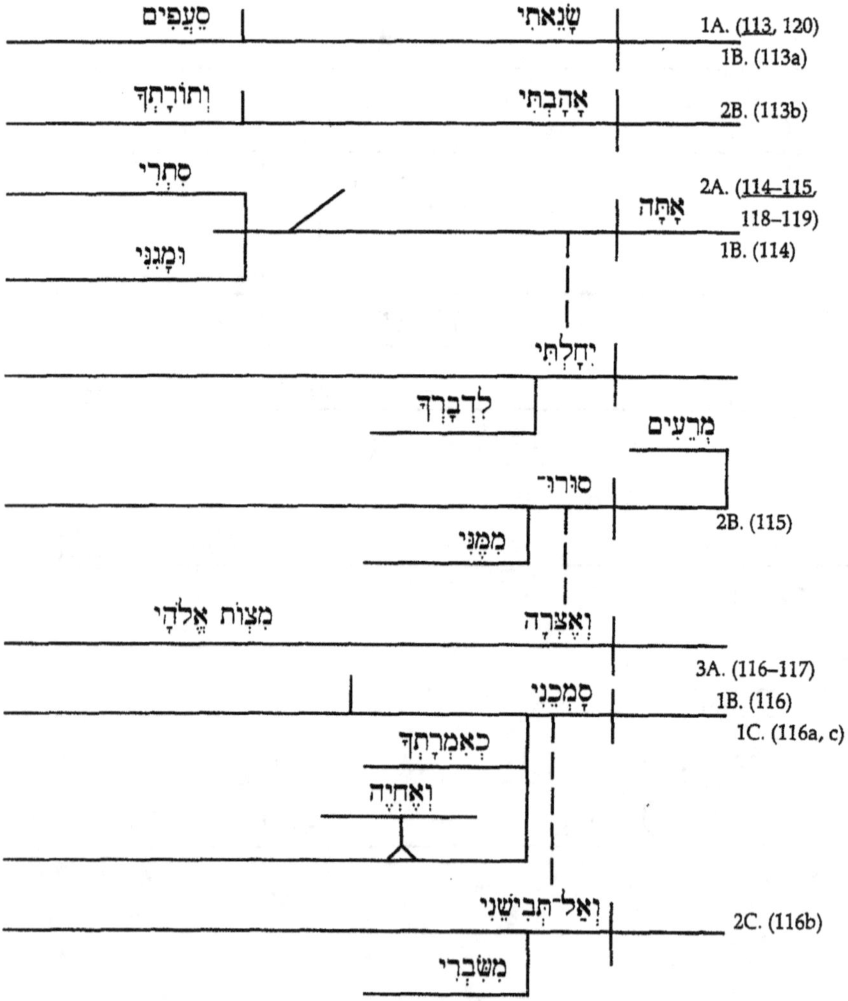

Psalm 119 : 117–120

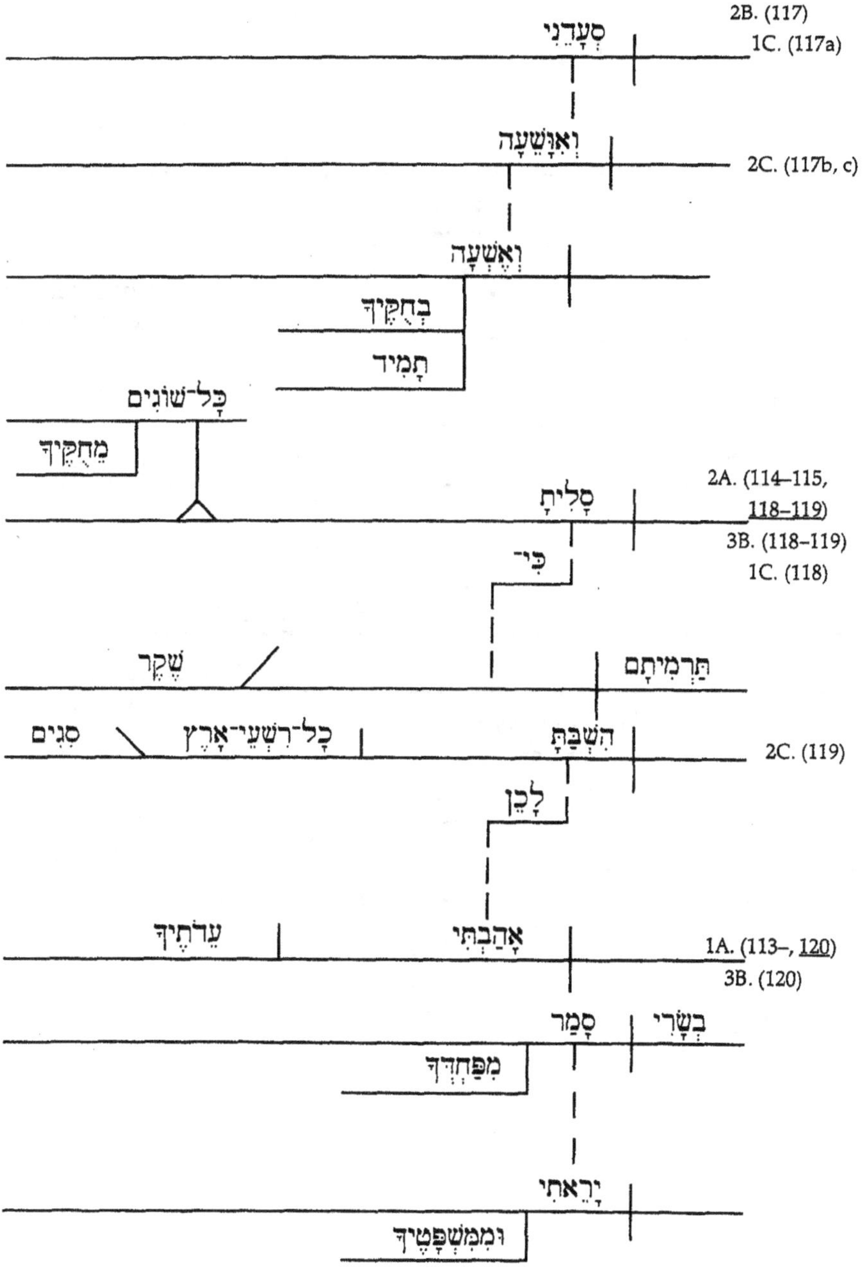

ע
Stanza

Psalm 119 : 121–128

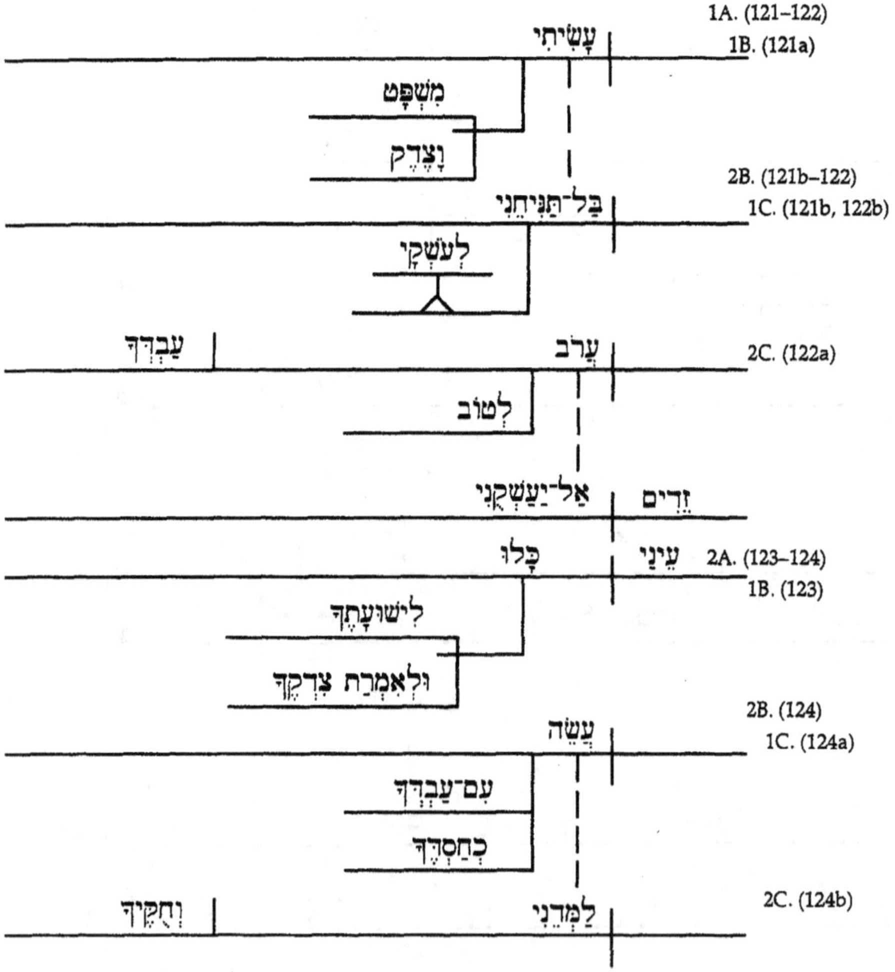

Psalm 119 : 125–128

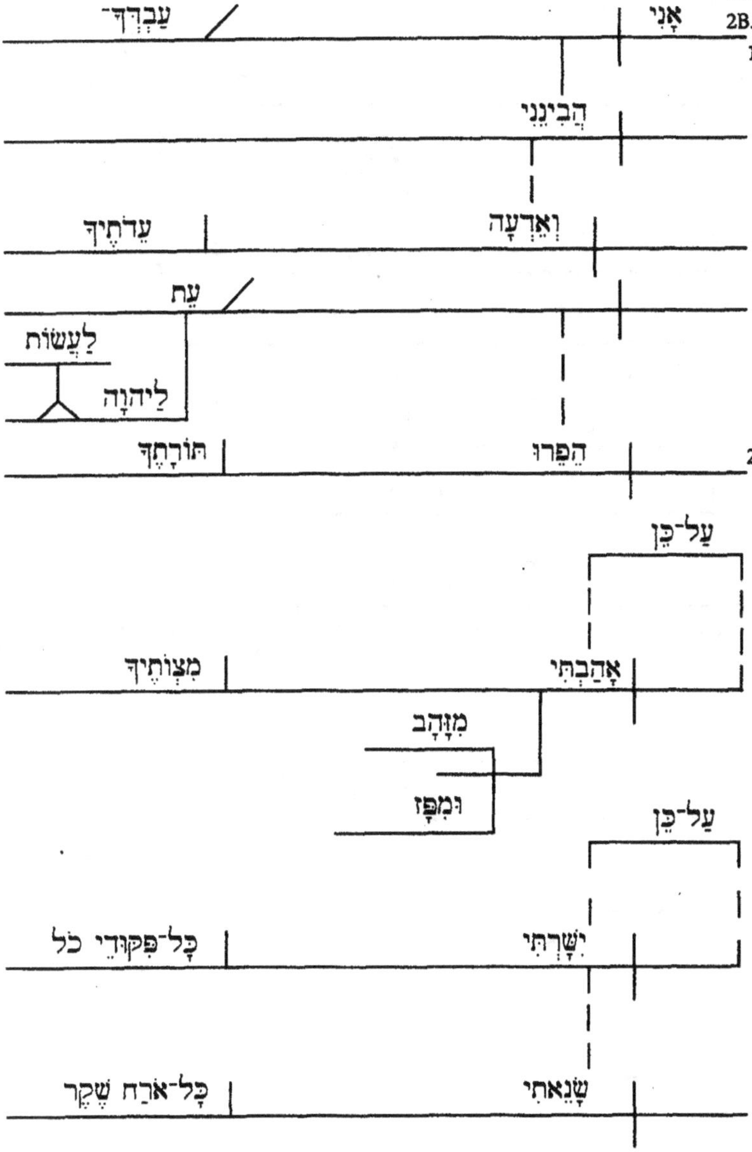

3A. (125–128)
1B. (125a)
2B. (125b–128)
1C. (125b–126a)
1D, (125b, c)
2D. (126a)
2C. (126b–128)
1D. (126b)
2D. (127–128)
1E. (127–128a)
2E. (128b)

פ
Stanza

Psalm 119 : 129–136

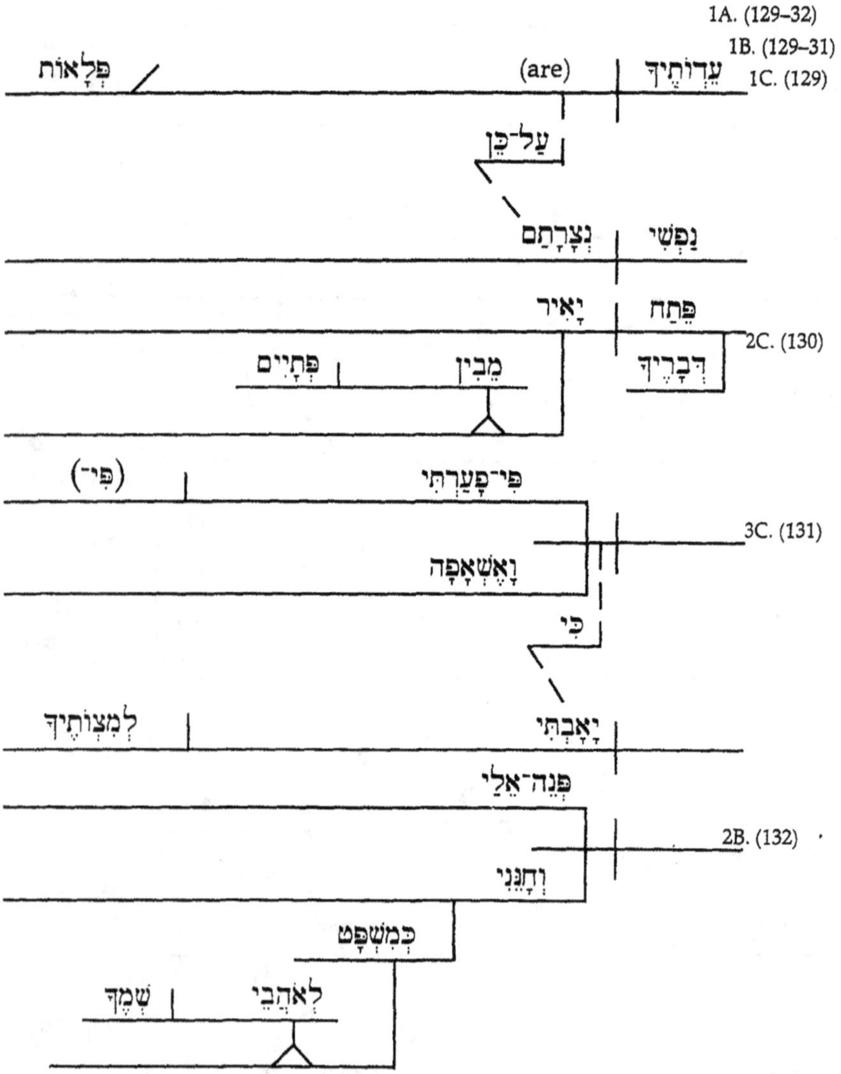

Psalm 119 : 133–136

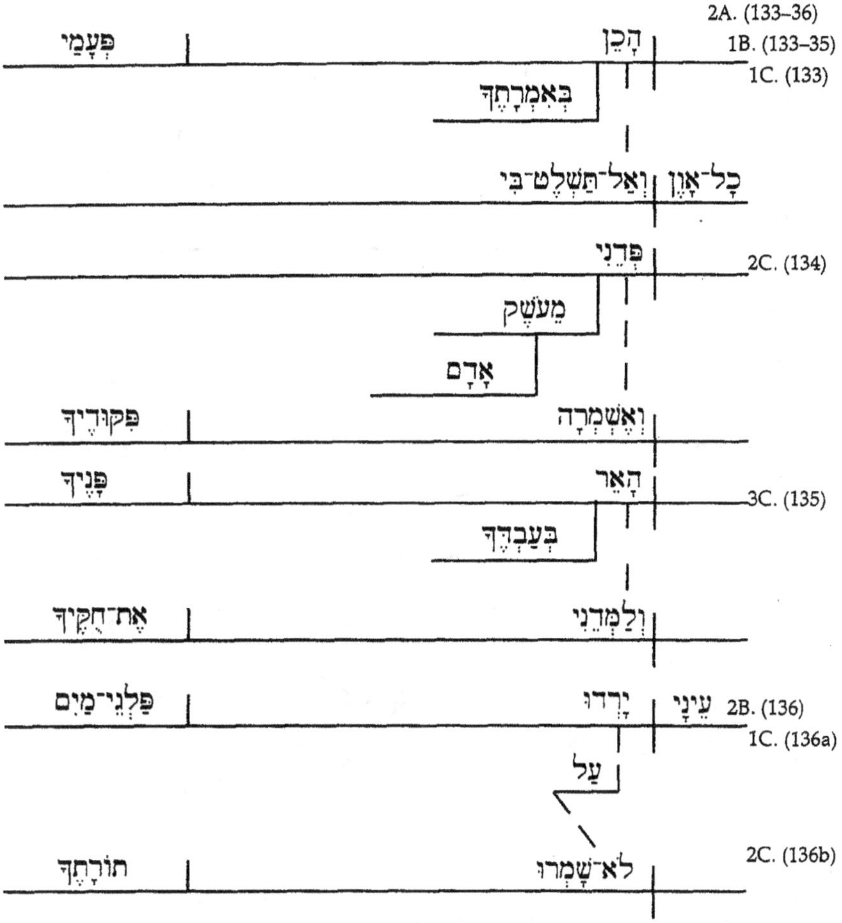

צ
Stanza

Psalm 119 : 137–144

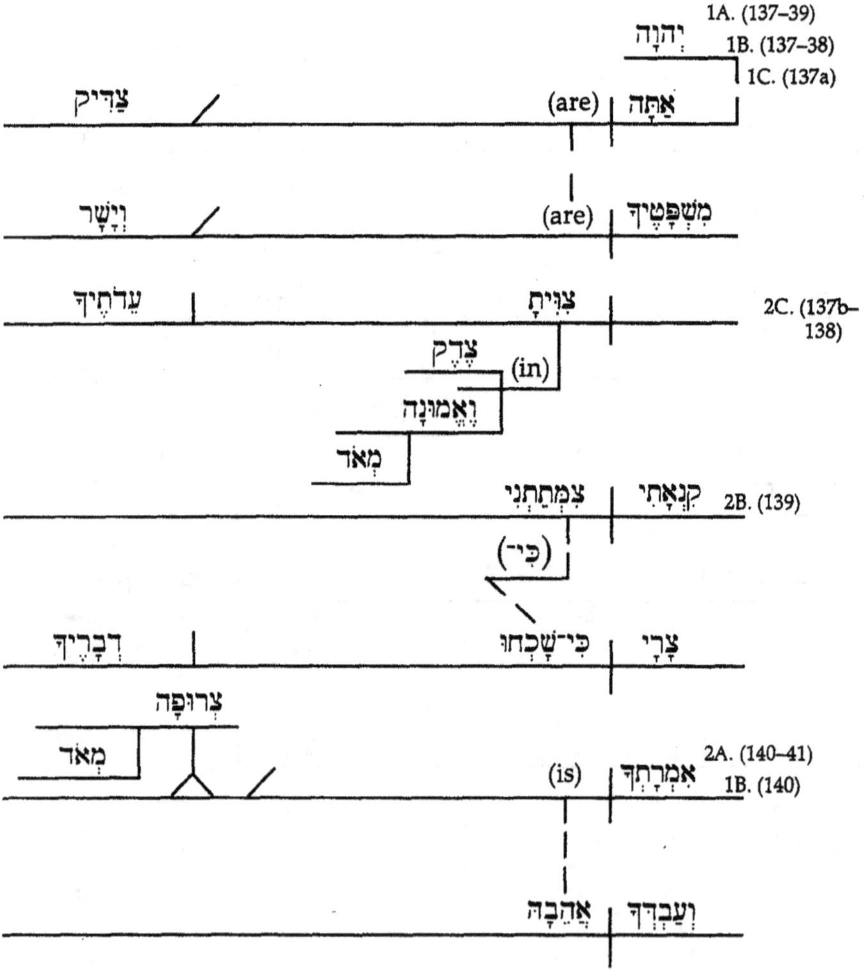

Psalm 119 : 141–144

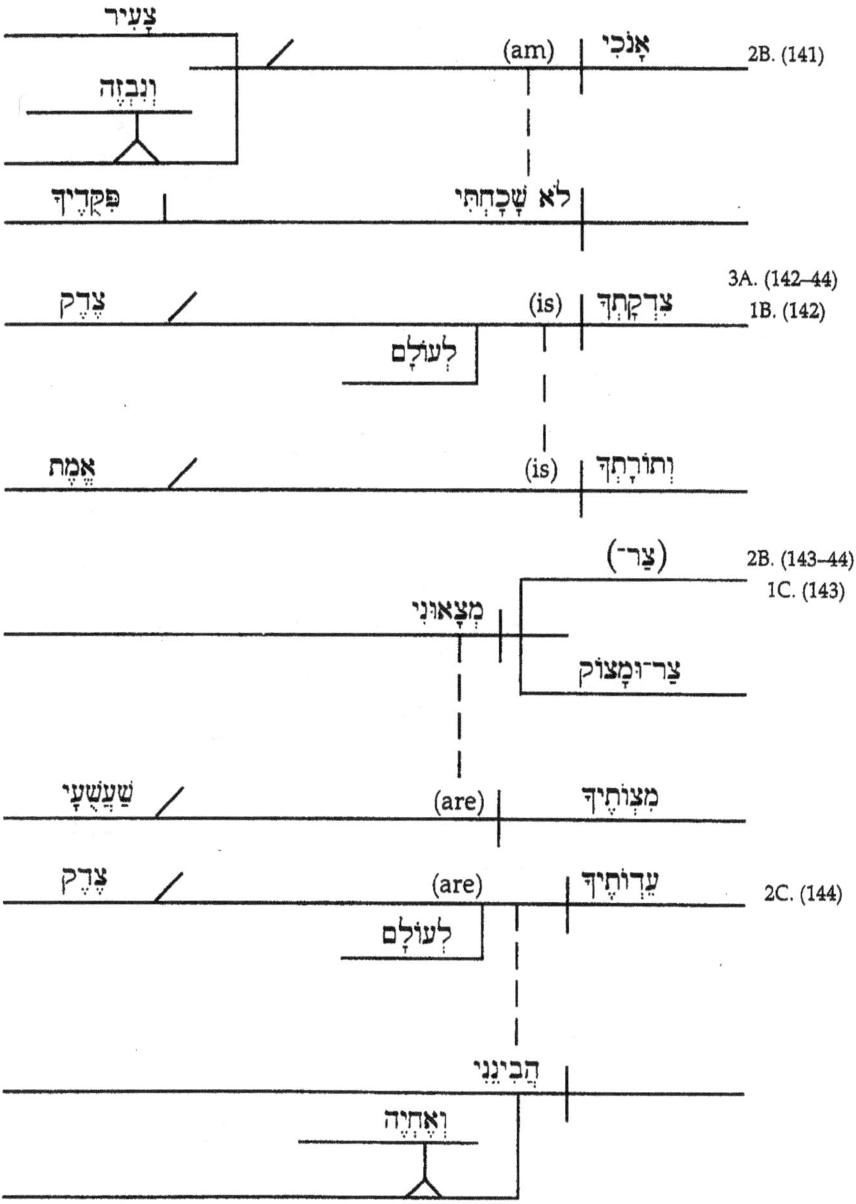

ק
Stanza
Psalm 119 : 145–152

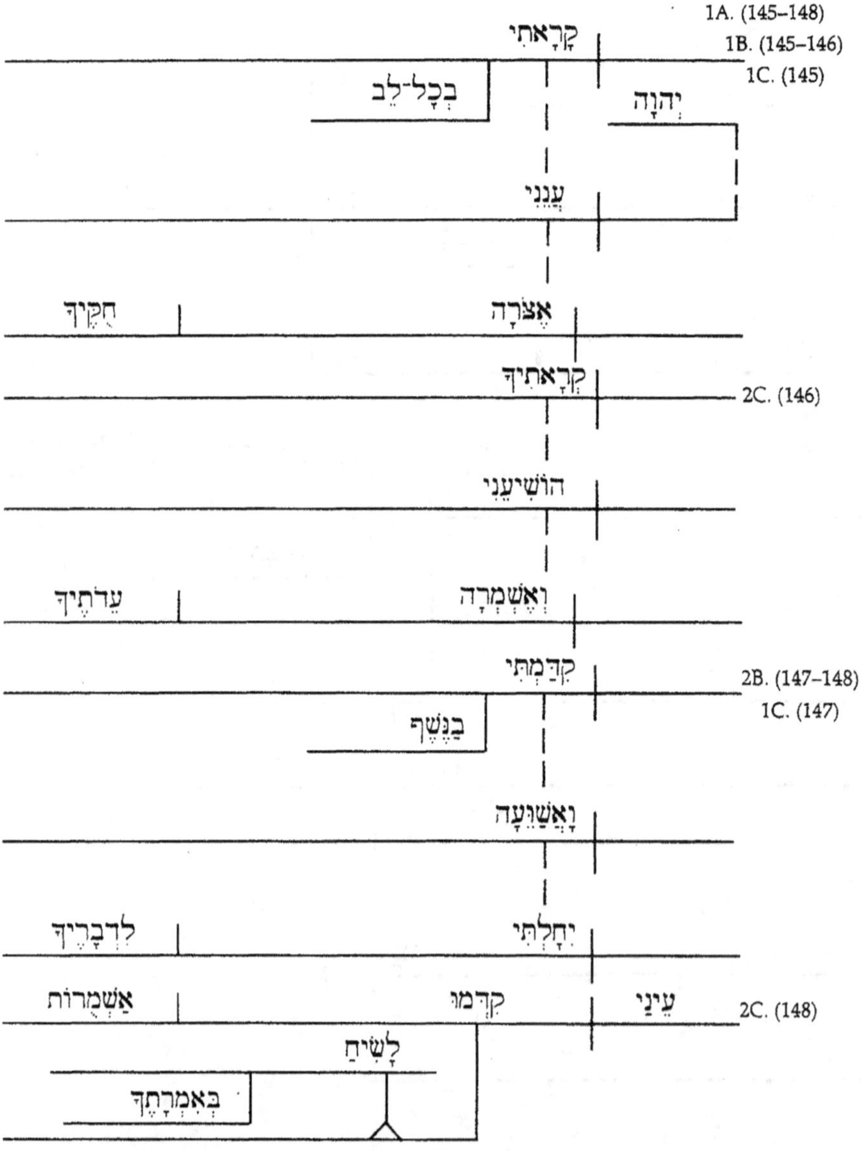

Psalm 119 : 149–152

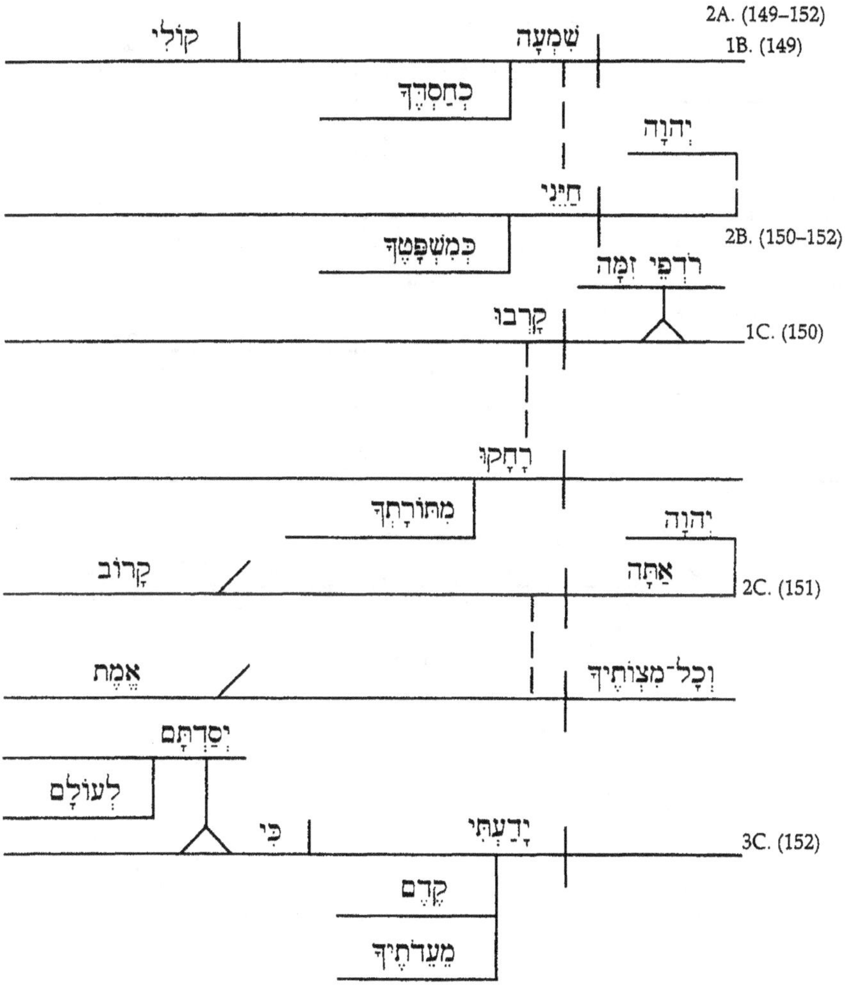

ר
Stanza
Psalm 119 : 153–160

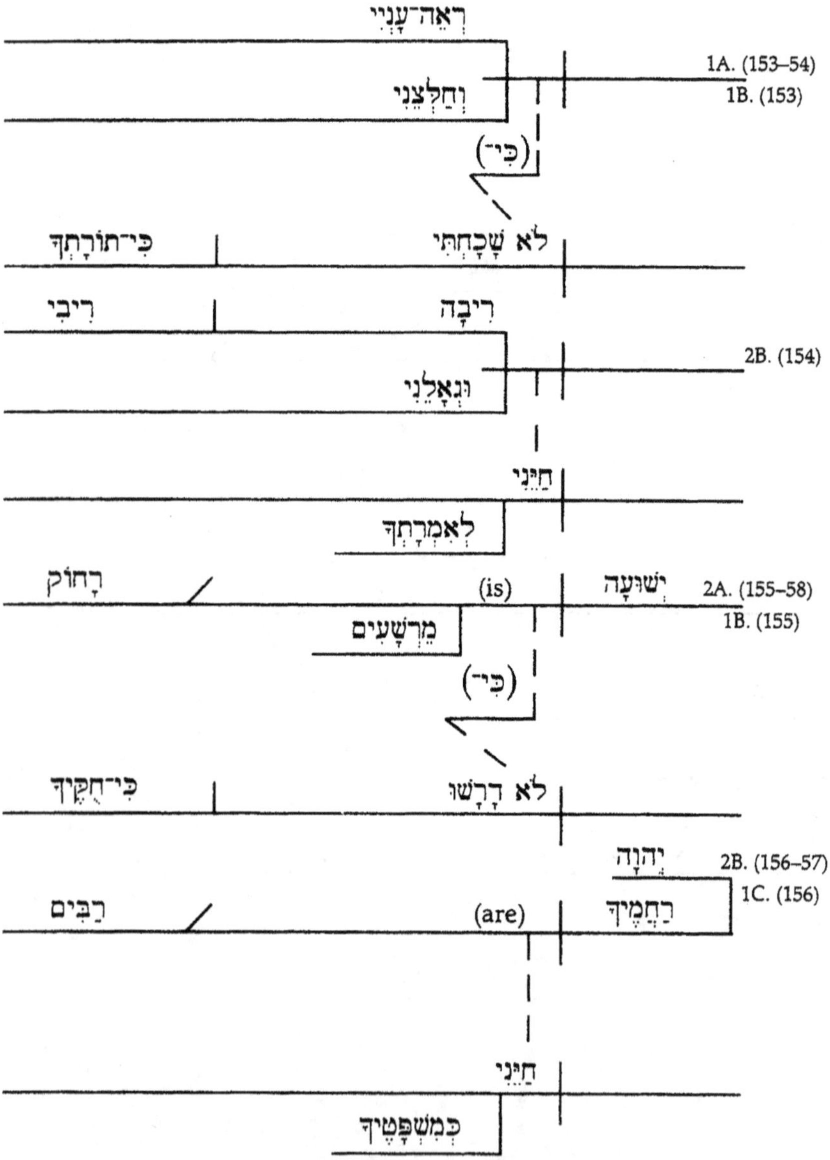

Psalm 119 : 157–160

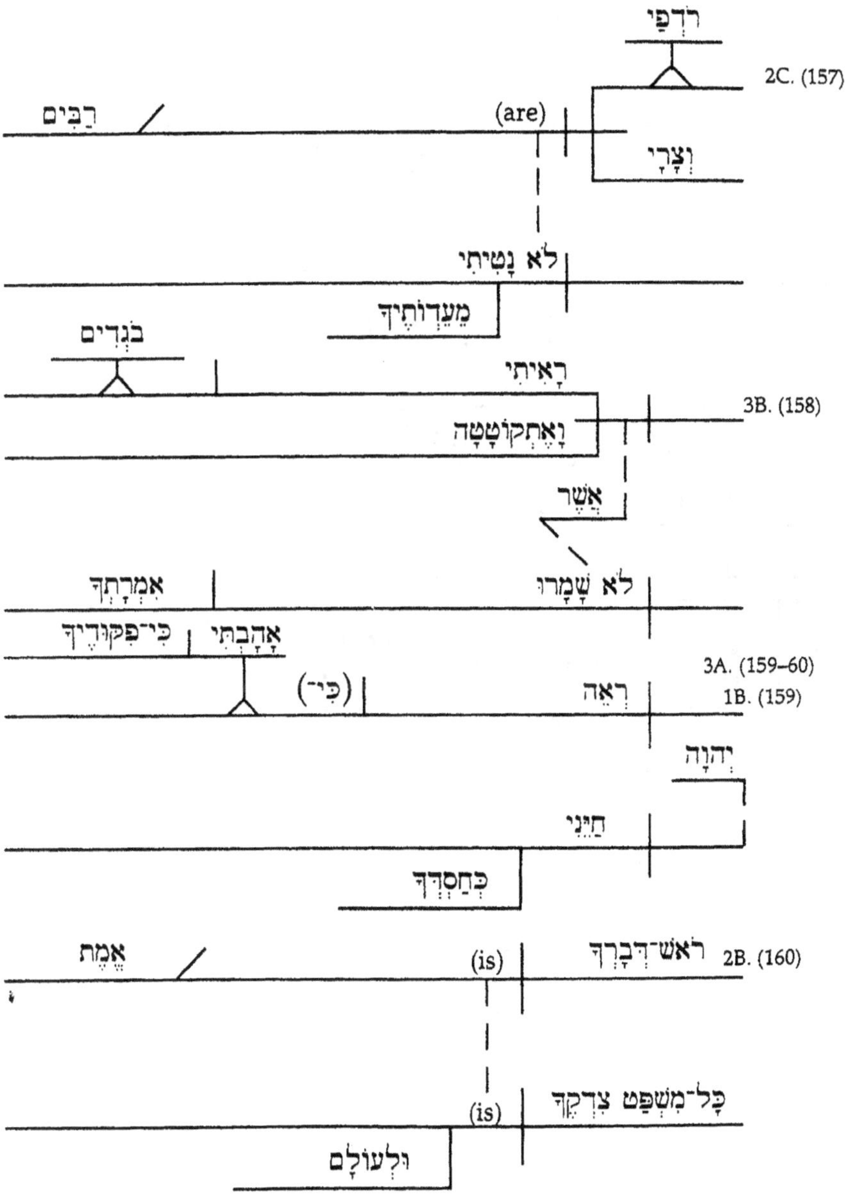

ש
Stanza
Psalm 119 : 161–168

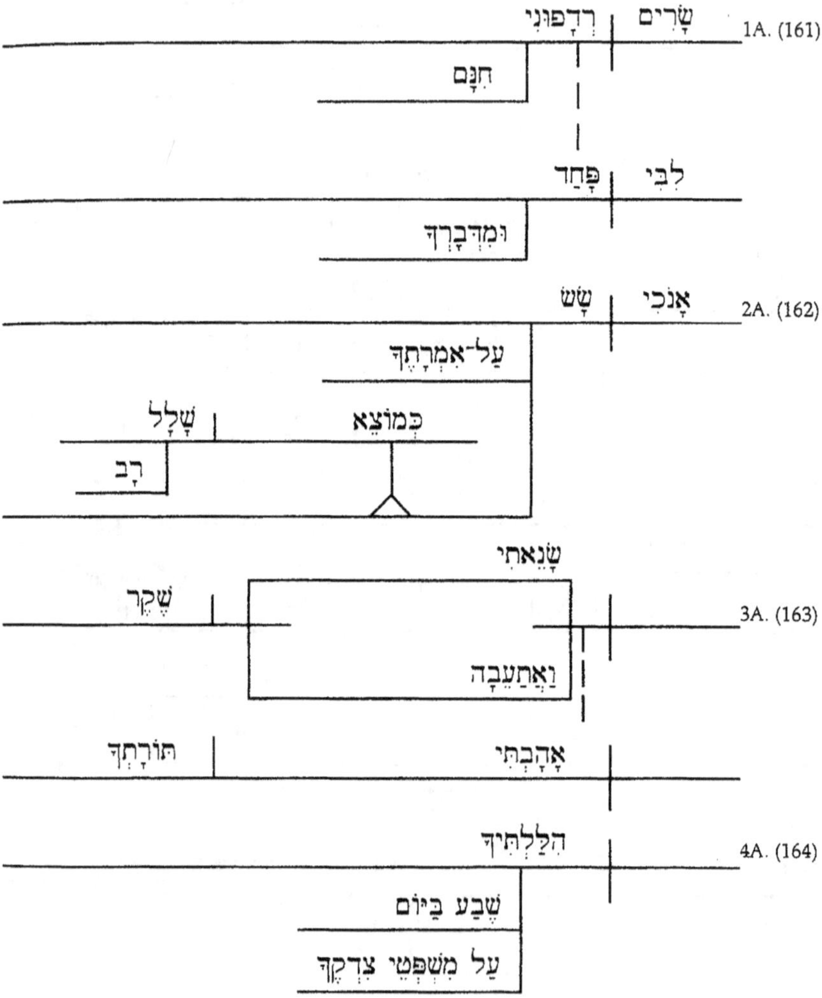

Psalm 119 : 165–168

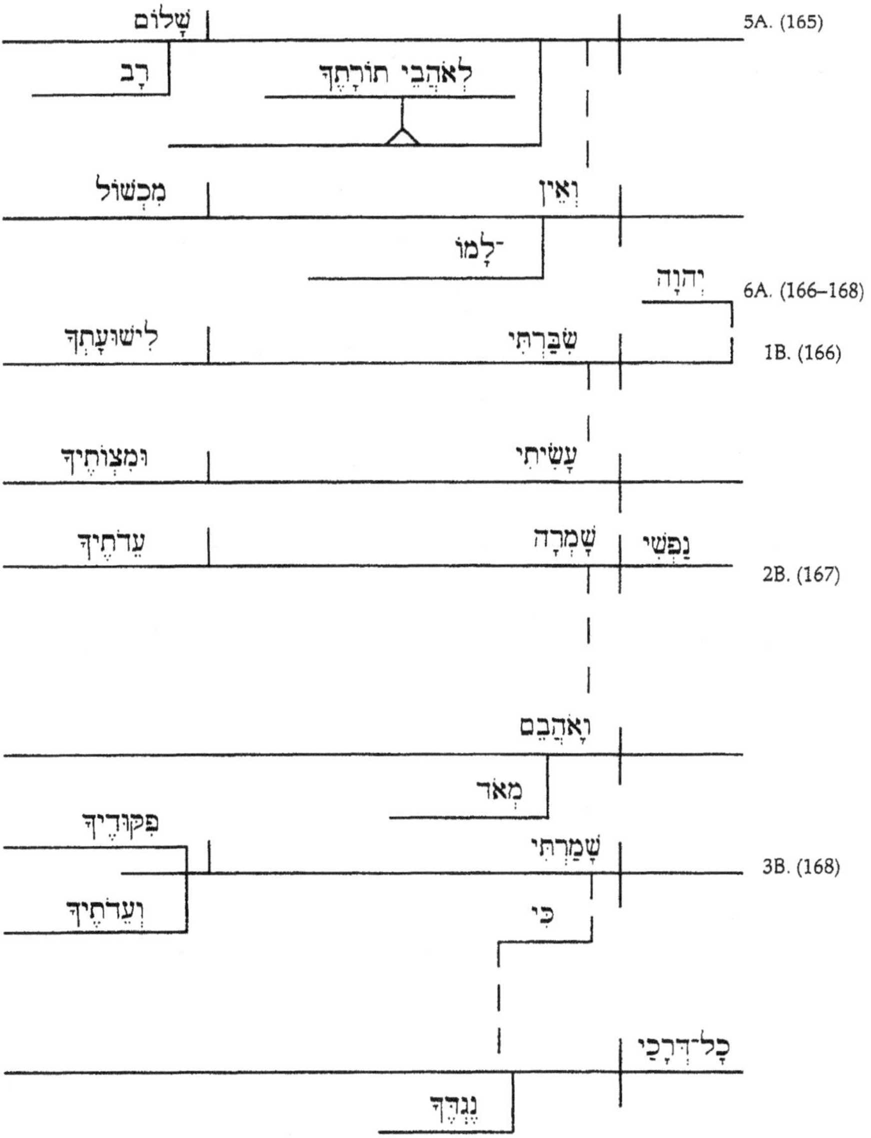

ת
Stanza
Psalm 119 : 169–176

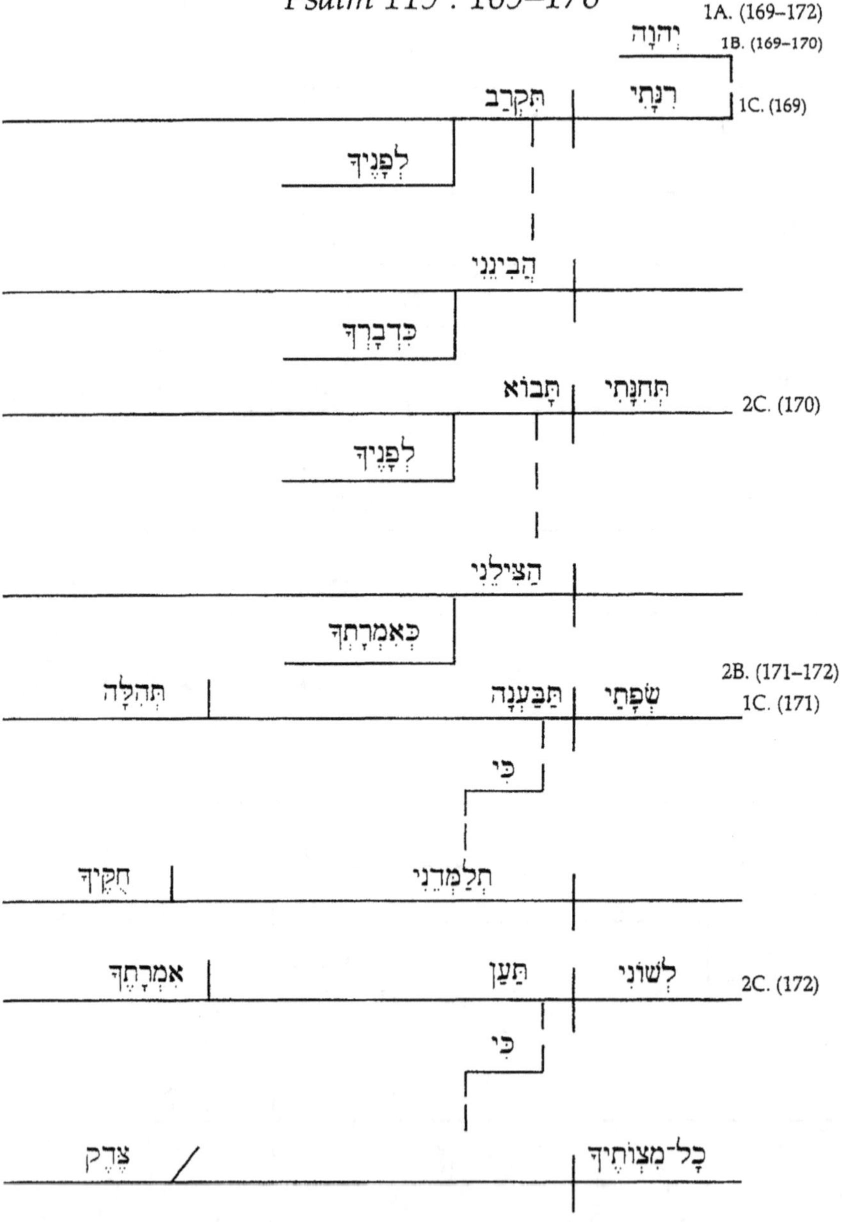

Psalm 119 : 173–176

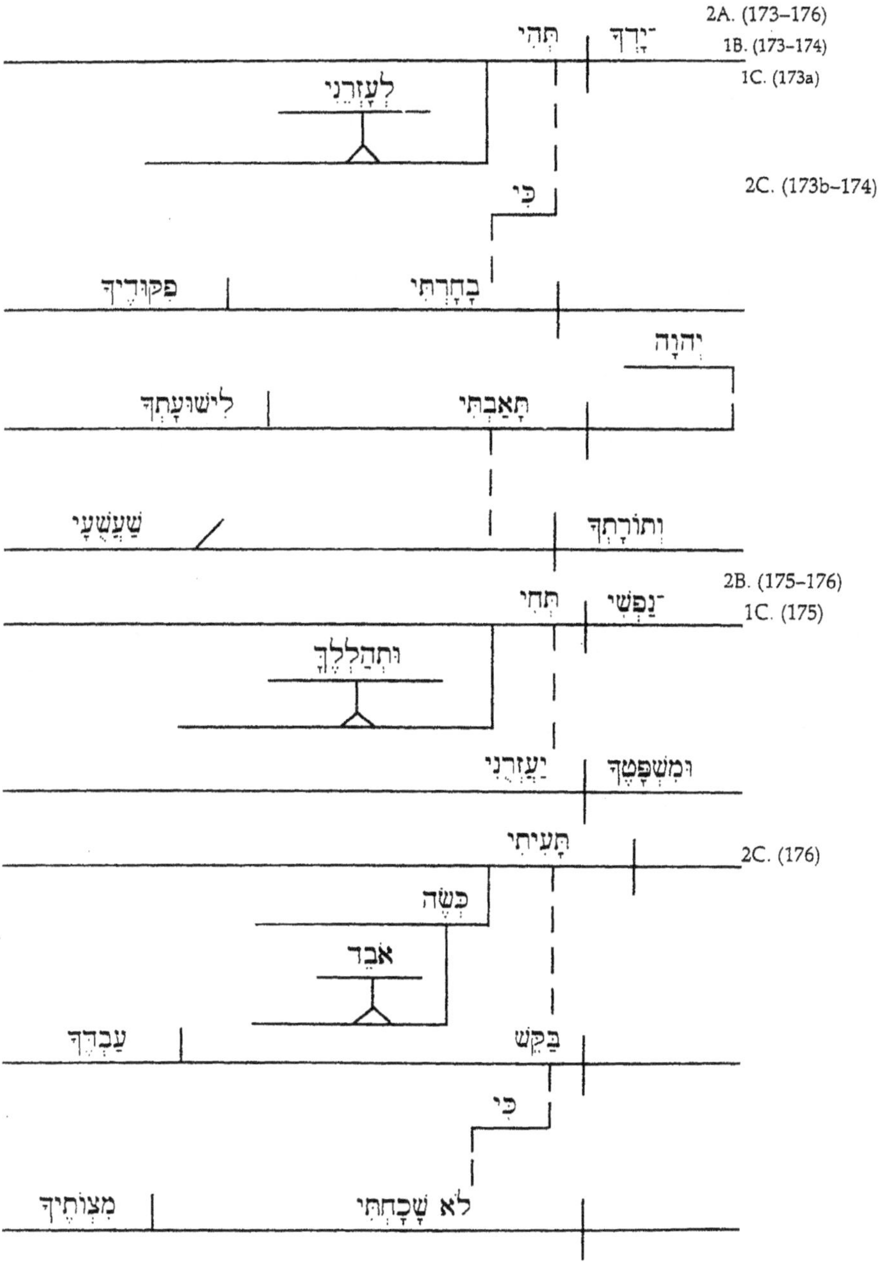

www.ingramcontent.com/pod-product-compliance
Lightning Source LLC
Chambersburg PA
CBHW071225290426
44108CB00013B/1293

* 9 7 8 1 5 9 7 5 2 3 8 0 6 *